W9-BQJ-147

MY SOUL LOOKS BACK, 'LESS I FORGET

MY SOUL LOOKS BACK, 'LESS I FORGET

A Collection of Quotations by People of Color

Dorothy Winbush Riley, editor

HarperCollinsPublishers

This book was previously published privately in 1991 by Winbush Publishing Company.

HarperCollins books may be purchased for educational, business, or sales promotional use. For information, please write: Special Markets Department, HarperCollins Publishers, Inc., 10 East 53rd Street, New York, NY 10022.

FIRST EDITION

Designed by C. Linda Dingler

Library of Congress Cataloging-in-Publication Data

My soul looks back, 'less I forget : a collection of quotations by people of color / edited by Dorothy Winbush Riley. — 1st ed.

p. cm.

Includes index.

ISBN 0-06-270086-3

1. Quotations, English. 2. Afro-Americans—Quotations. 3. Blacks—Quotations. I. Riley, D. Winbush (Dorothy Winbush)

PN6081.3.R5M9 1993

081'.08996073—dc20 92-25754

---

93 94 95 96 97 ❖/RRD 10 9 8 7 6 5 4 3 2 1

CONTENTS

INTRODUCTION

On April 23, 1991 I received 1,000 copies of my self-published edition of *My Soul Looks Back, 'Less I Forget* from the printer. I was not prepared for seventy-four cartons of books. I was not prepared to store them or even to move them from the transport truck. Seeing my bewildered look, the driver asked me, "Is this your first time doing this?" I was speechless and could only stare in wide-eyed amazement as I bobbed my head. He smiled and said, "Well, I guess I have to help you." The two of us managed to carry seventy-four thirty-pound cartons from the truck into my home. (The driver laughingly suggested I rent a warehouse the next time.) Later, when my children came home from school they had to slither past the cases which filled every empty space in the hall, kitchen, bathroom, living, and dining rooms.

This driver was just one of many who offered a word of encouragement, advice, or a listening ear during the eight years I spent attempting to compile, edit, finance, and publish the book. Althea Gibson said, "No matter what accomplishments you make, somebody helps you," and the publishing of the first edition of this book was no exception.

By April 27, I had sold twenty copies of *My Soul Looks Back, 'Less I Forget* and I was ecstatic. But at midnight on April 29, my entire life changed. A hospital called to tell me that one of my younger sisters was deathly ill. I forgot about the book and the cartons. I filled my days with my work as an assistant principal and my evenings at the hospital, hovering, hoping, and praying for my sister's recovery.

Though I lacked time to promote *My Soul Looks Back, 'Less I Forget,* it refused to be pushed aside and took on a life of its own. During the early part of May telephone calls requesting the book filled my answering machine. The natural grapevine of the Aframerican (a term used by Claude McKay during the Harlem Renaissance) community had spread the news about it. On May 8, the *Michigan Chronicle* published a feature, "A Convention of Quotations: Detroit Woman Publishes Book of Black Quotations," that highlighted the publication of *My Soul Looks Back, 'Less I Forget.* Orders for the book poured in from Colorado, Washington, and California; subscribers for the *Chronicle* had seen the article. Meanwhile, my sister's illness so occupied my thoughts and actions that my fifteen-year-old daughter, Tiaudra, did everything from taking orders over the phone to shipping the books through United Parcel Service.

On June 12, two days after we buried my sister, the *Detroit Free Press* featured *My Soul Looks Back, 'Less I Forget* in an article entitled "Source of Pride." Soon newspapers from Columbus, Ohio, to Atlanta, Georgia, were publishing articles about the book, emphasizing its importance as a source of pride and heritage for people of color. An avalanche of orders poured into my house.

By early July, I planned to print a hardcover edition when David Streitfeld of the *Washington Post* called and wanted to review the book. On July 21, 1991, the review appeared in "Book Report," generating hundreds of orders from the East Coast and queries from several publishers. One of the first publishers to call was HarperCollins, and after several conversations, we began negotiations for an expanded edition, which they would publish and distribute.

I had originally hoped this book of quotations would stimulate, inform, amuse, and awaken middle-school students. I did not expect the overwhelming response from politicians, writers, trainers, educators, speakers, doctors, lawyers, and many other professional and non-professional workers. The original targeted market widened significantly from middle-school adolescents to include practically everyone.

My life—and the book—has changed drastically since that April day in 1991. My immediate family has increased to include my sister's three sons. *My Soul Looks Back, 'Less I Forget* has grown from 5,000 citations to more than 7,000.

A. G. Gaston said, "Successful businesses are founded on needs," and this book is no exception. The writing of this book started when I was a middle-school teacher searching for materials to meet the needs of my students. For almost twenty-five years of teaching I have used quotations extensively. I began collecting sayings, maxims, proverbs, quips, and quotations during my first year as an elementary-school librarian. In 1984–85, when budget cuts forced the Detroit Public Schools to close all elementary- and middle-school libraries, I had the opportunity to teach language arts, literature, and writing at Durfee Middle School. The students were given the annual task of completing a paper or project during African-American History Month. In one assignment, students were directed to use the words of their ancestors at least twice in a research paper. They searched but were unable to find suitable quotations. I then began to look through anthologies and quotation books to see what I could find.

Despite my efforts and skills, I could only locate quotations by Martin Luther King, Jr., James Baldwin, and Muhammad Ali. Not once in the conventional reference anthologies did I find Paul Robeson, Frantz Fanon, Malcolm X, Toni Morrison, Gwendolyn Brooks, Alice Walker, and especially not David Walker.

Quotations have served writers and speakers, preachers and politicians, and students and teachers for centuries. Yet, in the more familiar, conventional quotation books, there is an astonishing scarcity of quotations by people of color. These people have affected every facet of society—the arts, politics, theater, and the family—yet there was no encyclopedic book illuminating and illustrating their witticisms, thoughts, and instructions. Many people of color have been pivotal in the fight for justice and humanity, risking their lives and the lives of their families. Where were the revolutionaries? Douglass? Gandhi? Where were the educators? Bethune? Washington? Where were the people of color?

I gathered my files and the students were able to use them to complete their research, but my project was just beginning. I began earnestly collecting words of wisdom, opinions, and humor from books, magazines, newspapers, and television. Originally, the only criteria for selecting a citation was that the speaker be a person of color. As the files evolved from a collection of index cards into files on a hard drive, I became more selective in choosing quotes, carefully considering their usefulness and eloquence.

Some quotations were chosen for their lyricism, some for the point they make, others for the uniqueness and ingenuity of expression. Many quotations reveal the ideals and character of the speaker. Other quotations were chosen because they presented such a memorable image. I also gathered quotations from people in various careers, including politicians, writers, ministers, abolitionists, musicians, educators, poets, doctors, and entertainers.

My Soul Looks Back, 'Less I Forget has evolved into a broader compilation of quotations than I had originally foreseen. Since I am an Aframerican, I started with quotes by Aframericans and was then enthralled by African writers. In 1989, I was transferred to a school that is truly multicultural and met people of color from Central America, Mexico, the Caribbean Islands, and the Middle East. I searched for literature and writings representative of their cultures and began to catalogue them. I've been limited by sources available and consequently some groups are underrepresented in this edition. As my reading expands and accessibility of material improves, more quotations by South Americans, Indians, Latin Americans, and Middle Easterners will be included in future editions of this book.

Since this is an eclectic compilation of inspiring quotes of pride and heritage about people of color, it is important to include the more controversial ones. After all, some of the nonconformists who dared to speak their minds regardless of the consequences have become our greatest heroes.

One of the first quotations I catalogued into my brain was that of Ptah Hotep who urged, "Follow in the footsteps of your ancestors for the mind is trained through knowledge. Behold their words endure in books. Open and read them and follow their wise counsel." Consequently, the chief goal of this new edition is to provide a representative selection of "words of the ancestors" in a readable, enjoyable reference format. A second purpose was to remind the readers to "look back" into the past with pride at the triumphs and victories of those who came before us.

The reader must remember that this is not a book of "firsts": Often the original source of a quotation has been lost but not the words themselves, which were then popularized by others. However, the cataloguing of the words of people of color must begin somewhere, and this book is a starting point.

The book took more than eight years to compile. Some of the original notes and quotes were lost during the transcription. Readers, I invite you to send any corrections, changes, or additions to me for revisions in following editions. I welcome your support and contributions.

The most difficult part of the entire writing process was stopping. Again, I thank my daughter, Tiaudra, for simply saying, "Mom, you have to stop, you have enough for two books. You must end this book!" *My Soul Looks Back, 'Less I Forget* will never be complete; it will never truly end. The book will continue to grow and change as it has from April 1991 to now. This task is unfinished and will remain so until the thoughts and ideals of people of color from all nations are looked upon with respect and value.

HOW TO USE THIS BOOK

Senusret II of Egypt cried, "Would I have words that are unknown, utterances and sayings in new languages, that have not yet passed away, and that have not already been said repeatedly by the ancestors." The ancient ones knew as we know that original thought is limited, and many ideas are repeated from generation to generation. They also knew the importance of keeping historical records detailing their deeds and accomplishments.

The standard practice of organizing quotations chronologically is used here. This was done to project a sense of history, as well as reveal the changing mood of our nation and the many ways of expressing feelings and thoughts over a period of time. The book also chronicles how an idea, once born, is planted in generation after generation. For example, under FREEDOM, Jean Dessalines said in 1840, "We have dared to be free; let us dare to be so by ourselves and for ourselves." Alice Walker repeats a similar sentiment in 1983 with these words, "For in the end, freedom is a personal and lonely battle and one faces down fears of today so that those of tomorrow might be engaged."

For magazines and newspapers, the issue date is used. Some quotations where the dates are unknown are given approximate dates shown as c. (circa). Dates for books are the publication date, and do not necessarily reflect when a particular quote was given.

Poetry and song lyrics are printed in complete lines with oblique strokes showing the poet's line breaks.

The first index lists speakers, and the second, subjects and cross-references. Each quotation was placed under its key subject heading. Since many quotations refer to secondary subjects they are included as cross-references in the index.

Lastly, a bibliography is also included for further reference to books used to compile *My Soul Looks Back, 'Less I Forget.*

ACKNOWLEDGMENTS

This is a book of positive learning, sharing, and understanding, I want to thank the following people who made it possible:

To the principal of Longfellow School, Shirley Lusby, who made this encyclopedic volume possible. If she had not taught me the rudiments of the personal computer, *My Soul Looks Back, 'Less I Forget* would still be a box of file cards.

To Mike Laramee, my second teacher, who never tired of my endless questions about Microsoft Works and Word.

To my children, Schiavi, Ted, Robert, and especially my youngest daughter, Tiaudra, for running the house while I read, researched, and edited.

To my friend Andrew Anyanonyou, for his inspiration, comfort, positive thinking, and visualization on how to turn an idea into an actuality.

To my colleagues and friends Louise Kirks, Rosa Williams, Doris Jones, and Mord-Essie Ingram, who supported and advised me.

To my editor, Nancy Peske, who has edited and shaped the book into its present Harper-Collins format.

To the librarians in the Detroit Public Schools and the Detroit Woodward Branch Library for their patience and help.

To all readers, especially my siblings: Lee, Ronnie, John, Darlene, Deborah, Shirley, and Antoinette, who made me feel that my efforts were truly useful and appreciated.

ABILITY

The price of your hat isn't the measure of your brain.

TRADITIONAL

Man's ability depends on the surrounding circumstances.

H. FORD DOUGLASS, c. 1860

Whatever the white man has done, we have done, and often better.

MARY MCLEOD BETHUNE, in the *Journal of Negro History,* January 1938

If initiative is the ability to do the right thing, then efficiency is the ability to do the thing right.

KELLY MILLER, *Out of the House of Bondage,* 1944

The ability to know what is the right thing to do in a given circumstance is a sheer gift of God.

HOWARD THURMAN, *Meditations of the Heart,* 1953

Our ability to create has outreached our ability to use wisely the products of our inventions.

WHITNEY YOUNG, *To Be Equal,* 1964

You have the ability, now apply yourself.

BENJAMIN MAYS, *Born to Rebel,* 1971

We all have ability. The difference is how we use it.

STEVIE WONDER, in Haskins, *Growing Up in a World of Darkness,* 1976

ABORTION

Abortions will not let you forget./ You remember the children you got that you did not get.

GWENDOLYN BROOKS, "The Mother," *A Street in Bronzeville,* 1945

The damp small pulps with a little or with no hair,/ The singers and workers that never handled the air./ You will never neglect or beat/ Them, or silence or buy with a sweet./ You will never wind up the sucking-thumb/ Or scuttle off ghosts that come./ You will never leave them, controlling your luscious sigh,/ Return for a snack of them, with gobbler mother-eye.

Ibid.

If men could get pregnant, abortion would be a sacrament.

FLORYNCE KENNEDY, *Sisterhood Is Powerful,* 1970

Is abortion right, is a question each of us must answer individually.

SHIRLEY CHISHOLM, *Unbought and Unbossed,* 1970

Abortion [is not the] solution to the problems that still plague us.

PAMELA CARR, in "Which Way Black America: Anti-Abortion or Pro Choice?" *Ebony,* October 1989

Those who argue that abortions are necessary for the poor will not argue for economic empowerment.

FLOYD FLAKE, in *ibid.*

ACCEPTANCE

I've never accepted any inferior role because of my race or color. And by God, I never will.

PAUL ROBESON, "For Freedom and Peace," speech given at Rockland Palace, New York City, 19 June 1949

We want to be accepted just as we are, but at the same time we want the other person to *win* the right to our acceptance of him.

HOWARD THURMAN, *Disciplines of the Spirit,* 1963

The Negro's so-called "revolt" is merely an asking to be *accepted* into the existing system!

MALCOLM X, *The Autobiography of Malcolm X,* 1965

The only person who can organize the man in the streets is the one who is unacceptable to the white community. They don't trust the other kind.

MALCOLM X, in the *Village Voice,* 25 January 1965

Too many of us have a need to be accepted no matter what the cost.

SHIRLEY CHISHOLM, speech given at Federal College, Washington, D.C., 1969

A slave is one who recognizes and accepts his status. The real slave needs no chains.

DICK GREGORY, *No More Lies,* 1971

Forced to accept an alien language, alien and hostile gods, and an alien view of the world, our imaginations were shackled to those of our rulers, with the result that we continued for a considerable time the work they had begun in their manner.

ADAM DAVID MILLER, "Some Observations on a Black Aesthetic," in Gayle, ed., *The Black Aesthetic,* 1971

For above all, in behalf of an ailing world which sorely needs our defiance, may we never accept the notion of "our place."

LORRAINE HANSBERRY, *Black Women in White America,* 1972

"You're mine." And Blackness—the red of it, the milk and cream of it, the tan and yellow-tan of it, the deep-brown middle-brown high-brown of it, the "olive" and the ochre of it!—Blackness marches on.

GWENDOLYN BROOKS, *Report From Part One,* 1972

[Zora Neale Hurston] took the trouble to capture the beauty of rural black expression. She saw poetry where other writers merely saw failure to cope with English. She was so at ease with her blackness it never occurred to her that she should act one way among blacks and another among whites.

ALICE WALKER, *In Search of Our Mothers' Gardens,* 1983

I don't want to be the boss. I just want to be the accepted emperor.

HAROLD WASHINGTON, in "Mayor Washington Eulogized as Symbol of Hope for Blacks," *Jet,* 14 December 1987

ACHIEVEMENT/ACCOMPLISHMENT

Up, you mighty race, you can accomplish what you will.

MARCUS GARVEY, *Philosophy and Opinions of Marcus Garvey,* 1923

All of us may not live to see the higher accomplishments of an African empire, so strong and powerful as to compel the respect of mankind, but we in our lifetime can so work and act as to make the dream a possibility within another generation.

Ibid.

Dissatisfaction with possession and achievement is one of the requisites to further achievement.

JOHN HOPE, c. 1925

One race has not accomplished any more than any other race, for God could not be just and at the same time make one race the inferior of the other.

CARTER G. WOODSON, in the *Journal of Negro History,* 1925

To struggle and battle and overcome and absolutely defeat every force designed against us is the only way to achieve.

NANNIE BURROUGHS, in "Unload Your Uncle Toms," *Louisiana Weekly,* 23 December 1933

For despite their achievements, the world has not been willing to accept the contributions that women have made.

MARY MCLEOD BETHUNE, speech given before the National Council of Negro Women, 5 December 1935

No matter what accomplishments you make, somebody helps you.

ALTHEA GIBSON, in *Time,* 26 August 1957

What great achievement has been performed by the person who told you it couldn't be done.

MELVIN CHAPMAN, speech given at Miller Junior High, Detroit, Michigan, 1959

The many of us who attain what we may and forget those who help us along the line—we've got to remember that there are so many others to pull along the way. The further they go, the further we all go.

JACKIE ROBINSON, *Baseball Has Done It,* 1964

Negro History Week reminds us of the achievements that [were] made in the Western hemisphere under the tutelage of the white man.

MALCOLM X, speech given at the Organization of Afro-American Unity Rally, Audubon Ballroom, New York City, 24 January 1965

Achieving the education and going higher is something that I wanted to do for myself, and to show my children that although their father does one thing it is possible to do many things because humans have a brain capable of doing three or four things at once.

BILL COSBY, in "Interview," *Scholastic,* November 1977

I learned that along with the towering achievements of the cultures of ancient Greece and China there stood the culture of Africa, unseen and denied by the imperialist looters of Africa's material wealth.

PAUL ROBESON, "How I Discovered Africa," in Foner, *Paul Robeson Speaks,* 1978

I am awed at man's ingenuity and what he can achieve. I recognized what a beautiful and fragile planet we live on. Seeing Earth from 170 miles out in space is not like standing on Earth and looking at the moon.

GUION BLUFORD, in *USA Today,* 1 February 1983

As I stood there at the top of the world and thought of the hundreds of men who had lost their lives in the effort to reach it [North Pole], I felt profoundly grateful that I had the honor of representing my race.

MATTHEW HENSON, in "Matt Henson: Arctic Explorer Featured in Film," *Ebony,* November 1983

Tell our children they're not going to jive their way up the career ladder. They have to work their way up hard. There's no fast elevator to the top.

MARIAN WRIGHT EDELMAN, "We Must Convey to Children That We Believe in Them," *Ebony,* August 1988

To be the best you have to be cocky, arrogant and conceited. Conceited is just loving yourself. If you don't love yourself, you can never achieve anything. And I love myself.

MIKE TYSON, in "Mike Tyson Talks About His Future and Says, 'I'm a Dreamer,'" *Jet,* 14 November 1988

Use missteps as stepping stones to deeper understanding and greater achievement.

SUSAN TAYLOR, c. 1989

I feel no flattery when people speak of my voice. I'm simply grateful that I found a way to work around my impairment. Once a stutterer, always a stutterer. If I get any credit for the way I sound, I accept it in the name of those of us who are impaired.

JAMES EARL JONES, 1990

You can have it all. You just can't have it all at one time.

OPRAH WINFREY, in *Ladies' Home Journal,* May 1990

For a man not to achieve the things he has an opportunity to do is such a waste of life.

JAKE SIMMONS, *Staking a Claim,* 1991

ACT/ACTION

Words are nothing but words; power lies in deeds. Be a man of action.

MALI GRIOT MAMADOU KOUYATE, *Sundiata, An Epic of Old Mali,* 1217–1237 A.D.

When you pray, move your feet.

AFRICA

A little subtleness is better than a lot of force.

CONGO

God gives nothing to those who keep their arms closed.

MALI

When a needle falls into a deep well, many people will look into the well, but few will be ready to go down after it.

GUINEA

He who can do nothing, does nothing.

SENEGAL

When you ain't never done nothing you don't have to undo.

TRADITIONAL

Those who are agitated must be chastened, the fainthearted must be consoled, the feeble must be sustained, the argumentative must be refuted, the treacherous must be guarded against, the untutored must be taught, the indolent must be goaded, the conscientious must be restrained, the proud must be held in check, the quarrelsome must be placated, the impoverished must be aided, the oppressed must be delivered, the good must be commended, the evil must be endured, and all must be loved.

ST. AUGUSTINE, on the anniversary of his ordination

There shall be no peace to the wicked . . . this guilty nation shall have no peace . . . we will do all that we can to agitate! AGITATE! AGITATE!

FREDERICK DOUGLASS, "Resolution of the National Convention of Colored People and Friends," speech given in Troy, New York, 1847

For it is not light that is needed, but fire; it is not the gentle shower, but thunder. We need the storm, the whirlwind, and the earthquake. The feeling in the nation must be quickened, the conscience of the nation must be roused, the propriety of the nation must be startled, the hypocrisy of the nation must be exposed: and its crimes against God and man must be denounced.

FREDERICK DOUGLASS, "What to the Slave is the Fourth of July?" speech given in Rochester, New York, 5 July 1852

Do not do that which others can do as well.

BOOKER T. WASHINGTON, *Up from Slavery,* 1901

Men must not only know, they must act.

W. E. B. DU BOIS, *The Souls of Black Folk,* 1903

According to the commonest principles of human action, no man will do as much for you as you will do for yourself.

MARCUS GARVEY, *Philosophy and Opinions of Marcus Garvey,* 1923

We must do something and we must do it now. We must educate the white people out of their two hundred fifty years of slave history.

IDA B. WELLS, in Duster, ed., *Crusade for Justice,* 1928

God never appears to you in person but always in action.

MOHANDAS GANDHI, in *Young India,* 1928

Nothing counts but pressure, pressure, more pressure, and still more pressure through broad organized aggressive mass action.

A. PHILIP RANDOLPH, speech given to March on Washington Movement, Detroit, Michigan, 26 September 1942

The purpose of direct action is to create a situation so crisis-packed that it will inevitably open the door to negotiation.

MARTIN LUTHER KING, JR., *Letter from a Birmingham City Jail,* 1963

Revolutions are brought about by men who think as men of action and act as men of thought.

KWAME NKRUMAH, *Consciencism,* 1964

Do whatever you do so well that no man living and no man yet unborn could do it better.

BENJAMIN MAYS, "What Man Lives By," in Philpot, ed., *Best Black Sermons,* 1972

When do any of us do enough?

BARBARA JORDAN, *Barbara Jordan,* 1977

Every man is born into the world to do something unique and something distinctive and if he or she does not do it, it will never be done.

BENJAMIN E. MAYS, "I Knew Carter G. Woodson," *Negro History Bulletin,* January–March 1981

[God] is not just a talking God. . . . He acted. He showed Himself to be a doing God. . . . He takes sides. He is not a neutral God. He took the side of the slaves, the oppressed, the victims.

DESMOND TUTU, *Hope and Suffering,* 1983

I never regret anything I don't do.

GEOFFREY HOLDER, in "Geoffrey Holder Grabs for the Gusto," *Class,* April 1984

Love in action is the answer to every problem in our lives and in this world. Love in action is the force that helped us make it to this place, and it's the truth that will set us free.

SUSAN TAYLOR, c. 1985

Napoleon was not different from the slum kid who tries to take over the block, he just had big armies through which to amplify his aggression.

RALPH ELLISON, "What These Children Are Like," *Going to the Territory,* 1986

What I do goes beyond myself. It can have an influence on those who have the opportunity to come afterwards. There may be significance in being the first, but there is more significance in being the second, third, fourth, and fifth.

CLIFTON WHARTON, in "Clifton Wharton: The Nation's Highest Paid Black Executive," *Ebony,* September 1987

I don't base my actions on popularity. If you're in a position of leadership, you can't wait to determine how it's going to affect you in terms of good or bad. You have to lead and do what you think is good.

L. DOUGLASS WILDER, in the *Detroit News,* 28 April 1991

ACTOR/ACTRESS

I was thinking about all the honors that are showered on me in the theatre, how everyone wishes to shake my hand or get an autograph; a real hero, you'd naturally think. However, when I reach a hotel, I am refused permission to ride on the passenger elevator, I cannot enter the dining room for my meals, and am Jim Crowed generally.

BERT WILLIAMS, c. 1922

To expect the Negro artist to reject every role with which he is not ideologically in agreement, is to expect the Negro artist under our present scheme of things to give up his work entirely.

PAUL ROBESON, in the *Amsterdam News,* 5 October 1935

They will never let me play a part in which a Negro is on top.

PAUL ROBESON, in "Paul Robeson Tells Us Why," *Cine-Technician,* London, September–October, 1938

It is a sad fact that I have rarely seen a Negro actor really well used on the American stage or screen, or on television.

JAMES BALDWIN, *The Fire Next Time,* 1963

We are all tempted to become actors and when we forget who we are and where we are from, our phony selves take command.

RALPH ELLISON, lecture on "Education for Culturally Different Youth," Dedham, Massachusetts, September 1963

Blacks should be used to play whites. For centuries we had probed their faces, the angles of their bodies, the sounds of their voices and even their odors. Often our survival had depended upon the accurate reading of a white man's chuckle or the disdainful wave of a white woman's hand.

MAYA ANGELOU, *The Heart of a Woman,* 1981

It is very, very difficult for a Black actor to do anything for Black people . . . [and] because they are extremely sensitive, we can't laugh it up too much. We can't be too serious. We can't be too light or too dark. We can't be too ugly [and] we can't be too nice looking. It's ridiculous.

ROBERT GUILLAUME, in "Behind the Scenes with TV's 'Benson,'" *Ebony,* November 1983

I'm fighting the label of "Black" actress simply because it's very limiting in people's eyes, especially people who are making movies.

WHOOPI GOLDBERG, in "What's Whoopi Goldberg Doing on Broadway?" *Ebony,* March 1985

The art of acting is to be other than what you are.

Ibid.

Thirty seconds. That's what somebody said we get to respond. No longer than thirty seconds. But look at me. Look at the given condition: Black actress for over a quarter of a century. Still waiting for my big break. Tired of neglect, of the indifference to material of substance about Black people. And I can only have thirty seconds.

RUBY DEE, *My One Good Nerve,* 1987

Black actors and actresses have won Oscars throughout the 60 years. Hattie McDaniels won the first one. Then Sidney Poitier won one and Lou Gossett won one.

EDDIE MURPHY, in "Celebrities," *Jet,* 2 May 1988

It is incumbent upon us—Black actors, directors, writers—to push for more projects, more dynamic casting, interchangeable roles, and to develop projects for ourselves that deal with Black issues and themes.

GREGORY HINES, 1989

I have been offered Black quasi-heroes who get hanged at the end. I won't do a part like that. If I do a hero, he's going to live to the end of the movie.

MORGAN FREEMAN, 1990

Film is about nuances. That's why when you see a good film, it's a miracle.

COURTNEY B. VANCE, 1990

[G]rowing as an actor is about learning to stand on your own two feet.

WESLEY SNIPES, in Lee, *Mo' Better Blues,* 1990

On those few occasions when a movie has focused on a Black jazz performer as star or lead character, I think Black audiences often have been dismayed and shocked that such a movie had been made not to speak to them but to reach some large White audience instead. The history of jazz in the movies . . . has been a long, sorry tale that reads like one of cultural displacement or arrested development.

DONALD BOGLE, in *ibid.*

ADVICE

It's a bad child who does not take advice.

ASHANTI

'I know, I know' surpasses everything.

CONGO

As your mother has advised you, so has our mother advised us, too.

GHANA

Keep your counsel: the world knowing your plans will seek to destroy them.

WILLIAM TECUMSEH VERNON, sermon given at Western University, Qindaro, Kansas, c. 1900

There are those who advise the black man to pay little or no attention to where he is going so long as he keeps moving. . . . They assume that God will attend to the steering. This is arrant nonsense. The feet of those that aimlessly wander land as often in hell as heaven.

W. E. B. DU BOIS, "Socialists of the Path," *Horizon,* 1–2 February 1907

It is no more use to give advice to an old man than to give a tonic to a corpse.

ZORA NEALE HURSTON, *Moses, Man of the Mountain,* 1939

Good advice is needed and appreciated from wherever it comes, but our actions cannot be decisive, if the advisor and helper hold the guiding rein.

PAUL ROBESON, *Here I Stand,* 1958

Those who can serve us as examples are not qualified to offer us advice, much less give us orders.

CHEIKH ANTA DIOP, *The Cultural Unity of Black Africa,* 1978

My major advice to young black artists would be [to] shut themselves up somewhere away from all the debates about who they are and what color they are and just turn out paintings and poems and stories and novels.

ALICE WALKER, *In Search of Our Mothers' Gardens,* 1983

I was advised to "go and try" physics because in the words of one counselor, "You're good enough."

RON MCNAIR, in *Choosing to Succeed,* 1986

Get into the profession you think you want to be and do more than is expected of you.

JOSHUA SMITH, in *Jet,* 22 June 1987

Listen and learn from people who have already been where you want to go. Benefit from their mistakes instead of repeating them. Read good books . . . because they open up new worlds of understanding.

BENJAMIN CARSON, *Gifted Hands,* 1990

AFRICA

I am of the African race, and in the colour which is natural to them of the deepest dye, and it is under a sense of the most profound gratitude to the Supreme Ruler.

BENJAMIN BANNEKER, letter to Thomas Jefferson, 1791

Oh, Africa, land of my fathers, my heart bleeds for thy children.

Black Chronicle, January 1794

The map of Africa is no longer a Chinese puzzle. Its geographical mysteries have been solved. Its mighty lakes and rivers have been traced to their source . . . from the vastness of the Atlantic's waste of waters to the smallest stream that, like a silver thread, wanders down the mountain side and sighs itself away into the sands of the desert.

T. THOMAS FORTUNE, "The Nationalization of Africa," speech given at the Africa and the Africans Congress, Atlanta, Georgia, December 1896

Painting and sculpture have felt Africa's influence and so may the theater and decorative arts. In its own setting African Art was a vital part of life—masks and costumes for the ritual dances, the festivals, the initiations, the pageants of a primitive but wholesome civilization. Africa produced things imperishably beautiful.

ALAIN LOCKE, in *Theatre Arts Monthly,* 3 February 1920

He is an African of the African and is working for Africa.

JOHN E. BRUCE, letter to Dr. Rochas, in Schomburg Collection, 29 July 1920

I know no national boundary where the Negro is concerned. The whole world is my province until Africa is free.

MARCUS GARVEY, *Philosophy and Opinions of Marcus Garvey,* 1923

When Europe was inhabited by a race of cannibals, a race of savage man, heathens and pagans, Africa was peopled with a race of cultured Black men who were masters in art, science, and literature.

Ibid.

Wake up Ethiopia! Wake up Africa! Let us work towards the one glorious end of a free, redeemed and mighty nation. Let Africa be a bright star among the constellation of nations.

Ibid.

Africa is not only our mother, but in the light of most recent science is beginning to appear as the mother of civilization.

ALAIN LOCKE, "Apropos of Africa," *Opportunity,* February 1924

What is Africa to me:/ Copper sun or scarlet sea,/ Jungle star or jungle track,/ Strong bronzed men, or regal black/ Women from whose loins I sprang/ When the birds of Eden sang?/ *One three centuries removed/ From the scenes his father loved,/ Spicy grove, cinnamon tree,/ What is Africa to me?*

COUNTEE CULLEN, "Heritage," *Color,* 1925

Africa is a Dark Continent not merely because its people are dark-skinned or by reason of its extreme impenetrability, but because its history is lost.

PAUL ROBESON, "I Want to Be African," *What I Want From Life,* 1934

Africa, I have kept your memory, Africa,/ you are within me.

JACQUES ROUMAIN, *Ebony Wood,* 1939

In America, one heard little or nothing about Africa. I hadn't realized that until we went to live in England.

ESLANDA ROBESON, *African Journey,* 1945

The ladder of survival dawn men saw/ In the quicksilver sparrow that slips/ The eagle's claw!/ Liberia?

MELVIN B. TOLSON, "Do," *Libretto for the Republic of Liberia,* 1953

Africa is a rubber ball;/ The harder you dash it to the ground/ the higher it will rise.

Ibid.

Africa is my heart, the heart of all of us who are Black. Without her we are nothing: while she is not free we are not men. That is why we must free her or die.

PETER ABRAHAMS, *A Wreath for Udomo,* 1956

Dry your tears, Africa! Your children come back to you, their hands full of playthings and their hearts full of love. They return to clothe you in their hopes.

BERNARD DADIÉ, "Dry Your Tears Africa," *Dance of the Days,* 1956

Africa, my Africa/ . . . I have never known you/ But my face is filled with your blood.

DAVID DIOP, "Africa," *Poundings,* 1956

As a boy I knew little of Africa save legends and some music in my family. The books which we studied in the public schools had almost no information about Africa, save Egypt.

W. E. B. DU BOIS, speech given to the All African Conference, 1958

Africa is marching forward to freedom, and no power on earth can halt her now.

KWAME NKRUMAH, speech given to National Assembly, Accra, Ghana, 16 December 1959

Africa, help me to go home, carry me like an aged child in your arms. Undress me and wash me. Strip me of all of these garments, strip me as a man strips off dreams when the dawn comes. . . .

AIMÉ CÉSAIRE, *The Tragedy of King Christophe,* 1963

We're an African people/ hard softness burning black/ the earth's magic color our veins,/ an African people are we;/ burning blacker softly, softer.

HAKI MADHUBUTI, "African Poem," *We Walk the Way of the New World,* 1970

In all your Turnings and your Churnings/ remember Africa./ You have to call your singing and your bringing,/ your pulse, your intimate booming . . . / you have to call all that, that is your Poem/AFRICA

GWENDOLYN BROOKS, *Report From Part One,* 1972

It is still yesterday in Africa. It will take millions of tomorrows to rectify what has been done here.

LORRAINE HANSBERRY, *Les Blancs,* 1972

Africa would if Africa could. America could if America would. But Africa can't and American ain't.

JESSE JACKSON, in Smitherman, *Talkin' and Testifying,* 1977

We had sung it in our blues, shouted it in our gospels and danced the continent in our breakdown. As we carried it to Philadelphia, Boston and Birmingham we had changed its color, modified its rhythm, yet it was Africa which rode in the bulges of our high calves, shook in our protruding behinds and crackled in our wide open laughter.

MAYA ANGELOU, *All God's Children Need Traveling Shoes,* 1986

The Afro-American approach to dance which was uprooted from Africa is at the very core of the dance in America.

TEVIS WILLIAMS, in "Black Dance in Perspective," *City Arts Quarterly,* Spring 1987

Being in Africa, the kind of reception you get as a visitor and even after you make your home there is more than hospitality. It's a natural extension and an expression of their gratitude for plenty, that they have something to share with you.

ALI ABDULLAH, in "An Interview with Ali Abdullah," *City Arts Quarterly,* Spring 1987

The original people of Africa, "the blue people," they were full of color, blue-black color, and they were the keepers of the earth.

ANDERSON PIGATT, in *Black Art: Ancestral Legacy,* 1989

Here man was truly one with nature . . . so much was he a part of the surroundings, the same as the trees, the birds, the lower animals that moved on four feet. These people possessed an obvious pride, but it could not be associated with conceit, selfishness, pretentiousness; it was a pride . . . born simply of being, of sharing in nature's immensity. Upon this land man lived with the rhythm of the seasons.

JOHN BIGGERS, in *ibid.*

All people of African descent—the Latin, the Jamaican, the Haitian, the Brazilian, the Caribbean, and the African American—all must realize that, although they were not born in Africa, they are still African people and *all* of us have been through the experience of slavery.

D'JIMO KOUYATE, "The Role of the Griot," in Goss and Burnes, eds., *Talk That Talk,* 1989

AGE

The harder we work to conceal our age, the more we reveal it.

TERTULLIAN, *The Apparel of Women,* c. 200 A.D.

Every age is reminded by what it hears, that what has been done can be done again. Transgressions never die from the passage of age; crime is never erased by time; vice is never buried in oblivion.

SAINT CYRIAN, *To Donatus,* c. 246 A.D.

Man is like palm-wine: when young, sweet but without strength, in old age, strong but harsh.

CONGO

It is easy to become a monk in one's old age.

CONGO

The young cannot teach tradition to the old.

NIGERIA

The body perishes, the heart stays young. The platter wears away with serving food. No log retains its bark when old, no lover peaceful while the rival sleeps.

ZULU

A woman who will tell her own age will tell anything.

TRADITIONAL

Act your age and not your shoe size.

TRADITIONAL

The changes of many summers have brought old age upon me, and I cannot expect to survive many moons. . . .

BLACK HAWK, *Farewell, My Nation! Farewell,* 1833

We're all mortal and the old must make way for the young, otherwise there would be no promotion.

ALEXANDRE DUMAS, *The Count of Monte Cristo,* 1844

I am above eighty years old; it is about time for me to be going. I have been forty years a slave and forty years free, and would be here forty years more to have equal rights for all. I suppose I am kept here because something remains for me to do; I suppose I am yet to help break the chain.

SOJOURNER TRUTH, *Narrative of the Life of Sojourner Truth,* 1867

I am an aged tree, that when I was growing,/ uttered a vague sweet sound when the breeze caressed me./ The time for youthful smiles has now passed by;/ now, let the hurricane swirl my heart to song!

RUBEN DARIO, *In Autumn,* 1898

If no use were made of the labor of the ages, the world would remain always in the infancy of knowledge.

CARTER G. WOODSON, *The Mis-education of the Negro,* 1933

[My] head is ole and tilted toward [the] grave.

ZORA NEALE HURSTON, *Their Eyes Were Watching God,* 1937

When one is too old for love, one finds great comfort in good dinners.

ZORA NEALE HURSTON, *Moses, Man of the Mountain,* 1939

I have lived to an age in life which is increasingly distasteful to this nation. Unless by sixty a man has gained possession of enough money to support himself, he faces the distinct possibility of starvation. He is liable to lose his job and meet with refusal if he seeks another. At seventy he is frowned upon by the church and if he is foolish enough to survive until ninety, he is often considered a freak.

W. E. B. DU BOIS, *The Autobiography of W. E. B. Du Bois: A Soliloquy on Viewing My Life from the Last Decade of Its First Century,* 1964

Age is nectar.

WOLE SOYINKA, *Kongi's Harvest,* 1967

Radical in their teens, liberal in their twenties, conservative in their thirties, and reactionary in their forties.

WHITNEY YOUNG, in *Parks and Recreation,* April 1969

The trouble with most women is they get old in their heads. They think about it too much.

JOSEPHINE BAKER, 1970

At my age and in my condition I'm going to do what I want and I haven't got time for anything else.

FLORYNCE KENNEDY, *Sisterhood is Powerful,* 1970

As you get older, you find that often the wheat, disentangling itself from the chaff, comes out to meet you.

GWENDOLYN BROOKS, *Report From Part One,* 1972

To those incurable optimists among you the age of miracles is over. The age of slogan is over. The age of progress without a plan is over. The age of studying without a strategy, of running without a reason and flying without a flight plan is over. The waters of reaction are not going to turn into the wine of justice. Not today. Not tomorrow. Not ever, if we do not come together.

RICHARD HATCHER, speech given at the National Black Political Convention, Little Rock, Arkansas, 16 March 1974

I am too past youth/ too strong/ too black/ to cry/
still/ need comes; a steadied profuseness/
insensitive/ spreading/ spreading.

JOHARI AMINI, "Let's Go Somewhere," in *Black Poetry Writing,* 1975

How old would you be if you didn't know how old you are?

SATCHEL PAIGE, in Kanin, *It Takes Time To Become Young,* 1978

I wish I had started out at the age of ninety-six, look how much fun I would have had.

EUBIE BLAKE, *Eubie,* 1979

My mother used to send me to the movies with my birth certificate, so I wouldn't have to pay the extra fifty cents [the adult had to pay].

KAREEM ABDUL JABBAR, in "Words of the Week," *Jet,* 19 March 1984

I feel old for some reason, I really feel like an old soul.

MICHAEL JACKSON, c. 1985

Age has made Baldwin neither bitter nor mellow. It has given his face the damaged purity of an Ife mask and his mind the edge of a bored chess master.

JOE JOHNSON, in "Books," *Crisis,* February 1986

I don't feel old, just downright worn out.

WILL SMITH (110-year-old man), in *Jet,* 22 June 1987

Nothing depresses me anymore. For a while in your life you worry about the passage of time and getting old and . . . after a while you just say, "My God, does it matter? Get on with it."

BOBBY SHORT, in "Words of the Week," *Jet,* 30 May 1988

If a man can reach the latter days of his life with his soul intact, he has mastered life.

GORDON PARKS, in "A Passion for Living," *Modern Maturity,* June–July 1989

When I was forty and looking at sixty, it seemed like a thousand years away. But sixty-two feels like a week and a half away from eighty. I must now get on with those things I always talked about doing but put off.

HARRY BELAFONTE, in the *Washington Post,* 15 December 1989

[T]hey were a remarkably *old* people. About them was the smell of old temples. Cities lost when Europe was embryonic. Looking at them, at their dark skin soft as black leather against knee-length gowns similar to Greek chitons, you felt they had run the full gamut of civilized choices, or played through every political and social possibility and now had nowhere to *go.*

CHARLES JOHNSON, *Middle Passage,* 1990

ALCOHOL

Don't indulge in drinking beer, lest you utter evil speech . . . and fall down and hurt your body . . . one finds you lying on the ground as if you were a child.

SCRIBE ANY of the Palace of Nefertari

When man drunk, him walk and stagger; when woman drunk, him sit down and consider.

JAMAICA

He drinks so much he staggers in his sleep.

TRADITIONAL

If the blues was whiskey, I'd stay drunk all the time, stay drunk, baby just to wear you off my mind.

BLUES

You are full of the white man's devil water. You are like dogs in the Hot Moon when they run mad and snap at their own shadows.

LITTLE CROW OF THE SIOUX, speech given before Congress, 1862

I don't mind playin' anytime y'all can get me drunk,/ But Mr. Pinetop is sober now./ I been playing the piano round here all night long/ And y'all ain't brought the first drink somehow.

CLARENCE "PINE TOP" SMITH, "I'm Sober Now," c. 1920

Nothing but ruin stares a nation in the face that is a prey to the drink habit.

MOHANDAS GANDHI, in *Young India,* 1929

Here's the man with the dream machine. I want it to hit me around the edges and get to every point.

FATS WALLER, 1945

Whiskey just naturally likes me but beer likes me better. By the time I got married . . . a cold beer was as good as a warm bed, especially when the bottle could not talk and the bed warmer could.

LANGSTON HUGHES, "Feet Live Their Own Lives," *Tales of Simple,* 1950

If the ocean was whiskey/ And I was a duck/ I'd dive right in/ And never come up.

RICHARD WRIGHT, *The Outsider,* 1953

He drank from the bottle and was grateful for the sense of depression caused by the alcohol which made him feel less of pleasure, pain, anxiety, and hope.

Ibid.

The wine of life was sweet/ And drink came first;/ Here lies a fool who drank/ But died of thirst.

NAOMI L. MADGETT, "Epitaph," *One and the Many,* 1956

One needs the clarity/ the comma gives the eye/ not the head of the hawk/ swollen with rye.

MELVIN B. TOLSON, "Beta," *Harlem Gallery,* 1965

My mother could smell whiskey on your breath if she was in the market and you were home in bed.

EUBIE BLAKE, *Eubie,* 1979

Like alcohol, sports doesn't lie. What it reveals about a person under its influence was just hiding. People sometimes use sports as a way of denying responsibility for what they really are.

BILL RUSSELL, *Second Wind,* 1979

[He] was in that advanced stage of alcoholic stupor that severs mind from body, both his eyeballs large as eggs, and glaring blankly into a mug of warm beer, as drunks often do, talking to his reflection.

CHARLES JOHNSON, *Middle Passage,* 1990

ALONE

One who runs alone can't be outrun by another.

ETHIOPIA

It's better to travel alone than with a bad companion.

SENEGAL

If a man sought a companion who acted entirely like himself, he would live in solitude.

NIGERIA

Alas, the journey of life is beset with thorns to those who have to travel it alone.

ALEXANDRE DUMAS, *Le Demi-Monde,* 1855

If you see him plowing in the open field, traveling the forest at work with a spade, a rake, a hoe, a pick-axe, or a bill—let him alone, he has a right to work. If you see him on his way to school with spelling book, geography, and arithmetic in hand—let him alone. If he has a ballot in his hand and is on his way to the ballot box to deposit his vote for the man who he thinks will most justly and wisely administer the government which has the power of life and death over him—let him alone.

FREDERICK DOUGLASS, *Life and Times of Frederick Douglass,* 1892

Runnin' wild/ lost control/ Always showin' that I don't care/ Don't love nobody, it ain't worth while/ All alone runnin' wild.

NOBLE SISSLE AND EUBIE BLAKE, *Running Wild, Shuffle Along,* 1921

Everybody has some special road of thought along which they travel when they are alone to themselves. And his road of thought is what makes every man what he is.

ZORA NEALE HURSTON, *Moses, Man of the Mountain,* 1939

Poised in space, held between nothing and nothing, there floats a golden ball. Not only is it golden, it is blue, red, green, brown, and grey. Such is our earth. Only man is on the outside, alone and out of touch, not a part of the preconceived pre-planned order. . . . Only man is alone, haunted by fear and the echoes that float from fear.

PETER ABRAHAMS, *Wild Conquest,* 1950

Suddenly the world has run amok and left you alone and sane behind.

WOLE SOYINKA, *Kongi's Harvest,* 1967

Free? Is that to be alone/ remembering loves of yesterday,/ look beyond home?

CONRAD KENT RIVERS, "The Death of a Negro Poet," *Still Voice of Harlem,* 1968

We of the black intelligentsia for the most part are already set apart. We have trained scholars with black skins secluded in the ivory towers, the ebony towers.

NATHAN HARE, in *The Black Scholar,* November 1969

The foremost enemy of the Negro intelligentsia has been isolation.

LORRAINE HANSBERRY, *Les Blancs,* 1972

God bursts in violently the moment the soul is alone, horribly alone, detached from the whole created universe, suspended in the sort of void between creation and God. Then the soul is flooded by God.

ERNESTO CARDENAL, "Love," *Vida en al Amor,* 1974

God teach him to be used to being alone, for a person who put ambition first at the expense of his family was always a loner.

BUCHI EMECHETA, *The Joys of Motherhood,* 1979

For winter's not the roads we looked upon, now empty: not the angry blast and froze, It is the sunless heart, the spirit dark and dim, It is what I shall be when you are there no more.

ALEXANDER DUMAS, "Lady of the Pearls," in *Quotations in Black,* 1981

I saw myself as if on a boat which the nations would allow to put up at no port. I could come in for food and supplies. This done, I'd have to put out to sea again . . . never having a harbor which I could call my own, never knowing a port in which I could come to rest—always at sea . . . by order of the government of the universe.

JEAN TOOMER, in Kerman and Eldridge, *The Lives of Jean Toomer,* 1987

In my culture, there is no such thing as a single woman alone with children. There is no such thing as "alone" at all. There is the family.

MIRIAM MAKEBA, *My Story,* 1987

Alone in an alien world. Wanting to belong somewhere and to someone.

CHARLES JOHNSON, *Middle Passage,* 1990

I had learned to live with myself and for myself. Living as a prisoner in solitary confinement for four years had not destroyed my personality, nor poisoned my attitude toward people.

BENJAMIN DAVIS, JR., *Benjamin Davis, Jr.: An Autobiography,* 1991

AMBITION

A man with too much ambition cannot sleep in peace.

AFRICA

A big fish is caught with big bait.

SIERRA LEONE

If you never reach, you're never going to grab what you're after.

TRADITIONAL

Jump at the sun, you may not land on the sun, but at least you'll be off the ground.

TRADITIONAL

If you don't grab for yourself then nothing is going to help you.

TRADITIONAL

If slaves have a bad master, his ambition is to get a better one, when he gets a better, he aspires to have the best; and when he gets the best, he aspires to be his own master.

FREDERICK DOUGLASS, "An Appeal to the British People," speech given in Moorfield, England, 12 May 1846

Strive to make something of yourself; then strive to make the most of yourself.

ALEXANDER CRUMMELL, speech to high school graduating class, Washington, D.C., 6 June 1884

The treacheries of ambition never cease.

RUBEN DARIO, *To Columbus,* 1892

We have sat on the river bank and caught catfish with pin hooks. The time has come to harpoon a whale.

JOHN HOPE, c. 1900

People mistake their limitations for high standards.

JEAN TOOMER, *Remember and Return,* 1931

Aspire to be, and all that we are not God will give us credit for trying.

NANNIE BURROUGHS, in "Unload Your Uncle Toms," *Louisiana Weekly,* 23 December 1933

No matter how far a person can go the horizon is still way beyond you.

ZORA NEALE HURSTON, *Their Eyes Were Watching God,* 1937

Most of us who aspire to be tops in our fields don't really consider the amount of work required to stay tops.

ALTHEA GIBSON, *So Much To Live For,* 1968

I rise above my self/ like a fish flying.

LUCILLE CLIFTON, *Good News About the Earth,* 1972

Always aim high, never aim low. If you aspire to lofty things, you have accomplished much even though you have not reached the topmost round.

WILLIAM HASTIE, *Grace Under Pressure,* 1984

AMERICA

Let no man of us budge one step, and let slaveholders come to beat us from our country. America is more our country, than it is the whites—we have enriched it with our *blood and tears.* The greatest riches in all America have arisen from our blood and tears.

DAVID WALKER, *Appeal to the Coloured Citizens of the World,* 1829

They came to our shores a lone shelterless few,/ They drank of our cup, and they e'er found us true,/ But the serpent we cherished and warmed at our breast,/ Has coiled round our vitals; let time tell the rest.

MIAMI INDIAN, "This Soil Shall Be Ours," written during the Seminole Wars, 1837

This is called "the land of the free and the home of the brave"; 'it is called the "asylum of the oppressed," and some have been foolish enough to call it the "Cradle of Liberty." If it is the "Cradle of Liberty," they have rocked the child to death.

WILLIAM WELLS-BROWN, speech given to Female Anti-Slavery Society, Salem, Massachusetts, 14 November 1847

You degrade us and then ask why we are degraded. You shut our mouths and ask why we don't speak. You close your colleges and seminaries against us and then ask why we don't know.

FREDERICK DOUGLASS, "Country, Conscience and the Anti-Slavery Course," 1847

It is idle—worse than idle, ever to think of our expatriation, or removal. . . . We are here, and here we are likely to be. To imagine that we shall ever be eradicated is absurd and ridiculous. We can be remodified, changed and assimilated, but never extinguished. We repeat, therefore, that we are here; and that this is our country; and the question for the philosophers and statesmen of the land ought to be, "What principles should dictate the policy of action toward us?" We shall neither die out, nor be driven out, but shall go with these people, either as a testimony against them, or as evidence in their favor throughout their generation. . . .The white man's happiness cannot be purchased by the Black man's misery.

FREDERICK DOUGLASS, "The Destiny of Colored Americans," *North Star,* 16 November 1849

I know this was the soil on which I was born: but I have nothing to glorify this as my country. I have no pride of ancestry to point back to. Our forefathers did not come here as did the Pilgrim fathers, in search of a place where they could enjoy civil and religious liberties.

AUGUSTUS WASHINGTON, "African Colonization—By A Man of Color," *New York Daily Tribune,* July 1851

America, it is to thee/ Thousands hast boasted land of liberty/ It is to thee I raise my song/ Though land of blood and crime and wrong.

JAMES WHITFIELD, "America," 1853

Let the greedy foreigners know that a part of this country belongs to us: and that we assert the right to live and labor here; . . . Our fathers have fought for this country, and helped free it from the British yoke. We are now fighting to free it from the combined conspiracy of Jeff Davis and Co.; we are doing so with the distinct understanding that WE ARE TO HAVE ALL OUR RIGHTS AS MEN AND CITIZENS, and there will be no side issues, NO RESERVATIONS, either political, civil, or religious.

JAMES PENNINGTON, speech given in Poughkeepsie, New York, August 1863

It appears to me that America has become like the great city of Babylon. . . . She is indeed a seller of slaves and the souls of men.

MARIA W. STEWART, *Meditations from the Pen of Mrs. Maria W. Stewart,* 1879

There is nothing so indigenous, so completely "made in America" as we Blacks.

WILLIAM WELLS-BROWN, *My Southern Home,* 1880

As an American citizen I feel it born in my nature to share in the fullest measure all that is American. I sympathize in all my hopes, aspirations, and fruitions of my country. In a word, I am an American citizen, I have a heritage in each and every provision incorporated in the Constitution of my country.

T. THOMAS FORTUNE, *Black and White Lands: Politics in the South,* 1884

I have no patriotism. I have no country. What country have I? The institutions of this country do not recognize me as a man. I am not thought of, spoken of, in any direction, out of the anti-slavery ranks, as a man. I am not thought of, spoken of, except as a piece of property belonging to some *Christian* slaveholder, and all the religious and political institutions of this country alike pronounce me a slave and a chattel.

FREDERICK DOUGLASS, "The Right to Criticize American Institutions," speech given to Anti-Slavery Society, 11 May 1887

America cannot always sit as queen in peace and and repose. Prouder and stronger governments than hers have been shattered by the bolts of a just God.

FREDERICK DOUGLASS, "Government and Its Subjects," *North Star,* 9 November 1889

America will destroy herself and revert to barbarism if she continues to cultivate things of the flesh and reject the higher virtues.

NANNIE BURROUGHS, in *The Southern Workman,* July 1927

The white man does not understand the Indian for the reason that he does not understand America. He is too far removed from its formative processes. The roots of the tree of his life have not yet grasped the rock and soil.

LUTHER STANDING BEAR, *Land of the Spotted Eagle,* 1933

The meaning of America is the possibilities of the common man. It is a refutation of that widespread assumption that the real makers of the world must always be a small group of exceptional men, while most men are incapable of assisting civilization or achieving culture. The United States of America proves, if it proves anything, that the number of men who may be educated and may achieve is much larger than the world has hitherto assumed.

W. E. B. DU BOIS, "What the Negro Has Done for the

United States and Texas," address given at the opening of the Hall of Negro Life, 1936

We're no more or less than other Americans . . . we're just people . . . white, black, yellow, brown. . . . In our working, our loving, our sorrowing, and our dying we are making America of Now and Tomorrow, just as we helped make it Yesterday.

WALTER TURPIN, *These Low Grounds,* 1937

America was the land of education and opportunity. It was a new land to which all people who had youth and a youthful mind turned.

CLAUDE MCKAY, *My Green Hills of Jamaica,* 1946

O, yes,/ I say it plain,/ America never was America to me,/ And yet I swear this oath—/ America will be!

LANGSTON HUGHES, "Let America Be America Again," in Bontemps, ed., *Poetry of the Negro,* 1949

I love America more than any other country in the world, and, exactly for this reason, I insist on the right to criticize her perpetually.

JAMES BALDWIN, *Notes of a Native Son,* 1955

America is essentially a dream, a dream as yet unfulfilled. It is a dream of a land where men of all races, of all nationalities and of all creeds can live together as brothers.

MARTIN LUTHER KING, JR., "The American Dream," speech given at Lincoln University, Oxford, Pennsylvania, 6 June 1961

But oh! I was reluctant coming back,/ I felt like one expelled from heaven to hell./ To the arena packed of black and white,/ America's heart-breaking spectacle.

CLAUDE MCKAY, "Note on Harlem," in Wagner, *Black Poets of the United States,* 1963

America is a great nation, but—. That but is a commentary on two hundred and more years of chattel slavery and on twenty million Negro men and women deprived of life, liberty and the pursuit of happiness. That but stands for practical materialism that is often more interested in things than values.

MARTIN LUTHER KING, JR., *Strength to Love,* 1963

America is not the world and if America is going to become a nation, she must find a way . . . to use the tremendous potential and tremendous energy which this [black] child represents. If this country does not find a way to use that energy, it will be destroyed by that energy.

JAMES BALDWIN, "A Talk to Harlem Teachers," in Clarke, *Harlem, USA,* 1964

The American Negro people is North American in origin and has evolved under specifically American conditions: climatic, nutritional, historical, political and social. It takes its character from the experience of American slavery and the struggle for, and the achievement of, emancipation; from the dynamics of American race and caste discrimination, and from living in a highly industrialized society. . . .

RALPH ELLISON, "Some Questions and Some Answers," *Shadow and Act,* 1964

We have to undo the millions of little white lies that America told itself and the world about the American Black man.

JOHN KILLENS, "Black Revolution and the White Backlash," speech given at Town Hall Forum, New York City, 15 June 1964

This country does not know what to do with its black population, now that they are no longer a source of wealth, are no longer to be bought and sold and bred like cattle.

JAMES BALDWIN, c. 1965

Until the moment comes when we, the Americans, are able to accept the fact that my ancestors are black and white, that on that continent we are trying to forge a new identity, that we need each other, that I am not a ward of America, I am not an object of missionary, I am one of the people who built this country . . . there is scarcely any hope for the American Dream. If they are denied participation in it, by their very presence they will wreck it.

JAMES BALDWIN, "The American Dream Is at the Expense of the American Negro," speech given in Cambridge, England, February 1965

Americans take their vices with them wherever they go.

JOHN WILLIAMS, *Beyond the Angry Black*, 1966

America is a nation that lies to itself about who and what it is. It is a nation of minorities ruled by a minority of one—it thinks and acts as if it were a nation of white Anglo-Saxons and Protestants.

HAROLD CRUSE, *The Crisis of the Negro Intellectual*, 1967

The Black man must find himself as a Black man before he can find himself as an American. He must now become a hyphenated American discovering the hyphen so that he can eventually lose it.

JAMES FARMER, in *Progressive*, January 1968

America is reaping the harvest of hate and shame planted through generations of educational denial, political disfranchisement and economic exploitation of its black population.

MARTIN LUTHER KING, JR., in "Showdown for Nonviolence," *Look*, 16 April 1968

America, our native land, is but a hopeful weed.

CONRAD KENT RIVERS, "Wordsworth for a Native Son," in *The Still Voice of Harlem*, 1968

Being black in America has nothing to do with skin color. To be black means that your heart, your soul, your mind and your body are where the dispossessed are.

JAMES CONE, *Black Theology and Black Power*, 1969

America is both racist and anti-feminist.

SHIRLEY CHISHOLM, speech given before Congress, 1970

Before you people ever crossed the ocean to come to this country, and from that time to this, you have never proposed to buy a country that was equal to this in riches. My friends, this country that you have come to buy is the best country that we have . . . this country is mine, I was raised in it, my forefathers lived and died in it; and I wish to remain in it.

KANGI WIYAKA (CROW FEATHER), in Brown, *Bury My Heart at Wounded Knee*, 1971

America is our oven, but there are ways to survive in ovens, too. The oven's heat makes metal stronger.

JOHN O'NEAL, "Black Arts: Notebook," in Gayle, ed., *The Black Aesthetic*, 1971

What a man does to his own kids he will do to everybody else. By attacking her own kids, America has finally given full sway to her suicidal tendencies.

DICK GREGORY, *No More Lies*, 1971

America is me. It gave me the only life I know so I must share in its survival.

GORDON PARKS, *Born Black*, 1971

The American—a titan enamored of progress, a fanatical giant who worships "getting things done" but never asks himself what he is doing or why he is doing it. His activity is not creative play but mindless sport; he drops bombs in Vietnam and sends messages home on Mother's Day; he believes in sentimental love and his sadism goes by the name of mental hygiene; he razes cities and visits his psychiatrist. He is still tied by his umbilical cord even though he is the explorer of outer space. . . . He does not suffer from hubris; he is simply lawless, perpetually repentant and perpetually self-satisfied.

OCTAVIO PAZ, *Alternating Currents*, 1973

America's made bigger promises than almost any other country in history. We're told that everyone's entitled to this and to that. We've got this hip Constitution and this precious Bill of Rights. We make the promises, we talk and talk, but often we don't do the deed.

RAY CHARLES, *Brother Ray*, 1978

[America] masquerades as the leader of the so-called free world in the campaign against communism.

NELSON MANDELA, *The Struggle Is My Life*, 1978

In America the government took the land from the Indians and then established laws protecting private property. So to set Blacks free with no money or resources and then sit back and wait for them to succeed results in all kinds of difficulties.

ALVIN POUSSAINT, "The Challenge of the Black Family," *Message,* October 1987

[R]acial strains do not exist separately in a man but blend to form a new product ... [and] are creating a new people in this world, a people to whom all Americans, without exception, belong.

JEAN TOOMER, in Kerman and Eldridge, *The Lives of Jean Toomer,* 1987

A few generations from now, the Negro will still be dark, and a portion of his psychology will spring from this fact, but in all else he will be a conformist to the general outlines of American civilization, or of American chaos.

Ibid.

America has abandoned the strong woman of spirituality and is shacking up with the harlot of materialism.

JOSEPH LOWERY, c. 1989

America is the greatest nation in history. Measure it however you like. We are a mere five percent of the world's population, but produce thirty percent of the goods and services. In science, mathematics, and medicine, we walk away with most of the Nobel Prizes. In the Olympics, our amateurs defeat the state-supported athletic elite of other nations. And with America doing eighty-five percent of all world giving, you'd think we invented charity.

WALTER E. WILLIAMS, "Why We're Number One," *Success,* March 1989

America is sorely in need of a renewed effort to eliminate racist attitudes. One symptom of these persistent attitudes is the nomenclature applied to Greek Americans, Italian Americans, Turkish Americans, Black Americans, and other ethnic groups.... We are all simply Americans ... the unnecessary labeling of people by race ... or ethnicity does nothing to bring the many diverse groups of American society together.

BENJAMIN DAVIS, JR., *Benjamin Davis, Jr.: An Autobiography,* 1991

[A]merica is a rainbow.... America is European and African and *much more.* It is the "much more"—Indians, Asians, Latinos, and others—which makes this country a rainbow.

JAMES CONE, *Martin and Malcolm and America,* 1991

The future of America and the world depends upon the ability and determination of the majority to manage diversity, sustain pluralism, celebrate differences and achieve equality and justice for all.

CHARLES G. ADAMS, sermon given at Hartford Church, Detroit, Michigan, 15 January 1991

ANCESTORS

See also BRIDGES

Follow in the footsteps of your ancestors for the mind is trained through knowledge. Behold, their words endure in books. Open and read them and follow their wise counsel.

PTAH HOTEP, c. 2340 B.C.

There are no unknown words, utterances, or sayings in new languages that have not already been said by the ancestors.

SENUSRET II, 2150 B.C.

I have told you what future generations will learn about your ancestors, but what will we be able to relate to our sons so that your memory will stay alive, what will we have to teach our sons about you? What unprecedented exploits, what unheard-of feats? By what distinguished actions will our sons be brought to regret not having lived in the time of Sundiata?

MALI GRIOT MAMADOU KOUYATE, *Sundiata: An Epic of Old Mali,* 1217–37 A.D.

Ancestors, ancestors guide me to whatever I'm looking for whatever it may be.

ETHIOPIA

My father was a Creole, his father a Negro, and his father a monkey; my family, it seems, begins where yours left off.

ALEXANDRE DUMAS (when asked of his ancestry)

Years ago I resolved that because I had no ancestry myself I would leave a record of which my children would be proud, and which might encourage them to still higher effort.

BOOKER T. WASHINGTON, *Up From Slavery,* 1901

We need the historian and philosopher to give us with trenchant pen, the story of our forefathers and let our soul and body with phosphorescent light, brighten the chasm that separates us. We should cling to them just as blood is thicker than water.

ARTHUR SCHOMBURG, *Racial Integrity,* 1913

Meanwhile, the men with vestiges of pomp,/ Race memories of king and caravan,/ High priests, an ostrich and a juju-man,/ Go singing through the footpaths of the swamp.

JEAN TOOMER, "Georgia Dusk," *Cane,* 1923

When one is on the soil of one's ancestors, most anything can come to one.

JEAN TOOMER, *Fern,* 1923

Teach your children they are direct descendants of the greatest and proudest race who ever peopled the earth.

MARCUS GARVEY, 1926

My ancestors were among the first to people America. Men and women of my family were brought over as slaves in 1620.

PAUL ROBESON, "I, Too, Am American," *Reynolds News,* London, 27 February 1949

We cry among the skyscrapers/ As our ancestors/ Cried among the palms in Africa. Because we are alone/ It is night and we're afraid.

LANGSTON HUGHES, "Afraid," *Montage of a Dream Deferred,* 1951

You wouldn't be in this country if some enemy hadn't kidnapped you and brought you here. On the other hand some of you think you came here on the Mayflower.

MALCOLM X, in *Malcolm X Speaks,* 1965

Who would not be wise on the path so long walked upon by my ancestors?

LIHOLIHO, KAMEHAMEHA IV, in *Hawaiian Reflections,* 1970

To acknowledge our ancestors means we are aware that we did not make ourselves, that the line stretches all the way back, perhaps, to God; or to Gods. We remember them because it is an easy thing to forget: that we are not the first to suffer, rebel, fight, love and die. The grace with which we embrace life, in spite of the pain, the sorrows, is always a measure of what has gone before.

ALICE WALKER, in *Revolutionary Petunias,* 1970

How many silent centuries sleep in my sultry veins?/ The cries of tribal dancers call from far off buried plains;/ The plaintive songs of India, the melodies of Spain;/ The rhythms of their tom-tom drums. . . .

MARGARET WALKER, "How Many Silent Centuries Sleep in My Sultry Veins?" *Prophets for a New Day,* 1970

Why are our ancestors/ always kings and princes/ and never the common people?

DUDLEY RANDALL, "Ancestors," *More to Remember,* 1971

Ancestors of mine came from the Ghanian coast and begat with some Englishman who was a blacksmith. Thus, my English name and my African loyalty.

LORRAINE HANSBERRY, *Les Blancs,* 1972

We, today, stand on the shoulders of our predecessors who have gone before us. We, as their successors, must catch the torch of freedom and liberty passed on to us by our ancestors. We cannot lose in this battle.

BENJAMIN E. MAYS, "I Knew Carter G. Woodson," *Negro History Bulletin,* March 1981

Our ancestors are an ever widening circle of hope.

TONI MORRISON, in "Rootedness: The Ancestor as Foundation," in Evans, ed., *Black Women Writers,* 1984

The griot symbolizes how all human ancestry goes back to some place, and some time where there was no writing. Then the memories and the mouths of ancient elders was the only way that early histories of government passed along for all of us to know who we are.

ALEX HALEY, in "We Must Honor Our Ancestors," *Ebony,* August 1986

My son, now is the time to tell you that every village has, actually, three different sets of people.

First there are those whom your grandmother has just joined in eternity. Then the second set of people are those like you and me, now here walking around and talking amidst our brothers and sisters within our village, and in neighboring villages. And our third set of people are those yet unborn, my son. They are seeds in your and your playmates' loins, who quicker than we can realize will replace first me and then you when also we will join your grandmother in eternity.

Ibid.

Your ancestors took the lash, the branding iron, humiliations and oppression because one day they believed you would come along to flesh out the dream.

MAYA ANGELOU, *All God's Children Need Traveling Shoes,* 1986

[D]eath does not separate us from our ancestors. The spirits of our ancestors are ever-present. We make sacrifices to them and ask for their advice and guidance. They answer us in dreams or through a medium like the medicine men and women we call *isangoma.*

MIRIAM MAKEBA, *My Story,* 1987

The traditional guidelines of our ancestors are the progressive directions and manifestations of our art today . . . a sacred living art that works towards promoting symbols and effects that are synonymous with spiritual progress . . . and blackness will be our accomplishment.

ADEMOLA OLUGEBEFOLA, in *Black Art: Ancestral Legacy,* 1989

ANGER

Swift is the speech of one who is angered.

INSTRUCTION OF AMENEMOPE, 18th dynasty, Egypt

If you wash yourself in anger you never have clean hands.

TRADITIONAL

Violence of language leads to violence of action. Angry men seldom fight if their tongues do not lead the fray.

CHARLES V. ROMAN, *American Civilization and the Negro,* 1916

All day long and all night through,/ One thing only must I do:/ Quench my pride and cool my blood,/ Lest I perish in the flood/ Lest a hidden ember set/ Timber that I thought was wet/ Burning like the dryest flax,/ Melting like the merest wax . . .

COUNTEE CULLEN, "Heritage," *Color,* 1925

I always feel/ about to foam with rage/ against what surrounds me/ against what prevents me/ ever/ from being/ a man.

LÉON DAMAS, "So Often," *Pigments,* 1937

You must be willing to suffer the anger of the opponent, and yet not return anger. No matter how emotional your opponents are, you must remain calm.

MARTIN LUTHER KING, JR., *Stride Toward Freedom,* 1958

When [people] get angry, they aren't interested in logic, they aren't interested in odds, they aren't interested in consequences. When they get angry, they realize that the condition that they're in—that their suffering is unjust, immoral, illegal, and that anything they do to correct or eliminate it, they're justified. When you and I develop that type of anger and speak in that voice, then we'll get some kind of respect and recognition, and some changes from these people who have been promising us falsely already for far too long.

MALCOLM X, "With Mrs. Fannie Lou Hamer," speech given 20 December 1964

Anger made us terribly aware that something is wrong because it does not spring wantonly out of air: it has an originating cause. But anger also blinds and therefore limits and weakens: it cripples those who suffer it, and in the end those who have caused it.

JOHN WILLIAMS, *Beyond the Angry Young Black,* 1966

In me there is a rage to defy/ the order of the stars/ despite their pretty patterns.

ALICE WALKER, "Rage," *Revolutionary Petunias,* 1970

Muffle your rage. Get smart instead of muscular.

ROY WILKINS, in "Interview: Roy Wilkins and Nikki Giovanni," *Encore,* May 1973

Every Black woman in America lives her life somewhere along a wide curve of ancient and unexpressed anger.

AUDRE LORDE, *Sister Outsider,* 1974

Outrage is born of resentment and implies the will to resist.

R. SARIF EASMON, "Heart of a Judge," *The Feud,* 1981

When a man angers you, he conquers you.

TONI MORRISON, "Rootedness: The Ancestor as Foundation," in Evans, ed., *Black Women Writers,* 1984

I believed in myself. I carried a burning anger in me at the advantage that people had taken of me—at the discrimination that I had suffered as a people. I find it difficult to understand why everyone does not burn with that same rage. You could be sustained by that resentment. I still have it. It makes you want to get whatever you have to get in order to improve yourself.

COLEMAN A. YOUNG, in *USA Today,* 31 January 1985

I always knew that fury was my natural enemy. It clotted my blood and clogged my pores. It literally blinded me so that I lost my peripheral vision.

MAYA ANGELOU, *All God's Children Need Traveling Shoes,* 1986

It's better to get smart than to get mad. I try not to get so insulted that I will not take advantage of an opportunity to persuade people to change their minds.

JOHN H. JOHNSON, in *USA Today,* 16 April 1986

Each knell of the clock/ hounds my growing rage.

EUGENE REDMOND, "My Study is a Battleground," in Finn, *Voices of Negritude,* 1988

[I]f people could make me angry they could control me. Why should I give someone else such power over my life?

BENJAMIN CARSON, *Gifted Hands,* 1990

Anger is like the blade of a sword. Very difficult to hold for long without harming oneself.

CHARLES JOHNSON, *Middle Passage,* 1990

Anger and humor are like the left and right arm. They complement each other. Anger empowers the poor to declare their uncompromising opposition to oppression, and humor prevents them from being consumed by their fury.

JAMES CONE, *Martin and Malcolm and America,* 1991

APARTHEID

The interest of humanity compels every nation to take steps against such inhumanity and barbarity and to act in concert to eliminate apartheid from the world.

KWAME NKRUMAH, speech given at the United Nations, 23 September 1960

Apartheid seems utterly indifferent to the suffering of individual persons, who lose their land, their homes, their jobs, in the pursuit of what is surely the most terrible dream in the world.

ALBERT LUTHULI, "The Dignity of Man," 1961 Nobel Peace Prize acceptance speech

Apartheid is simply one form of the division into compartments of the colonized world.

FRANTZ FANON, *The Wretched of the Earth,* 1963

And another man with no pass was led away. God bless us thy children, with a hoarse voice and a body that trembled all over. And then as the blue uniforms stood before him, the last triumphant role.

RICHARD RIVE, "God Bless Africa, Nkosi Sikele Africa," *African Song,* 1963

Apartheid stirs hatred and frustration among people. Young people who should be in school or learning a trade roam the streets, join gangs, and wreak their revenge on the society that confronts them with the dead end alley of crime or poverty.

NELSON MANDELA, c. 1968

They arrested the bedspread/ they and their friends are working/ to arrest the dreams in our heads/ and the women, accustomed to closing the eyes of the dead/ are weaving cloth still brighter/ to drape us in glory in a Free Azania.

LORNA GOODISON, "Bedspread," *I Am Becoming a Woman,* 1969

Every American moral, economic, and political force must be brought to bear to help influence the South African government to move toward dismantling the apartheid system.

LEON SULLIVAN, in the *Negro History Bulletin,* February 1986

Apartheid . . . is a combined creation of [religion and politics]. . . . The [Dutch Reformed] Church give[s] the Nationalist party its license to oppress.

CLARENCE GLOVER, in "Spirituality: An African View," *Essence,* December 1987

[In] 1948, . . . a new word enters our language: apartheid. It will become one of the most hated words the world has ever known. The Boers are going to create the type of country they always wanted, and to do this they must make us, the natives, invisible.

MIRIAM MAKEBA, *My Story,* 1987

Apartheid will only work if everything associated with black is worthless.

Ibid.

[Apartheid] is the only surviving ideology in the world with its roots still firmly planted in the old ideology of Adolf Hitler and Nazism.

ALLAN BOESAK, in "Boesak: South African Revolutionary," *Essence,* April 1988

[In apartheid] racial discrimination is legalized. It is written into the constitution . . . The system is so thoroughly evil that it cannot be reformed.

Ibid.

We declare to South Africa—Freedom is coming to us. We don't want apartheid to survive even one more day. So long as it survives, it will continue to kill and shed the blood of our people—even our children.

NELSON MANDELA, speech given in Detroit, Michigan, 28 June 1990

ART/ARTIST

No artist's skills are perfect.

PTAH HOTEP, c. 2340 B.C.

Oh, how great and glorious art is! It shows more devotion than a friend, it is more faithful than a mistress, more consoling than a confessor.

ALEXANDRE DUMAS, *My Memoirs,* 1822–25

Pictures come not with slavery and oppression and destitution, but with liberty, fair play, leisure, and refinement.

FREDERICK DOUGLASS, *Narrative of the Life and Times of Frederick Douglass,* 1845

Art is of great value to any people as a preserver of manners and customs—religious, political, and social. It is a record of growth and development from generation to generation. No one will do this for us: we must ourselves develop the men and women who faithfully portray the inmost thought and feelings with all the fire and romance which lie dormant in our history.

PAULINE HOPKINS, c. 1900

Art is not simply works of art; it is the spirit that knows Beauty, that has music in its soul and the color of sunsets in its handkerchief, that can dance on a flaming world and make the world dance too.

W. E. B. DU BOIS, *The Souls of Black Folk,* 1903

Art is signalling man's conquest of the world by its symbols of beauty, springing up in spots that were barren of all voices and colour. . . . Art is like the spread of vegetation to show how far man has reclaimed the desert of his own.

RABINDRANATH TAGORE, *Personality,* 1917

The road for the serious black artist, then, who would produce racial art is most certainly rocky and the mountain is high. Until recently he received almost no encouragement for his work from either white or colored people.

LANGSTON HUGHES, "The Negro Artist and the Racial Mountain," *The Nation,* 23 June 1926

An artist must be free to choose what he does, certainly, but he must also never be afraid to do what he might choose.

Ibid.

African art had done much to influence artistic productions of all people.

CARTER G. WOODSON, *Negro Makers of History,* 1928

It is only possible to render well in art what one understands thoroughly.

PAUL ROBESON, in "Paul Robeson Speaks Out About Art and the Negro," *The Millgate,* December 1930

Life is greater than all art . . . the man whose life comes nearest to perfection is the greatest artist; for what is art without the sure foundation and framework of a noble life?

MOHANDAS GANDHI, *Lenin and Gandhi*, 1930

To what end does the West rule the world if all art dies?

PAUL ROBESON, "I Am at Home," *Daily Worker*, 15 January 1935

I am producing strictly a Negro art, studying not the culturally mixed of the cities, but the more primitive types. Very few artists have gone into the history of the Negro in America, cutting back to the sources and the origins of the life of the race in this country.

SARGENT JOHNSON, in the *San Francisco Chronicle*, 6 October 1935

Every man has some element of the artist in him, and if this is pulled up by the roots he becomes suicidal and dies.

PAUL ROBESON, in "Primitives," *New Statesman and Nation*, 8 August 1936

The artist must elect to fight for Freedom or for Slavery.

PAUL ROBESON, "Why I Joined Labor Theater," *Daily Worker*, 24 November 1937

To be an artist, one must first be a man, vitally concerned with all problems of social struggle . . . never shirking from the truth as he understands it, never withdrawing from life.

DIEGO RIVERA, c. 1940

An artist deals with aspects of reality different from those which a scientist sees.

RICHARD WRIGHT, *12 Million Black Voices*, 1941

Art . . . cannot be an egotistic activity engulfed in the limits of pure creation, free of all human contaminations.

NICHOLAS GUILLÉN, speech given at the Cultural and Scientific Conference, New York City, 25 March 1949

Art is animated by invisible forces that rule the universe.

LEOPOLD SENGHOR, speech given at the First Congress of Negro Artists and Writers, Paris, 1956

Art must be functional, collecting, and committing.

Ibid.

Art is life.

Ibid.

All art is a kind of confession, more or less oblique. All artists, if they are to survive, are forced at least to tell the whole story; to vomit the anguish up.

JAMES BALDWIN, c. 1961

An artist's first responsibility is to himself.

MILES DAVIS, in *Ebony*, January 1961

Artists are at war with society and if the artist is a Black man in the Free World, he is doubly at war and the war's consequences are especially dangerous. But he/she must fight in any event, for the consequences of his temporizing are fraught with even greater danger.

JOHN KILLENS, "Black Revolution and the White Backlash," speech given at the Town Hall Forum, New York City, 15 June 1964

Our art has always been the art of the people, whose welfare has ever been our overriding care. We have always been close to the people, for we have come from them. For art is and must always remain a living, thinking, and serving part of the community to which it belongs.

KWAME NKRUMAH, c. 1965

All art is a communication of the artist's ideas, sounds, thoughts.

LIONEL HAMPTON, in the *New York Journal American*, 31 August 1965

The artist must draw out of his soul the correct image of the world. He must use this image to band his brothers and sisters together.

LEROI JONES, *Home, Social Essays*, 1966

Great art can only be created out of love.

JAMES BALDWIN, in "James Baldwin . . . in Conversation," *Arts in Society*, Summer 1966

Art for art's sake is an invalid concept; all art reflects the value system from which it comes; for if the artist created only for himself and not for others, he would lock himself up somewhere and paint and play just for himself.

RON KARENGA, in "Black Cultural Nationalism," *Negro Digest,* August 1968

Art is everyday life, given more form and color.

Ibid.

For all African art meaning flows plainly from the signs used to express it.

FRANCES BEBY, *African Music: A People's Art,* 1969

'Primitive' art is . . . vital art.

ELIO POMARE, in *Ebony,* December 1969

Art doesn't come from history or scholasticism. Art comes from life itself.

Ibid.

African art is an attempt to capture the energy or the essence of a thing.

JAMES BALDWIN, *A Rap on Race,* 1971

Art cannot disdain the gift of a natural irony, of a transfiguring imagination, of rhapsodic Biblical speech, of dynamic musical swing, of cosmic emotion such as only the gifted pagans knew . . . not by way of the forced and worn formula of Romanticism, but through the closeness of an imagination that has never broken kinship with nature. Art must accept such gifts, and revaluate the giver.

ALAIN LOCKE, "Negro Youth Speaks," in Gayle, ed., *The Black Aesthetic,* 1971

The artist and the political activist are one. They are both shapers of the future reality. Both understand and manipulate the collective myths of the race. Both are warriors, priests, lovers, and destroyers.

LARRY NEAL, in *ibid.*

The task of pointing out northern duplicity was left to the black artist.

ADDISON GAYLE, in *ibid.*

Art is inseparable from life, and form and content are one.

PAULE MARSHALL, in *New Letter,* Autumn 1973

The Europeans who went to Africa came back with "modern" art. What is more African than a Picasso?

DUKE ELLINGTON, *Music Is My Mistress,* 1973

The artist must say it without saying it.

Ibid.

The ultimate in art is self-expression, not escape.

Ibid.

We must invest in images that are important to us. Black people and institutions have got to learn and acknowledge our visual history. It is the seed of Western art as we know it.

DOROTHY DISNER, c. 1975

ART is refining and evocative translation of the materials of the world.

GWENDOLYN BROOKS, in *Black Poetry Writing,* 1975

The Black artist by defining and legitimizing his own reality becomes a positive force in the Black community.

HAKI MADHUBUTI, in *ibid.*

We look too much to museums. The sun coming up in the morning is enough.

ROMARE BEARDEN, "The Field of the Fever, the Time of the Tall Walker," *Ebony,* 1975

Art is really the realm of the ancestral world of images so confined as it were to creativity in a spiritual world.

BEN ENWONWE, in Paster, *The Roots of Soul,* 1982

The artist . . . is the voice of the people, . . . she is also The People.

ALICE WALKER, *In Search of Our Mothers' Gardens,* 1983

Art . . . reacts to or reflects the culture it springs from.

SONIA SANCHEZ, "Ruminations/Reflections," in Evans, ed., *Black Women Writers,* 1984

Art is not living. It is a use of living. The artist has the ability to take that living and use it in a certain way, and produce art.

AUDRE LORDE, "My Words Will Be There," in *ibid.*

An artist represents an oppressed people and makes revolution irresistible.

TONI CADE BAMBARA, "Salvation Is the Issue," in *ibid.*

Folkway is the basis of art.

Ibid.

Art is timeless.

TONI MORRISON, "Rootedness: The Ancestor as Foundation," in *ibid.*

Art [is] an assertive statement . . . of an evolving self.

SONDRA O'NEALE, "Reconstruction of the Composite Self," in *ibid.*

No artist should have to struggle. That went out with Modigliani.

GEOFFREY HOLDER, in "Geoffrey Holder Grabs for the Gusto," *Class,* April 1984

Great artists suffer for the people.

MARVIN GAYE, in Ritz, *Divided Soul,* 1985

Art is a way of possessing destiny.

Ibid.

The true artist destroys the accepted world by way of revealing the unseen, and creating that which is new and uniquely his own.

RALPH ELLISON, "The Art of Romare Bearden," *Going to the Territory,* 1986

The work of art is . . . an act of faith in our ability to communicate symbolically.

RALPH ELLISON, "The Little Man at Chehaw Station," in *ibid.*

An art form can influence your thinking, your feeling, the way you dress, the way you walk, how you talk, what you do with yourself.

WYNTON MARSALIS, "Why We Must Preserve Our Jazz Heritage," *Ebony,* February 1986

You have to have serious people to make serious art.

Ibid.

It is a poor people who don't support their culture.

ISHMAEL REED, in "The Visual Arts: Culture or Commodity? Truth or Artifice?" *Crisis,* February 1986

Perhaps at the root of American art is a rivalry between the oppressor and the oppressed, with a secret understanding that the oppressor shall always prevail and make off with the prizes, no matter how inferior his art is to that of his victims.

Ibid.

[A]rt in our day, other than its purely aesthetic phase, has a sort of religious function. It is a religion, a spiritualization of the immediate.

JEAN TOOMER, in Kerman and Eldridge, *The Lives of Jean Toomer,* 1987

Art is about life, art is about death.

GILDA SNOWDEN, in "Interview with Gilda Snowden," *City Arts Quarterly,* Fall–Winter 1987

One of the astonishing things about the artist of ancient times was the freshness with which they depicted Blacks. All Negroes may look alike to some whites, but not to the artist of antiquity.

FRANK SNOWDEN, in "Blacks in the Classical World: Frank Snowden's Fifty-year Search," *American Visions,* October 1987

I'm an artist because this is one aspect of life no one can control but me. Nothing can stop me from creating but the Creator.

BILL SANDERS, in "Bill Sanders," *City Magazine,* December 1987

A people who ignore their artists are placing themselves in grave jeopardy. No society or culture can afford to ignore the most creative among them without detrimental effects.

DANIEL ALDRIDGE, sermon given at the Mayflower Church, February 1988

I see myself as a Black man and as an artist, and when I think about art, I think about it in a broader scope. I explore it as a way of living, of transcending the hype that surrounds us, and I'm able to become a better human being.

DANNY GLOVER, in *Jet,* 15 August 1988

Without the artist we would not have anything.

ABBEY LINCOLN, in "Abbey Sings Billie," *City Arts Quarterly,* Summer 1988

The Lord puts pictures in my head and he means for me to paint them.

CLEMENTINE HUNTER, in *American Visions,* October 1988

The creative artist has always been a controversial figure in the politics of nations. Together with the intellectual and the scholar, he has been generally regarded as a threat to the establishment.

JOSEPH OKPAKU, *New African Literature and the Arts,* 1988

The obligation of being an artist is to tell the story as it was.

AVERY BROOKS, in *Essence,* April 1989

Being an artist is a continual unfolding.

LYNN WHITFIELD, in "People," *Essence,* May 1989

When the artist can make art the medium for a greater love, only triumph is possible.

EDMUND BARRY GAITHER, in *Black Art: Ancestral Legacy,* 1989

My [art] is serious fun.

CHARLES SEARLES, in *ibid.*

The role of art is to express the triumph of the human spirit over the mundane and material . . . to express the universal myths and archetypes of the universal family of man.

JOHN BIGGERS, in *ibid.*

[Art] allows me access into myself.

ED LOVE, in *ibid.*

Art is a creative connection to the past and the present.

SAM GILLIAM, in "Sam Gilliam: Working with His Seven League Boots on," *American Visions,* February 1989

I never painted dreams. I painted my own reality.

FRIDA KAHLO, in Herrera, *Frida Kahlo: The Paintings,* 1991

ATTACK

[A]ttacks against black leadership are going to multiply as the conflict increases in intensity. Witness what happened to the Three M's: Brothers Medgar, Malcolm and Martin.

JOHN OLIVER KILLENS, introduction to *An ABC of Color,* 1963

Those of us who manage to get before the public spend so much time tearing each other apart.

JULIAN MAYFIELD, in *Negro Digest,* September 1967

We never signed a pact either on paper or in our hearts to turn the other cheek forever and ever when we were assaulted.

ROY WILKINS, c. 1968

You pick only so many daggers from your back before you become anesthetized to them.

MARVA COLLINS, in "Marva Collins: Teaching Success in the City," *Message,* July 1987

ATTENTION

Give your brain as much attention as you do your hair and you'll be a thousand times better off.

MALCOLM X, in *Malcolm X on Afro-American History,* 1967

I was enfolded in the attention of the three women who figured so importantly in my childhood. What a wonderful womb to live in.

ADAM CLAYTON POWELL, JR., *Adam by Adam,* 1971

America really respects violence, and she only pays attention when someone is staring at her down the muzzle of a gun.

DICK GREGORY, *No More Lies,* 1971

People don't pay much attention to you when you are second best. I wanted to see what it felt like to be number one.

FLORENCE GRIFFITH JOYNER, in "Spotlight: Life in the Fast Lane," *Essence,* March 1989

ATTITUDE

Anything that is as old as racism is in the blood line of the nation. It's not any superficial thing—that attitude is in the blood and we have to educate it out.

NANNIE BURROUGHS, in "Unload Your Uncle Toms," *Louisiana Weekly,* 23 December 1933

I'm talking of millions of men who have been skillfully injected with the attitude of fear, inferiority complexes, trepidation, servility, despair, and abasement.

AIMÉ CÉSAIRE, 1956

You cannot legislate an attitude.

H. RAP BROWN, *Die Nigger Die,* 1970

Funny is an attitude.

FLIP WILSON, in *Black Stars,* February 1973

Attitude was the most important asset we had to break the back of racism.

TOM BRADLEY, *The Impossible Dream,* 1986

I removed myself from the "Age of the Shrug" with its "so what—it is not my problem" attitude because this is what I was taught to do in a Black college.

MARVA COLLINS, in *Choosing to Succeed,* 1986

AUDIENCE

He who could address this audience without a quailing sensation has stronger nerves than I do.

FREDERICK DOUGLASS, "What to the Slave Is the Fourth of July?" speech given at Corinthian Hall, Rochester, New York, 5 July 1852

My audience wants to see me beautifully gowned, and I have spared no expense or pains . . . for I feel that the best is none too good for the public that pays to hear a singer.

MA RAINEY, in *Norfolk Journal and Guide,* 1921

The main thing is to live for that audience. What you're there for is to please people the best you can. Those few moments belong to them.

LOUIS ARMSTRONG, in *Life,* 16 April 1956

I see their souls, and I hold them in my hands, and because I love them they weigh nothing.

PEARL BAILEY, *The Raw Pearl,* 1968

Imagine a symphony audience snapping its finger or saying, Yeah Baby!

ORTIZ WALTERS, *Music Black White and Blue,* 1980

The artist is free to choose, but cannot limit his audience.

RALPH ELLISON, "The Little Man at Chehaw Station," *Going to the Territory,* 1986

If it wasn't for Black audiences, we wouldn't be here. They are the backbone of our existence.

DOUGLASS TURNER WARD, in "The State of the Arts: Theater," *Crisis,* January 1986

My audience is my life. What I did and how I did it, was all for my audience.

CAB CALLOWAY, 1988

Hollywood perceives that audiences will be uncomfortable with anything that goes beyond Black folks singing and dancing and doing the ha ha hee hee number. That perception is incorrect.

SPIKE LEE, 1988

For years Blacks had no choice but to watch Shakespeare or Beaver Cleavers and see the universal humanity in those white faces. There's no reason white audiences can't make the same imaginative leap today with Black actors.

GEORGE WOLFE, 1991

BALDWIN, JAMES

The . . . literary talent of James Baldwin had no easy birth, and he did not emerge overnight. . . . For years this talent was in incubation in the ghetto of Harlem. . . .

JOHN HENRIK CLARKE, "The Alienation of James Baldwin," *Harlem, USA,* 1964

Speeches will be given, essays written and hefty books will be published on the various lives of James Baldwin. Some fantasies will be broadcast and even some truths will be told. Someone will speak of the essayist James Baldwin in his role as prophet Isaiah admonishing his country to repent from wickedness and create within itself a clean spirit and a clean heart. Others will examine Baldwin, the playwright and novelist who burned with righteous indignation over the paucity of kindness, the absence of love, and crippling hypocrisy he saw in the streets of the United States and sensed in the hearts of his fellow citizens.

MAYA ANGELOU, eulogy of James Baldwin, Cathedral of St. John the Divine, New York City, January 1988

This man traveled the earth like history and its biographer. He reported, criticized, made beautiful, analyzed, cajoled, lyricized, attacked, sang, made us think, made us better, made us consciously human or perhaps more acutely pre-human.

IMAMU AMIRI BARAKA, eulogy of James Baldwin, Cathedral of St. John the Divine, New York City, January 1988

You gave me a language to swell in, a gift so perfect it seems my own invention. No one possessed or inhabited language for me the way you did. You made American English honest—genuinely international. You had the gift of courage. The courage of love—to go as a stranger into the villages and transform the distance between people into intimacy with the world.

TONI MORRISON, eulogy of James Baldwin, Cathedral of St. John the Divine, New York City, January 1988

James Baldwin was a towering literary giant whose brilliant writings illuminated and interpreted the Black experience in a manner that will withstand the test of time. He was an artist with an all-consuming social conscience that exploded in the incandescence of his work. Honesty was in every word he wrote, and rarely has any writer presented a black perspective so eloquently as he. We will miss him, but his legacy is imperishable.

BENJAMIN HOOKS, in "Goodbye, James Baldwin," *Crisis,* January 1988

In his youth James Baldwin was a storefront preacher in Harlem. When he died at age 63, he was among America's most honored writers, and his funeral was held in the vaulted vastness of the Cathedral of St. John the Divine.

WALTER W. MORRISON, in *ibid.*

BATTLE

The battles of the future, whether they be physical or mental, will be fought on scientific lines and the race of the people who are able to produce the highest scientific developments will ultimately lead the world.

MARCUS GARVEY, *Philosophy and Opinions of Marcus Garvey,* 1923

This the American Black man knows: his fight is a fight to the finish. Either he dies or he wins. He will enter modern civilization in America as a Black man on terms of perfect and unlimited equality with any white man, or he will enter not at all. Either extermination root and branch or absolute equality. There can be no compromise. This is the last great battle of the west.

W. E. B. DU BOIS, *Black Reconstruction,* 1935

I was free only in battle, never free to rest—and he who finds no way to rest cannot long survive the battle.

JAMES BALDWIN, *Nobody Knows My Name,* 1961

When the battle is won, let history be able to say to each one of us: He was a dedicated patriot. Dignity was his country, Manhood was his government and Freedom was his land.

JOHN KILLENS, *And Then We Heard the Thunder,* 1963

The cutting edge of the battles will now become the sword's point of the new thrust.

JAMES FARMER, speech given at the Congress on Racial Equality, Durham, North Carolina, 1 July 1965

The battle we are waging now is the battle for the minds of Black people and if we lose this battle, we cannot win the violent one.

RON KARENGA, "Black Cultural Nationalism," *Black World,* 1 January 1968

Being a man is the continuing battle of one's life. One loses a bit of manhood with every stale compromise to the authority of any power in which one does not believe.

H. RAP BROWN, *Die Nigger Die,* 1969

[T]he battles that count aren't the ones for gold medals. The struggles within yourself—the invisible, inevitable battles inside all of us—that's where it's at.

JESSE OWENS, *Blackthink,* 1970

BEAUTY

'Twas then her beauties first enslaved my heart—/ Those glittering pearls and ruby lips,/ whose kiss was sweeter far than honey to the taste.

ANTAR, c. 650–c. 715 A.D.

She is like a road, pretty but crooked.

CAMEROON

You are beautiful; but learn to work, for you cannot eat your beauty.

CONGO

The blacker the berry, the sweeter the juice.

TRADITIONAL

I have gazed at your beauty from the beginning of my existence, that I have kept you in my arms for countless ages, yet it has not been enough for me.

RABINDRANATH TAGORE, *Personality,* 1917

Her skin is like the dusk on the eastern horizon,/ O cant you see it , O cant you see it,/ Her skin is like dusk on the far eastern horizon/ . . . When the sun goes down.

JEAN TOOMER, "Karintha," *Cane,* 1923

I aim to show the natural beauty and dignity in that characteristic lip and hair, bearing, and manner. I wish to show that beauty to the Negro himself. Unless I can interest my race, I am sunk, and this is not so easily accomplished.

SARGENT JOHNSON, in the *San Francisco Chronicle,* 6 October 1935

It must be recess in [heaven] if St. Peter is lettin[g] his angels out. . . .

ZORA NEALE HURSTON, *Their Eyes Were Watching God,* 1937

Zipporah of the tawny skin. Zipporah of the flowing body. Zipporah of the night-black eyes. Zipporah of the luxuriant, crinkly hair that covered her shoulders like a great ruff of feathers. Zipporah of the full, dark red lips. Zipporah of the warm, brown arms.

ZORA NEALE HURSTON, *Moses, Man of the Mountain,* 1939

And let me die suddenly, to be born again in the revelation of beauty. . . . And the revelation of beauty is the wisdom of the ancestors.

AIMÉ CÉSAIRE, "l'Afrique," *Poesie,* 1946

If this gentleman went to the battlefield, surely the enemy would not kill him or capture him and if bombers saw him in a town which was to be bombed, they would not throw bombs in his presence, and if they did throw it, the bomb itself would not explode until this gentleman left that town, because of his beauty.

AMOS TUTUOLA, *Palm Wine Drunkard,* 1952

A sealskin brown will make a preacher lay his Bible down.

TRADITIONAL, in *The Book of Negro Folklore,* 1958

Brown skin mama make a rabbit chase a hound.

Ibid.

The night is beautiful,/ So the faces of my people./ The stars are beautiful./ So the eyes of my people./ Beautiful, also, is the sun./ Beautiful, also, are the souls of my people.

LANGSTON HUGHES, "My People," *Selected Poems*, 1959

She wore big oval earrings like the queen in the picture, but she could not bring herself to wear her hair short and kinky; but sometimes she would look at the picture and see herself there and for the first time in her life, she began to think that she might be beautiful.

SAM GREENLEE, *The Spook Who Sat By the Door*, 1969

My blackness, tender and strong, wounded and wise. My blackness is the beauty of the land.

LANCE JEFFERS, "My Blackness is the Beauty of the Land," *My Blackness is the Beauty of the Land*, 1970

[Langston Hughes] believed in the beauty of blackness when belief in the beauty of blackness was not the fashion, not "the thing," not the sweet berry of the community tooth.

GWENDOLYN BROOKS, *Report From Part One*, 1972

A Satin Doll is a woman who is as pretty on the inside as she is on the outside.

DUKE ELLINGTON, *Music Is My Mistress*, 1973

Pretty can only get prettier, but beauty compounds itself.

J. KENNEDY ELLINGTON, in *ibid.*

We turn outward, attracted by the beauty we see in created things without realizing that they are only a reflection of the real beauty. And the real beauty is within us. And so paradoxically, the more we turn toward beauty, the more we turn away from it. For it is in the opposite direction. We turn outward and it is within.

ERNESTO CARDENAL, "Love," *Vida en al Amor*, 1974

The stranger took my beauty and placed it in my hand. Loveliness beyond the jewels of a throne.

WOLE SOYINKA, *The Lion and the Jewel*, 1975

The more blackness a woman has, the more beautiful she is.

ALEX HALEY, *Roots*, 1977

It was Martin, more than anyone, who exposed the hidden beauty of black people in the South, and caused us to look again at the land our fathers and mothers knew.

ALICE WALKER, *In Search of Our Mothers' Gardens*, 1983

The folk-spirit was walking in to die on the modern desert. That spirit was so beautiful. Its death was so tragic.

JEAN TOOMER, in Kerman and Eldridge, *The Lives of Jean Toomer*, 1987

I love beautiful things, beauty in anything, beauty in an athlete, or just getting up very early in the morning for rehearsals.

JESSYE NORMAN, in "The Norman Conquests," *American Visions*, April 1988

BEGINNING/ORIGINS

In the beginning this universe was nothing but the Self in the form of a man. It looked around and saw there was nothing but itself, whereupon its first shout was "It is I!" whence the concept I arose.

BRIHADARANYAKA UPANISHAD, c. 700 B.C.

We were here before the Anglo-Saxon evolved, and thick lips and heavy lidded eyes looked out from the inscrutable face of the sphinx across the sands of Egypt, while yet the ancestors of those who now oppress him were practicing human sacrifices and painting themselves with wood and the Negro is here yet.

CHARLES W. CHESTNUTT, *The Marrow of Tradition*, 1901

In the beginning there was neither nothing nor anything. Darkness hid in darkness—shrouded in nothingness.

ZORA NEALE HURSTON, *Moses, Man of the Mountain*, 1939

There were bizarre beginnings in old lands for the making of me.

MARGARET WALKER, "Dark Blood," *For My People*, 1942

Even the most incorrigible maverick has to be born somewhere. He may leave the group that produced him—he may be forced to—but nothing will efface his origins, the marks of which he carries with him everywhere.

JAMES BALDWIN, *Nobody Knows My Name,* 1961

Know whence you came. If you know whence you came, there is really no limit to where you can go.

JAMES BALDWIN, *The Fire Next Time,* 1962

Martyrdom does not end something; it is only the beginning.

INDIRA GANDHI, address to Parliament, New Delhi, 12 August 1971

A nation beginning is a proper source of reflective pride only to the extent that the subsequent and continuing process of its becoming deserves celebration.

WILLIAM HASTIE, speech given at Independence Hall, Philadelphia, Pennsylvania, 1976

Life has brought to an end so many things. Evidently it is demanding of me, "Start again. Begin new things. Again set to work to build your world."

JEAN TOOMER, in Kerman and Eldridge, *The Lives of Jean Toomer,* 1987

BEHAVIOR

Make no distinction in your behavior between those of ranks and the common people.

PTAH HOTEP, 2340 B.C.

"Ain't Misbehavin'" was written while I was lodged in the alimony jail, and I wasn't misbehaving, you dig?

FATS WALLER, c. 1930

Even while demonstrating that he is really an equal . . . [he] must never appear to be challenging white superiority. Climb up if you can—but don't act "uppity." Always show that you are *grateful.* (Even if what you have gained has been wrested from unwilling powers, be sure to be grateful lest "they" take it all away.) Above all, *do nothing to give them cause to fear you,* for then the oppressing hand . . . will surely become a fist to knock you down again!

PAUL ROBESON, *Here I Stand,* 1958

There is a code of social behavior among Southern blacks . . . which is as severe and distinct as a seventeenth-century minuet or an African initiation ritual. There is a moment to speak, a tone of voice to be used, words to be carefully chosen, a time to drop one's eyes, and a split-second when a stranger can be touched on the shoulder or arm or even knee without conveying anything more than respectful friendliness.

MAYA ANGELOU, *The Heart of a Woman,* 1981

Black people have no copyright on virtue. People are people; some behave badly and some don't.

RANDALL ROBINSON, in "Interview: Randall Robinson," *Crisis,* November 1986

I am to struggle with myself, first and last. . . . Not with something in you I do not like. And I am to thank you for giving me the opportunity—really thank you, inwardly, and on occasion perhaps outwardly too. This is not the way we usually behave. We merely react, according to which button is pushed.

JEAN TOOMER, in Kerman and Eldridge, *The Lives of Jean Toomer,* 1987

BEING

I, Isis, am all that has been, all that is or shall be, and no mortal man has ever unveiled me.

INSCRIPTION ON TEMPLE OF ISIS

I am not you but you will not give me a chance—will not let me be me.

ROLAND DEMPSTER, "Africa's Plea," *Song Out of Africa,* 1960

I can never be what I ought to be until you are what you ought to be. You can never be what you ought to be until I am what I ought to be.

MARTIN LUTHER KING, JR., "The American Dream," speech given at Lincoln University, Oxford, Pennsylvania, 6 June 1961

I am a part of Being to the degree that I go beyond it.

FRANTZ FANON, *Black Skin, White Masks,* 1967

To be a Negro in this country and to be relatively conscious is to be in rage almost all the time.

JAMES BALDWIN, in Noble, *Beautiful, Also, Are the Souls of My Black Sisters,* 1978

I am going to be a fighter. I am going to be somebody. It gave me a sense of pride and dignity to at least want to be somebody.

JOE LOUIS, *My Life,* 1981

It is difficult to be black and boring.

JANICE HALE BENSON, *Black Child in Education,* 1986

I feel, therefore I think, therefore I am.

Ibid.

We never know we are beings till we love. And then it is we know the powers and the potentialities of human existence, the powers and potentialities of organic, conscious, solar, cosmic matter and force. We, together, vibrate as one in harmony with man and with the cosmos.

JEAN TOOMER, in Kerman and Eldridge, *The Lives of Jean Toomer,* 1987

Be as you are and hope that it's right.

DIZZY GILLESPIE, in "Words of the Week," *Jet,* 23 November 1987

I am alive because of the blood of proud people who never scraped or begged or apologized for what they were. They lived asking only one thing of this world, to be allowed to be. And I learned through the blood of these people that Black isn't beautiful and it isn't ugly, Black is. It's not kinky hair and it's not straight hair—it just is.

GLORIA NAYLOR, *The Women of Brewster Place,* 1988

BELIEF

Whether you believe it or not, I tell you God will dash tyrants, in combination with devils, into atoms, and will bring you out from wretchedness and miseries under these *Christian People!*

DAVID WALKER, *Appeal to the Coloured Citizens of the World,* 1829

A universal human stupidity is the belief that our neighbor's success is the cause of our failure.

CHARLES V. ROMAN, "What the Negro May Reasonably Expect of the White Man," *American Civilization and the Negro,* 1916

Those who believe in ghosts always see them.

CHARLES V. ROMAN, *The Horoscope of Ham,* 1918

We have been believers believing in our burdens and our demigods too long.

MARGARET WALKER, "We Have Been Believers," *For My People,* 1942

My beliefs are now one hundred percent against racism and segregation in any form and I also believe that we don't judge a person by the color of his skin but rather by his behavior and by his deeds.

MALCOLM X, in *Malcolm X Speaks,* 1965

We believed—because we were young . . . and had nothing as yet to risk.

PAULE MARSHALL, "Reena," in Clarke, ed., *American Negro Short Stories,* 1966

Find the good. It's all around you. Find it, showcase it and you'll start believing in it.

JESSE OWENS, *Blackthink,* 1970

Do I believe I'm blessed? Of course, I do! In the first place, my mother told me so, many, many times, and when she did it was always quietly, confidently. . . . and I knew that anything she told me was true.

DUKE ELLINGTON, *Music Is My Mistress,* 1973

To be a great champion you must believe you are the best. If you're not, pretend you are.

MUHAMMAD ALI, speech given at Dacca, Bangladesh, 19 February 1978

My belief in [Martin Luther King] overcame even my disbelief in America.

ALICE WALKER, *In Search of Our Mothers' Gardens,* 1983

Whatever I believed, I did; and whatever I did, I did with my whole heart and mind as far as possible to do so—and thus I gained in intensity of experience what may have taken a less intense person a much longer time.

JEAN TOOMER, in Kerman and Eldridge, *The Lives of Jean Toomer,* 1987

It's very comfortable to pigeonhole someone, put them in a box and put a label on it so that you know what they are and what they do. Now, my belief is that human beings are basically—inherently—versatile. I stand for that versatility.

HERBIE HANCOCK, in "Words of the Week," *Jet,* 26 September 1988

BELONGING

I belong to this race, and when it is down I belong to a down race; when it is up I belong to a risen race.

FRANCES E. W. HARPER, in Still, *The Underground Railroad,* 1872

Nothing is more pathetic than to fit nowhere. Nothing is more pathetic than to be an outcast.

PETER ABRAHAMS, *Dark Testament,* 1942

He belongs someplace. The day he was given a name he was also given a place which no one but he himself can fill. And after his death, that place remains his.

MAYA ANGELOU, *All God's Children Need Traveling Shoes,* 1986

BIBLE

Have not the Americans the Bible in their hands? Do they believe it? Surely they do not. See how they treat us in open violation of the Bible! . . . Our divine Lord and Master said, "All things whatsoever ye would that men should do unto you, do ye even unto them." But an American minister, with the Bible in his hand, holds us and our children in the most abject slavery and wretchedness. . . . I tell you Americans! That unless you speedily alter your course, you and your country are gone!!! Will not that very remarkable Scripture be fulfilled on Christian Americans?

DAVID WALKER, *Appeal to the Coloured Citizens of the World,* 1829

Give a hungry man a stone and tell him that beautiful houses are made of it; give ice to a freezing man and tell him of its good properties in hot weather, throw a drowning man a dollar, as a mark of your good will, but do not mock the bondsman in his misery by giving him a Bible when he cannot read it.

FREDERICK DOUGLASS, *Bibles for Slaves,* 1847

There is a class of people who seem to believe that if a man should fall overboard into the sea with a Bible in his pocket it would hardly be possible to drown.

FREDERICK DOUGLASS, *North Star,* 18 June 1849

For if Cain was the progenitor of Noah and Cain's new peculiarities were perpetuated then as Noah was the father of the world's new population the question would be, not how to account for any of the human family being black, but how can we account for any being white.

WILLIAM WELLS-BROWN, *Rising Sun,* 10 August 1849

For my part I am not giving the slaves the Bible or anything else this side of Freedom. Give him that first and then you need not give him anything else. He can get what he needs.

HENRY BIBB, *Narrative of Life and Adventure of Henry Bibb,* 1849

Perhaps the most valuable thing I got out of my second year [at Hampton University] was an understanding of the use and value of the Bible. . . . Before this I had never cared a great deal about it, but now I learned to love to read the Bible, not only for the spiritual help which it gives, but on account of it as literature.

BOOKER T. WASHINGTON, *Up From Slavery,* 1901

The Bible ought to teach him that he will become a black angel and go home to a black God at death.

MARCUS GARVEY, *Philosophy and Opinions of Marcus Garvey,* 1923

It's a curious thing, that the Bible has been the sole law for two contrasting races—its originators, men of fiery action and inspired thought, and the enslaved Negroes.

PAUL ROBESON, in "The Source of the Negro Spiritual," *Jewish Tribune,* 22 July 1927

"Moses, my servant is dead. Therefore arise and go over Jordan." There are no deliverers. They're all dead. We must arise and go over Jordan. We can take the promised land.

NANNIE BURROUGHS, in "Unload Your Uncle Toms," *Louisiana Weekly,* 23 December 1933

"Whosoever," it said. No Jew, nor Gentile, no Catholic nor Protestant, no black nor white; just "whosoever." It meant that I, a humble Negro girl, had just as much chance as anybody in the sight and love of God. These words stored up a battery of faith and confidence and determination in my heart, which has not failed me to this day.

MARY MCLEOD BETHUNE, "Faith That Moved a Dump Heap," *WHO,* June 1941

Having mixed with the Egyptians for centuries, if the descendants of Jacob weren't black when they arrived in Egypt, which they may have been, they certainly were black when they left.

CHARLES FINCH, c. 1941

Them that's got, shall get/ Them that's not, shall love/ So the Bible said/ and it still is news/ Mama may have/ Papa may have/ But God bless the child/ that's got his own.

BILLIE HOLIDAY, "God Bless the Child," 1941

The Old Testament is devoted to what was right and just from the viewpoint of the Ancient Hebrews. All of their enemies were twenty-two carat evil. They, the Hebrews, were never aggressors. The Lord wanted His Children to have a country full of big grapes and tall corn. Incidentally, while they were getting it, they might as well get rid of some trashy tribes that He never did think much of anyway.

ZORA NEALE HURSTON, *Dust Tracks on a Road,* 1942

During the days of slavery, the white minister used as his text: "Slaves, be obedient to them that are your masters" . . . I promised my maker if I ever learned to read and if freedom ever came, I would not read that part of the Bible.

GRANDMOTHER OF HOWARD THURMAN, in *Jesus and the Disinherited,* 1949

When the white Christian missionaries went to Africa, the white folks had the Bible and the natives had the land. When the missionaries pulled out, they had the land and the natives had the Bibles.

DICK GREGORY, "Divine Libel," *Black Manifesto: Religion, Racism, and Reparations,* 1969

On becoming more acquainted with the word of the Bible, I began to understand so much more of what I had been taught, and of what I had learned about life and about the people in mine.

DUKE ELLINGTON, *Music Is My Mistress,* 1973

Black women "didn't know nothing" about Dr. Spock, but they did know the Bible. Raise up a child in the way he should go and when he is old he will not depart from it.

NA'IM AKBAR, 1975

Bible says that thou shalt not commit adultery. Moses got that law from God. It's a good law . . . because back in those Bible days, if a man could have six wives, three hundred concubines and still commit adultery, I'd kill him myself.

RAY CHARLES, *Brother Ray,* 1978

There's nothing written in the Bible, Old or New Testament, that says if you believe in Me, you ain't going to have no troubles.

Ibid.

The first recorded versions of the creation story, the flood story, the resurrection story, the story of Job, the story of the prodigal son, are to be found in ancient Egypt.

W. J. HARDEMAN, c. 1980

When you are a slave what you want most of all is to be set free, to be liberated. And so for the slave, the most important word that Moses brought to them was, "I will rescue you and set you free from bondage."

DESMOND TUTU, *Hope and Suffering,* 1983

BIRD

And 'tis an added grief that with my own feathers I am slain.

AESOP, "The Eagle and the Feathers," 570 B.C.

I know why the caged bird beats his wing/ Till its blood is red on the cruel bars.

PAUL L. DUNBAR, "Sympathy," *Selected Poems,* 1913

God has given as a gift a bird's two wings./ From the flash of feathery line and colour/ Spiritual joy springs.

RABINDRANATH TAGORE, *Flying Man,* 1940

BIRTH

There is only one genuine misfortune, not to be born.

JOAQUIM MACHADO DE ASSIS, *Epitaph for a Small Winner,* 1881

The childless lady despises/ her own exquisite figure/ when the cook comes by in the street with her six/ children and a seventh on the way.

RUBEN DARIO, "Thistles," c. 1900

You were born with a silver spoon in your mouth, I was born with an iron hoe in my hand.

KELLY MILLER, *The American Negro,* 1908

None of us are responsible for our birth. Our responsibility is the use we make of life.

JOSHUA HENRY JONES, *By Sanction of Law,* 1924

Most things are born in the mothering darkness and most things die. Darkness is the womb of creation. But the sun with his seven horns of flame is the father of life.

ZORA NEALE HURSTON, *Moses, Man of the Mountain,* 1939

Some say she was born with a veil on her face/ So she could look through unnatural space/ Through the future and through the past/ And charm a body or an evil place/ And every man could well despise/ The evil look in her coal black eyes.

MARGARET WALKER, "Molly Means," *For My People,* 1942

I wanted to be born, to be born again. I knew perfectly well that I was going to be hurt, but I wanted to be a man, and it seemed to me that nothing could be too painful if, by enduring it, I was to come to man's estate. My companions felt the same. Like me, they were prepared to pay for it with their blood. Our elders had paid for it thus; those who were born after us would pay for it in their turn. Why should we be spared? Life itself would spring from the shedding of our blood.

CAMARA LAYE, *The Dark Child,* 1954

Sometimes writing is like giving birth. You need someone to give a name, to say, push, baby, push.

JAMES BALDWIN, in "James Baldwin . . . in Conversation," *Arts in Society,* Summer 1966

Some are born into better circumstances than others, but we are not responsible for where we are born nor for what we are born with. We inherit a good mind by means we do not understand, a mind which we did nothing to get. We develop into a handsome boy or beautiful girl by nature and God's nature, but we did nothing to get the beauty or the comeliness.

BENJAMIN MAYS, "What Man Lives By," in Philpot, ed., *Best Black Sermons,* 1972

A newborn baby is an extraordinary event; and I have never seen two babies who looked exactly alike. Here is the breathing miracle who could not live an instant without you, with a skull more fragile than an egg, a miracle of eyes, legs, toenails, and lungs.

JAMES BALDWIN, *No Name in the Street,* 1972

Birth control is one thing, but the same amount of money that would make birth control work would give [poor women] twice as many healthy [babies].

DUKE ELLINGTON, *Music Is My Mistress,* 1973

Surrounded by life,/ a perfect picture of/ blackness blessed. . . .

LUCILLE CLIFTON, *An Ordinary Woman,* 1974

I saw her come here with no words,/ arms flailing air, past mother, thigh/ and blood. . . .

KEORAPETSE KGOSITSILE, "For Ipeleng," in *Black Poetry Writing,* 1975

[My daughter's] birth was the incomparable gift of seeing the world at quite a different angle than before, and judging it by standards that would apply far beyond my natural life.

ALICE WALKER, *In Search of Our Mothers' Gardens,* 1983

Not only was I not born to be a slave; I was not born to hope to become the equal of the slave master.

JAMES BALDWIN, *Price of the Ticket,* 1985

[T]here are three things I was born with in this world, and there are three things I will have until the day I die: hope, determination, and song.

MIRIAM MAKEBA, *My Story,* 1987

I was born with the music inside me. That's the only explanation I know of. Music was one of my parts . . . like my blood. It was a force already with me when I arrived on the scene. It was a necessity for me—like food or water.

RAY CHARLES, in "Words of the Week," *Jet,* 14 December 1987

Don't smile at me staff nurse/ I gatecrashed into this life/ You did not want me to be born/ I beat the barricades of your birth-control scheme/ I swallowed the pill/ In her womb/ I diluted the solution you distribute/ I was a tiny spermatozoon/ Wagging my tail/ Invisible invincible/ I glided past your loop/ Dashed straight to the ovule/ To mate you/ Check!

BICCA MASEKO, "Mate," in Chinweizu, ed., *Voices from Twentieth-Century Africa,* 1988

With the issue of surrogacy, there is a clear danger of Black women and poor women spending nine months pregnant while career women go on with their interests. During slavery, Black women served as wet nurses for white children. [Reviving a similar demeaning tradition is a giant step in the wrong direction.]

ANGELA DAVIS, in "Lifestyle: Angela Davis: Good-Health Advocate," *Essence,* January 1988

When do people stop being kids? The body is ready to have babies, that's why they are in a passion to do it. Nature wants it done then, when the body can handle it, not after 40, when the income can handle it.

TONI MORRISON, in "The Pain of Being Black," *Time,* 22 May 1989

If you are born on the bottom—in bondage—there are only two ways you can go: outright sedition or plodding reform.

CHARLES JOHNSON, *Middle Passage,* 1990

The only reason you were born was to be better than your parents and to make this world better for your children.

DREW BROWN, in the *Pittsburgh Courier,* 17 August 1991

BLESSINGS

Blessed is the man who to himself has kept the high creations of his soul.

ALEXANDER PUSHKIN, "Eugene Onegin," *Fame,* 1823

May hills lean toward you,/ Hills and windswept mountains,/ And trees be happy/ That have seen you pass.

DONALD JEFFREY HAYES, "Benediction," in Bontemps, ed., *Poetry of the Negro,* 1949

My mother told me I was blessed, and I have always taken her word for it. Being born of—or reincarnated from—royalty is nothing like being blessed. Royalty is inherited from another human being, blessedness comes from God.

DUKE ELLINGTON, *Music Is My Mistress,* 1973

To secure the blessings of liberty, we must secure the blessings of learning.

MARY FUTRELL, 1987

When we recognize where our power truly comes from, we become blessed.

BEN VEREEN, in "Dealing With Adversities," *Body Mind Spirit,* Summer 1991

BLUES

And every day I have the blues.

TRADITIONAL

I wish I was a catfish swimming in the deep blue sea.
I would have all you women swimming after me.

TRADITIONAL

Saint Louis woman with her diamond rings/ Pulls that man around by her apron strings,/ 'Twant for powder and for store bought hair/ The man I love would not gone nowhere.

W. C. HANDY, *St. Louis Blues,* 1914

The blues is where we came from and what we experience. The blues came from nothingness, from want, from desire.

W. C. HANDY, c. 1918

An everlasting song, a singing tree,/ caroling softly. . . .

JEAN TOOMER, "Song of the Son," *Cane,* 1923

You see me ravin', you hear me crying,/ Oh Lawd, this lonely heart of mine,/ Sometimes, I'm grieving from my hat down to my shoes./ I'm a good hearted woman that's a slave to the blues.

MA RAINEY, "Slave to the Blues," 1926

White folks hear the blues come out, but they don't know how it got there.

MA RAINEY, c. 1929

The spirituals and the blues were not created out of sweet deceit. Spirituals and blues contain sublimated bitterness and humility, pathos and bewilderment. And if the Negro is a little bitter, the white man should be the last person in the world to accuse him of bitterness. For the feelings of bitterness are a natural part of the black man's birthright. It matters not so much that one has an experience of bitterness but rather how one has developed out of it. To ask him to render up his bitterness is asking him to part with his soul. For out of his bitterness he has blossomed and created spirituals and conserved his racial attributes—his humor and ripe laughter and particular rhythm of life.

CLAUDE MCKAY, in "A Negro Writer to His Critics," *New York Herald Tribune,* 6 March 1932

I, who was borne away to become an orphan, carry my parents with me. So he groaned aloud in the ship and hid his drum and laughed.

ZORA NEALE HURSTON, *Jonah's Gourd,* 1934

I've got to keep moving, got to keep moving,/ Blues fallin' down like hail/ And the days keep mindin' me/ There's a hellhound on my trail.

ROBERT JOHNSON, "Hellhound On My Trail," 1937

Modern blues is the expression of the emotional life of the race.

W. C. HANDY, c. 1937

Somebody in Glasgow brought up to me an old "St. Louis Blues," record. This guy says, "In the middle of the record are two bars of a Bach chorale, how do you explain that?" Well, I just couldn't explain it. In fact I'm still trying to find out how two bars of a Bach chorale got into the "St. Louis Blues."

FATS WALLER, c. 1940

The most astonishing aspect of the blues is that, though replete with a sense of defeat and downheartedness, they are not intrinsically pessimistic; their burden of woe and melancholy is dialectically redeemed through sheer force of sensuality into an exultant affirmation of life, of love, of sex, of movement, of hope.

RICHARD WRIGHT, *12 Million Black Voices,* 1941

The blues can be real sad, else real mad, else real glad, and funny, too, all the same time. I ought to know. Me, I growed up with blues. I heard so many blues when I was a child until my shadow is blue.

LANGSTON HUGHES, *Simple Speaks His Mind,* 1950

I leaves tryin' to pray, but I cain't. I thinks and I thinks, until I thinks my brain go'n bust, 'bout how I ain't guilty. I don't eat nothin' and I don't drink nothin' and cain't sleep at night. Finally I starts singin'. I don't mean to, I didn't think 'bout it, just start singin'.. . . All I know is I ends up singin' the blues . . . and while I'm singing them blues I makes up my mind that I ain't nobody but myself and ain't nothing I can do but let whatever is gonna happen happen.

RALPH ELLISON, *The Invisible Man,* 1952

Blues jazz was the scornful gesture of men turned ecstatic in their state of rejection. It was the musical language of the satisfiedly amoral, the boasting of the contentedly lawless, the recreation of the innocently criminal.

RICHARD WRIGHT, *The Outsider,* 1953

Good morning blues/ Blues, how do you do?/ Yes, blues, how do you do?

TRADITIONAL, in *The Book of Negro Folklore,* 1958

Backwater blues done caused me/ To pack my things and go./ Cause my house fell down/ An I can't live there no mo'.

Ibid.

Now when a woman gets the blues./ Lord, she hangs her head and/ Cries. But when a man gets the blues,/ Lord, he grabs a train and rides.

Ibid.

You've taken my blues, and gone—/ You sing 'em on Broadway/ And you sing 'em in the Hollywood Bowl,/ And you mixed 'em up with symphonies/ and you fixed 'em/ So they don't sound like me./ Yes, you have taken my blues and gone.

LANGSTON HUGHES, *Selected Poems,* 1959

But softly/ As the tune comes from his throat/ trouble/ mellows to a golden note.

LANGSTON HUGHES, "Trumpet Player," *Selected Poems,* 1959

The blues sum up the universal challenge, the universal hope, the universal fear. . . . They contain the toughness that manages to make this experience articulate.

JAMES BALDWIN, "The Uses of the Blues," *Playboy,* June 1963

The blues occurs when the Negro is sad, when he is far from his home, his mother, or his sweetheart. Then he thinks of a motif or a preferred rhythm and takes his trombone, or his violin, or his banjo, or his clarinet, or his drum, or else he sings, or simply dances. And on this chosen motif, he plumbs the depths of his imagination. This makes his sadness pass away—it is the Blues.

ERNEST ANSERMET, in Jones, *Blues People,* 1963

Blues was conceived by freedmen and ex-slaves as the result of personal or intellectual experiences: an emotional confirmation of, and reaction to, the way in which most Negroes are still forced to exist in the United States.

LEROI JONES, in *ibid.*

The blues is an impulse to keep the painful details and episodes of a brutal experience alive in one's aching consciousness, to finger its jagged grain, and to transcend it, not by the consolation of philosophy but by squeezing from it a near-tragic, near-comic lyricism. As a form, the blues is an autobiographical chronicle of personal catastrophe expressed lyrically.

RALPH ELLISON, "Richard Wright's Blues," *Shadow and Act,* 1964

The blues is an art of ambiguity, an assertion of the irrepressibly human over all circumstances whether created by others or by one's own human failings.

Ibid.

The blues come from way back when they had to study something to try to give them some consolation, so they sang about what they felt.

JASPER LOVE, *Blues from the Delta,* 1970

Grew up in the singing of Bessie, Billie, in Satchmo's horn, on Duke's piano, in Langston's poetry, on Robeson's baritone. The point is the blues is grown.

GIL SCOTT HERON, "Bicentennial Blues," *It's Your World,* 1976

The blues slows you down and gives you time to think.

ALBERT KING, in "Albert King's Blue Funk," *Essence,* October 1977

I, too, have said that I would exchange all the blues to save one starving child. I was wrong, not only because the exchange is not in my power, but also because the singing of the Lord's song in so strange a land has saved more children than anyone will ever know.

JAMES BALDWIN, in the *New York Times,* 16 October 1977

Blues is a music of this earth and all its paradoxes, where both its joys and pains are synthesized and resolved into an emotional spiritual unity that helps make possible life.

ORTIZ WALTON, *Music Black White and Blue,* 1980

I'm not living the blues, I'm just singing for the women who think they can't speak out. Can't a man alive mistreat me, 'cause I know who I am.

ALBERTA HUNTER, c. 1985

Miles cried like a singer, and Billie sang like an instrumentalist, everything they did was wrapped in the blues.

MARVIN GAYE, in Ritz, *Divided Soul,* 1985

Women, cheating, getting caught, and stuff like that. It's the kind of blues that I can sing and it has a universal appeal. Sooner or later, somewhere down the line, you're going to be on at least one side of it.

ROBERT CRAY, in "Words of the Week," *Jet,* 16 December 1986

At this point in my career, it would be pretty silly for me to go in another direction. . . . The blues has been here since day one and will be here long after I'm gone.

BOBBY BLUE BLAND, in "Words of the Week," *Jet,* 22 August 1988

Blues is joyful. It's a celebration of having overcome bad times. A great blues line is, "You don't love me, and I don't even care. I'll find a good person for me in this world somewhere."

JOE WILLIAMS, in "Words of the Week," *Jet,* 14 November 1988

This is B. B. King, making a statement and a natural fact. All you got to do is sit back, and dig where it's coming from. Listen, not only with your ear, but with your heart. Everybody wants to know "Why I Sing the Blues."

JOE "BIG DADDY" LOUIS, in *Black Art: Ancestral Legacy,* 1989

It's never hard to sing the blues. Everyone in the world has the blues . . . poor people have the blues because they're poor and hungry. Rich people can't sleep at night because they're trying to hold on to their money and everything they have.

JOHN LEE HOOKER, in the *Detroit Free Press,* 8 September 1991

You don't have to be hungry and poor to sing the blues. When I was poor I sang the blues and I was happy singing them. Now the blues still picks me and makes me happy.

Ibid.

BOXING

The possession of muscular strength and the courage to use it in contests with other men for physical supremacy does not necessarily imply a lack of appreciation for the finer and better things of life.

JACK JOHNSON, *Jack Johnson In the Ring and Out,* 1927

Hurting people is my business.

SUGAR RAY ROBINSON, in a statement to the New York Boxing Commission, 23 May 1962

The fighter loses more than his pride in the fight, he loses part of his future. He's a step closer to the slum he came from.

FLOYD PATTERSON, c. 1970

In order for a prizefighter to be successful and come out with what belongs to him, he has to be two separate people in two different places—in the gym and in the lawyer's office. Since no one can be two people, a prizefighter must have a partner, a brother, a friend, a counsel, a twin in thinking and inspiration who will be the other self he needs.

MUHAMMAD ALI, *The Greatest,* 1975

There ain't nothing like being in the corner, and the trainer is whispering in your ear and another is putting in your mouthpiece. Five seconds to go, then boom! The bell. It's more exciting than looking down a cliff.

GEORGE FOREMAN, in *Newsweek,* 26 January 1976

Any fight and every fight is important.

JOE LOUIS, *My Life,* 1981

The only way for a fighter to get back in shape is to fight his way back.

SUGAR RAY LEONARD, c. 1988

Muhammad Ali enabled me to present him to the world and in so doing I had an opportunity to demonstrate that I had a talent to complement the greatest talent.

DON KING, in *Jet,* 30 May 1988

It's a business where everybody puts so many daggers in your back, you look like a porcupine.

DON KING, in the *Detroit News,* 24 February 1989

BOYCOTT

Don't ride the bus to work, to town, to school or anyplace Monday, December 5. Another Negro woman has been arrested and put in jail because she refused to give up her bus seat. Don't ride the buses to work, to town, to school, or anywhere on Monday. If you work, take a cab, or share a ride, or walk. Come to a mass meeting, Monday at 7:00 P.M. at the Hall Street Baptist Church for further instruction.

FLYER DISTRIBUTED IN BIRMINGHAM, ALABAMA

I'm just an average citizen. Many Black people were arrested for defying the bus laws. They prepared the way.

ROSA PARKS, c. 1960

We (NAACP) are quite capable of taking their money one day and boycotting the next.

BENJAMIN HOOKS, in *American Visions,* February 1987

BOYHOOD

As a boy in Princeton [New Jersey] I dreamed and dreamed of the land of my forefathers and mothers. And in reality my bonds were undoubtedly very close. My paternal grandfather or great-grandfather, torn from his ages-old continent, had survived the dreadful passage. My own father was the embodiment of the strength, warmth, and quiet dignity of the African people.

PAUL ROBESON, "A Word about African Languages," *Spotlight on Africa,* February 1955

I began plotting novels at about the time I learned to read. The story of my childhood is the usual bleak fantasy, and we can dismiss it with the restrained observation that I certainly would not consider living it again.

JAMES BALDWIN, *Notes of a Native Son,* 1955

The glory of my boyhood was my father. . . . Just as in youth he had refused to remain a slave, so in all the years of his manhood he disdained to be an Uncle Tom.

PAUL ROBESON, *Here I Stand,* 1958

If I were a teacher . . . I would try to teach [children] that those streets, those houses, those dangers, those agonies by which they are surrounded, are criminal . . . the results of a criminal conspiracy to destroy him. I would teach him that if he intends to get to be a man, he must at once decide that he is stronger than this conspiracy and that he must never make his peace with it. And that one of his weapons for refusing to make his peace with it and for destroying it depends on what he decides he is worth.

JAMES BALDWIN, "A Talk to Harlem Teachers," in Clarke, *Harlem, USA,* 1964

[S]ince I was a little boy I learned that one of the things that made you grow into manhood are tests and trials and tribulations.

MALCOLM X, speech given at the Organization of Afro-American Unity Rally, Audubon Ballroom, New York City, 24 January 1965

[M]ost of the time I played by myself. Even then I was a loner, and I have stayed a loner all my life. I'm not particularly proud of this trait—it can make a man seem a little distant or even aloof—but it has helped pull me through some tight spots and hard times.

ROY WILKINS, *Standing Fast,* 1982

When my mother went to work, my older sister took care of us, and wherever she went, we had to go, including choir practice. I was the only boy in a choir of 36 girls because to sing in a choir was considered sissy.

BILLY OCEAN, in "The Man Behind the Voice," *Ebony,* August 1987

Some kids' parents took them fishing. When I was a kid, my dad took me on the road.

SAMMY DAVIS, JR., in *Jet,* 13 June 1988

And the male children were deaf to the pleas of the mothers, and they couldn't see no men nowhere, they had no respect.

ANEB KGOSITSILE, in *City Arts Quarterly*, Fall–Winter 1989

BRAINWASHING

The tendency has really been, insofar as this was possible, to dismiss white people as the slightly mad victims of their own brainwashing.

JAMES BALDWIN, *The Fire Next Time*, 1963

The challenge of this age is to resist and conquer in each of our own beings the racist brainwashing that is still active in our minds.

WYATT T. WALKER, "Crime, Vietnam and God," *Negro Digest*, December 1967

They are sick in the way all brainwashed people are sick. They don't know what they are doing. So much of their humanity, their dignity has been destroyed that they are afraid of standing on their own.

PETER ABRAHAMS, "Pluralia," in *English Studies*, February 1969

In my preaching the shafts are ever aimed at the brainwashed horde.

ADAM CLAYTON POWELL, JR., *Adam by Adam*, 1971

Brainwashing of children and adults in America is the worst in the world, and it's always done by those with complexes.

DUKE ELLINGTON, *Music Is My Mistress*, 1973

Youth too often succumb to a sort of brainwashing which drains their ego strength that comes from self awareness, self knowledge, and the security of group identity.

I. A. NEWBY, c. 1981

BREAD

Having been given, I must give. Man shall not live by bread alone, and what the farmer does I must do. I must feed the people with my song.

PAUL ROBESON, "Paul Robeson Speaks about Art and the Negro," in *The Millgate*, December 1930

Bread cast upon the water comes back buttered toast.

SONNY GREER, c. 1950

Although she feeds me bread of bitterness,/ And sinks into my throat her tiger's tooth,/ Stealing my breath of life, I will confess/ I love this cultured hell that tests my youth!

CLAUDE MCKAY, "America," *Selected Poems*, 1953

BRIDGES

See also ANCESTORS

Never despise a bridge which carries you safely over.

GULLAH SAYING

Let's build bridges here and there, Or sometimes just a spiral stair.

GEORGIA DOUGLASS, "Interracial," in Bontemps, ed., *Poetry of the Negro*, 1949

My mother, religious-negro, proud of having waded through a storm, is, very obviously, a sturdy bridge that I have crossed over on.

TONI CADE BAMBARA, *Gorilla, My Love*, 1972

We, today, stand on the shoulders of our predecessors who have gone before us. We as their successors, must catch the torch of freedom and liberty passed on to us by our ancestors. We cannot lose in this battle.

BENJAMIN MAYS, "I Knew Carter G. Woodson," *Negro History Bulletin*, March 1981

I am where I am because of the bridges that I crossed. Sojourner Truth was a bridge. Harriet Tubman was a bridge. Ida B. Wells was a bridge. Madame C.J. Walker was a bridge. Fannie Lou Hamer was a bridge.

OPRAH WINFREY, in "An Intimate Talk With Oprah," *Essence*, August 1987

On the front porch of a home, beside a stove in a country store, or gathered . . . outside a church, these elders constantly evoke memory to bridge past times with the present.

WILLIAM FERRIS, in *Black Art: Ancestral Legacy*, 1989

In climbing through the Army's ranks from 1898 to 1932, my father had overcome what seemed almost impossible odds. In spite of the attitude of whites in the United States toward all people of color, he had managed to buck the system and accomplish his goals. He had made life easier for me. Now it was my turn to make things better for those who would come after me.

BENJAMIN DAVIS, JR., *Benjamin Davis, Jr.: An Autobiography,* 1990

I don't know much about history, but I know those players from the old Negro Leagues opened doors for those who came later.

BO JACKSON, *Bo Knows Bo,* 1990

BROTHER

He is a fool who treats his brother worse than a stranger.

NIGERIA

A brother is like one's shoulder.

SOMALIA

A man has to act like a brother before you can call him a brother.

MALCOLM X, speech given in Paris, 1964

One day somebody should remind us that, even though there may be political and ideological differences between us, the Vietnamese are our brothers, the Russians are our brothers, the Chinese are our brothers; and one day we've got to sit down together at the table of brotherhood.

MARTIN LUTHER KING, JR., sermon given at Ebenezer Baptist Church, New York City, 4 April 1967

All life is interrelated. The agony of the poor impoverishes the rich; the betterment of the poor enriches the rich. We are inevitably our brother's keeper because we are our brother's brother. Whatever affects one directly affects all indirectly.

MARTIN LUTHER KING, JR., *Where Do We Go From Here?* 1968

I was the older brother. And when I was growing up I didn't like all those brothers and sisters. No kid likes to be the oldest. . . . But when they turn to you for help—what can you do?. . . [T]hey kept me so busy caring for them . . . that I had no time . . . to become a junkie or an alcoholic.

JAMES BALDWIN, in "Why I Left America," *Essence,* October 1970

If I cud ever write a/ poem as beautiful as u/ little 2/yr/ old/ brother, i wud laugh, jump, leap/ touch the stars.

SONIA SANCHEZ, "To P.J.," *It's a New Day,* 1971

We need to stop idealizing and idolizing the brother on the block. He is no hero. He is a casualty, a victim. And he will remain a pawn, like all of us, until we *live* together, until we all work together to rebuild our family.

KEORAPETSE KGOSITSILE, in *Black Poetry Writing,* 1975

My brothers . . . never understood they must represent half the world to me, as I must represent the other half to them.

ALICE WALKER, *In Search of Our Mothers' Gardens,* 1983

Black women may find lovers on street corners and even in church pews, but brothers are hard to come by and are as necessary as air and as precious as love. Black women in this desolate world, Black women in this cruel time have a crying need for brothers.

MAYA ANGELOU, eulogy for James Baldwin, Cathedral of St. John the Divine, New York City, 1988

BROWN V. BOARD OF EDUCATION

When you put a white child in a school with a whole lot of colored children, the child would fall apart or something. Everybody knows that is not true. Those same kids in Virginia and South Carolina—and I have seen them do it—they play in the streets together, they play on the farms together, they separate to go to school, they come out of school and play ball together . . . They have to be separated in school. . . . Why, of all the multitudinous groups of people in this country, [do] you have to single out the Negroes and give them this separate treatment?

THURGOOD MARSHALL, arguments before the Supreme Court, *Brown* v. *Board of Education,* 1953

For all men of good will 17 May 1954 marked a joyous end to the long night of enforced segregation. In unequivocal language the Supreme Court affirmed that "separate but equal" facilities are unequal, and that to segregate a child on the basis of his race is to deny that child equal protection of the law.

MARTIN LUTHER KING, JR., *Stride Toward Freedom,* 1958

Having fought the issue to the highest court in the land and seen the decision given in their favor, Negroes experienced the most shameless perversion of justice. In state after state, and school district after school district, human ingenuity was employed to defy the clear statement of the court. And where elusive action failed to nullify the court decision, violence, intimidation, legislative evasion and even assassination were employed.

WHITNEY YOUNG, *To Be Equal,* 1964

We are still a racist society. Some of the litigants in that 1954 decision never saw a day of desegregated education. They saw evasion, circumvention, massive resistance and a generation of litigation.

CARL ROWAN, c. 1975

The wording of the 1954 Supreme Court decision says, in essence, that segregated schools are damaging to Black children and what they really need is to be in a school with white children. This is the message our parents heard. Nowhere does it say that segregated schools are also damaging to white children.

NA'IM AKBAR, in "Growing Up Integrated (Did Momma Do the Right Thing?)" *Crisis,* March 1988

My most vivid childhood memory of the Supreme Court was the "Impeach Earl Warren" signs which lined Highway 17 near Savannah. I didn't quite understand who this Earl Warren fellow was, but I knew he was in some kind of trouble.

CLARENCE THOMAS, in *Jet,* July 1990

BURDEN

They call it "love, love,"/ Slighting its name./ But it's heavier than a stone/ For the one who has to bear it.

ETHIOPIA

[A]s long as this burden of race is borne by any of my brothers, I, too, bear it.

PAUL ROBESON, in "Robeson Finds a Natural Link to the Songs of African Tribes," *New York Herald-Tribune,* 27 October 1935

The burden of suffering that must be borne, impose it upon one generation! Do not, with false kindness of the missionaries and businessman, drag out this agony for another five hundred years.

RICHARD WRIGHT, *Black Power: A Record of Reactions in a Land of Pathos,* 1954

My burden's so heavy I can hardly see/ Seems like everybody is down on me/ An' that's all right, I don't worry, oh/ There will be a better day.

TRADITIONAL, in Jones, *Blues People,* 1963

What a great burden you bear, little people, here's to all your parents' stillborn dreams of greatness.

MARY E. VROMAN, "See How They Run," in Clarke, ed., *American Negro Short Stories,* 1966

History tells us a nation can survive for years by shifting the burdens of life to the people confined by force and violence to the bottom.

LERONE BENNETT, *The Challenge of Blackness,* 1968

We are capable of bearing a great burden, once we discover that the burden is reality and arrive where reality is.

ROBERT SLATER, *The Pursuit of Loneliness,* 1971

Ours is the burden of proving that our system is suited to human needs.

WILLIAM HASTIE, *Grace Under Pressure,* 1984

Everything you buy is an added burden.

BILLY OCEAN, in "The Man Behind the Voice," *Ebony,* August 1987

I am burdened daily with showing whites that Blacks are people, I am in the old vernacular, "a credit to my race"—my brother's keeper and my sister's though many have abandoned me because they think I have abandoned them.

LEANITA MCNAIR, in *Ebony,* March 1988

May their burdens be lighter, and their stars shine brighter.

EARL GRAVES, c. 1989

BUSINESS

He who has goods can sell them.

NIGERIA

Your reputation is only as good as what you did yesterday.

TRADITIONAL

Friendship is one thing, business is another.

TRADITIONAL

Business? That's very simple—it's other people's money.

ALEXANDRE DUMAS, c. 1850

Do you ask what we can do? Unite and build a store of your own. . . . Do you ask where is the money? We have spent more than enough for nonsense.

MARIA STEWART, *Meditations from the Pen of Mrs. Maria W. Stewart,* 1872

The conviction grew upon me that the pursuit of business, money, civic, or literary position was like building a house upon sands; if race prejudice and persecution and public discrimination for mere color was to spread up from the South.

MONROE TROTTER, c. 1901

If you obtain and hold the confidence of the business world, you will be in a position to conquer more prejudice than we have been able to estimate.

FANNIE BARRIER WILLIAMS, speech given to the National Negro Business League, Tuskegee, Alabama, 1903

Business pays. . . . Philanthropy begs.

W. E. B. DU BOIS, "Business and Philanthropy," *Crisis,* June 1911

We must keep our business to ourselves. We must be as wise as the serpent and appear to be harmless as the dove. We must strike at the right moment.

MARCUS GARVEY, *Philosophy and Opinions of Marcus Garvey,* 1923

Don't shop where you can't work. Buy where you can work.

CHICAGO WHIP SLOGAN, c. 1930

There is no other American community in which the huge bulk of local business, from the smallest to the largest, is operated by outsiders.

CLAUDE MCKAY, *Harlem: Negro Metropolis,* 1940

Successful businesses are founded on needs.

A. G. GASTON, c. 1974

What people want in the world is not ideology, they want goods and services.

ANDREW YOUNG, in "Outspoken Andy Young," *Newsweek,* 28 March 1977

Black-owned businesses don't want charity. We have never asked for it. We don't want corporate handouts. We don't want to be treated as second-class business. And above all, we don't want to be treated as if doing business with us fulfills some sort of goodwill.

EARL GRAVES, speech at the Blacks in Government Conference, Washington, D.C., February 1981

The Black community's commitment to Black business is lax. There is too little faith in minorities. We're going to have to stop running from ourselves so hard and so fast.

DON DAVIS, 1984

The first Black man at the White House, Fred House, had a difficult time even getting a secretary to work for him. Today we have passed that stage of problems. But, after leaving the perch near the seat of power at the White House, many of the Blacks find little opportunity in the business and corporate world.

MELVIN BRADLEY, 1985

Dirt [land] is much more valuable than diamond rings.

EARTHA KITT, c. 1985

Wherever you spend your money is where you create a job. If you live in Harlem, and spend your money in Chicago, you create jobs for people in Chicago. If you are Black and the businesses are run by people who are not Black, then those people come in at 9:00 A.M.; leave at 5:00 P.M. and take the wealth to the communities in which they live.

TONY BROWN, c. 1986

You don't have to be a Phi Beta Kappa to figure out some things in this world. Sure, it's a business decision. And there are no Black head coaches in the NFL. That's a business decision, too. Who can argue if you say it's not racism, it's a business decision. You can cut it up anyway you want to.

DOUG WILLIAMS, c. 1986

Blacks will never succeed in white corporations because [white] America is about dominance and control. They're not going to share their secrets of oppression with African-American men. Those secrets are going to stay in "the Club!" We have to form our own corporations and our own institutions because only those will provide jobs for us.

DENNIS RAHIIM WATSON, in "In Review," *Ebony*, December 1986

I wasn't forced into this business, I did it because I enjoyed it and because it was to me as drawing breath and exhaling it. I did it because I was compelled to do it, not by my parents or family, but by my own inner life in the world of music.

MICHAEL JACKSON, 1987

I rarely hear Black preachers and politicians talk about business. Economics. We talk about politics. Politics without economics is lunatics.

JOSHUA SMITH, 1988

The world of business represents still virgin territory for black Americans.

BENJAMIN HOOKS, in *Crisis*, February 1988

I've watched the talented ones who were supposed to change the world make a lifetime commitment to business as usual for the price of a Rolex watch and a new BMW.

PEARL CLEAGE, in "Introduction," *Catalyst*, Summer 1988

America has achieved greatness because her citizens are free to compete with each other, and free to keep the fruits of their victories. The benefits reach to every shore of human endeavor.

WALTER E. WILLIAMS, "Why We're Number One," *Success*, March 1989

Black businesses don't need any more banquets and plaques with inscriptions telling how great they are—they need more contracts.

GLENN WASH, speech given to the National Association of Black Organizations, Detroit, Michigan, 19 November 1990

We have to be accountable for the state of our race. Our bondage and our battle is economic. We're not slaves but servants. We have to spend more time at economic conferences, be producers and provide jobs. The answer is economic self-sufficiency.

SHIRLEY CHISHOLM, speech given to the National Association of Black Organizations, Detroit, Michigan, 19 November 1990

I don't cross over. I expand. I'm expanding my market just like any other business. I don't know of one business that caters only to one people. If they did most of the businesses would go bankrupt.

HAMMER, c. 1991

Educate yourself about the music business. If you have the opportunity, go to college and become knowledgeable about the capitalist system, because economics is the key to maintaining financial stability.

KOOL MOE DEE, in "Words of the Week," *Jet*, 11 March 1991

CALL

Unless you call out who will open the door?

CONGO

My lord calls us/ He calls us by the thunder/ The trumpet sounds it in my soul.

SPIRITUAL

[O]ften we must sit dumb before the golden calf, but is not this the greater call for a voice to cry in the wilderness . . . ?

W. E. B. DU BOIS, "The Truth," *Crisis,* 1912

It is a political calling for me to redeem Africa. It is like asking Napoleon to take the world. He failed and died at St. Helena. But may I not say that the lessons of Napoleon are but stepping stones by which we shall guide ourselves to African liberation.

MARCUS GARVEY, *Philosophy and Opinions of Marcus Garvey,* 1923

Calling black people/ Calling all black people, man, woman child/ Wherever you are, calling you, urgent, come in/ Black People, come in, wherever you are, urgent, calling/ you, calling all black people/ calling all black people, come in, black people, come/ on in.

AMIRI BARAKA, "SOS," *Selected Poetry of Amiri Baraka/ LeRoi Jones,* 1979

The Black college has a special calling to reach the unreachable, teach the unteachable, embrace the rejected and be patient with the late bloomer.

JESSE JACKSON, in *Choosing to Succeed,* 1986

My calling to the ministry will be the perpetuation of the flame, the spirit of my father living on.

BERNICE KING, in "Whatever Happened to Bernice King?" *Ebony,* August 1987

CAPITALISM

The history of the capitalist era is characterized by the degradation of my people: despoiled by their lands . . . denied equal protection of the law, and deprived of their rightful place in the respect of their fellows.

PAUL ROBESON, "The Artist Must Take Sides," *Daily Worker,* 4 November 1937

Capitalism is development by refinement from feudalism, just as feudalism is a development by refinement from slavery.

KWAME NKRUMAH, *Consciencism,* 1964

You show me a capitalist, I'll show you a bloodsucker.

MALCOLM X, speech given in New York City, 20 December 1964

Capitalism used to be like an eagle, but now it's more like a vulture.

MALCOLM X, interview in *Young Socialist,* March–April 1965

We have deluded ourselves into believing the myth that capitalism grew and prospered out of the Protestant ethic of hard work and sacrifices. Capitalism was built on the exploitation of black slaves and continues to thrive on the exploitation of the poor, both black and white, both here and abroad.

MARTIN LUTHER KING, JR., speech given at the National Conference for a New Politics, Chicago, Illinois, August 1967

Whenever the dollar is held supreme and capitalistic interests dominate, a higher value will always be placed upon property rights than upon human rights.

DICK GREGORY, *No More Lies,* 1971

Racism cannot be separated from capitalism.

ANGELA DAVIS, "An Open Letter to Students," Marin County Jail, Marin County, California, 23 March 1971

Capitalism always and everywhere drives its victims to the end of endurance so that one must either break under the strain of the society or salvage some dignity from the general confusion.

SELWYN CUDJOE, "Maya Angelou and the Autobiographical Statement," in Evans, ed., *Black Women Writers,* 1984

CAUSE

We wish to plead our own cause. Too long have others spoken for us.

JOHN RUSSWURM, in *Freedom's Journal,* 16 March 1827

Remember that our cause is one, and that we must help each other, if we would succeed.

FREDERICK DOUGLASS, in *North Star,* 3 December 1847

We trace the real cause of this World War to the despising of the darker races by the dominant groups of men, and the consequent fierce rivalry among European nations in their efforts to use darker and backward people for the purposes of selfish gain regardless of the ultimate good of the oppressed. We see permanent peace only in the extension of the principle of government by the consent of the governed, not simply among the smaller nations of Europe, but among the natives of Asia and Africa, the West Indies and the Negroes of the United States.

W. E. B. DU BOIS, *Dusk of Dawn: An Essay Toward an Autobiography of Race Concept,* 1940

A devotion to humanity . . . is too easily equated with a devotion to a Cause; and Causes . . . are notoriously bloodthirsty.

JAMES BALDWIN, *Notes of a Native Son,* 1955

When you know the origin, you know the cause.

MALCOLM X, speech given at the Organization of Afro-American Unity Rally, Audubon Ballroom, New York City, 24 January 1965

Cause and effect are in fact joined and if you build a sufficient cause then not all the talk or all the tears in God's creation can prevent the effect from presenting itself one morning as the now ripened fruit of your labors.

WILLIAM GRIER AND PRICE COBB, *Black Rage,* 1968

It's a blessing to die for a cause, because you can so easily die for nothing.

ANDREW YOUNG, in "Interview," *Playboy,* July 1977

CHAINS

The legs in chains with friends is better to be with than strangers in a garden.

AFRICA

You can take the chains off arms, but not off minds.

TRADITIONAL

The heavy hanging chains will fall. The walls will crumble at a word, and Freedom greet you in the light, Brothers give you back the sword.

ALEXANDER PUSHKIN, *Message to Siberia,* 1824–25

When I alone thought myself lost my dungeon shook, my chains fell off.

WILLIAM WELLS-BROWN, *Narrative,* 1847

No man can put a chain about the ankle of his fellowman, without at last finding the other end of it about his own neck.

FREDERICK DOUGLASS, *Life and Times of Frederick Douglass,* 1895

Along the way of life, someone must have the sense enough and morality enough to cut off the chain of hate.

MARTIN LUTHER KING, JR., speech given at Hall Street Baptist Church, Montgomery, Alabama, 5 December 1955

They supported their chains only so long as they did not know any condition of life more happy than that of slavery. But today . . . if they had a thousand lives they would sacrifice them all rather than be forced into slavery again.

TOUSSAINT L'OUVERTURE, in James, *The Black Jacobins,* 1963

Ellis Island is for the people who came over on ships. My people came in chains.

DAVID DINKINS, in "Being There," *Vanity Fair,* January 1991

CHALLENGE

Through the destruction, in certain countries, of the greatest of man's literary heritage, through the propagation of false ideas of racial and national superiority, the artist, the scientist, the writer is challenged.

PAUL ROBESON, in "The Artist Must Take Sides," *Daily Worker,* 4 November 1937

It is the hour of the common man. May we rise to the challenge to struggle for our rights. Come what will or may and let us never falter.

A. PHILIP RANDOLPH, speech given to March on Washington Movement, Detroit, Michigan, 26 September 1942

We are students in a segregated institution, and while certainly we must work within the frame work of the laws of our state, let it be realized by every student that the challenge facing us is not the defense of any system, be it segregated or integrated; the challenge facing us is to equip ourselves that we will be able to take our place wherever we are in the affairs of men.

BARBARA JORDAN, c. 1951

Our task, then always, is to challenge the apparent forms of reality—that is, the fixed manner and values of the few, and to struggle with it until it reveals its mad, vari-implicated chaos, its false face, and so on until it surrenders its insight, its truth.

RALPH ELLISON, 1953

You who stoop, you who weep,/ You who'll one day die, and not know why,/ You who fight to guard Another's sleep,/ You whose eyes no longer laugh,/ You, my brother with the face of fear and pain,/ Rise up and cry out: NO!

DAVID DIOP, "Challenge," *Poundings,* 1956

There is never time in the future in which we will work out our salvation. The challenge is in the moment, the time is always now.

JAMES BALDWIN, *Nobody Knows My Name,* 1961

We are challenged to see that the barriers of yesterday—the barriers built by prejudice, fear and indifference which are now crumbling—are not replaced by new barriers of apathy, of underdeveloped skills, of lack of training. If this happens, our gains will be but temporary, our victories hollow.

WHITNEY YOUNG, "Social Revolution: Challenge of the Nation," speech given at the Urban League Conference, New York City, 1963

The great challenge is to prepare ourselves to enter these doors [of opportunity].

MARTIN LUTHER KING, JR., *Where Do We Go From Here?* 1968

When someone is taught the joy of learning, it becomes a life-long process that never stops, a process that creates a logical individual. That is the challenge and joy of teaching.

MARVA COLLINS, in "Marva Collins: Teaching Success in the City," *Message,* February 1987

My challenge to the young people is to pick up where this generation has left off to create a world where every man, woman, and child is not limited, except by their own capabilities.

COLIN POWELL, in *Jet,* 11 September 1989

CHANCE

Chance comes to those who know what they want.

ASHANTI

There were some doubts . . . about admitting me as a student. . . . After some hours had passed, the head teacher said to me, "The adjoining recitation-room needs sweeping. Take the broom and sweep it." It occurred to me at once that here was my chance. . . . I swept the recitation-room three times and I dusted it four times. . . . When I was through I reported to the head teacher. . . . She went into the room and inspected the floor and closets; then she took her handkerchief and rubbed it on the woodwork about the walls. . . . When she was unable to find one bit of dirt on the floor, or a particle of dust on any of the furniture, she quietly remarked, "I guess you will do to enter this institution."

BOOKER T. WASHINGTON, *Up From Slavery,* 1901

[T]he drums of Africa still beat in my heart. They will not let me rest while there is a single Negro boy or girl without a chance to prove his worth.

MARY MCLEOD BETHUNE, "Faith That Moved A Dump Heap," *WHO,* June 1941

Colored men in a camp by themselves would get a fair chance at promotions. Opposition is helping the South, which does not want the Negroes to have any kind of military training.

JOEL SPINGARN, *Slavery to Freedom,* 1947

America has had chance after chance to show that it really meant that "all men are endowed with certain inalienable rights." America has had precious chances in this decade to make it come true.

JULIUS LESTER, "The Angry Children of Malcolm X," *Sing Out,* November 1966

One chance is all you need.

JESSE OWENS, *Blackthink,* 1970

The American creed of democratic equality encourages the belief in a second chance that is to be achieved by being born again—and not simply in the afterlife, but here and now, on earth. Change your name and increase your chances.... Alter the shape of your nose, tint of skin, or texture of hair. Change your sexual identity by dress or by surgery.... The second self's hope for a second chance has now been extended even beyond... death.

RALPH ELLISON, "An Extravagance of Laughter," *Going to the Territory,* 1986

I thanked God that through a Black university, I had the chance to develop, the desire to be, and the opportunity to do.

RONALD MCNAIR, in *Choosing to Succeed,* 1986

We're a society that's not about perfection, but about rectifying mistakes. We're about second chances.

HARRY EDWARDS, in "Hardline," *Detroit Free Press,* 8 May 1988

The guy who takes a chance, who walks the line between the known and unknown, who is unafraid of failure, will succeed.

GORDON PARKS, in "A Passion for Living," *Modern Maturity,* June–July, 1989

Risks, big and small, are the way those of us not born to wealth can pursue it and achieve success.

CLARENCE PAGE, in the *Detroit News,* 13 February 1989

CHANGE

Wood may remain ten years in the water, but it will never become a crocodile.

CONGO

Seven year no 'nough to wash speckles off guinea hen back. (Human nature never changes.)

JAMAICA

Change the joke and slip the yoke.

TRADITIONAL

Change your mind, and you will change your life. Usually what we travel miles to see is closer than we think.

TRADITIONAL

They endeavor to make you as much like brutes as possible. When they have blinded the eyes of your mind—when they have embittered the sweet waters of life—when they have shot out the light which shines from the word of God, then and not till then, has American slavery done its perfect work.

HENRY HIGHLAND GARNET, "An Address to the Slaves of the United States of America," speech given at the National Negro Convention, Buffalo, New York, 1843

We can be remodified, changed, and assimilated, but never extinguished. We shall never die out, nor be driven out. We are here and this is our country.

FREDERICK DOUGLASS, in "The Destiny of the Colored American," *North Star,* 16 November 1849

He was against all change, except the kind he jingled in his pocket.

WILLIAM HASTIE, in *Person and Affairs,* 28 April 1934

Our brains receive and nourish new ideas, our hands develop new abilities. In the past we were slaves; in the future God knows what, but today we exist in a state of almost incredibly rapid change.

PAUL WILLIAMS, *American Magazine,* 1937

The world changes, but men are always the same.

RICHARD WRIGHT, *The Outsider,* 1953

The spark became a flame and it changed everything.

E. D. NIXON, on the Montgomery Bus Boycott, Montgomery, Alabama, December 1955

Change does not roll in on the wheels of inevitability, but comes through continuous struggle. And so we must straighten our backs and work for our freedom. A man can't ride you unless your back is bent.

MARTIN LUTHER KING, JR., "The Death of Evil upon the Seashore," sermon given at the Cathedral of St. John the Divine, New York City, 17 May 1956

Open my flesh to the ripe blood of the tumult, the true sperm adds me as breath to the ferment of the leaves and the tornado.

TCHICAYA U TAM'SI, *Brush Fire,* 1957

Christians should be ready for a change because Jesus was the greatest changer in history.

RALPH ABERNATHY, c. 1962

Now, there is simply no possibility of a real change in the Negro's situation without the most radical and far-reaching changes in the American political and social structure. And it is clear that white Americans are not simply unwilling to effect these changes; they are, in the main, so slothful have they become, unable even to envision them.

JAMES BALDWIN, *The Fire Next Time,* 1963

World-changing is a hazardous pursuit. The lives of men who would dare to change the world and challenge the Gods of Power and the Status Quo are never smooth, indeed are always fraught with great danger.

JOHN KILLENS, introduction to *An ABC of Color,* 1963

The danger is that people may mistake what is basically a change of vocabulary for a change in behavior, practices, and attitudes. While practically all Americans have learned to talk inoffensively, not enough have learned to think differently, or to act positively.

WHITNEY YOUNG, *To Be Equal,* 1964

[Macmillan] came back crying to the other Europeans about the winds of change that are sweeping down across the African continent, meaning that the people who formerly had permitted Europeans or whites to oppress them had changed their minds.

MALCOLM X, speech given at the Organization of Afro-American Unity Rally, Audubon Ballroom, New York City, 24 January 1965

Every time I sit down to the typewriter, with every line I put on paper I am out to change the world, to capture reality, to melt it down and forge it into something entirely different.

JOHN KILLENS, *Beyond the Angry Black,* 1966

When a people are mired in oppression, they realize deliverance only when they have accumulated the power to enforce change.

MARTIN LUTHER KING, JR., in "Martin Luther King Defines Black Power," *New York Times Magazine,* 11 June 1967

What matters is not to know the world but to change it.

FRANTZ FANON, *Black Skin, White Masks,* 1967

Unless America changes drastically within the next few years, most American readers will continue to look at literature through the eyes of the white critic rather than the black.

DARWIN T. TURNER, in *College English,* April 1970

How most of us dread change, fight against it, or refuse to acknowledge it, even unto the last look in the coffin. We stand there, forcing ourselves to "see" that everything is as it was, that "he" really still looks the same, looks "just as he did in life." Of course "he" does not. What we [know] is gone forever. And did we ever know it. For even in the moment, moments, of our knowing, it was changing: was never the same from moment to moment, from second to second: was always leaving.

GWENDOLYN BROOKS, *Report From Part One,* 1972

When you start dealing with real change, you are talking about interfering with those who are in possession of something.

KWAME NKRUMAH, *Promise of Power,* 1973

A title is in jeopardy every time a champion steps into the ring.

JOE LOUIS, c. 1974

If you're going to bring about change, do it and be done with it.

MELVIN CHAPMAN, 1976

You can change the lyrics, but it's still the same song.

RAY CHARLES, *Brother Ray,* 1978

The first part of the '60s when Martin Luther King and Malcolm X were turning on the faucet and the pressure. That's when it turned around, it changed.

DICK (NIGHT TRAIN) LANE, *Blacks in Detroit,* 1980

Our moral leaders have been murdered, our children worship power and drugs, our official leadership is frequently a joke, usually merely oppressive. Our chosen and most respected soul singer—part of whose unspoken duty is to remind us who we are—has become a blonde.

ALICE WALKER, *In Search of Our Mothers' Gardens,* 1983

Everything will change. The only question is growing up or decaying.

NIKKI GIOVANNI, "An Answer to Some Questions on How I Write: In Three Parts," in Evans, ed., *Black Women Writers,* 1984

At times it may be better for the Omnipotent One to give men the wit and the will to continue to plan purposely and to struggle as best they know how to change things that seem immutable.

WILLIAM HASTIE, *Grace Under Pressure,* 1984

Where we stand today, everything has changed and nothing has changed. We have honored King with a national holiday, but we haven't talked enough of what he stood for and what we believed ourselves in those days.

JAMES LAWSON, speech given to the Southern Christian Leadership Council, Los Angeles, California, 28 May 1984

I have forgiven myself; I'll make a change. Once that forgiveness has taken place you can console yourself with the knowledge that a diamond is the result of extreme pressure. Less pressure is crystal, less than that is coal, less than that is fossilized leaves or plain dirt. Pressure can change you into something quite precious, quite wonderful, quite beautiful and extremely hard.

MAYA ANGELOU, in *USA Today,* 5 March 1985

[After the invasions of white settlers] there no longer was that wealth, that livestock, and our men had to head for urban areas, had to go to the mineon contract. That alone shattered the traditional lifestyle of the Black man.

WINNIE MANDELA, in "The Soul of Nonzamo Winnie Mandela," *Crisis,* November 1985

We are faced with endless possibilities for change, for metamorphosis. We change our environment, our speech, our style of living, our dress, and often our values. . . . We become somebody else.

RALPH ELLISON, "What These Children Are Like," *Going to the Territory,* 1986

There is no brilliant single stroke that is going to transform the water into wine or straw into gold.

COLEMAN YOUNG, in the *Detroit News,* 5 January 1986

[W]hen we learned to play by the rules, they changed the rules.

CALVIN BUTTS, in "Quest for Power," *Crisis,* February 1986

I'm starting with the man in the mirror./ I'm asking him to change his ways./ No message could get any clearer;/ if you want to make the world a better place take a look at yourself and make a change.

MICHAEL JACKSON, "Man In the Mirror," 1988

People create social conditions and people can change them.

TESS ONWUEME, in "The Broken Calabash," *City Arts Quarterly,* Fall 1988

People underestimate their capacity for change. There is never a right time to do a difficult thing. A leader's job is to help people have vision of their potential.

JOHN PORTER, speech given in Detroit, Michigan, June 1990

ple: with them stands the destiny of democracy in America.

PAUL ROBESON, *Here I Stand,* 1958

[God] did give us children to make [our] dreams seem worth while.

LORRAINE HANSBERRY, *A Raisin in the Sun,* 1959

What shall I tell my children?/ . . . You tell me—/
'Cause freedom ain't freedom when a man ain't free.

LANGSTON HUGHES, "Freedom Train," *Selected Poems,* 1959

I have never felt myself to be an honest part of anything since the world of childhood deserted me.

GEORGE LAMMING, *Season of Adventure,* 1960

Children have never been very good at listening to their elders, but they have never failed to imitate them.

JAMES BALDWIN, *Nobody Knows My Name,* 1961

A child cannot, thank Heaven, know how vast and how merciless is the nature of power, with what unbelievable cruelty people treat each other. He reacts to the fear in his parents' voices because his parents hold up the world for him and he has no protection without them.

JAMES BALDWIN, *The Fire Next Time,* 1963

If we are good to the child and to other people, he will get from us directly a conception of goodness more profound and significant than all the words we may use about goodness as an ideal. If we lose our temper and give way to hard, brittle words which we fling around and about, the child learns more profoundly and significantly than all the formal teaching about self control.

HOWARD THURMAN, *Disciplines of the Spirit,* 1963

I have a dream my four little children will one day live in a nation where they will not be judged by the color of their skin but by content of their character.

MARTIN LUTHER KING, JR., "I Have A Dream," speech given at Lincoln Memorial, Washington, D.C., 28 August 1963

A child is the root of the heart.

CAROLINA MARÍA DE JESUS, *Child of the Dark: The Diary of Carolina María de Jesus,* 15 July 1966

Any and every child born into the world deserves all the dignity and respect there is—in short, love, which is not a privilege, but a natural right.

KEORAPETSE KGOSITSILE, in "The Impulse Is Simple," *Negro Digest,* July 1968

sweet baked apple dappled cinnamon speckled sin of mine/ freckled peach brandy and amber wine woman.

EVERETT HOAGLUND, "Love Child," *Black Velvet,* 1970

A child must learn early to believe that he is somebody worthwhile and that he can do many praiseworthy things. The baby must be made to know that he or she is wanted. The child must have the love of [the family] and the protection they give . . . in order to live and flourish.

BENJAMIN MAYS, "What Man Lives By," in Philpot, ed., *Best Black Sermons,* 1972

I was happy to have children. I had always intended to have children. Not only because having "my own"—and "our own": because I knew that my husband, whoever he was to be, would want and care for and richly love them too—would stand up at such a joyous thing, but also because I respected and marveled at and admired my body. I wanted my body to do something its composition suggested it was supposed to do. I did not want my body to fail. I wanted my body, as well as my mind and spirit, to succeed, to reach an appropriate glory.

GWENDOLYN BROOKS, *Report From Part One,* 1972

There's a time when you have to explain to your children why they're born, and it's a marvelous thing if you know the reason by then.

HAZEL SCOTT, in "Great (Hazel) Scott!" *Ms.,* November 1974

But what's more important. Building a bridge or taking care of a baby.

JUNE JORDAN, *New Life, New Room,* 1975

Children make you want to start life over.

MUHAMMAD ALI, *The Greatest,* 1975

Just because a child's parents are poor or uneducated is no reason to deprive the child of basic human rights to health care, education, proper nutrition. We ignore the needs of Black children, poor children, and handicapped children in this country.

MARGARET WRIGHT EDELMAN, in "Society's Pushed-Out Children," *Psychology Today,* June 1975

Your child does not belong to you, and you must prepare your child to pick up the burden of his life long before the moment when you must lay your burden down.

JAMES BALDWIN, *The Devil Finds Work,* 1975

My heart leaps when I look into the face of my beautiful Indian child, wrapped in the strength of his father's arms: together we are the flag of North America. We are growing free and joyous.

BUFFY SAINTE-MARIE, in *Akwesasne Notes,* Winter 1976

Everywhere I go, kids walk around not with books under their arms, but with radios up against their heads. Children can't read or write but they can memorize whole albums.

JESSE JACKSON, in "Education," *Newsweek,* 27 June 1977

You may be a pain in the ass, you may be bad, but child, you belong to me.

RAY CHARLES, *Brother Ray,* 1978

If you don't have children the longing for them will kill you, and if you do, the worrying over them will kill you.

BUCHI EMECHETA, *The Joys of Motherhood,* 1979

Childhood is the incubation for the contaminants of civilization in the Western world.

ALFRED PASTER, *The Roots of Soul,* 1982

When a child has no sense of how he should fit into the society around him, he is culturally deprived.

RALPH ELLISON, "What These Children Are Like," *Going to the Territory,* 1986

When will children stop wanting, when will they be, when will they accomplish—not as children but as beings.

NURIDDIN FARAH, *Maps,* 1986

Adults admire children—they see angels in the infants they spy and marvel at God's generosity, some because they have no children and envy those who are thus blessed.

Ibid.

A child is a quicksilver fountain/ spilling over with tomorrows and tomorrows/ and that is why/ she is richer than you and I.

TOM BRADLEY, *The Impossible Dream,* 1986

Nowadays babies get up and walk soon's you drop 'em, but twenty years ago when I was a girl babies stayed babies longer.

TONI MORRISON, *Beloved,* 1987

Grown don't mean nothing to a mother. A child is a child. They get bigger, older, but grown. In my heart it don't mean a thing.

Ibid.

In Yoruba, we don't count our children. We just say the Gods have been kind to us.

WOLE SOYINKA, in "Wole Soyinka," *Ebony,* April 1987

Save the children!/ Save the children from dope, miseducation and poverty./ Save the children from gang warfare and adult abuse./ Save the children from the apathy and indifference and timidity of their elders.

JOHN H. JOHNSON, "Publisher's Statement," *Ebony,* August 1988

She was nurturing within her what had gone before and would come after. This child would tie her to that past and future as inextricably as it was now tied to her every heartbeat.

GLORIA NAYLOR, *The Women of Brewster Place,* 1988

Kids lived in such an insulated world, where the smallest disturbance was met with cries of protest.

Ibid.

We are starving our children to death at every level. And what we provide for them in the way of sedation, in the way of pacification, ultimately poisons the human spirit and makes them permanent spiritual cripples.

OSSIE DAVIS, "It's On Us," *City Arts Quarterly,* Spring 1988

Every child's sense of himself is terrifyingly fragile. He is at the mercy of his elders, and when he finds himself totally at the mercy of his peers, who know as little about themselves as he, it is because his elders have abandoned him. I am talking, then, about morale, that sense of self with which the child must be invested. No child can do it alone. Children, I submit, cannot be fooled. They can only be betrayed by adults.

JAMES BALDWIN in "Dark Days," *City Arts Quarterly,* Spring 1988

Our children's allegiance to high goals and standards will be principally established and enforced, not on the campus, but in the home.

HARRY EDWARDS, in "Hardline," *Detroit Free Press,* 8 May 1988

Your children need your presence more than your presents.

JESSE JACKSON "Down with Dope, Up with Hope," c. 1988

When I was a child I had these strange things I'd see and feel and now I'm putting them in wood . . . and just about everything I touch is Africa.

BESSIE HARVEY, in *Black Art: Ancestral Legacy,* 1989

We must teach our young girls to honor and respect the temples of their bodies. We must make our boys understand the difference between making a baby and being a father.

WILLIAM RASPBERRY, in the *Detroit News,* 9 June 1990

If you wish children well, deliver them to themselves, the ultimate reward for a parent is reflected glory.

VIVIAN AYERS-ALLEN, in "On Raising Creative Children," *McCall's,* February 1990

There's a child in all of us, a person who believes in a glorious future.

JASMINE GUY, in "Spotlight: Jasmine Guy," *Essence,* September 1990

Children are the only future of any people. If the children's lives are squandered, and if the children . . . are not fully developed at whatever cost and sacrifice, the people will have consigned themselves to certain death.

FRANCES CRESS WELSING, *The Isis Papers,* 1991

CHOICE

A slave has no choice.

EGYPT

I have made my choice. I had no alternative.

PAUL ROBESON, "The Artist Must Take Sides," *Daily Worker,* 4 November 1937

The choice is no longer between violence and nonviolence; it is either nonviolence and nonexistence.

MARTIN LUTHER KING, JR., "The American Dream," speech given at Lincoln University, Oxford, Pennsylvania, 6 June 1961

I would rather go to hell by choice than to stumble into Heaven by following the crowd.

BENJAMIN MAYS, *Born to Rebel,* 1971

It does not matter where we were born, what kind of rearing we had, who our friends were, what kind of trouble we got into, how low we sank, or how far behind we fell. When we add it all up, we still have some options left, we still have some choices we can make.

SAMUEL D. PROCTOR, in *Sermons from the Black Pulpit,* 1984

In the land of my choice, I was bluntly made to understand that because of the pigmentation of my skin, I was denied even the elementary necessities of life—food and shelter.

JOHN SOMERVILLE, in *American Visions,* February 1988

CHRIST/CHRISTIAN/CHRISTIANITY

The first dealings we had with men calling themselves Christians exhibited the worst features of corrupt and sordid hearts, and convinced us that no cruelty is too great, no villainy and no robbery too abhorrent for even enlightened men to perform.

HENRY HIGHLAND GARNET, "An Address to the Slaves of the United States of America," speech given at the National Negro Convention, Buffalo, New York, August 1843

The Christianity of America is a Christianity of whose votaries it may be truly said, as it was of the ancient scribes and Pharisees, "They bind heavy burdens and grievous to be borne, and lay them on men's shoulders, but they themselves will not move them with one of their fingers. All their works they do for to be seen of men." . . . Dark and terrible as is this picture, I hold it to be strictly true of the overwhelming mass of professional Christians in America. . . . They would be shocked at fellowshipping a sheep-stealer; and at the same time they hug to their communion a man-stealer, and brand me an infidel. They attend the Pharisees' strictness to the outward forms of religion, while neglecting the weightier matters of law, judgment, mercy and faith.

FREDERICK DOUGLASS, speech given at Wesleyan Chapel, Cork, Ireland, 17 October 1845

Here a Christian writhes in bondage still,/ Beneath his brother Christian's rod,/ And pastors trample down at will,/ The image of the living God.

JAMES WHITFIELD, "America," 1853

Great damage was done the cause of Christianity by the position assumed on slavery by the American churches. . . . Think of a religious kidnapper! A Christian slave-breeder! A slave-trader, loving his neighbor as himself, receiving the sacraments . . . , then the next day selling babies by the dozen. . . . Imagine a religious man selling his own children into eternal bondage! Think of a Christian defending slavery out of the Bible, and declaring there is no higher law, but atheism is the first principle of a Republic Government.

WILLIAMS WELLS-BROWN, *The Negro in the American Rebellion,* 1880

Where and when has the Christianity of the land recorded its protest against mob violence, lynchings, and outrages?

H. I. JOHNSON, in the *Christian Recorder,* 1893

That great Christian body which expresses itself in opposition to card playing, athletics, sports, and promiscuous dancing, protested against saloons, inveighed against tobacco, wholly ignored the seven million colored people whose plea was for a word of sympathy and support.

IDA B. WELLS, in Duster, ed., *Crusade for Justice,* 1928

You can't make a good Christian out of a hungry man.

BOOKER T. WASHINGTON, *Selected Speeches of Booker T. Washington,* 1932

Christianity was on its way to world power that would last. That was only the beginning. Military Power was called in time and time again to carry forward the gospel of peace. There is not apt to be any difference of opinion between you and a dead man.

ZORA NEALE HURSTON, *Dust Tracks on a Road,* 1942

The most devastating answer to this business of ascribing guilt by association is when we are reminded that it was said of Christ "that he conspired with publicans and sinners," and therefore must be guilty.

WILLIAM HASTIE, c. 1945

Christianity is an adjunct of the armed-to-the teeth Nordic exploiters, and is carrying out God's will to dispossess others and to exterminate them by segregation to clear the way for their enjoyment of the whole earth.

CARTER G. WOODSON, "African Superiority," c. 1945

No one can say that Christianity has failed. It has never been tried.

ADAM CLAYTON POWELL, JR., *Marching Blacks,* 1945

The earliest Christians pictured the Virgin Mary and Christ as black, both being an evolution of the worship of Isis and Horus which was once common in Rome.

J. A. ROGERS, *Nature Knows No Color Line,* 1952

Unfortunately Christianity came to the black man through white oppressors who demanded that he reject his concern for the world as well as his blackness and affirm the next world and whiteness.

JAMES CONE, *Black Theology and Black Power,* 1969

Christian love means giving no ground to the enemy but relentlessly insisting on one's dignity as a person.

Ibid.

Once a man walked this earth and spoke with such uncommon power that He separated history into B.C. and A.D.;... the teachings He proclaimed become newer and more challenging as the centuries roll.

ADAM CLAYTON POWELL, JR., *Adam by Adam,* 1971

America is not a Christian country. It is a country of pretensions, of "churchianity," where the institution of Christianity has been perverted to propagate the doctrines of segregation and discrimination.

Ibid.

We are made of star, or rather the whole cosmos is made of our own flesh. And when the Word was made flesh and dwelt among us, as Adam said of Eve: "This now is flesh of our flesh and bone of my bones." In Christ's body, as in ours, there is all creation. And the whole creation is also in the mystical body of Christ, which is all of us and all creation too....

ERNESTO CARDENAL, "Love," *Vida en al Amor,* 1974

Christianity is a good philosophy if you live it, but it's controlled by white people who preach it but don't practice it. They just organize it and use it any which way they want to.

MUHAMMAD ALI, in "Playboy Interview," *Playboy,* November 1975

The white Christian church never raised to the heights of Christ. It stayed within the limits of culture.

JESSE JACKSON, on "McNeil-Lehrer Report," 10 March 1977

It is difficult to see all the religions in the world and then come back to Christianity thinking it has all the answers.

ARTHUR ASHE, in *USA Today,* 24 November 1985

Christianity was based upon the life and activity of an African (Black) prophet named Jesus.

FRANCES CRESS WELSING, *The Isis Papers,* 1991

CHURCH

The giant crime committed by the Founders of the African Methodist Episcopal Church, against the prejudiced white American and the timid Black—the crime which seems unpardonable—was that they dared to organize a Church of men, men to think for themselves, men to talk for themselves, men to act for themselves.

BENJAMIN T. TANNER, "An Apology for African Methodism," *AME Review,* 1867

Go to our churches and see the silk, the satins, the velvet, and the costly feathers, and talk with the wearers and you will see at once the main hindrance of self evaluation.

WILLIAM WELLS-BROWN, *My Southern Home,* 1880

The church among black people has been a social cosmos; it has provided an emotional outlet, a veritable safety valve for people caught up in the whirling storms of life. She has been a source of inspiration and entertainment of movements, and plans which have moved the entire nation.

KELLY MILLER, *Race Adjustment,* 1908

By accepting segregation and emphasizing other worldly matters, the church tended to play an accommodating role and to stimulate the sentiments of racial solidarity.

RALPH BUNCHE, *Concepts and Ideologies of Negro Problems,* 1940

The church is the door through which we first walked into Western civilization; religion is the form in which America first allowed our personalities to be expressed.

RICHARD WRIGHT, *12 Million Black Voices,* 1941

The Negro Church has known how far it can safely instruct its people to go in righting their wrongs, and this conservation has no doubt saved the Negro from the fate of the oppressed groups who have suffered extermination because of their failure to handle their cause more diplomatically.

CARTER G. WOODSON, *The History of the Negro Church,* 1945

They stopped me from swinging in church, so I had to swing outside.

FATS WALLER, c. 1945

The doctrine of brotherly love which the white man preached from his god was like the wings of the ostrich. No ostrich has ever flown by his wings.

VICTOR REID, *New Day,* 1949

I went to church when I was very young, but when I was six, I asked my mother why the church kept calling me a sinner when I hadn't done anything wrong.

MILES DAVIS, in *Esquire,* 1956

Where people have been oppressed as a race group, the Church has sought safeguards and concessions for the individual, evading the necessity and responsibility of group action. And while it fixed its eyes on Calvary or kept up an aloofness from political realities, the road has been slipping back under its feet.

EZEKIEL MPHAHLELE, *Down Second Avenue,* 1959

The Church in the colonies is the white people's Church, the foreigner's Church. She does not call the native to God's ways but to the ways of the white man, of the master, of the oppressor. And as we know, in this matter many are called but few chosen.

FRANTZ FANON, *Wretched of the Earth,* 1963

The church once changed society. It was then a thermostat of society. But today . . . the church is merely a thermometer, which measures rather than molds popular opinion.

MARTIN LUTHER KING, JR., in "Playboy Interview," *Playboy,* January 1965

Portuguese Catholic priests had sprinkled holy water on slave ships, entreating God to give safe passage to the crews and cargoes on journeys across the Atlantic. American slave owners had used the Bible to prove that God wanted slavery, and even Jesus Christ had admonished slaves to "render unto their masters" obedience. As long as the black man looked to the white man's God for his freedom, the black man would remain enslaved.

MAYA ANGELOU, *The Heart of a Woman,* 1981

When it came to action we were in the church where we had been baptized. We knew when to moan, when to shout, and when to start speaking in tongues.

Ibid.

A Church that is in solidarity with the poor can never become a wealthy Church.

DESMOND TUTU, *Hope and Suffering,* 1983

The black church became not merely the means through which Western thoughts from Plotinus to Buber entered indirectly into the lived experience of black people, but a common spiritual, economic, and political experience.

CHARLES JOHNSON, *Being and Race,* 1988

Every Sunday, black congregations sing and perform the music of slave masters and the captains of slave ships while ignoring the music of Ellington, Monk, Coltrane, Tyner, Johnson, Shorter, Byrd, Mingus, Roach, McKinney, and hundreds of others.

DAN ALDRIDGE, in "Mayflower Piano Festival," *City Arts Quarterly,* Summer 1988

CITY

It is one of the defects of the provincial mind that it can never see any good in a great city. It concludes that as many people are wicked, where large numbers are gathered there must be a much greater amount of evil than in a smaller place. It overlooks the equally obvious reasoning that some people are good and there must be a larger amount of goodness.

PAUL LAURENCE DUNBAR, *The Uncalled,* 1898

Let us spend less time talking about the part of the city that we cannot live in and more time in making the part of city that we can live in beautiful and attractive.

BOOKER T. WASHINGTON, speech given to the Convention of National Negro Business League, 1914

The city has conquered me/ Though it causes me pain,/ I love its bewitching spell/ That's rampant in my brain.

JOHN HENRIK CLARKE, "The City's Conquest," *Rebellion in Rhyme,* 1948

If Atlanta succeeds, the South will succeed. If Atlanta fails, the South will fail, for Atlanta is the South in the miniature.

MARTIN LUTHER KING, JR., speech at the Southern Christian Leadership Conference Crusade, 12 January 1958

[A]ll cities [have] different personalities, which [are] modified by the people you [meet] in them.

DUKE ELLINGTON, *Music Is My Mistress,* 1973

A city is dying when it has an eye for real estate value but has lost its heart for personal values, when it has an understanding of traffic flow, but little concern about the flow of human beings, when we have increasing competence in buildings, but less and less time for housing and ethical codes, when human values are absent at the heart of a city's decision making, planning, and the execution of its plans in the processes like relocation.

HOWARD MOODY, c. 1974

If the cities go down, the suburbs go down, if the suburbs go down, the nation goes down.

COLEMAN YOUNG, *Current Biography,* 1977

In a great city, City Hall must be a beacon to the people's aspirations, not a barrier.

TOM BRADLEY, *The Impossible Dream,* 1986

CIVILIZATION

The Creator gave all nations arts and sciences. Where nations have turned aside to idolatry, they have lost their civilization.

GEORGE WASHINGTON WILLIAM, c. 1876

Civilization is handed from one people to another, its great foundation source God, our father.

WILLIAM WELLS-BROWN, c. 1877

Old civilizations die hard, and old prejudices die harder.

WILLIAM CROGMAN, speech given at the 26th Anniversary of the Emancipation Proclamation Convention, Atlanta, Georgia, 1889

Our boasted civilization is but a veneer which cracks and scrubs off at the first impact of primal passions.

CHARLES W. CHESTNUTT, *The Marrow of Tradition,* 1901

No one can say, who has any respect for the truth, that the United States is a civilized nation, especially if we take the daily papers and inspect them for a few moments and see the deeds of horror.

H. M. TURNER, *20th Century Negro Literature or a Cyclopedia of Thought on the Vital Topics Relating to the American Negro,* 1902

Being worked meant degradation; working means civilization.

BOOKER T. WASHINGTON, *The Story of My Life,* 1907

White man's civilization is as much a misnomer as the white man's multiplication table. It is the equal inheritance of anyone who can appropriate and apply it.

KELLY MILLER, "As To The Leopard's Spots," *Race Adjustment,* 1908

Civilization is not a spontaneous generation with any race or nation known to history, but the torch to be handed from race to race from age to age.

KELLY MILLER, *The American Negro,* 1908

No civilization can become worldwide and enduring if a white skin is the indispensable passport to justice and distinction. This would exclude the majority of mankind.

CHARLES V. ROMAN, *Sciences and Ethics,* 1912

The march of civilization is attended by strange influences.

WILLIAM ALLISON SWEENEY, *The Great War,* 1919

By the time Alexander the Great was sweeping the civilized world with conquest after conquest from Chaeronicia to Gaza, from Babylon to Cabal, by the time the first Aryan conquerors were learning the rudiments of war and government at the feet of Aristotle, and by the time Athens was laying down the foundations of European civilization, the earliest and greatest Ethiopian culture had already flourished and dominated the civilized world for over four centuries and a half. Imperial

Ethiopia had conquered Egypt and founded the XXVth Dynasty.

JOSEPH B. DANQUAH, 1927

When I look at the rest of the world, I wonder if perhaps Africa is not more civilized.

RICHMOND BARTHE, 1939

We had our own civilization in Africa before we were captured and carried off to this land. We smelted iron, danced, made music and folk poems; we sculpted, worked in glass, spun cotton and wool, wove baskets and cloth. We invented a medium of exchange, mined silver and gold, made pottery and cutlery, we fashioned tools and utensils of brass, bronze, ivory, quartz, and granite. We had our own literature, our own systems of law, religion, medicine, science, and education.

RICHARD WRIGHT, *12 Million Black Voices,* 1941

[G]reat slashes of civilization [spit]/ holy water on domesticated brows.

DAVID DIOP, "Vultures," *Poundings,* 1956

When you civilize a man, you only civilize an individual, but when you civilize a woman, you civilize a whole people.

PATRICE LUMUMBA, *Congo, My Country,* 1961

Civilization lies first in the mind.

JAMES BALDWIN, *Nobody Knows My Name,* 1961

A nation or a civilization that continues to produce softminded men purchases its own spiritual death on an installment plan.

MARTIN LUTHER KING, JR., *The Strength to Love,* 1963

Form is what counts, my friend. That's what civilization is . . . the forming of man.

AIMÉ CÉSAIRE, *Tragedy of King Christophe,* 1963

What would civilization resemble if all revolutionaries, inventors, adventurers, and scientists had heeded the inevitable voice of the doubting Thomases, who perennially admonish that every daring and novel exploit is predestined to fail?

ROBERT WILLIAMS, in "USA: The Potential of a Minority Revolution," *The Crusader Monthly Newsletter,* May–June, 1965

The humanism of the twentieth century which can only be the Civilization of the Universal, would be impoverished if it excluded a single value of a single person, a single race, a single continent.

LEOPOLD SENGHOR, speech given at the World Festival of Negro Arts, Dakar, Senegal, 1966

Cities are the jewels, the showplaces of any civilization.

COLEMAN YOUNG, *Current Biography,* 1977

Out of the encounter with oppression have emerged the trauma of a Black skin in a white world, and the culture of Black survival, and the influence of black aesthetics on Western civilization.

MARTHA COBB, *Africa In Latin America,* c. 1978

Mankind's prohibition against incest marked a starting point toward civilization.

CHEIKH ANTA DIOP, in "Civilization or Barbarism: the Legacy of Cheikh Anta Diop," *Journal of African Civilization,* November 1982

A civilization is always judged in its decline.

MELVIN TOLSON in Giovanni, "An Answer to Some Questions on How I Write," in Evans, ed., *Black Women Writers,* 1984

The supreme fact of mechanical civilization is that you become a part of it, or get sloughed off (under).

JEAN TOOMER, in Kerman and Eldridge, *The Lives of Jean Toomer,* 1987

If you knew what civilization was about, we wouldn't kill the animals, including the human animal.

KRIS PARKER A.K.A. KRS-ONE, in the *Detroit Free Press,* 8 March 1992

CLASS

What I call middle-class society is any society that becomes rigidified in predetermined forms, forbidding all evolution, all gains, all progress, all discovery . . . a closed society in which life has no taste, in which the air is tainted, in which ideas and men are corrupt.

FRANTZ FANON, *Black Skin, White Masks,* 1967

We have developed an underclass in this nation. And unless this underclass is made a working class, we are going to continue to have problems.

MARTIN LUTHER KING, JR., speech given at Poor People's Campaign, Memphis, Tennessee, March 1968

Blacks are part of the middle class to the degree that they can find someplace to flee beyond the perimeter of the central city.

COLEMAN YOUNG, c. 1975

A competitive society needs an underclass—a class of the unemployed who function as targets for the displacement of frustrations, anxieties, and fears by those others who are employed.

JOHN CONYERS, 1978

CLOTHES

Naked came we into the world, and naked shall we depart from it.

AESOP, *Fables,* 600 B.C

Clothes put on while running, come off while running.

CONGO

He who wears too fine clothes shall go about in rags.

MAURITANIA

Put on that red dress, baby, 'cause we're going out tonight.

BLUES

She all dressed up so till it would take a doctor to tell her how near she is dressed to death.

ZORA NEALE HURSTON, *Moses, Man of the Mountain,* 1939

I wouldn't enjoy being all dressed up in Paris gowns, mink coat and presiding over a gorgeous mansion, if any old un-American could come along and lynch or rape or kill me, as they tried to kill Paul at Peekskill—or could bomb or dynamite me and my mansion. I'd rather be dressed up and living in Civil Rights. I would feel safe and very well dressed if I wore my first-class citizenship; that would be more stylish and becoming and more comfortable than anything else any American could wear.

ESLANDA GOODE ROBESON, in "Here's My Story," *Freedom,* July 1953

To President Johnson's Presidential Scholars' reception I went, beautifully gowned in blue chiffon: for surely, I fancied, White House guests don their "best." I arrived to find all the other ladies in knits, tweeds, linen. . . . But I stayed.

GWENDOLYN BROOKS, *Report From Part One,* 1972

A man does not choose as his boon companion an individual whom he never sees in dress clothes except when carrying a tray at his banquet.

WILLIAM HASTIE, *Grace Under Pressure,* 1984

What I didn't have in suits, I tried to make up for in cleanliness.

TOM BRADLEY, *The Impossible Dream,* 1986

Nobody ever asked what kind of car Ralph Bunche drove or what kind of designer suit Martin Luther King, Jr., bought.

MARIAN WRIGHT EDELMAN, "Save the Children: They Are Our Most Precious Resource," *Ebony,* August 1986

We are a wave of fine, impeccably dressed sameness.

RACHEL BROWN, in "Window on the Park," *City Arts Quarterly,* Fall–Winter 1987

COLLEGE

Not only do we recruit you, we graduate you.

LANGSTON UNIVERSITY MOTTO

[College provides] a glimpse of the higher life, the broader possibilities of humanity, which is granted to the man who, amid the rush and roar of living, pauses four short years to learn what living means.

W. E. B. DU BOIS, speech given at Fisk University commencement, 1898

Perhaps the most valuable thing I got out of my second year [at Hampton University] was an understanding of the use and the value of the Bible. . . . Before this I never cared a great deal about it, but now I learned to love the Bible, not only for the spiritual help which it gives, but on account of it as literature.

BOOKER T. WASHINGTON, in *Up From Slavery,* 1901

All men cannot go to college but some men must; every isolated group or nation must have its yeast, must have for the talented few centers of training where men are not so mystified and befuddled by the hard and necessary toll of earning a living, as to have no aims higher than their bellies, and no God greater than Gold.

W. E. B. DU BOIS, "The Talented Tenth," *The Negro Problem,* 1903

A university is a human invention for the transmission of knowledge and culture from generation to generation.

Ibid.

Go with me tonight to the Tuskegee Institute . . . in an old plantation where a few years ago my people were bought and sold, and I will show you an industrial village with nearly eight hundred young men and women working . . . preparing themselves that they may prepare thousands of others of our race that they may contribute their full quota of virtue, of thrift and intelligence to the prosperity of our beloved country.

BOOKER T. WASHINGTON, *Selected Speeches of Booker T. Washington,* 1932

There would be no prejudiced white officials out of whom appropriations must be wheedled by way of various and sundry forms of "bootlicking"! There would be no "Simon Legrees" constantly brandishing a psychological whip over its purposeful and sincere faculty. Our youth would be taught the true meaning of manhood and womanhood; they would leave this institution bubbling over with enthusiasm and initiative—ready to grapple with, and solve, the vital problems of their race.

O'WENDELL SHAW, *Greater Need Below,* 1936

Just because you have colleges and universities doesn't mean you have education. The colleges and universities in the American educational system are skillfully used to mis-educate.

MALCOLM X, in interview for *Young Socialist,* 18 January 1965

Black colleges have been menders, healers for wounded minds and restless souls. They have produced sterling talent which benefited the Republic beyond measures of calculation, not only in material contributions but intellectual, cultural, moral, and spiritual offerings.

HOWARD UNIVERSITY BULLETIN, 1982

Ignorance, arrogance, and racism have bloomed as Superior Knowledge in all too many universities.

ALICE WALKER, *In Search of Our Mothers' Gardens,* 1983

It was from Howard, Morehouse, Fisk, and those predominantly Black colleges that the Martin Luther Kings, Thurgood Marshalls, Andrew Youngs, Langston Hughes and Toni Morrisons came.

LERONE BENNETT, c. 1986

At a Black college, a student has the greatest choice of opportunity for self-expression and leadership without the racial factor coming into the picture.

FREDERICK PATTERSON, in *Choosing to Succeed,* 1986

Black colleges can dare our students to not only dream of buying that dream house with the two car garage, but also of owning the car franchise itself.

MARVA COLLINS, in *ibid.*

Fisk should continue as a shining monument to education rather than in a tombstone with a flame in front of it.

BILL AND CAMILLE COSBY, in *Message,* February 1987

In that rich enclave [Sarah Lawrence] of white people and snow, any Black face, any place, was likely to be a sun.

ALICE WALKER, 1988

All that I learned at Howard with their outstanding faculty is the reason I have had the success that I have.

ROBERTA FLACK, in *Jet,* 27 August 1988

I believe in desegregation and I would like to see the white schools do as good a job of desegregating as the Black schools. The average Black college has a white faculty anywhere from thirty to eighty percent. You can't find a white college in America with a Black faculty of that percent.

TONY BROWN, 1989

Tuskegee Institute was an island within which blacks could live and move about comfortably, surrounded by whites, who handicapped themselves and poisoned their own individual and collective lives by the virulence of their hatred for Blacks.

BENJAMIN DAVIS, JR., *Benjamin Davis, Jr.: An Autobiography,* 1990

I went to college because my daddy gave me two choices. One was college, the other was death.

DREW BROWN, in the *Pittsburgh Courier,* 17 August 1991

COLONIZATION

It is the sleepless agent of colonization. It has penetrated the utmost bounds of the globe. It has wrenched from the weak their fertile valleys and luxuriant hillsides; and when theyprotested, when they resisted, it has enslaved them or cut their throats.

T. THOMAS FORTUNE, "The Nationalization of Africa," speech given at the Africa and the Africans Congress, Atlanta, Georgia, 12–13 December 1896

Colonialism is an abomination; it is a sin; it is an evil. It brings about the degradation and the demoralization of the human spirit, of the personality of the people who are the victims of it.

A. PHILIP RANDOLPH, speech given in Atlantic City, New Jersey, 11 December 1937

[I]n the past the white world was in power. . . . They called it European history, or colonialism. They ruled all the dark world. . . . They didn't call that racism, they called it colonialism.

MALCOLM X, speech given at the Organization of Afro-American Unity Rally, Audubon Ballroom, New York City, 24 January 1965

The times have passed when any nation sitting three or four thousand miles away could give orders to Indians on the basis of their color superiority to do as they wished. India has changed and she is no more a country of natives.

INDIRA GANDHI, speech given to the Workers' Congress, New Delhi, India, 2 December 1971

COLOR

The color of the skin is in no way connected with strength of the mind or intellectual powers.

BENJAMIN BANNEKER, preface to *Banneker's Almanac,* 1796

They think because they hold us in infernal chains we wish to be white, or of their color, but they are dreadfully deceived—we wish to be just as it pleased our Creator to have made us.

DAVID WALKER, *Appeal to the Coloured Citizens of the World,* 1829

Because the brood-sows left side pigs were black/ Whose sable tincture was by nature struck,/ Were you by justice bound to pull them back/ And leave the sandy colored pigs to suck.

GEORGE HORTON, "The Slave," *Liberator,* 29 March 1834

Color is made to obscure the brightest endowments, to degrade the fairest character, and to check the highest and most praiseworthy aspirations.

CHARLES REMOND, in the *Liberator,* 25 February 1842

The nearer a slave approaches an Anglo Saxon in complexion, the more he is abused by both owner and fellow slaves. The owner flogs him "to keep him in his place" and the slaves hate him on account of his being whiter than themselves. Thus the complexion of the slave became a crime, and he is made to curse his father for the Anglo-Saxon blood that courses through his veins.

WILLIAM WELLS-BROWN, *Narrative of the Life of William Wells-Brown,* 1856

There are persons of complexion as dark as any mulatto, and often with frizzy hair, who are recognized as white, but they are not of African origin, nor descendants of a race of slaves. If it were color they would suffer the same indignations, and be subject to the same unrighteous laws which we are.

PHILIP BELL, 1862

I am held to answer for the crime of color when I was not consulted in the matter. Had I been consulted in the matter and my future fully described, I think I should have objected to being born in this gospel land.

James Rapier, in the *Congressional Record,* 9 June 1874

Don't be afraid to show your colors and to own them.

William Wells-Brown, *My Southern Home,* 1880

Though all call Krishna black,/ He is not black./ He is the glow of the moon—/ the black moon,/ And there is no other moon to equal him. . . .

Lalan, c. 1885

I am the Smoke King/ I am black/ I am darkening with song/ I am hearkening with wrong/ I will be black as blackness can/ the blacker the mantle the mightier the man.

W. E. B. Du Bois, "The Song of the Smoke," *The Horizon,* 1899

Most men in the world are colored. A belief in humanity means a belief in colored men. The future world will, in all reasonable possibility, be what colored men make it.

W. E. B. Du Bois, c. 1902

The problem of the twentieth century is the problem of the color line, the question is how far differences of a race which show themselves chiefly in the color of the skin and the texture of the hair will hereafter be made the basis of denying over half the world the right of sharing to their utmost ability the opportunities and privileges of modern civilization.

W. E. B. Du Bois, "Of the Training of Black Men," *Atlantic Monthly,* September 1902

Black contains by absorption all the colors of the rainbow though it does not reflect them, we have in us all the elements of civilization and may yet reflect them as brilliantly as any man.

Charles W. Roman, "A Knowledge of History Conducive to Racial Solidarity," speech given in Wilberforce, Ohio, 24 February 1911

His color had been the mark of enslavement and was taken to be also the mark of inferiority; for prejudice does not reason, or it would not be prejudice.

William Pickens, *The New Negro,* 1916

. . . so blacks have their chocolate, chocolate-to-the-bone, brown, low brown, teasing-brown, high brown, yellow, high yellow and so on.

Claude McKay, in review of *Shuffle Along, Liberator,* December 1921

I have been taught that color counts for nothing. It is what we are—therefore I forget color. Besides, of what color am I?

Joshua Henry Jones, *By Sanction of Law,* 1924

Black queen of beauty, thou hast given color to the world./ Among other women thou art the fairest.

Marcus Garvey, "The Black Woman," 1927

I tell you if I have any taint to be ashamed of at all, it is the taint of white blood.

Ida B. Wells, in Duster, ed., *Crusade for Justice,* 1928

I am not tragically colored. There is no great sorrow damned up in my soul, nor lurking behind my eyes. I do not mind at all. I do not belong to the sobbing school of Negrohood who hold that nature somehow has given them a lowdown dirty deal and whose feelings are all hurt about it. No, I do not weep at the world—I am too busy sharpening my oyster knife.

Zora Neale Hurston, "Colored Me," *World Tomorrow,* 1928

As long as there lurks deep down in the consciousness of any Negro a feeling that white is better than black, just so long is that person a hindrance to human advancement.

William Hastie, in *Person and Affairs,* 10 February 1934

We've got Chinese, white, black and mixed; but remember that our colors are cheap, for after many years of contracts and tricks nobody's purity runs very deep.

Nicolas Guillén, *West Indies Ltd,* 1934

And Cuba has long known that she is a mulatto.

Ibid.

Color consciousness was the fundamental of my restlessness. And it was something with which my fellow expatriates could sympathize, but which they could not altogether understand. For they were not Black like me. Not being Black and unable to see deep into the profundity of blackness, some even thought that I preferred to be white like them. They couldn't imagine that I had no desire merely to exchange my Black problems for their white problem. For all their knowledge and sophistication, they couldn't understand the instinctive and animal and purely physical pride of a Black person resolute in being himself and yet living a simple civilized life like themselves. Because their education in the white world had trained them to see a person of color either as an inferior or as an exotic.

CLAUDE MCKAY, *A Long Way from Home,* 1937

[M]y blackness is neither tower nor cathedral/ It takes root in the red flesh of the soil/ It takes root in the ardent flesh of the sky/ It breaks through the opaque prostration with its upright patience.

AIME CÉSAIRE, *Notes on a Return to the Native Land,* 1947

Marcus Garvey exalted everything Black. He insisted Black stood for strength and beauty.

JOHN HOPE FRANKLIN, *From Slavery to Freedom,* 1947

No one color can describe the various and varied complexions in our group. They range from the deep black to the fairest white with all the colors of the rainbow thrown in for good measure. When twenty or thirty of us meet, it is as hard to find three or four with the same complexion as it would be to catch greased lightning in a bottle.

MARY CHURCH TERRELL, in the *Washington Post,* 14 May 1949

We are blossoms of the sun, and as blossoms owe their color to sunlight so do human beings.

J. A. ROGERS, *Nature Knows No Color Line,* 1952

This world is white no longer, and it will never be white again.

JAMES BALDWIN, *Notes of a Native Son,* 1955

I thank you, Lord, for having made me Black./ I have carried the World since the dawn of time/ and in the night my laughter at the World/ creates the day.

BERNARD DADIÉ, "I Thank You, Lord," *Dance of the Days,* 1956

I thank you, Lord, for having made me Black,/ for having made me/ the sum of all pain./ A thousand swords have pierced my heart./ A thousand brands have burned me./ And my blood has reddened the snow of all the calvaries,/ and my blood, at each dawn, has reddened all horizons.

Ibid.

Color is an act of God that neither confers privileges nor imposes a handicap. A man's skin is like the day: day is neither clear or dark. There is nothing more to it until external agencies come in and invest it with special meaning and importance.

PETER ABRAHAM, in *Holiday Magazine,* 1959

All token Blacks have the same experience. I have been pointed at as a solution to things that have not yet begun to be solved, because pointing at us token Blacks eases the consciences of millions, and this is dreadfully wrong.

LEONTYNE PRICE, in *Divas: Impressions of Six Opera Superstars,* 1959

To remain neutral in a situation where the laws of the land virtually criticized God for having created men of color was the sort of thing I could not, as a Christian, tolerate.

ALBERT LUTHULI, "The Dignity of Man," Nobel Peace Prize Acceptance Speech, 1961

We live surrounded by white images, and white in this world is synonymous with the good, light, beauty, success, so that, despite ourselves sometimes, we run after whiteness and deny our darkness. . . .

PAULE MARSHALL, "Reena," in Clarke, ed. *American Negro Short Stories,* 1966

I am black: I am the incarnation of a complete fusion with the world, an intuitive understanding of the earth, an abandonment of my ego in the heart of the cosmos.

FRANTZ FANON, *Black Skin, White Masks,* 1967

To us, the man who adores the Negro is as "sick" as the man who abominates him. [And] conversely, the black man who wants to turn his race white is as miserable as he who preaches hatred for the white man.

Ibid.

We must never be ashamed of our heritage . . . [or] the color of our skin. Black is as beautiful as any color. . . . I am Black and beautiful.

MARTIN LUTHER KING, JR., "Some Things We Must Do," speech given in Cleveland, Ohio, 9 April 1967

Ultimately Dr. King's dream still has fascination for me. I shall keep as the ideal an open society where men are brothers—color-blind if you will—for eventually humanity must transcend color.

JAMES FARMER, *Black Is Becoming*, 1968

Blackness is the same as whiteness as far as God and truth is concerned. God has all kinds of colors in his universe and has not condemned any color.

C. L. FRANKLIN, "The Preacher Who Got Drunk," 1969

Men were not created for separation and color is not the essence of man's humanity.

JAMES CONE, *Black Theology and Black Power*, 1969

Blackness is no longer a color, it is an attitude.

DICK GREGORY, c. 1970

Black people have freed themselves from the dead weight albatross of blackness that once hung about their neck. They have done it by picking it up in their arms and holding it out with pride for all the world to see. They have done it by embracing it—not in the dark but in the searing light of the white sun. They have said "Yes" to it and found that the skin that was once seen as symbolizing their shame is in reality their badge of honor.

SHIRLEY CHISHOLM, *Unbought and Unbossed*, 1970

Children are vari-colored—tea, coffee, chocolate, mocha, honey eggplant, coated with red pepper, red pepper dipped in eggplant—but the shades of color now count for nothing.

JAMES BALDWIN, c. 1971

Color is the crucial ingredient in the recipe of America's melting pot.

DICK GREGORY, *No More Lies*, 1971

It is not only in the Orient that white is the color of death.

LERONE BENNETT, *Challenge of Blackness*, 1972

Virtue itself and prudence are color free; there is no color in an honorable mind, no color in skill. Why does thou fear or doubt that the blackest man may scale the lofty house of the Western Caesar?

FRANCIS WILLIAMS "Ode," in *Quotations in Black*, 1976

All we want is the equal opportunity to compete fairly in the marketplace—without the color of human skin making a bit of difference in the business decisions that are made in that marketplace.

EARL GRAVES, "Black Reflections," *Negro History Bulletin*, June 1981

[A]t first color doesn't mean very much to little children, black or white. Only as they grow older and absorb poisons from adults does color begin to blind them.

ROY WILKINS, *Standing Fast*, 1982

The problem of the twenty-first century will still be the problem of the color line, not only "the relation of the darker to the lighter races of men [sic] in Asia and Africa, in America and the islands of the sea," but the relations between the darker and the lighter people of the same races, and of the women who represent both dark and light within each race.

ALICE WALKER, *In Search of Our Mothers' Gardens*, 1983

The colored race is just like a flower garden, with every color flower represented.

Ibid.

"What is a people that props itself up on the color of its skin? And what is a people that excludes the womb-source of its own genetic heritage?" For certainly every Afro-American is descended from a black black woman.

TRELLIE JEFFERS, in *ibid.*

The challenge we all face is to be judged by the body of our work rather than by the color of our bodies.

ED BRADLEY, c. 1986

We were Black Americans in West Africa, where for the first time in our lives the color of our skin was accepted as correct and normal.

MAYA ANGELOU, *All God's Children Need Traveling Shoes,* 1986

I've been called by Whites a yellow nigger, a light-skinned nigger, a red uppity nigger, a fair-skinned seditious nigger.

MALCOLM X, in *ibid.*

The ancients didn't fall into the error of biological racism; black skin color was not a sign of inferiority. Greek and Roman didn't establish color as an obstacle to integration. Color was not the basis for judging a man.

FRANK SNOWDEN, in "Blacks in the Classical World," *American Visions,* October 1987

She was tall and her skin was the color of black coffee with a tad of sweet cream added. She had on a Rastafarian beret, and her clothes were the mystic blend of all colors, textures, and radical ideas. She looked to me like a peacock in a woman's clothing. Her eyes were the color of tiger-eye stones, and her lips were painted bright, happy sunshine orange.

RACHEL BROWN, in "Window on the Park," *City Arts Quarterly,* Fall–Winter 1987

Color can be a cage and color consciousness can become a terminal condition.

JOHN WIDEMAN, in "The Divisible Man," *Life,* Spring 1988

What my color is, is somebody else's problem not mine. People will say, "You're a terrific Black general." I'm trying to be the best general I can be.

COLIN POWELL, 1990

I am proud of my heritage and happy to represent my people of color. Being Black is one of the advantages I had in the pageant. It made me stand out.

CAROLE ANN GIST, speech given at Cass Technical High School, 1990

[At West Point] I got stared at [as] the "brown curiosity" [and] always attracted lots of attention.

BENJAMIN DAVIS, JR., *Benjamin Davis, Jr.: An Autobiography,* 1990

I refuse to let my nation's fixation with color deter me from fulfilling myself.

BERNARD SHAW, in *USA Weekend,* 1 March 1991

I've been "not Black enough." When I became the first Black Miss America, there was feedback that I wasn't representative of Black America because I didn't have true African-American features—my eyes are green, I have lighter skin.

VANESSA WILLIAMS, in *USA Weekend,* 28 June 1991

COMMITMENT

My guitar is half my life and my wife is the other half.

LEADBELLY, c. 1926

Teacake has asked, not commanded; his request stems from a desire to be with Janie, to share every aspect of his life with her, rather than from a desire to coerce her into some mindless submission.

SHIRLEY WILLIAMS, introduction to *Their Eyes Were Watching God,* 1937

To act is to be committed, and to be committed is to be in danger.

JAMES BALDWIN, *The Fire Next Time,* 1963

Commitment means that it is possible for a man to yield the nerve center of his consent to a purpose or cause, a movement or an ideal, which may be more important to him than whether he lives or dies.

HOWARD THURMAN, *Disciplines of the Spirit,* 1963

I won't have any money to leave behind. I won't have the fine and luxurious things of life to leave behind. But I just want to leave a committed life behind.

MARTIN LUTHER KING, JR., "I Have Been to the Mountaintop," speech given in Memphis, Tennessee, 3 April 1968

You have to give yourself entirely, then you are prepared to do anything that serves the Cause. I have reached that point. I have no options anymore. I have given myself fully.

MARTIN LUTHER KING, JR., in *My Life With Martin Luther King,* 1969

Palomine/ throw your arm/ around my shoulder/
Wrap my soul/ in the bearhug of/ reassurance/ i'm for YOU.

NAOMI MADGETT, "Brothers at the Bar," in Chapman, *New Black Voices,* 1972

It is time we rolled up our sleeves and put ourselves at the top of our commitment list.

MARIAN WRIGHT EDELMAN, in *USA Today,* 18 November 1982

Zora [Neale Hurston] was committed to the survival of her people's cultural heritage. . . .

ALICE WALKER, *In Search of Our Mothers' Gardens,* 1983

I made a commitment to completely cut out drinking and anything that might hamper me from getting my mind and body together. And the floodgates of goodness have opened upon me—spiritually and financially.

DENZEL WASHINGTON, in "Spotlight: Denzel," *Essence,* November 1986

When you grow up in an environment where that kind of commitment and dedication is not just talked about but lived so fully, so honestly, there is no way that it does not take root in your being.

YOLANDA KING, in *Ebony,* August 1987

Whatever I'm doing, I don't think in terms of tomorrow.

ANITA BAKER, in "Spotlight: Anita Baker," *Essence,* December 1987

Commitment is when you perform a note like it's the last note you'll ever play on earth. And you play every note that way.

THAD JONES, c. 1988

The "me" generation is not committed to anything but themselves.

AMINDA WILKINS, in "Interview: Aminda Wilkins," *Crisis,* January 1988

COMMUNICATION

He who chatters with you will chatter of you.

EGYPT

Confiding a secret to an unworthy person is like carrying grain in a bag with a hole.

CONGO

If the tongue and the mouth quarrel, they invariably make it up because they have to live in the same head.

NIGERIA (IBO)

A dog who will bring a bone will carry one.

TRADITIONAL

Evil communication corrupts good manners. I hope to live to hear that good communication corrects bad manners.

BENJAMIN BANNEKER, *Banneker's Almanac,* 1800

Some of the . . . big picture talkers were using a side of the world for a canvas.

ZORA NEALE HURSTON, *Their Eyes Were Watching God,* 1937

I would rediscover the secret of great communications and great combustions. I would say storm. I would say river. I would say tornado. . . . I would say tree.

AIMÉ CÉSAIRE, *Notes on a Return to the Native Land,* 1947

If we sit down together, shake hands and talk things over and get to know one another, world peace will change from a growing hope to a positive fact.

PAUL ROBESON, "The Constitutional Right to Travel," *Freedom,* July–August 1955

Communication and reconciliation introduces harmony into another's life by sensing and honoring the need to be cared for and understood.

HOWARD THURMAN, *Disciplines of the Spirit,* 1963

In order to have a conversation with someone you must reveal yourself.

JAMES BALDWIN, 1965

Reunions are the conveyor belts of our individual histories. They reaffirm the thread of continuity, establish pride in self and kin, and transmit a family's awareness of itself, from the youngest to the oldest. Reunions are a means of communicating with our living kin and that in turn is testament to our heritage. Reunions are nothing less than a family's roots brought to the surface.

ALEX HALEY, in "We Must Honor Our Ancestors," *Ebony,* August 1986

The human subject is the most important thing. My work is abstract, but not in the sense of having no human contact. I want to communicate the idea to strike right away.

JACOB LAWRENCE, in "Jacob Lawrence: Chronicler of the Black American Experience," *American Visions,* February 1987

These natives are unintelligent—/ We can't understand their language.

CHINWEIZU, "Colonizer's Logic," in *Voices from Twentieth-Century Africa,* 1988

COMMUNITY

We have the right and, above all, we have the duty to bring strength and support of our entire community to defend the lives and property of each individual family.

PAUL ROBESON, *Here I Stand,* 1958

[T]he Black community [is] under a microscope just like in a scientist's laboratory, to find out how you're thinking on the beat of your pulse—are you beating too hot, or is your temperature running too hot, or is it too cool.

MALCOLM X, speech given at the Organization of Afro-American Unity Rally, Audubon Ballroom, New York City, 24 January 1965

Community cannot feed for long on itself, it can only flourish with the coming of others from beyond, their unknown and undiscovered brothers.

HOWARD THURMAN, *Search for a Common Ground,* 1971

An individual who can't relate to the Black community, understand and be understood by her own people, isn't well educated.

JOHNETTA COLE, "Culture: Negro, Black and Nigger," in Chapman, *New Black Voices,* 1972

In Nigeria, you are simply not allowed to commit suicide in peace, because everyone is responsible for the other person. Foreigners may call us a nation of busybodies, but to us an individual life belongs to the community and not just to him or her. So a person has no right to take it while another member of the community looks on. He must interfere, he must stop it from happening.

BUCHI EMECHETA, *The Joys of Motherhood,* 1979

Start where you are and move to positions of control in your own community.

HAKI MADHUBUTI, "Black Nationalism," *Crisis,* February 1988

The Black community should take the lead in demanding a hard line on crime because we're most victimized by it.

HARRY EDWARDS, in "Hardline," *Detroit Free Press,* 8 May 1988

COMPLAINT

We have enough and more than enough to complain of, and in the face of the notorious facts everywhere pronounced and obtrusive, the editor who dares to ask why we do complain must be regarded as either an ignoramus or a wise man made mad by too much society.

T. THOMAS FORTUNE, in *Freeman,* 9 October 1886

If we expect to gain our rights by nerveless acquiescence in wrong then we expect to do what no other nation ever did. What must we do then? We must complain. Yes, plain, blunt, complain, ceaseless agitation, unfailing exposure of dishonesty and wrong—this is the ancient, unerring way to liberty, and we must follow it.

W. E. B. DU BOIS, c. 1910

An inch of progress is worth more than a yard of complaint.

BOOKER T. WASHINGTON, *Selected Speeches of Booker T. Washington,* 1932

I started thinking about the unfortunate children who, even being tiny, complain about their condition in the world. They say Princess Margaret of

England doesn't like being a princess. Those are the breaks in life.

CAROLINA MARÍA DE JESUS, 1958

There is no point in complaining over the past or apologizing for one's fate.

RALPH ELLISON, "Portrait of Inman Page," *Going to the Territory,* 1986

CONFIDENCE

I have confidence not only in my country and her institutions but in the endurance, capacity and destiny of my people.

BLANCHE K. BRUCE, speech given before the United States Senate, 31 March 1876

I was cool and perfectly at ease. I never had any doubts of the outcome.

JACK JOHNSON, c. 1920

You see, being at Barnard and measuring arms with others known to be strong increases my self-love and stiffens my spine. They don't laugh in French when I recite, and one of those laughers has asked to quiz with me. I know getting mad would not help any; I had to get my lessons so well that their laughter would seem silly.

ZORA NEALE HURSTON, 10 November 1925

Nobody in town can bake a sweet jelly roll like mine.

BESSIE SMITH, c. 1926

[He] walked like he knew where he was going.

ZORA NEALE HURSTON, *Their Eyes Were Watching God,* 1937

I was going to beat Schmeling. The mind is a powerful thing. From the tip of my toes to the last hair on my head, I had complete confidence.

JOE LOUIS, *My Life,* 1981

The years of familial adoration, the compliments of strangers, and the envy of plain women had given her a large share of confidence.

MAYA ANGELOU, *The Heart of a Woman,* 1981

I've always had confidence. It came because I have lots of initiative. I wanted to make something of myself.

EDDIE MURPHY, c. 1982

The first time I shot the hook, I was in fourth grade, and I was about five feet eight inches tall. I put the ball up and felt totally at ease with the shot. I was completely confident it would go in and I've been shooting it ever since.

KAREEM ABDUL JABBAR, in *Star,* May 1986

If you don't have confidence, you'll always find a way not to win.

CARL LEWIS, c. 1988

Once I get the ball you're at my mercy. There's nothing you can say or do about it. I own the ball, I own the game, I own the guy guarding me. I can actually play him like a puppet.

MICHAEL JORDAN in "Michael Jordan in His Own Orbit," *GQ,* March 1989

People are intimidated by anyone of color who has an idea of what he wants and says it—not in any mean way—but just says it.

COURTNEY B. VANCE, c. 1990

I'm a good neurosurgeon. That's not a boast but a way of acknowledging the innate ability God has given to me. Beginning with determination and using my gifted hands, I went on for training and sharpening of my skills.

BENJAMIN CARSON, *Gifted Hands,* 1990

CONFUSION

Black people have been mis-educated into confusing their interests with those of the dominant society.

CARTER G. WOODSON, *The Mis-education of the Negro,* 1933

[H]ow is it that we, the people, the great majority of the people, struggling as we have for generation after generation . . . how can it happen that everywhere in history a few seem to take the power in their hands, confuse the people themselves and there they remain?

PAUL ROBESON, speech given at the International Fur and Leather Workers Union Convention, New Jersey, 20 May 1948

What is wrong with the United States? We are an intelligent, rich and powerful nation. Yet today we are confused and frightened.

W. E. B. DU BOIS, "What Is Wrong with the United

States?" speech given to the American Labor Party, Madison Square Garden, New York City, 13 May 1952

The moral vacuum of any society creates an actual social chaos. This vacuum is that space of confusion in which the word is not suited to the action, nor intended to be—in which the action is not suited to the word, nor intended to be. It is that space in which everyone, helplessly, has something to hide, in which every man's hand—helplessly—is against his brother; that space in which we dare not recognize that our birthright is to love each other.

JAMES BALDWIN, *Evidence of Things Not Seen,* 1985

Whenever there is chaos, it creates wonderful thinking. Chaos is a gift.

SEPTIMA CLARK, c. 1986

If confusion exists anywhere today, it exists within human beings . . . within those of us who are not in harmony.

SUSAN TAYLOR, c. 1987

CONNECTION

[T]here was something which all black men held in common, something which cut across opposing points of view, and placed in the same context their widely dissimilar experience. What they held in common was their precarious, their unutterably painful relation to the white world. What they held in common was the necessity to remake the world . . . and no longer be controlled by the vision of the world, and of themselves, held by other people. What, in sum, black men held in common was their ache to come into the world as men. And this ache united people who might otherwise have been divided as to what a man should be.

JAMES BALDWIN, *Nobody Knows My Name,* 1961

I felt more relaxed among Negroes who were being their natural selves and not putting on airs. Even though I did live on the Hill, my instincts were never . . . to feel myself any better than any other Negro.

MALCOLM X, *The Autobiography of Malcolm X,* 1965

[W]hen you begin to connect yourself on the world stage with the whole of dark mankind, and you see that you're the majority and this majority is waking up and rising up and becoming strong, then you deal with this man.

MALCOLM X, speech given at the Organization of Afro-American Unity Rally, Audubon Ballroom, New York City, 24 January 1965

The close links forged between Africans and people of African descent over half a century of common struggle continue to inspire and strengthen us. For although the outward forms of our struggle may change, it remains in essence the same, a fight to death against oppression, racism, and exploitation.

KWAME NKRUMAH, *The Spectre of Black Power,* 1968

We are an African people. We sit back and watch the Jews in this country make Israel a powerful state in the Middle East, but we are not concerned actively about the plight of our brother in Africa.

JAMES FORMAN, 26 April 1969

Imagery becomes the magic denominator . . . the connective currents that nod Black heads from Maine to Mississippi to Montana.

MARI EVANS, "My Father's Passage," in Evans, ed., *Black Women Writers,* 1984

It is not culture which binds the people who are of partially African origin now scattered throughout the world, but an identity of passions. We share a hatred for the alienation forced upon us by Europeans during the process of colonization and empire, and we are bound more by our common suffering than by our pigmentation.

RALPH ELLISON, *Going to the Territory,* 1986

A special mission of the Black college is to keep our roots and fruits connected.

JESSE JACKSON, in *Choosing to Succeed,* 1986

CONSCIENCE

The conscience of some men is never calm.

ALEXANDRE DUMAS, *The Count of Monte Cristo,* 1844

Eighteen ninety-four marked the awakening of the public conscience to a system of anarchy and outlawry which was so common that scenes of unusual brutality failed to have any visible effect upon human sentiments.

IDA B. WELLS, *A Red Record: Tabulated Statistics and Alleged Causes of Lynchings in the United States, 1892–1894,* 1894

Individual shocks stir the individual and conscience. Great world shocks are necessary to stir the world conscience and heart to start those movements to right the wrongs in the world.

WILLIAM ALLISON SWEENEY, *The Great War,* 1919

In matters of conscience the Law of Majority has no place.

MOHANDAS GANDHI, *From Yeravda Mandir,* 4 August 1920

Conscience is solid convicting and permanently demonstrative; belief is only a matter of opinion changed by superior reasoning.

MARCUS GARVEY, *Philosophy and Opinions of Marcus Garvey,* 1923

We merely bring to the surface the hidden tension that is already alive. We bring it out in the open where it can be seen and dealt with. Like a boil that can never be cured as long as it is covered up but must be opened with all its pus-flowing ugliness to the natural medicines of air and light, injustice must likewise be exposed, with all of the tension its exposing creates, to the light of human conscience and the air of national opinion before it can be cured.

MARTIN LUTHER KING, JR., *Letter from a Birmingham City Jail,* 1963

I am strong in my conscience and I dare to say with truth that among all of the servants of the State none is more honest than I.

TOUSSAINT L'OUVERTURE, in James, *The Black Jacobins,* 1963

We feel that we are the conscience of America—we are its troubled souls—we will continue to insist that right be done because both God's will and the heritage of our nation speak through our echoing demands.

MARTIN LUTHER KING, JR., Noble Peace Prize Acceptance Speech, 10 December 1964

Few things are as bad as a guilty conscience.

BUCHI EMECHETA, *The Joys of Motherhood,* 1979

When aroused the American conscience is a powerful force for reform.

CORETTA SCOTT KING, c. 1983

Black America has been the nation's conscience for two hundred years. It is time to help guide its conscious activities as well.

HAROLD WASHINGTON, in "Mayor Washington Eulogized as Symbol of Hope for Blacks," *Jet,* 14 December 1987

CONSTITUTION

I would have the Constitution torn in shreds and scattered to the four winds of heaven. Let us destroy the Constitution and build on its ruins the temple of liberty. I have brothers in slavery. I have seen chains placed on their limbs and beheld them captive.

WILLIAM WELLS-BROWN, in the *Liberator,* 18 May 1855

In its language and in its spirit, the Constitution welcomes the Black man to all the rights which it was intended to guarantee to any class of the American people. Its preamble tells us for whom and for what it was made.

FREDERICK DOUGLASS, *Douglass Monthly,* 1863

The Constitution of the United States knows no distinction between citizens on account of color. Neither does it know any difference between a citizen of a state and a citizen of the United States.

FREDERICK DOUGLASS, "Reconstruction," *Atlantic Monthly,* December 1866

The Constitution is a very flexible instrument and it cannot be anything more than the controlling elements that the American society wish it to be.

RALPH BUNCHE, "Critical Analysis of the Tactics and Programs of Minority Groups," *Journal of Negro Education,* July 1935

The Constitution confers complete equality on all citizens, he must rest his case on the proposition that there is only one side: his side, the constitutional side.

LOREN MILLER, "Farewell to Liberals," *The Nation,* 20 October 1962

When the architects of our republic wrote the magnificent words of the Constitution and Declaration of Independence, they were signing a promissory note to which every American was to fall heir . . . that all men . . . would be guaranteed the unalienable rights of life, liberty, and the pursuit of happiness.

MARTIN LUTHER KING, JR., "I Have a Dream," speech given at the Lincoln Memorial, Washington, D.C., 28 August 1963

We know we are citizens because it is written in an amendment to the Constitution.

SEPTIMA P. CLARK, "Literacy and Liberation," *Freedomways,* April 1964

"We, the people"; it is a very eloquent beginning. But when the Constitution of the United States was completed on the seventeenth of September, 1787, I was not included in that "We, the people." I felt for many years that somehow George Washington and Alexander Hamilton just left me out by mistake.

BARBARA JORDAN, *Barbara Jordan,* 1977

If we keep this up, it'll be like we shredded the Constitution. The Constitution is the full intent of this nation to be, and you to be, before you can become. What we need is action, on the part of every one of us.

PEARL BAILEY, c. 1980

While I have no desire to use hindsight to criticize the values of men who lived two centuries ago, I think it downright insensitive to ask that any Black man salute the memory of men who recognized each of them as only three-fifths of a whole man.

BRYANT GUMBEL, in *We The People,* 1987

Today's Constitution is a realistic document of freedom only because of several corrective amendments. Those amendments speak to a sense of decency and fairness that I and other Blacks cherish.

THURGOOD MARSHALL, in *ibid.*

Our Constitution is the envy of the world, as it should be for it is the grand design of the finest nation on earth.

Ibid.

I do not believe that the meaning of the Constitution was forever "fixed" at the Philadelphia Convention. . . . The government they devised was defective from the start, requiring several amendments, a civil war, and momentous social transformation to attain the system of constitutional government, and its respect for the individual freedoms and human rights, we hold as fundamental today.

THURGOOD MARSHALL, "The Real Meaning of the Constitutional Bicentennial," *Ebony,* September 1987

CONTRIBUTION

No race that has anything to contribute to the marketplace of the world is long in any degree ostracized.

BOOKER T. WASHINGTON, speech given at the Atlanta Exposition, Atlanta, Georgia, 1896

Always Africa is giving us something new. On its black bosom arose one of the earliest, if not the earliest, of self-protecting civilizations and grew so mighty that it still furnishes superlatives to thinking and speaking man. Out of its darker and more remote forest fastness, came the first welding of iron—we know that agriculture and trade flourished when Europe was a wilderness. Nearly every empire that has arisen in the world, material and spiritual, has found some of its greatest crises in Africa.

W. E. B. DU BOIS, *The African Roots of the War,* 1915

Having been given I must give. Man shall not live by bread alone. And what the farmer does I must do. I must feed the people with my song.

PAUL ROBESON, in "Paul Robeson Speaks about Art and the Negro," *The Millgate,* December 1930

Any genuine artistic expression can transcend a fad. The Negroes' contribution to literature and art should have a permanent place in American life, American life would be richer by the content and it should find an outlet and a receptive audience.

CLAUDE MCKAY, c. 1934

This is our contribution—our blood. Not only did we give of our free labor, we gave of our blood. Every time [we] had a call to arms, we were the first ones in uniform. We died on every battlefield the white man had. We have made a greater sacrifice than anybody who's standing up in America today.

MALCOLM X, "The Ballot or the Bullet," speech given at Cory Methodist Church, Cleveland, Ohio, 3 April 1965

It is not an accident that there is a blackout on the Black man's contribution to America.

MELVIN CHAPMAN, speech given at Mercy College, Detroit, Michigan, July 1976

Long before the paleolithic period and white men came here thinking that the world was flat your forefathers made contributions to advance world culture.

BETTY SHABAZZ, c. 1980

CONTROL

Restraint is a brief moment.

INSTRUCTION TO KAGEMNI, c. 2650–2135 B.C.

The man who never submitted to anything will soon submit to a burial mat.

NIGERIA

The one who divides and distributes and who knows how to have his own way, every time he makes divisions, can get the best part for himself.

NEW MEXICO

The sun has been hot on my head and made me as in a fire; my blood was on fire, but now I have come into this valley and drunk of these waters and washed myself in them and they have cooled me.

COCHISE OF THE CHIRICAHUA APACHES, in "Recollections of an Interview with Cochise, Chief of the Apaches," *Collections,* 1915

We of the less-favored race realize our future lies chiefly in our hands.

PAUL ROBESON, valedictory speech given at Rutgers University, New Brunswick, New Jersey, 1919

Nothing will do me any good unless I learn to control this body of mine.

ALICE NELSON DUNBAR, in *Give Us Each Day,* 12 August 1921

Each race should be proud and stick to its own/ and the best of what they are should be shown./ This is no shallow song of hate to sing/ But over Blacks there should be no white king/ Every man in his own foothold should stand./ Claiming a nation and a fatherland/ White, Yellow, and Black should make their own laws/ And force no one-sided justice with flaws.

MARCUS GARVEY, *Philosophy and Opinions of Marcus Garvey,* 1923

When you determine that a man shall think you do not have to concern yourself with what he will do. If you make a man feel that he is inferior, you do not have to compel him to accept inferior status, for he will seek it himself. If you make a man think he is justly an outcast, you do not have to order him to the back door. He will go without being told; and if there is no back door, his very nature will demand one.

CARTER G. WOODSON, *The Mis-education of the Negro,* 1933

As we Blacks continued to multiply and spread, the Lords of the Land sought to distribute us on the plantation so that our population would never exceed that of the whites or grow so great in any one area as to constitute an insurrectionary danger.

RICHARD WRIGHT, *12 Million Black Voices,* 1941

Let the martial songs be written, let the dirges disappear. Let a race of men now rise and take control.

MARGARET WALKER, "For My People," *For My People,* 1942

People don't understand the fight it takes to record what you want to record the way you want to record it.

BILLIE HOLIDAY, *Lady Sings the Blues,* 1956

In the midst of our own crises, our own life problems, the power of our deliverance is in our own power in our own possession.

C. L. FRANKLIN, "The Moses and the Red Sea," c. 1957

All my life people have been at my soul, tugging at it in different directions. I have chafed under unrelenting controls, enthusiastic evangelizing, ruthful police watchfulness. So many hands have been reaching out for me, and so many voices have been babbling about my ears like idiotic rattling of wheels of a moving train, and I must scream, leave me alone.

EZEKIEL MPHAHLELE, *Down Second Avenue,* 1959

Toussaint L' Ouverture was as completely master of his body as of his mind. He slept but two hours every night and for days would be satisfied with two bananas and a glass of water.

C. L. R. JAMES, *The Black Jacobins,* 1963

Having complete control over Africa, the colonial powers of Europe projected the image of Africa negatively . . . jungle savages, cannibals, nothing civilized.

MALCOLM X, "After the Bromberg," speech given 14 February 1965

He who can control image controls minds, and he who controls minds has little or nothing to fear from bodies.

LERONE BENNETT, *Challenge of Blackness,* 1972

You must learn to be still in the midst of activity and to be vibrantly alive in repose.

INDIRA GANDHI, in "Indira's Coup," *New York Review of Books,* 18 September 1975

We are still not free even after the loosening of bonds. We will never be allowed to select a political and social regime different from those of the Western world without running the risk of having to fight or seeing ourselves overthrown by intrigues, making use of local parties of Western allegiances. This is the last camouflaged line of retreat for the battles, the imperialist West alleging that its own economic fate and "civilization as we know it" depend on retaining control of Africa.

CHEIKH ANTA DIOP, *The Cultural Unity of Black Africa,* 1978

Constant harassment is an important tool for the authorities so they can keep us preoccupied and subjugated.

MIRIAM MAKEBA, *My Story,* 1987

Being sensitive, being a father, being a grandfather, seeing the things that happen, waiting, bragging, crying, feeling frustrated, almost abandoned, it becomes almost too much for an individual to carry on his shoulders. You need something to happen in your life that restores the foundation of hope; that gives you back a sense of belonging, some control over your destiny.

OSSIE DAVIS, "It's On Us," *City Arts Quarterly,* Spring 1987

As soon as we get control, the criticism becomes, "Oh, you just want to be another boss."

HAROLD WASHINGTON, in "Mayor Washington Eulogized as a Symbol of Hope for Blacks," *Jet,* 14 December 1987

It is time for Blacks to take charge of their fate and to refuse to permit White liberals and Black sycophants to continue leading the race down a primrose path to ultimate oblivion.

JOE CLARK, "It's Time for Blacks to Take Charge of Their Fate," *Ebony,* August 1988

Go to school. I play sports because I love it. But after sports, I'm going into the real world, and the real world is controlling this country. You have to be a businessman, a doctor, a lawyer, or a scientist like Carver.

MIKE TYSON, in "Mike Tyson Talks About His Future And Says 'I'm A Dreamer,'" *Jet,* 14 November 1988

Our greatness, our talent has never been the question. It's been a matter of grappling for control over what we do.

SPIKE LEE, in *Savvy Woman,* October 1989

COOPERATION

One head does not go into council.

AFRICA

Two small antelopes can beat a big one.

ASHANTI

Living together is an art.

WILLIAM PICKENS, sermon given at the Oak Park, Illinois Congregational Meeting, 2 November 1932

Either we get along with the Communists, jump in the ocean, or blow up the whole world. Saying you can't get along with the Communists is like saying you can't get along with birds.

PAUL ROBESON, "The United Nations Position on South Africa," *New Africa,* December 1946

We must all learn to live together as brothers. Or we will all perish together as fools.

MARTIN LUTHER KING, JR., speech given at the National Cathedral, Washington, D.C., 31 March 1968

COST

When a thing is abundant, it is always cheap.

TERTULLIAN, *The Apparel of Women,* c. 200

Never buy wit, when you can have it at another man's cost.

TERENCE, *The Self-Tormentor,* c. 200

There is no cure that does not cost.

IVORY COAST

Nobody buys pebbles which can be picked up on the beach, but diamonds sell high.

A. PHILIP RANDOLPH, in "Our Reason for Being," *Messenger,* August 1919

The cost of developing the kind of mind by which the discoveries of science were made has been one which now threatens the discoverer's very life.

PAUL ROBESON, c. 1948

COURAGE

I am a good American, the colored people are good people. The valor of the colored people was tested on many battlefields and today their bones lie bleaching beside every hill and every valley from the Potomac to the Gulf.

JAMES RAPIER, in the *Congressional Record,* 9 June 1874

Lose not courage, lose not faith, go forward.

MARCUS GARVEY, *Philosophy and Opinions of Marcus Garvey,* 1923

Always our deepest love is for those children of ours who turn their backs upon our way of life, for our instincts tell us that those brave ones who struggle against death are the ones who bring new life into the world, even though they die to do so, even though . . .

RICHARD WRIGHT, *12 Million Black Voices,* 1941

Never let your head hang down. Never give up and sit and grieve. Find another way. And don't pray when it rains if you don't pray when the sun shines.

SATCHEL PAIGE, c. 1945

It is brave to be involved/ To be not fearful to be unresolved.

GWENDOLYN BROOKS, "do not be afraid of no," *Annie Allen,* 1949

Walk in peace, walk alone, walk tall, walk free, walk naked.

DAVID DIOP, "Listen Comrades . . . ," *Poundings,* 1956

These are the days for strong men to courageously expose wrong.

ADAM CLAYTON POWELL, JR., "Can Any Good Thing Come Out of Nazareth?" baccalaureate address, Howard University, Washington, D.C., 29 May 1966

Bravery lies in his words, his telling the truth; some say he's a poet.

HAKI MADHUBUTI, in "Only a Few Left," *Negro Digest,* September 1967

Courage [is] the determination not to be overwhelmed by any object, that power of the mind capable of sloughing off the thingification of the past.

MARTIN LUTHER KING, JR., *Where Do We Go From Here?* 1968

He who is not courageous enough to take risks will accomplish nothing in life.

MUHAMMAD ALI, c. 1972

Courage is one step ahead of fear.

COLEMAN YOUNG, c. 1978

Yours was the courage to live life, in and from its belly as well as beyond its edges, to see and say what it was to recognize and identify evil, but never fear or stand in awe of it.

TONI MORRISON, eulogy of James Baldwin, Cathedral of St. John the Divine, New York City, January 1988

One isn't necessarily born with courage, but one is born with potential. Without courage, we cannot practice any other virtue with consistency. We can't be kind, true, merciful, generous, or honest.

MAYA ANGELOU, in *USA Today,* 5 March 1988

We had no more courage than Harriet Tubman or Marcus Garvey had in their times. We just had a more vulnerable enemy.

STOKELY CARMICHAEL, in "What Became of the Prophets of Rage," *Life,* Spring 1988

COWARD

Caution is not cowardice; even the ants march armed.

EGYPT

A coward is without precaution.

SOMALIA

We want no cowards in our band/ We call for valiant hearted men,/ You shall gain the victory, you shall gain the day.

TRADITIONAL

Vice is a coward; to be truly brave, a man must be truly good.

IGNATIUS SANCHO, letter to Mrs. S, 1772

If he wasn't a coward, he wouldn't gang up on you. That is how they function. They function in mobs.

MALCOLM X, speech given in Selma, Alabama, 1965

They don't come by ones/ They don't come by twos/ But they come by tens.

STERLING BROWN, "Old Lem," in Bontemps, ed., *Poetry of the Negro,* 1970

Patience has its limits. Take it too far and it's cowardice.

GEORGE JACKSON, in *Soledad Brothers,* 1971

What he might call cowardice other people called common sense.

TONI MORRISON, *Beloved,* 1987

CREATE

The male embraced the female, and from that the human race arose. She reflected: "How can he unite with me, who am produced from himself? Let me hide!" She became a cow, he a bull and united with her; and from that cattle arose. She became a mare, he a stallion; she an ass, he a donkey and united with her; and from that solid hoofed animals. She became a goat, he a buck. . . . Thus he poured forth all pairing things, down to the ants. Then he realized: "I, actually, am creation; for I have poured all this." Anyone understanding this becomes, truly, himself a creator in this creation.

BRIHADARANYAKA UPANISHAD, c. 700 B.C.

We must consider not only by whom all things were created but also by whom they were perverted.

TERTULLIAN, *The Spectacle,* c. 198 A.D.

Then he descended/ while the heaven rubbed against the earth./ They moved among the four lights,/ among the four layers of the stars./ The world was not lighted;/ there was neither day nor night nor moon./ Then creation dawned upon the world.

MAYA, *The Book of Chilam Balam of Chumayel,* 1933

The great I AM took the soul of the world and wrapped some flesh around it and that made you.

ZORA NEALE HURSTON, *Moses, Man of the Mountain,* 1939

We made the world we're living in and we have to make it over.

JAMES BALDWIN, *Nobody Knows My Name,* 1961

Potential powers of creativity are within us and we have the duty to work assiduously to discover these powers.

MARTIN LUTHER KING, JR., c. 1963

We must use time creatively, and forever realize that the time is always ripe to do right.

MARTIN LUTHER KING, JR., *Letter from a Birmingham City Jail,* 1963

In the world through which I travel, I am endlessly creating myself.

FRANTZ FANON, *Black Skin, White Masks,* 1967

Create, and be true to yourself, and depend only on your own good taste.

DUKE ELLINGTON, *Music Is My Mistress,* 1973

People don't really give much credit to the creative element. I've known them to say the imitation was better than the original. Are you going to say the son has better blood than the father?

Ibid.

For creation is transparent and the splendor of God shines through it.

ERNESTO CARDENAL, "Love," *Vida en al Amor,* 1974

My net is spread, my net is spread. Come close to me, wrap yourself around me. Only God knows which moment makes the child.

WOLE SOYINKA, *The Lion and the Jewel,* 1975

Idols are created in order to be broken.

JAMES BALDWIN, c. 1976

And so our mothers and grandmothers have, more often than not anonymously, handed on the creative spark, the seed of the flower they themselves never hoped to see: or like a sealed letter they could not plainly read.

ALICE WALKER, *In Search of Our Mothers' Gardens,* 1983

It becomes almost second nature to be on guard against the creative pattern of our own thought.

ALICE CHILDRESS, "A Candle in a Gale Wind," in Evans, ed., *Black Women Writers,* 1984

Once a man has tasted creative action, then thereafter, no matter how safely he schools himself in patience, he is restive, acutely dissatisfied with anything else. He becomes as a lover to whom abstinence is intolerable.

JEAN TOOMER, in Kerman and Eldridge, *The Lives of Jean Toomer,* 1987

We are all creative, but by the time we are three or four years old, someone has knocked creativity out of us. Some people shut up the kids who start to tell stories. Kids dance in their cribs, but someone will insist they sit still. By the time the creative people are ten or twelve, they want to be like everyone else.

MAYA ANGELOU, in *USA Today,* 5 March 1988

I try not to repeat myself. It's the hardest thing in the world to do—there are only so many notes one human being can master.

PRINCE, in "Spotlight: Prince—What U See Is What U Get," *Essence,* November 1988

We are here, charged with the task of completing (one might say creating) ourselves.

WILLIAM COOK, in "The Meaning of Life," *Life,* December 1988

CREDIT

Buying on credit is robbing next year's crop.

TRADITIONAL

You can get a lot done in this world, if you don't mind doing the work and letting other people take the credit.

TRADITIONAL

It's a foolish elder who becomes a creditor, since he must wait until the other world to outlive his debtors.

NIGERIA

Take the cash, forget the credit.

COLEMAN YOUNG, in "The Survivor," *Detroit Monthly,* February 1981

CRIME

And turmoil will not cease tomorrow./ Everyone is mute about it,/ The whole land is in great distress,/ Nobody is free from crime.

ANKHU, "The Complaint of Khakheperre-Sonb," 1550–1305 B.C.

If you wish to discover the guilty person, first find out to whom the crime might be useful.

ALEXANDRE DUMAS, *The Count of Monte Cristo,* 1844

For men perpetrate lawless acts, revolting deeds, disgraceful and brutal crimes, regardless of nationality, language, or color.

H. M. TURNER, *20th Century Negro Literature or a Cyclopedia of Thought on the Vital Topics Relating to the American Negro,* 1902

Crime has no color, the criminal no race. He is the common enemy of society.

KELLY MILLER, *The American Negro,* 1908

In times of acute crisis the finest individual thoughts and feelings may be reduced to nothing before the blind brute forces of tigerish tribalism which remains at the core of civilized society.

CLAUDE MCKAY, "Another White Friend," 1934

The crime was not stealing, but rather getting caught.

FRANK YERBY, 1952

I have faced during my life many unpleasant experiences: the growl of a mob, the personal threat of murder, the scowling distaste of an audience. But nothing so cowed me as that day, November 8, 1951, when I took my seat in a Washington courtroom as an indicted criminal.

W. E. B. DU BOIS, *Battle for Peace; The Story of My 83rd Birthday*, 1952

I knew that I was a convicted criminal, but I was proud of my crime. It was the crime of joining my people in a nonviolent protest against injustice. It was the crime of seeking to instill within my people a sense of dignity and self-respect. It was the crime of desiring for my people the inalienable rights of life, liberty, and the pursuit of happiness. It was above all the crime of seeking to convince my people that non-cooperation with evil is just as much a moral duty as is the cooperation with good.

MARTIN LUTHER KING, JR., "The Violence of Desperate Men," *Stride Toward Freedom*, 1958

[C]rime often grows out of a sense of futility and hopelessness.

MARTIN LUTHER KING, JR., *Where Do We Go From Here?* 1968

The major crime of the society . . . is the inherent homicidal tendency of an oppressive and racist society which pushes . . . young people to the brink of spiritual waste and physical destruction.

SELWYN CUDJOE, "Maya Angelou and the Autobiographical Statement," in Evans, ed., *Black Women Writers*, 1984

Who is the greater sinner, one must ask, the individual who commits a crime and must experience the shame and guilt of the action, or the individual who can enjoy a crime committed by another while maintaining a sense of moral superiority?

DARWIN T. TURNER, "Theme, Characterization, and Style in the Works of Toni Morrison," in *ibid.*

The Black community as a whole has to take a much harder line toward the criminals among us even though they may be thirteen, thirteen-year-olds are murdering people.

HARRY EDWARDS, in "Hardline," *Detroit Free Press*, 8 May 1988

CRISIS

We must establish our own organ, for then we could publish whatever we wished; whereas if we sent articles to other magazines we would have to depend upon their good will, to say nothing of the disposition to change our views to suit their own ideas. This view prevailed and the *Crisis* was born.

IDA B. WELLS, in Duster, ed., *Crusade for Justice*, 1928

To your tents, Americans! We have gone far enough into this morass of fear, war, hate, lying and crime. We face a crisis and our first duty is here and now. For the time being, never mind the Soviet Union; forget China. . . . Come back home and look at America.

W. E. B. DU BOIS, "Let's Restore Democracy to America," *National Guardian*, 2 January 1956

The Crisis became the only magazine in the country devoted to social service that was not dependent upon subsidy.

LANGSTON HUGHES, *Fight for Freedom: Story of the NAACP*, 1962

CRITICISM

And now, my chubby critic, fat burly cynic,/ forever mocking and deriding my sad muse,/ Draw near, and take a seat, I pray, close beside me,/ And let us come to terms with this accursed spleen.

ALEXANDER PUSHKIN, *A Study*, 1830

A critic advises/ not to write on controversial subjects/ like freedom or murder,/ but to treat universal themes/ and timeless symbols/ like the white unicorn./ *A white unicorn?*

DUDLEY RANDALL, "Black Poet, White Critic," in *Black Poetry Writing*, 1949

Honest men may and must criticize America. Describe how she has ruined her democracy, sold out her jury system, and led her seats of justice astray.

W. E. B. DU BOIS, *The Autobiography of W. E. B. Du Bois: A Soliloquy on Viewing My Life from the Last Decade of Its First Century*, 1964

It is not a sign of weakness, but a sign of high maturity, to rise to the level of self-criticism.

MARTIN LUTHER KING, JR., *Where Do We Go From Here?* 1968

Critics have their purposes, and they're supposed to do what they do, but sometimes they get a little carried away with what they think someone should have done, rather than concerning themselves with what he did.

DUKE ELLINGTON, *Music Is My Mistress,* 1973

If you go down the list and look at the critics from those of Bernard Shaw on to Shakespeare, when it was happening, the critics didn't know what was happening and wrote about each offering like it was a piece of trash.

BILL COSBY, c. 1980

Every Black person who rises is subject to a greater degree of criticism and more than any other segment of the population.

COLEMAN YOUNG, c. 1984

The greatest threat to freedom is the absence of criticism.

WOLE SOYINKA, in "Nobel Laureate: Wole Soyinka," *Essence,* August 1987

Critics often impose their theories on works of art without exploring ideas with the artists themselves.

WILLIAM FERRIS, in *Black Art: Ancestral Legacy,* 1989

Only false prophets shun criticism, because they do not want their real motives revealed.

JAMES CONE, *Martin and Malcolm and America,* 1991

CRY

If you knock the nose, the eye cries.

AFRICA

The start of weeping is hard.

AFRICA

Oh Mary, don't you weep, don't mourn; / Pharaoh's army got drowned; Mary, don't weep and don't mourn.

TRADITIONAL

I have borne thirteen children and seen them all sold into slavery, and when I cried out with all my mother's grief none but Jesus heard.

SOJOURNER TRUTH, *Narratives of Sojourner Truth, A Northern Slave,* 1850

The man who suffered the wrong is the man to demand redress—the man struck is the man to cry out.

FREDERICK DOUGLASS, "What to the Slave is the Fourth of July?" speech given at Corinthian Hall, Rochester, New York, 5 July 1852

Out of the depths we have cried unto the deaf and dumb masters of the world. Out of the depths we cry to our own sleeping souls.

W. E. B. DU BOIS, speech given at the Second Pan African Congress, 1921

I cry my woe to the whirling world, but not in despair. For I understand the forces that doom the race into which I was born to lifelong discrimination and servitude. And I know that these forces are not eternal, they can be destroyed and will be destroyed.

CLAUDE MCKAY, in review of "He Who Gets Slapped," *Liberator,* 5 May 1922

Would it please you if I strung my tears/ In pearls for you to wear?

NAOMI MADGETT, "The Race Question," *Star by Star,* 1965

Oh, it's crying time again, you gonna leave me.

RAY CHARLES, c. 1965

Crying is an act which one should perform only in private, for crying is a private way of groping for truth.

ADDISON GAYLE, "The Son of My Father," in Chapman, *New Black Voices,* 1972

Each tear that fell/ from the crushed/ moons of your face,/ stabbed me,/ broke and split into a thousand pains.

HENRY DUMAS, "If I Were Earth," *Play Ebony Play Ivory,* 1974

When a man is hanging on a tree and he cries out, should he cry out unemotionally? When a man is sitting on a hot stove and he tells you how it feels to be there, is he supposed to speak without emotions? This is what you began to tell black people in this country when they begin to cry out against the injustices that they're suffering.

MALCOLM X, in Franklin and Meir, eds., *Black Leaders of the 20th Century,* 1982

CULTURE

A man without culture is like a grasshopper without wings.

AFRICA

I couldn't see it [culture] for wearing it. It was only when I was off in college, away from my native surroundings, that I could see myself like somebody else and stand off and look at my garment. I had to have the spy-glass of Anthropology to look through at that.

ZORA NEALE HURSTON, 1925

It was like homecoming, and I felt I had penetrated to the core of African culture when I began to study the legendary traditions, folk-song and folklore of the West African.

PAUL ROBESON, in "African Culture," *The African Observer, a Review of Contemporary Affairs,* 5 March 1935

We do not choose our cultures, we belong to them.

AIMÉ CÉSAIRE in Baldwin, *Nobody Knows My Name,* 1961

Music, dance, religion, do not have artifacts as their end products so they were saved. These nonmaterial aspects of the African culture were impossible to eradicate. And these are the most apparent legacies of the African past, even to the contemporary Black American blues, jazz, and the adaptation of the Christian religion, all rely heavily on African culture.

LEROI JONES, *Blues People,* 1963

Culture is how one lives and is connected to history by habit.

Ibid.

Destroy the culture and you destroy the people.

FRANTZ FANON, *Wretched of the Earth,* 1963

Culture is the first requisite and the final objective of all development.

LEOPOLD SENGHOR, speech given at First World Festival of Negro Arts, Dakar, Senegal, 1966

You do not inherit culture and artistic skill through your genes. These come as a result of personal conquest, of the individual's applying himself to that art, that music . . . which helps him to realize and complete himself.

RALPH ELLISON, "The Little Man at Chehaw Station," *Going to the Territory,* 1986

To keep the race and keep the culture moving ahead, and that means lifting up those ships that are stuck deepest in the mud, because then we lift up the whole flotilla.

HARRY EDWARDS, in "Hardline," *Detroit Free Press,* 8 May 1988

Politics create the environment that shapes culture; slavery and segregation, for instance, saved the seeds that grew into jazz and the blues. At the same time, culture sends powerful messages to the American people about what our country is about and which direction we should take.

JOHN CONYERS, 1989

[C]ulture [is] a quilt of intricate geometrical design in which all of the many colored pieces, their shapes and stitching flow into one another, constitute the whole.

FRANCES CRESS WELSING, *The Isis Papers,* 1991

DANCE

If the dance is pleasing, even the lame will crawl to it.

AFRICA

He who cannot dance will say: The Drum is bad.

AFRICA

Tell me, woman, I ask you/ Can your husband dance?/ Tell me, woman, answer me,/ How does your husband dance? Oh my God, all he can do is sit and eat./ Ever since I married him/ He hasn't moved his feet.

SUDAN, "Mocking Song"

And the Negro dancers who will dance like flames and the singers who will continue to carry our songs to all who listen—they will be with us in even greater numbers tomorrow.

LANGSTON HUGHES, "The Negro Artist and the Racial Mountain," *The Nation,* 23 June 1926

Jungle jazzing, Orient wriggling, civilized stepping. Shake that thing. Sweet dancing thing of primitive joy, perverse pleasure, prostitute ways, many adored variations of the rhythm, savage, barbaric, refined-eternal rhythm of the mysterious, magical, magnificent—the dance divine of life. Oh, shake that thing.

CLAUDE MCKAY, *Banjo,* 1929

Americans will be amazed to find how many of the modern dance steps are relics of the African heritage.

PAUL ROBESON, in the *London Observer,* 29 July 1934

We must never forget that the dance is the cradle of Negro music.

ALAIN LOCKE, c. 1937

Mine is a proud village, such as it is,/ We are best when dancing.

MAKAH, *Bulletin of American Ethnology,* 1939

[The] break-yoke dance/ jail-break dance/ it-is-fine-and-good-and-right-to-be-a-Negro dance.

AIMÉ CÉSAIRE, *Notes on a Return to the Native Land,* 1947

[A]ll dances have a cumulative tendency, because each beat of the tom-tom has an almost irresistible appeal. Soon, those who were just spectators would dance too.

CAMARA LAYE, *The Dark Child,* 1954

You are the dance in the naked joy of your smile/ Through the offering of your breast and your secret powers/ You are the dance by the golden legend of wedding nights/ In the new times and the age-old rhythm.

DAVID DIOP, "To a Black Dancer," *Poundings,* 1956

The dance is strong magic. The dance is a spirit. It turns the body to liquid steel. It makes it vibrate like a guitar. The body can fly without wings. It can sing without voice. The dance is strong magic. The dance is life.

PEARL PRIMUS, "African Dance," speech given to American Society of African Culture, 1964

All Indians must dance, everywhere keep on dancing. . . . Indians who don't dance, who don't believe will grow little, just about a foot high. Some of them will be turned into wood and burned in fire.

WOVOKA, THE PAIUTE MESSIAH, in Brown, *Bury My Heart at Wounded Knee,* 1971

Blacks and whites here whirl in a fantastic *dance macabre,* a pure fandango, feverish at one moment, then as pale and bloodless as a formal waltz; but each partner expertly knows his role, keeps in step, never loses the proper beat.

HOYT FULLER, in Brooks, *Report From Part One,* 1972

Dancing is our Negritude. It's us and we shouldn't try to deny that.

SPIKE LEE, in *Essence,* 1987

You dance because you have to. Dance is an essential part of life that has always been with me.

KATHERINE DUNHAM, in "She Danced to Teach—and They Loved It," *American Visions,* February 1987

To dance is to give channel to the Creator.

ALI ABDULLAH, in "An Interview with Ali Abdullah," *City Arts Quarterly,* Spring 1988

I come alive alone, in front of the mirror, skipping and dancing and acting the fool. Dance is both escape and excitement.

JODY WATLEY, *Essence,* May 1988

Dancing is being trusted with other people's guts; choreographing is trusting other people with yours. When I choreograph I'm giving a dancer something to do and trusting the dancer to do it and build on it.

JUDITH JAMISON, in interview, "Dancing on Air," WDET (radio), 1988

Each time a dancer moves devoutly or a composer faithfully searches the silence for the veiled melodies, eternity is engaged.

MAYA ANGELOU, in "The Jamison Spirit," *Essence,* December 1990

DANGER

The cat always eats the mouse it plays with.

AFRICA

No matter how hardened to danger a man may be, he always realizes from the pounding of his heart and the shivering of his flesh, the enormous difference there is between a dream and reality, between a plan and its execution.

ALEXANDRE DUMAS, *The Count of Monte Cristo,* 1844

All generations are dangerous, even this one.

ALEXANDRE DUMAS, 1850

Today, our heads are in the lion's mouth, and we must get them out the best way we can. To contend against the government is as difficult as it is to sit in Rome and fight the Pope.

JOHN S. ROCK, speech given to the Massachusetts Anti-Slavery Society, 23 January 1862

A little learning, indeed, may be a dangerous thing, but the want of learning is a calamity to any people.

FREDERICK DOUGLASS, commencement address, The Colored High School, Baltimore, Maryland, 22 June 1894

Our greatest danger in the great leap from slavery is that we may overlook the fact that the masses live by the productions of our hands, and fail to keep in mind that we shall prosper in proportion as we learn to dignify and glorify common labor and put brains and skills into common occupations of life.

BOOKER T. WASHINGTON, *Speeches of Booker T. Washington,* 1932

Until we conquer ourselves I make no empty statements when I say that we shall have a cancer gnawing at the heart of this republic that shall someday prove to be as dangerous as an attack from an army without or within.

Ibid.

Common danger [makes] common friends.

ZORA NEALE HURSTON, *Their Eyes Were Watching God,* 1937

We have allowed our civilization to outrun our culture, and so we are in danger now of ending up with guided missiles in the hands of misguided men.

MARTIN LUTHER KING, JR., "The American Dream," speech given at Lincoln University, Oxford, Pennsylvania, 6 June 1961

We have known how to face dangers to obtain our liberty, we shall know how to brave death to maintain it.

TOUSSAINT L'OUVERTURE, in James, *The Black Jacobins,* 1963

Let's begin by saying that we are living through a very dangerous time. . . . The society in which we live is desperately menaced . . . from within.

JAMES BALDWIN, "A Talk to Harlem Teachers," in Clarke, *Harlem, USA,* 1964

Irrationality is dangerous, perhaps the most dangerous force stalking through the world today.

FRANK YERBY, *Judas, My Brother,* 1967

The Lord has laid his hands on you, and that is a dangerous, dangerous thing.

BAYARD RUSTIN, *Down the Road Chicago,* 1970

No one is more dangerous than he who imagines himself pure in heart: for this purity by definition is unassailable.

JAMES BALDWIN, "Why I left America," *Essence,* October 1970

You simply find your situation intolerable and you set about to change it, and when you do that, you place yourself in a certain kind of danger: the danger of being excessive, the danger of being wrong.

JAMES BALDWIN, *A Rap on Race,* 1971

It is dangerous for white America to insist that basic American documents be read by the black, poor and oppressed, because such people are just naive enough to go out and do what the founding fathers said oppressed people should do.

DICK GREGORY, *No More Lies,* 1971

Our demonstrations, murder, political chicanery, hatred, and strife are but symptoms of a psychopath who has forgotten his name. The pain, the guilt, and the frustration break us.

HERMAN WATTS, "What Is Your Name?" in Philpot, ed., *Best Black Sermons,* 1972

To be born Black and male in America is a double jeopardy. [We are] a threat to those who control this society.

LELAND HALL, in "The Black Male in Jeopardy," *Crisis,* March 1986

[I]n a dangerous world, a realm of disasters, a place of grief and pain, a sensible man made *himself* dangerous. . . .

CHARLES JOHNSON, *Middle Passage,* 1990

DAY

Every dog has his day; there is time for all things.

TERENCE, *The Eunuch,* 167 B.C.

Even one day is a donation to eternity and every hour is a contribution to the future.

KING KHETI of Egypt

No day dawns like another.

AFRICA

Come all! Stand up!/ Just over there the dawn is coming./ Now I hear/ Soft laughter.

PAPAGO

See in the east the illustrious king of day!/His rising radiance drives the shades away.

PHILLIS WHEATLEY, "A Hymn to Morning," in *Poems on Various Subjects, Religious and Moral,* 1773

The fight is longer than a span of life; the test is great. Gird your loins, sharpen your tools! Time is on our side. Carry on the organizing and the conserving of your forces, my dear brother, grim with determination, for a great purpose—for the Day.

CLAUDE MCKAY, in review of "He Who Gets Slapped," *Liberator,* 5 May 1922

Try to make each day reach as nearly as possible the high water mark of pure, unselfish, useful living.

BOOKER T. WASHINGTON, *Speeches of Booker T. Washington,* 1932

Each of my todays has eyes that/ look upon my yesterdays.

LÉON DAMAS, "The Black Man's Lament," *Pigments,* 1937

Over the land was the shadow of a new day.

PETER ABRAHAMS, *Wild Conquest,* 1950

All of us know a better day is coming . . . when we go home to Paradise . . . we also realize that the things practiced in Paradise are not practiced here.

MARCUS GARVEY, *Garvey and Garveyism,* 1963

To each day its own resources.

FRANK YERBY, c. 1965

The day will not save them and we own the night.

LEROI JONES, *Home: Social Essays,* 1966

They wake up each morning knowing that no day is a good day to die, but that one day is as good as any other as long as they do not die alone.

JULIAN MAYFIELD, "You Touch My Black Aesthetic and I'll Touch Yours," in Gayle, *The Black Aesthetic,* 1971

Any day I wake up is a good day.

DUKE ELLINGTON, *Music Is My Mistress,* 1973

The good old days were horrible. They were not good.

WILLIS WARD, *Blacks in Detroit,* 1980

At the end of the day, give up your worries and give thanks for the journey.

BEN VEREEN, in "Dealing With Adversities," *Body Mind Spirit,* Summer 1991

DEATH

When the messenger of death comes to take you, let him find you ready to go to your resting place saying, "Here comes one prepared before you." Do not say, "I am too young to be taken." For death comes and seizes the baby at his or her mother's breast as well as the man or woman who have reached an old age.

PTAH HOTEP, c. 2340 B.C.

O Prince my Lord, the end of life is at hand; old age descendeth upon me; feebleness cometh and childishness is renewed; he that is old lieth down in misery every day. The eyes are small, the ears are deaf. Energy is diminished, the heart has no rest.

Ibid.

Death is in my eyes today. Like the desire of a man to see his home when he has passed many years in captivity. Death is before me today/ like a well trodden way/ like a man coming home from warfare.

"The Dispute Between a Man and His Ba," c. 1990–1785 B.C.

Though this may be play to you, 'Tis death to us.

AESOP, "The Boys and the Frog," 570 B.C.

Pray learn first what it is to live. When you have tried that and don't like it, then die if you will.

TERENCE, *The Self-Tormentor,* 161 B.C.

For soon or late we yield our vital breath,/ And all our worldly troubles end in death.

SHAHNAMAH OF FIRDAUSI, 932–1020 A.D.

There is no occasion for our rejoicing at a foe's death, because our own life will also not last forever.

The Gulistan of Sadi, 1184–1292 A.D.

What is said of the dead lion's body could not be said to him alive.

CONGO

If a dead tree falls, it carries with it a live one.

IVORY COAST

Sleep is the cousin of death.

CONGO

Many dogs are the death of the lion.

AFRICA

Death is a great cold.

AFRICA

When brothers fight to death a stranger inherits their father's estate.

NIGERIA

One dies in fire, one dies in water. So do we all belong to death and go to our place.

TOGO

I could tell better where my father's shadow groans tonight. I could tell better where he groans.

ZAIRE

O sun, you remain forever, but we Kaitsenko must die. O earth, you remain forever, but we Kaitsenko must die.

DEATH SONG OF THE KIOWA SOLDIER SOCIETY

Ax the trunk, the limb dies.

TRADITIONAL

Before I'd be a slave/ I'd be buried in my grave/ And go home to my Lord and be free.

SPIRITUAL

Soon one mornin' death came knocking at my door.

SPIRITUAL

I have nothing more to offer than what George Washington would have had to offer had he been taken by the British officers and put to trial by them. I have ventured my life in an endeavor to obtain the freedom of my countrymen. I know that you have predetermined to shed my blood. Why then all the mockery of a trial?

SLAVE IN GABRIEL'S REVOLT, 1800

Beneath the deep blue sky of her own native land,/ She weary grew, and drooping, pined away./ She died and passed, and over me I oft-times feel/ Her youthful shadow fondly hovering/ And all the while a gaping chasm divides us both./ In vain I would my aching grief awake.

ALEXANDER PUSHKIN, "Elegy," 1826

Death is . . . an ordeal, . . . not an expiation.

ALEXANDRE DUMAS, *The Count of Monte Cristo,* 1844

Nothing lives long/ Only the earth and the mountains.

CHEYENNE DEATH SONG, 1851

No chance for me to live, Mother mourn for me.

SITTING BULL, c. 1877

We have slumbered and slept too long already; the day is far spent; the night of death approaches.

MARIA STEWART, *Meditations from the Pen of Mrs. Maria W. Stewart,* 1879

I am not going to die, I'm going home like a shooting star.

SOJOURNER TRUTH, 1883

Someone must show that the Afro-American race is more sinned against than sinning, and it seems to have fallen to me to do so. The awful death roll called every week is appalling, not only because of the lives taken, the cruelty and outrage to the victims, but because of the prejudice it fosters.

IDA B. WELLS, *A Red Record,* 1895

Death is a phenomenon like life; perhaps the dead live.

JOAQUIM MACHADO DE ASSIS, *Esau and Jacob,* 1901

Because I had loved so deeply,/ Because I had loved so long,/ God in His great compassion/ Gave me the gift of song./ Because I had loved so vainly,/ And sung with such faltering breath,/ The Master in infinite mercy/ Offers the boon of Death.

PAUL LAURENCE DUNBAR, "Compensation," *Complete Poems,* 1913

Why must you always come like a thief, Death./ . . . Leaving only tears? Come to me festively,/ Make the whole night ring with your triumphant blow/ Your victory-conch, dress me in blood-red robes,/ Grasp me by the hand and sweep me away!/ Pay no heed to what others may think, Death,/ For I shall of my own free will/ Resort to you if you but take me graciously.

RABINDRANATH TAGORE, *Death-wedding,* 1914

When I was young I walked over this country, east and west, and saw no other people than the Apaches. After many summers I walked again and found another race of people had come to take it. How is it? Why is it that the Apaches wait to die—that they carry their lives on their fingernails? They roam over the hills and plains and want the heavens to fall on them. The Apaches were once a great nation; they are now but few, and because of this they want to die and so carry their lives on their fingernails.

CHOCHISE OF THE CHIRICAHUA APACHES, in "Recollections of an Interview with Cochise, Chief of the Apaches," *Collections,* 1915

The first dying to be done by the black man will be done to make himself free.

MARCUS GARVEY, *Philosophy and Opinions of Marcus Garvey,* 1923

And Death heard the summons,/ And he leaped on his fastest horse,/ Pale as a sheet in the moonlight./ Up the golden street Death galloped.

JAMES WELDON JOHNSON, "Go Down Death—A Funeral Sermon," *God's Trombones,* 1927

But how were we to die? What should we dare and do so that there would be nothing before us except a choice of victory or death? An impenetrable wall was before me, as it were, and I could not see my way through.

MOHANDAS GANDHI, *Satyagraha in South Africa,* 1929

I die if I don't work,/ and if I do, I die./ Either way I die,/ Either way I die.

NICOLAS GUILLÉN, *Blues,* 1934

If a nation were perfect it would not die.

CARTER G. WOODSON, *The Story of the Negro Retold,* 1935

[Death] stands watchful and motionless all day with his sword drawn back, waiting for the messenger to bid him come.

ZORA NEALE HURSTON, *Their Eyes Were Watching God,* 1937

So the beginning of this was a woman and she had come back from burying the dead. Not the dead of sick and ailing with friends at the pillow and the feet. She had come back from the sodden and the bloated; the sudden dead, their eyes flung wide open in judgment.

Ibid.

He had seen Death coming and had stood his ground and fought it . . . to the last breath. Naturally he didn't have time to straighten himself out. Death had to take him like it found him.

Ibid.

You may bury my body down by the highway side/ So my old evil spirit/ Can catch a Greyhound bus and ride.

ROBERT JOHNSON, "Me and the Devil Blues," 1937

What has been done in my country I did not want did not ask for it; white people going through my country. When the white man comes to my country he leaves a trail of blood behind him.

MAHPIUA LUTA (RED CLOUD) OF THE OGLALA SIOUX, in Hyde, *Red Cloud's Folk,* 1937

The Master-Maker in His making had made Old Death. Made him with big, soft feet and square toes. Made him with a face that reflects the face of all things, but neither changes itself, nor is mirrored anywhere. Made the body of death out of infinite hunger. Made a weapon of his hand to satisfy his needs. This was the morning of the day of the beginning of things.

ZORA NEALE HURSTON, *Dust Tracks on a Road,* 1942

[Y]our fathers await you without impatience.

JACQUES ROUMAIN, "Guinea," *Masters of the Dew,* 1944

Once again this life hobbling before me, what am I saying life, *this death,* this death without sense or piety, this death that so pathetically falls short of greatness, the dazzling pettiness of this death, this death hobbling from pettiness to pettiness, . . . and all these deaths futile.

AIMÉ CÉSAIRE, *Notes on a Return to the Native Land,* 1947

Death traces a shining circle/ above this man/ death stars softly above his head/ death breathes, crazed, in the ripened canefield of his arms/ death gallops in the prison like/ a white horse/ death gleams in the dark like/ the eyes of a cat/ death hiccups like the water under the keys/ death is a struck bird . . . death expires in a white pool/ of silence.

Ibid.

No one can escape death. Then why be afraid of it? In fact, death is a friend who brings deliverance from suffering.

MOHANDAS GANDHI, speech given on an All India Radio Broadcast, 16 January 1948

"Starved to death,"/ He died of hunger,/ but it won't be written on his tomb/ for they put him in an unmarked grave,/ it won't be written there in stone/ for the government rejects the truth.

BERNARD DADIE, "In Memoriam," *Africa Arise!* 1950

I was coming home from Fa'oye, having drunk there deeply at the solemn/ tomb/ . . . And [it is] the watching hour [when] one sees spirits, when the light becomes transparent.

LEOPOLD SENGHOR, *Ethiopics,* 1956

The only possible death is to lose belief in this truth simply because the great end comes slowly, because time is long.

W. E. B. DU BOIS, "Last Message to the World," speech given 26 June 1957

Who dares say no when the Angel of Death calls? You can be in your grocery store ringing up a hundred-dollar sale on the cash register and Death will call and you'll have to drop the sale and go. You can be riding around in your Buick and Death will call and you'll have to go. You are about to get out of your bed to go down to your job and old Death will call and you'll have to go. Mebbe you are building a house and called the mason and the carpenter and then Death calls and you have to go. Death's asking you to come to your last home.

RICHARD WRIGHT, *The Long Dream,* 1958

There is no better time to talk about the living than when we remember the dead.

CHINUA ACHEBE, *Things Fall Apart,* 1959

Bear in mind/ That death is a drum/ Beating forever/ Till the last worms come/ To answer its call,/ Till the last stars fall,/ Until the last atom/ Is no atom at all,/ Until time is lost/ And there is no air/ And space itself/ Is nothing nowhere. . . .

LANGSTON HUGHES, "Drum," *Selected Poems,* 1959

He rose up on his dying bed/ and asked for fish./ His wife looked it up in her dream book/ and played it.

LANGSTON HUGHES, "Hope," in *ibid.*

Listen to Things/ More often than Beings,/ Hear the voice of fire,/ Hear the voice of water./ Listen in the wind,/ To the sighs of the bush;/ This is the ancestors breathing./ Those who are dead are not ever gone.

BIRAGO DIOP, "Spirits," *Gleams and Glimmers,* 1960

Those who are dead are never gone;/ They are in the darkness that grows lighter/ And in the darkness that grows darker./ They are in the trembling of the trees,/ In the groaning of the woods,/ In the water that runs,/ In the water that sleeps.

Ibid.

I said to prune the tree, not to uproot it.

TOUSSAINT L'OUVERTURE, in James, *The Black Jacobins,* 1963

When I am dead wrap the mantle of the Red, Black, and Green around me, for in the new life I shall rise . . . to lead the millions up the heights of triumph with the colors that you well know. Look for me in the whirlwind or storm, look for me all around you, for, with God's grace, I shall come and bring with me countless millions of black slaves who have died in America and the West Indies and the millions in Africa to aid you in the fight for Liberty, Freedom, and Life.

MARCUS GARVEY, *Garvey and Garveyism,* 1963

Last year I looked death in the face and found its lineaments not unkind. But it was not my time. Yet in nature time comes soon and in the fullness of days I shall die, quietly, I trust with my face turned south and eastward; and dream or dreamless I shall death enjoy as I have life.

W. E. B. DU BOIS, *The Autobiography of W. E. B. Du Bois: A Soliloquy on Viewing My Life from the Last Decade of Its First Century,* 1964

If I die or am killed before making it back to the States, you may rest assured that what I've already set in motion will never be stopped. The foundation has been laid and no one can hardly undo it.

MALCOLM X, letter from Cairo, 29 May 1964

If physical death is the price I must pay to free my white brothers and sisters from the permanent death of the spirit, then nothing could be more redemptive.

MARTIN LUTHER KING, JR., speech given in St. Augustine, Florida, 5 June 1964

Man dies when he refuses to stand up for that which is right. A man dies when he refuses to take a stand for that which is true.

MARTIN LUTHER KING, JR., 1965

It is a time for martyrs now, and if I am to be one, it will be for the cause of brotherhood. That's the only thing that can save this country.

MALCOLM X, speech given in New York City, 19 February 1965

The quality, not the longevity, of one's life is what is important. If you are in a moment that is designed to save the soul of a nation, then no other death could be more redemptive.

MARTIN LUTHER KING, JR., "I Have Been to the Mountaintop," speech given in Memphis, Tennessee, 3 April 1968

The only way we can really achieve freedom is to somehow conquer the fear of death. For if a man has not discovered something that he will die for he isn't fit to live.

MARTIN LUTHER KING, JR., in Coretta Scott King, *My Life With Martin Luther King, Jr.,* 1969

It is better to die on one's feet than to live on one's knees, but some individuals appear actually to believe that it is better to crawl around on one's bare belly.

NATHAN HARE, in *The Black Scholar,* November 1969

I came here to die—not to make a speech.

CHEROKEE BILL in Gregory, *No More Lies,* 1971

Brother, brother, there are too many of us dying.

MARVIN GAYE, "What's Going On," 1971

Each man's death is fated from the beginning of time.

FRANK YERBY, 1972

It frightens me to realize that, if I had died before the age of fifty, I would have died a "Negro" fraction.

GWENDOLYN BROOKS, *Report From Part One,* 1972

Malcolm died in the sound of explosion, lying on a public platform for all the world to see, his life flowing in crimson rivulets from bullet punctures.

JULIUS LESTER, in Hansberry, *Les Blancs,* 1972

When you've lost your identity, when you've lost your purpose, when you've lost your hope, when you've lost your integrity . . . you are sick unto death. . . . [W]hen you destroy another man's dignity, . . . when you've slaughtered another man's dream, you are more than sick unto death.

OTIS MOSS, JR., "Going from Disgrace to Dignity," in Philpot, ed., *Best Black Sermons,* 1972

If you're afraid to die, you will not be able to live.

JAMES BALDWIN, on "Assignment America" (television program), 13 May 1975

Death mattered not—It was a mere punctuation.

NATHAN HUGGINS, *Black Odyssey,* 1977

Hadn't been for your daddy, I wouldn't be here today. I would have died in the womb. And died again in the woods. But he saved me and here I am boiling eggs. Our papa was dead, you see. They blew him five feet up into the air. He was sitting on the fence waiting for 'em, and they sneaked up from behind and blew him five feet in the air.

TONI MORRISON, *Song of Solomon,* 1977

What will die with me when I die, what pathetic or fragile form will the world lose?

JOSÉ LUIS BORGES, "The Witness," *Latin American Tales,* 1977

I imagine death to be like sleep. When death comes to you, you just pass out, just the way you passed out last night.

RAY CHARLES, *Brother Ray,* 1978

It is said that those about to die, be it by drowning or by a gradual terminal illness, use their last few moments of consciousness going through their life kaleidoscopically.

BUCHI EMECHETA, *The Joys of Motherhood,* 1979

Who told you that the dead are not with us? Who told you that they do not see? A good person does not die and go forever; he goes to another world, and may even decide to come back and live his life again. But one must be good in this world to have that choice.

Ibid.

It may get me crucified, I may even die. But I want it said even if I die in the struggle that "He died to make men free."

MARTIN LUTHER KING, JR., in Oates, *Let the Trumpet Sound,* 1982

Some of the children have been shot, some have been stabbed, some strangled. Some are naked, some are clothed, some are decomposing. You don't know all of them, but you know some. The last time you saw this one or that one, he was in the kitchen with your child. You begin waiting for your child to come home.

JAMES BALDWIN, *Evidence of Things Not Seen,* 1985

Death cannot put the brakes on a good dream.

MARVA COLLINS, in "The Most Unforgettable Person in My Family," *Ebony,* August 1986

South African police shot to death a four-year-old little girl. They told her father they were sorry, but they thought that she was a dog.

ALLAN BOESAK, "Who Can Speak for South Africa?" *Crisis,* November 1986

[T]he mainspring of . . . life on this earth is wound like the mainspring of a clock to work not endlessly but for a definite brief time and then stop.

JEAN TOOMER, in Kerman and Eldridge, *The Lives of Jean Toomer,* 1987

What can you do about death. You have to go on. I work on the basis that I'm doing God's work, and it's his business to look after me. Nobody is indispensable.

DESMOND TUTU, *Message,* Freedom Issue, 1987

The death angel can make the very important irrelevant in the winking of an eye and can change agendas and alternatives.

JESSE JACKSON, in "National Report," *Jet,* 14 December 1987

When you look death in the face you make up your mind that if you're going to die you're going to go fighting.

JOHNNY FORD, c. 1988

Too often in the black community when the family dies the company dies.

A. G. GASTON, 1988

When death comes/ to fetch you/ She comes unannounced,/ She comes suddenly/ Like the vomit of dogs,/ And when She comes/ The wind keeps blowing/ The birds go on singing/ And the flowers/ Do not hang their heads.

OKOT P'BITEK, "When Death Comes To Fetch You," in Chinweizu, *Voices from Twentieth-Century Africa,* 1988

The clock stops, and is rewound or sent to the handyman/ But your clock has stopped, your arms are still/ Your vast maze of dials and rotaries, sensors and generators are/ forever motionless.

ONWUCHEKWA JEMIE, "Lament for Ellsworth Janifer," in *ibid.*

Death should be like an extended sojourn/ In some foreign country/ During which hope is kept alive/ With occasional letters, photographs and gifts/To us loved ones waiting at home/ Sent through some wayfarer/ Who saw you in exile prosperous and happy. . . .

Ibid.

There is no reason why the angel of death should bypass sports.

HARRY EDWARDS, in "Hardline," *Detroit Free Press,* 8 May 1988

When we die, it's sure enough for the first time. I'll be interested to see how it comes out, but I'm in no hurry.

RAY CHARLES, in "Ray Charles Sees the Beauty," *Parade,* 10 October 1988

In those days everyone died of a heart attack, no matter what it really was. Well, it's hard to disagree with, because everybody's heart stops when they're dead.

Ibid.

The day I no longer go on stage will be the day I die.

JOSEPHINE BAKER in Rose, *Jazz Cleopatra,* 1989

Death climbed in through every portal.

CHARLES JOHNSON, *Middle Passage,* 1990

There is a skeleton of death that flees in the face of my will to live.

FRIDA KAHLO, in Herrera, *Frida Kahlo: The Paintings,* 1991

I hope the exit is joyful—and I hope never to come back.

Ibid.

The order to open fire disciplined them into juggernauts of death; from that moment on there was no excitement, only death. The rifles and the sten guns were crackling death, spitting at anything which moved—anything black. The police selected their targets at random with persistent accuracy. . . . The shooting, the screaming, the dying, continued for what seemed like the whole day, and the snap staccato of the guns echoed from all around Sophiatown; and the smell and the decay of death spread over the township, over the burning cinders and smog.

YOUTH LEAGUER, in Mandela, *Higher Than Hope,* 1991

One never should seek independence from those upon whom one feels permanently dependent, for that would be an act of suicide.

FRANCES CRESS WELSING, *The Isis Papers,* 1991

If you're going to die, die doing what you love to do.

BERNARD SHAW, in *USA Weekend,* 1 March 1991

I stared death in the face and blinked. I don't expect to get more chances like that.

Ibid.

DECISION

If it is to be, it's up to me.

TRADITIONAL

Every artist, every scientist must decide now where he stands. . . . There is no standing above the conflict on Olympian heights. There are no impartial observers.

PAUL ROBESON, "The Artist Must Take Sides," *Daily Worker,* 4 November 1937

When I got up to "speak" I suddenly decided that to "speak" was irrelevant. I was a poet, and . . . so I merely read a few poems from my book.

GWENDOLYN BROOKS, *Report From Part One,* 1972

We've got to decide if it's going to be this generation or never.

DAISY BATES, c. 1975

Making a decision to write [is] a lot like deciding to jump into a frozen lake.

MAYA ANGELOU, *The Heart of a Woman,* 1981

I decided to box my way out of the ghetto.

LARRY HOLMES, c. 1982

The thing is to never deal yourself out. . . . Opt for the best possible hand. Play with verve and sometimes with abandon, but at all times with calculation.

L. DOUGLAS WILDER, in "Virginia's Lieutenant Governor: L. Douglas Wilder is First Black to Win Office," *Ebony,* April 1986

I didn't have it in my head to do bad things, I did them because everyone else was doing them.

MIKE TYSON, in *Star,* May 1986

The people making the decisions now are not in charge of the future.

OSSIE DAVIS, "It's On Us," *City Arts Quarterly,* Spring 1988

DEFEAT

You can't hold a man down without staying down with him.

BOOKER T. WASHINGTON, *Speeches of Booker T. Washington,* 1932

Defeat is like a mis-cue on a pool table. In any game there's got to be a mis-cue.

MUHAMMAD ALI, *The Greatest,* 1975

A true champion never forgets a real defeat.

Ibid.

Defeat should not be the source of discouragement, but a stimulus to keep plotting.

SHIRLEY CHISHOLM, in *USA Today,* 26 August 1987

Defeat is not bitter unless you swallow it.

JOE CLARK, "It is Time for Blacks to Take Care of Their Fate," *Ebony,* 1988

DEFINITION

All of Bigger's life is controlled, defined by his hatred and his fear.

JAMES BALDWIN, "Everybody's Protest Novel," *Notes on a Native Son,* 1955

You must begin to define for yourself; you must begin to define your Black heritage.

H. RAP BROWN, c. 1970

[Image is] central to a man's self-definition.

CAROLYN GERALD, "The Black Writer and His Role," in Gayle, *The Black Aesthetic,* 1971

American society cannot define the role of the individual, or at least not that of the *responsible* individual. For it is our fate as Americans to achieve that sense of self-consciousness through our own efforts.

RALPH ELLISON, "On Initiation Rites and Power," *Going to the Territory,* 1986

All people have a major task, from cradle to grave, of defining who they are.

WILLIAM LYLES, in "The Black Male in Jeopardy," *Crisis,* March 1986

Diaspora does not describe the Black experience. We came here as slaves, not as a diaspora people.

YOSEF BEN JOCHANNON, in "Interview: Dr. Yosef ben Jochannon, PhD," *Crisis,* June 1986

Definitions belonged to the definer—not the defined.

TONI MORRISON, *Beloved,* 1987

I'm black. I don't feel burdened by it and I don't think it's a huge responsibility. It's part of who I am. It does not define me.

OPRAH WINFREY, in "Opinionated Oprah," *Woman's Day,* 4 October 1988

When we play to the demands of others, we are putting through our heads what we think they want and we are using our energies to do that. When we are freed from that, we are free to move on to the job of defining ourselves.

CAMILLE COSBY, in *Delta Newsletter,* 22 April 1989

DEMOCRACY

A democracy cannot long endure with the head of a God and the tail of a demon.

JOSEPHINE YATES, *The Voice of the Negro,* 1904

The real argument for democracy is, then, that in the people we have the source of that endless life and unbounded wisdom which the rulers of men must have. A given people today may not be intelligent, but through a democratic government that recognizes not only the worth of the individual to himself, but the worth of his feelings and experiences to all, they can educate, not only the individual unit, but generation after generation, until they accumulate vast stores of wisdom. Democracy alone is the method of showing the whole experience of the race for the benefit of the future and if democracy tries to exclude women or Negroes or the poor or any class because of innate characteristics which do not interfere with intelligence, then that democracy cripples itself and belies its name.

W. E. B. DU BOIS, *Darkwater,* 1920

Strip American democracy and religion of its verbiage and you find the Neanderthal.

J. A. ROGERS, in "Critical Excursions and Reflections," *The Messenger,* 5 May 1924

He had no illusions about American democracy. He had learned as a porter how America was ruled. He knew the power of organized crime, of self-indulgence, of industry, of business, corporations, finance, commerce. They all paid for what they wanted the government to do for them—for their immunity, their appetites, for their incomes, for justice and the police.

W. E. B. DU BOIS, *Dark Princess,* 1928

This country can have no more democracy than it accords and guarantees to the humblest and weakest citizen.

JAMES WELDON JOHNSON, *Along This Way,* 1933

It was the Black man that raised a vision of democracy in America such as neither American nor European conceived in the eighteenth century and they have not even accepted in the twentieth century, and yet a conception which every clear-sighted man knows is true and inevitable.

W. E. B. DU BOIS, *Black Reconstruction,* 1935

World history points out clearly that modern democracy, conceived in the womb of the middle-class revolution, was early put out to work in support of the those ruling middle-class interests of capitalistic society which fathered it. It has remained their loyal child and has rendered profitable service for them.

RALPH BUNCHE, "A Critical Analysis of the Tactics and Programs of Minority Groups," *Journal of Negro Education,* 7 July 1935

We are anxious for you to know that we want to be and insist upon being considered a part of our American democracy, not something apart from it. We know from experience that our interests are too often neglected, ignored, or scuttled unless we have effective representation in the formative stages. . . . We are not blind to what is happening. We are not humiliated. We are incensed.

MARY MCLEOD BETHUNE, speech given to the National Council of Negro Women, 26 November 1938

A great state is a well-blended mash of something of all the people and all of none of the people. The liquor of statecraft is distilled from the mash you got.

ZORA NEALE HURSTON, *Moses, Man of the Mountain,* 1939

A born democrat is a born disciplinarian. Democracy comes naturally to him who is . . . willing to yield willing obedience to all laws, human or divine.

MOHANDAS GANDHI, in *Harijan,* 27 May 1939

Democracy was fought for and taken from political royalists, the kings. Industrial democracy is being won and taken from the economic royalist, big business.

A. PHILLIP RANDOLPH, address to Policy Conference of the March on Washington Movement, Detroit, Michigan, 26 September 1942

Democracy is not tolerance. Democracy is a prescribed way of life erected on the premise that all men are created equal.

CHESTER HIMES, *If You're Scared, Go Home,* 1944

I want to congratulate you for doing your bit to make the world safe for democracy and unsafe for hypocrisy.

A. PHILIP RANDOLPH, in *The Messenger,* 1 December 1948

[A]ny Negro, if he were honest, would have to say that in our democracy at present, that he is never, for any one second, unconscious of the fact that he is a black American. He can never be unconscious of it in any part of the United States.

PAUL ROBESON, interview, Pacifica Radio San Francisco, 15 March 1958

Democracy must be something African to have permanence; something lively to have attractiveness; something creative to have appeal; something now—here, to have promise, something practiced to have realism, to draw faith; something altruistic to draw a future, and it must be godly to merit reverence.

A. A. NWAFOR, in "Democracy and Africa," *Negro Digest,* December 1961

History has thrust on our generation an indescribably important destiny—to complete a process of democratization which our nation has developed too slow.

MARTIN LUTHER KING, *Where Do We Go From Here?* 1968

I have cherished the ideal of a democratic and free society. . . . [i]t is an ideal for which I am prepared to die.

NELSON MANDELA, *The Struggle Is My Life,* 1978

Democracy is a collectivity of individuals.

RALPH ELLISON, "Perspective of Literature," *Going to the Territory,* 1986

Democracy is a leveling process which moves in any direction along the scale of taste.

Ibid.

DEMONSTRATION

We must develop huge demonstrations, because the world is used to big dramatic affairs. They think in terms of hundreds of thousands and millions and billions. Billions of dollars are appropriated at the twinkling of an eye. Nothing little counts.

A. PHILIP RANDOLPH, address to Policy Conference of the March on Washington movement, Detroit, Michigan, 26 September 1942

We are gathered here in the largest demonstration in the history of this nation. Let the nation and the world know the meaning of our numbers. We are not pressure groups, we are not an organization or a group of organizations, we are not a mob. We are the advance guard of a massive moral revolution for jobs and freedom.

A. PHILIP RANDOLPH, speech given at Lincoln Memorial, Washington, D.C., 28 August 1963

Massive civil disobedience is a powerful weapon under civilized conditions where the law safeguards the citizens' right of peaceful demonstration.

ROBERT WILLIAMS, in "USA, The Potential of a Minority Revolution," *The Crusader Monthly Newsletter,* May–June 1965

DEPENDENCE

No people that has solely depended on foreign aid or rather upon the efforts of those in any way identified with the oppressor to undo the heavy burdens, ever gained freedom.

FREDERICK DOUGLASS, *Life and Times of Frederick Douglass,* 1881

Let the Afro-American depend on no party, but on himself, for his salvation. Let him continue toward education, character, and above all, put money in his purse.

IDA B. WELLS, in Duster, ed., *Crusade for Justice,* 1928

A race that is solely dependent upon another for its economic existence sooner or later dies.

MARCUS GARVEY, *Garvey and Garveyism,* 1963

We can't rely on anyone but ourselves to define our existence, to shape the image of ourselves.

SPIKE LEE, c. 1988

DEPRIVATION

Whom the gods would destroy they first deprive of a sense of history.

WILLIAM HASTIE, speech given to National Bar Association, Atlanta, Georgia, 1971

Material deprivation is horrible, but it does not compare to spiritual deprivation.

OSSIE DAVIS, "It's On Us," *City Arts Quarterly,* Spring 1988

DESIRE

It is very difficult to crush in man his natural desire for liberty.

CARTER G. WOODSON, *Negro Makers of History,* 1928

Desire is the germ of the mind. There is no creation without it. Desire is a woman who is little understood and much slandered when her back is turned.

ZORA NEALE HURSTON, *Moses, Man of the Mountain,* 1939

Though I can re-grieve the night-stained caresses/ I can never not want you/. . . I can never unlove you.

EUGENE REDMOND, "I Can Never Unlove You," in Finn, *Voices of Negritude,* 1988

DESPAIR

If you ever been down you know just how I feel/ Like a broken down engine, got no driving wheel/ Like a poor soldier boy left on the battlefield.

BLUES

Been down so long, down don't worry me.

TRADITIONAL

Only a man who has felt ultimate despair is capable of feeling ultimate bliss.

ALEXANDRE DUMAS, *The Count of Monte Cristo,* 1844

I got stones in my pass way and my road seems dark as night.

ROBERT JOHNSON, 1937

Lord, I need all my strength against despair/—How sweet the dagger thrust to its hilt into the heart.

LEOPOLD SENGHOR, "Midnight Elegy," *Ethiopics,* 1956

Despair? Did someone say despair was a question in the world? Well then, listen to the sons of those who have known little else if you wish to know the resiliency of this thing you would so quickly resign to mythhood, this thing called the human spirit.

LORRAINE HANSBERRY, *To Be Young, Gifted and Black,* 1959

There comes a time when the cup of endurance runs over, and men are no longer willing to be plunged into an abyss of injustice where they experience the blackness of corroding despair.

MARTIN LUTHER KING, JR., *Letter From a Birmingham City Jail,* 1963

Despair sits on this country in most places like a charm, but there is a special gray death that loiters in the streets.

IMAMU AMIRI BARAKA, *Cold Hurt and Sorrow,* 1966

I have come to the center of a stagnant pool where I drift aimlessly around a slow oozy backwash of putrid nothingness.

ALICE NELSON DUNBAR, in *Give Us Each Day,* 1984

Difficulty need not foreshadow despair or defeat. Rather achievement can be all the more satisfying because of obstacles surmounted.

WILLIAM HASTIE, *Grace Under Pressure,* 1984

DESTINY

No matter how many rivers the crab may ford, it will end up in a soup pot.

NIGERIA

Every people should be the originators of their own designs, the projectors of their own schemes, and creators of the events that lead to their destiny—the consummation of their own desires.

MARTIN DELANY, *The Condition, Elevation, Emigration, and Destiny of the Colored People of the United States,* 1852

The laws which determine the destinies of individuals and nations are impartial and eternal. We shall reap as we shall sow.

FREDERICK DOUGLASS, "The Negro Exodus from the Gulf States," *Journal of Social Science,* May 1880

Destiny is not only a dramatist, it is also its own stage manager.

JOAQUIM MACHADO DE ASSIS, *Dom Casmurro,* 1900

We have lived in darker hours than those of today; we have seen American justice and fair play go through fire and death and devastation and come out purified by the faith that abides in the God of Destiny.

BOOKER T. WASHINGTON, *My Life and Work,* 1917

I went to Paris during the the Peace Conference because the destiny of mankind for hundreds of years was being decided by the Big Four because they had the power through their armed forces, capital, and propaganda machines to do so.

W. E. B. DU BOIS, "My Mission," *Crisis,* 4 April 1919

One God! One Aim! One Destiny! Let justice be done to all mankind.

MARCUS GARVEY, *Philosophy and Opinions of Marcus Garvey,* 1923

It's too big for us to be mere people. We've got to give up being people and feel like the tools of destiny, that's a big honor in itself.

ZORA NEALE HURSTON, *Moses, Man of the Mountain,* 1939

Each one follows his own destiny, my son. Men can not change what is decreed.

CAMARA LAYE, *The Dark Child,* 1954

Stars in profusion/ Pure/ As the eyes of/ Wise men/ Will be as brilliant/ As the destiny of men.

BERNARD DADIE, "A World to Come," *Dance of the Days,* 1956

To be free—to walk the good American earth as equal citizens, to live without fear, to enjoy the fruits of our toil, to give our children every opportunity in life—that dream which we have held so long in our hearts is today the destiny that we hold in our hands.

PAUL ROBESON, *Here I Stand,* 1958

[T]he human race does command its own destiny and that destiny can eventually embrace the stars.

LORRAINE HANSBERRY, *To Be Young, Gifted and Black,* 1959

We are caught in an inescapable network of mutuality, tied in a single garment of destiny. Whatever affects one directly affects all indirectly. As long as there is poverty in this world, no man can be totally rich even if he has a billion dollars. As long as diseases are rampant and millions of people cannot expect to live more than twenty or thirty years, no man can be totally healthy, even if he just got a clean bill of health from the finest clinic in America.

MARTIN LUTHER KING, JR., "The American Dream," speech given at Lincoln University, Oxford, Pennsylvania, 6 June 1961

I know very well that Columbus suffered ingratitude from Spain, and that such is the destiny of men who serve their country well; they have powerful enemies. As for me, it is the fate which is reserved for me, and I know I shall perish a victim of calumny.

TOUSSAINT L'OUVERTURE, in James, *The Black Jacobins,* 1963

I am not a prisoner of history. I should not seek there for the meaning of my destiny.

FRANTZ FANON, *Black Skin, White Masks,* 1967

We must all learn to live together as brothers. Or we will all perish as fools.

MARTIN LUTHER KING, JR., speech given at National Cathedral, Washington, D.C., 31 March 1968

You and I will never reach our potential. We'll never gain full control of our destinies. Man can't handle everything.

RAY CHARLES, *Brother Ray,* 1978

What then can be the destiny of a people that pampers and cherishes the blood of the white slaveholder who maimed and degraded their female ancestors? What can be the future of a class of descendants of slaves that implicitly gives slaveholders greater honor than the African women they enslaved? What can be the end of a class that pretends to honor blackness while secretly despising working class blackskinned women whose faces reveal no trace of white blood.

TRELLIE JEFFERS, in Walker, *In Search of Our Mothers' Gardens,* 1983

Never in my life have I experienced utter despair. . . . Something in me has always been convinced that I am a child of great destiny, that I have a star, that I am led on by it toward great fulfillment. . . . Nature in America experimented for three hundred years and with millions of blood-crossings to produce one man.

JEAN TOOMER, in Kerman and Eldridge, *The Lives of Jean Toomer,* 1987

I wasn't concerned about the hardships, because I always felt I was doing what I had to do, what I wanted to do and what I was destined to do.

KATHERINE DUNHAM, in "She Danced to Teach—and They Loved it," *American Visions,* February 1987

We create our own destiny by the way we do things. We have to take advantage of opportunities and be responsible for our choices.

BENJAMIN CARSON, *Gifted Hands,* 1990

DESTROY

To imagine that we shall ever be eradicated is absurd and ridiculous. We can be remodified, changed, and assimilated, but never extinguished.

FREDERICK DOUGLASS, in "The Destiny of Colored Americans," *North Star,* 16 November 1849

Destruction is not the law of humans. Man lives freely by his readiness to die, if need be, at the hands of his brother, never by killing him. Every murder, no matter for what cause . . . is a crime against humanity.

MOHANDAS GANDHI, in the *Harijan,* 20 July 1935

They have decided to destroy me out of hand. They are ready to do anything to confirm them in their position, and to do that, they have to prostitute the language. They must blow out the sun and switch on a spotlight.

ZORA NEALE HURSTON, *Moses, Man of the Mountain,* 1939

For the past several years a vicious effort has been made to destroy my career. Hall-owners, sponsors and even audiences have been intimidated.

PAUL ROBESON, in "Robeson on Records Again," *Freedom,* December 1952

It's self-destructive to save bitterness. Bitterness is meant to be used as part of the long term vision to understand how we've been victimized, but the trick is to break the cycle.

BUFFY SAINTE-MARIE, in *Akwesasne Notes,* Winter 1976

We should not be the first to destroy God's world.

JESSE JACKSON, 1988

DETERMINATION

Though a chicken does not have spurs, it can dig in.

AFRICA

We will either find a way or make one.

HANNIBAL

There was never a time in my youth, no matter how dark and discouraging the days might be, when one resolve did not continually remain with me, and that was a determination to secure an education at any cost.

BOOKER T. WASHINGTON, *Up From Slavery,* 1901

There is in this world no such force as the force of a man determined to rise.

W. E. B. DU BOIS, "Race Prejudice," speech given at the Republican Club, New York City, 5 March 1910

It is our intention to carry on an intelligent, persistent and aggressive agitation until we educate this nation, more than educate it, until we whip and sting its conscience, until we awaken it, until we startle it into a realization that we know what we want, we know what we are entitled to, and that we are determined by all that is sacred to have it and be satisfied with nothing less.

JAMES WELDON JOHNSON, "Africa at the Peace Table and the Descendants of Africans in our American Democracy," speech given at NAACP Annual Conference, 1919

The determination of Negro Americans to win freedom from all forms of oppression springs from the same deep longing that motivates oppressed people from all over the world. The rumblings of discontent in Asia and Africa are expressions of a quest for freedom and human dignity by people who have been the victims of colonialism and imperialism.

MARTIN LUTHER KING, JR., *Stride Toward Freedom,* 1958

When the sun is shining I can do anything; no mountain is too high, no trouble too difficult to overcome.

WILMA RUDOLPH, 6 September 1960

At the core of life is a hard purposefulness, a *determination* to live.

HOWARD THURMAN, *Disciplines of the Spirit,* 1963

You have to be tough and stick it out, or you wind up being nothing but a wino or a junkie.

JOE LOUIS, *My Life,* 1981

Largely through [Carter Woodson's] own efforts, [he] mastered the fundamentals of common school subjects by the time [he was] seventeen. Because one difficulty after another was thrown across [his] path, [he] was not able to enter high school until [he was] twenty, the time the average young man, in 1946, graduates from college. Entering high school at twenty, only a man of rare insight and prophetic vision would have been able to predict that [he] would earn an M.A. at Chicago, a Ph.D. at Harvard, become a Historian of national renown, and achieve the facilities to speak fluently three languages.

BENJAMIN MAYS, in "I Knew Carter G. Woodson," *Negro History Bulletin,* March 1981

Determination and perseverance move the world; thinking that others will do it for you is a sure way to fail.

MARVA COLLINS, in *Choosing to Succeed,* 1986

I may not work here, but I'm going to work somewhere, even if I have to go to the moon.

L. SCOTT CALDWELL, in *Jet,* 1 August 1988

I was determined to achieve the total freedom that our history lessons taught us we were entitled to, no matter what the sacrifice.

ROSA PARKS, in "The Meaning of Life," *Life,* December 1988

When I'm on my game, I don't think there's anybody that can stop me.

MICHAEL JORDAN, in "Michael Jordan in His Own Orbit," *GQ,* March 1989

The stubbornness I had as a child has been transmitted into perseverance. I can let go but I don't give up. I don't beat myself up about negative things.

PHYLICIA RASHAD, in "The Cosby Show's Phylicia Rashad," *McCall's,* February 1990

DETROIT

Most precious of recollections is Cadillac Square, Detroit . . . to stand there and sing to thousands of auto workers, massed in a historic demonstration, as the CIO took over Ford [Motor].

PAUL ROBESON, "The UAW Should Set the Pace," *Freedom,* March 1951

Douglass, Tubman and hundreds of our folk escaped into Canada around Detroit.

PAUL ROBESON, in *Freedom,* March 1953

Detroit is a bellwether, economically, in this nation, an early warning of economic trouble.

COLEMAN YOUNG, in *Detroit Monthly,* July 1979

Detroit turned out to be heaven, but it also turned out to be hell.

MARVIN GAYE, in Ritz, *Divided Soul,* 1985

I am a Detroit Piston, why shouldn't I live in Detroit?

JOHN SALLEY, 1989

In 1760, Detroit became a jewel in the British Crown.

NORMAN MCRAE, *Second Baptist Commemorative Book,* 1989

Detroit is not only famous for its motor and steel industries, but also for enriching the culture of the United States and the world. When we were in prison, we appreciated and avidly listened to the sound of Detroit, Motor Town. It is Motor Town that gave to the world that great singer, Steve Wonder.

NELSON MANDELA, speech given in Detroit, Michigan, 28 June 1990

DEVELOPMENT

The idea of constructive development of Negro communities commercially, politically, and culturally should be actively prosecuted, in spite of intellectual opposition. The Negro minority has been compelled of necessity to create its own preachers, teachers, doctors, and lawyers. If these were proportionately complemented by police, judges, principals, landlords, and businessmen, etc. the Negro American would take on the social aspects of its white counterpart.

CLAUDE MCKAY, *Harlem: Negro Metropolis,* 1940

The most crucial time in my own development came when I was forced to recognize that I was a kind of bastard of the West; when I followed the line of my past I did not find myself in Europe but in Africa.

JAMES BALDWIN, *Notes of a Native Son,* 1955

You don't invent a tree, you plant it. You don't extract the fruit, you let it grow. A nation isn't a sudden creation, it's a slow ripening, year after year, ring after ring.

AIMÉ CÉSAIRE, *Tragedy of King Christophe,* 1963

I'm a late bloomer. Ten years ago, twenty years ago I never opened my mouth to tell them how I felt or thought.

LENA HORNE, in "Great God Almighty, Lena Horne Is 'Me at Last,'" *Encore,* 15 August 1977

[Drive] makes us enter a world, not because . . . it is good or bad or indifferent, but because it suits our needs of catharsis—development as of that time. So we enter a world, develop in it, develop through it, and, in time, develop out of it.

JEAN TOOMER, in Kerman and Eldridge, *The Lives of Jean Toomer,* 1987

In the past the schools, the church, the neighborhood itself supported the development of the Black child. [Desegregation] destroyed that support system, and we were left only with the *opportunity* to *assimilate.*

NA'IM AKBAR, in "Growing Up Integrated (Did Momma Do the Right thing?)" *Crisis,* March 1988

The '60s are that period in which a generation went from consciousness to cynicism without passing through compassion.

NIKKI GIOVANNI, in "Episodes," *Catalyst,* Summer 1988

There's a pattern to my life. I do everything to the absolute ultimate. I grow. I grow until I can't grow anymore in a certain position. And then another door opens for me.

OPRAH WINFREY, in *Ladies' Home Journal,* May 1990

DEVIL

Diligence outdoes the devil.

TERENCE, *The Self-Tormentor,* 161 B.C.

When the devil speaks the truth even his truth does damage.

ORIGEN, *On Jeremiah,* c. 240

If Satan says I don't have grace, I'll take him back to the starting place.

TRADITIONAL

A mirror on the front porch would frighten the devil out of the front yard, since his reflection is even horrifying to himself.

TRADITIONAL

An idle mind is the devil's workshop.

TRADITIONAL

Had the devil come to our first parents personally and unmasked, they would have more easily seen the deception. The reality of a future punishment is so clearly impressed on the human mind that even Satan is constrained to own that there is a hell.

LEMUEL B. HAYNES, "Universal Salvation—A Very Ancient Doctrine," 1795

The devil is not dead, but still lives, and is able to preach as well as ever. "He shall not surely die."

Ibid.

In some places in America black is supposed to symbolize the devil and white symbolize God. But this is wrong for the devil is white and never was black.

HENRY MCNEAL TURNER, in the *Baltimore Afro-American,* 16 May 1888

Race prejudice is the devil unchained.

CHARLES W. CHESTNUTT, *Marrow of Tradition,* 1901

The favorite device of the devil, ancient and modern, is to force a human being into a more or less artificial class, accuse the class of unnamed and unnameable sin, and then damn any individual in the alleged class, however innocent he may be.

W. E. B. DU BOIS, "The Jim Crow Argument," *Crisis,* 1913

I believe in the Devil and his angels, who wantonly work to narrow the opportunity of struggling human beings, especially if they be Black; who spit in the faces of the fallen, strike them that cannot strike again, believe the worst and work to prove it, hating the image which their Maker stamped on a brother's soul.

W. E. B. DU BOIS, *Darkwater,* 1920

I vision God standing on the height of Heaven,/ Throwing the Devil like a burning torch over the gulf into the valleys of Hell.

ZORA NEALE HURSTON, *Jonah's Gourd Vine,* 1934

When the Devil is too busy to bug a man he sends a woman.

LANGSTON HUGHES, ed., *Book of Negro Humor,* 1966

A devil is a mental attitude born out of false pride and self-exalting lies. One who goes against the natural order of creation and creates an adversary in the minds of the people against the creator and His laws.

HERBERT MUHAMMAD, in Ali, *The Greatest,* 1975

I have seen the devil, by day and by night, and have seen him in you and in me: in the eyes of the cop and the sheriff and the deputy, the landlord, the housewife, the football player: in the eyes of some junkies, eyes of preachers, governors, wardens, orphans, presidents, and in the eyes of my father, and in my mirror.

JAMES BALDWIN, *The Devil Finds Work,* 1975

Oh, Satan sweet-talked her,/ and four bullets hushed her./ Lord's lost Him His diva,/ His fancy warbler's gone./ Who would have thought,/ who would have thought she'd end that way?

ROBERT HAYDEN, "Mourning Poem for the Queen of Sunday," *Collected Poems,* 1985

DIGNITY

You will see that from the start we tried to dignify our race. If I am to be condemned for that I am satisfied.

MARCUS GARVEY, *Philosophy and Opinions of Marcus Garvey,* 1923

Human dignity is more precious than prestige.

CLAUDE MCKAY, "Race and Color in East Asia," *Opportunity,* August 1939

Life should be lived with dignity, the personalities of others shouldn't be violated, that men should be able to confront other men without fear or shame, and that if men were lucky in their living on earth, they might win some redeeming meaning for their having struggled and suffered here beneath the stars.

RICHARD WRIGHT, *12 Million Black Voices,* 1941

With all the energy I command, I fight for the rights of the Negro people and other oppressed labor driven Americans to have a decent home, decent job, and the dignity that belongs to every human being.

PAUL ROBESON, c. 1945

Your door is shut against my tightened face,/ And I am sharp as steel with discontent;/ But I possess the courage and the grace/ To bear my anger proudly and unbent.

CLAUDE MCKAY, "The White House," *Selected Poems,* 1953

Mankind through the ages has been in a ceaseless struggle to give dignity and meaning to human life. It is that quest which separates it from the animal.

MARTIN LUTHER KING, JR., speech given at District 65 30th Anniversary, October 1963

There is a battle to be fought, there are obstacles to be overcome. There is a world struggle for human dignity to be won. Let us address ourselves seriously to the supreme tasks that lie ahead.

KWAME NKRUMAH, Address to the National Assembly, 26 March 1965

The willingness to die for human dignity is not novel; indeed, it stands at the heart of Christianity.

JAMES CONE, *Black Theology and Black Power,* 1969

Christian love means giving no ground to the enemy, but relentlessly insisting on one's dignity as a person.

Ibid.

I have struggled all my life for the kind of world all people can live in in dignity and reasonable comfort.

COLEMAN YOUNG, in the *Detroit Free Press*, 8 August 1973

There is no dignity without freedom. For any subjection, any coercion, dishonors the man who submits, deprives him of part of his humanity and arbitrarily turns him into an inferior being.

SEKOU TOURE, c. 1976

Begging strips me of my dignity.

MARVA COLLINS, in "Marva Collins: Teaching Success in the City," *Message*, July 1987

Dignity is fighting weakness and winning.

LOLA FALANA, in "Lola Falana's Valiant Fight," *Ebony*, 7 May 1988

DISAPPOINTMENT

Disappointment drives men to desperate lengths.

MARTIN LUTHER KING, JR., c. 1963

Like all of us I've had difficulties and disappointments. I've got a long way to go. I seem to be marking time, but I'm crouching, in order to leap.

JAMES BALDWIN, in "James Baldwin . . . in Conversation," *Arts in Society*, Summer 1966

All have disappointments, all have times when it isn't worthwhile.

JOHN H. JOHNSON, in "Interview: John H. Johnson," *Crisis*, January 1987

DISCIPLINE

Without discipline true freedom cannot survive.

KWAME NKRUMAH, *Autobiography of Kwame Nkrumah*, 1957

Self-discipline, as a virtue or an acquired asset, can be valuable to anyone.

DUKE ELLINGTON, *Music Is My Mistress*, 1973

Don't blame children for being bad. Blame those who failed to discipline them.

MELVIN CHAPMAN, speech given at Mercy College, Detroit, Michigan, July 1976

We put a sense of structure and discipline in their lives to offset the negatives in the street.

ARTHUR MITCHELL, in "Structure and Discipline through Dance," *Smithsonian*, July 1987

DISCORD

Crow and corn can't grow in the same field.

TRADITIONAL

Tattling woman can't make the bread rise.

TRADITIONAL

Black snake knows the way to the hen house.

TRADITIONAL

Liquor talks loud when it gets loose from the jug.

TRADITIONAL

There is no peace with you/ Nor any rest!/ Your presence is a torture to the brain./ Your words are barbed arrows to the breast.

JESSIE REDMOND FAUSET, "Enigma," in Bontemps, ed., *Poetry of the Negro*, 1949

DISCOVERY

The urge to explore, the push toward the unknown—this is inherent in the life of the child. It does not seem to be a response to something from without but rather the expression of some deep urge that wells up from within.

HOWARD THURMAN, *Disciplines of the Spirit*, 1963

I came into the world imbued with the will to find a meaning in things . . . and then I found I was an object in the midst of other objects.

FRANTZ FANON, *Black Skin, White Masks*, 1967

That he had found it did not necessarily mean it had been lost.

RICHARD PERRY, *Montgomery's Children*, 1984

DISCRIMINATION

Discrimination once permitted cannot be bridled: recent history in the South shows that in forging chains for Negroes the white voters are forging chains for themselves.

Kansas City Call, 1909

Students in our colleges and universities can do much to eradicate prejudice by starting a crusade which has for its slogan—Down with discrimination against human beings on account of race, color, sex, or creed.

MARY CHURCH TERRELL, c. 1920

The people who invented discrimination in public places to ostracize people of a different race or nationality or color or religion are the direct descendants of medieval torturers. It is the most powerful instrument in the world that may be employed to prevent rapprochement and understanding between different groups of people. It is a cancer in the universal human body and poison to the individual soul.

CLAUDE MCKAY, c. 1936

Hate demands existence, and he who hates has to show his hate in appropriate actions and behaviors; in a sense, he has to become hate. That is why the Americans have substituted discrimination for lynching.

FRANTZ FANON, *Black Skin, White Masks,* 1967

In the courts, we were treated courteously by many officials but we were very often discriminated against by some and treated with resentment and hostility by others. We were constantly aware that no matter how well, how correctly, how adequately we pursued our career of law we could not become a prosecutor, or a magistrate, or a judge. We became aware of the fact that the competence and attainments of the attorneys we often dealt with were no higher than ours, but their superior position was maintained and protected by white skins.

NELSON MANDELA, *The Struggle Is My Life,* 1978

The black middle class has for generations excluded the black, black woman from the mainstream of black middle-class society, and it has, by its discrimination against her, induced in itself a divisive cancer that has chopped the black race in this country into polarized sections; consequently the black middle class has devoured its own soul and is doomed . . . to extinction.

TRELLIE JEFFERS, in Walker, *In Search of Our Mothers' Gardens,* 1983

Discrimination and intolerance will eat you up and destroy whatever creativity was in you if you let it.

GORDON PARKS, in *Voices in the Mirror,* 1990

DISEASE

If you desire that your conduct is good, fight against the fault of greed, a severe disease which is incurable. It alienates fathers, mothers, as well as uncles and makes a dear friend bitter.

EGYPT

He who conceals his disease can't expect to be cured.

CONGO

The bug disease kills more people than any other disease in the world, and that is why it is important not to let anything bug you.

DUKE ELLINGTON, *Music Is My Mistress,* 1973

DOOR

A door has been sealed up for two hundred years. You can't open it overnight but little crevices are coming.

MARY MCLEOD BETHUNE, speech given at the National Council of Negro Women, 26 November 1938

When a person walks through doors of opportunity, he is not going to be the same when he walks out the other end.

MELVIN CHAPMAN, speech given at Miller Junior High School, Detroit, Michigan, June 1960

Who can deny that years of my life have been spent knocking in vain, patiently, moderately, modestly at a closed and barred door?

ALBERT LUTHULE, *Negro Digest,* June 1961

Openings are made in a life by suffering that are not made in any other way.

HOWARD THURMAN, *Disciplines of the Spirit,* 1963

Check your ego at the door.

QUINCY JONES, at the taping of "We Are the World," 1985

The only thing worse than a revolving door is a closed door.

FRANK W. HALE, JR., speech given at Ohio State University, Columbus, Ohio, November 1988

DOWN

If you have been down, you know just how I feel, feel like an engine, ain't got no driving wheel.

BLUES

You can't hold a man down without staying down with him.

BOOKER T. WASHINGTON, c. 1900

The world ought to know that it could not keep four hundred million Negroes down forever.

MARCUS GARVEY, *Philosophy and Opinions of Marcus Garvey,* 1923

Let no man pull you down, let no man destroy your ambition.

Ibid.

It is when you're down that you learn about your faults.

CLAUDE MCKAY, letter to Max Eastman, 13 August 1942

You can't get too high for somebody to bring you down.

BILLIE HOLIDAY, *Lady Sings the Blues,* 1956

Don't let them get you down to the level of dealing with their attitude problem.

TOM BRADLEY, *The Impossible Dream,* 1986

I've had so many downs that I knew the law of averages would be in my favor one day.

DOUG WILLIAMS, in "Triumphs and Tragedies of Doug Williams," *Ebony,* October 1988

DREAM

Thousands of men have been destroyed for the pleasure of a short moment, which passes like a dream and then brings death to those who have indulged in it.

PTAH HOTEP, 2340 B.C.

I have a cow in the sky, but I can't drink her milk.

CONGO

A man has to saddle his dreams before he can ride them.

TRADITIONAL

It is a hard thing to live haunted by the ghost of an untrue dream.

W. E. B. DUBOIS, *The Souls of Black Folk,* 1903

Oh, that we cannot see the dreams of one another.

JOAQUIM MACHADO DE ASSIS, *A Woman's Arms,* c. 1905

The dream is lovelier than the song.

JAMES D. CORROTHERS, *The Dream and the Song,* 1914

The dream of the dreamer/ Are life-drops that pass/ The break in the heart/ To the Soul's hour-glass.

GEORGIA DOUGLAS JOHNSON, *The Heart of a Woman,* 1918

I shall try to lay my dreaming aside. Try hard. But Oh, if you knew my dreams, my vaulting ambition! How I constantly live in fancy seven-league boots, taking mighty strides across the world, but conscious all the time of being a mouse on a treadmill.

ZORA NEALE HURSTON, January 1926

Prometheus on his rock with his liver being continually consumed as fast as he grows another is nothing to my dreams. I dream such wonderfully complete ones, so radiant in astral beauty. I have not the power yet to make them come true. They always die. But even as they fade I have others. All this is a reason, not an excuse. There is no excuse for a person who lives on Earth, trying to board in Heaven.

Ibid.

Hold fast to dreams/ For if dreams die/ Life is a broken-winged bird/ That cannot fly./ Hold fast to dreams/ For when dreams go/ Life is a barren field/ Frozen with snow.

LANGSTON HUGHES, "Dreams," *The Dream Keeper and Other Poems,* 1932

Most people think I am a dreamer. . . . We need visions for larger things, for the unfolding and reviewing of worthwhile things.

MARY MCLEOD BETHUNE, speech given at the National Council of Negro Women, 5 December 1935

Dreams [can be] mocked to death by Time.

ZORA NEALE HURSTON, *Their Eyes Were Watching God,* 1937

I am, indeed, a practical dreamer. My dreams are not airy nothings. I want to convert my dreams into realities as far as possible.

MOHANDAS GANDHI, c. 1940

The impulse to dream was slowly beaten out of me by experience. Now it surged up again and I hungered for books, new ways of looking and seeing.

RICHARD WRIGHT, *12 Million Black Voices,* 1941

Is this real, this fascination? Are my dreams holding you fast?

FATS WALLER, c. 1946

It was a long time ago/ I have almost forgotten my dream/ But it was there then/ In front of me,/ Bright like a sun—My dream. And then the wall rose./ Rose slowly,/ slowly/ Between me and my dream./ Rose slowly, slowly/ Dimming, Hiding/ the light of my dream./ Rose until it touched the sky— The Wall.

LANGSTON HUGHES, "As I Grew Older," *Montage of a Dream Deferred,* 1951

What happens to a dream deferred?/ Does it dry up/ like a raisin in the sun?/ Or fester like a sore—/ And then run?/ Does it stink like rotten meat?/ Or crust and sugar over—/ like a syrupy sweet?/ Maybe it just sags/ like a heavy load./ *Or does it explode?*

LANGSTON HUGHES, "Harlem," in *ibid.*

Many have changed so much that they have lost the magic of the dream that carried them on that uphill journey till they lifted themselves up by their own bootstraps.

PETER ABRAHAMS, *Return to Goli,* 1953

Like any other American I dreamed of going into business and making money, I dreamed of working for a firm that would allow me to advance to an important position.

RICHARD WRIGHT, *Eight Men,* 1961

We are simply seeking to bring into full realization the American dream—a dream yet unfulfilled. A dream of equality of opportunity, of privilege and property widely distributed; a dream of a land where men no longer argue that the color of a man's skin determines the content of his character; the dream of a land where every man will respect the dignity and worth of human personality—this is the dream. When it is realized, the jangling discords of our nation will be transformed into a beautiful symphony of brotherhood, and men everywhere will know that America is truly the land of the free and the home of the brave.

MARTIN LUTHER KING, JR., speech given in Washington, D.C., 19 July 1962

[A] dream [is] the bearer of a new possibility, the enlarged horizon, the great hope.

HOWARD THURMAN, *Disciplines of the Spirit,* 1963

To dreamers Truth is an unlovely thing.

FRANK YERBY, *Judas, My Brother,* 1967

Another weaver of Black dreams has gone.

ETHERIDGE KNIGHT, "For Langston Hughes" *Poem from Parson,* 1967

Dreams are deferred on American shores to frustration, dope, and wine.

DON SIMMONS, in "Farewell to Langston Hughes," *Negro Digest,* 1967

The soft grey hands of sleep/ Toiled all night long/ To spin a beautiful garment/ Of dreams.

EDWARD SILVERIA, "Forgotten Dreams," in Bontemps, ed., *The Poetry of the Negro,* 1970

Walk with the sun,/ Dance at high noon;/ And dream when night falls black;/ But when the stars/ Vie with the moon,/ Then call the lost dream back.

LEWIS ALEXANDER, "Dream Song," in *ibid.*

Man is what his dreams are.

BENJAMIN MAYS, *Born to Rebel,* 1971

It isn't a calamity to die with dreams unfulfilled, but it is a calamity not to dream.

BENJAMIN MAYS, "What Man Lives By," in Philpot, ed., *Best Black Sermons,* 1972

[G]reat men of history are great not because of the abundance of the things they possessed but because of their dreams and the contributions they made to mankind.

Ibid.

I am cotton candy on a rainy day/ the unrealized dream of an idea unborn.

NIKKI GIOVANNI, *Cotton Candy on a Rainy Day,* 1978

Sometimes my dreams are so deep that I dream that I'm dreaming.

RAY CHARLES, *Brother Ray,* 1978

[D]reams, if they're any good, are always a little crazy.

Ibid.

Life at times could be so brutal that the only thing that made it livable were dreams.

BUCHI EMECHETA, *The Joys of Motherhood,* 1979

The dream is real, my friends. The failure to make it work is the unreality.

TONI CADE BAMBARA, *The Salt Eaters,* 1980

I dream and make a ballet out of it.

GEOFFREY HOLDER, in "Geoffrey Holder Grabs for the Gusto," *Class,* April 1984

I have a dream. This dream must, alas, be disentangled from whatever nightmare controls this fearfully White Republic. Difficult it is to make bricks without straw. We may be doomed to discover that it is not impossible; we may, indeed, be on the edge of the recognition that making bricks without straw is, precisely, our historical and actual specialty.

JAMES BALDWIN, *The Evidence of Things Not Seen,* 1985

The dreams have been cashed in for reality and reality is so much sweeter than the dream.

PHILIP MICHAEL THOMAS, in "Spotlight: The Spice of Vice," *Essence,* November 1985

The only thing that will stop you from fulfilling your dreams is you.

TOM BRADLEY, *The Impossible Dream,* 1986

Life is for dreaming dreams, but few have the courage or will to realize them.

CRENNER BRADLEY, in *ibid.*

Today, my ambitions and my dreams are focused on trying to become as much like Momma as I can.

LEONTYNE PRICE, in "The Most Unforgettable Person In My Family," *Ebony,* August 1986

We need to dream big dreams, propose grandiose means if we are to recapture the excitement, the vibrancy, and pride we once had.

COLEMAN YOUNG, in the *Native Detroiter,* 1987

We are the first generation of Black people in four hundred years who can live our dreams.

SUSAN TAYLOR, c. 1988

We don't have an eternity to realize our dreams, only the time we are here.

SUSAN TAYLOR, 1988

True. I talk of dreams,/ Which are the children of an idle brain/ Begat of nothing but vain fantasy.

GLORIA NAYLOR, *The Women of Brewster Place,* 1988

[W]hat do you pack when you pursue a dream? And what do you leave behind?

SANDRA SHARP, in "Growing Up Integrated (Did Momma Do the Right Thing?)" *Crisis,* March 1988

It's naive to think that King's dream is going to be totally realized in twenty-five years in light of three hundred and fifty years of slavery, segregation, and institutionalized racism.

WILLIAM GRAY, III, in "The Next Step: Constituencies that are Truly Colorblind," *Life,* Spring 1988

I've seen the dream deferred and its defenders discredited or entombed in monuments that encourage us to honor the memories and forget their struggles and their enemies.

PEARL CLEAGE, in "Introduction," *Catalyst,* Summer 1988

I'm a dreamer and I dream all the time.

MIKE TYSON, in "Mike Tyson Talks About His Future and Says 'I'm a Dreamer,'" *Jet,* 14 November 1988

You can't just sit there and wait for people to give you that golden dream, you've got to get out there and make it happen for yourself.

DIANA ROSS, in "Diana Ross: Down to Earth," *Essence,* October 1989

I don't allow anyone to put a limit on my dreaming, and I dream big. Always.

GORDON PARKS, *Voices in the Mirror,* 1990

I believe in the American proposition, the American Dream, because I've seen it in my own life.

CLARENCE THOMAS, July 1990

DROPOUTS

See also EDUCATION

In every city ghetto tens of thousands of yesterday's and today's dropouts are keeping body and soul together by some form of hustling.

MALCOLM X, *The Autobiography of Malcolm X,* 1965

These dropouts . . . are living critics of their environment, of our society, and of our educational system . . . and their teachers.

RALPH ELLISON, "What These Children Are Like," *Going to the Territory,* 1986

Millions of dropouts and pushouts are wandering the mean streets of urban America looking for the inspiration that can only be found in institutions (Black colleges) conceived in hope and organized specifically for the disadvantaged and the misunderstood.

LERONE BENNETT, in *Choosing to Succeed,* 1986

DRUGS

Self-pity is a drug.

TRADITIONAL

Few people are able to face the realities of life without a stimulant.

GEORGE S. SCHUYLER, in "Lights and Shadows of the Underworld," *Messenger,* 8 August 1923

It's all in the mind. You can get just as high if you did deep breathing.

SIDNEY BECHET, c. 1946

Drugs and drink are at the two arms of the devil with which he strikes his helpless victims into stupefaction and intoxication.

MOHANDAS GANDHI, in *Young India,* 12 April 1946

I had the white gowns and the white shoes. And every night they'd bring me the white gardenias and the white junk. When I was on, I was on and nobody gave me trouble. No cops, no treasury agents, nobody. I got into trouble when I tried to get off.

BILLIE HOLIDAY, c. 1955

All dope can do is kill you the long hard way. And it can kill the people you love right along with you.

BILLIE HOLIDAY, c. 1956

When a person is a drug addict, he's not the criminal; he's a victim of the criminal. The criminal is the man who brings the drugs into the country.

MALCOLM X, speech given at the Organization for Afro-American Unity Rally, New York City, 28 June 1964

Narcotics is the traditional way out for many of the frustrated young in the asphalt jungle of the North.

CHARLAYNE HUNTER, c. 1967

One day in their midst one will tell of a new sickness among the children.

HOWARD THURMAN, *Search for a Common Ground,* 1971

In 1946, the term "dope dealer" would have given birth in most people's minds to the confusing image of a man who trafficked in imbeciles.

RICHARD PERRY, *Montgomery's Children,* 1984

Blood may be thicker than water, but it is not thicker than crack cocaine.

DOROTHY RILEY, *Family Reunion,* 1984

We've sacrificed babies/ and burnt our mothers/ as payment to some viridian eyed God dread/ who works in cocaine/ under hungry men's head.

LORNA GOODISON, "Jamaica, 1980," *I Am Becoming My Mother,* 1985

Today we are having great trouble with young people of educated, sheltered, and financially well-heeled backgrounds who ... have not been taught they shouldn't play with heroin.... We [s]hould develop a special rite of initiation for dealing with the availability of drugs.

RALPH ELLISON, "On Initiation Rites and Power," *Going to the Territory,* 1986

Self-deception is like a drug.

RICHARD PRYOR, in *Jet,* 28 April 1986

Drug addiction is a cry for immediate gratification.

LORRAINE HALE, in "Massive Abuse of Illegal Drugs Must Be Stopped," *Ebony,* August 1986

No one is forcing anyone to snort anything through their nose, or inject anything into their veins or swallow anything to get high. That's coming from people's own needs and inner weakness.

TIM REID, in *ibid.*

We need to see drug pushers as terrorists, and neither age, race, status nor sex should be sanctuary. ... Drugs are a national security issue.

JESSE JACKSON, in *ibid.*

There is a new Ku Klux Klan out there called "Killer Crack and Coke." And the new lynch mob is sweeping all through the black neighborhood.

JOSEPH LOWERY, in "NAACP Focus," *Crisis,* November 1986

The most deadly thing about cocaine is that it separates you from your soul.

QUINCY JONES, c. 1987

Drug dealers don't get rich buying from each other or by selling their wares to their poverty-stricken neighbors.

WILLIAM RASPBERRY, c. 1988

Don't get hooked on drugs which have destroyed actors, politicians, and heroes and have decreased bank accounts from millions to zeroes.

ROEBUCK "POPS" STAPLES, in "Words of the Week," *Jet,* 28 March 1988

Our minds and our morals do not reject dope to the degree that we reject the rope. Yet we are losing more of our young people to dope than we ever lost to the rope.

JESSE JACKSON, in "Down With Dope, Up With Hope," *Ebony,* August 1988

The whole country is becoming addicted to something.

WILLIAM JUDSON KING, in the *Detroit News,* 3 September 1988

Drugs cannot be legalized. It will make it too easy. We need an all-out war on drugs because drugs are out of control.

OPRAH WINFREY, in *Woman's Day,* 4 October 1988

Weed does nothing but cloud your mind and make you think you are something you are not.

SMOKEY ROBINSON, c. 1989

Cocaine told me she loved me, but never said she'd lead me to the county jail.

TODD BRIDGES, c. 1989

We have a generation enslaving itself to drugs, young men and women doing to our race what slavery couldn't.

LUCILLE CLIFTON, in "Letter to Fred," *Essence,* November 1989

I hungered—literally *hungered*—for life in all its shades and hues: I was hooked on sensation....

CHARLES JOHNSON, *Middle Passage,* 1990

There are too many addictions out there in the world today. We can't evolve as human beings if we constantly latch onto fads and trends. When you get locked into fads, spin-offs, and sequels, you suffer poverty of the imagination. It's a poverty of the mind and soul.

JAMES EARL JONES, in *New Dimensions,* April 1990

DUALITY

A bull does not enjoy fame in two herds.

AFRICA

There is no phrase without a double meaning.

IVORY COAST

Face a grin, but knife at throat.

JAMAICA

An Indian as bad as the white men could not live in our nation; he would be put to death, and eaten by the wolves. The white men are bad schoolmasters; they carry false looks, and deal in false actions; they smile in the face of the poor Indian to cheat him; they shake him by the hand to gain their confidence, to make them drunk, to deceive them, and to ruin their wives. We told them to let us alone, and keep away from us; but they followed on, and beset our paths, and they coiled themselves among us, like the snake. They poisoned us by their touch.

BLACK HAWK, speech given at Prairie de Chien, Wisconsin, August 1835

Me an my captain don't agree,/ But he don't know 'cause he don't ask me/ He don't know, he don't know my mind/ When he see me laughing/ Just laughing to keep from crying./ Got one mind for white folks to see,/ 'Nother for what I know is me.

LAWRENCE GILLERT, c. 1845

It is a peculiar sensation, this double-consciousness, this sense of always looking at one's self through the eyes of others, of measuring one's soul by the tape of a world that looks on in amused contempt and pity. One ever feels his twoness,—an American, a Negro; two souls, two thoughts, two unreconciled strivings; two warring ideals in one dark body, whose dogged strength alone keeps it from being torn asunder.

W. E. B. DU BOIS, *The Souls of Black Folk,* 1903

I have lived among the two race groups. Now white, now colored. From my own point of view I am naturally an American. I have strived for a spiritual fusion analogous to the fact of racial intermingling. Without denying a single element in me, with no desire to subdue one to the other, I have sought to let them live in harmony. Within the last two or three years, however, my growing need for artistic expression has pulled me deeper and deeper into the Negro group. And as powers of receptivity increased, I found myself loving it in a way that I could never love the other.

JEAN TOOMER, in the *Liberator,* August 1922

The double obligation of being both Negro and American is not so unified as we are often led to believe.

COUNTEE CULLEN, c. 1924

Father, Son, and Holy Ghost,/ So I make an idle boast;/ Jesus of the twice-turned cheek,/ Lamb of God, although I speak/ With my mouth thus, in my heart/ Do I play a double part.

COUNTEE CULLEN, "Heritage," *Color,* 1925

Everybody is two beings: one lives and flourishes in the daylight and stands guard. The other being walks and howls at night.

ZORA NEALE HURSTON, *Moses, Man of the Mountain,* 1939

I will always protest the double standard of morals.

MARY CHURCH TERRELL, *Confessions of a Colored Woman in a White World,* 1940

Equality is the heart and essence of democracy, freedom, and justice, equality of opportunity in industry, in labor unions, schools and colleges, government, politics, and before the law. There must be no dual standards of justice, no dual rights, privileges, duties, or responsibilities of citizenship. No dual forms of freedom.

A. PHILIP RANDOLPH, speech given to the March on Washington Movement, Detroit, Michigan, 26 September 1942

My position is a split one. I'm a Black man of the West . . . but I also see and understand the non- or anti-Western point of view . . . Being a Negro living in a white Western Christian society, I've never been allowed to blend in a natural and healthy manner with the culture and civilization. . . .

RICHARD WRIGHT, speech given at the First International Conference of Negro Artists and Writers, Paris, 1956

Poised between two civilizations. I'm tired of hanging in the middle way, but where can I go?

MABEL SEGUN, "Conflict," in *Reflections: Nigerian Prose and Verse,* 1962

I am a man concerned with truth, not flattery, who shares a dual culture that is unwilling to deny the Harlem where I grew up or the Harlem of the Dutch masters that contributed its element to my understanding of art.

ROMARE BEARDEN, in *Art News,* October 1964

This time I can forget my Otherness,/ Silence my drums of discontent awhile/ And listen to the stars.

NAOMI MADGETT, "The Race Question," *Star by Star,* 1965

No educational program or institution can serve two cultural and political masters, two contradictory causes, whether freedom and oppression or racism and Black liberation.

NATHAN HARE, c. 1968

Each of us is two selves, and the great burden of life is to always try to keep that higher self in command. Don't let the lower self take over.

MARTIN LUTHER KING, JR., in "The Martin Luther King I Knew," *Evergreen Review,* January 1970

Black professionals labor under a double handicap. He finds it difficult, if not impossible, to crash the white world and simultaneously faces the problem of proving himself to his own. The vestiges of slavery endure.

BENJAMIN MAYS, *Born to Rebel,* 1971

They may have used the same words, the same Bible, and the same creeds, but the Lord knew that they longed for a higher goodness, a truer truth, a more immediate salvation, and a more authentic church than Massa conceived of or would permit.

GAYRAUD S. WILMORE, "Black Theology," in Philpot, ed., *Best Black Sermons,* 1972

The equilibrium you admire in me is an unstable one, difficult to maintain. My inner life was split early between the call of the Ancestors and the call of Europe, between the exigencies of black-African culture and those of modern life.

LEOPOLD SENGHOR, in Kennedy, *The Negritude Poets,* 1975

The student of Black poetry should arm himself with the tools of criticism and a knowledge of Black culture. He must understand the part "duality" plays in the lives of Blacks and how much "twoness" is manifested in the poetry.

EUGENE REDMOND, *Drumvoice,* 1976

Day after day, my white-dipped childhood stuck me with little needles, painful little needles piercing me in places where I should have known joy—my heart, my eyes, my woman place, my sleep—giving me little doses of hate regularly, frequently, silently.

BUFFY SAINTE-MARIE, in *Akwesasne Notes,* Winter 1976

A woman may be ugly and grow old, but a man is never ugly and never old. He matures with age and is dignified.

BUCHI EMECHETA, *The Joys of Motherhood,* 1979

I've never been to Africa. It is a faraway situation I dream about; I am not truly African. I am African and Western.

LESTER JOHNSON, *Blacks in Detroit,* 1980

Our young brothers need to know how to live in both worlds.

ALVIN POUSSAINT, in "The Black Male in Jeopardy," *Crisis,* 3 March 1986

We live like pebbles in a creek, tossed from one bank to the other. When the African side suits our needs of the moment, we cling to it. But as soon as it hinders us, we fling ourselves in the stream to cross to the modernity imported from Europe. We are forever fleeing our African realities.

SEMBANE OUSMANE, "The President's Wife," in Chinweizu, ed., *Voices from Twentieth-Century Africa,* 1988

We learned to speak two languages every day. On the bus going home from school we spoke to whites in their language. Soon as we crossed 96th Street going uptown, we changed back to street language. . . . It was a schizophrenic existence.

PEGGY PREACELY, in "Growing up Integrated (Did Momma Do the Right Thing?)" *Crisis,* March 1988

We do not have a double standard of justice. What is illegal in the street is illegal in the dorm room.

L. DOUGLASS WILDER, in the *Detroit News*, 28 April 1991

DUTY

Be master of yourself, if you will be the servant of Duty.

Mahabharata, 5–1 B.C.

Neither gods nor angels, or just men, command you to suffer for a single moment. Therefore it is your imperative duty to use every means, moral, intellectual, and physical, that promise success.

HENRY HIGHLAND GARNET, "An Address to the Slaves of the United States of America," speech given at the National Negro Convention, Buffalo, New York, August 1843

It is our duty to conserve our physical powers, our intellectual endowments, our spiritual ideals.

W. E. B. DU BOIS, "The Conservation of Races," speech given before the American Negro Academy, Washington, D.C., 1897

What should be your first duty? Will you pardon us for suggesting membership in the NAACP as your first and greatest duty?

W. E. B. DU BOIS, "Free, White and Twenty-One," *Crisis*, 1914

I tell you, we who have been better privileged are forsaking our duty to the downtrodden,

PAUL JOHNSON, *O Canaan*, 1932

To civilize is the university's first real duty.

RON KARENGA, in "Black Cultural Nationalism," *Black World*, January 1968

He owes the men who have come before him, the ones who helped him personally and the many more who helped by standing up and not copping out when it counted. . . . He owes it to a lot of men, as yet unborn, who'll stand up in the future in a world that isn't gutted by hatred. . . .

JESSE OWENS, *Blackthink*, 1970

For where my duty as a black poet, writer, and teacher would take me, people would have little need of Keats, Byron or even Robert Frost, but much need of Hughes, Bontemps, Gwendolyn Brooks, and Margaret Walker.

ALICE WALKER, *In Search of Our Mothers' Gardens*, 1983

Unless a sense of service and duty is instilled, our upward mobility will only be measured by cars and styling.

NIARA SUDARKASA, in "Niara Sudarkasa: Educator for the 1990s," *Essence*, May 1989

EARS

Even the night has ears.

AFRICA

It is only by closing the ears of the soul, or by listening too intently to the clamors of the sense, that we become oblivious of their utterances.

ALEXANDER CRUMMELL, "Rightmindedness," speech given at Lincoln University, Oxford, Pennsylvania, 1897

I always hear, I seldom see. I hear my way through the world.

PAUL ROBESON, in "An Exclusive Interview with Paul Robeson," *West African Review,* 8 August 1936

Traveling round the world opened up my ears.

RAY CHARLES, *Brother Ray,* 1978

Years ago I had the affliction of muteness for five years. I listened to everything and I memorized. The Black Southern minister influenced and informed my ear.

MAYA ANGELOU, in *USA Today,* 5 March 1985

My ear is so sensitive that every time I hear something that disagrees with me musically I almost feel physical pain.

ANITA BAKER, in *Essence,* June 1990

EDUCATION

See also DROPOUTS

It takes a whole village to educate a child.

NIGERIA

Education in the past has been too much inspiration and too little information. Therefore today Negro educators face a crisis. Educational institutes can no longer be prizes in church politics or furnish berths for failure in other walks of life.

E. FRANKLIN FRAZIER

It is by the wisdom of our conduct, our success in the arts and sciences, that we shall secure the triumph of respected and illustrious patrons. . . .

HENRI CHRISTOPHE, *Proclamation,* 1 January 1816

For colored people to acquire learning in this country makes tyrants quake and tremble in their sandy foundation.

DAVID WALKER, *Appeal to the Coloured Citizens of the World,* 1829

Prejudice is not so much dependent upon natural antipathy as upon education.

DAVID RUGGLES, *The "Extinguisher" or the Extinguished,* 1834

. . . whom I have taught with sacred zeal. . . . Oh, who shall now your rising talents guide. . . .

DANIEL PAYNE, *Preceptor's Farewell,* 1835

. . . what a burning shame it is that many of the pieces on the subject of slavery and the slave trade, contained in different school books, have been lost sight of, or been subject to the pruning knife of the slaveholding expurgatorial system! To make me believe that those men who have regulated education in our country have humanity in their hearts, is to make me believe a lie.

ROBERT PURVIS, letter to William Garrison, 5 March 1842

One's work may be finished some day, but one's education never.

ALEXANDRE DUMAS, c. 1856

How is it that little children are so intelligent and men so stupid? It must be education that does it.

Ibid.

Education is a ladder.

MANUELITO OF THE NAVAHOS, speech given to Congress, 1865

The combined opposition cannot prevent us from advancing so long as we have the road to books and schools open to us. Even the snub given to our political condition is as nothing compared with what it would be to shut the doors of the school against us.

BENJAMIN LEE, in the *Christian Recorder,* 1877

Educate your sons and daughters, send them to school and show them that beside the cartridge box, the ballot box, and the jury box, you have also the knowledge box.

FREDERICK DOUGLASS, *Life and Times of Frederick Douglass,* 1892

I plead for industrial education and development for the Negro, not because I want to cramp him, but because I want to free him. I want to see him enter the all-powerful business and commercial world.

BOOKER T. WASHINGTON, speech given at the Atlanta Exposition, Atlanta, Georgia, 1895

Education was feared by slave owners because slaves might read of their national rights.

Black Chronicle, 1 June 1896

For years to come the education of my people should be so directed that the greatest proportion of the mental strength of the masses will be brought to bear upon the practical things of life, upon something that is needed to be done, and something which they will be permitted to do in their community.

BOOKER T. WASHINGTON, *Up From Slavery,* 1901

Whether you like it or not the millions are here, and here they will remain. If you do not lift them up, they will pull you down. . . . Education must not simply teach work—it must teach life.

W. E. B. DU BOIS, "The Talented Tenth," *The Negro Problem,* 1903

Education is the development of power and ideal.

W. E. B. DU BOIS, *Resolutions, Niagara Movement,* 1906

Education is the key to unlock the golden door of freedom.

GEORGE WASHINGTON CARVER, c. 1912

The modern school without systematic lectures turns out many graduates who lack retention. No sooner has the sound of the word left their teacher's lips, the subject has been forgotten; and if they are called to explain, it is reduced to an incomprehensible mass of meaningless words.

A. A. SCHOMBURG, *Racial Integrity,* July 1913

In truth, school is a desperate duel between new souls and old to pass on facts and methods and dreams from a dying world . . . without letting either teacher or taught lose for a moment faith and interest. It is hard work. . . . It is never wholly a success without the painstaking help of the parent.

W. E. B. DU BOIS, "Education," *Crisis,* 1922

I got my education from many sources, private tutors, public schools, two grammar or high schools, and two colleges. Between school and work, at fourteen, I had under my control several men. I was strong and manly. I made them respect me.

MARCUS GARVEY, *Philosophy and Opinions of Marcus Garvey,* 1923

One system of education could not fit the needs of an entire race; to sneer at and discourage higher education would mean to rob the race of leaders which it so badly needed; and that all of the industrial education in the world could not take the place of manhood.

IDA B. WELLS, in Duster, ed., *Crusade for Justice,* 1928

Education fits us for the work around us and demanded by the time in which we live.

BOOKER T. WASHINGTON, *Selected Speeches of Booker T. Washington,* 1932

One of the most striking evidences of the failure of higher education among Negros is their estrangement from the masses, the very people upon whom

[they] must eventually count for carrying out a program of progress.

CARTER G. WOODSON, *The Mis-education of the Negro,* 1933

The same educational process which inspires and stimulates the oppressor with the thought that he is everything and has accomplished everything worth while, depresses and crushes at the same time the spark of genius in the Negro by making him feel that his race does not amount to much and never will measure up to the standards of other peoples.

Ibid.

The only question which concerns us here is whether these "educated" persons are actually equipped to face the ordeal before them or unconsciously contribute to their own undoing by perpetuating the regime of the oppressor.

Ibid.

Truth must be dug up from the past and presented to the circle of scholastics in scientific form and then through stories and dramatizations that will permeate our educational system.

Ibid.

Is the ability to master and converse in foreign languages, to travel through all the intricacies of geometry and trigonometry education or the end we seek? No, they are but the means to an end . . . nor shall the end be reached till every passion, every appetite be controlled, every prejudice, all malice, all jealousy be banished from the heart.

Ibid.

If education is of any practical value it should serve to guide us to living, to fit us for the work around us and demanded by the times in which we live. It should aid us into putting the most into life in the age, country, and into the position we are to fill.

Ibid.

At a very early age I began to thump on the piano alone, and it was not long before I was able to pick out a few tunes. When I was seven years old I could play by ear all of the hymns and songs that my mother knew. I also learned the names of the notes in both clefs, but I preferred not to be hampered by notes.

JAMES WELDON JOHNSON, *Along This Way,* 1933

Real education consists in drawing the best out of yourself. What better book can there be than the book of humanity?

MOHANDAS GANDHI, in *Harijan,* 30 March 1934

You can be educated in some vision and feeling, as well as in mind. To see your enemy and know him is part of the complete education of man; to spiritually regulate oneself is another form of the higher education that fits man for a nobler place in life, and still to approach your brother by the feeling of your own humanity, is an education that softens the ills of the world and makes us kind indeed.

MARCUS GARVEY, c. 1939

Education came to be one of the great preoccupations, enlightenment was viewed as the greatest single opportunity to escape the indignities that whites were heaping upon Blacks. Children were sent to school even when it was a great inconvenience to their parents. Parents made untold sacrifices to secure the learning for their children that they had been denied.

JOHN HOPE FRANKLIN, *From Slavery to Freedom,* 1947

The function of education is to teach one to think intensively and to think critically. Intelligence plus character—that is the goal of true education.

MARTIN LUTHER KING, JR., *What Manner of Man,* c. 1958

We real cool. We/ Left school. We/ Lurk late. We / Strike straight. We/ Sing sin. We/ Thin gin. We/ Jazz June. We/ Die soon.

GWENDOLYN BROOKS, "We Real Cool," *The Bean Eaters,* 1960

And then the division came. I got a public scholarship which started my migration into another world, a world whose roots were the same, but whose style of living was entirely different from what my childhood knew. It had earned me privilege. . . .

George Lamming, *Season of Adventure,* 1960

Integration and education are not synonymous.

James Baldwin, *Nobody Knows My Name,* 1961

The education and training of our children must not be limited to the "Three Rs" only. It should instead include the history of the black nation, the knowledge of civilizations of man and the Universe, and all sciences.

Elijah Muhammad, in Essien-Udom, *Black Nationalism,* 1962

Education consists not only in the sum of what a man knows, or the skill with which he can put this to his own advantage. A man's education must also be measured in terms of the soundness of his judgment of people and things, and in his power to understand and appreciate the needs of his fellow man and to be of service to them. The educated man should be so sensitive to the conditions around him that he makes it his chief endeavor to improve those conditions for the good of all.

Kwame Nkrumah, speech given at the Institute of African Studies, 25 October 1963

Schools have to be infused with a mission if they are to be successful: rapid improvement of the school performance of children. If this does not happen, America will suffer for decades to come. Where a missionary zeal has been demonstrated by school administrators and teachers, and where . . . [there is] a desire to involve parents, much has been accomplished.

Martin Luther King, Jr., *Why We Can't Wait,* 1963

The purpose of education . . . is to create in a person the ability to look at the world for himself, to make his own decisions. . . .

James Baldwin, "A Talk to Harlem Teachers," in Clarke, ed., *Harlem, USA,* 1964

You can't legislate good will—that comes through education.

Malcolm X, in the *Amsterdam News,* 28 March 1964

Without education, you are not going anywhere in this world.

Malcolm X, speech given at the Militant Labor Forum, 29 May 1964

I had to constantly overcome the disadvantage of having no academic training by inventing my own way of doing things.

Gordon Parks, *A Choice of Weapons,* 1965

Education is indoctrination if you're white; subjugation if you're black.

James Baldwin, c. 1968

The purpose of education is to transmit from one generation to the next, the accumulated wisdom and knowledge of the society and to prepare the young people for their future membership in society and active participation in its maintenance and development.

Julius Nyerere, *Ujamaa,* 1968

Nothing should be overlooked in fighting for better education. Be persistent and ornery; this will be good for the lethargic educational establishment and will aid the whole cause of public education.

Roy Wilkins, speech given at the NAACP Convention, 1969

Inner city education must change. Our responsibility is not merely to provide access to knowledge, we must produce educated people.

James L. Farmer, in *Today's Education,* April 1969

You don't have to teach people to be human. You have to teach them how to stop being inhuman.

Eldridge Cleaver, *Conversation with Eldridge Cleaver,* c. 1970

Education means to bring out wisdom. Indoctrination means to push in knowledge.

Dick Gregory, *No More Lies,* 1971

A writer should get as much education as possible, but just going to school is not enough; if it were, all owners of doctorates would be inspired writers.

Gwendolyn Brooks, *Report From Part One,* 1972

Education is creating, not limiting and destroying.

MELVIN CHAPMAN, speech given in Detroit, Michigan, June 1972

Custodial education does not have as its objective the education of youth but rather social control over them. It suppresses rather than stimulates their intellectual and physical energies.

JOHN CONYERS, in "The Politics of Unemployment: Lost—Another Generation of Black Youth," *Freedomways,* 1975

Education serves to prepare people to be clear about their roles, to tap their potential so that their lives can be meaningful; so they can better consolidate their resources and be productive in, and useful to, their communities.

KEORAPETSE KGOSITSILE, c. 1976

Getting through isn't a laughing matter. If they drop out, they're going to miss out.

BILL COSBY, in "Interview," *Scholastic,* 17 November 1977

She and her husband were ill-prepared for a life like this, where only pen and not mouth could really talk. Her children must learn.

BUCHI EMECHETA, *The Joys of Motherhood,* 1979

We need education in the hands to work in a new kind of job environment, we need education of the head to help think through the complex problems of today's world, and we need education of the heart to work together with one another.

LEON SULLIVAN, in the *Negro History Bulletin,* March 1983

Education is the jewel casting brilliance into the future.

MARI EVANS, "My Father's Passage," in *Black Women Writers,* 1984

Education is all a matter of building bridges.

RALPH ELLISON, "What These Children Are Like," *Going to the Territory,* 1986

What did you learn today? Did anyone tell you how
to meet tomorrow/ did anyone tell you why there are
people/ who don't know you/ did anyone seem to
know who you were/ did anyone know that you have
the blood of Africa in your veins/ or did they
pretend to be blind to your color and thereby deny
its value/ Did anyone explain the nature of
freedom,/ the nature of racism,/ the nature of love/
what did you learn today?

RONALD COLEMAN, in *Black Child in Education,* 1986

Black males negotiate white and female cultures and are getting wiped out in school.

JANICE HALE BENSON, in *ibid.*

It is becoming increasingly clear that urban high schools are graduating hundreds of thousands of undereducated Black students who need the motivation that only Black colleges can provide.

LERONE BENNETT, in *Choosing to Succeed,* 1986

Getting [the] degree meant more to me than an NCAA title, being named All-American or winning an Olympic gold medal.

PATRICK EWING, in *Ebony,* February 1986

I don't expect white people to educate our kids. . . . We are responsible. The power structure will not address issues that are at the root. The challenge falls back on us.

GIL NOBLE, in "Footnotes of a Culture at Risk," *Crisis,* March 1986

[O]ur children learn best when taught by teachers who groom them in their history and give them the special attention they sometimes require.

FAUSTINE JONES-WILSON, in "NAACP Focus," *Crisis,* November 1986

Parents often speak of sending their children to the "integrated school"; they say, "My child is going to the white school." No white children are "integrated" into Negro schools. Since integration is only a one-way street that Negroes travel to a white institution, then inherent in the situation itself is the implied inferiority of the Black man.

ALVIN POUSSAINT, c. 1987

[I had never before worked in school, but now I] became regenerated at once . . . studied seriously . . . won prizes for excellence, and fulfilled her expectations . . . [a teacher who believed in me].

JEAN TOOMER, in Kerman and Eldridge, *The Lives of Jean Toomer,* 1987

As a Black child, just attending school is almost an act of sedition. Education is considered "bad" for us . . . unnecessary.

MIRIAM MAKEBA, *My Story,* 1987

Education is an important element in the struggle for human rights, our passport to the future, in that tomorrow belongs to the people who prepare for it today. It is a torch with which to burn down a decadent world of corruption and oppression so that the green grass of freedom and justice grow.

NATHAN HARE, 1988

In the educational section, break down the walls that surround our schools and universities, and let the people who know our culture teach our people. Let us Africanize our curriculum in a meaningful manner. Let African culture form the core of our curriculum and foreign culture be at the periphery.

OKOT P'BITEK, "Africa's Cultural Revolution," in Chinweizu, ed., *Voices from Twentieth-Century Africa,* 1988

Education must serve a consciousness-raising function to prepare Black people to make a contribution to a struggle that began centuries before they were born and will extend centuries after their death.

JANICE HALE BENSON, in *Black Child in Education,* 1988

An education is the first step in preparing yourself for a job.

COLEMAN YOUNG, in *Native Detroiter,* 1988

An education opens a person's mind to the entire world. And there is nothing more important than to make sure everyone has the opportunity for an education.

MICHAEL JACKSON, in "Michael Jackson Gives A Big Piece of Action," *Jet,* 28 March 1988

Education heals, giving new information, new knowledge of who they are and what they are.

NA'IM AKBAR, in *Essence,* April 1988

Education takes place in the combination of the home, the community, the school and the receptive mind.

HARRY EDWARDS, in "Hardline," *Detroit Free Press,* 8 May 1988

Education is painful and not gained with playing games or being average.

MARVA COLLINS, in *Ebony,* August 1988

Before we even attempt to teach children, we want them to know each of them is unique and very special. We want them to like themselves, to want to achieve and care about themselves.

MARVA COLLINS, in *Working Woman,* October 1988

The army provides an educational system that is better than the public schools in many cities.

ALVIN POUSSAINT, c. 1989

Education is the foundation of governance.

JACOB H. CARRUTHERS, *Pedagogy of Kemet,* 1989

Modern schools aren't set up to help children develop themselves. They assume the children get this development at home. We are creating a generation of people who can't fit into the mainstream of society.

JAMES COMER, in the *Detroit News,* 11 January 1989

Urban school settings are cold and ungiving to Black male youngsters.

WILLIAM LYLES, in *Crisis,* March 1989

All education is self-acquired, since no one can educate another.

CHARLES G. ADAMS, sermon given at Hartford Church, Detroit, Michigan, June 1989

The purpose of "Education" is to allow a people to systematically guide the reproduction and refinement of the best of themselves.

WADE NOBLES, speech given at the Black Child Conference, Detroit, Michigan, 20 January 1990

Education remains the key to both economic and political empowerment. That is why the schools charged with educating African-Americans have, perhaps, the greatest, the deepest challenge of all.

BARBARA JORDAN, in *Black Collegian,* June 1990

I only went through tenth grade, but you'll see all kinds of textbooks around me. The more popular I become, the more I miss education. Whether you play blues or whatever, don't let people keep you like you were.

B. B. KING, c. 1991

You must defend the rights of African parents to decide the kind of education that shall be given to their children. . . . Establish your own community schools. . . . If it becomes dangerous or impossible to have alternative schools, then you must make every home, every shack, every rickety structure a center of learning for our children. Never surrender to the inhuman and barbaric theories of Verwoerd.

NELSON MANDELA, *Higher Than Hope,* 1991

There are too many people who get degrees and think that they're educated. In order to be a truly knowledgeable person one has got to be engaged in serious, systematic, lifelong learning.

BENJAMIN PAYTON, speech given at Tuskegee Institute, Tuskegee, Alabama, 25 February 1991

We have a stake in educating and socializing our children. But if we really expect to see a change, men have to get involved, because it takes a Black man to prepare a Black boy for whatever he's going to face out there.

SPENCER HOLLAND, speech given at Morgan State College, Baltimore, Maryland, March 1991

Pluralism in the curriculum is not a matter of trivial pursuit, nor is it primarily about self-esteem. . . . It's about truth.

ASA HILLIARD, speech given for the Association for Supervisors and Curriculum Developers Bulletin, May 1991

There are very few educated poor people. Everything hinges on education. Without it, you can't advocate for proper health care, for housing, for a civil rights bill that ensures your rights.

SUSAN TAYLOR, in *USA Weekend,* 28 June 1991

We must always go the second mile. When we go the first mile, we simply do what is required of us. It is when we go the second mile that excellence is achieved and minor miracles happen.

DEBORAH MCGRIFF, in *The Detroit Teacher,* 9 September 1991

EFFORT

By trying often, the monkey learns to jump from the tree.

CAMEROON

To try and to fail is not laziness.

SIERRA LEONE

Talk, without effort, is nothing.

MARIA W. STEWART, *Meditations from the Pen of Mrs. Maria W. Stewart,* 1879

In America, the Negro stands alone as a race. No people has borne oppression like him, and no race has been so much imposed upon. Whatever progress he makes, it must be mainly by his own efforts.

WILLIAM WELLS-BROWN, *My Southern Home,* 1880

By patience and hard work, we brought order out of chaos, just as will be true of any problem if we stick to it with patience and wisdom and earnest effort.

BOOKER T. WASHINGTON, *Up From Slavery,* 1901

Let us not try to be the best or worse of others, but let us make the effort to be the best of ourselves.

MARCUS GARVEY, in *Negro World,* October 1923

Man attempt[s] to climb to painless heights from his dung hill.

ZORA NEALE HURSTON, *Their Eyes Were Watching God,* 1937

Since 1619 Negroes have tried every method of communication, of transformation of their situation from petition to the vote, everything. There isn't anything that hasn't been exhausted.

LORRAINE HANSBERRY, "Black Revolt and the White Backlash," speech given at Town Hall Forum, New York City, 15 June 1964

It is through the effort to recapture the self and to scrutinize the self, it is through the lasting tension of their freedom that men will be able to create the ideal conditions of existence for a human world.

FRANTZ FANON, *Black Skin, White Masks,* 1967

Every try will not succeed. If you live, your business is trying.

JOHN KILLENS, in Angelou, *The Heart of a Woman,* 1981

I try to do the right thing at the right time. They may just be little things, but usually they make the difference between winning and losing.

KAREEM ABDUL JABBAR, in *Star,* May 1986

Some of us are timid. We think we have something to lose so we don't try for that next hill.

MAYA ANGELOU, in *USA Today,* 5 March 1988

EGO

The pretender sees no one but himself,/ Because he has the veil of conceit in front;/ If he were endowed with a God-discerning eye,/ He would see that no one is weaker than himself.

The Gulistan of Sadi, 1184–1292 A.D.

Vanity is the beginning of corruption.

JOAQUIM MACHADO DE ASSIS, *Dom Casmurro,* 1900

I shall not regard my swelled head as a sign of real glory.

AIMÉ CÉSAIRE, *Notes on a Return to the Native Land,* 1947

People wind up making God in their own image, and they rarely notice how strange it is that their God looks at things from their point of view.... That is the ego, a symbol of our pretensions.

BILL RUSSELL, *Second Wind,* 1979

[T]he ego has always been a paradox—it is the point from which you see, but it also makes you blind.

Ibid.

...we shrink your heads down to that of normal man, we cleanse your minds of the abnormal conceit and love of self that has caused you to walk blindly among the dark people of the world.

"Fourteen Strings of Purple Wampum to Writers About Indians," First Convocation of Indian Scholars, Princeton University, March 1979

I needed that championship. I am not a man without ego and pride.

JOE LOUIS, *My Life,* 1981

Ego is a killer. Humility is probably the greatest power that one can study, to understand that you didn't create anything. God created it all.

MELBA MOORE, in *USA Today,* 17 September 1987

People try to criticize artists for having an ego and arrogance. But if you want to get to the place where I want to go, you'd better have some ego or you'll be crushed like a grapefruit seed.

TERENCE TRENT D'ARBY, in "Words of the Week," *Jet,* 12 September 1988

ELECTION

We are here to celebrate a resounding victory. We have fought a good fight. We have finished our course and we have kept the faith. We fought it with unseasoned weapons and a phalanx of people who had mostly never been involved in a political campaign before. This has truly been a pilgrimage. We never stopped believing that we were part of something good that has never happened before.

HAROLD WASHINGTON, in "Mayor Washington Eulogized as Symbol of Hope for Blacks," *Jet,* 14 December 1987

Whether or not America is ready to elect a Black president remains to be seen.

SPIKE LEE, in "National Report," *Jet,* 2 May 1988

We cannot go on electing actors to the presidency, or consider electing preachers to the presidency. We have to get serious statesmen into the position of authority.

HARRY EDWARDS, in "Hardline," *Detroit Free Press,* 8 May 1988

EMANCIPATION

The progress of emancipation is certain. It is certain because God has made of one blood all nations of men, and who is said to be no respecter of persons, has so decreed. Did I believe that it would always continue and that men to the end of time would be permitted with impunity to usurp the same undue authority over his fellows? Ridicule the religion of the Savior of the world? I would consider my Bible as a book of false and delusive fables and commit it to flames; nay, I would still go further; I would at once confess myself an atheist, and deny the existence of holy God.

NATHANIEL PAUL, speech given at the Antislavery Convention, New York City, 5 April 1827

The proclamation of President Lincoln reaches the most forlorn condition, in which our people are placed. The first day of January, 1863, is destined to form one of the most memorable epochs in the history of the world. The seeds of freedom which are never rejuvenescent in themselves, have now been scattered where despotism and tyranny ranked and ruled, will be watered by the enlivening dews of God's clemency, till the reapers [abolitionists] shall shout the harvest home.

HENRY TURNER, 1863

Unquestionably, for weal or for woe, the First of January is to be the most memorable day in American Annals. The Fourth of July was great, but the First of January, when we consider it in all its relations and bearings, is comparatively greater. The one had respect to the mere political birth of a nation; the last concerns the national life and character, and is to determine whether that life and character shall be radiantly glorious with all high and noble virtues, or infamously blackened, forever.

FREDERICK DOUGLASS, in the *Douglass Monthly,* January 1863

It shall flash through coming ages,/ It shall light the distant years;/ And eyes now dim with sorrow/ Shall be brighter through the years.

FRANCES E. W. HARPER, *Emancipation Proclamation,* c. 1865

The wild rejoicing on the part of the emancipated coloured people lasted but for a brief period. . . . The great responsibility of being free, of having charge of themselves, of having to think and plan for themselves and their children, seemed to take possession of them. It was very much like suddenly turning a youth of ten or twelve years out into the world to provide for himself.

BOOKER T. WASHINGTON, *Up From Slavery,* 1901

Abolition is the dawn of liberty, we await the sun: the black emancipated, it remains to emancipate the white.

JOAQUIM MACHADO DE ASSIS, *Esau and Jacob,* 1904

The Emancipation Proclamation does not fail to evoke the Black man's grateful emotions because he is told it was merely an incident of a larger policy. It is sufficient for him that the slave has been transformed into a freeman, the chattel into a citizen.

KELLY MILLER, *The American Negro,* 1908

When emancipation was the inevitable result of the Civil War, but one decent and logical path faced the nation and that was to educate the freed men for full citizenship in the land which they had helped to build and free.

W. E. B. DU BOIS, in *Crisis,* June 1930

We shall never secure emancipation from the tyranny of the white oppressor until we have achieved it in our own soul.

W. E. B. DU BOIS, in "Economic Disfranchisement," *Crisis,* 1937

WAKE UP! The emancipation which was given was only an opportunity. Real emancipation lies in your own intellectual efforts.

PAUL WILLIAMS, in *American Magazine,* 1937

We like to speak of Lincoln as the great Emancipator in thinking of the liberation of the slaves. But Lincoln was a much greater emancipator than that. It was the whole American nation he liberated to measure itself and take its stride as a leader in the general progress of the world.

CLAUDE MCKAY, in "Pact Exploded Communist Propaganda Among Negroes," *New Leader,* 13 February 1943

Emancipation means out of . . . the hands of former masters and oppressors. And I've spent my life finding out how to use my own hands—my own talents. . . .

PAUL ROBESON, in "The Road to Real Emancipation," *Freedom,* January 1951

You say you love Lincoln [because he freed us]. He is your emancipator. . . . Lincoln was not your brother. He was not your friend any more than George Washington.

ELIJAH MUHAMMAD, in Essien-Udom, *Black Nationalism,* 1962

If our nation has done nothing more in its whole history than to create just two documents, its contribution to civilization would be imperishable. The first of these documents is the Declaration of Independence and the other is the Emancipation Proclamation. All tyrants, past, present, and future, are powerless to bury the truths in these declarations, no matter how extensive their legions, how vast their power and how malignant their evil.

MARTIN LUTHER KING, JR. speech given at District 65 30th Anniversary, October 1963

In theory, the Emancipation Proclamation had been a wonderful thing. But in 1915 in Alabama it was only a theory. The Negro had been set . . . free to work eighteen hours a day, free to see all his labor add up to a debt at the year's end, free to be chained to the land he tilled but could never own any more than if he were still a slave.

JESSE OWENS, *Blackthink,* 1970

After three drafts Lincoln finally signed the Proclamation which freed the slaves—some of which were white—after being threatened with a race war; and Reconstruction began.

YOSEF BEN JOCHANNON, in "Interview: Dr. Yosef ben Jochannon," *Crisis,* June 1986

We should never make any apologies for doing what our times and circumstances compel us to do. The first emancipation was the burden of the white man, and it remained only a proclamation. But the second emancipation is the burden of the Black man, and that is why it must be made a reality.

DAMON J. KEITH, c. 1989

ENCOURAGEMENT

We must encourage creative dissenters. We must demonstrate, teach, and preach, until the foundations of our nation are shaken.

MARTIN LUTHER KING, JR., c. 1967

The people in the church did not contribute one dime to help me with my education. But they gave me something far more valuable. They gave me encouragement.

BENJAMIN MAYS, *Born to Rebel,* 1971

My grandfather encouraged me by saying, "Why don't you do what only you can do? Tell about the kids in the neighborhood. Tell about things that happened to you when you were a child."

BILL COSBY, in "Interview," *Scholastic,* 17 November 1977

END

See also FAREWELL

My journey's done. My labors in your vineyards are over.

RICHARD WRIGHT, "An Open Letter to Kwame Nkrumah," *Black Power,* 1954

I did not known then how much was ended. When I look back from this high hill of my old age, I can still see the butchered women and children lying heaped and scattered all along the crooked gulches plain as when I saw them with eyes still young. And I can see that something else died there in the bloody mud, and was buried in the blizzard. A people's dream died there. It was a beautiful dream . . . the nation's hoop is broken and scattered. There is no center any longer, and the sacred tree is dead.

BLACK ELK, in Neihardt, *Black Elk Speaks,* 1959

I'm coming to the end of the tunnel. I will get out of it.

JAMES BALDWIN, in "James Baldwin . . . in Conversation," *Arts in Society,* Summer 1966

The end of a thing,/ is never the end,/ something is always being born like/ a year or a baby

LUCILLE CLIFTON, "December," *Everett Anderson's Year,* 1974

All things come to pass/ When they do, if they do/ All things come to their end/ When they do, as they do. . . .

KEORAPETSE KGOSITSILE, in *Black Poetry Writing,* 1975

Theology is not eternal nor can it ever hope to be perfect. There is no final theology.

DESMOND TUTU, *Hope and Suffering,* 1983

I hope at the end of my life I can be certain that I have done the right things, that I have invested in the truly worthy causes.

WILLIAM HASTIE, *Grace Under Pressure,* 1984

ENEMY

If there is no enemy within, the enemy without cannot get in.

TRADITIONAL

I have only three adversaries. The first two are distance and time, but with persistence I am able to overcome them. The third one is the most terrible: the fact that I am mortal.

ALEXANDRE DUMAS, *The Count of Monte Cristo,* 1844

The golden opportunity had passed. They had been blind at the opportune time; they had played into their enemies' hand.

New York Tribune, 22 November 1862

We need not waste time by seeking to deceive our enemies into thinking we are going to be content with half of a loaf, or by [being] willing to lull our friends into a false sense of our indifferences and present satisfactions.

W. E. B. DU BOIS, "The Immediate Program of the American Negro," *Crisis,* April 1915

To see your enemy and know him is a part of the complete education of man.

MARCUS GARVEY, *Philosophy and Opinions of Marcus Garvey,* 1923

Mr. Moderator, Brother Lomax, brothers and sisters, friends and enemies: I just can't believe everyone in here is a friend and I don't want to leave anybody out.

MALCOLM X, "The Ballot or the Bullet," speech given at Cory Methodist Church, Cleveland, Ohio, 3 April 1964

It is impossible for a people to rise above their aspirations. If we think we cannot, we most certainly cannot. Our greatest enemy is our defeatist attitude.

ROBERT WILLIAMS, "USA: The Potential of a Minority Revolution," *The Crusader Monthly Newsletter,* May–June 1964

You get freedom by letting your enemy know that you'll do anything to get your freedom; then you'll get it. . . . [D]on't run around . . . trying to make friends with somebody who's depriving you of your rights. They're not your friends . . . they're your enemies.

MALCOLM X, "To Mississippi Youth," speech given at Hotel Theresa, New York City, 31 December 1964

The longer we keep at each others' throat, our real enemies would have nothing to worry about.

JULIAN MAYFIELD, in the *Negro Digest,* September 1967

The enemy was never to be understood in terms of color—but in the more difficult and abstract terms of human irrationality, ignorance, superstition, rigidity, and arbitrary cruelty.

KENNETH B. CLARK, in the *Journal of Negro History,* January 1968

The enemies of Black people have learned something from history and they're discovering new ways to divide us faster than we are discovering new ways to unite.

ELDRIDGE CLEAVER, open letter to Stokely Carmichael, 1969

The man who shoots and burns and drowns us is surely our enemy, but so is he who cripples our children for life with inferior public education.

ROY WILKINS, speech given at the NAACP Convention, 1969

The oppressor is the enemy and he attacks while we argue and continue to play bid whist.

NATHAN HARE, "A Torch to Burn Down a Decadent World," *The Black Scholar,* September 1970

Never completely encircle your enemy. Leave him some escape, for he will fight even more desperately if trapped.

ALEX HALEY, *Roots,* 1977

We are being seduced by the forces that make us enemies of each other.

RUBY DEE, in "With Ossie and Ruby: Creative Family at Work," *Black Stars,* April 1981

Our enemies don't show their colors as they once did. Today's Bull Connors smile a lot, don't have hoses, and may even invite you to lunch.

CAMILLE COSBY, in the *Delta Newsletter,* April 1989

ENVY

Envy—what a plague of one's thoughts, how great a rust of the heart, to be jealous of another.

ST. CYPRIAN, *On Jealousy,* 246 A.D.

Jealousy arises often from a narrow heart.

AFRICA

Compete, don't envy.

LIBYA

Better to die by blows than by jealousy fade away.

ZUNI

The will to humble a man more powerful than themselves was stronger than the . . . wish for the common brotherhood of man. It was the cruelty of chickens—fleeing with great clamor before superior force but merciless towards the helpless.

ZORA NEALE HURSTON, *Moses, Man of the Mountain,* 1939

Men in general are so inclined to envy the glory of others, are so jealous of good which they have not themselves accomplished, that a man often makes himself enemies by the simple fact that he has rendered great service.

TOUSSAINT L'OUVERTURE, in James, *The Black Jacobins,* 1963

EQUALITY

Only equals can be friends.

ETHIOPIA

I am not in favor of caste, nor a separation of the brotherhood of mankind, and would as willingly live among white men as Black, if I had an equal possession and enjoyment of privileges, but I shall never be reconciled living among them subservient to their will.

MARTIN DELANY, "The Condition, Elevation, and Destiny of the Coloured People of the United States," 1852

The American Negro demands equality—political eqality, industrial equality and social equality; and he is never going to rest satisfied with anything less. He demands this in no spirit of braggadocio and with no obsequious envy, but with as an absolute measure of self defense and the only one to assure the darker races their ultimate survival on earth.

W. E. B. DU BOIS, in "The Immediate Program of the Negro," *Crisis,* April 1915

Bone is bone and flesh is flesh,/ When worms come out to dine:/ For they will feast on your remains,/ Just as they'll feast on mine.

ANDREA RAZAFKERIEFO, "Equality," in Kerlin, *Negro Poets and Their Poems,* 1923

The only way to get equality is for two people to get the same thing at the same time at the same place.

THURGOOD MARSHALL, Murray case, 1934

To make our way, we must have firm resolve, persistence, tenacity. We must gear ourselves to work hard all the way. We can never let up. We can never have too much preparation and training. We must be a strong competitor. We must adhere staunchly to the basic principle that anything less than full equality is not enough. If we compromise on that principle our soul is dead.

RALPH BUNCHE, "A Critical Analysis of the Tactics and Programs of Minority Groups," *Journal of Negro Education,* July 1935

Equality is the heart and essence of democracy, freedom, and justice.

A. PHILIP RANDOLPH, speech given at the March on Washington Movement Conference, Detroit, Michigan, 26 September 1942

All men have the same rights. . . . But some men have more duties than others. That's where the inequality comes in.

AIMÉ CÉSAIRE, *The Tragedy of King Christophe,* 1963

Equality cannot be seized any more than it can be given. It must be a shared experience.

JAMES FARMER, *All About CORE,* 1963

People are not . . . terribly anxious to be equal (equal . . . to what and to whom?) but they love the idea of being superior.

JAMES BALDWIN, *The Fire Next Time,* 1963

[T]he liberation of Afro-Americans . . . ultimately lies in an understanding, appreciation, and assertion of his Afro-American and African cultural heritage. It is the exploitation and assertion of cultural and spiritual heritage that will help to usher him into freedomland during the second century of emancipation.

E. U. ESSIEN-UDOM, "The Nationalist Movements of Harlem," in Clarke, *Harlem, USA,* 1964

The victims of apartheid in South Africa were created equal: those victimized by United States imperialism in Southeast Asia were created equal; and those oppressed by United States sponsored dictators were created equal.

MARTIN LUTHER KING, JR., in "Interview: Dr. Martin Luther King, Jr.," *New York Times,* 2 April 1967

There are two places on earth where human equality is absolute: in the grave and in a prison cell.

FRANK YERBY, c. 1970

We're fighting for the right to be different and not be punished for it. Equal means sameness.

MARGARET WRIGHT, in *West Magazine, Los Angeles Times,* 7 June 1970

The Declaration of Independence was not meant for me: that its chief architect, Thomas Jefferson, was a slave owner; that the Thirteenth, Fourteenth, and Fifteenth Amendments have not been fully implemented and that the "land of the free" and "sweet land of liberty" are not equally applicable to Black and white.

BENJAMIN MAYS, *Born To Rebel,* 1971

Unlike the gentle rain, unemployment does not fall on everyone equally. It falls first on the poor, longest on the Black, and hardest on Black youth.

JOHN CONYERS, in "The Politics of Unemployment: Lost—Another Generation of Black Youth," *Freedomways,* Third Quarter, 1975

In Africa, including Egypt and Ethiopia, the woman enjoyed a liberty equal to the man, had a legal individuality, and could occupy any function. She was already emancipated and no public act was alien to her.

CHEIKH ANTA DIOP, *The Cultural Unity of Black Africa,* 1978

We have tried to create a nation where all men would be equal in the eyes of the law, where all citizens would be judged on their own abilities, not their race. . . . We have believed in our Constitution. We have believed that the Declaration of Independence meant what it said. All my life I have believed in these things, and I will die believing them.

ROY WILKINS, *Standing Fast,* 1982

While the Union survived the Civil War, the Constitution did not. In its place arose a new, more promising basis for justice and equality, the 14th Amendment, ensuring protection of the life, liberty, and property of *all* persons against deprivations without due process, and guaranteeing equal protection of the laws. And yet another century would pass before . . . black Americans [obtained the right] to share equally . . . and have their votes counted, and counted equally.

THURGOOD MARSHALL, in "The Real Meaning of the Constitutional Bicentennial," *Ebony,* September 1987

Head Start should have been called 'Equal Start' and not 'Head Start.'

ASA HILLIARD, in Benson, *Black Child in Education,* 1988

You learn about equality in history and civics, but you find out life is not really like that.

ARTHUR ASHE, c. 1988

We must fight the mainstream to establish Black authority and to achieve full equality or be overwhelmed in the attempt.

HARRY EDWARDS, in "Hardline," *Detroit Free Press,* 8 May 1988

I never thought of myself as the sidekick. I've never been the side of anything. I just assumed that I was equal.

AVERY BROOKS, in "Spotlight: Not Just Another Pretty Face," *Essence,* April 1989

ESCAPE

When I thought of slavery, with its democratic whips, its republican chains, its evangelical bloodhounds and its religious slaveholders—when I thought of all this paraphernalia of American democracy and religion behind me, and the prospect of liberty before me, I was encouraged to press forward, my heart was strengthened and I forgot that I was tired and hungry.

WILLIAM WELLS-BROWN, *Narrative of the Life of William Wells-Brown,* 1856

Run, you can run/ Tell my friend Willie Brown/ That I'm standing at the crossroads/ Believe I'm sinking down.

ROBERT JOHNSON, "Me and the Devil Blues," 1937

It is impossible and unnatural to escape into something that doesn't matter.

GEORGE LAMMING, *The Emigrants,* 1954

Nowhere can a Black man escape. On land, on sea, at home and abroad, the same stupid and cruel discrimination spreads its tentacles.

BENJAMIN MAYS, *Born to Rebel,* 1971

If you escape from people too often, you wind up escaping from yourself.

MARVIN GAYE, *Divided Soul,* 1985

For the Black manchild his only hope of escape has traditionally been believed to lie in the dream of a successful athletic career.

HARRY EDWARDS, in "Hardline," *Detroit Free Press,* 8 May 1988

EUROPE

For four hundred years the avarice, fraud, and oppression of Europeans and their descendants have been preying upon the children of Africa and her descendants in America.

AUGUSTUS WASHINGTON, in "African Colonization—By A Man of Color," *New York Daily Tribune,* 9–10 July 1851

The only reason I stay in Paris is because I can work.

SIDNEY BECHET c. 1940

Europe is an empty python hiding in grass.

MELVIN B. TOLSON, *Libretto for the Republic of Liberia,* 1953

When the Europeans came to this country, embarked upon these shores, America to them was a land of promise, was a mountaintop of possibilities. But to the Negro, when he embarked upon these shores, America to him was a valley: a valley of slave huts, a valley of slavery and oppression, a valley of sorrow.

C. L. FRANKLIN, "The Prophet and Dry Bones in the Valley," c. 1957

European reason is abstract mainly because it has willfully forsaken spiritual values.

LEOPOLD SENGHOR, speech given at Fordham University, New York City, 2 November 1961

I went away to Paris and found myself. I met a lot of people in Europe. I even encountered myself.

JAMES BALDWIN, c. 1963

[I]n the past the white world was in power. This is history, this is fact. They called it European History, or colonialism.

MALCOLM X, *On Afro-American History,* 1967

It is too often forgotten that when the Europeans gained enough maritime skills and gunpowder to conquer most of the world, they not only colonized the bulk of the world's people but they colonized the interpretation of history itself. Human history was rewritten to favor them at the expense of other people. The roots of modern racism can be traced to this conquest and colonization.

JOHN HENRIK CLARKE, in "Race: An Evolving Issue in Western Thought," *Journal of Human Relations,* 1970

I had gone to Europe . . . to reach for a place as a serious artist, but I never doubted that I must return. I was—and am—an American.

MARIAN ANDERSON, in Stoddard, *Famous American Women,* 1970

. . . we take away the dark clouds from the face of the sun, that its rays may purify your thoughts, that you may look forward and see America, instead of looking backward toward Europe.

"Fourteen Strings of Purple Wampum to Writers About Indians," First Convocation of Indian Scholars, Princeton University, March 1979

The United States spends more on the defense of Europe than the Europeans themselves.

GEORGE CROCKETT, JR., in Hatchett, "Is There a Black Foreign Policy?" *Crisis,* 25 November 1986

A baby is a European/ *he does not eat our food:/* he drinks from his own water-pot./ A baby is a European/ *he does not speak our tongue:/* he is cross when the mother understands him not./ A baby is a European/ *he cares very little for others:/* he forces his will upon his parents./ A baby is a European/ *he is always very sensitive:/* the slightest scratch on his skin results in an ulcer.

EWE, "A Baby is a European," in Chinweizu, *Voices from Twentieth-Century Africa,* 1988

Europeans had once been members of their tribe—rulers even, for a time—but fell into what was . . . the blackest of sins. The failure to experience the unity of Being. . . .

CHARLES JOHNSON, *Middle Passage,* 1990

Whether Europeans are discussing world peace, writing history and theology, or organizing for the next revolution, they often act as if other peoples' viewpoints do not have to be taken seriously.

JAMES CONE, *Malcolm and Martin and America,* 1991

EVIDENCE

The truth is: *I am not and never have been involved in any international conspiracy.* . . . It should be plain to everybody . . . that if the government officials had a shred of evidence to back up that charge, you can bet your last dollar they would have tried their best to put me *under* their jail. . . . [T]he charge is a lie.

PAUL ROBESON, *Here I Stand,* 1958

Say there are gods. What evidence have you ever had that they care about what happens to men? Have you ever seen virtue rewarded—in any considerable way I mean—or evil punished? What's punished in life is stupidity and weakness; and morality is an irrelevancy to your hypothetical gods.

FRANK YERBY, *Goat Song,* 1967

I have proven that children labeled "unteachable" can learn.

MARVA COLLINS, in "Marva Collins: Teaching Success in the City," *Message,* July 1987

EVIL

Look at this land, from which you have sprung! When there is silence before evil,/ And when what should be chided is feared./ Then the great is overthrown in the land of your birth.

NEFERTARI, 2600–2450 B.C.

If you wish to be free from evil, guard against the vice of greed for material things.

PTAH HOTEP, 2340 B.C.

Although anyone may become evil, not everyone can persevere in good.

TERTULLIAN, *Patience,* c. 200 A.D.

Evil begins within them secretly at first, to draw them into open disobedience afterwards. For there would have been no evil work, but there was an evil will before it: and what could begin this evil will but pride.

ST. AUGUSTINE, *City of God,* c. 391 A.D.

There is in God a principle called "Evil" and it lies in the north of God, of it is written (Jeremiah 1:4) out of the north the evil shall break forth upon all the inhabitants of the land. And what principle is this? It is the form of the hand, one of the seven forms which represent God as the original man, and it has many messengers and all are named "Evil." And they that fling the world into guilt for the *Tobu* is in the north and the *Tobu* means precisely the evil that confuses men until they sin, and it is the source of all men's evil impulses.

THE BOOK BAHIA, 1180 A.D.

If relatives help each other, what evil can hurt them?

CONGO

Evil enters like a needle and spreads like an oak tree.

ETHIOPIA

Evil deeds are like perfume—difficult to hide.

GHANA

He who does evil, expects evil.

GUINEA

And there are evil faces that ten coats of mail cannot conceal.

INDIA

Evil knows where evil sleeps.

NIGERIA

Deception is your bicycle and you'll ride it all the way over a cliff, proclaiming you are on the straight path.

NIGERIA

The three evils of the world that a man can suffer are to live in another's house, to beg, and to be a pauper.

ZUNI

For every evil there are two remedies: time and silence.

ALEXANDRE DUMAS, *The Count of Monte Cristo,* 1844

Poverty, ignorance, and degradation are the combined evils [which] constitute the social disease of the free colored people of the United States.

FREDERICK DOUGLASS, letter to Harriet Beecher Stowe, 8 March 1853

Slavery, like all other systems of wrong, founded in the depths of human selfishness and existing for ages, has not neglected its own conservation.

FREDERICK DOUGLASS, "Reconstruction," *Atlantic Monthly,* December 1866

Those who set in motion the forces of evil cannot always control them afterwards.

CHARLES W. CHESTNUTT, *The Marrow of Tradition,* 1901

Lynch laws, peonage, whitecapping, and all kindred evil have their root in the rape of the ballot.

R. L. SMITH, speech given to Farmer's Improvement Society of Texas, 1902

We must remember because if once the world forgets evil, evil is reborn; because if the suffering of the American Negro is once forgotten, then there is no guerdon, down to the last pulse of time, that Devils will not again enslave and maim and murder and oppress the weak and the unfortunate.

W. E. B. DU BOIS, in "Three Hundred Years," *Crisis,* 1919

Of all the evils for which man has made himself responsible, none is so degrading, so shocking, or so brutal as his abuse of the better half of humanity, the female sex, not the weaker sex.

MOHANDAS GANDHI, in *Yeravda Mandir,* 15 September 1921

The evil of internal division is wrecking our existence as a people, and if we do not seriously and quickly move in the direction of readjustment, it simply means our doom becomes imminently conclusive.

MARCUS GARVEY, *Philosophy and Opinions of Marcus Garvey,* 1923

The mother of malice had trifled with men.

ZORA NEALE HURSTON, *Their Eyes Were Watching God,* 1937

He stood before Pharaoh and felt as if he stood in the presence of the evil dead. And he was glad that he stood facing them at last. The past and the future were pouring out of time.

ZORA NEALE HURSTON, *Moses, Man of the Mountain,* 1939

It's much easier to show compassion to animals. They are never wicked.

HAILE SELASSIE, c. 1940

It is not a persuasive argument that an evil should continue because it has existed in the past.

WILLIAM HASTIE, *Washington Star,* 30 October 1945

Be loving enough to absorb evil and understanding enough to turn an enemy into a friend.

MARTIN LUTHER KING, JR., *Stride Toward Freedom,* 1958

The wicked do prosper. When a man who has an evil heart gives the nerve center of his consent to evil, he does receive energy and strength.

HOWARD THURMAN, *Disciplines of the Spirit,* 1963

Past evils are the cause of present chaos.

ADAM CLAYTON POWELL, JR., "The Courage to Repent," *Keep the Faith, Baby,* 1967

Structures of evil do not crumble by passive waiting. If history teaches anything, it is that evil is recalcitrant and determined, and never voluntarily relinquishes its hold short of an almost fanatical resistance.

MARTIN LUTHER KING, JR., *Where Do We Go From Here?* 1968

Man takes in vice more readily than virtue.

MOHANDAS GANDHI, in Herikson, *Gandhi's Truth,* 1969

To turn their evil backward is to live.

IMAMU AMIRI BARAKA, "Sacred Chants for the Return of Black Spirit and Power," *Black Magic Poetry,* 1969

We must not be frightened or cajoled/ into
accepting evil as deliverance from evil./ We must go
on struggling to be human,/ though monsters of
abstraction / police and threaten us.

ROBERT HAYDEN, "Words in the Mourning Time," *Words in the Mourning Time,* 1970

Evil never appears in its own face to bargain, nor does impotence, nor does despair. After all, who believes anymore in the devil buying up souls?

AUDRE LORDE, 1975

The purpose of evil was to survive it.

TONI MORRISON, *Sula,* 1975

I am on the thin side of evil and trying not to break through.

TONI MORRISON, *Song of Solomon,* 1977

Overcome evil with good. The command does not suggest that to overcome evil is to eradicate it.

JAMES BALDWIN, in Oates, *Let the Trumpet Sound,* 1982

We shall see no evil. We shall strangle it.

NTOZAKE SHANGE, *See No Evil,* 1984

Who isn't fascinated by evil?

MARVIN GAYE, in Ritz, *Divided Soul,* 1985

There is no stability anywhere and there will not be for many years to come, and progress now insistently asserts its tragic side; the evil now stares out of the bright sunlight.

RALPH ELLISON, "Society, Morality, and the Novel," *Going to the Territory,* 1986

The protection of evil must be the most self-destructive job.

ALICE WALKER, *Living With the Wind,* 1988

EXCEL

The highest excellence which an individual can attain must be to work according to the best of his genius and to work in harmony with God's creation.

J. H. SMYTH, "Africa and the American Negro," speech given at Congress on Africa, Atlanta, Georgia, 13–15 December 1896

In the long run, the world is going to have the best, and any difference in race, religion, or previous history will not long keep the world from what it wants.

BOOKER T. WASHINGTON, *Up From Slavery,* 1901

There is nothing magical about attending a Black university. No matter where you go to school, there are many ways to fail and only a few ways to excel.

JESSE JACKSON, in *Choosing to Succeed,* 1986

You can be anything you want to be if you're willing to pay the price. One of these men could be the President of the United States. They have the right to think that way and we have the right to coach that way.

EDDIE ROBINSON, c. 1987

Excellence is no respecter or persons or places or races.

JOHN H. JOHNSON, in "Interview: John H. Johnson," *Crisis,* January 1987

Excellence is not an act but a habit. The things you do the most are the things you will do best.

MARVA COLLINS, in "Marva Collins: Teaching Success in the City," *Message,* July 1987

Try to pursue excellence with no excuses.

BILL CAMPBELL, in "Words of the Week," *Jet,* 26 September 1988

Excellence is the best deterrent to racism or sexism.

OPRAH WINFREY, c. 1990

EXCUSE

A horse thief pleading that the existence of the horse is the apology for his theft, or a highwayman contending that the money in the traveler's pack is the sole cause of his robbery are not entitled to respect.

FREDERICK DOUGLASS, 1862

Make no excuses. You don't have time because if you use energy that way, you won't have any energy to deal with what you need to deal with, which is overcoming obstacles and obtaining your goals.

FRANCES WILLIAMS, c. 1970

Write as well as you rap; teach as well as you dress; build as well as you dance; study as well as you condemn others and we will not have to make excuses.

HAKI MADHUBUTI (Don Lee), *Dynamite Voices,* 1971

If people could make it in the darkness of slavery, there is no excuse for us in the light of today's alleged freedom.

MARVA COLLINS, in *USA Today,* 7 March 1983

My teachers reinforced what I was taught at home: that nothing—not poverty, race, sex, nor peer pressure would ever be enough of an excuse for my not achieving in school.

MARY FUTRELL, c. 1989

EXISTENCE

Commoner exists where there is no king, but a kingdom cannot exist without commoners. Grass exists where there is nothing that eats grass, but what eats grass cannot exist where no grass is. Water exists where there is nothing that drinks water, but what drinks water cannot exist where no water is.

NIGERIA

. . . Forget not/ that your body contains the whole of existence.

GOSAIN GOPAL, c. 1910

The real *leap* consists in introducing invention into existence.

FRANTZ FANON, *Black Skin, White Masks,* 1967

No one is any more than the context to which he owes his existence.

RON KARENGA, in "Black Cultural Nationalism," *Black World,* January 1967

I am the hope/ and tomorrow/ of your unborn./ Truly, when there is no more of me,/ there shall be no more of you.

CONRAD KENT RIVERS, "The Still Voice of Harlem," *The Still Voice of Harlem,* 1968

The Black church was the creation of a Black people whose daily existence was an encounter with the overwhelming and brutalizing reality of white power.

JAMES CONE, *Black Theology and Black Power,* 1969

We don't ask a flower to give us any special reasons for its existence. We look at it and we are able to accept it as being something different, and different from ourselves.

GWENDOLYN BROOKS, *Report From Part One,* 1972

[E]xistence . . . is knowing the difference between what I am now and what I was then. It is being capable of looking after myself intellectually as well as financially. It is being able to tell when I am being wronged and by whom. It means being awake to protect myself and the ones I love. It means being a part of the world community . . . knowing how to change. . . .

ALICE WALKER, *In Search of Our Mothers' Gardens,* 1983

I ceased a long time ago to exist as an individual.

WINNIE MANDELA, in "A Part of My Soul Went With Him," *Ebony,* December 1985

I believe we are here on the planet Earth to live, grow up and do what we can to make this world a better place for all people to enjoy freedom.

ROSA PARKS, in "The Meaning of Life," *Life,* December 1988

EXPECTATION

Anticipate the good so you may enjoy it.

CONGO

Those who sow the wind may expect to reap the whirlwind.

KELLY MILLER, *The American Negro,* 1908

Children respond to the expectations of their environment.

WILLIAM GRIER AND PRICE COBB, *Black Rage,* 1968

They expected nothing, gave little, and got the same in return.

CHARLAYNE HUNTER, *Resurrection City,* Washington, D.C., 1968

Our future expectations must be turned into present realities.

JAMES CONE, *Black Theology and Black Power,* 1969

Never, not even in death. I am a prisoner of my own flesh and blood. Is it an enviable position? The men make it look as if we must aspire for children or die. That's why when I lost my first son I wanted to die, because I failed to live up to the standard expected of me by the males in my life, my father and my husband—and now I have to include my sons. But who made the law that we should not have hope in our daughters? We women subscribe to that law more than anyone. Until we change all this, it's still a man's world which women will always help to build.

BUCHI EMECHETA, *The Joys of Motherhood,* 1979

It was in a climate of expectancy created at Black colleges that generations of Black youth learned that they were, in fact, human beings, and that no one could limit their horizons and hope.

LERONE BENNETT, in *Choosing to Succeed,* 1986

You can't base your life on other people's expectations.

STEVIE WONDER, c. 1988

When you expect good, it's available constantly, and it makes itself a reality in your life.

ALFRE WOODARD, in "Spotlight: Alfre Woodard, Power Player," *Essence,* April 1988

You have to expect things of yourself before you can do them.

MICHAEL JORDAN, in "Michael Jordan: In His Own Orbit," *GQ,* March 1989

EXPERIENCE

As for the man who lacks experience and listens not, he nothing good can do, knowledge he seems to see in ignorance, profit in loss—to mischief he will go, and running in the error of his ways, chooses the opposite of what man praises.

PTAH HOTEP, *On the Unteachable and Fools,* c. 2400 B.C.

One writes out of one thing only—one's own experiences. Everything depends on how relentlessly one forces from this experience the last drop, sweet or bitter, it can possibly give. This is the only real concern of the artist, to recreate out of the disorder of life that order which is art.

JAMES BALDWIN, *Notes of a Native Son,* 1955

History and experience should not be ignored.

ROY WILKINS, speech given to the NAACP, Jackson, Mississippi, 7 June 1961

To be alive is to be involved in events some of which take their rise uniquely in the individual's experience and some of which flow into life apparently without rhyme or reason.

HOWARD THURMAN, *Disciplines of the Spirit,* 1963

People are always speculating—why am I as I am? To understand that of any person, his whole life, from birth, must be reviewed. All our experiences fuse into our personality. Everything that ever happened to us is an ingredient . . . an objective reader may see how in the society to which I was exposed as a black youth here in America, for me to wind up in a prison was really just about inevitable.

MALCOLM X, *The Autobiography of Malcolm X,* 1965

The twisted circumstances under which we live is grist for the writing mill, the loving, hating and discovering, finding new handles for old pitchers, and realizing there is no such thing as *the* Black experience. . . . Time and events allow for change on both sides.

ALICE CHILDRESS, "A Candle in a Gale Wind," in Evans, ed., *Black Women Writers,* 1984

Close your eyes as I take you on the experience of my life, the experience of hearing many different sounds from many different cultures from around the world. We hear the energy, the sound of musics, the sound of someone saying, "I love you."

STEVIE WONDER, c. 1987

Because of my personal experience, my ups and downs, my I-am-I states, and my I-am-nothing states, I was fairly well convinced that in man there was a curious duality—and "I," a something that was not I; an inner being, an outer personality. . . . [T]he inner being was the real thing . . . the outer personality the false thing.

JEAN TOOMER, in Kerman and Eldridge, *The Lives of Jean Toomer,* 1987

Nobody should be a teenager. . . . But since science has not yet found a cure for adolescence, the best we can do is give the only real antidote for immaturity—experience.

THOMAS SOWELL, *Compassion vs. Guilt,* 1987

Experience is sometimes better than money.

MIKE TYSON, in "Mike Tyson Talks About His Future And Says 'I'm A Dreamer,'" *Jet,* 14 November 1988

My writing is a lens into the possibilities of the American experience.

CHARLES JOHNSON, in "Interview with Charles Johnson," *The World and I,* 1990

I have twenty-six years. . . . Would you prefer to be administered for your brain tumor by the surgeon who graduated this year or by the surgeon who has been practicing for ten years and never lost a patient?

WILLIE BROWN, 29 October 1990

How you perceive experience and how you handle it determine how your life turns out in the long run.

BILL COSBY, in "Bill and Camille Cosby: Five Kids, Two Careers, Love, Work, Fame, and Happiness," *Lear's,* April 1991

EXPLOITATION

The exploitation that goes on in the world cannot go on forever—great spiritual uprising against the proscription, the defamation, and the violence of the preceding years.

BENJAMIN BRAWLEY, *A Social History of the Negro,* 1921

Exploitation is not always humane, but it is human and universal.

CLAUDE MCKAY, in "Race and Color in East Asia," *Opportunity,* August 1939

It is incorrect to to classify the revolt of the Negro as simply a racial conflict of Black against white or as a purely American problem. Rather, we are today seeing a global rebellion of the oppressed against the oppressor, the exploited against the exploiter.

Columbia Daily Spectator, 19 February 1965

The lion does not lie down peacefully with the lamb. The exploiters do not suffer a change of heart and cease to exploit. The great powers do not suddenly discover a morality that tells them it is wrong to manipulate small countries and use their lands as bases and battlegrounds and their people as living targets in the power game of showing muscle.

PETER ABRAHAMS, in "Pluralia," *English Studies,* February 1969

We are not against Jews. We are against exploitation. I cannot tolerate Black exploitation of Black people any more than I can tolerate it from white people.

LOUIS FARRAKHAN, *The Honorable Louis Farrakhan: Minister of Progress,* 1984

EXPRESSION

The only place Blacks felt they could maintain an element of self-expression was the church.

RICHARD ALLEN, *The Life Experience and Gospel Labors of Richard Allen,* 1887

We younger Negro artists who create now intend to express our individual dark-skinned selves without fear or shame. If white people are pleased we are glad. If they are not, it doesn't matter.

LANGSTON HUGHES, "The Negro Artist and the Racial Mountain," *The Nation,* 23 June 1926

The first time I heard the expression "baby" used by one cat to address another was in 1951. The term had a hip ring to it, a colored ring—I knew right away I had to start using it. It was like saying, "Man, look at me. I've got masculinity to spare." If you could say it, this meant that you really had to be sure of yourself, of your masculinity.

CLAUDE BROWN, *Manchild in the Promised Land,* 1965

All Blacks are militant in their guts, but militancy is expressed in different ways.

BARBARA JORDAN, *Barbara Jordan,* 1977

Jazz is an important expression of the twentieth century: Black experience in America, the nobility of the race put into sound.

WYNTON MARSALIS, VH-1 interview (television), 14 November 1989

EYES

The eye which sees the smoke will look for fire.

AFRICA

You must be blind in one eye and can't see out of the other.

TRADITIONAL

Fern's eyes desired nothing that you could give her; . . . Men saw her eyes and fooled themselves.

JEAN TOOMER, *Fern,* 1923

Each of my todays has eyes that/ look upon my yesterdays/ with rancor/ and with shame.

LÉON DAMAS, "The Black Man's Lament," *Pigments,* 1937

My eyes and my mind keep taking me where my old legs can't keep up.

ZORA NEALE HURSTON, *Moses, Man of the Mountain,* 1939

[Toussaint L'Ouverture] had eyes like steel and no one ever laughed in his presence.

C. L. R. JAMES, *The Black Jacobins,* 1963

[E]yes that refuse you are really seeking you out; those that open up for you have nothing to promise you.

ES'KIA MPHAHLELE, "Tirenje or Monde?" in Chinweizu, ed., *Voices from Twentieth-Century Africa,* 1988

FACE

We know the face, but we don't know the heart.

ANGOLA

Ashes fly back into the face of him who throws them.

TRADITIONAL

If our black face, O King, seems to your ministers odious,/ We Ethiops find your white ones no more to our taste.

JUAN LATINO, c. 1530

Moses looked at the mask of her face. It looked like nothing had moved in it for years. Nothing had gone in its portals and nothing had come out. It seemed to have finished with everything and just to have been waiting on time.

ZORA NEALE HURSTON, *Moses, Man of the Mountain,* 1939

Our faces do not change. Our cheekbones remain as unaltered as the stony countenance of the sphinx.

RICHARD WRIGHT, *12 Million Black Voices,* 1941

O face as God made you even before the memory of the ages,/ Face of the world's dawn, show no tender throat to rouse my flesh.

LEOPOLD SENGHOR, "Negro Mask," *Song of Darkness,* 1945

[A] face like all of the African masks held captive in all of the museums in the Western world.

JAMES BALDWIN, *Go Tell It on the Mountain,* 1953

One can only face in others what one can face in oneself.

JAMES BALDWIN, *Nobody Knows My Name,* 1961

. . . we take away the fog that surrounds your eyes and obstructs your view, that you may see the truth concerning our people.

"Fourteen Strings of Purple Wampum to Writers About Indians," First Convocation of Indian Scholars, Princeton University, March 1979

In the face of one's victim one sees oneself.

JAMES BALDWIN, *Price of the Ticket,* 1985

My face and my name are known all over because of the history of the Chicago political machine and the movement that brought it down.

HAROLD WASHINGTON, in "Mayor Washington Eulogized as Symbol of Hope for Blacks," *Jet,* 14 December 1987

FAILURE

Our own people seem to stand in the way of any accomplishment of federal intervention against lynching, by failing to organize their forces and raise money to lobby for desired results.

IDA B. WELLS, in Duster, ed., *Crusade for Justice,* 1928

The army officials want the camp to fail. The last thing they want is to help colored men to become commissioned officers. The camp is intended to fight segregation, not encourage it.

JOEL SPINGARN, *From Slavery to Freedom,* 1947

Growth always involves the risk of failure. . . .

HOWARD THURMAN, *Disciplines of the Spirit,* 1963

We will not be guaranteed against failure, but we will learn that we may fail again and again and yet be assured always that we are not mistaken in what we affirm with all our hearts and minds.

Ibid.

The greatest failure for any man is to fail with a woman.

CHESTER HIMES, *The Quality of Hurt,* 1972

We live in a distraught present. Although we have had the courage to deplore it, we have failed to heal the gap between the middle-class Black lawyer and the Black slum dweller, who hates us almost as much as he hates whitey.

BARBARA JORDAN, *Barbara Jordan,* 1977

I don't really know the exact formula for success, but I do know the formula for failure: trying to please everybody.

BILL COSBY, in "Interview with Bill Cosby," *Scholastic,* 17 July 1977

I despair at our failure to wrest power from those who have it and abuse it; our reluctance to reclaim our old powers lying dormant with neglect; our hesitancy to create new power in areas where it never before existed.

TONI CADE BAMBARA, "Salvation Is the Issue," in Evans, ed., *Black Women Writers,* 1984

At fourth grade, if young males do not receive constant reinforcement and nurturing at this point they will evolve into adults who are socially and politically impotent.

JAWANZA KUNJUFU, *The Conspiracy to Destroy Fourth Grade Boys,* 1984

Failure is a word that I simply don't accept.

JOHN H. JOHNSON, in *USA Today,* 16th April 1986

Whites are beginning to realize that the entire culture is at stake if Blacks and other minorities are not educated and included in this country's business community. It is all tied together; if Blacks fail, the whole culture will fail.

CORETTA SCOTT KING, in *Crisis,* November 1986

None of you has ever failed. School may have failed you. Goodbye to failure, children. Welcome to success.

MARVA COLLINS, in "Marva Collins: Teaching Success in the City," *Message,* October 1987

Failure is not a fatal disease.

EARL G. GRAVES, in *Black Enterprises,* March 1988

For some odd reason, when Blacks fail, there seems to be a collective failure. And I don't think I have a right to fail.

ROY ROBERTS, in "Words of the Week," *Jet,* 29 August 1988

All of our Mercedes Benzes and Halston frocks will not hide our essential failure as a generation of Black "haves" who did not protect the Black future during our watch.

MARIAN WRIGHT EDELMAN, in "We Must Convey to Children That We Believe in Them," *Ebony,* August 1988

There must be a sense that we will *not* promote failure through the school system.

RICHARD GREEN, in "Dr Richard Green: Chancellor of New York City Schools," *Ebony,* August 1988

If you deal with failure all your life, you'll never know how to succeed.

BARBARA REYNOLDS, c. 1989

[There is] no competition for the bottom of the class.

BENJAMIN CARSON, *Gifted Hands,* 1990

[F]ailure was not in my scheme of things . . . I would perform at West Point exactly as I had performed in my life up to this time—with considerable routine and expected success.

BENJAMIN DAVIS, JR., *Benjamin Davis, Jr.: An Autobiography,* 1991

Treat failure as practice shots.

DEBORAH MCGRIFF, in the *Detroit Teacher,* 9 September 1991

FAITH

Hold fast to Faith. Desert not the ranks, but as brave soldiers march on to victory. I am happy and shall remain so as long as you keep the flag flying.

MARCUS GARVEY, *Philosophy and Opinions of Marcus Garvey,* 1923

I opened the doors of my school . . . with an enrollment of five little girls . . . whose parents paid me fifty cents' weekly tuition. . . . Though I hadn't a penny left, I considered cash money as the smallest part of my resources. I had faith in a living God, faith in myself, and a desire to serve.

MARY MCLEOD BETHUNE, in "Faith That Moved a Dump Heap," *WHO,* June 1941

We must have faith that this society divided by race and class, and subject to profound social pressure, can one day become a nation of equals.

A. PHILIP RANDOLPH, a speech given to the March on Washington Movement, Detroit, Michigan, 26 September 1942

As I reflect down the vistas of the past, as I think about all the problems and all the experiences I have had; without a faith in God, a faith in prayer, and a disposition of loyalty to God, I don't know what I would have done.

C. L. FRANKLIN, "Hannah, the Ideal Mother," 1958

Before the ship of your life reaches its last harbor, there will be long drawn-out storms, howling and jostling winds, and tempestuous seas that make the heart stand still. If you do not have a deep and patient faith in God, you will be powerless to face the delay, disappointment, and vicissitudes that inevitably come.

MARTIN LUTHER KING, JR., *Strength to Love,* 1963

In the spirit of the darkness, we must not despair, we must not become bitter—we must not lose faith.

Ibid.

Faith can give us courage to face the uncertainties of the future.

Ibid.

We live by faith in others. But most of all we must live by faith in ourselves—faith to believe that we can develop into useful men and women.

BENJAMIN MAYS, "What Man Lives By," in Philpot, ed., *Best Black Sermons,* 1972

I always had a lot of faith in my ability not to break my neck.

RAY CHARLES, *Brother Ray,* 1978

[A] man [can] get along if he ha[s] faith in the goodness of other people . . . and believe[s] in himself.

ROY WILKINS, *Standing Fast,* 1982

Faith is the flip side of fear.

SUSAN TAYLOR, 1988

Living on faith is a mental exercise.

Ibid.

FALL

If you fall you don't have to wallow.

TRADITIONAL

It is much easier to pick oneself up from a fall, than to get up when one has always lain supine.

PAUL ROBESON, in "The Source of the Negro Spirituals," *Jewish Tribune,* 22 July 1927

If a person is hit hard enough, even if she stands, she falls.

ALICE WALKER, *Meridian,* 1976

Manute's so tall if he falls down, he'd be halfway home.

DARRYL DAWKINS, 1987

There was nothing more to lose. Being that far down he was no longer afraid to fall.

CHARLES JOHNSON, *Middle Passage,* 1990

FAME

Notoriety is often mistaken for fame.

AESOP, "The Mischievous Dog," 300 B.C.

The pathway to glory is rough, and many gloomy hours obscure it.

BLACK HAWK, *Farewell, My Nation! Farewell,* 1833

The little praises I have received does not affect me unless it be to make me work furiously. Instead of a pillow to rest upon, it is a goad to prod me. I know that I can only get into the sunlight by work and only remain there by more work.

ZORA NEALE HURSTON, letter to Annie Meyer, 12 May 1925

One must glow before one can glorify.

JEAN TOOMER, *Essentials,* 1931

The price that one has to pay in public life is that of being misquoted, misrepresented, and misunderstood.

MARTIN LUTHER KING, JR., 1961

But within his heart of hearts he could still feel the passionate longing for the bright lights for the limelight, for adulation.

CHESTER HIMES, *Prison Mass,* May 1961

He had wanted the renown more than the money; wanted to see his name on the pages of popular magazines . . . I shall be no forgotten man.

Ibid.

However famous a man is outside, if he is not respected inside his own home, he is like a bird with beautiful feathers, wonderful on the outside, but ordinary within.

CYPRIAN EKWENSI, *Beautiful Feathers,* 1963

Fame is no good, I can have no peace.

MUHAMMAD ALI, in the *New York Post,* 18 May 1965

I feel terribly menaced by this present notoriety because it is antithetical to the kind of an endeavor which has to occur in silence and over a great period of time and which by definition is extremely dangerous precisely because one has to smash at all the existing definitions.

JAMES BALDWIN, in "James Baldwin . . . in Conversation," *Arts in Society,* Summer 1966

Fame is a flippant lover.

WOLE SOYINKA, *Kongi's Harvest,* 1967

I got fame and fortune and I lost my sense of reasoning.

LITTLE RICHARD, in "Little Richard," *Jet,* 26 November 1984

It isn't at all easy, when you have lived . . . in complete obscurity, to adjust yourself in a matter of hours to the role of celebrity.

BARBARA KIMENYE, "The Winner," in Obradovic, ed., *Looking for a Rain God,* 1990

FAMILY

See also MOTHER, FATHER

Poor is he who shuns his kin.

PTAH HOTEP, c. 2340 B.C.

None but a mule deserves his family.

AFRICA

Adam's sons are limbs of each other, having been created of one essence. When the calumny of time afflicts one limb the other limbs cannot remain at rest. If you have no sympathy for the troubles of others, you are unworthy to be called by name of man.

The Gulistan of Sadi, 1184–1292 A.D.

The only thing that links me to this land is my family, and the painful consciousness that here there are three million of my fellow creatures, groaning beneath the iron rod of the worst despotism that could be devised, even in Pandemonium.

FREDERICK DOUGLASS, "The Right to Criticize American Institutions," speech given to the Anti-Slavery Society, 11 May 1887

I have not father nor mother; I am alone in the world. No one cares for Cochise; that is why I do not care to live, and wish the rocks to fall on me and cover me up. If I had a father or a mother like you, I would be with them and they with me.

COCHISE OF THE CHIRICAHUA APACHES, in "Recollections of an Interview with Cochise, Chief of the Apaches," *Collections,* 1915

For purpose of the novel I created around myself what seemed to me a more typical family than my own had been. I gave myself aunts I didn't have, modeled after other children's aunts.

LANGSTON HUGHES, *Not Without Laughter,* 1930

The shooting star is my sister,/ my brother is the shattered glass,/ my brother is the blood kiss of the cut head/ on the plate of silver, and my sister the epizooty/ and my sister the epilepsy, and my friend is the chicken hawk,/ my beloved the fire's lust. . .

AIMÉ CÉSAIRE, *Miraculous Weapons,* 1946

What I most remember was an abiding sense of comfort and security. I got plenty of mothering not only from Pop and my brothers and sisters when they were home, but from the whole of our close-knit community.

PAUL ROBESON, *Here I Stand,* 1958

I have learnt too much of the heart of man not to be certain that it is only in the bosom of my family that I shall find happiness.

TOUSSAINT L' OUVERTURE, in James, *The Black Jacobins,* 1963

[I]t is the family that gives us a deep private sense of belonging. Here we first begin to have our self defined for us.

HOWARD THURMAN, *Disciplines of the Spirit,* 1963

Nearly everyone in Ibuza was related. They all knew each other, the tales of one another's ancestors, their ancestors, their histories and heroic deeds. Nothing was hidden. It was the duty of every member of the town to find out and know his neighbor's business.

BUCHI EMECHETA, *The Bride Price,* 1976

The uneasy world of family life—where the greatest can fail and the humblest succeed.

MELVIN CHAPMAN, speech given at Mercy College, Detroit, Michigan, 1976

Over many generations, all the way back to slavery, black families had developed customs for the sheltering and releasing of stray children. There seemed to be intricate rules about which relative would take what child under every circumstance. The taking in was to be done in the closest possible imitation of a natural family, and the giving up was to be done quickly with stoic smiles and a chorus of farewells that it was best for all.

BILL RUSSELL, *Second Wind,* 1979

I come from a family of very gifted laughers. . . . My mama taught me the power of the word, the importance of the resistance tradition, and the high standards our community has regarding verbal performance.

TONI CADE BAMBARA, "Salvation Is the Issue," in Evans, ed., *Black Women Writers,* 1984

The function of the family is to celebrate the triumphs and heroes of the Black struggle and to remember the defeats.

JANICE HALE BENSON, *Black Child in Education,* 1986

Black family endures. It survived forced separation of husbands and wives, parents and baby, brother and sister during slavery. Adverse social forces and the stress of urban life have battered it for generations, yet it remains intact, strong, perhaps because of the annealing process imposed by hard times.

JOHN H. JOHNSON, in "Publisher's Statement," *Ebony,* August 1986

Your relationships with people begin in the home, where you learn values. It's the responsibility of the family.

MELBA MOORE, 1988

You leave home to seek your fortune and when you get it you go home and share it with your family.

ANITA BAKER, 1988

Anyone else can go home and see their family, but for me to do so would require changing the political system of South Africa.

MIRIAM MAKEBA, in "Makeba: My Story," *Essence,* May 1988

The institution primarily responsible for the survival and advancement of Black people from slavery to present times has been the extended family.

ROBERT HILL, in *Life*, December 1988

When we realize we are part of the same family then we'll come up with real solutions.

CHARLES WRIGHT, speech given at Detroit Afro-American Museum, 1989

In the church, we think of ourselves as all part of God's family. That means we think of the people where we worship as brothers and sisters—part of our family.

BENJAMIN CARSON, *Gifted Hands*, 1990

I was barely ten when our father died . . . Yet a member of our clan educated me and never expected any refund. According to our custom, I was his child and his responsibility. I have a lot of praise for this institution . . . it caters to all those who are descended from one ancestor and holds them together as one family.

NELSON MANDELA, *Higher Than Hope*, 1991

All people throughout the world have, at one time or another, had clans and some clans were certainly mightier and better known in history than ours . . . ours is the whole world, our umbrella, the source of all our strength and efforts, the navel that links us together as a family.

Ibid.

FAREWELL

See also END

Every shut-eye ain't sleep and every good-bye ain't gone.

TRADITIONAL

If you want to see how much folks are going to miss you, just stick your finger in a glass of water, then pull it out and look at the hole.

TRADITIONAL

Let the door hit you where the good Lord split you.

TRADITIONAL

Farewell, my nations. Black Hawk tried to save you, and avenge your wrongs. . . . He can do no more. He is near his end. His sun is setting, and he will rise no more.

BLACK HAWK, *Farewell, My Nation, Farewell!* 1833

I am well in body and soul.

JOHN ANTHONY COPELAND, on the day of his execution, 16 December 1859

I leave my parents here behind/ And all my friends to love resigned/ 'Tis grief to go, but death to stay/ Farewell—I'm gone with love away.

GEORGE MOSES HORTON, "The Lover's Farewell," 1865

This is perhaps the Negroes' temporary farewell to the American Congress; but, Phoenix-like, he will rise up some day and come again.

GEORGE WHITE, c. 1901

I am for sleeping and forgetting/ All that has gone before;/ I am for lying still and letting/ Who will beat at my door;/ I would my life's cold sun were setting/ To rise for me no more.

COUNTEE CULLEN, "Requiescam," *Color*, 1925

Didn't he ramble?/ He rambled,/ Rambled all around/ In and out the town./ Didn't he ramble?/ He rambled/ He rambled till the butchers cut him down.

JELLY ROLL MORTON, in Hughes, ed., *Book of Negro Humor*, 1958

Today you bid farewell to the friendly security of the academic environment, a setting that will remain dear to you as long as the cords of memory shall lengthen.

MARTIN LUTHER KING, JR., "The American Dream," speech given at Lincoln University, Oxford, Pennsylvania, 6 June 1961

Farewell, Beloved Comrade,/ We make this solemn vow:/ The fight will go on,/ The fight must still go on/ Until we win, until we, the people, win.

PAUL ROBESON, eulogy of Benjamin Davis, New York City, 27 August 1964

Sometimes I feel like an eagle in the air; as Lorraine (Hansberry) says farewell, she bids us keep our heads high and to hold on to our strength and powers, to soar like the eagle.

PAUL ROBESON, eulogy of Lorraine Hansberry, 1965

Whenever you want to see me, always look at the sunset; I will be there.

GRACE OGOT, "Unwinding Thread," *The Rain Came,* 1968

We've got some difficult days ahead. But it doesn't matter with me now. Because I've been to the mountaintop. And I don't mind. Like anybody, I would like to live a long life. Longevity has its place. But I'm not concerned about that now. I just want to do God's will. And he's allowed me to go up to the mountain. And I've looked over. And I've seen the promised land.

MARTIN LUTHER KING, JR., "I Have Been to the Mountaintop," speech given in Memphis, Tennessee, 3 April 1968

The worst thing in the world is to say good-bye to someone and they don't go.

BILL COSBY, in *Jet,* 23 February 1987

And so with hymns and prayers, trumpets and drums, above all rich and compelling language, New York has said its goodbye to a native son. The mortal was consigned to the earth, but James Baldwin had long before put on immortality.

IMAMU AMIRI BARAKA, eulogy of James Baldwin, Cathedral of St. John the Divine, New York City, January 1988

FATE

Everyone is more or less the master of his own fate.

AESOP, "The Traveler and the Fortune," c. 300 B.C.

[There are] those returns of good fortune which announce to a man that fate has at last grown weary of attacking him.

ALEXANDRE DUMAS, *The Count of Monte Cristo,* 1844

My fate as far as man can seal it, is sealed; but let this not occasion you misery. Remember this cause I engaged, remember that it was a holy cause.

JOHN ANTHONY COPELAND, letter to his family on the day of his execution, 26 November 1859

We are all puppets in the hands of Fate and seldom see the strings that move us.

CHARLES W. CHESTNUTT, *The Marrow of Tradition,* 1901

Fate is being kind to me. Fate doesn't want me to be too famous too young.

DUKE ELLINGTON, *Music Is My Mistress,* 1973

Fate will lay enough unhappiness on me; I don't need to look for any of my own.

RAY CHARLES, *Brother Ray,* 1978

Fate is determined by what one does and what one doesn't do.

RALPH ELLISON, "Remembering Richard Wright," *Going to the Territory,* 1986

FATHER

See also MOTHER, FAMILY

Happy the sons whom fathers educate. There is no error in their being's plan.

PTAH HOTEP, c. 2340 B.C.

How good for a son to grasp his father's words. He will reach old age through them.

PTAH HOTEP, c. 2340 B.C.

When you follow in the path of your father, you learn to walk like him.

ASHANTI

"The ugliest child he had ever seen," his own father said that to his face, but he was not destroyed by it. Was hurt, of course. Scarred. But was not destroyed. Used it in fact, whether consciously or not, as the threshing floor from which he took wings. Soared. It gave him the key to understand hatred, whether directed in or out, whether from a man or a society.

And miraculously, gave him the key to understand love, self love, family love.

JAMES BALDWIN, *Go Tell It On the Mountain,* 1953

Of all the different kinds of work my father engaged in, none fascinated me so much as his skill with gold. No other occupation was so noble, no other needed such a delicate touch.

CAMARA LAYE, *The Dark Child,* 1954

My father was a slave and my people died to build this country and I am going to stay here and have a part of it just like you.

PAUL ROBESON, testimony given before the House Un-American Activities Committee, June 12, 1956

He was my first teacher in public speaking, and long before my days as a class orator and college debater there were the evenings or recitations at home, where his love for the eloquent and meaningful word and his insistence on purity of diction made their impress.

PAUL ROBESON, *Here I Stand,* 1958

My father gave me a trumpet because he loved my mother so much.

MILES DAVIS, in *Downbeat,* 6 March 1958

Sundays too my father got up early/ and put his
clothes on in the blueblack cold,/ then with cracked
hands that ached/ from labor in the weekday
weather made/ banked fire blazes. No one ever
thanked him./

ROBERT HAYDEN, "Those Winter Sundays," *A Ballad of Remembrance,* 1962

My father, besides being an active worker in the Marcus Garvey movement, was a Christian clergyman—a Baptist minister. He was lynched in Lansing, Michigan, in 1954, by being thrown under a streetcar.

MALCOLM X, in the *Daily Gleaner* (Jamaica), 12 July 1964

The image of him that made me the proudest was his crusading and militant campaigning with the words of Marcus Garvey. . . . I can remember hearing . . . "Africa for Africans," "Ethiopians, Awake!" And my father would talk about how it would not be much longer before Africa would be completely run . . . "by Black men."

MALCOLM X, *The Autobiography of Malcolm X,* 1965

I would sit goggle-eyed at my father [a minister] jumping and shouting as he preached, with the congregation jumping and shouting behind him. . . .

Ibid.

There is a man in my house/ He's so big and
strong/ He goes to work each day and stays all day
long/ Comes home at night, looking tired and
beat . . . I think I'll color him Father . . . I think I'll
color him love.

O. C. SMITH, *O. C. Smith at Home,* c. 1970

As there were no Black founding fathers, there were no Black founding mothers—a great pity on both accounts.

SHIRLEY CHISHOLM, in the *Congressional Record,* 10 August 1970

My father was a kingdom seeker. He believed that the mere act of seeking the kingdom brought all things unto you. . . .

ADAM CLAYTON POWELL, JR., *Adam by Adam,* 1971

And he was a commanding figure . . . all his proportions and measurements were the exact same ones I have today. I am not a chip off the old block, I am "the block itself," living again, a reincarnation.

Ibid.

His age was showing in his face. . . . he looked a great deal like his father, a small, Black man who had faded to a parchment-colored mummy in his old age.

CHESTER HIMES, *Black on Black,* 1973

[My father] always acted as though he had money, whether he had it or not. He spent and lived like a man who had money, and he raised his family as though he were a millionaire. The best had to be carefully examined to make sure it was good enough for my mother. Maybe he was richer than a millionaire? I'm not sure that he wasn't.

DUKE ELLINGTON, *Music Is My Mistress,* 1973

My daddy's face is a study. Winter moves into it and presides there. His eyes become a cliff of snow threatening to avalanche, his eyebrows bend like black limbs of leafless trees. His skin takes on the pale cheerless yellow of winter sun; for a jaw he has the edges of a snowbound field dotted with stubble; his high forehead is the frozen sweep of the Erie.

TONI MORRISON, "The Coming of Maureen Peal," c. 1975

My father was a statesman, I'm a political woman. My father was a saint, I'm not.

INDIRA GANDHI, in "Indira's Coup," *New York Review of Books,* 18 September 1975

God is love and God is a father, we are pictured as his children. Thus I cannot think of God being a father, the epitome of love, and just because his children happen to be contrary and unruly sometimes, that he will put them into eternal punishment. I can't see that. I'm a better father than that.

C. L. FRANKLIN, "Give Me This Mountain," c. 1976

It is so even today in Nigeria—when you have lost your father you have lost your parents.... A fatherless family is a family without a head, a family without a shelter, a family without parents, in fact a non-existing family. Such traditions do not change very much.

BUCHI EMECHETA, *The Bride Price,* 1976

He wondered how his father and other men ever found time to learn so much about everything there was to know.

ALEX HALEY, *Roots,* 1977

My father is a strong man. My earliest memories of him come from days when our whole family played together in the fields near our home in Monroe, Louisiana. He worked hard in a paperbag factory, but he'd still come home full of energy and call out for my brother and mother and me. We would follow him to the fields where the grass grew tall as wheat, and the four of us would play hide-and-seek there.... When it was time to go home, my father would reach down and pick me up under one arm, my brother under the other, lean down so my mother could crawl up on his back, and then run all the way home, carrying his whole family as if we weighed nothing.

BILL RUSSELL, *Second Wind,* 1979

My father had enough education to realize that the equality of all men as set forth in the Declaration of Independence wasn't exactly common policy around Marshall County [Mississippi]; he became the family's first hell-raiser. Since he talked back to white people whenever he felt like it, people around Holly Springs began to worry about him. They said he was on his way to becoming a troublemaker, bum ... [and] I have the same traits buried somewhere in my chromosomes. I don't like to be mistreated.... I believe in fighting back.

ROY WILKINS, *Standing Fast,* 1982

My father's gifts ... are daily surprises: my love of naturalness, the tone of my voice, my very face, eyes, and hair.

ALICE WALKER, *In Search of Our Mothers' Gardens,* 1983

I never really knew my father, and the biggest problem that I have had in growing up is missing that fatherly love.

BERNICE KING, in "Whatever Happened to Bernice King?" *Ebony,* October 1983

I met "Dr. King" as "Dr. King" just the very way you did. I never really met him as "Daddy." I never had that experience of a real father-daughter relationship.

Ibid.

No single living entity really influenced my life as did my father.... An oak of a man, his five feet eight loomed taller than Kilimanjaro. He lived as if he were poured from iron, and loved his family with a vulnerability that was touching.... [O]ne could not spend a lifetime in his presence without absorbing something beautiful and strong and special.

MARI EVANS, "My Father's Passage," in *Black Women Writers,* 1984

My old man provided me not only with money, but with care. He gave me a vision of myself, and a foundation to build on.

QUINCY TROUPE, in "The Black Male in Jeopardy," *Crisis,* March 1986

[My father and I] have the same hands. We have the same dreams. We write the same lyrics, sometimes.

PRINCE, in "Interview with Prince," *Ebony,* July 1986

He is perhaps not listed in the history books. Few people have heard of him, and no front-page stories heralded his demise, but I shall always remember that it was he who influenced my life. His name will not matter to most readers because . . . he never made the "Ten Most Admired" list. But in my book, he is the greatest man that I have ever known.

MARVA COLLINS, in "The Most Unforgettable Person in My Family," *Ebony,* August 1986

I feel privileged to be his son. I am happy to have had him, if only for a little while.

JULIUS GARVEY, "Remembering Marcus Garvey," *Essence,* November 1986

As a teenager, I rebelled and wanted to break out of the confines of my strict upbringing. But now I've mellowed and I'm becoming more like my father.

DENZEL WASHINGTON, in "Spotlight: Denzel," *Essence,* November 1986

He had tremendous belief in holding to one's values, whatever the cost; never [become] shaken from your belief, except through logic, but never by crowds. He said have the courage to stand up even against majorities if our position is right.

RANDALL ROBINSON, in "Interview: Randall Robinson," *Crisis,* November 1986

Way back in me he became a sort of mystery, part real, part legendary, a kindly portentous figure quite outside the ordinary run of life.

JEAN TOOMER, in Kerman and Eldridge, *The Lives of Jean Toomer,* 1987

Fathers are by historic design the heads of the family, the protectors of wives, mothers, and children. Whenever a society has turned away from the patriarchal design, it has faded away.

RAYMOND S. MOORE, in "Mind Over Belt," *Message,* February 1987

Dad had a wonderful habit of talking to everybody the same way. A briefcase and a three-piece suit didn't impress him. "The guy with the mop may have the answer you need," my father told me, "but if you're holding your head too high, you're going to miss what he's saying."

LIONEL RICHIE, in "Words of the Week," *Jet,* 23 February 1987

My father used to tell me stories before I fell asleep. When the children would gather, at a certain point, I had a tendency to make up my own elementary variations on stories I had heard, or to invent totally new ones.

WOLE SOYINKA, in "Wole Soyinka: Nigerian Playwright Is First Black Nobel Laureate in Literature," *Ebony,* April 1987

Fatherhood is responsibility, it's definitely humility, a lot of love and the friendship of a parent and child.

DENZEL WASHINGTON, in "Father's Day," *Jet,* 22 June 1987

My father said never look up to any other person and never look down to any person.

DORIAN HAREWOOD, in "Father's Day," *Jet,* 22 June 1987

[T]he most important thing my father did for me was exude a belief in himself, a confidence in himself that I knew I could not override.

OPRAH WINFREY, in "An Intimate Talk with Oprah," *Essence,* August 1987

If I went into the U.S. Foreign Service and did well, I would never know whether it was because I'm good or because I'm my father's son.

CLIFTON WHARTON, in "Clifton Wharton: The Nation's Highest-Paid Black Executive," *Ebony,* September 1987

Black men must make a special effort to become spiritual and psychological fathers to needy Black children within their extended families and community.

ALVIN POUSSAINT, in "The Challenge of the Black Family," *Message*, September–October 1987

I was given incentive by my dad, who always says, "If you're going to do it, get it done."

CHARLEY PRIDE, in "Words of the Week," *Jet*, 25 April 1988

My father was a man who never thought he was going to be more than a good performer. He lived the good life. If I have any class, it's from watching him. He was touched by God and touched other people mainly out of love. He was very proud of his family.

SAMMY DAVIS, JR., in "Census," *Jet*, 13 June 1988

When I look in the mirror I see my father. It's not that I resemble him, I look identical.

LIONEL HAMPTON, *Hamp*, 1989

I just feel fortunate, especially watching a musician like my father struggle from day to day, not having the right gigs.

WYNTON MARSALIS, 1989

My father is my idol, so I always did everything like him. He used to work two jobs and still come home happy every night. He didn't do drugs or drink, and he wouldn't let anyone smoke in his house. Those are rules I adopted, too.

MAGIC JOHNSON, in *Michigan Living*, April 1989

When I was little I always found it amusing that my father, a small man, played such a big instrument, the bass. My earliest recollection of my father is of him lugging that bass around. Other kids, my friends in particular, had fathers with regular nine-to-five jobs, but I had a musician for a father, and it's been a great influence.

SPIKE LEE, *Mo' Better Blues*, 1990

How lucky I was to have a father who, in spite of formidable obstacles, would fight for his beliefs and ambitions and win!

BENJAMIN DAVIS, JR., *Benjamin Davis, Jr.: An Autobiography*, 1990

FAULT(S)

All men have faults. Small men are blind to their own, and therefore remain small.

JEAN TOOMER, *Essentials*, 1931

FEAR

While the best men are well guided by love, most men need to be goaded by fear. Many people profit by a preliminary dose of force which makes it possible for them to be taught something, or to put into practice what had previously been only words to them.

ST. AUGUSTINE, *Appeal to the Secular Arms*, c. 409 A.D.

Sometimes when we are afraid of the future, we cling to the past.

TRADITIONAL

He who is bitten by a snake fears a lizard.

BUGANDA

The dog's bark is not might, but fright.

MADAGASCAR

The fear of the Lord does not consist of protecting devils. Should the lives of such creatures be spared? Are God and mammon in league? What has the Lord to do with a gang of desperate wretches who go sneaking about the country like robbers?

DAVID WALKER, *Appeal to the Coloured Citizens of the World*, 1829

Fearlessness is the first requisite of spirituality. Cowards can never be moral.

MOHANDAS GANDHI, 1910

We have allowed cowardice and fear to take possession of us for a long time, but that will never take us anywhere. It is no use being afraid of these nations and their people. They are human beings just like us. We have blood, feelings, passions, and ambitions. Why should we allow them to trample down our rights and deprive us of our liberty?

MARCUS GARVEY, *Africa's Wealth,* 1923

Men are apt to idolize or fear that which they cannot understand, especially if it be a woman.

JEAN TOOMER, *Fern,* 1923

Fear is a noose that binds until it strangles.

JEAN TOOMER, *Essentials,* 1931

Because they are afraid of us, we are afraid of them.

RICHARD WRIGHT, *12 Million Black Voices,* 1941

I am one of those troubled hearts,/ Fearing the night, fearing the day.

RENÉ MARAN, "Human Soul," *Five French Negro Poets,* 1943

There can be no courage without fear, and fear comes only from the imagination.

PETER ABRAHAMS, *Mine Boy,* 1954

No man lives in safety as long as his brother is in fear.

WILLIAM BRANCH, *In Splendid Error,* 1954

When he has conquered fear, a new dimension is added to his personality. He has lived this period. He has experienced the terror and the exultation. At the root of his being, he has experienced deep ecstasy. He is a human volcano.

PEARL PRIMUS, "African Dance," American Society of African Culture, 1959

You fear and love the white Christian though you are even disgraced and killed by them—from your ministers of their slavery religion down to the lowly, ignorant man in the mud.

ELIJAH MUHAMMAD, *Black Muslims in America,* 1961

To defend oneself against a fear is simply to insure that one will, one day, be conquered by it; fears must be faced.

JAMES BALDWIN, *The Fire Next Time,* 1963

I have seen these fears of social change operate many times, where, under the influence of mob psychology, rational people became irrational, and some of the same people who in other periods had suffered severely because of hate and bigotry became the perpetrators of injustice to others.

WHITNEY YOUNG, *To Be Equal,* 1964

Fear is a two-edged sword that sometimes cuts the wielder.

JACKIE ROBINSON, *Baseball Has Done It,* 1964

If you are not afraid to look back, nothing you are facing can frighten you.

JAMES BALDWIN, in "Why I Left America," *Essence,* October 1970

Our greatest fears are often of things that do not happen.

BENJAMIN MAYS, *Born to Rebel,* 1971

To be afraid is to behave as if the truth were not true.

BAYARD RUSTIN, "Meaning of Birmingham," *Liberator,* June 1973

Fear of losing is what makes competitors so great. Show me a gracious loser and I'll show you a perennial loser.

O. J. SIMPSON, c. 1976

Animals can sense fear. They feel it. . . . Never, never let a person know you're frightened . . . and absolutely never [a group]. Fear brings out the worst thing in everybody.

MAYA ANGELOU, *The Heart of a Woman,* 1981

I was frightened, but I figured we needed help to get us more jobs and better education.

ROSA PARKS, in Oates, *Let The Trumpet Sound,* 1982

I sometimes fear for the future. I fear for the wave of violence that may engulf us and sweep away whatever dreams we may have for our children. I fear for that insidious destruction of violence that destroys the soul, even as much as it has destroyed the soul of white South Africa.

ALLAN BOESAK, "Who Can Speak for South Africa?" *Crisis*, November 1986

Fear cannot live with faith.

CHARLES G. ADAMS, sermon given at Hartford Church, Detroit, Michigan, 1987

Fear and terror scrape out the bottom of one's soul.

ANTHONY SLOANE, *A Mystic Wind*, 1988

[I]f you let them,/ They will use your fears against you,/ Your lack of daring against you,/ Your respectability against you,/ . . . Your craving for trinkets against you,/ Your thirst for their praise against you,/ Your hunger for their world against you,/ Your contempt for your own against you, / . . . Your sense of self-shame against you,/ . . . Your legendary patience against you,/ . . . And they'll stuff your mouths once more/ With glass shards of defeat, / And force you to swallow them.

CHINWEIZU, "Admonition to the Black World," in *Voices from Twentieth-Century Africa*, 1988

You tend to be afraid when someone seems foreign to you. But if you aren't careful, that can lead to bigotry.

JASMINE GUY, in "Spotlight: Jasmine Guy," *Essence*, August 1988

For Bleek, every moment of his life is mapped out. He can only give so much to other people. He's afraid that someone, mainly one of his women friends, will take away his God-given talent.

JOIE LEE, in Spike Lee, *Mo' Better Blues*, 1990

FEELING

Every man who wishes to master his house must first master his emotions.

EGYPT

[T]here is nothing in the world so monstrously vast as our indifference.

JOAQUIM MACHADO DE ASSIS, *Epitaph for a Small Winner*, 1881

Have some sympathy . . . put me down easy . . . I'm a cracked plate.

ZORA NEALE HURSTON, *Their Eyes Were Watching God*, 1937

More than anything else, as a writer, I was fascinated by the similarity of the emotional tensions of Bigger in America and Bigger in Nazi Germany and Bigger in old Russia. All Bigger Thomases, white and black, felt tense, afraid, nervous, hysterical, and restless.

RICHARD WRIGHT, "How Bigger Was Born," *Saturday Review*, 1 June 1940

[W]atch the real bourgeois Black American. He never wants to show any sign of emotion. You can have some of that real soul music, and he won't even tap his feet . . . like it doesn't move him.

MALCOLM X, speech given at the Organization of Afro-American Unity Rally, Audubon Ballroom, New York City, 24 January 1965

Feelings may twist, but the lack of it may twist it even more.

JAMES CONE, *Black Theology and Black Power*, 1969

Ecstasy is a full deep involvement in life.

JOHN LOVELL, *Black Song*, 1972

I used to be very cold. When you are cold you miss passion in your life. I went for years just like ice. I was killing myself. I was not loving back.

LENA HORNE, in *USA Today*, 27 May 1983

Folks bring their pain, their insecurities, and their crazies with them wherever they go—to work, to church, to meetings, to relationships. How we treat one another reflects how we feel about ourselves.

SUSAN TAYLOR, c. 1987

If a dear one dies I weep without shame;/ If someone jokes I laugh with all my heart./ They stifle a tear as if to cry was something wrong/ But they also stifle a laugh,/ As if to laugh was something wrong, too. No wonder they need psychiatrists!

PAUL CHIDYAUSIKU, "Grandpa," in Chinweizu, ed., *Voices from Twentieth-Century Africa,* 1988

FIGHT

I am the mongrel Antar! Every man defends his woman, whether she be black or white, whether she be smooth or hairy.

ANTAR, 600 B.C.

If two refuse, no one fights.

JOAQUIM MACHADO DE ASSIS, *Esau and Jacob,* 1904

And the oppressed, groaning under the lash, evinced the same despicable hate and harshness toward the weaker fellows. I ceased to think of people and things in the mass—why should I fight with mad dogs only to be bitten and transformed into a mad dog myself?

CLAUDE MCKAY, "A Negro Poet Writes," *Pearson's Magazine,* September 1918

We are not fighting any race, we are simply looking for our own. The first law of nature is self-preservation.

MARY WASHINGTON, in the *Union Paper,* 16 September 1922

Never in the world should we fight against association with ourselves.

W. E. B. DU BOIS, "Separation and Self-Respect," *Crisis,* March 1935

Fighting is a game where everybody is the loser.

ZORA NEALE HURSTON, *Moses, Man of the Mountain,* 1939

We must fight as a race for everything that makes for a better country and a better world. We are dreaming idiots and trusting fools to do anything less.

RALPH BUNCHE, c. 1944

We Negroes are not fighting against . . . slavery. That fight is won. . . . [W]e are fighting . . . desperately the economic battle for the right to work and to get from our work food, housing, education, health and a chance to live as human beings.

W. E. B. DU BOIS, "On the Future of the American Negro," 1953

And in his fight to be free he would not counter bigotry with more bigotry, prejudice with more prejudice. He would know that to do so would be to lose for his fight its contact with history, with the two-thousand-year-old journey of man from darkness to the stars. And if he loses that contact, the battle will be lost, though won.

PETER ABRAHAMS, *Return to Goli,* 1953

Like men we'll face the murderous, cowardly pack, / Pressed to the wall, dying, but fighting back!

CLAUDE MCKAY, "If We Must Die," *Selected Poems,* 1953

Sometimes it's worse to win a fight than to lose.

BILLIE HOLIDAY, *Lady Sings the Blues,* 1956

If it cost me my life in the morning I will tell you tonight that the time has come for the Black man to die fighting. If he's going to die, die fighting.

MALCOLM X, C. 1964

Along with the fight to desegregate schools, we must desegregate the entire cultural statement of America, we must desegregate the minds of the American people or we will find that we have won the battle and lost the war.

JOHN KILLENS, "White Backlash and the Black Revolution," speech given at Town Hall Forum, New York City, 15 June 1964

If something is yours by right, then fight for it or shut up. If you can't fight for it, then forget it.

MALCOLM X, speech given at the London School of Economics, February 1965

It is in the nature of the American Negro, the same as all other men, to fight and try to destroy those things that block his path to a greater happiness in life.

ROBERT WILLIAMS, "USA, The Potential of a Minority Revolution," *The Crusader Monthly Newsletter,* May–June 1965

Our people fight daily and magnificently for a more comfortable material base for their lives, clean homes, decent food, and dignity.

LORRAINE HANSBERRY, *Les Blancs,* 1972

Early on in the music business I learned to enter certain fights, swinging with all I got, and to avoid others, knowing that I wouldn't accomplish anything even if I won.

RAY CHARLES, *Brother Ray,* 1978

We have had to fight because we couldn't switch.

JANICE HALE BENSON, *Black Child in Education,* 1986

FINANCE

See also MONEY

At the bottom of education, at the bottom of politics, even at the bottom of religion, there must be economic independence.

BOOKER T. WASHINGTON, C. 1903

Black colleges took students no other college would accept, and created teachers and preachers and healers because they did this work for one hundred years with inadequate funds and because they are still doing it with inadequate funds our Black institutions have a claim on our attention and our resources.

LERONE BENNETT, in *Choosing to Succeed,* 1986

We must take the profit out of prejudice.

COLEMAN YOUNG, c. 1987

I was able to convince a loan company to loan me $500 on my mother's furniture, which we used as collateral. I used it to buy direct mail literature which I sent out to 20,000 names from insurance companies. Three thousand answered and sent me $2.00 each and with $6,000 I published my first edition of *Negro Digest* in November, 1942.

JOHN H. JOHNSON, in "Interview: John H. Johnson," *Crisis,* January 1987

Black entrepreneurs start backing Black films, Black independent filmmakers need financial backers.

SPIKE LEE, in *Ebony,* August 1987

You're under incredible financial pressure to make something work. It's a very delicate process to write something, put it on its feet, and not make mistakes.

NTOZAKE SHANGE, in *American Visions,* October 1987

FLOWER(S)

I come to the Garden alone/ while the dew is still on the roses/ And the voice I hear falling on my ear / The son of God discloses . . .

SPIRITUAL

The flowers take the tears/ of the weeping night/ And give them to the sun/ for the day's delight.

JOSEPH S. COTTER, SR., c. 1900

Somehow we feel that through a rose the language of love reaches our heart. Do we carry a rose to our beloved because in it is already embodied a message which cannot be analyzed.

RABINDRANATH TAGORE, *Sidhana,* 1912

How shall we crown her bright young head?/ Crown it with roses, rare and red;/ Crown it with roses, creamy white,/ As the lotus blooms that sweetens the night./ Crown it with roses as pink as shell/ In which the voices of ocean dwell.

ANGELINA W. GRIMKÉ, *From a June Song,* 1921

A slight pretty flower that grows on any ground, and flowers pledge no allegiance to banners of any man.

ALICE WALKER, "The Child Who Favored Daughter," *In Love and Troubles: Stories of Black Women,* 1973

For thirty-one years he planted roses,/until the withered structure of the house/became thorned flesh,/At night he would lie/exhausted and crucified.

HENRY DUMAS, "Rose Jungle," *Play Ebony Play Ivory,* 1974

Paul D . . . was the first to smell the doomed roses . . . the closer the roses got to death, the louder their scent . . . but it did nothing to extinguish the eagerness of the colored people filing down the road.

TONI MORRISON, *Beloved,* 1987

FLY

Stretch your mind and fly.

TRADITIONAL

Airplanes may kill you, but they ain't likely to hurt you.

LEROY "SATCHEL" PAIGE, c. 1959

Drifting night in the Georgia pines,/ coonskin drum and jubilee banjo./ Pretty Malinda, dance with me. . . ./ O fly away home fly away.

ROBERT HAYDEN, "O Daedalus, Fly Away Home," *A Ballad of Remembrance,* 1962

Every time I take a flight I am always mindful of the many people who make a successful journey possible, the known pilots and the unknown ground crew.

MARTIN LUTHER KING, JR., Nobel Prize Acceptance Speech, 10 December 1964

I'd fly if you tell me what happens in the second hour on a plane that doesn't happen in the first.

DUKE ELLINGTON, August 1972

Sugarman done fly away/ Sugarman done gone/Sugarman cut across the sky/ Sugarman gone home.

TONI MORRISON, *Song of Solomon,* 1977

I was ninety when I started flying; and that did so much for me.

EUBIE BLAKE, *Eubie,* 1979

We have already done so much that people call dynamics. Look at the bumblebee being unaware of scientific truths, goes ahead and flies anyway. If it is possible, we will do it here.

TOM BRADLEY, *The Impossible Dream,* 1986

Most of the details of [my] first flight are lost to me. . . . About all I really remember are the takeoff and the feeling of exhilaration, . . . looking down on the city of Washington and up at the white clouds. . . . And I remember a sudden surge of determination to become an aviator.

BENJAMIN DAVIS, JR., *Benjamin Davis, Jr.: An Autobiography,* 1990

FOOL

When a fool is told a proverb its meaning has to be explained to him.

ASHANTI

By the time the fool has learned the game, the players have dispersed.

ASHANTI

The fool is thirsty in the midst of water.

ETHIOPIA

He who attempts to shake a stump only shakes himself.

IBO

My mama didn't raise no fool.

TRADITIONAL

The Americans say that we are ungrateful—but I ask them for heaven's sake, what should we be grateful to them for—for murdering our fathers and mothers?—Or do they wish us to return thanks to them for chaining and handcuffing us, branding us, cramming fire down our throats, or for keeping us in slavery, and beating us nearly or quite to death to make us work in ignorance and miseries, to support them and their families. They certainly think that we are a gang of fools.

DAVID WALKER, *Appeal to the Coloured Citizens of the World,* 1829

You are fools. You cannot see the face of your chief; your eyes are full of smoke. You cannot hear his voice; your ears are full of roaring waters. Braves, you are little children—you are fools. You will die like the rabbits when the hungry wolves hunt them in the Hard Moon of January.

WAMDITANKA (BIG EAGLE) OF THE SANTEE SIOUX, "Big Eagle's Story of the Sioux Outbreak of 1862," *Collections,* 1894

Angels rush in when fool is almost dead.

RUDOLPH FISHER, *Blades of Steel,* 1927

Silence is all the genius a fool has.

ZORA NEALE HURSTON, *Moses, Man of the Mountain,* 1939

Above all don't become know-alls, for nothing is more objectionable and nothing makes us look more a fool.

KWAME NKRUMAH, speech given at Adisodel College, 10 November 1955

There are some people that if they don't know, you can't tell 'em.

LOUIS ARMSTRONG, c. 1956

I wanted to be a comedian. But what does that mean to people? My mother would always cry, "Oh, he makes a fool of himself and gets paid for it."

BILL COSBY, in *Scholastic,* 11 November 1977

Gambling is basically a foolish vice. It's like diving into an empty swimming pool. The chances that you'll hit bottom are about the same.

MUHAMMAD ALI, c. 1978

When you come across a fool who can't help himself, always remember that he's a fool. Don't bother with him. On up the road he's liable to run into another fool, and one of them will destroy the other.

CHARLIE RUSSELL, in Bill Russell, *Second Wind,* 1979

People do not wish to appear foolish; to avoid the appearance of foolishness, they were willing actually to remain fools.

ALICE WALKER, *In Search of Our Mothers' Gardens,* 1983

FREEDOM

He who is free of faults will never die.

CONGO

A fish that once frees itself from the hook/ Will swim away never to return.

AFRICA

Oh freedom oh freedom, oh freedom over me/ And before I'd be a slave I'll be buried in my grave/ And go home to my Lord and be free.

TRADITIONAL

We have dared to be free; let us dare to be so by ourselves and for ourselves.

JEAN DESSALINES, Proclamation of Haitian Liberation, 1 January 1840

I was free, but there was no one to welcome me to the land of freedom. I was a stranger in a strange land.

HARRIET TUBMAN, c. 1845

O Freedom! Freedom! Oh, how oft/ Thy loving children call on thee!/ In wailings loud and breathing soft,/ Beseeching God, thy face to see.

CHARLES L. REASON, *Freedom,* 1847

In passing from place to place, and seeing new faces every day, and knowing they could go as they pleased, I soon became unhappy, and thought of leaving the boat . . . and making my escape to Canada.

WILLIAM WELLS-BROWN, *Narrative of the Life of William Wells-Brown,* 1856

While at the wheel of the Planter as pilot in the rebel service, it occurred to me that I could not only secure my own freedom but that of numbers of my comrades in bonds, and I thought the Planter might be of some use to Uncle Abe.

ROBERT SMALLS, c. 1864

I freed thousands of slaves, I could have freed thousands more, if they had known they were slaves.

HARRIET TUBMAN, c. 1865

The Fourth of July—memorable in the history of our nation as the great day of independence to its countrymen—had no claim upon our sympathies. They made a flag and threw it to the heavens and bid it float forever; but every star in it was against us.

HENRY MCNEAL TURNER, speech given on the anniversary of Emancipation Day, Augusta, Georgia, 1 January 1866

You might as well expect the rivers to run backward as that any man who was born a free man should be contented when penned up and denied liberty to go where he pleases . . . I have asked some of the white chiefs where they get their authority to say to the Indian that he shall stay in one place, while he sees white men going where they please. They cannot tell me.

HIGHN'MOOT TOOYALAKET (CHIEF JOSEPH) OF THE NEZ PERCES, "An Indian's View of Indian Affairs," *North American Review,* 1879

Let me be a free man—free to travel, free to stop, free to work, free to trade where I choose, free to choose my own teachers, free to follow the religion of my fathers, free to think and talk and act for myself—and I will obey your laws, or submit to the penalty.

Ibid.

Freedom is a state of mind: a spiritual unchoking of the wells of human power and superhuman love.

W. E. B. DU BOIS, "Free, White and Twenty-One," *Crisis,* 1914

Freedom is the most precious of our treasures, and it will not be allowed to vanish so long as men survive who offered their lives for it.

PAUL ROBESON, valedictory speech, Rutgers University, New Brunswick, New Jersey, 1919

Black men and Black men alone, hold the key to the gateway leading to their freedom.

MARCUS GARVEY, *Philosophy and Opinions of Marcus Garvey,* 1923

I can come when I please/ I can go when I please/ I can flit, fly, and flutter, like the birds in the trees.

ETHEL WATERS, *His Eye Is on the Sparrow,* 1925

No man may make another free. Freedom was something internal. The outside signs were just signs and symbols of the man inside. All you could do was to give the opportunity for freedom and the man himself must make his own emancipation.

ZORA NEALE HURSTON, *Moses, Man of the Mountain,* 1939

The song of freedom must prevail.

PAUL ROBESON, c. 1942

Upright and free and the lustral ship advance unafraid.

AIMÉ CÉSAIRE, *Notes on a Return to the Native Land,* 1947

Freedom is a precarious thing, a sometime thing, a completely unpredictable quantity.

SAUNDERS REDDING, *They Came in Chains,* 1950

I refuse to answer under the First Amendment provision of speech, sanctity, and privacy of political beliefs and since I have no purpose of being a stool pigeon.

COLEMAN YOUNG, testimony before the House Un-American Activities Committee, 28 February 1952

Songs of liberation—who can lock them up? The spirit of freedom—who can jail it? A people's unity—what lash can beat it down? Civil rights—what doubletalk can satisfy our need?

PAUL ROBESON, "A Lesson from Our South African Brothers and Sisters," *Freedom,* September 1952

Freedom is a precious thing, and the inalienable birthright of all who travel this earth.

PAUL ROBESON, foreword to *Born of the People,* 1953

To be free means the ability to deal with the realities of one's situation so as not to be overcome by them.

HOWARD THURMAN, *Meditations of the Heart,* 1953

It is only those who are free inside who can help those around them.

PETER ABRAHAMS, *Mine Boy,* 1954

How long this night when no man walks in freedom, without fear in this cradle of democracy, no man who's Black? How will it happen, and what will we have to do? Nat Turner tried it with guns and he failed. Dred Scott went to the high courts and they hurled him back into slavery. Old John said it must be by blood, and tonight he lies wounded in a Virginia prison. When will it end—how long this night?

WILLIAM BRANCH, *In Splendid Error,* 1954

Let us make our intentions crystal clear. We must and we will be free. We want freedom now. We do not want our freedom fed to us in teaspoons over another one hundred fifty years. Under God we were born free. Misguided men robbed us of our freedom. We want it back.

MARTIN LUTHER KING, JR., speech given at the Southern Christian Leadership Conference Crusade for Citizenship, 12 February 1958

I, breathing the new air of freedom, and now the barrel of gall has no bottom any more. I shall soon know what to do with this freedom.

EZEKIEL MPHAHLELE, *Down Second Avenue,* 1959

Freedom is not free.

MARTIN LUTHER KING, JR., speech given in Montgomery, Alabama, 3 December 1959

[F]reedom is the fire which burns away illusion.

JAMES BALDWIN, *Nobody Knows My Name,* 1961

To a degree academic freedom is a reality today because Socrates practiced civil disobedience.

MARTIN LUTHER KING, JR., "Love, Law, and Civil Disobedience," speech given to Fellowship of the Concerned, 16 November 1961

We are seeking an open society of freedom where people will be accepted for what they are worth, will be able to contribute fully to the total culture and life of the nation.

JAMES FARMER, in "Malcolm and James Farmer: A Debate," *Dialogue,* May 1962

One can give nothing whatever without giving oneself.... If one cannot risk oneself, then one is simply incapable of giving. And, after all, one can give freedom only by setting someone free.

JAMES BALDWIN, *The Fire Next Time,* 1963

The most rewarding freedom is freedom of the mind.

AMY GARVEY, *Garvey and Garveyism,* 1963

Toussaint L'Ouverture and the Haitian slaves brought into the world more than the abolition of slavery. When Latin Americans saw that small and insignificant Haiti could win and keep independence they began to think that they ought to be able to do the same.

C. L. R. JAMES, *The Black Jacobins,* 1963

The price of freedom is death.

MALCOLM X, speech given in New York City, 5 June 1964

One thing I became aware of in traveling recently through Africa and the Middle East . . . usually the degree of progress can never be separated from the woman. If you're in a country that's progressive, the woman is progressive. If you're in a country that reflects the consciousness toward the importance of education, it's because the woman is aware of the importance of education. But in every backward country . . . where education is not stressed it's because the women don't have education. So . . . I [am] convinced of . . . the importance of giving freedom to the woman, giving her education, and giving her the incentive to . . . put that same spirit and understanding in [her] children.

MALCOLM X, interview given in Paris, November 1964

What we are seeing now is a freedom explosion.... The deep rumbling of discontent that we hear today is the thunder of the disinherited masses, rising from dungeons of oppression to the bright hills of freedom.... All over the world, like a fever, the freedom movement is spreading in the widest liberation in history.

MARTIN LUTHER KING, JR., "Quest for Peace and Justice," Nobel Lecture, 11 December 1964

You don't have to be a man to fight for freedom. All you have to do is be an intelligent human being.

MALCOLM X, "with Mrs. Fannie Hall Hamer," speech given in New York City, 20 December 1964

What a tiresome place America would be if freedom meant we had to think alike and be the same color and wear the same gray flannel suit. That road leads to the conformity of the graveyard!

JOHN KILLENS, *Black Man's Burden,* 1965

Only when it is dark enough can you see the stars. And I see God working in this period of the twentieth century in a way that men are responding. Something is happening in our world. The masses of people are rising up, whether they are in Johannesburg, Nairobi, Atlanta, Jackson, or Memphis, the cry is always the same: We want to be free.

MARTIN LUTHER KING, JR., c. 1966

To be born in a free society and not be born free is to be born into a lie. To be told by co-citizens and co-Christians that you have no value, no history, have never done anything that is worthy of human respect destroys you because in the beginning you believe it.

JAMES BALDWIN, in "James Baldwin . . . in Conversation," *Arts in Society,* Summer 1966

A piece of freedom is no longer enough for human beings; freedom is like life. It cannot be had in installments.

Ibid.

A man is free or he is not. There cannot be any apprenticeship for freedom.

LEROI JONES, *Home: Social Essays,* 1966

Our freedom was not won a century ago, and it is not won today; but some small part of it is in our hands, and we are marching no longer by ones and twos but in legions of thousands, convinced it cannot be denied by any human force.

MARTIN LUTHER KING, JR., c. 1967

Freedom is an internal achievement rather than an external adjustment.

ADAM CLAYTON POWELL, JR., "Man's Debt to God," *Keep the Faith, Baby,* 1967

No attempt must be made to encase man, for it is his destiny to be set free.

FRANTZ FANON, *Black Skin, White Masks,* 1967

It is by risking life that freedom is obtained.

Ibid.

When I liberate others, I liberate myself.

FANNIE LOU HAMER, c. 1969

A man is free when he can determine the style of his existence in an absurd world. A man is free when he sees himself for what he is and not as others define him.

JAMES CONE, *Black Theology and Black Power,* 1969

I was born upon the prairie, where the wind blew free and there was nothing to break the light of the sun. I was born where there were no enclosures and where everything drew a free breath. I want to die there and not within walls of a reservation.

PARRA-WA SAMEN (TEN BEARS) OF THE UAMPARIKA COMMANCHES, in Brown, *Bury My Heart at Wounded Knee,* 1971

If a person is to be freed from his frustrations and insecurities, he must surrender to something larger than himself.

HERMAN WATTS, *"What Is Your Name?* in Philpot, ed., *Best Black Sermons,* 1972

Freedom from hate unconditionally, freedom from self pity. Freedom from the fear of doing something that would help someone else more than me. Freedom from the kind of pride that makes me feel I am better than my brother.

DUKE ELLINGTON, *Music Is My Mistress,* 1973

Who ever walked behind anyone to freedom? If we can't go hand in hand, I don't want to go.

HAZEL SCOTT, in "Great (Hazel) Scott!" *Ms.,* November 1974

The price of freedom is not only eternal vigilance, but eternally to have the necessary manpower in terms of your alliances to maintain your freedom.

COLEMAN YOUNG, c. 1977

Those who would be called tyrants cannot be called free men.

NATHAN HUGGINS, *Black Odyssey,* 1977

Only through hardship, sacrifice, and militant action can freedom be won. The struggle is my life. I will continue fighting for freedom until the end of my days.

NELSON MANDELA, *The Struggle Is My Life,* 1978

The desire for freedom is overpowering, like a drowning man's need for air. You have to reach inside yourself for all the strength and independence you have. It takes a lot of strength not to drown and not to be a slave, and the fight can be lonely.

BILL RUSSELL, *Second Wind,* 1979

All my limitations are self-imposed, and my liberation can only come from true self-love.

MAX ROBINSON, c. 1981

For in the end, freedom is a personal and lonely battle and one faces down fears of today so that those of tomorrow might be engaged.

ALICE WALKER, *In Search of Our Mothers' Gardens,* 1983

Freedom is indivisible. Whites can't enjoy their separate freedoms. They spend too much time and resources defending those freedoms instead of enjoying them.

DESMOND TUTU, *Hope and Suffering,* 1983

Freedom is only sweet when it is won. When it is forced, it is called responsibility.

TONI MORRISON, "Rootedness: The Ancestor as Foundation," in Evans, ed., *Black Women Writers,* 1984

The color of freedom is green.

TONY BROWN, IN *USA Today,* 22 October 1985

Unless we understand freedom in terms other than achieving, materially, what our oppressors have achieved, we may be guilty of actively working for our own demise. What we may spend a whole history struggling to obtain may prove to have little ultimate meaning.

BILL HOWARD, in "Where Have All the Heroes Gone?" *Essence,* November 1985

Freeing yourself was one thing, claiming ownership of that freed self was another.

TONI MORRISON, *Beloved,* 1987

The struggle for freedom is part of our common heritage.

STEVEN BARBOZOA, in *American Visions,* February 1987

All of us are free as long as no one tramples on us.

TESS ONWUEME, in "The Broken Calabash," *City Arts Quarterly,* Spring 1988

What's beautiful about America is the freedom.

RAY CHARLES, in "Ray Charles Sees the Beauty," *Parade,* 10 October 1988

I don't want to be trapped into one particular thing.

PRINCE, in "What U See Is What U Get," *Essence,* November 1988

[F]reedom was the fact that no leaf fell, no word was uttered or deed executed that did not echo eternally throughout the universe.

CHARLES JOHNSON, *Middle Passage,* 1990

I cherish my own freedom dearly but I care even more for your freedom. Too many have died since I went to prison. Too many have suffered for the love of freedom. I owe it to their widows, to their orphans, to their mothers and to their fathers who have grieved and wept. Not only I have suffered during these long, lonely, wasted years.

NELSON MANDELA, *Higher Than Hope,* 1991

FRIENDS

Equals make the best friends.

AESOP, "The Two Pots," c. 300 B.C.

Friendship takes fear from the heart.

Mahabharata, 5–1 B.C.

The friends of our friends are our friends.

CONGO

A close friend can become a close enemy.

ETHIOPIA

The enemy of my enemy is my friend.

NIGERIA

An intelligent enemy is better than a stupid friend.

SENEGAL

When you know who his friend is, you know who he is.

SENEGAL

When I had money,/ had friends for miles around/ now ain't got no money,/ friends cannot be found.

TRADITIONAL

Everybody that grins in your face ain't no friend to you.

TRADITIONAL

He has nothing but "friends" and may the good God deliver him from most of them for they are like to lynch his soul.

W. E. B. DU BOIS, "The Philosophy of Mr. Dole," *Crisis,* 1914

True friendship is an identity of souls rarely to be found in the world. Only between like natures can friendships be altogether worthy and enduring.

MOHANDAS GANDHI, in Erikson, *Gandhi's Truth,* 1937

A person without friends might as well be dead.

BILLIE HOLIDAY, c. 1945

I wore out a couple of generations of friends, but I've still got so many.

EUBIE BLAKE, *Eubie,* 1979

No person is your friend (or kin) who demands your silence, or denies your right to grow and be perceived as fully blossomed as you were intended.

ALICE WALKER, *In Search of Our Mothers' Gardens,* 1983

Being a friend means mastering the art of timing. There is a time for silence. A time to let go and allow people to hurl themselves into their own history. And a time to pick up the pieces when it's all over.

GLORIA NAYLOR, *The Women of Brewster Place,* 1988

Friends are my heart and my ears.

MICHAEL JORDAN, in "Michael Jordan in His Own Orbit," *GQ,* March 1989

FUNERAL

Let us hold up our heads and with firm and steady tread go manfully forward. No one likes to feel that he is continually following a funeral procession.

BOOKER T. WASHINGTON, speech given in Louisville, Kentucky, 1903

Black people have always clung to a genuine love for each other. That's why a funeral said so much. You can't let this person die as though it was nothing happening. A great loss had been suffered. I learned to cry at funerals.

VERNON JARRETT, c. 1979

Once the band starts, everybody starts swaying from one side of the street to the other, especially those who drop in and follow the ones who have been to the funeral. These are known as the second line and they may be anyone passing along who wants to hear the music. The spirit hits them and they follow.

LOUIS ARMSTRONG, *Autobiography,* 1979

At the end,/ One day I shall shut my eyes and close my mouth/ . . . And my feet shall be made ready for a journey./ On that day shall I be an object of public display/ . . . Both in the sky and on earth./ On that day I shall refuse food/ That there might be enough for the living./ On that day my kinfolk shall assemble./ Those who do not know me shall come to know me;/ My enemies shall come to see/ . . . / And those who do not know me/ Shall call out my praise names. . . .

NNAMDI OLEBARA, "At the End," in Chinweizu, ed., *Voices from Twentieth-Century Africa,* 1988

FUTURE

Where there is no future, there is no hope.

EDWARD WILMOT BLYDEN, "Our Origins, Dangers, and Duties," speech given on Independence Day, Monrovia, Liberia, 26 July 1865

Leave it to the future. When the war is over, the country saved, peace established, and the Black man's rights are secured, as they will be, history with an impartial hand will dispose of that and sundry other questions.

FREDERICK DOUGLASS, *Life and Times of Frederick Douglass,* 1892

[M]y future depends mostly upon myself.

PAUL ROBESON, in "An Actor's Wanderings and Hopes," *The Messenger,* October 1924

Nothing the future brings can defeat a people who have come through three hundred years of slavery and humiliation and privation with heads high and eyes clear and straight.

PAUL ROBESON, "We Must Come South," speech given in New Orleans, Louisiana, 29 October 1942

The future of American Negroes is in the South. Here three hundred twenty-seven years ago, they began to enter what is now the United States of America; . . . here they have suffered the damnation of slavery, the frustration of Reconstruction and the lynching of emancipation.

W. E. B. DU BOIS, "Behold the Land," speech given to Southern Town Legislature, Columbia, South Carolina, 20 October 1946

The future is uncertain to us. We are blinded by the night, we are blinded by the mystery of history, we are blinded by the density of time.

C. L. FRANKLIN, "Watchman, What of the Night?" c. 1953

Sometimes, I can see the future stretched out in front of me—just as plain as day. The future hanging over there at the edge of my days. Just waiting for me.

LORRAINE HANSBERRY, *A Raisin in the Sun,* 1959

[T]he future is like heaven—everyone exalts it but no one wants to go there now.

JAMES BALDWIN, *Nobody Knows My Name,* 1961

Whatever future America will have will be directly related to the solving of its racial dilemma, which is a human dilemma.

JOHN WILLIAMS, *Beyond the Angry Black,* 1966

The present will always contribute to the building of the future.

FRANTZ FANON, *Black Skin, White Masks,* 1967

If there is no future for the Black ghetto, the future of all Negroes is diminished. What affects it, affects me, for I am a child of the ghetto.

STANLEY SANDERS, "I'll Never Escape the Ghetto," in *Black Voices,* 1971

He had no future in the past, because once you leave, you cannot really go back.

JAMES BALDWIN, *A Rap on Race,* 1971

If a young man tells me what he aspires to be, I can almost predict his future

BENJAMIN MAYS, *Born to Rebel,* 1971

Only an omniscient God can predict the future.

Ibid.

The perfection of the white future was a white death: the death of a culture based on a central human nature, exclusive of all things that did not fit its optimism, its abolishment of the tragic sphere, its religion of progress, its disregard for both the fullness of the instant and the presentness of the past, its deliberate ignorance of the cultures foreign to its particular reason.

CARLOS FUENTES, "Central and Eccentric Writing," *The American Magazine,* 21 October 1974

I don't believe in planning for the future. I believe in planning for now.

RAY CHARLES, *Brother Ray,* 1978

I'm into now and the future.

COLEMAN YOUNG, c. 1980

All futures are erected out of a past.

ASA HILLIARD, "Pedagogy of Ancient Kemet" in Karanga and Carruthers, eds., *Kemet and the African Worldview,* 1986

When I look at the future it's so bright it burns my eyes.

OPRAH WINFREY, "Quotable Quotes," *Reader's Digest,* February 1988

The future must be planned today. We may never see it in our lifetime, but the success of our ventures will impact future generations.

L. DOUGLASS WILDER, in "Virginia's Lieutenant Governor L. Douglass Wilder Is First Black to Win Office," *Ebony,* April 1988

The future of the nation is on the shoulders of teachers and how they teach kids; the future of the world is in the classroom where the teachers are. And if we have any chance to guarantee a positive bridge to the 21st century, it is how we educate the children in the classrooms today.

RICHARD GREEN, in "Dr. Richard Green: Chancellor of New York City Schools," *Ebony,* August 1988

GARVEY, MARCUS

What [Garvey] is trying to say and do is this: American Negroes can, by accumulating and ministering their own capital, organize industry, join the black centers of the south Atlantic by commercial enterprise and in this way ultimately redeem Africa as a fit and free home for black men. This is true. It is *feasible*. It is, in a sense, practical. . . .

W. E. B. Du Bois, "Marcus Garvey," *Crisis*, December 1920

Outsiders will never understand the psychology of these they call Garveyites. We doubt if we who are thus nicknamed understand it ourselves. The binding spell, the indefinable charm which Mr. Garvey exercises over us. . . . But we find reason for it in our conviction that no man has spoken to us like this man, inculcating pride and nobility of race, and clearly pointing out the Star of Hope to a discouraged and downtrodden people.

George Alexander McGuire, in *The Negro Churchman*, September 1923

Marcus Garvey opened windows in the minds of Negroes.

Garveyite, 1925

Garvey made thousands think who had never thought before. Thousands who merely dreamed, now see visions.

Garveyite, 1925

Garveyism may be a transient, if spectacular, phenomenon, but the possible role of American Negroes in the future development of Africa is one of the most constructive and universally helpful missions that any modern people can lay claim to.

Alain Locke, *Enter the New Negro*, 1925

Marcus Garvey made Black people proud of their race. In a world where black is despised, he taught them that Black is beautiful, he taught them to admire and praise Black things and Black people. They rallied to him because he heard and responded to the heartbeat of his race.

Amsterdam News, 2 February 1925

Garvey failed; but he might have succeeded with more than moderate success. He had energy and daring and the Napoleonic personality, the personality that draws masses of followers. He stirred the imagination of the Negro masses as no Negro ever had. He raised more money in a few years than any other Negro organization had ever dreamed of. He had power and great possibilities within his grasp.

James Weldon Johnson, *Black Manhattan*, 1930

The banishment of Garvey was epochal in its significance since it was the first time in American history that the federal government "paid a Negro the compliment" of banishment on account of his ideas or enterprise.

Kelly Miller, in the *Negro World*, 21 May 1932

Garvey's idea of a Black God aroused the Negroes to a sense of deep appreciation for his race and stimulated the Negro to work to improve his social and economic conditions.

Benjamin Mays, *The Negro's God as Reflected in His Literature*, 1938

There has never been a Negro leader like Garvey. None ever enjoyed a fraction of his universal popularity. He winged his way into the firmament of the white world holding aloft a black star and exhorting the Negro people to gaze upon and follow. His aspirations to reach dizzy heights and dazzle the vision of the Negro world does not remain monumental like the rugged path of the pioneer or of the hard calculating builder. But it survives in the memory like the spectacular swath of an unforgettable comet.

CLAUDE MCKAY, *Harlem: Negro Metropolis,* 1940

Garvey is regarded as a Black George Washington, the father of Jamaican Independence.

JOHN HOPE FRANKLIN, *From Slavery to Freedom,* 1947

The basis for Garvey's wide popularity was his appeal to race pride at a time when Negroes generally had so little to be proud of.

Ibid.

For thy redemption brave Garvey fell,/ But yet in the gang of the immortals,/ Thy sons shall fight unseen by mortals,/ And ere long regain thy pride, oh, Nigeria.

OSITA EGBUNIWE, "Nigeria, Oh My Nigeria," *Daily Comet,* 23 November 1948

Garvey was easily the most colorful figure to appear in America since the historic times of Frederick Douglass and Booker T. Washington.

CHICAGO DEFENDER, in Cronon, *Black Moses: The Story of Marcus Garvey,* 1955

Marcus Garvey captured the imagination of thousands, because he personified the possibility of the fulfillment of a dream latent in the heart of every Negro. I remember as a lad in Cleveland, Ohio, during the hungry days of 1921, standing on Central Avenue, watching a parade one Sunday afternoon when thousands of Garvey Legionnaires, resplendent in their uniforms, marched by. When Garvey rode by in his plumed hat, I got an emotional lift, which swept me up above the poverty and prejudice by which my life was limited.

JAMES H. ROBINSON, in the *Christian Century,* 8 June1955

Marcus Garvey gave . . . a sense of self-awareness, a sense of pride and dignity that largely overcame the inferiority complex bred by centuries of racial and color oppression. And since the first stage in any kind of liberation is the liberation of the mind, Marcus Garvey can justly be regarded as a primary source of the great freedom movements in the colonial world today.

PETER ABRAHAMS, *Public Opinion,* 3 November 1956

Long before any of us were conscious of our own degradation, Marcus Garvey fought for African national and racial equality.

KWAME NKRUMAH, speech given at All African People's Conference, Accra, Ghana, 13 December 1958

Garvey is giving my people backbones where they had wishbones.

GARVEYITE, in *Garvey and Garveyism,* 1963

Every time we see another nation on the African continent become independent, you know that Marcus Garvey is alive. It was Garvey's philosophy of Pan Africanism that initiated the entire freedom movement. . . . All freedom movements that are taking place right here in America today were initiated by the work and teachings of Marcus Garvey.

MALCOLM X, in the *Daily Gleaner* (Jamaica), 12 July 1964

Garvey was the first man of color in the history of the United States on a mass scale and level to give millions a sense of dignity and destiny . . . and make him feel like he was somebody.

MARTIN LUTHER KING, JR., speech given in Kingston, Jamaica, June 1965

Marcus Garvey was the first man to ever make "black" Negroes proud of their color.

ADAM CLAYTON POWELL, JR., *Adam by Adam,* 1971

GENIUS

My genius from a boy,/ Has fluttered like a bird within my heart;/ But could not thus confined her powers employ,/ Impatient to depart.

GEORGE MOSES HORTON, "Myself," *Poems by a Slave,* 1829

The man of genius does not steal, he conquers.

ALEXANDRE DUMAS, *My Memoirs,* 1831–32

Genius has no age, no country, no race; it belongs to mankind.

KELLY MILLER, *The American Negro,* 1908

Somehow we must harness man's genius for the purpose of making peace and prosperity a reality for all.

MARTIN LUTHER KING, JR., 1968

It was Charlie Parker's revolutionary approach to self, society, and existence that illuminates those brilliant arpeggios and lays the basis of his genius.

A. B. SPELLMAN, "Not Just Whistling Dixie," in Jones and Neal, eds. *Black Fire,* 1968

Black people have shown a genius for surviving under the most deadly circumstances. They have survived because of their close attention to reality.

WILLIAM GRIER and PRICE COBB, *Black Rage,* 1968

Through our scientific and technological genius, we have made of this world a neighborhood.

MARTIN LUTHER KING, JR., "Remaining Awake Through a Great Revolution," sermon given at National Cathedral (Episcopal), Washington, D.C., 31 March 1968

[G]enius [is] a person so locked in on one area of thought that he is consumed by it. One thought, one loyalty, one purpose is his. Indeed, he no longer holds an interest, but an interest seizes him and holds and claims him.

HERMAN W. WATTS, "What Is Your Name?" in Philpot, ed. *Best Black Sermons,* 1972

Pushkin . . . was a genius. In spite of all the obstacles he confronted throughout his life, through his writings he developed the standards and styles for Russian language and literature.

JAMES D. LOCKETT, "Alexander Sergevich Pushkin," *Negro History Bulletin,* July–September 1982

We are a people. A people do not throw their genius away. And if they are thrown away, it is our duty . . . *as witnesses for the future* to collect them again for the sake of our children, and, if necessary, bone by bone.

ALICE WALKER, *In Search of Our Mothers' Gardens,* 1983

How many geniuses do you get *anywhere*? And where *do* you find a first-class imagination? . . . Imagination is where you find it; thus we must search the whole scene.

RALPH ELLISON, "What These Children Are Like," *Going to the Territory,* 1986

Alvin Ailey is a generous genius and he's passed that on to his dancers.

JUDITH JAMISON, in interview on WDET (radio program), 1987

God didn't sprinkle genius on only one side of the race or the gender.

CLARENCE GLOVER, in "Spirituality: An African View," *Essence,* December 1987

If there is touch of genius in me, it's probably there because God gave it to me. The ability to hear chord structures, to take them out of my mind, pull them together, and make them work. That is a gift.

GORDON PARKS, *Voices in the Mirror,* 1990

GENOCIDE

When you first came we were very many and you were few; now you are many, and we are getting very few, and we are poor.

RED CLOUD, speech given at Cooper Union, New York City, 16 July 1870

We have been south and suffered a great deal down there. Many have died of diseases which we have no name for. Our hearts looked and longed for this country where we were born. There are only a few of us left, and we only wanted a little ground, where we could live. We left our lodges and ran away in the night. . . . The troops followed. We only wanted to go north . . . all we got was a volley. . . . the whites killed them all.

OHCUMGACHE (LITTLE WOLF) OF THE NORTHERN CHEYENNES, speech given to Congress, 1878

You have driven me from the East to this place, and I have been here two thousand years or more. . . . if you took me away from this land it would be very hard for me. I wish to die in this land. I wish to be an old man here . . . I have not wished to give even a part of it to the Great Father. Though he were to give me a million dollars I would not give him this land. . . . When people want to slaughter cattle they drive them along until they get them to a corral, and then they slaughter them. So it was with us. . . . My children have been exterminated; my brother has been killed.

STANDING BEAR OF THE PONCAS, speech given to Congress, 1879

We, the people, charge genocide. We . . . declare that Jim Crow and segregation are a genocidal policy of government. . . . The proof is all in . . . the lynchings condoned and encouraged by government officials, the killings by police. . . , the legal lynchings by the courts of our land, the racist laws. The violence and murder are all stamped with the government seal.

PAUL ROBESON, "Genocide Stalks the U.S.A," *New World Review,* February 1952

[E]conomic genocide [is] the silent, cruel killer.

Ibid.

By historical genocide, the Black man in the world and western civilization has been removed.

WYATT T. WALKER, "Crime, Vietnam and God," *Negro Digest,* December 1967

Genocide is the logical conclusion of racism.

JAMES CONE, *Black Theology and Black Power,* 1969

Genocide is the substitute for conversion.

DICK GREGORY, *No More Lies,* 1971

If it had not been for the massacre, there would have been a great many more people here now; but after that massacre who could have stood it?

ESKIMINZIN OF THE ARAVAIPA APACHES, in Brown, *Bury My Heart at Wounded Knee,* 1971

Where today are the Pequot? Where are the Narragansett, the Mohican, the Pokanet, and many other once powerful tribes of our people? They have vanished before the avarice and the oppression of the White Man, as snow before a summer sun. Will we let ourselves be destroyed in our turn without a struggle, give up our homes, our country bequeathed to us by the Great Spirit, the graves of our dead and everything that is dear and sacred to us? I know you will cry with me, "Never! Never!"

TECUMSEH OF THE SHAWNEES, in *ibid.*

[Apartheid is] a subtle form of genocide.

ALLAN BOESAK, in "Allan Boesak: South African Revolutionary," *Essence,* April 1988

We must take control of ourselves and come out of our own Black racism. We must believe in ourselves, in our God, to lead us out of this forest where they are performing genocide.

NETTIE JONES, in the *Detroit News,* 31 March 1989

We . . . do not see the war being waged against us because we don't want to and because we are afraid. We are engaging in behavior specifically designed to *block out* any awareness of the war—our true reality.

FRANCES CRESS WELSING, *The Isis Papers,* 1991

GHETTO

. . . a sinister noose runs around our necks/ And we hang like the Jews in the Ghetto/ waiting for them to hook us up.

EDWARD ROUMER, in *Poemes d'Haiti et de France,* 1925

The echoes we hear in the ghetto of "liberate me or exterminate me" are sincere.

WHITNEY YOUNG, c. 1961

A ghetto can be improved in one way only: out of existence.

JAMES BALDWIN, *Nobody Knows My Name,* 1961

Time was when it was sad to be a man/ every color of the body was a ghetto.

TCHICAYA U TAM'SI, "Communion II," *Bow Harp,* 1962

We cannot be satisfied as long as the Negro's basic mobility is from a smaller ghetto to a larger one.

MARTIN LUTHER KING, JR., "I Have a Dream," speech given at the Lincoln Memorial, Washington, D.C., 28 August 1963

The dark ghettos are social, political, educational and—above all—economic colonies. Their inhabitants are subject peoples, victims of the greed, cruelty, insensitivity, guilt, and fear of their masters.

KENNETH B. CLARK, *Dark Ghetto,* 1965

The ghettos in America are like the native reserves in South Africa. They symbolize the Negro as unacceptable, inferior and kept apart.

RALPH BUNCHE, in *Newsweek,* 20 November 1967

The ghetto terror kneeling thief-like on my back.

LANCE JEFFERS, "The Night Rains Hot Tar," in *New Black Voices,* 1968

The needs of the society determine its ethics, and in the ghetto the hero is that man who is offered only the crumbs from his country's table but by ingenuity and courage is able to take for himself a Lucullan feast.

MAYA ANGELOU, *I Know Why the Caged Bird Sings,* 1969

The section where a nickel costs a dime.

LANGSTON HUGHES, *Vital Speeches,* 15 August 1970

It's a kind of concentration camp, and not many people survive it.

JAMES BALDWIN, *A Rap on Race,* 1971

The hot winds of change, blowing through the central city ghettos of just about every major city, are producing an articulate group of young people whose rhetoric may possess the seeds of hope for tomorrow.

SAMUEL B. MCKINNEY, "The Hot Winds of Change," in Philpot, ed., *Best Black Sermons,* 1972

. . . Six blocks of cruelty.

NTOZAKE SHANGE, *For Colored Girls Who Have Considered Suicide When the Rainbow Is Enuf,* 1975

GIFTS

He who receives a gift doesn't measure.

IVORY COAST

One does not give a gift without motive.

MALI

Cleverness and cunning are gifts of Heaven.

INDIA

One cannot give to a person that which he already possesses.

TOUSSAINT L'OUVERTURE, *Proclamation,* 1 March 1802

Here we have brought our three gifts and mingled them with yours: a gift of story and song—soft, stirring melody in an ill-harmonized and unmelodious land; the gift of sweat and brawn to beat back the wilderness, conquer the soil, and lay the foundation of this vast economic empire two hundred years earlier than your weak hands could have done it; the third, a gift of the Spirit. Around us the history of the land has centered for thrice a hundred years; out of the nation's heart we have called all that was best to throttle and subdue all that was worst.

W. E. B. DU BOIS, *The Souls of Black Folk,* 1903

I do not say that the only person who can write of England must be an Englishman, or that only the Japanese should write of Japan, but I would insist that if a person is writing of a group to which he is socially and culturally alien, he must have some extraordinary gifts of insight.

W. E. B. DU BOIS, *Dusk of Dawn: An Essay Toward an Autobiography of Race Concept,* 1940

Every one has a gift for something, even if it is the gift of being a good friend.

MARIAN ANDERSON, *Marian Anderson, A Portrait,* 1970

The greatest gift is not being afraid to question.

RUBY DEE, in "With Ossie and Ruby: Creative Family at Work," *Black Stars,* April 1981

I don't ask for much. Just a birthday strip-a-gram with choreography, and a serenade in three-part harmony by Magic Johnson, Smoky and Clifton Davis.

MARSHA WARFIELD, 1987

I took an inventory and looked into my little bag to see what I had left over. I had one jewel left in the bag, the brightest jewel of all. I had the gift of faith.

LOLA FALANA, in "Lola Falana's Valiant Fight Against Multiple Sclerosis," *Ebony,* May 1988

Once you've danced, you always dance. You can't deny the gifts that God sends your way.

JUDITH JAMISON, in "About People," *Essence,* December 1988

There is no Santa Claus. I'm Santa Claus.

JOSEPHINE BAKER, in Rose, *Jazz Cleopatra,* 1989

It's my belief that God gives us all gifts, special abilities that we have the privilege of developing to help us serve Him and humanity.

BENJAMIN CARSON, *Gifted Hands,* 1990

If you benefit from the gift of a thief, you're a thief.

KRIS PARKER A.K.A KRS-ONE, in the *Detroit Free Press,* 8 March 1992

GOAL

Humanity is the goal of all good, and no single race, whatever its color or deed, can disinherit God's anointed people.

W. E. B. DU BOIS, "The Coronation," *Crisis,* 1911

To get where you want to go you can't only do what you like.

PETER ABRAHAMS, *Tell Freedom,* 1954

We will build a democratic America in spite of undemocratic Americans. We have rarely worried about the odds or the obstacles before—we will not start worrying now. We will have both of our goals—Peace and Power!

SHIRLEY CHISHOLM, speech given at Federal City College, Washington, D.C., 1969

A goal that is the basis of true democracy above the law; A child born to a Black mother in a state like Mississippi—born to the dumbest, poorest, sharecropper—by merely drawing its first breath in the democracy has exactly the same rights as a white baby born to the wealthiest person in the United States. It's not true, but I challenge anyone to say it is not a goal worth working for.

THURGOOD MARSHALL, c. 1980

Did you ever have a goal and still not know where you're going? I knew I wasn't going to stay where I was but I wasn't sure just where I was going.

JOE LOUIS, *My Life,* 1981

Never give up. Keep your thoughts and your mind always on the goal.

TOM BRADLEY, *The Impossible Dream,* 1986

I wasn't concerned about the hardships, because I always felt I was doing what I had to do, what I wanted to do and what I was destined to do.

KATHERINE DUNHAM, in "She Danced to Teach—And They Loved It," *American Visions,* February 1987

People think I'm . . . temperamental because I know what I want.

ANITA BAKER, in "Spotlight: Anita Baker," *Essence,* December 1987

Being a runner was my biggest goal. Now I'm the fastest woman in the world on a track.

EVELYN ASHFORD, c. 1988

I always had something to shoot for each year: to jump one inch farther.

JACKIE JOYNER KERSEE, in "Spotlight: Life in the Fast Lane," *Essence,* 1989

Be Black, shine, aim high.

LEONTYNE PRICE, in "The 1990 *Essence* Awards," *Essence,* October 1990

I was . . . silenced solely because cadets did not want Blacks at West Point. Their only purpose was to freeze me out. What they did not realize was that I was stubborn enough to put up with their treatment to reach the goal I had come to attain.

BENJAMIN DAVIS JR., *Benjamin Davis, Jr.: An Autobiography,* 1991

Focus so strongly on your goal that disappointments don't shatter you.

JOLYN ROBICHAUX, in "Words of the Week," *Jet*, 14 January 1991

GOD

I am He who when He opens His eyes, it becomes light and when He closes His eyes, it becomes dark. He at whose command the waters of the Nile rise and whose name the Exalted Ones do not know.

SELF-DEFINITION OF RA

God sells knowledge for labor, honor for risk.

AFRICA

If God made him, man can find some use for him.

AFRICA

The Giver of Life/ Placed the sun in great space,/
And said: No hand Shall be the length to reach it;/
Though clouds disappear, And we become a
mountain Immovable and high,/ It will not be that
the hand obeys not.

DAHOMEY

Do not scheme against people. God punishes accordingly. People's schemes do not prevail. God's commands is what prevails.

EGYPT

One who recovers from a sickness forgets about God.

ETHIOPIA

When one is in trouble, one remembers God.

NIGERIA

Even God is not ripe enough to watch me and catch me if I really want to love another man. What is wrong with falling in love with others anyway? I was not born to hate people.

YORUBA

He guides the eagle through the pathless air.

TRADITIONAL

God has no grandchildren.

TRADITIONAL

There is no god like one's throat; we have to sacrifice to it every day.

NIGERIA

I am in the hand of God and at your disposal. My life is not dear unto me, but I am ready to be offered at any moment.

DAVID WALKER, *Appeal to the Coloured Citizens of the World*, 1829

God punishes the indifference of men who remain cold and proud before the terrible spectacles He presents to them.

ALEXANDRE DUMAS, *The Count of Monte Cristo*, 1844

God helps me wherever I shall be, at home, abroad, on land, on sea, in public or private walks. As a Black man, my labors will be antislavery labors.

SAMUEL WARD, *Autobiography of a Fugitive Negro*, 1855

Having God for my friend and portion, what have I to fear? As long as it is the will of God, I rejoice that I am as I am; for man, in his best estate, is altogether vanity.

MARIA STEWART, *Meditations from the Pen of Mrs. Maria W. Stewart*, 1879

Say to us if you can say it, that you were sent by the Creative Power to talk to us. Perhaps you think the Creator sent you here to dispose of us as you see fit. If I thought you were sent by the Creator I might be induced to think you had a right to dispose of me.

HIGHN'MOOT TOOYALAKET (CHIEF JOSEPH) OF THE NEZ PERCES, "An Indian's View of Indian Affairs," *North American Review*, 1879

He who would be friends with God must remain alone or make the whole world his friend.

MOHANDAS GANDHI, 1888

Poor, blind conceited humanity! Interpreters of God, indeed! We reduce the deity to vulgar fractions. We place our own little ambitions before a shrine and label them "Divine Messages." We set up our own Delphian tripod, and we are the priests and oracles. We despise the plans of Nature's Ruler and substitute our own. With our short sight we affect to take a comprehensive view of eternity. Our horizon is the universe. We spy on the Divine and try to surprise his secrets, or to sneak into his confidence by stealth. We make God the eternal puppet.

PAUL LAURENCE DUNBAR, *The Uncalled,* 1898

We have as much right biblically and otherwise to believe that God is a Negro as white people have to believe that God is a fine-looking symmetrical and ornamented white man. Every race of people since time began who have attempted to describe God by words or painting, or by carvings, have conveyed the idea that the God who made them and shaped their destinies was symbolized in themselves, and why should not the Negro believe that he resembles God as much as other people?

HENRY MCNEAL TURNER, "God Is a Negro," *The Voice of Mission,* February 1898

We have lived in darker hours than those of today; we have seen American justice and fair play go through fire and death and devastation and come out purified by the faith that abides in the God of Destiny.

ALEXANDER WALTERS, speech given to Afro-American Council, December 1898

God made us men long before man made us citizens.

CHARLES T. WALKER, 1900

In His good time America shall rend the Veil and the prisoned shall go free. Free, free as the sunshine trickling down the morning into these high windows . . . free as yonder fresh young voices welling up to me from the caverns of brick and mortar below—swelling with song. . . .

W. E. B. DU BOIS, *The Souls of Black Folk,* 1903

We have gradually won our way back into the confidence of the God of Africa, and He shall speak with a voice of thunder, that shall shake the pillars of a corrupt and unjust world, and once more restore Ethiopia to her ancient glory.

MARCUS GARVEY, *Philosophy and Opinions of Marcus Garvey,* 1923

How can I give up when in every part of the world I see my people being exploited and treated as if they're dregs of the earth? I could never do it. I could never compromise my conscience. What could I tell my God?

Ibid.

Black men are not going to cringe before anyone but God.

Ibid.

Young man—/ Young man—/ Your arm's too short to box with God.

JAMES WELDON JOHNSON, "The Prodigal Son," *God's Trombones,* 1927

God gave them [the discoveries] to me; how can I sell them to someone else?

GEORGE WASHINGTON CARVER, c. 1932

If God don't think no mo' 'bout 'em then Ah do, they's a lost ball in de high grass.

ZORA NEALE HURSTON, *Their Eyes Were Watching God,* 1937

Negroes were first worshiped in Greece and Rome. White masses bowed to Black deities. The rites of Apollo were founded by Delphos and his Negro mother, Melainis; and the worship of Black Isis and Horus was popular in Rome and the Roman colonies as far north as Britain. When this latter evolved into the worship of the Black Madonna and Black Christ, whites also bowed down to them.

J. A. ROGERS, *Nature Knows No Color Line,* 1952

Many things have been used as symbolic expressions to give us a picture of God or some characteristics of one of his attributes. The ocean, with her turbulent majesty, the mountain, the lion—many things have been employed as pictures of either God's strength or God's power or God's law or God's mercy. So the eagle is used here as a symbol of God. The eagle symbolizes God because there is something about an eagle that is a fitting symbol of God. The eagle is the king of the birds. It is a regal, kingly bird.

C. L. FRANKLIN, "The Eagle Stirs His Nest," 1953

God became a living being for me: a brown old man with a long beard who wore black clothes and who liked singing and laughter.

PETER ABRAHAMS, *Tell Freedom,* 1954

You say that there is one supreme God who made heaven and earth. We also believe in Him and call Him Chukwa. He made all the world and the other gods.

CHINUA ACHEBE, *Things Fall Apart,* 1959

To be with God is really to be involved with some enormous, overwhelming desire, and joy, and power which you cannot control, which controls you. God is a means of liberation and not a means to control others.

JAMES BALDWIN, *Nobody Knows My Name,* 1961

I cannot see everything, but nothing escapes God.

TOUSSAINT L'OUVERTURE, in James, *The Black Jacobins,* 1963

He who governs all is alone immortal.

Ibid.

Without God, all of our efforts turn to ashes and our sunrise into the darkest of nights. Without him, life is a meaningless drama in which the decisive scenes are missing.

MARTIN LUTHER KING, JR., c. 1963

God has been profoundly real to me in recent years. In the midst of outer dangers, I have felt an inner calm. In the midst of lonely days and dreary nights I have heard an inner voice saying, "Lo, I will be with you."

MARTIN LUTHER KING, *Strength to Love,* 1963

What is against life will be destroyed by life, for what is against life is against God.

HOWARD THURMAN, *Disciplines of the Spirit,* 1963

As I look into each different face, I am exalted./ I am exalted to recognize His Grace/ shimmering
through the varied pattern lace.

MARGARET DANNER, "through the varied patterned lace," *to flower,* 1963

This country can seduce God . . . —it has that seductive power—the power of dollarism. You can cuss out colonialism, imperialism and all the other kinds of isms, but it's hard to for you to cuss that dollarism. When they drop those dollars on you, your soul goes.

MALCOLM X, answer to question, Militant Labor Forum, New York City, 7 January 1965

In the pre-Christian slave period, all the Blacks that were brought here brought their god. If he was from Dagomba, he brought the god Wuni. If he was a Fo, he brought the god Mawa. If he was a Kikuyu, he brought the god Ngui.

JIMMY STEWART, 1966

[A]rtists of all . . . races have painted whatsoever God they worship to resemble themselves. . . . After all, Christ was born in that part of the world that had always been predominantly populated by colored people.

JOHN H. CLARKE, "The Boy Who Painted Christ Black," in Clarke, ed., *American Negro Short Stories,* 1966

God is man idealized.

LEROI JONES, *Home: Social Essays,* 1966

I call for more arrogance of power among Black people, but an arrogance of power that is God-inspired, God-led and God-daring.

ADAM CLAYTON POWELL, JR., baccalaureate speech given at Howard University, Washington, D.C., 29 May 1966

When reading all those books on the life of God, it should be noted that they were all written by men.

BOB KAUFMAN, "Heavy Water Blues," *Golden Sandals,* 1967

He's the comfort/and wine and piccalilli for my soul.

GWENDOLYN BROOKS, "In the Mecca," *In the Mecca,* 1968

What price would God demand from the churches for having the audacity to lighten the color of his son's skin, and straighten out his nappy hair?

DICK GREGORY, *Black Manifesto: Religion, Racism, and Reparations,* 1968

To be the God of black people, he must be against the oppression of black people.

JAMES CONE, *Black Theology and Black Power,* 1969

God of our weary years,/ God of our silent tears,/ Thou who hast brought us this far on the way;/ Thou who hast by Thy might/ Let us into the light,/ Keep us forever in the path, we pray.

JAMES W. JOHNSON, "Lift Every Voice and Sing," in Bontemps, ed., *Poetry of the Negro,* 1970

God is the Old Repair Man./ When we are junk in Nature's storehouse he takes us apart./ What is good he lays aside; he might use it someday./ What has decayed he buries in six feet of sod to nurture the weeds./ Those we leave behind moisten the sod with their tears.

FENTON JOHNSON, "The Old Repair Man," in *ibid.*

Man lives in God, and the circumference of life cannot be rightly drawn until the center is set.

BENJAMIN MAYS, "What Man Lives By," in Philpot, ed., *Best Black Sermons,* 1972

Every group of people, every race, thinks about God out of its own state of being, its own understanding of itself, out of its own condition of life. Look at the various racial pictorializations of God—the northern European, the medieval Italian, the Japanese, the Chinese, the American Indian.

GAYNAUD WILMORE, "Black Theology," in *ibid.*

Theology is man's thought about God in the light of what God is doing about man. If you are black and you were created in the image of God, then for you, in more than a superficial sense, God is black and your thoughts about him—your theology, in order to be authentic—must be black theology.

Ibid.

Self-imposed deification is as deceiving as a rooster which thinks that day breaks because he crows.

D. E. KING, "The God Who Takes off Chariot Wheels," in *ibid.*

I believe I have had a glimpse of God many times. I believe because believing is believable, and no one can prove it unbelievable.

DUKE ELLINGTON, *Music Is My Mistress,* 1973

It is logical that although we all know God is a spirit, yet all religions more or less visualize Him in a likeness akin to their own race. It was most vital that pictures of God should be in the likeness of the [Negro] race.

AMY JACQUES GARVEY, in "Mrs. Marcus Garvey Talks with Ida Lewis," *Encore,* May 1973

i found god in myself/ and i loved her fiercely.

NTOZAKE SHANGE, *For Colored Girls, Who Have Considered Suicide When the Rainbow Is Enuf,* 1975

Behold—the only thing greater than yourself.

ALEX HALEY, *Roots,* 1977

There is the firm commitment to the triumph of the human spirit over adversity, the certainty that there's a God on high who may not move mountains but will give you the strength to climb.

GENEVA SMITHERMAN, *Talkin' and Testifying,* 1977

There is hope for the future because God has a sense of humor, and we are funny to God.

BILL COSBY, c. 1978

We live inside this unbelievable cosmos, inside our unbelievable bodies—everything so perfect, everything so in tune. I got to think God had a hand in it. . . . There's got to be something greater than us.

RAY CHARLES, *Brother Ray,* 1978

People from almost every culture in history have decided that they were God's chosen people. Cultural bias gets strong when a group claims to be on intimate terms with God. They've got a pipeline to Him. Whatever they don't like, God doesn't like either. People wind up making God in their own image, and they rarely notice how strange it is that their God looks at things from their point of view.

BILL RUSSELL, *Second Wind*, 1979

In the beginning God, . . . in the end God.

DESMOND TUTU, *Hope and Suffering*, 1983

Who learned the first man on Earth? God. He is unchangeable, and if he learned the first man he can learn you.

ALICE WALKER, *In Search of Our Mothers' Gardens*, 1983

Duke [Ellington was] an example of the mysterious way in which God showed His face in music.

RALPH ELLISON, "Homage to Duke Ellington on His Birthday," *Going to the Territory*, 1986

If . . . every man and woman is an object of wonder and joy in the heart of the Superior Being, then it is not too much to expect that some day all wrongs will be righted, and justice will prevail.

MIRIAM MAKEBA, *My Story*, 1987

My old world suddenly and completely collapsed. I found myself in a world without a God. I felt that the foundation of the earth had been pulled out from under me. I felt like a condemned man swinging with a rope about his neck. For several days I was so stunned and broken that I could hardly do more than lay [sic] on my bed in a darkened room and feel I was dying. Also, I felt as if I had been somehow betrayed. I didn't want to see anyone. I didn't want to see the light. In truth, I did not want to live.

JEAN TOOMER, in Kerman and Eldridge; *The Lives of Jean Toomer*, 1987

I do not know which of our afflictions God intends that we overcome and which He means for us to bear. . . . But this is certain: Some I have overcome, some I continue to bear.

Ibid.

There isn't a certain time we should set aside to talk about God. God is part of our every waking moment.

MARVA COLLINS, in "Marva Collins: Teaching Success in the City," *Message*, February 1987

You fools, you forsake your own ancestors to worship a foreign deity. You turn your back on your own religion to worship something you have stumbled across.

VUSAMAZULA MUTWA "The Rout of the Arabi," *Africa Is My Witness*, 1988

We've moved God out of the stained-glass prison that so many religious leaders have locked Him into.

MARVIN WINANS, in "The Glory of Gospel," *Ebony*, May 1988

My mother knew her polio was not a curse but a test that God gave her to triumph over, and she instilled in me a love of Him that I will always have.

MICHAEL JACKSON, in *Jet*, 16 May 1988

I always thank God. I'm here because this is what I love to do. When they say come and sing, that's the medicine.

ELLA FITZGERALD, in *Jet*, 27 June 1988

Others try to worship things that are less than God; it may be money, or ambition, or drugs, or sex. In the end they find that they are worthless idols. To worship means to give due worth to someone or something.

DESMOND TUTU, in *Jet*, 26 September 1988

When one finds himself, one finds God. You find God and you find yourself.

PRINCE, in "Spotlight: Prince—What U See Is What U Get," *Essence*, November 1988

Reach for God. Don't reach for stars. You might get a cloud and nothing is in clouds. Reach for God. Reach to shake God's hand.

MIKE TYSON, in "Mike Tyson Talks About His Future and says 'I'm a Dreamer,'" *Jet*, 14 November 1988

There is something in the nature of God that corresponds to our maleness and our femaleness. We have tended to speak much more of the maleness, so we refer to the Fatherhood of God, which is as it should be. But we have missed out on the fullness that is God when we have ignored that which corresponds to our femaleness. We have hardly spoken about the Motherhood of God, and consequently we have been the poorer for this.

DESMOND TUTU in Naomi Tutu, *The Words of Desmond Tutu,* 1989

The ultimate evil of oppression, and certainly of that policy of South Africa called apartheid, is when it succeeds in making a child of God begin to doubt that he or she is a child of God.

Ibid.

GOOD

The constant virtues of the good are tenderness and love/ To all that lives—in earth, air, sea—great, small—below, above.

Mahabharata, 5–1 B.C.

GOVERNMENT

The governing of the world, is it done with guns? Is it done with swords?

NIGERIA

To change the character of the government at this point is neither possible nor desirable. All that is necessary to be done is to make the government consistent with itself, and render the rights of the states compatible with the sacred rights of human nature.

FREDERICK DOUGLASS, "Reconstruction," *Atlantic Monthly,* December 1866

A government which has power to tax a man in peace, draft him in war, should have power to defend his life in the hour of peril. A government which can protect and defend its citizens from wrong and outrage and does not is vicious. A government which would do it and cannot is weak; and where human life is insecure through either weakness or viciousness in the administration of law, there must be a lack of justice and where this is wanting, nothing can make up the deficiency.

FRANCES E. W. HARPER, in Avery, ed., *Transactions of the National Council of Women of the United States assembled in Washington, D.C.,* 22 February 1891

The day will come when Americans realize that a government that will not protect its citizens cannot demand protection for itself.

Black Chronicle, 1 June 1896

I asked, Where is the black man's Government. . . . Where is his President, his country, and his ambassador, his army, his navy, and his big men of affairs? I could not find them and I declared, I will help make them.

MARCUS GARVEY, *Philosophy and Opinions of Marcus Garvey,* 1923

The days of the nineteenth century dwarf states are gone.

ALIOUNE DIOP, c. 1965

Capitalism fails to realize that life is social. Marxism fails to realize that life is individual.

MARTIN LUTHER KING, JR., speech given at Southern Christian Leadership Retreat, Frogmore, South Carolina, 14 November 1967

Some members of Congress are the best actors in the world.

SHIRLEY CHISHOLM, *Unbought and Unbossed,* 1970

The stakes . . . are too high for government to be a spectator sport.

BARBARA JORDAN, speech given at Harvard University, Cambridge, Massachusetts, 16 June 1977

I am aware of the penalties attached to this call. I am not defying the government, I am obeying God.

DESMOND TUTU, 1984

[The] rewriting of history makes us . . . cry. . . . [We] cry because we know a government that can make up a lie can lie about anything.

MIRIAM MAKEBA, *My Story,* 1987

No form of government makes anybody omniscient.

THOMAS SOWELL, in the *Detroit News,* 13 February 1987

Authority is always dangerous, selfish, inexplicable. It looks after its own mysterious affairs in a dark privacy. It never explains. Its servants, even the most approachable, resent nothing so much as a request for explanation. Even when they do give it, it is generally false.

JOYCE CARY, *Mister Johnson,* 1988

Government does not own men's goods and liberties; it has no right to distribute justice and the freedom to succeed by race, sex, or religion.

WALTER E. WILLIAMS, "Why We're Number One," *Success,* March 1989

The problem with depending on a government is that you can't depend on it.

TONY BROWN, in the *Pittsburgh Courier,* 19 August 1991

GRANDPARENTS

Great-grandmother hobbles in on crutches, her garment pinned across her chest with a safety pin, and her cap tied on with a black ribbon. But it takes more than crutches and discarded ribbons to abash a colored grandmother. In fact, they are the only grandmothers whom I have ever known to come into their own. They are still persons. They never quail before a stylish granddaughter by so much as a fraction of an inch. . . . They have drunk at the fount of youth and never lost its flavor.

ELEANOR WEMBRIDGE, *Life Among the Lowbrows,* 1931

On my various errands I passed my grandmother's house and she always had something to spare for me. I was frequently threatened with punishment if I stopped there; and my grandmother, to avoid detaining me, often stood at the gate with something for my breakfast or dinner. I was indebted to her for all my comforts, spiritual or temporal.

SLAVE, in Frazier, *The Negro Family in the United States,* 1939

My grandmothers were strong./ They followed
plows and bent to toil./ They moved through fields
sowing seed./ They touched earth and grain grew./
They were full of sturdiness and singing./ My
grandmothers were strong./ My grandmothers
are full of memories. . .

MARGARET WALKER, "Lineage," *For My People,* 1942

I am a product of the sustained indignation of a branded grandfather, the militant protest of my grandmother, the disciplined resentment of my father and mother, and the power of mass action of the church. . . . I am a marching Black.

ADAM CLAYTON POWELL, JR., *Marching Blacks,* 1945

All my life I had heard she was a great beauty and no one ever remarked that they had meant half a century before! The woman that I met was as wrinkled as a prune and . . . always seemed to be thinking of other times. But she could still rock and talk and even make wonderful cupcakes which were like cornbread, only sweet. . . . She died the next summer and that is all that I remember about her, except that she was born in slavery and had memories of it and they didn't sound anything like *Gone With the Wind.*

LORRAINE HANSBERRY, *To Be Young, Gifted and Black,* 1959

My grandmother thinks only of me. The food that
people bring her comes to/ me. The chicken newly
caponed is for me./ Already she is thinking of my
future.

FILY-DABO SISSOKO, "Grandmother," *Poems from Black Africa,* 1963

My hand was in my grandmother's a good part of the time. If we were not standing outside the picket gate waiting for my uncles to come home from school, we were waiting under the tree in the front yard picking pecans. If we were not decorating a backyard bush with eggshells, we were driving our buggy across the bridge to Pineville.

ARNA BONTEMPS, in "The South Today," *Harper's,* April 1965

He cast his spell over me and I was affected by him more profoundly, because I loved him. I loved him first as my grandfather and then as the great and famous man he was.

SUSAN ROBESON, *The Whole World in His Hand,* 1981

Our grandmother would tell the story of her life and how she had married Osip Hannibal, the son of the Moor; he was handsome, he was black.

ALEXANDER PUSHKIN, in "Alexander Sergevich Pushkin: An Interpretation of the Russian Renaissance," *Negro History Bulletin,* October 1982

The true accolade was not only my father saying he was pleased, but that my grandmother would have been proud of me.

WILLIAM H. HASTIE, in *Grace Under Pressure,* 1984

Grandparents instilled in me a great belief in the power of the individual through his own industry, determination, and courage to achieve.

Ibid.

Hug [your] grandparents and say "I want to thank you for what you've done to make me and my life possible."

ALEX HALEY, in "Words of the Week," *Jet,* 4 February 1985

Grandparents somehow sprinkle a sense of stardust over grandchildren.

ALEX HALEY, "We Must Honor Our Ancestors," *Ebony,* August 1986

I pray every day. Not only do I pray, but I pray on my knees. Like my grandmother taught me.... "As long as God allows you to bend, you bend." And I've bent every day of my life.

OPRAH WINFREY, in "An Intimate Talk with Oprah," *Essence,* August 1987

Knowing as a child how to care for my grandfather, being told what to do for him, gave me a lot of information about growing old, respecting people.

TONI MORRISON, in "Toni Morrison Now," *Essence,* October 1987

My grandfather was the most influential person in my life. He affected the lives of many.... He was born in ... poverty, and on top of that was crippled by a bone disease. It never hindered him from achieving the things he did.

BILL LEE in Spike Lee, *Mo' Better Blues,* 1990

GREAT

Oh, small, small fire, who takes the great and devours them.

DAHOMEY

You see nothing but the springs of the machine and not the sublime workman who makes it function. You recognize around you only those whose positions have been assigned to them by some minister or king; you are unable to see those men whom God has placed above kings and ministers by giving them a mission to fulfill, rather than a position to occupy.

ALEXANDRE DUMAS, *The Count of Monte Cristo,* 1844

Man's greatness consists in his ability to do and the proper application of his powers to things needed to be done.

FREDERICK DOUGLASS, 1886

There is no great education which one can get from books and costly apparatus that is equal to that which can be gotten from contact with great men and women.

BOOKER T. WASHINGTON, *Up From Slavery,* 1901

Great men cultivate love ... only little men cherish a spirit of hatred.

Ibid.

Greatness is largely a social accident, and almost always socially supported.

MARY MCLEOD BETHUNE, C. 1902

A people may become great through many means, but there is only one measure by which its greatness is recognized and acknowledged. The final measure of the greatness of all peoples is the amount and standard of the literature and art they have produced. The world does not know that a people is great until that people produces great literature and art.

JAMES WELDON JOHNSON, preface to *The Book of Negro Poetry,* 1931

Gabriel will say ... "I'd be the greatest trumpeter in the Universe, if old Satchmo had never been born!"

MELVIN TOLSON, "Lamda," *Harlem Gallery,* 1965

Greatness has nothing to do with goodness.

FRANK YERBY, *Goat Song,* 1967

When you're as great as I am, it's hard to be humble.

MUHAMMAD ALI, c. 1970

The rich man who achieves a degree of greatness achieves it not because he hoards his wealth but because he gives it away in the interest of good causes—his concern for humanity, his concern for the poor, and his desire to improve the quality of education. The truly great men of history are great not because of the abundance of things they possessed but because of their dreams and the contributions they made to mankind.

BENJAMIN MAYS, "What Man Lives By," in Philpot, ed., *Best Black Sermons,* 1972

The great are those who in their lives fought for life.

STEPHEN HENDERSON, introduction to Evans, ed., *Black Women Writers,* 1984

The great turn stumbling blocks into stepping stones on their way to a singular achievement.

GILBERT WARE, *Grace Under Pressure,* 1984

Black men are ten times greater than they appear against the backdrop of today's world. If equity prevailed, Jesse Jackson would be president, Michael Jackson a movie star, Bill Cosby would *own* a network. If there was equity . . . in the world, South Africa would still be Azania and Nelson Mandela would be in charge.

SUSAN TAYLOR, c. 1985

[G]reatness isn't determined by how many people know you, it's determined by service to other people.

OPRAH WINFREY, in "An Intimate Talk with Oprah," *Essence,* August 1987

A great soul serves everyone all the time. A great soul never dies. It brings us together again and again.

MAYA ANGELOU, "Goodbye James Baldwin," *Crisis,* January 1988

It doesn't mean anything to me to be called "the greatest." I've heard that word "great" so much. What is great?

BO JACKSON, "Bo Knows Bo," *GQ,* March 1990

GREED

Excessive greed should ne'er be cherished. Have greed—but keep it moderate.

PANCHATANTRA, 2 A.D.

Greed fortifies prejudice.

TOUSSAINT L'OUVERTURE, c. 1800

If there were no greed, there would be no occasion for armaments. Nonviolence necessitates complete abstention from exploitation in any form.

MOHANDAS GANDHI, in *Harijan,* 12 November 1938

GRIOT

I am a Griot. It is I, Djeli Mamoudou Kouyate, son of Bintou Kouyate and Djeli Kedian Kouyate, master in the art of eloquence. Since time immemorial the Kouyates have been in the service of the Keita princes of Mali; we are vessels of speech, we are the repositories which harbor secrets many centuries old. Without us the names of kings would vanish into oblivion; we are the memory of mankind; by the spoken word we bring to life the deeds and exploits of kings for younger generations. History holds no mystery for us, we teach to the vulgar just as much as we want to teach them, for it is we who keep the keys to the twelve books of Mali. I teach the kings of their ancestors so the lives of the ancients might serve them as an example, for the world is old but the future springs from the past.

MALI GRIOT MAMADOU KOUYATE, *Sundiata: An Epic of Old Mali,* 1217–1237

Griots are men of spoken word, and by the spoken word we give life to the gestures of kings. But words are nothing but words; power lies in deeds. Be a man of action, do not answer me any more with your mouth, but tomorrow show me what you will have me recount to coming generations.

Ibid.

I heard recalled the lofty deeds of my father's ancestors and their names from the earliest times. As the couplets were reeled off it was like watching the growth of a great genealogical tree that spread its branches far and wide and flourished its boughs and twigs before my eyes.

CAMARA LAYE, *The Dark Child,* 1954

When I returned, having forgotten nothing which I learned as a child, I had the great happiness of meeting the old Amadou Koumba, the Griot of my family who told me the same stories which had cradled my childhood and others containing the wisdom of the ancestors.

BIRAGO DIOP, "The Stories Which Cradled My Childhood," *Tales of Amadou Koumba,* 1966

Few Black Americans grew up without guidance from a sort of Griot (uncle, grandmother, brother, sister, preacher, etc.). The job of the Griot in African societies was so important that an error could cost him his life. The Griot began at a very early age to master his technique and information. Like the master drummer, he understudied an elder statesman of the tribe. His training demanded a certain psychological adjustment to the significance of his job—which was to contain and give advice to the cultural "heirlooms of the community."

EUGENE REDMOND, *Drumvoice,* 1976

When a Griot dies, it is as if a library has burned to the ground.

ALEX HALEY, "We Must Honor Our Ancestors," *Ebony,* August 1986

The word griot . . . has come to be used to denote a specialist musician-cum-narrator of the type found in the Malinke culture zone of West Africa. . . . For millennia, and in all parts of Africa, counterparts . . . have enlightened and entertained their audiences with songs, stories, admonitions, histories and moral instructions. They have transmitted the classics of African societies and . . . have served as traditional Africa's informal academy of the humanities.

CHINWEIZU, introduction to *Voices from Twentieth-Century Africa,* 1988

Griot singers and storytellers are compared to kings and princes because their memory is a sacred trust that touches every person in their culture.

WILLIAM FERRIS, "Black Art," *Black Art: Ancestral Legacy,* 1989

There is the person who has exhibited the genius of tale telling from childhood. . . . Among many people he is known as the Griot. According to the Wolof people of Senegal, the true name is gewel. The term Griot is a European adaptation. The Griot (gewel) is that revered individual in the society who is entrusted with the exact cultural history. This exalted position is inherited.

PEARL PRIMUS, *The Storyteller,* 1989

The art of the Griot requires music and song skill and also an unerring memory. The spiritual life of the citizens of the community, past and present, and future, rest on the virtuosity and unerring exactness of the Griot. The songs of the Griot are more precise than any history book.

Ibid.

Transforming words were placed in the mouths of folk poets from the earliest times in America. Africans in the Americas remembered the storytellers, the griots, who stood in the midst of the children and adults at night and told them rhythmic stories that possessed the special quality of moral and verbal resolution.

MOLEFI ASANTE, "Folk Poetry in the Storytelling Tradition," in Goss and Barnes, eds., *Talk That Talk,* 1989

The griot was the oral historian and educator in any given society. The griot was well respected and very close to kings—in fact, closer to the king than the king's own wife.

D'JIMO KOUYATE, "The Role of the Griot," in *ibid.*

GROWTH

No matter how full the river, it still wants to grow.

CONGO

If a little tree grows in the shade of a larger tree, it will die.

SENEGAL

One might as well try to stop the progress of a mighty railroad train by throwing his body across the tracks; as to try to stop the growth of the world in the direction of giving mankind more intelligence, more culture, and more liberty.

BOOKER T. WASHINGTON, c. 1903

Nations, like plants and human beings, grow. And if the development is thwarted they are dwarfed and overshadowed.

CLAUDE MCKAY, "Out of the War Years: Lincoln, Apostle of a New America," *New Leader,* 13 February 1943

My soul has grown deep like the rivers.

LANGSTON HUGHES, "The Negro Speaks of Rivers," *Selected Poems,* 1959

Growing is the reward of learning.

MALCOLM X, interview given in Ghana, 11 May 1964

Growth is the surviving influence in all our lives. The tree will send up its trunk in thick profusion from land burned black by atom bombs. Children will grow from poverty and filth and oppression and develop honor, develop integrity, contribute to all mankind.

CHESTER HIMES, *Beyond the Angry Black,* 1966

So much of growing up is an unbearable waiting. A constant longing for another time. Another season.

SONIA SANCHEZ, "Graduation Notes," *From Under a Soprano Sky,* 1987

Common sense is all we had when I was growing up.

GRANDMA, *Michigan Chronicle,* 22 August 1987

In growth, one is first interested in oneself, one's family, one's community. Whenever we stop growing we start deterioating.

LOUIS FARRAKHAN, c. 1988

It is impossible to grow up Black in today's society without a very keen awareness of Black history, of the injustices done to Black people in the recent and distant past, of the prejudices that still exist, of the civil rights movement, of apartheid.

MALCOLM JAMAL-WARNER, c. 1988

I don't pull the flower from the pot after each primary or caucus and see how much it has grown.

JESSE JACKSON, in "National Reports," *Jet,* 25 April 1988

HABITS

She's got her habits on.

TRADITIONAL

Vile habits acquired in a state of servitude are not easily thrown off.

RICHARD ALLEN, *The Life Experience and Gospel Labors of Richard Allen,* 1887

Sins, like snakes, die hard. The habits and customs of a people were not to be changed in a day, nor by the stroke of a pen.

CHARLES W. CHESTNUTT, *The Marrow of Tradition,* 1901

Only where things mattered could they breathe and suffer . . . for the habit of making things matter had become an instinct, human, and it would seem eternal.

GEORGE LAMMING, *The Emigrants,* 1954

I don't have any bad habits. They might be bad habits for other people, but they're all right for me.

EUBIE BLAKE, *Eubie,* 1979

I have always found myself repelled by the Euro-American habit of telling all, even the intimate details of dirty little affairs.

WOLE SOYINKA, in "Wole Soyinka: Nigerian Playwright Is First Black Nobel Laureate in Literature," *Ebony,* April 1987

HAIR

God made us in his perfect creation. He made no mistake when he made us black with kinky hair.

MARCUS GARVEY, *Philosophy and Opinions of Marcus Garvey,* 1923

The spreading of the hair-straightening custom among Negro males has spawned that singular phenomenon of the stocking on heads.

CLAUDE MCKAY, *Harlem: Negro Metropolis,* 1940

My first time in Boston made me marvel at how Negro hair was straight and shiny like white men's hair. And I was among the millions who were insane enough to feel it was some kind of status symbol.

MALCOLM X, *The Autobiography of Malcolm X,* 1965

You could tell the clan, the village by the style of hair they wore. Then the Yoruba people were wearing thirty braids and more. You know the princess, queen, and bride by the number of braids. You know the gods they worshipped by the pattern they made.

CAMILLE YARBROUGH, *Cornrows,* 1979

Style it fancy/ style it simple/ style it with seeds in cowry shells/ style it with ribbons/ style it with ivory/ style it with beads on tinkle bells

Ibid.

She refused to cut those dreadlocks off, talking some stuff about her sense of purpose and thought process and rationale and happiness would be messed up if it wasn't dreaded.

RACHEL BROWN, "The Window on the Park," *City Arts Quarterly,* Fall–Winter 1987

They cook their hair/ with hot iron/and pull it hard/ So that it may grow long./ Then they rope the hair on wooden pens/ like a billy goat/ brought for the sacrifice/ struggling to free itself./ They fry their hair/ in boiling oil/ as if it were locusts/ and the hair sizzles/ It cries aloud in sharp pain/ as it is pulled and stretched/ and the vigorous and healthy hair/Curly, springy and thick/ that glistens in the sunshine/ Is left listless and dead.

OKOT P 'BITEK, "The Graceful Giraffe Cannot Become a Monkey," *Song of Lawino and Song of Ocol,* 1988

They told me my hair wasn't beautiful because I have the typical African strand; it's coiled and it's airborne. It's different from everybody else's. They said my ancestors were cannibals who didn't contribute anything to the world. That's why I form my hair styles.

ABBEY LINCOLN, in "Abbey Sings Billie: Interview," *City Arts Quarterly,* Summer 1988

My hair would be a badge, a symbol of my pride, a statement of self-affirmation.

GLORIA WADE GAYLES, "The Pilgrimage," *Catalyst,* Summer 1988

Hair still works on the minds of many anglicized Africans.

TONY BROWN, *Tony Brown's Journal,* 4 September 1989

HAND

One hand washes the other.

AFRICA

Allow him a handshake and he wants to embrace.

NIGERIA

My hands were weak, but I reached them out/ To feebler ones than mine,/ and over the shadow of my life/ Stole the light of a peace divine.

FRANCES E. W. HARPER, *Go Work in My Vineyard,* c. 1870

He lifted his right hand. . . . He lifted his right hand and the thing come upon me. I felt it when it come. His right hand was clothed in light.

ZORA NEALE HURSTON, *Moses, Man of the Mountain,* 1939

Free hands/ Living hands/ made/ for waking/ and not for smothering/ for giving/ enriching/ and not for taking away/ for keeping time/ and for conquering hate.

BERNARD DADIÉ, "Hands," *Dance of the Days,* 1956

You cannot shake hands with a clenched fist.

INDIRA GANDHI, address given to Parliament, New Delhi, 12 August 1971

A fighter's only weapons are his hands. If they go he goes. I've been using my hands for twenty-five years striking against the hardest thing on a man's body, the head.

MUHAMMAD ALI, *The Greatest,* 1975

In your hands . . . we saw how it was meant to be: neither bloodless or bloody, and yet alive.

TONI MORRISON, eulogy of James Baldwin, Cathedral of St. John the Divine, New York City, January 1988

I don't arrive at the rehearsal waiting to have the hand of the director, which is the direct hand of God, to explain to me what it is I'm supposed to be doing.

JESSYE NORMAN, in "The Norman Conquest," *American Visions,* April 1988

Open hands beckon our youth to higher thought and achievement, while the closed ones signify pathways which are dead ends, unclaimed or leading to destruction.

CAROLYN WARFIELD, in "Carolyn Warfield: Rising to the Light Within," *City Arts Quarterly,* Spring 1988

HANDICAP

Sitting is being crippled.

CONGO

All classes of a people under social pressure are permeated with a common experience; they are emotionally welded as others cannot be. With them, even ordinary living has epic depth and lyric intensity, and this, their material handicap, is their spiritual advantage.

ALAIN LOCKE, *The New Negro,* 1925

Nothing is more desirable than to be released from an affliction, but nothing is more frightening than to be divested of a crutch.

JAMES BALDWIN, *Nobody Knows My Name,* 1961

Handicaps are really to be used another way to benefit yourself and others.

STEVIE WONDER, in Haskins, *Growing Up in a World of Darkness,* 1976

Probably one of the most serious psychological handicaps young people have today is the notion that it is "cool" to be a non-achiever, that it is "hip" to put down hard work in school.

BILL COSBY, c. 1977

A handicap can be a blessing.

WILLIAM HOLMES BORDERS, SR., "Handicapped Lives," in Philpot, ed., *Best Black Sermons,* 1972

A negative attitude is a true handicap.

CRENNER BRADLEY, in *The Impossible Dream,* 1986

By accepting the traditional Hollywood attitude about Black characters, Black actors end up crippling themselves. If the part doesn't actually say "black sergeant," they won't even go up for it.

LOUIS GOSSETT, "I Was Swallowing a Kind of Poison," *Parade,* 17 July 1988

I was dirt poor, blind, you name it. Yet here I am today.

RAY CHARLES, in "Ray Charles Sees the Beauty," *Parade,* 10 October 1988

HAPPINESS

Better are loaves when the heart is joyous, than riches in unhappiness.

AMENENOPE, 950 B.C.

Happiness is like those palaces in fairy tales whose gates are guarded by dragons: we must fight in order to conquer it.

ALEXANDRE DUMAS, *The Count of Monte Cristo,* 1844

[T]here is neither happiness nor unhappiness in this world; there is only the comparison of one state with another.

Ibid.

The white man's happiness cannot be purchased by the black man's misery.

FREDERICK DOUGLASS, "The Destiny of Colored Americans," *North Star,* 16 November 1849

Let no one trust the happiness of the moment, there is in it a drop of gall.

JOAQUIM MACHADO DE ASSIS, *Epitaph for a Small Winner,* 1881

To increase abiding satisfaction for the mass of our people, and for all people, someone must sacrifice something of his own happiness. This is a duty only to those who recognize it as a duty. . . . It is silly to tell intelligent human beings: Be good and you will be happy. The truth is today, be good, be decent, be honorable and self-sacrificing and you will not always be happy. You will often be desperately unhappy. You may even be crucified, dead and buried, and the third day you will be just as dead as the first. But with the death of your happiness may easily come increased happiness and satisfaction and fulfillment for other people—strangers, unborn babies, uncreated worlds. If this is not sufficient incentive, never try it—remain hogs.

W. E. B. DU BOIS, "Education and Work," Commencement address, Howard University, Washington, D.C., 6 June 1930

Happiness is perfume, you can't pour it on somebody else without getting a few drops on yourself.

JAMES VAN DER ZEE, c. 1935

There is no short cut to utopia.

CLAUDE MCKAY, c. 1938

I have a true happiness/ and a happiness betrayed,/ the one like a rose,/ the other like a thorn.

GABRIELA MISTRAL, "Richness," *Tala,* 1938

There must always be the continuing struggle to make the increasing knowledge of the world bear some fruit in increasing understanding and in the production of human happiness.

CHARLES R. DREW, c. 1940

Oh mother, mother, where is happiness?/ They took my lover's tallness off to war,/ Left me lamenting. Now I cannot guess/ What I can use an empty heart-cup for./ He won't be coming back here any more.

GWENDOLYN BROOKS, "the sonnet-ballad," *Annie Allen,* 1949

When we said that men are endowed with certain inalienable rights, among those are life, liberty, and the pursuit of happiness, we did not pause to define happiness. That is the unexpressed quality in our quest, and we never tried to put it into words. That is why we say, "Let each man serve God in his own fashion."

JAMES BALDWIN, *Notes of a Native Son,* 1955

I do not deal in happiness. I deal in meaning.

RICHARD WRIGHT, c. 1956

I am content with the shape of my head/ made to carry the World./ Satisfied/ with the shape of my nose/ made to inhale the four winds of the world.

BERNARD DADIÉ, "I Thank You, Lord," *Dance of the Days,* 1956

People who make a living doing something they don't enjoy wouldn't even be happy with a one-day work week.

DUKE ELLINGTON, *Music Is My Mistress,* 1973

The Declaration of Independence declares the right of life, liberty, and the pursuit of happiness. The catch is that it doesn't give you the chance to catch up with happiness.

NATHAN HARE, JR., c. 1976

I could never live happily in Africa—or anywhere else—until I could live freely in Mississippi.

ALICE WALKER, *In Search of Our Mothers' Gardens,* 1983

Winnie, your love and support, the raw warmth of your body, the charming children you have given the family, the many friends you have won, the hope of enjoying that love and warmth again is what life and happiness mean to me.

NELSON MANDELA, February 1985

I'm fulfilled in what I do. . . . I never thought that a lot of money or fine clothes—the finer things of life—would make you happy. My concept of happiness is to be fulfilled in a spiritual sense.

CORETTA SCOTT KING, in "The King Family," *Ebony,* January 1987

Happiness is a gift bestowed upon/ the mortal,/ Even stars as they twinkle/ remind us that this is so./ When clouds clear away, the stars/ in Heaven smile at us,/ Light is shed upon the earth,/ bringing waves of happiness,/ To the big and small, that happiness/ is both destined.

SHABAAN ROBERTS, "Laugh with Happiness," in Chinweizu, ed., *Voices from Twentieth-Century Africa,* 1988

What we need is a happiness bridge where two hearts that are strangers can make an exchange of their gifts . . . ding!

ANTOINE LAMBA BOLAMBA, "Esanzo," in *ibid.*

HARD-HEAD

If you make your bed hard, you're going to lie in it.

TRADITIONAL

A hard head makes a soft behind.

TRADITIONAL

You don't believe fat meat is greasy.

TRADITIONAL

HARLEM

Harlem is the precious fruit in the Garden of Eden, the big apple.

ALAIN LOCKE, c. 1919

I sit on my stoop on Seventh Avenue and gaze at the sunkissed folks strolling up and down and think that surely Mississippi is here in New York, in Harlem, yes right on Seventh Avenue.

HARLEMNITE, in the *Messenger,* 1923

Ever since a traveling preacher had first told him about the place, King Solomon Gillis had longed to come to Harlem . . . In Harlem, black was white. You had rights that could not be denied you; you had privileges protected by law. And you had money. Everybody in Harlem had money. It was a land of plenty.

RUDOLPH FISHER, "City of Refuge," *Atlantic Monthly,* February 1925

Harlem is the largest plantation in this country—all sharecroppers: sharecropping on a mean plantation.

JOHN KILLENS, in *McClure's,* June 1928

Within the past ten years Harlem has acquired a world-wide reputation. . . . It is known as being exotic, colorful, and sensuous: a place where life wakes up at night.

JAMES WELDON JOHNSON, *Black Manhattan,* 1930

Harlem is still in the process of making. It is still new and mixed; so mixed that one may get many different views—which is all right so long as one view is not taken to be the whole picture.

Ibid.

There is the real and overshadowing Harlem, the commonplace, work-a-day Harlem. The Harlem of doubly handicapped Black masses engaged in the grim daily struggle for existence in the midst of this whirlpool of white civilization.

JAMES WELDON JOHNSON, *Along This Way,* 1933

Harlem did not have a "race" riot, it had a human revolt.

HARLEMNITE in *Afro-American,* 13 April 1935

Negro writers, both poets and novelists, centered their attention so exclusively upon life in the great urban centers that the city, especially Harlem, became an obsession with them. Now Harlem life is far from typical of Negro life; indeed life there is lived on a theatrical plane that is far from true of Negro life elsewhere. The writers' mistake lay in the assumption that what they saw was Negro life, when in reality it was just Harlem life.

J. SAUNDERS REDDING, *To Make a Poet Black,* 1939

Harlem still has a much greater number of the miserable than any other place I know. This is inspiring. Where can you find so many people in pain and so few crying about it?

CLAUDE MCKAY, *Harlem: Negro Metropolis,* 1940

Harlem is the queen of the Black belt, drawing Aframericans together into a vast humming hive.

Ibid.

Harlem was my first positive reaction to American life—it was like entering a paradise of my own people; the rhythm of Harlem still remains one of the most pleasurable sensations of my blood.

Ibid.

Ah, heart of me, the weary, weary feet/ In Harlem wandering from street to street.

CLAUDE MCKAY, "Harlem Shadows," *Selected Poems,* 1953

I could take the Harlem night/ and wrap around you,/ Take the neon lights and make a crown . . .

LANGSTON HUGHES, "Juke Box Love Song," *Selected Poems,* 1959

Harlem [is] a six-square-mile area in Manhattan's geographical center, containing over half of New York's million-plus black people. It [is] a community in transition, searching for its proper place in the black revolution.

JOHN HENRIK CLARKE, *Harlem, USA,* 1964

The colored people are in Harlem to stay, and they are coming each year by the thousands.

JOHN ROYALL, in *ibid.*

[In Harlem] we discovered the best "fishing" audience of all, by far the best-conditioned for Mr. Muhammad's teachings: the Christian churches.

MALCOLM X, *The Autobiography of Malcolm X,* 1965

Where, O Harlem, do you sleep? Perhaps you pluck the leaves of the last star in your fragile cup, and find again at the portals of the dawn the trouble, the weariness.

JEAN BRIERE, "Harlem," in Finn, ed., *Voices of Negritude,* 1988

Everybody thought I was absolutely insane. They said it would never work, a ballet school in Harlem. Minority kids, Black kids, a European art-form, a classical dance. Inside of two months I had four hundred kids, four months, eight hundred.

ARTHUR MITCHELL, in "Structure and Discipline Through Dance," *Smithsonian,* July 1988

HARLEM RENAISSANCE

The year 1928 represents probably the flood-tide of the present Negrophile movement. More books have been published about Negro life by white and Negro authors than the normal output of more than a decade in the past. More aspects of Negro life have been treated than were ever dreamed of, the typical curve of a major American fad.

ALAIN LOCKE, "1928: A Retrospective View," *Opportunity,* August 1929

That spring for me was the end of the Harlem Renaissance. Sophisticated New Yorkers turned to Noel Coward. Colored actors began to go hungry, publishers politely rejected new manuscripts, and patrons found other uses for their money. The cycle that had charlestoned into being on the dancing heels of *Shuffle Along* now ended in *Green Pastures* and *de Lawd.* The generous 1920s were over.

Ibid.

Melting pot Harlem—Harlem of honey and chocolate and caramel and rum and vinegar and lemon and lime and gall. Dusky dream Harlem rumbling into a nightmare tunnel where the subway from the Bronx keeps right on downtown, where the money from the nightclubs goes right on back downtown, where the jazz is drained to Broadway, whence Josephine goes to Paris, Robeson to London, Jean Toomer to a Quaker Meeting House. . . .

LANGSTON HUGHES, "My Early Days in Harlem," in Clarke, ed., *Harlem,* 1969

HATE

There is no medicine to cure hatred.

ASHANTI

When you are rich, you are hated, when you are poor, you are despised.

ASHANTI

Don't try to make someone hate the person he loves, for he will go on loving, but he will hate you.

SENEGAL

What an ever-present demon the spirit of hate is.

SAMUEL WARD, *Autobiography of a Fugitive Negro,* 1833

Hatred is blind, anger is foolhardy, and he who pours out vengeance risks having to drink a bitter draft.

ALEXANDRE DUMAS, *The Count of Monte Cristo,* 1844

I wonder that every colored person is not a misanthrope. Surely we have something to make us hate mankind.

CHARLOTTE FORTEN, 1856

When, oh When shall this cease?

Ibid.

I shall never permit myself to stoop so low as to hate any man.

BOOKER T. WASHINGTON, c. 1896

Those who become inoculated with the virus of race hatred are more unfortunate than the victim of it. Race hatred is the most malignant poison that can afflict the mind. It freezes up the fount of inspiration and chills the higher faculties of the soul.

KELLY MILLER, *The American Negro,* 1908

Hatred is the ever-handy dynamic of the demagogue.

Ibid.

Hatred is one long wait.

RENÉ MARAN, *Bataoula,* 1921

Vengeance is not a food which is eaten hot,/ It is a good thing to hide your hatred under the most warmhearted cordiality; cordiality being the ash with which you damp the fire, in order to allow it to hatch.

Ibid.

[A]ny man who walks in the way of power and property is bound to meet hate.

ZORA NEALE HURSTON, *Their Eyes Were Watching God,* 1937

It don't make no difference where you go, they always hating somebody somewhere. All along from Texas through New Mexico they hate Mexes worse'n a snake; down in lower California they get like mad dogs if you mention Japs; I ain't never been far east, but they say that out there everybody hates everybody else.

WILLIAM ATTAWAY, *Let Me Breathe Thunder,* 1939

What do you get out of hating people, out of having this bitterness in your heart always?

PETER ABRAHAMS, *Dark Testament,* 1942

Men often hate each other because they fear each other; they fear each other because they do not know each other; they do not know each other because they cannot communicate; they cannot communicate because they are separated.

A. PHILIP RANDOLPH, speech given at March on Washington Movement, Detroit, Michigan, 26 September 1942

But in so doing, my heart, preserve me from all
hatred/ do not make me turn into that man of
hatred of whom I feel only hatred/ for entrenched as
I am in this unique race/ you still know my tyrannical
boundless love/ you know that it is not from hatred
of other races/ that I demand a dinger for this
unique race.

AIMÉE CÉSAIRE, *Notes on a Return to the Native Land,* 1947

There is no sense in hate; it comes back to you; therefore, make your history so laudable, magnificent, and untarnished, that another generation will not seek to repay your seeds for the sins inflicted upon their fathers.

MARCUS GARVEY, in *Garvey and Garveyism,* 1963

Hate is consuming and weakening. Hateful thinking breeds negative actions.

Ibid.

When a man is despised and hated by other men and all around are the instruments of violence in behalf of such attitudes, then he may find himself resorting to hatred as a means of salvaging a sense of self, however fragmented.

HOWARD THURMAN, *Disciplines of the Spirits,* 1963

When you have taught a man to hate himself, you've really got it and gone.

MALCOLM X, speech given at Economic Club, London, 1965

The colonial powers of Europe ... always project Africa in a negative light: jungle savages, cannibals, nothing civilized.... [I]t was negative to you and me, and I began to hate it.... In hating Africa and in hating the Africans, we ended up hating ourselves, without ever realizing it.

MALCOLM X, "After the Bombing," speech given in Detroit, Michigan, 14 February 1965

[W]e have been a people who hated our African characteristics. We hated our heads, we hated the shape of our nose, we wanted one of those long dog-like noses.... we hated the color of our skin, hated the blood of Africa that was in our veins; we had to end up hating ourselves.

Ibid.

Hate is not inborn; it has to be constantly cultivated, to be brought into being, in conflict with more or less recognized guilt complexes. Hate demands existence, and he who hates has to show his hate in appropriate actions and behaviors; in a sense, he has to become hate. That is why the Americans have substituted discrimination for lynching.

FRANTZ FANON, *Black Skin, White Masks,* 1967

Depression and grief are hatred turned on the self.

WILLIAM GRIER and PRICE COBB, *Black Rage,* 1968

Men must be carefully taught to hate, and the lessons learned by one generation must be relearned by the next.

LERONE BENNETT, *Challenge of Blackness,* 1968

[O]ne could not create a world of hatred because invariably that world becomes a suspicious one, an isolated one; and, finally, one so infected by disease that life, any life, trapped within it was worthless.

ADDISON GAYLE, JR., "The Son of My Father," in Chapman, ed., *New Black Voices,* 1971

Up to the age thirty-one I had been hurt emotionally, spiritually, and physically as much as thirty-one years can bear: I had lived in the South, I had fallen down an elevator shaft, I had been kicked out of college, I had served seven and one half years in prison, I had survived the Depression; and still I was entire, complete, functional and my mind was sharp, my reflexes were good, and I was not bitter. But under the mental corrosion of race prejudice in Los Angeles I had become bitter and saturated with hate.

CHESTER HIMES, *The Quality of Hurt,* 1972

The price of hating other human beings is loving oneself less.

ELDRIDGE CLEAVER, c. 1975

Hate is an ugly word. It is an ugly emotion. It would be wonderful to say there is no hate; to say we do not hate. But to merely speak the words would not make it so.

CHESTER HIMES, 1976

We can no longer afford the luxury of bigotry and hatred.

COLEMAN YOUNG, c. 1977

Only those who permit themselves to be are despised.

ALEX HALEY, *Roots,* 1977

[T]he opposite of love was not hate but indifference, and the opposite of hate was also indifference.

BILL RUSSELL, *Second Wind,* 1979

Pushkin's antipathy toward autocracy began in his infancy. He encountered three czars during his short life: the first snatched the bonnet off his head; the second exiled him; the third censored him.

JAMES LOCKETT, "Alexander Sergevich Pushkin," *Negro History Bulletin,* July–September 1982

Our youth do not want our hate, our youth want to live in a world in understanding, fellowship, and unity.

LEON SULLIVAN, "Dreams of the Future," *Negro History Bulletin,* January–March 1982

[Hate] once spread about . . . becomes a web in which [one] sit[s] caught and paralyzed like the fly who stepped into the parlor.

ALICE WALKER, *In Search of Our Mothers' Gardens,* 1983

No one can hate their source and survive. . . .

Ibid.

We have more hatred now because we've entered a new era: a competition for jobs, attention, power. We've come a long way, but it's like nibbling at the edge of darkness.

BENJAMIN HOOKS, publisher's foreword, *Crisis,* March 1987

There is a greater antipathy toward Blacks than any other ethnic group.

AMINDA WILKINS, in "Interview: Aminda Wilkins," *Crisis,* January 1988

HEALING

Truth is healing.

FRANK YERBY, c. 1969

The sickness of the Church in America is intimately involved with the bankruptcy of American theology. When the Church fails to live up to its appointed mission, it means that theology is partly responsible.

JAMES CONE, *Black Theology and Black Power,* 1969

The healing/ of all our wounds/ is forgiveness/ that permits a promise/ of our return/ at the end.

ALICE WALKER, *Good Night Willie Lee, I'll See You in the Morning,* 1975

Mankind must realize that it is in need of healing, not from the outer world, but from within.

CAROLYN WARFIELD, "Rising to the Light Within," *City Arts Quarterly,* Spring 1988

Whatever we can do to facilitate learning on the one hand and loving on the other is important, because those are the most healing forces available to us.

NA'IM AKBAR, in *Essence,* April 1988

HEALTH

A healthy ear can stand hearing sick words.

SENEGAL

Sickness come di gallop, but e tek e own time fo' walk 'way. (Sickness comes suddenly, but goes slowly.)

WEST INDIES

You'll never catch a cold if you catch the first rain of spring.

TRADITIONAL

A society that [treats] a whole race of people as flotsam and jetsam in the river of life cannot expect all of them to grow up healthy and well-balanced.

MARTIN LUTHER KING, JR., *Where Do We Go From Here?* 1968

Health is a human right, not a privilege to be purchased.

SHIRLEY CHISHOLM, address given to Congress, 1970

Good health is a duty to yourself, to your contemporaries, to your inheritors, to the progress of the world.

GWENDOLYN BROOKS, *Report from Part One,* 1972

Though ill health has compelled my retirement, you can be sure that in my heart I go on singing. . . .

PAUL ROBESON, in *Daily World*, 22 April 1973

I had an easy life and that makes me healthy.

EUBIE BLAKE, *Eubie,* 1979

My mind is like a general, and my body is like an army. I keep the body in shape and it does what I tell it to do.

HERSCHEL WALKER, in "Herschel Walker: Pro Football's New Million-Dollar Man," *Ebony,* November 1986

In a sick world, it is the first duty of an the artist to get well.

JEAN TOOMER, in Kerman and Eldridge, *Lives of Jean Toomer,* 1987

I had a series of childhood illnesses. The first was scarlet fever. Then I had pneumonia. Polio followed. I walked with braces until I was at least nine years old. My life wasn't like the average person who grew up and decided to enter the world of sports.

WILMA RUDOLPH, in *USA Today,* 6 August 1987

The key to Black mental health is awareness, a clear picture of who you are as a contemporary historical being.

NA'IM AKBAR, in "Growing Up Integrated (Did Momma Do the Right Thing?)" *Crisis,* March 1988

Clean living. I don't do anything that would injure my health. That's why I'm eighty-one years old and I've been able to work this long.

CAB CALLOWAY, c. 1988

God gave me this physical impairment to remind me that I'm not the greatest, He is.

MUHAMMAD ALI, in *Jet,* 16 May 1988

As long as I have breath in my body, a little good health, I can get success again.

RAY CHARLES, in "Ray Charles Sees the Beauty," *Parade,* 10 October 1988

I am not sick. I am broken.

FRIDA KAHLO, in Herrara, *Frida Kahlo: The Paintings,* 1991

I thought education should be the priority until four or five years ago, but if you're not healthy and well-fed, you are not going to do well even in a private school. If a child comes to school hungry, the best school in the world won't help. You have not seen many civil rights groups marching for medical and nutrition rights for children.

ARTHUR ASHE, in *USA Weekend,* 28 June 1991

HEART

When the eyes see, the ears hear, and the nose breathes, they report to the heart. It is the heart that brings forth every issue, and the tongue that repeats the thoughts of the heart.

PTAH HOTEP, c. 2350 B.C.

Do not reveal your heart to a stranger. He might use your words against you.

SCRIBE ANY of the Palace of Nefertari, 1554–1070 B.C.

Break not your heart; sorrow will roll away the mists at sunrise.

AFRICA

Be careful what you set your heart upon, for it will surely be yours.

AFRICA

The heart of a man is a gift of god. Beware of neglecting it.

EGYPT

The heart is more dangerous than the river with its nine bends.

INDIA

The heart is not a knee that can be bent.

SENEGAL

When the heart overflows, it comes out through the mouth.

CONGO

Hearts do not meet one another like roads.

IVORY COAST

Oh doctor, I have a pain in my heart, give me a treatment, but don't put me in the hospital.

SOMALIA

The heart "eats" what it desires.

KENYA

Make some muscle/ in your head but/ use the muscle in your heart.

TRADITIONAL

The human heart is a strange mystery.

ALEXANDRE DUMAS, *Le Demi-Monde,* 1855

My heart was like a tiger's when a hunter tries to seize her young.

LINDA BRENT, *Incidents in the Life of a Slave Girl,* 1861

An envious heart makes a treacherous ear.

ZORA NEALE HURSTON, *Their Eyes Were Watching God,* 1937

Our going to church on Sunday is like placing one's ear to another's chest to hear the unquenchable murmur of the human heart.

RICHARD WRIGHT, *12 Million Black Voices,* 1941

To walk with treachery all day is painful. It puts a weight on a man's heart.

PETER ABRAHAMS, *Wild Conquest,* 1950

As long as man has a dream in his heart, he cannot lose the significance of living.

HOWARD THURMAN, *Meditations of the Heart,* 1953

[T]he individual human heart [is] more revolutionary than any political party or platform.

AL YOUNG, "Statement on Aesthetics, Poetics, Kinetics," in Chapman, ed., *New Black Voices,* 1972

The human heart is limited and only capable of loving and caring for but a few people. If this were not so, we'd all be saints and really take care of our brothers.

ROMARE BEARDEN, in *Encore,* October 1972

His heart is a lion.

MUHAMMAD ALI, *The Greatest,* 1975

My heart is a laughing gland.

TONI CADE BAMBARA, "Salvation Is the Issue," in Evans, ed., *Black Women Writers,* 1984

A good head and good heart are always a formidable combination.

NELSON MANDELA, *Higher Than Hope,* 1991

Can't nobody but God handle your whole heart without messing it up.

JEREMIAH WRIGHT, sermon given at Hartford Church, Detroit, Michigan, October 1991

HEAVEN

Everybody talking about Heaven ain't going there.

SPIRITUAL

Bread of Heaven, Bread of Heaven, feed me till I want no more.

SPIRITUAL

I heard a loud noise in the heavens and the Spirit instantly appeared to me and said the Serpent was loosened, and Christ had laid down the Yoke he had borne for the sins of man, and that I should take it on and fight against the Serpent, for the time was fast approaching when the first should be last and the last should be first.

NAT TURNER, *Confessions of Nat Turner,* Southampton County, Virginia, November 1831

The shortness of time, the certainty of death, and the instability of all things here induce me to turn my thoughts from earth to heaven.

MARIA STEWART, *Meditations from the Pen of Mrs. Maria W. Stewart,* 1879

We have tried all the courts of the land with no avail; now let us try the courts of Heaven, with an unshaken confidence in Him, with patience to wait until change comes.

REVERDY RANSOM, in *AME Church Review,* 1895

Heavenly witnesses are a tricky lot, to be used by whoever is closest to Heaven at that time.

JAMES BALDWIN, *The Fire Next Time,* 1963

Only a "dry as dust" religion prompts a minister to extol the glories of Heaven while ignoring the social conditions that cause men to live in earthly hell.

MARTIN LUTHER KING, JR., *Why We Can't Wait,* 1963

Art of meekness is the science of Heaven.

JOHN B. RAYNER, in Meier, ed., *Negro Thought in America,* 1964

Heaven is a place where you get an opportunity to use all the millions of sensitivities you never knew you had before.

DUKE ELLINGTON, *Music Is My Mistress,* 1973

My job as a minister is not only to make heaven my home, but to make my home on earth sheer heaven.

JOSEPH LOWERY, in *USA Today,* 8 March 1985

HELL

A bad wife in a good man's house is his hell in this world already.

The Gulistan of Sadi, 1184–1292 A.D.

Purgatory is a pawnshop which lends on all virtue for high interest and short terms.

JOAQUIM MACHADO DE ASSIS, *Don Casmuro,* 1900

The man who believes his neighbor is foreordained to hell, is prone to raise hell for him.

CHARLES V. ROMAN, *American Civilization and the Negro: The Solution,* 1916

If hell is what we are taught it is, then there will be more Christians there than all the days in creation.

MARCUS GARVEY, *Philosophy and Opinions of Marcus Garvey,* 1923

The very idea of hell is a helluvanidea.

WILLIAM PICKEN, "Things Nobody Believes," *Messenger,* February 1923

The Hell that Sherman knew was a physical one—of rapine, destruction and death. The other is a purgatory for the mind, for the spirit, for the soul of men. Not only War is Hell.

VICTOR DALY, *Not Only War,* 1932

It is hell to belong to a suppressed minority.

CLAUDE MCKAY, *A Long Way from Home,* 1937

What if this were Hell, this absence of sleep, this poet's desert,/ This pain of living, this dying of not dying,/ This anguish of shadows, this passion over death and light.

LEOPOLD SENGHOR, "Midnight Elegy," *Ethiopics,* 1956

To live without roots is to live in hell and no man chooses voluntarily to live in hell.

PETER ABRAHAMS, "The Blacks," *Holiday Magazine,* 1959

Now beauty hides a vandal's face./ Yours stripped my tall heart bare,/ Still hell is an entrancing place/ Because you're going there.

SAMUEL ALLEN, "Love Song," *New Negro Poets: USA,* 1964

And you wonder why you're catching so much hell. Why, the money you spend for whiskey will run a government.

MALCOLM X, *The Autobiography of Malcolm X,* 1965

It's harder to defeat/ Than it is to spell,/ Revenge is not sweet,/ It's bitter as Hell.

DUKE ELLINGTON, "Sacred Concert," 1965

There is no heaven or hell in the sense that they are places one goes after death. The heaven or hell to which one goes is right there in the span of years that we spend in this body on earth.

ADAM CLAYTON POWELL, JR., *Adam by Adam,* 1971

HELP

Self-help is the best help.

AESOP, "Hercules and the Wagon," c. 300 B.C.

He could be helped in a certain way only because he was hurt in a certain way; and his help is simply to be enabled to move from one conundrum to the next . . . from one disaster to the next.

JAMES BALDWIN, *Notes of a Native Son,* 1955

If help is given to us let us accept it, but let us not sit down and say nothing can be done until the rest of the world out of the goodness of its heart willing to grant us charity.

ARTHUR LEWIS, speech given at the Study Conference of Economic Development, 5–15 August 1957

The day has arrived that you will have to help yourselves or suffer the worst.

ELIJAH MUHAMMAD, in the *Pittsburgh Courier,* 3 September 1958

Elijah Muhammad has been able to do what generations of welfare workers and committees and resolutions and reports and housing projects . . . have failed to do: to heal and redeem drunkards, and junkies to convert people who have come out of prison and to keep them out, to make men chaste and women virtuous, and to invest both the male and the female with a pride and a serenity that hang about them like an unfailing light.

JAMES BALDWIN, *The Fire Next Time,* 1963

[T]here always seems [to have] been someone . . . to point out the way for me to go. When I got to the next corner, there would be someone else standing there to tell me where to go. And that's how my whole life has been all along.

DUKE ELLINGTON, *Music Is My Mistress,* 1973

In the early years, Richard Allen, Peter Williams, Absalom Jones, Prince Hall, Paul Cuffee and Daniel Coker took up projects of mutual aid for Africans. Their work set the stage for missionary abolitionist and self help programs undertaken by such people as Frederick Douglass, Martin Delaney, Sojourner Truth, and Alexander Crummell.

EUGENE REDMOND, *Drumvoice,* 1976

Help those who have kicked the habit and paid their dues because if we don't help them to get on their feet, the dope man will.

GEORGE KIRBY, c. 1979

When we have someone in the White House like Mr. Reagan, he helps us, not because he wants to help us, but his wickedness helps us to find each other.

LOUIS FARRAKHAN, 1984

What Africa needs is help. After centuries of slavers taking her strongest sons and daughters, after years of colonialism—Africa needs her progeny to bring something to her.

MAYA ANGELOU, *All God's Children Need Traveling Shoes,* 1986

An error means a child needs help, not a reprimand or ridicule for doing something wrong.

MARVA COLLINS, in "Marva Collins: Teaching Success in the City," *Message,* February 1987

If a Black person gets in trouble, he calls out two names, Jesus and the NAACP.

JOE MADISON, in "The NAACP in Search of a Great Future," *American Visions,* February 1987

If you and I don't build a bridge back, throw out some strong lifelines to our children, youth and families whom poverty, unemployment are engulfing, they're going to drown, pull many of us down with them and undermine the future our forbears dreamed, struggled, and died for.

MARIAN WRIGHT EDELMAN, speech given at the Congressional Black Caucus, 26 September 1987

If you don't look out for others, who will look out for you?

WHOOPI GOLDBERG, in "People Are Talking About . . . " *Jet,* 11 January 1988

Jesus said, "If you love me, feed my sheep." I want to feed the sheep.

MELBA MOORE, in *Essence,* April 1988

HERITAGE

Only a fool points to his heritage with his left hand.

GHANA

I do not for a moment doubt that my Negro descent and narrow group culture have in many cases predisposed me to interpret my facts too favorably for my race; but there is little danger of long misleading here, for the champions of white folk are legion. The Negro has long been the clown of history, the slave of industry. I am trying to show that the truth of history lies not in the mouths of partisans, but rather in the calm Science that sits between. Her cause I seek to serve, and wherever I feel, I am at least paying for Truth the respect of earnest effort.

W. E. B. DU BOIS, C. 1903

It is a heritage of which they would be proud to know how their fathers and grandfathers handled their brief day of power during the Reconstruction period.

IDA B. WELLS, in Duster, ed., *Crusade for Justice,* 1928

Our only chance to be ourselves is to repudiate no part of the ancestral heritage. Well, for eight-tenths of us this heritage is the gift of Africa.

JEAN PRICE MARS, *Thus Spake Our Uncle,* 1928

Nothing had been done in Negro folklore when the greatest cultural wealth of the continent was disappearing without the world ever realizing it had ever been.

ZORA NEALE HURSTON, *Mules and Men,* 1935

With some of us, militancy against discrimination and racial indignity is a heritage from our forbears.

WILLIAM HASTIE, speech given at the University of Rochester, Rochester, New York, 1950

Of my heritage I [am] very very, proud. I early learned to orate, to develop my speaking voice. I sang the songs of my people—in many ways, especially rhythmically, still full of African turns of musical phrase and forms.

PAUL ROBESON, "A Word about African Languages," *Spotlight on Africa,* February 1955

We must recapture our heritage and our ideals if we are to liberate ourselves from the bonds of white supremacy. We must launch a cultural revolution to unbrainwash an entire people.

MALCOLM X, speech given to the Organization of Afro-American Unity, 28 June 1964

My great-grandmama told my grandmama the part she lived through that my grandmama didn't live through and my grandmama told my mama what they both lived through and we were supposed to pass it down like that from generation to generation so we'd never forget.

GAYL JONES, *Corregidora,* 1975

[Martin Luther King] gave us back our heritage. He gave us back our homeland; the bones and dust of our ancestors, who may now sleep within our caring *and* our hearing. He gave us the blueness of the Georgia sky in autumn as in summer; the colors of the Southern winter as well as glimpses of the green of vacation-time spring. He gave us full-time use of our own words, and restored our memories to those of us who were forced to run away, as realities we might each day enjoy and leave for our children. He gave us continuity of place, without which community is ephemeral. He gave us home.

ALICE WALKER, *In Search of Our Mothers' Gardens,* 1983

Heritage . . . must continually be renewed rather than fixed in the past.

BARBARA CHRISTIAN, "Alice Walker: The Black Woman Artist as Wayward," in Evans, ed., *Black Women Writers,* 1984

I had the burning need to know where I came from. But apartheid had long adulterated my heritage and tradition.

MARK MATHABANE, *Kaffir Boy,* 1986

When I do a routine I am usually playing three fathers all the time—my grandfather, my father, and myself.

BILL COSBY, c. 1988

Whenever people refer to me as someone "who happens to be black," I wonder if they realize that both my parents are black. If I had turned out to be Scandinavian or Chinese, people would have wondered what was going on.

THOMAS SOWELL, in the *Detroit News,* 13 February 1989

Far from being ciphers, we are, have been, dreamers, witnesses, and lovers. The most pervasive evidence on the scene is that we endured and created out of the miracle of our survival jazz and the blues and the cakewalk and "Little Sally Walker" and "For Once In My Life" and "Fine and Mellow" and "Satin Doll" and "When Malindy Sings" and "When Sue Wears Red."

LERONE BENNETT, JR., in *Ebony,* August 1989

HERO

I am not terrified by the gallows upon which I am soon to stand and suffer death for doing what George Washington was made a hero for.

JOHN ANTHONY COPELAND, on his execution, 12 December 1859

Old John Brown's body lies a mouldering in the grave. While weep the sons of bondage, whom he ventured to save; But though he lost his life in struggle for the slave, His soul is marching on. Glory, glory, Hallelujah! Glory, glory, Hallelujah! Glory, glory, Hallelujah! His soul is marching on.

WILLIAM WELLS-BROWN, in *The Negro in the Rebellion,* 1867

Remember Denmark Vesey, . . . remember Nathaniel Turner, . . . remember Shields Green and Copeland, who followed noble John Brown, and fell as glorious martyrs for the cause of the slave. Remember that in a contest with oppression, the Almighty has no attribute which can take sides with oppressors.

FREDERICK DOUGLASS, *Life and Times of Frederick Douglass,* 1881

John Brown worked not simply for Black men—he worked with them, and he was a companion of their daily life, knew their faults and virtues, and felt as few white Americans have felt the bitter tragedy of the lot.

W. E. B. DU BOIS, c. 1910

There are those who go down in the blood and dust of battle. They say ugly things to an ugly world. They spew the lukewarm fence straddlers out of their mouths, like God of old; they cry aloud and spare not; they shout from the housetops, and they make this world so damned uncomfortable with its nasty burden of evil that it tries to get good and does get better.

W. E. B. DU BOIS, "The Philosophy of Mr. Dole," *Crisis,* May 1914

You have been tremendously tested. Your record sent a thrill of joy and satisfaction to the hearts of millions of Black and white Americans, rich and poor, high and low. You will go back to America, heroes, as you really are. You will go back as you carried yourself over here—in a straightforward, manly, and modest way. Do nothing to spoil the magnificent record you have made in war.

ROBERT R. MOTON, *Finding a Way Out,* 1920

Du Bois by his full participation and dedication to the people's struggle, gives new meaning to the history of the Negro on his long and courageous fight for all liberation.

PAUL ROBESON, "A Tribute to W. E. B. Du Bois," *Freedom,* March 1951

Heroes can be found less in large things than in small ones, less in public than in private.

JAMES BALDWIN, *Nobody Knows My Name,* 1961

None of our heroes fail because of progressive perfection. They did as much as they could given the time and the circumstancees.

RON KARENGA, speech given at Yale University, New Haven, Connecticut, 1967

There will not be found in anyone/ nor will there be
in two or more another one who will have or place
at our hand/ as he did./All of the attributes at his
command.

MARGARET DANNER, "There Will Not Be Found," *Negro Digest,* June 1967

Malcolm is an authentic hero, indeed the only universal Black hero. In his unrelenting opposition to the viciousness in America, he fired the imaginations of Black men all over the world.

WILLIAM GRIER AND PRICE COBB, *Black Rage,* 1968

Joe Louis . . . Champion of the world. A Black boy. Some Black mother's son. He was the strongest man in the world. People drank Coca-Colas like ambrosia and ate candy bars like Christmas. . . . It wouldn't do for a Black man and his family to be caught on a lonely country road on the night when Joe Louis had proved that we were the strongest people in the world.

MAYA ANGELOU, *I Know Why the Caged Bird Sings,* 1969

Booker T. Washington was the idol of Marcus Garvey.

AMY GARVEY, in " Mrs. Marcus Garvey Talks with Ida Lewis," *Encore,* May 1973

They had the impossible dream of becoming pilots, fighting for their country. Believe me, it was almost impossible. The country created a special air force for the Tuskegee Airmen.

LENA HORNE, 1976

Mary McLeod Bethune's visionary crusade gave a view of possibilities to be realized in some distant future.

HOWARD THURMAN, *With Head and Heart,* 1979

Henri Christophe was my first hero after my mother. To me, he was just the opposite of a slave: *he would not be one.* He was indomitable. . . . [H]is life brought home to me for the first time that being Black was not just a limiting feeling. Christophe could not be held back by anything, and his power reminded me of my mother.

BILL RUSSELL, *Second Wind,* 1979

Booker T. Washington was born a slave in 1856 and lived as one for nine years. But, despite poverty, illiteracy, and other disadvantages, he always imagined a purposeful life for himself.

DAVID SMITH, c. 1980

Timmie Smith and John Carlos were beautiful on the victory stand raising their fist in the Black power salute while the "Star Spangled Banner" played. They showed how displeased they were about how Americans were treating them. . . . Duke was royalty. Good-looking, dressed like a king, and easygoing. He could just as soon talk to the King of England as he would some jive hustler. I listened to his mellow tones.

JOE LOUIS, *My Life,* 1981

I wouldn't be forgotten, maybe one hundred years from now some little boy would be thumbing some book and be glad that I was born.

Ibid.

If Frederick Douglass had not run away from slavery into freedom and thereby become a greater emancipator than Garrison and went to Europe and pleaded our cause for freedom, nobody else would have done it.

BENJAMIN E. MAYS, "I Knew Carter G. Woodson," *Negro History Bulletin,* March 1981

He was The One, The Hero, The One Fearless Person for whom we had waited. I hadn't even realized before that we *had* been waiting for Martin Luther King, Jr., but we had. And I knew it for sure when my mother added his name to the list of people she prayed for every night.

ALICE WALKER, *In Search of Our Mothers' Garden,* 1983

Duke was a culture hero, a musical magician who worked his powers through his mastery of form nuance, good style. A charismatic figure whose personality influenced even those who had no immediate concern with jazz.

RALPH ELLISON, "Homage to Duke Ellington on His Birthday," *Going to the Territory,* 1986

Duke Ellington touched a very special place in the soul of this country. The fact that he has not and will not be recognized has left us with a gigantic cultural void.

WYNTON MARSALIS, "Why We Must Preserve Our Jazz Heritage," *Ebony,* February 1986

[From my school principal]... I learned to dream that I could be more than I was permitted to be in the segregated society about me. He taught me that if I was to be all that I was capable of being, I must work hard and study hard. But, most of all ... he taught me that work and learning could be fun.

PERCY SUTTON, in "The Most Unforgettable Person in My Family," *Ebony,* August 1986

Mayor Harold Washington knew how to talk to Black people, how to talk about Black people and you better believe, he knew how to talk for black people.

HERBERT MARTIN, in "Mayor Washington Eulogized as Symbol of Hope for Blacks," *Jet,* 14 December 1987

Those who stand tall in our presence appear to be of unusual height because, in most cases, they stand on the shoulders of giants who have preceded them.

JOHN HOPE FRANKLIN, 1988

Roy Wilkins and his NAACP family changed America. This was done with a faith and understanding of American society and the fighting spirit of Afro-Americans and their allies.

JOE JOHNSON, 1988

The Patriots are Malcolm X, Martin, Gandhi, Selassie, Sadat, Garvey, and Satchel Paige. They were men who loved a people, had a conviction and a belief in self-reliance. They were of a universal spirit.

CAROLYN WARFIELD, in "Rising to the Light Within," *City Arts Quarterly,* Spring 1988

Muhammad Ali visited kids when I was in juvenile, he changed my life. I reshaped my life. I decided then I was going to be a champion of the world.

MIKE TYSON, in "Mike Tyson Talks About His Future And Says 'I'm a Dreamer,'" *Jet,* November 1988

A hero is simply someone who rises above his own human weaknesses, for an hour, a day, a year, to do something stirring.

BETTY DERAMUS, 1989

HISTORY

They recreated history, giving it life through the word and voices.

KENYA

Kingdoms and empires are in the likeness of man; like him they are born, they grow and disappear. Each sovereign embodies one moment of that life. Formerly, the kings of Ghana extended their kingdom over all the lands inhabited by the Black man, but the circle has closed and they are nothing more than petty princes in a desolate land.

MALI GRIOT MAMADOU KOUYATE, *Sundiata; An Epic of Old Mali,* 1217–1237 A.D.

The first thing to do is to get into every school, private, public, or otherwise, Negro literature and history. We aren't trying to displace other literature but trying to acquaint all children with Negro history and literature.

BOOKER T. WASHINGTON, c. 1900

All great people glorify their history and look back upon their early attainments with a spiritual vision.

KELLY MILLER, *Voice of the Negro,* 1906

Many histories of our people in slavery, peace, and war are written and each serves a purpose. These books have disseminated the fragmentary knowledge where the spark of learning has awakened the soul to thirst for more and better food.

ARTHUR A. SCHOMBURG, in *Racial Integrity,* July 1913

All these books are like meat without salt, they bear no analogy to our own, it would be a wise plan for us to lay down a course of study in Negro History and achievements.

Ibid.

We should emphasize not Negro History, but the Negro in history. What we need is not a history of selected races or nations, but the history of the world, void of national bias, race, hate, and religious prejudice. There should be no indulgence in undue eulogy of the Negro. The case of the Negro is well taken care of when it is shown how he has far influenced the development of civilization.

CARTER G. WOODSON, 1927

Every student must take a course in Negro History. Recitation every day for two months is held, then an examination, written and oral. The students then write orations on our achievements.

NANNIE BURROUGHS, in the *Pittsburgh Courier,* 8 June 1929

Facts are mere dross of history. It is from the abstract truth which interpenetrates them and lies latent among men, like gold in the ore, that the mass derives its whole value. The precious particles are generally combined with the baser in such a manner that the separation is a task of the utmost difficulty.

CARTER G. WOODSON, *The Story of the Negro Retold,* 1935

The historian is the prophet looking backward.

Ibid.

History is a record of the progress of mankind rather than of racial or national achievements.

Ibid.

The course of history can be changed but not halted.

PAUL ROBESON, "The Artist Must Take Sides," *Daily Worker,* 4 November 1937

As a historian, I know that Hitlers come and go; they are never permanent fixtures.

CARTER G. WOODSON, *Journal of Negro History,* c. 1945

I brought to Shakespeare, Bach, Rembrandt, to the stones of Paris, to the cathedral at Chartres, and to the Empire State Building, a special attitude. These were not really my creations, they did not contain my history; I might search in them in vain forever for any reflection of myself. I was an interloper; this was not my heritage.

JAMES BALDWIN, *Notes of a Native Son,* 1955

History is God's big clock. For a day is but a thousand years in terms of eternity.

C. L. FRANKLIN, "Watchman, What of the Night?" c. 1956

History and freedom should not be ignored.

JAMES M. LAWSON, "From a Lunch Counter Stool," speech given at SNCC Conference, Raleigh, North Carolina, 17 April 1960

Sometimes history offers only one path. And all are obliged to take it.

AIMÉ CÉSAIRE, *Tragedy of King Christophe,* 1963

The settler makes history and is conscious of making it. And because he constantly refers to the history of his mother country, he clearly indicates that he himself is the extension of that mother country. Thus the history which he writes is not the history of the country which he plunders but the history of his own nation in regard to all that she skims off, all that she violates and starves.

FRANTZ FANON, *Wretched of the Earth,* 1963

We are not makers of history. We are made by history.

MARTIN LUTHER KING, JR. *Strength to Love,* 1963

History is the long and tragic story of the fact that privileged groups seldom give up their privileges voluntarily.

MARTIN LUTHER KING, JR., *Letter from a Birmingham City Jail,* 1963

Of all our studies, history is best qualified to reward our research. When you see you have problems . . . examine the historic method used all over the world by others who have problems similar to yours. Once you see how they got theirs straight, then you know how you can get yours straight.

MALCOLM X, "Message to the Grass Roots," speech given in Detroit, Michigan, 10 November 1963

Western man wrote "his" history as if it were the history of the entire human race.

JOHN KILLENS, "Explanation of the Black Psyche," *New York Times,* 7 June 1964

History furnishes innumerable proofs of one of its own major laws, that the budding future is always stronger than the withering past. This has been amply demonstrated during every major revolution throughout history.

KWAME NKRUMAH, *Neocolonialism,* 1965

The Black man's history—when you refer to him as the black man you go way back, but when you refer to him as a Negro, you can only go as far back as the Negro goes. And when you go beyond the shores of America you can't find a Negro.

MALCOLM X, speech given at Organization for Afro-American Unity Rally, Audubon Ballroom, New York City, 24 January 1965

History is a people's memory and without a memory, man is demoted to the level of the lower animals.

MALCOLM X, speech given to the Organization of Afro-American Unity Rally, Audubon Ballroom, New York City, 14 February 1965

Native Son was a foremost example of the novelist as historian; the prying in the past could clue him in to the future. America had not seen the likes of Bigger Thomas before; perhaps it dreamed of him, but Wright produced this oppression-activated man whose cousins still stalk the American streets.

JOHN WILLIAMS, *Beyond the Angry Black,* 1966

I want American history taught. Unless I'm in that book, you're not in it either. History is not a procession of illustrious people. It's about what happens to a people. Millions of anonymous people is what history is about.

JAMES BALDWIN, "James Baldwin . . . in Conversation," *Arts in Society,* Summer 1966

History give[s] eloquent testimony to the fact that conflicts are never resolved without trustful give and take on both sides.

MARTIN LUTHER KING, JR., "A Time to Break Silence," speech given at Riverside Church, New York City, 4 April 1967

The final interpretation of African history is the responsibility of scholars of African descent.

JOHN HENRIK CLARKE, "A New Approach to African History," speech given at Afro-American Conference, Detroit, Michigan, 13 May 1967

Rob a people of their sense of history and you take away hope.

WYATT T. WALKER, "Crime, Vietnam and God," *Negro Digest,* December 1967

History takes still more from those who have lost everything, and gives more to those who have taken everything. For its sweeping judgments acquit the unjust and dismiss the pleas of their victims. History never confesses.

Negro Digest, August 1968

It is ironical that America with its history of injustice to the poor, especially the Black man and the Indian, prides itself on being a Christian nation.

JAMES CONE, *Black Theology and Black Power,* 1969

American history is a myth and can only be accepted when read with blinders that block out the facts.

DICK GREGORY, *No More Lies,* 1971

History informs us of past mistakes from which we can learn without repeating them. It also inspires us and gives confidence and hope bred of victories already won.

WILLIAM HASTIE, speech given in Atlanta, Georgia, 1971

History is written by the winners.

ALEX HALEY, interview on "David Frost Show," 20 April 1972

No Black history becomes significant and meaningful unless it is taught in the context of world and national history. In its sealed off, black-studies centers, it will be simply another exercise in racial breast-feeding.

ROY WILKINS, c. 1975

As long as we rely on white historians to write Black history for us, we should keep silent about what they produce.

CHANCELLOR WILLIAMS, *The Destruction of Black Civilization,* 1975

What became of the Black people of Sumer the traveler asked the old man, for ancient records show that the people of Sumer were Black. What happened to them? "Ah," the old man sighed, "they lost their history, so they died."

Ibid.

The African historian who evades the problem of Egypt is neither modest nor objective, nor unruffled; he is ignorant, cowardly, and neurotic. Imagine, if you can, the uncomfortable position of a Western historian writing the history of Europe without referring to Greco-Latin antiquity and try to pass that off as a scientific approach.

CHEIKH DIOP, *The African Origins of Civilization: Myth or Reality,* 1978

History is calling us to rule again and you lost dead souls are standing around doing the freakie-deakie.

TONI CADE BAMBARA, *The Salt Eaters,* 1980

There is a tension in Black America. And it has its roots in the general history of race. The manner in which we see this history determines how we act. How should we see this history? What should we feel about it? This is important to know, because the sense of how that history should be felt is what either unites or separates us.

LARRY NEAL, c. 1981

It is not a coincidence that the history of Black business in this country is a history of wave after wave of Black accomplishment being blocked by wall after wall of racism and backlash.

EARL GRAVES, "Black Reflections: Visions of the Future," *Negro History Bulletin,* June 1981

History reminds us that our life traditions were wholly encompassed by our kinships and tribes. No children and mothers were ever unsheltered and unprotected.

DOROTHY HEIGHT, 1982

History offers us a peculiar irony: the idea, the value of equality is probably nurtured most by the protests of the very people who do not have it.

ROY WILKINS, *Standing Fast,* 1982

Sometimes history takes things into its own hands.

THURGOOD MARSHALL, 1983

Not having been taught black history—except for the once-a-year-hanging up of the pictures of Booker [T.] Washington, George Washington Carver, and

Mary McLeod Bethune that marked Negro History Week—we did not know how much of the riches of America we had missed.

ALICE WALKER, *In Search of Our Mother's Gardens,* 1983

History, like beauty, depends largely on the beholder. So, when you read that . . . David Livingstone discovered the Victoria Falls, you might be forgiven for thinking that there was nobody around the Falls until Livingstone arrived on the scene.

DESMOND TUTU, *Hope and Suffering*, 1983

History tells us it was Africa and not Asia that gave martial arts to the world. And that those same African roots are deeply embedded in the martial arts of India and China.

KILINDI IYI, *African Presence in Asia,* 1985

A good history will contain speeches, excerpts, people and the debates of legislators. A good history covers not only what was done, but the thought that went into the action. You can read the history of a country through its actions.

BENJAMIN HOOKS, "75 Years on the Cutting Edge," *Crisis,* December 1985

History has no vacuum. There are transformations, there are lesions, there are metamorphoses, and there are mysteries that cloak the clashing of individual wills and private interests.

RALPH ELLISON, "Remembering Richard Wright," *Going to the Territory,* 1986

There should be no "Negro History Corner" or "Negro History Week." There should be an integration of African American culture in all of its diversity throughout the curriculum.

JANICE HALE BENSON, *Black Child in Education,* 1986

I glanced at the North Carolina A&T banner proudly affixed to the wall of the Challenger, and four hundred years of history quickly raced through my mind.

RONALD MCNAIR, in *Choosing to Succeed,* 1986

Historically there has been the Age of Reason, the Age of Analysis, and the Age of Ideology. Perhaps we, as a people, need to return to the "Age of Analysis."

MARVA COLLINS, in *ibid.*

If we had a better sense of art and a stronger sense of history, we wouldn't have to accept the idea that entertainers are artists.

WYNTON MARSALIS, "Why We Must Preserve Our Jazz Heritage," *Ebony,* February 1986

One never knows how history will treat one individual, but the magazines will live forever because they are a record that cannot be erased. They're on microfilm: they're in the libraries of the world. They live forever.

JOHN H. JOHNSON, in "Interview," *Crisis,* January 1987

Woe to them who forget their history/ And drug their hearts with false memories.

CHINWEIZU, "Admonition to the Black World," *Voices From Twentieth-Century Africa,* 1988

Our history goes back thousands of years. You start with the Ashanti, the ancient kingdom of Ghana, ancient kingdom of black pharaohs, then bring it up to date.

TEVIS WILLIAMS, "Black Dance in Persepctive," *City Arts Quarterly,* Spring 1988

By understanding history we have a common ground to understand each other. If we keep looking at ourselves as ethnic groups, how can we have a country without prejudice or mistrust of each other?

MAURICE BARBOZOA, speech given to American Bar Association, 29 August 1988

Whether people call us names or not, somebody has to speak and somebody has to change. History is made, not by accepting it as it is, but by people writing it. We have to write history, for the continuity and without this kind of revolution there would be no history.

TESS ONWUEME, in "The Broken Calabash," *City Arts Quarterly,* Fall 1988

One has to grasp one's place in history. You cannot wait for others to hand it to you.

KASSHUN CHEVIOLA, in *Essence,* March 1989

We must explain the family by the history and not the history by the family.

LERONE BENNETT, JR., in *Ebony,* August 1989

Steep yourself in Black history, but don't stop there. I love Duke Ellington and Count Basie, but I also listen to Bach and Beethoven. Do not allow yourself to be trapped and snared in limits set for you by someone else.

GORDON PARKS, *Voices in the Mirror,* 1990

HOME/HOUSE

Live in the house of kindliness and men shall come and give gifts of themselves.

PTAH HOTEP, c. 2340 B.C.

The ruin of a nation begins in the homes of its people.

ASHANTI

If you burn a house, can you conceal the smoke?

BUGUNDA

You live in de cement house, and no worry de hurricane.

WEST INDIES

Do not leave your host's house throwing mud in his well.

ZULU

Sometimes I'm tossed and driven, Lord/ Sometimes I don't know what to do/ I've heard of a city called Heaven/ I'm trying to make it my home.

SPIRITUAL

It's a sorry house where the hen crows and the cock is silent.

TRADITIONAL

I left my baby standing in the back door/ She said, baby, you got a home just as long as I got mine.

BLUES

My God and my mother live in the West, and I will not leave them. It is a tradition of my people that we never cross the three rivers—the Grande, the San Juan, the Colorado. Nor could I leave the Chuska Mountains, I was born there. I shall remain. I have nothing to leave but my life, but I will not move.

MANUELITO OF THE NAVAHOS, speech given to Congress, 1865

Home, did I say. I forgot I have no home.

IDA B. WELLS, in Duster, ed., *Crusade for Justice,* 1928

Carry me/ O these feet of mine,/ Carry me to there/ To where the road meets/ The road that's overhung/ With leaves both thick and moving:/ It is a long time since I have seen/ My father and mother.

FLAVIEN RANAIVO, "Carry Me," *Return to the Fold,* 1955

This is our home and this is our country. Beneath its soil lie the bones of our fathers; for it some of them fought, bled, and died. Here we were born and here we will stay.

PAUL ROBESON, testimony before the House Un-American Activities Committee, 13 July 1956

Home with people who shared their next-to-nothing things and their more-than-hoped for wealth.

TONI CADE BAMBARA, *Sea Birds Are Still Alive,* 1974

Home is the place you can go when you're whipped.

MUHAMMAD ALI, *The Greatest,* 1975

We were all Black and we were all poor and we were all right there in place. For us, the larger community didn't exist.

BARBARA JORDAN, *Barbara Jordan,* 1977

I've never been homesick. I always knew when I was well off.

EUBIE BLAKE, *Eubie,* 1979

Home is where the hope is.

JOHN MCCLUSKEY, "And Called Every Generation Blessed," in Evans, ed., *Black Women Writers,* 1984

The ache for home lives in all of us, the safe place where we can go as we are and not be questioned.

MAYA ANGELOU, *All God's Children Need Traveling Shoes,* 1986

Whether you're a woman or a man, when you're out there fighting the world, you want to come home and find peace.

JOHN H. CLARKE, in *Essence,* May 1989

HOMELESS

Poverty can be a stranger/ In a far off land:/ an alien face/ . . . An empty rice bowl/. . . Until one bleak day you look out the window—/ And poverty is the squatter/ In your own backyard.

LUCY SMITH, "Face of Poverty," in Bontemps, ed, *Poetry of the Negro,* 1970

. . . [n]othing about the emptied rooms/ nothing about the emptied family.

LUCILLE CLIFTON, *Good Times,* 1970

The dissolution of the family unit is more than just a minority problem. Every family needs the love and input from grandma, grandpa, and mom and dad—and these homeless kids need the attention, love, and consistency only a family can bring.

LOUIS GOSSETT, in *Jet,* 14 December 1987

HONEST

We must learn to be honest with ourselves, and know our shortcomings. We will acquire cohesion but we will pay dearly for being a slow pupil.

ZORA NEALE HURSTON, 23 June 1925

To be profoundly dishonest, a person must have one of two qualities: either he is unscrupulously ambitious, or he is unswervingly egocentric.

MAYA ANGELOU, *I Know Why the Caged Bird Sings,* 1969

Speaking honestly is a fundamental principle of today's black artist. He has given up the futile practice of speaking to whites, and has begun to speak to his brothers.

ADDISON GAYLE, JR., *The Black Aesthetic,* 1971

We must be honest though the *truth,* or the stench of our lives, be painful.

KEORAPETSE KGOSITSILE, in *Black Poetry Writing,* 1975

You [James Baldwin] made American English honest—genuinely international. You exposed its secrets and reshaped it until it was truly modern dialogue representing humans. You stripped it of ease and false comfort and fake innocence, evasion, and hypocrisy. In place of deviousness was clarity. In place of soft plump lies was a lean targeted power. In place of intellectual disingenuousness and exasperating eccentrics, you gave us undecorated truth.

TONI MORRISON, eulogy of James Baldwin, Cathedral of St. John the Divine, New York City, January 1988

HONOR

A brave war chief would prefer death to dishonour.

BLACK HAWK OF THE SACS, *Farewell, My Nation! Farewell,* 1833

If we must die, O let us nobly die,/ So that our precious blood may not be shed/ In vain; then even the monsters we defy/ Shall be constrained to honor us though dead!

CLAUDE MCKAY, "If We Must Die," *Selected Poems,* 1953

I accept the Nobel Prize for Peace at a moment when twenty-two million Negroes of the United States of America are engaged in a creative battle to end the long night of racial injustice.

MARTIN LUTHER KING, JR., Nobel Prize Acceptance Speech, 10 December 1964

A "poet laureate" should do more than wear a crown—should be of service to the young.

GWENDOLYN BROOKS, *Report from Part One,* 1972

A jam session is a polite encounter, or an exchange of compliments, but in the old days they had cutting contests, where you defended your honor with your instrument.

DUKE ELLINGTON, *Music Is My Mistress,* 1973

Black people giving George Wallace an award is like the Anti-Defamation League giving a posthumous award to Hitler.

JOHN LEWIS, in the *Atlanta Inquirer,* 25 January 1975

Everywhere I go, I'm being honored and I don't really deserve it. It makes me scared. Is my plane going to blow up?

MUHAMMAD ALI, 1979

The prize has given fresh hope to many in the world that has sometimes had a pall of despondency cast over it by the experience of suffering, disease, poverty, famine, hunger, oppression, injustice, evil, and war.

DESMOND TUTU, Nobel Prize Acceptance Speech, 10 December 1984

Never give in, never, never never—in nothing great or small, large or petty—never give in—except in convictions of honor and good sense.

TOM BRADLEY, *The Impossible Dream,* 1986

I regard [the Nobel Prize for Literature] as a prize, not merely for me personally, but for the Black world, the African world.

WOLE SOYINKA, in "Wole Soyinka," *Ebony,* April 1987

I don't deserve the Songwriters Hall of Fame Award, but fifteen years ago I had a brain operation and I didn't deserve that either. So I'll keep it.

QUINCY JONES, c. 1991

HOPE

Sun going to shine in my back door some day.

BLUES

The sister of misfortune, hope./ In the under darkness dumb,/ Speaks joyful courage to your heart./ The day desired will come.

ALEXANDER PUSHKIN, "Letter to Siberia," c. 1824–1825

This very attempt to blot out forever the hopes of an enslaved people may be one of the necessary links in the chain of events preparatory to the complete overthrow of the whole slave system.

FREDERICK DOUGLASS, reaction to Supreme Court's decision in the Dred Scott case, 11 May 1857

Let not the shining thread of hope become so enmeshed in the web of circumstance that we lose sight of it.

CHARLES W. CHESTNUTT, *Wife of His Youth,* 1899

Out of the sighs of one generation are kneaded the hopes of the next.

JOAQUIM MACHADO DE ASSIS, *Education of a Stuffed Shirt,* 1906

It is easy to be hopeful in the day when you can see the things you wish on.

ZORA NEALE HURSTON, *Their Eyes Were Watching God,* 1937

It is only a straw, but we have nothing else to catch hold of.

WILLIAM HASTIE, in *Afro-American,* 29 January 1945

This is the faith that I go back to the South with. With this faith we will be able to hew out of the mountain of despair a stone of hope and to transform the jangling discords of our nation into a beautiful symphony of brotherhood.

MARTIN LUTHER KING, JR., "I Have a Dream," speech given at the Lincoln Memorial, Washington, D.C., 28 August 1963

I'm here, I exist and there's hope.

VERNON JARRETT, c. 1965

Hope is a delicate suffering.

LEROI JONES, *Home: Social Essays,* 1966

I am the hope of your unborn,/ truly, when there is no more of me . . . / there shall be no more of you.

CONRAD KENT RIVERS, *The Still Voice of Harlem,* 1968

I must slide down like a great dipper of stars/ and lift men up.

LUCILLE CLIFTON, *Good News About the Earth,* 1972

Malcolm is gone and Martin is gone and it is up to all of us to nourish the hope they gave us.

LENA HORNE, c. 1975

We've buried our hope/too long/as the anchor to our navel strings/ we are rooting at the burying spot/ we are recovering hope.

LORNA GOODISON, *I Am Becoming My Mother,* 1986

Many . . . who do not have a sense of hope will cite all the negatives that get [them] into deeper holes.

WILLIAM LYLES, in "The Black Male in Jeopardy," *Crisis,* March 1986

There's no hope without kids.

HARRY EDWARDS, in "Hardline," *Detroit Free Press,* 8 May 1988

Where there is hope there is life, where there is life there is possibility and where there is possibility change can occur.

JESSE JACKSON, in *Ebony,* August 1988

HUMAN

I have seen the human tragedy from a veiled corner.

ALEXANDRE DUMAS, *The Count of Monte Cristo,* 1844

The intolerance of the few, or the risk of it, carries the day against the wider humanity of the many.

PAUL ROBESON, "Thoughts on the Color Bar," *The Spectator,* London, 8 August 1931

Providence conceals itself in the details of human affairs, but becomes unveiled in the generalities of history.

CARTER G. WOODSON, c. 1935

You must not lose faith in humanity. If a few drops are dirty, the ocean does not become dirty.

MOHANDAS GANDHI, letter to Rajkumari Amrit, 29 August 1947

It's hard enough to be a human being under any circumstances, but when there is an entire civilization determined to stop you from being one, things get a little more desperately complicated.

LEROI JONES, *Home: Social Essays,* 1966

Man is human only to the extent to which he tries to impose his existence on another man in order to be recognized by him.

FRANTZ FANON, *Black Skin, White Masks,* 1967

Now I understand, if the good Lord doesn't like to behold the misery on earth, He takes the clouds and covers it from His sight: but where human beings dwell there is always a dark shadow.

MARIAN ANDERSON, *Marian Anderson, A Portrait,* 1970

[T]he only bond worth anything between human beings is their humanness.

JESSE OWENS, *Blackthink,* 1970

Nothing human is alien to me.

DUDLEY RANDALL, in *Black Poetry Writing,* 1975

You don't have to teach people how to be human. You have to teach them how to stop being inhumane.

ELDRIDGE CLEAVER, 1976

Each human is uniquely different. Like snowflakes, the human pattern is never cast twice.

ALICE CHILDRESS, "A Candle in a Gale Wind," in Evans, ed., *Black Women Writers,* 1984

There is no simplistic approach to worthwhile achievement in human affairs.

WILLIAM HASTIE, *Grace Under Pressure,* 1984

. . . it is a terrible, an inexorable law that one cannot deny the humanity of another without diminishing one's own. In the face of one's victim one sees oneself.

JAMES BALDWIN, *Price of the Ticket,* 1985

We brought you inside and slept and fed you because you are humans. You cannot pay us. We did not make you human. God did that.

MAYA ANGELOU, *All God's Children Need Traveling Shoes,* 1986

I am that mere human shell in which the revolt of Africa sealed its cry of bursting hope.

NOEMIA DE SOUSA, in Finn, ed., *Voices of Negritude,* 1988

I'm a human being before I am a race, a religion, and an occupation.

KRIS PARKER, A.K.A. KRS-ONE, in the *Detroit Free Press,* 8 May 1992

HUMOR

Humor may not be laughter, it may not even be a smile; it is a point of view, an attitude toward experience.

HOWARD THURMAN, *Meditations of the Heart,* 1953

Anything that's paradoxical has to have some humor in it or it'll crack you up. You put hot water in a cold glass, it'll crack. Because it's a contrast, a paradox. And America is such a paradoxical society, hypocritically paradoxical, that if you don't have some humor, you'll crack up.

MALCOLM X, 1965

Humor is laughing at what you haven't got when you ought to have it. Humor is when the joke's on you but hits the other fellow first before it boomerangs. Humor is what you wish in your secret heart were not funny, but it is and you must laugh. Humor is your own unconscious therapy.

LANGSTON HUGHES, *Book of Negro Humor,* 1966

Humor cleanses the heart and keeps it good.

ALFRED PASTER, *The Roots of Soul,* 1982

Verbal comedy [is] a way of confronting social ambiguity.

RALPH ELLISON, *Going to the Territory,* 1986

HUNGER

Hunger is felt by a slave and hunger is felt by a king.

ASHANTI

A too-modest man goes hungry.

CONGO

He whose stomach is empty is evil and becomes an opponent and grumbler.

EGYPT

One who is hungry does not care about taboos, does not care about death.

NIGERIA

Hunger makes a person climb up to the ceiling and hold on to the rafters. It makes a person lie down but not feel at rest.

NIGERIA

He who doesn't cultivate his fields will die of hunger.

GUINEA

Hunger is beating me./ The soapseller hawks her goods about./ But I cannot wash my inside, / how can I wash my outside?

YORUBA

The fact that I have eaten yesterday does not concern hunger. There is no god like one's stomach: we must sacrifice to it every day.

YORUBA

How can you teach book learning to people who are hungry and without proper shelter and know nothing about good living?

BOOKER T. WASHINGTON, *Up From Slavery,* 1901

Men can starve from a lack of self-realization as they can from a lack of bread.

RICHARD WRIGHT, *12 Million Black Voices,* 1941

[A] hunger which can no longer climb to the rigging of his voice/ a sluggish flabby hunger, a hunger buried in the depth of the Hunger of this famished morne.

AIMÉ CÉSAIRE, *Notes on a Return to the Native Land,* 1947

Hunger and lack of freedom always go hand in hand.

PAUL ROBESON, c. 1950

It's impossible to eat enough if you're worried about the next meal.

JAMES BALDWIN, *Notes of a Native Son,* 1955

America is concerned more with the possibility of moon folks than the reality of hungry poor folks.

DICK GREGORY, c. 1970

You can't run hungry. You can't learn nothing hungry. You can't even *think good* hungry.

CHARLES RUSSELL in Bill Russell, *Second Wind,* 1979

If you have never been hungry, you cannot know the *either/or* agony created by a single biscuit—either your brother gets it or you do. And if you *do* eat it, you know in your bones that you have stolen the food straight from his mouth. . . . This was the daily, debilitating side of poverty . . . the perpetual scarcity that makes . . . the simplest act a moral dilemma.

CHARLES JOHNSON, *Middle Passage,* 1990

HURRY

If one is not in a hurry, even an egg will start walking.

CONGO

[My] mama didn't tell me [I was] born in no hurry. So wh[a]t business I got rushin[g] now?

ZORA NEALE HURSTON, *Their Eyes Were Watching God,* 1937

HURSTON, ZORA NEALE

Zora Neale Hurston was ahead of her time. She was one witty, brave and bold person. One of the first women to wear trousers in public, she also wore turbans, and hats and scarves, and bangles, and beads, and bright colors and didn't care how cullud people thought she looked or acted.

VERTA MAE GROSVENOR, c. 1978

Zora Hurston . . . went to Barnard to learn how to study what she really wanted to learn: the ways of her own people, and what ancient rituals, customs, and beliefs had made them unique.

ALICE WALKER, *In Search of Our Mothers' Gardens,* 1983

Zora is too big, too bold, too outdoors, too downhome, to capture and release at a desk with a notebook.

TONI CADE BAMBARA, "Salvation Is the Issue," in Evans, ed., *Black Women Writers,* 1984

Called "free and courageous and foolish," Magical Zora, our truth-telling fore-mother, has taught an entire generation to celebrate the beauty and diversity of Black culture. Now, thirty years after her death in poverty, perhaps in despair, the American artistic world seeks frenetically to honor her as an anthropologist and novelist.

RUTH T. SHEFFEY, foreword to Proceedings of the First Annual All About Zora Conference, Eatonville, Florida, 26–27 January 1990

HYPOCRISY

The teeth are smiling, but is the heart?

CONGO

One camel does not make fun of the other camel's hump.

GUINEA

He acts like a dog who drives the flies away from food it has spurned.

LIBERIA

The white men are bad school-masters; they carry false looks, and deal in false actions; they smile in the face of the Indian to cheat him, they shake them by the hand to gain confidence, to make them drunk, to deceive them. . . . They coiled among us and poisoned us by their touch. . . . We were becoming like them hypocrites, and liars, adulterers, lazy drones, all talkers and no workers.

BLACK HAWK OF THE SACS, c. 1804

What to the American Slave is your Fourth of July? I answer: a day that reveals to him, more than all other days of the year, the gross injustice and cruelty to which he is the constant victim. To him, your celebration is a sham, your boasted liberty an unholy license, your national greatness, swelling vanity; your sounds of rejoicing are empty and heartless; your denunciation of tyrants, brass-fronted impudence; your shouts of liberty and equality, hollow mockery; your prayers and hymns, your sermons and thanksgiving, with all your religious parade and solemnity, are to him mere bombast, fraud, deception, impiety, and hypocrisy—a thin veil to cover up crimes which would disgrace a nation of savages.

FREDERICK DOUGLASS, "What to the American Slave Is Your Fourth of July," speech given at Corinthian Hall, Rochester, New York, 5 July 1852

Death is the one democracy/ That's truly real and fine,/ The end of all hypocrisy,/ a friend of yours—and mine.

ANDREA RAZAFKERIEFO, "Equality," in Kerlin, ed., *Negro Poets and their Poems,* 1921

I defy any errand boy Uncle Toms of the Negro people to challenge my Americanism because by word and deed I challenge this vicious system to death, because I refuse to let my personal success as part of a fraction of one percent of the Negro people explain away injustice to fourteen million of my people.

PAUL ROBESON, speech given at the Rockland Palace, New York City, 1945

America must begin the struggle for democracy at home. The advocacy of free elections in Europe by American officials is hypocrisy when free elections are not held in great sections of America.

MARTIN LUTHER KING, JR., speech given at the Southern Christian Leadership Conference Crusade for Citizenship, 12 February 1958

Swearing his love and devotion to the Omnipotent One on the one hand, yet defying and cursing him with rank impudence on the other; worshipping a Jew as the son of God on the one hand, yet persecuting all other Jews as enemies of God on the other hand; historically placing the same Jew on the African continent on the one hand, and describing him as a European in physical appearance on the other hand . . .

ABBEY LINCOLN, in *Negro Digest,* September 1966

Next to our foreign policy no institution in American life is more hypocritical and therefore does more to hurt the cause of God and the cause of democracy than our so-called Christian church.

ADAM CLAYTON POWELL, JR., *Adam by Adam,* 1971

Stay alert to the hypocrites, both Black and white. Sleep with one eye open and certainly keep both open while you are awake.

MAYNARD H. JACKSON, c. 1986

Whites from the small Alabama town would sneak into our home at night to borrow money from my father. Men who were respected and thought to be wealthy. I knew better. I learned first hand the hypocrisy of white supremacy.

MARVA COLLINS, in "Marva Collins: Teaching Success in the City," *Message,* July 1987

IDEA

Nothing is more unseemly than to give very long legs to very brief ideas.

JOAQUIM MACHADO DE ASSIS, 1900

Talk about it only enough to do it. Dream about it only enough to feel it. Think about it only enough to understand it. Contemplate it only enough to be it.

JEAN TOOMER, *Essentials,* 1931

If some half-dozen men at any time earnestly set their hearts on something coming about which is not discordant with nature, it will come to pass one day because it is not by accident that an idea comes into the heads of a few. Rather they are pushed on, and forced to speak or act by something stirring in the heart of the world which would otherwise be left without expression.

WILLIAM MORRIS, c. 1940

Ideas are the glory of man alone. No other creature can have them. Only man can get a vision and an inspiration that will lift him above the level of himself and send him forth against all opposition.

MATTHEW HENSON, c. 1950

Individual ideas—like breaths—are waiting to be drawn from unlimited supply.

MARGARET DANNER, "like breaths," *to flower,* 1963

Let's trace the birth of an idea. It's born as rampant radicalism, then it becomes progressivism, then liberalism, then it becomes moderate conservative, outmoded, and gone.

ADAM CLAYTON POWELL, JR., in Warren, *Who Speaks for the Negro?* 1966

Ideas rise with new morning but never die . . . only names, places, people change. . . .

FRANK MARSHALL DAVIS, "I Sing No New Songs," *Black Voices,* 1968

Ideas and knowledge are instruments for activity and not spectators of an outside realm.

ADAM CLAYTON POWELL, JR., *Adam by Adam,* 1971

One cannot kill an idea but it may be delayed for a long while.

ALICE CHILDRESS, "A Candle in a Gale Wind," in Evans, ed., *Black Women Writers,* 1984

Relying upon race, class, and religion as guides, we underestimate the impact of ideas and the power of life-styles and fashion to upset custom and tradition.

RALPH ELLISON, "On Initiation Rites and Power," *Going to the Territory,* 1986

IDEAL

Idealism is like a castle in the air if it is not based on a solid foundation of social and political realism.

CLAUDE MCKAY, "Out of the War Years: Lincoln, Apostle of a New America," *New Leader,* 13 February 1943

Blind idealism is reactionary.

FRANTZ FANON, *Wretched of the Earth,* 1963

He who will not use his office to fight for the ideals written into our basic law is false to his oath to support that law. He is the true subversive and deserves to be branded as such.

WILLIAM HASTIE, *Grace Under Pressure,* 1984

IDENTITY

See also IMAGE, IMITATION, SELF

A blade won't cut another blade, a cheat won't cheat another cheat.

CONGO

A cat goes to a monastery, but she still remains a cat.

CONGO

He who lives with an ass, makes noises like an ass.

ETHIOPIA

Nobody will think you're somebody, if you don't think so yourself.

TRADITIONAL

I am a Shawnee. My forefathers were warriors. Their son is a warrior. From them I take only my existence, from my tribe I take nothing, I am the maker of my own fortune. . . .

TECUMSEH OF THE SHAWNEES, in *The Book of the Indians of North America,* 1836

We have native hearts and virtues just as other nations. We are a nation within a nation as the Poles in Russia, the Hungarians in Austria, the Welsh, Irish, and Scotch in the British Dominion.

MARTIN DELANEY, *The Condition, Elevation, and Destiny of the Colored People of the United States,* 1852

The earth and myself are of one mind. The measure of the land and the measure of our bodies are the same.

HIGHN'MOOT TOOYALAKET (CHIEF JOSEPH) OF THE NEZ PERCES, in "An Indian's View of Indian Affairs," *North American Review,* 1879

The Negro must preserve his identity. Unity and harmony of sentiment and feeling are the levers that must of necessity overturn American caste-prejudice. In organization, cooperation, and agitation, the Negro will come nearer to the solution of the white man's problem than by merely submitting to injustice.

J. E. BRUCE, speech given to Washington, D.C., Protective League, 1887

We must have a nationality before we can become anybody.

J. MERCER LANGSTON, *From the Virginia Plantation to the National Capital,* 1894

Am I an American or am I a Negro? Can I be both? Or is it my duty to cease to be a Negro as soon possible and be an American? If I strive as a Negro, am I not perpetuating the very cleft that threatens and separates black and white America?

W. E. B. DU BOIS, "The Conservation of Races," speech given before the American Negro Academy, March 1897

So mixed are we that we know not who we are or what we are, and cannot even agree upon a suitable name for ourselves—so mixed that all were counted to us who bear our blood we would have at least 25 million rather than 10 million charged to our census account.

WILLIAM SCARBOROUGH, in *Race Integrity,* 1907

I am a Negro:/ Black as the night is black,/ Black like the depth of my Africa.

LANGSTON HUGHES, *The Weary Blues,* 1926

In my music, my plays, my films, I want always to carry the central idea: to be African.

PAUL ROBESON, "I Want to Be African," *The Millgate,* 1934

You cannot assume a nationality as you would a new suit of clothes.

Ibid.

If a man is not faithful to his own individuality, he cannot be loyal to anything.

CLAUDE MCKAY, *A Long Way From Home,* 1937

She wanted me to be primitive and know the intuitions of the primitive. But unfortunately, I did not feel the rhythm of the primitive surging through me, and so I could not live and write as though I did. I was only an American Negro—who had loved the surface of Africa and the rhythms of

Africa—but I was not Africa. I was Chicago and Kansas City and Broadway and Harlem.

LANGSTON HUGHES, *The Big Sea,* 1940

In the whole world no poor devil is lynched, no wretch is tortured, in whom I too am not degraded and murdered.

AIMÉ CÉSAIRE, *Miraculous Weapons,* 1946

I am a Negro. My skin is white, my eyes are blue, my hair is blond.

WALTER WHITE, *Man Called White,* 1948

I, the child of all races/ soul of India, Europe,/ my identity branded in the cry of Mozambique.

EDOUARD MAUNICK, "Seven Sides and Seven Syllables," *Carousels of the Sea,* 1955

Too great a sense of identity makes a man feel he can do no wrong. And too little does the same.

DJUNA BARNES, in Baldwin, *Nobody Knows My Name,* 1961

Most people guard and keep; they suppose that it is they themselves and what they identify with themselves that they are guarding and keeping is their system of reality and what they assume themselves to be.

JAMES BALDWIN, *The Fire Next Time,* 1963

I am not sure who I am, but I have given all of me that I can find to the pursuit of this consuming purpose, and the answer to the question is beginning to make itself known even to me.

HOWARD THURMAN, *Disciplines of the Spirit,* 1963

What passes for identity in America is a series of myths about one's heroic ancestors. It's astounding . . . that so many people really appear to believe that the country was founded by a band of heroes who wanted to be free. That happens not to be true. What happened was that some people left Europe because they couldn't stay there any longer and had to go some place else to make it. . . . They were hungry, they were poor, they were convicts.

JAMES BALDWIN, "A Talk to Harlem Teachers," in Clarke, ed., *Harlem, USA,* 1964

I am neither a fanatic nor a dreamer. I am a Black man who loves peace and justice and loves his people.

MALCOLM X, *Malcom X Speaks,* 1965

I am still a Muslim, I am still a minister, I am still Black.

MALCOLM X, "A Declaration of Independence," speech given in New York City, 12 March, 1965

If the young are to avoid the unnecessary burden of self-hatred (through identification with the aggressor) they will have to develop a keen faculty for identifying, fractionating out, and rejecting the absurdities of the conscious as well as the unconscious white racism in American society from what is worthwhile in it.

CHARLES A. DELEON, in the *Journal of the American Medical Association,* Fall 1967

Black consciousness is the state of being conscious of one's blackness vis-a-vis white racism. . . . awareness of membership in the Black race and the struggle including the state of being void of dreams of one day waking up white.

NATHAN HARE, c. 1968

Say that I was a drum major for justice; say that I was a drum major for peace; I was a drum major for righteousness.

MARTIN LUTHER KING, JR., "The Drum Major Instinct," sermon given at Ebenezer Baptist Church, Atlanta, Georgia, 4 February 1968

It is certain that all Africans are not Negroes, nor are all who are Negroes, African. Why should the race name of millions of African descent in America be derived from color only?

J. C. EMBRY, *Negro History Bulletin,* March 1969

For us, as a People, to try to find our Peopleness within the context of the American nation or the values of the West on which the nation is founded, would be like a chicken trying to find his chickenness in an oven.

JOHN O'NEAL, "Black Arts: Notebook," in Gayle, ed., *The Black Aesthetic,* 1971

I am a mystic because I have touched the intangible . . . heard the inaudible . . . and seen the invisible.

ADAM CLAYTON POWELL, JR., *Adam on Adam,* 1971

In her emotion she was sprung from the Southern Zulu and the Central Pygmy, the Eastern Watusi and the treacherous slave-trading Ashanti themselves. She was Kikuyu and Masai, ancient cousins of hers had made the exquisite forged sculpture at Benin, while surely even more ancient relatives sat upon the throne at Abu Simbel watching over the Nile.

LORRAINE HANSBERRY, *Les Blancs,* 1972

You are a reflection of your people—regardless of what anybody says.

HAKI MADHUBUTI, in *Black Poetry Writing,* 1975

It is hard in a revolutionary age to identify the real revolutionaries.

LERONE BENNETT, JR., *Challenge of Blackness,* 1976

Who one was, where one came from, what one was expected to be, the height of courage and character that were to be achieved, were woven into the fabric that linked oneself to all, touching, at last, the one who through superhuman power and character had pulled together the people in the birth of the tribe itself.

NATHAN HUGGINS, *Black Odyssey,* 1977

The mind of the intelligent Black child revolts against the descriptions of Blacks given in elementary books, geographies, travel histories.

ED BLYDEN, in "W. E. B Du Bois: The Scholar Reconsidered," *Negro History Bulletin,* July–September 1979

The Africans who came as slaves started their attempts to reclaim their lost African heritage soon after they arrived in this country. They were searching for the lost identity that the slave system had destroyed. The Black man's search for an identity has been his search for an identity in the world . . . his identity as a human being with a history before and after slavery that can command respect.

W. E. B. DU BOIS, in *ibid.*

In the old South there was no such thing as an anonymous person.

VERNON JARRETT, in Terkel, *American Dreams, Lost and Found,* 1980

I am a fighter, not a politician. I am no superman in any way.

JOE LOUIS, *My Life,* 1981

There is no person who is not a member of a race, a group, a family of humankind. Nobody exists alone. We are each part of a specific collective past, to which we respond in a way in which no person outside the group can respond.

EUGENIA COLLIER, "The Closing of the Circle: Movement from Division to Wholeness in Paule Marshall's Fiction," in Evans, ed., *Black Women Writers,* 1984

[W]ho I really am keeps surprising me.

NIKKI GIOVANNI, "An Answer to Some Questions on How I Write," in *ibid.*

She knows who she is because she knows who she isn't.

Ibid.

Ten or fifteen years ago, you could tell the brothers from the cousins. Not anymore. Everybody (sounds) Black—except for John Denver.

SAMMY DAVIS, JR., in "Words of the Week," *Jet,* 1 April 1985

Black male writers have contributed to who I am in the way that parents and church have contributed. Each has added to my knowledge of the craft of writing and, more important, has enhanced the way in which I view the world. [They have helped me] further define what it means to be a Black man, father, son, lover, writer, and friend.

RICHARD PERRY, in "Grapevine," *Essence,* November 1985

All people have a major task, from cradle to grave, of defining who they are.

NA'IM AKBAR, c. 1986

To see yourself as an American first and a Black man second means you're kind of crazy because the social realities don't define you in that way. The choices you must make, the decisions you have to make, the things you have to do, require that you see yourself first as an African-American within this context.

Ibid.

There is a mystery in this country because we live where we are; we wear the same clothing; we listen to the same television programs; we worship the same God; we read the same textbooks; we have the same heroes in sports, in politics, in music. We are at once very, very unified, and at the same time diversified.

RALPH ELLISON, "The Novel as a Function of American Democracy," *Going to the Territory,* 1986

If I cannot look at the most brutalized Negro on the street, even when he irritates me and makes me want to bash his head in because he's goofing off, I must still say within myself, "Well, that's you too, Ellison." And I'm not talking about guilt, but of an identification which goes beyond race.

RALPH ELLISON, "A Very Stern Discipline," in *ibid.*

Madame Toussaud's will have my statue. I just hope they don't make me look like James Brown.

LITTLE RICHARD, c. 1987

Living in the inner city is the same as living in the suburbs or surviving in the world. You have to know who you are, set goals in life, and maintain a self-image.

MARVA COLLINS, in "Marva Collins: Teaching Success in the City," *Message,* February 1987

Now people choose their identities. Now people choose to be Black. They used to be born Black. You can be Black genetically and choose not to be. You just change your mind . . . change anything. It's just a mind-set.

TONI MORRISON, in "Toni Morrison Now," *Essence,* October 1987

I've been like the Statue of Liberty. I haven't moved. I still have the same militancy.

HARRY EDWARDS, in "Covering All the Bases," *Ebony Man,* October 1987

When I was a child, you really had to search a store's shelves to see a reflection of yourself and then you found Aunt Jemima.

LLOYD RICHARDS, "Salute," *Life,* Spring 1988

I had always thought of myself as a Jamaican. I knew I was of mixed blood, but so was my father, and Alexander Dumas and Pushkin, Coleridge Taylor and Alexander Hamilton. These men by their contributions to the world progress, transcended the feeble delineation of race of color.

JOHN SOMERVILLE, in *American Vision,* February 1988

My generation was the last to make an all-out effort to be white, and as the last in line of this thrust we traveled the farthest and suffered the most when we were eventually, inevitably, brought up short. We went to Ivy League schools; we spoke almost too-perfect English as well as French; we traveled to Europe; we socialized with whites: some of us even married them. Then came the inevitable day when we realized individually and collectively that it had all been to no avail.

KRISTIN HUNTER, in "Growing Up Integrated (Did Momma Do the Right Thing?)" *Crisis,* March 1988

Sometimes I'm looked upon as not just a Black person but as a person. That's totally new ground for us—and for society.

MICHAEL JORDAN, in "Michael Jordan: In His Own Orbit," *GQ,* March 1989

One of the most difficult aspects of being a Black American is that in addition to my ever pervasive otherness, I have also become identityless.

CHERYL MCCOURTIE, "Where I Enter," *Essence,* April 1989

IGNORANCE

The ignorant and the fool will be thrown over.

PTAH HOTEP, 2340 B.C.

Men remain in ignorance as long as they hate, and they hate unjustly as long they remain in ignorance.

TERTULLIAN, *Apology,* c. 197

My life has elapsed in ignorance, I have done nothing; be on your guard.

The Gulistan of Sadi, 1184–1292

Ignorance doesn't kill you, but it makes you sweat a lot.

HAITI

An ignorant man without force can be made a slave.

AFRICA

People in their rashness and ignorance like to condemn things that are difficult and obscure, rather than learn their meaning by diligent painstaking study.

ORIGEN

You're so dumb, you can't throw rain water out of a boot and the directions say how.

TRADITIONAL

Either the United States will destroy ignorance or ignorance will destroy the United States.

W. E. B. DU BOIS, address given to the Niagara Movement, 1906

No human folly can surpass the conceit of ignorance.

CHARLES V. ROMAN, "Racial Differences," *American Civilization and the Negro,* 1912

The ignorant are always prejudiced and the prejudiced are always ignorant.

CHARLES V. ROMAN, *Science and Ethics,* 1912

Like most of Africa's children in America I had known little about the land of our father.

PAUL ROBESON, c. 1920

The blindness of contempt is more hopeless than the blindness of ignorance; for contempt kills the light which ignorance merely leaves unignited.

RABINDRANATH TAGORE, *Creative Unity,* 1922

Intolerance can grow only in the soil of ignorance: from its branches grow all manner of obstacles to human progress.

WALTER WHITE, *The Rope and the Faggot,* 1929

The realization of ignorance is the first act of knowing.

JEAN TOOMER, *Essentials,* 1931

Ignorance is in the saddle and we ride America.

JAMES BALDWIN, in *Negro Digest,* August 1968

I had gone from being ignorant of being ignorant to being aware of being aware.

MAYA ANGELOU, *I Know Why the Caged Bird Sings,* 1969

[W]e have not been scuffling in this waste-howling wildness for the right to be stupid.

TONI CADE BAMBARA, *The Salt Eaters,* 1980

ILLUSION

Of all the forms of illusion, woman is the most important.

BUDDHA

Honey outside, ice within.

ANGOLA

We possess only what we really love. We possess things only to the extent that we love them. All other possession is illusory.

VICTORIA OCAMPO, "The Lakes of the South," *The Green Continent,* 1944

Give me the illusion I'll no longer/ have to satisfy the sprawling need/ for mercy/ snoring beneath the world's disdainful nose.

LEON DAMAS, "Blues: For Robert Romain," *Pigments* 1956

Mornings of illusion and the remnants of ideas
And sleep inhabited by alcohol. . . .

DAVID DIOP, "With You," *Poundings,* 1956

[Y]ou had embraced only a chimera. You thought you would gain, you have only lost.

TOUSSAINT L'OUVERTURE, in James, *The Black Jacobins,* 1963

If one supposes things to be constant that are not safety, for example, or money or power, one clings then to a chimera, by which one can only be betrayed. And the entire hope, the entire possibility of freedom disappears.

ROBERT SLATER, *The Pursuit of Loneliness,* 1971

We cannot continue to live illusions. For us to do so is only a prologue to death.

HAKI MADHUBUTI, c. 1975

IMAGE

See also IDENTITY, IMITATION, SELF

That which you sense of the world goes with you.

DAHOMEY

Bull horn nebber too heavy for him head. (We always see ourselves in a favorable light.)

WEST INDIES

Man is a peculiar creature—he is the image of his God, though he may be subject to the most wretched conditions upon earth, yet the spirit and feeling which constitute the creature, man, can never be entirely erased from his breast, because the God who made him after his own image, planted it in his heart.

DAVID WALKER, *Appeal to the Coloured Citizens of the World,* 1829

I am black all over, and proud of my beautiful black skin.

JOHN E. BRUCE, c. 1902

God made us in His own image, and He had some purpose when He thus created us; then why should we seek to destroy our identity? Let us not divide ourselves in castes. To change our race is no credit . . . why should we want to be somebody else?

MARCUS GARVEY, in *Negro World,* August 1923

I am invisible, understand, simply because people refuse to see me. . . . When they approach me they see only my surroundings, themselves, or figments of their imagination—indeed, everything and anything except me.

RALPH ELLISON, *Invisible Man,* 1952

It's a shock to meet famous men—for the famous man cannot possibly feel the image which has evolved of him.

JAMES BALDWIN, 1955

I create social images within the work so far as the human condition is social. I create social identities so far as the subjects are Negro, but I have not created protest images because the world within the collage, if it is authentic, retains the right to speak for itself.

ROMARE BEARDEN, in *Art News,* October 1964

It's impossible for you and me to have a balanced mind in this society . . . because . . . as we function and fit into it right now, we're such an underdog, we're trampled upon, we're looked upon as almost nothing.

MALCOLM X, speech given at Organization for Afro-American Unity rally, Audubon Ballroom, New York City, 24 January 1965

I always said that Floyd [Patterson] was too meek and humble and gentle to be a good fighter. And I called him The Rabbit and the Hare, half for fun, but I meant it too.

MUHAMMAD ALI, "The Hare Was No Rabbit," *Life,* 12 February 1965

White men are not what they take themselves to be, and Blacks are very different—to say the very least—from the popular image of them.

CHESTER HIMES, *Beyond the Angry Black,* 1966

We can cry "Black Power" until doomsday, but until Black children stop saying, "You are blacker than me and so is your mama"; until grown Black men stop using black as a curse word; until *Ebony* stops asking such asinine questions as: "Are Negro Women Getting Prettier?" and carrying bleaching cream advertisements; until Black people stop saying such things as: "She's dark, but pretty"; in short, until black people accept values meaningful to themselves, there can be no completely effective organizing for the development of Black Power.

ROY INNISS, "Black Power—Phase 1: Psychological Warfare," *Rights and Reviews*, Winter 1966–1967

A belief in oneself is the antidote to implanted seeds of insecurity.

BARBARA CO (ANN) MACNEILL, "The Scandal of Black Social Knots," *Negro Digest*, December 1967

i only want to reclaim myself/ i even want you/ to reclaim yourself.

NIKKI GIOVANNI, "The Dance Committee," *Black Judgement*, 1968

To manipulate an image is to control a peoplehood. Zero image has for a long time meant the repression of our peoplehood.

CAROLYN GERALD, "The Black Writer and His Role," in Gayle, ed., *The Black Aesthetic*, 1971

There is indeed a new black today. He is different from any the world has known. He's a tall-walker. Almost firm.

GWENDOLYN BROOKS, *Report from Part One*, 1972

I am not a metaphor or a symbol.

CALVIN HERNTON, "The Distant Drum," in Lomax and Raoal, eds., *3000 Years of Black Poetry*, 1975

Image is what colonizes the mind.

JOHN HENRIK CLARKE, speech given at the Friends of Like It Is seminar, City College of New York, New York City, 11 October 1980

I come out of a tradition where those things are valued; where you talk about a woman with big legs and big hips and black skin. I come out of a black community where it was all right to have heavy hips and to be heavy. You didn't feel that people didn't like you. The values that imply you must be skinny come from another culture . . . Those are not the values that I was given by the women who served as my models. I refuse to be judged by the values of another culture. I am a black woman, and I will stand as best I can in that imagery.

BERNICE REAGON, "Black Women and Liberation Movements," in Walker, *In Search of Our Mothers' Gardens*, 1983

I see myself as becoming. I am a has-been, would perhaps, going to be. Underneath, I'm a dot. With no i's.

CAROLYN RODGERS, "An Amen Arena," in Evans, ed., *Black Women Writers*, 1984

If you want to see a positive image, it's in your house. It's standing there washing your underwear. If you want to see a positive image, it's cooking dinner and has a job to go to in the morning.

BILL COSBY, speech given at the Morehouse College graduation, Atlanta, Georgia, 10 February 1985

People think of me as close to royalty. . . . I carry myself the way I do because I am royalty within myself.

IMAN, in "Words of the Week," *Jet*, 2 February 1987

If we want to see the likes of ourselves, our talents, our rituals, our drama, our music, and our dance, we must build our own institutions.

CECILIA SLOANE, "Theater: A Look Back . . . A Look Ahead," *Crisis*, February 1987

I'm not combative. I just don't like being pushed around. . . . the press is [not] used to seeing Black men who stand up for their rights. That's because they don't know that many Black men. But Black people don't call me combative. They call me strong, which lets me know I'm on the right track.

HAROLD WASHINGTON, in "Mayor Washington Eulogized as Symbol of Hope for Blacks," *Jet*, 14 December 1987

He's just so smart. All I can see in him [Mark Jackson] is myself.

MAGIC JOHNSON, in "People Are Talking About . . ." *Jet,* 2 May 1988

Even though one is involved in the production of artistic works, one must be careful of the reflection left there because that is all the reader sees, our reflection.

JOHN WILLIAMS, in "Interview," *Catalyst,* Summer 1988

As a people, we must remember that we are not as weak as we have allowed ourselves to be painted, and we are not as strong as we can be.

JOHN EDWARD JACOB, c. 1989

I didn't think of myself as gifted. I just know I had things to do. You don't think of it as being gifted when you're Black and you're poor. You think of it as moving on.

ROBERTA FLACK, in "An Intimate Talk with Roberta," *Essence,* February 1989

To be Black and accept consciously or unconsciously the image of God as a white man is the highest possible form of self-negation and lack of self-respect. . . .

FRANCES CRESS WELSING, *The Isis Papers,* 1991

IMAGINATION

It is good to know truth, but it is better to speak of palm trees.

AFRICA

The artist must bow to the monster of his own imagination.

RICHARD WRIGHT, *12 Million Black Voices,* 1941

The imagination of the novelist determines what happens to his material.

JAMES BALDWIN, c. 1970

A man who has no imagination has no wings.

MUHAMMAD ALI, c. 1975

A lot of living is done in the imagination.

RALPH ELLISON, *Going to the Territory,* 1986

Your ammunition is your imagination and your technique.

WYNTON MARSALIS, "Why We Must Preserve Our Jazz Heritage," *Ebony,* February 1986

What God has intended for you goes far beyond anything you can imagine.

OPRAH WINFREY, c. 1987

Imagine how free we would feel and what we could accomplish if we could live without fear.

SUSAN TAYLOR, c. 1988

If we can reach in with the art and touch the imagination of the child, no matter who, we have affected that child.

OSSIE DAVIS, "It's on Us," *City Arts Quarterly,* Spring 1988

Imagination is something people use twenty-four hours a day . . . it's a universal thing.

MR. IMAGINATION, in *Black Art: Ancestral Legacy,* 1989

What stimulates my imagination is not actually knowing. Because there is a mystery, there are no rules set, I am free to use my own imagination.

RENEE STOUT, in *ibid.*

The power of imagination created the illusion that my vision went much farther than the naked eye could actually see. I could survey vast regions behind the long mountain range where I have never been. I walked out into the courtyard and the few living things there, the seagulls, wagtails, the plants, small trees, and even grass blades were gay and full of smiles. I looked into the vast dome of blue emptiness that stretched out above me in all directions and the illusion was still there, the size and speed, and what information they were sending to mother earth.

NELSON MANDELA, *Higher Than Hope,* 1991

IMITATION

See also IDENTITY, IMAGE, SELF

From the first generation to those who come after, they imitate what is past.

ANKHU, "The Complaint of Khakheperre-Sonb," 1550–1305 B.C.

Copying everybody else all the time, the monkey then cut his throat.

ZULU

If there is any fault with us it is that we are always aping somebody else. The Negro has not this love for his country [Africa] and it is unfortunate; even his virtue and his vices are the white man's. Race allegiance is comparable with the highest patriotism. The Negro is now a distinct, and ever will be a distinct race in this country.

JOHN H. SMYTHE, in the *Bee,* 25 June 1887

We are therefore bound by every drop of blood that flows in our being and by whatever of self-respect you and I individually and collectively possess, to make ourselves—not in the pattern of any other race, but actuated by our peculiar genius in literature, religion, commerce, and social intercourse—a great people.

Ibid.

Roll your eyes in ecstasy and ape his every move, but until we have placed something up on [the] street corner that is our own, we are right back where we were when they filed [the] iron collar off.

ZORA NEALE HURSTON, *Moses, Man of the Mountain,* 1939

The imitator is the most pitiful phenomenon, since he is like a man who eats garbage. A saxophonist who continues to "play like" Charlie Parker cannot understand that Charlie Parker wasn't certain what had happened to sound like that.

LEROI JONES, c. 1966

There may be some few/ Who remind us of thee/ But they are imitations/ As your friends will see.

WENDELL DABNEY, in Hughes, ed., *Book of Negro Humor,* 1966

A lotta cats copy the Mona Lisa, but people still like to see the original.

LOUIS ARMSTRONG, c. 1967

Nature's God is so resourceful that he breaks the mold and destroys it forever. We waste our energies and torture our years trying to be like someone else.

HERMAN WATTS, "What Is Your Name?" in Philpot, ed., *Best Black Sermons,* 1972

If two people are playing identically, one is an imitator.

DUKE ELLINGTON, *Music Is My Mistress,* 1973

Imitate Harriet Tubman's escape to become something unheard of.

ALICE WALKER, *Meridian,* 1976

You go to school to find out what other people have done, and then you go in life to imitate them.

MELVIN CHAPMAN, speech given at Mercy College, Detroit, Michigan, 1976

Success and failure are both impostors and I take them both lightly.

JOE CLARK, "It's Time for Blacks to Take Charge of Their Fate," *Ebony,* August 1988

IMPOSSIBLE

Sharp spur mek maugre horse cut caper. (The pinch of circumstances forces people to do what they thought impossible.)

JAMAICA

Nothing is impossible for those who love the Lord.

TRADITIONAL

It is impossible to raise and educate a race in the mass. All revolutions and improvements must start with individuals.

JOHN WESLEY BROWN, sermon, Asbury Methodist Episcopal Church, 31 January 1892

When reform becomes impossible, revolution becomes imperative.

KELLY MILLER, *The Negro in the New World Order,* 1919

We specialize in the wholly impossible.

NANNIE BURROUGHS, motto of National Training School for Girls, Washington, D.C., 1929

When a man has lived by the spear, it is difficult, sometimes impossible, to learn to live by his head.

PETER ABRAHAMS, *Wild Conquest,* 1950

It is impossible to compromise with Jim Crowism and anti-Semitism.

PAUL ROBESON, "Bonds of Brotherhood," *Jewish Life,* November 1954

[I]t's impossible for a chicken to produce a duck egg—even though they belong to the same family of fowl. . . . It's impossible for this system, as it stands, to produce freedom right now for the black man in this country.

MALCOLM X, "The Harlem 'Hate-Gang' Scare," speech given to the Militant Labor Front, 29 May 1964

It is impossible for people to rise above their aspirations.

ROBERT WILLIAMS "USA, the Potential of a Minority Revolution," *The Crusader Monthly Newsletter,* May–June 1965

Like a child, I had always believed that nothing was impossible until it could be proven impossible.

DUKE ELLINGTON, *Music Is My Mistress,* 1973

[It is impossible] for teachers to teach "blackness" to small children if they [have] no grasp of what black history was. . . .

ALICE WALKER, *In Search of Our Mothers' Gardens,* 1983

It is just about impossible to make a positive contribution to the world if one cannot read, write, compute, think, and articulate one's thoughts.

HAKI MADHUBUTI, "Lucille Clifton: Warm Water, Greased Legs and Dangerous Poetry," in Evans. ed., *Black Women Writers,* 1984

Don't doubt me because that's when I get stronger. I like to see the smiles on people's faces when I show them I can do the impossible.

MARVIN HAGLER, c. 1985

Voyagers discover that the world can never be larger than the person who is in that world, but it is impossible to foresee this, it is impossible to be warned. It is only when time has begun spilling through his fingers like water or sand carrying with it forever dreams, possibilities, challenges, and hope that the young man realizes he will not be young forever.

JAMES BALDWIN, "The New Lost Generation," in *City Arts Quarterly,* Spring 1988

INCLUSION

Our highest ambition is to be included in the stream of American life, to be permitted to "play the game" as any other American; and is opposed to anything that aids in the exclusion; the face may be of Africa, but the heart has the beat of Wall Street.

CHESTER HIMES, *Beyond the Angry Black,* 1966

For a real end to exclusion in American society, that society would have to be so radically changed that the goal cannot really be defined as inclusion.

STOKELY CARMICHAEL, c. 1976

[D]emocracy is not simply material well-being but the extension of the democratic process in the direction of perfecting itself. And that the most obvious test and clue to that perfection is the inclusion—not assimilation—of the black man.

RALPH ELLISON, "What America World Be Like Without Blacks," *Going to the Territory,* 1986

INDEPENDENCE

Every tub must sit on its own bottom.

TRADITIONAL

Mama may have/ Papa may have/ But god bless the child that's got his own.

BILLIE HOLIDAY, "God Bless the Child," 1941

Though I am independent, I have a debt to my slave father. I have a debt to my relatives in North Carolina who are very poor sharecroppers today, I won't allow my independence to be used against them.

PAUL ROBESON, testimony before the House Un-American Activities Committee, 31 May 1948

[Y]ou need self-independence. Not servants, not workers for another one. You need now to turn and go work for yourself.

ELIJAH MUHAMMAD, in Essien-Udom, *Black Nationalism,* 1962

It's easy to be independent when you've got money. But to be independent when you haven't got a thing—that's the Lord's test.

MAHALIA JACKSON, *Movin' On Up,* 1966

I am my own foundation.

FRANTZ FANON, *Black Skin, White Masks,* 1967

Without money of one's own in a capitalist society, there is no such thing as independence.

ALICE WALKER, *In Search of Our Mothers' Gardens,* 1983

[M]any of our pressing racial problems will be taken care of when we who are among the minorities will stand on our own feet and refuse to look to anybody else to save us from our situations. The culture in which we live stresses looking out for number one. Without adopting such a self-centered value system, we can demand the best of ourselves while we are extending our hands to help others.

BENJAMIN CARSON, *Gifted Hands,* 1990

INFERIORITY

The mere fact of separation does not necessarily involve inferiority.

FRANCIS L. CARDOZA, in *AME Review,* October 1806

Inferior race! It is an old argument. All nations have been compelled to meet it in some form or other since mankind has been divided into stronger and weak oppressed.

FREDERICK DOUGLASS, *Douglass Monthly,* 1886

We refuse to allow the impression to remain that we assent to inferiority, are submissive under oppression, and apologize before insults.

W. E. B. DU BOIS, Niagara Platform, 1906

If you make a man feel that he is inferior, you do not have to compel him to accept inferior status, for he will seek it himself.

CARTER G. WOODSON, *The Mis-education of the Negro,* 1933

This was my first really big step toward self-degradation: when I endured all that pain, literally burning my flesh to have it look like a white man's hair. I had joined that multitude of Negro men and women in America who are brainwashed into believing that the black people are "inferior"—and white people "superior"—that they will even violate and mutilate their God-created bodies to try to look "pretty" by white standards.

MALCOLM X, *The Autobiography of Malcolm X,* 1965

Day after day we are treated like dirt and told we are inferior. It is drummed into our heads. First, your self-respect disappears. . . . [then] you begin to hate yourself.

MIRIAM MAKEBA, *My Story,* 1987

INFLATION

What is inflated too much will burst into fragments.

ETHIOPIA

The frog wanted to be as big as the elephant and burst.

NIGERIA

INFLUENCE

When one begins looking for influences one finds them by the score . . . the King James Bible, the rhetoric of the store-front church, something ironic and violent and perpetually understated in Negro speech—and something of Dickens' love for bravura . . . the fact that I was born a Negro.

JAMES BALDWIN, *Notes of a Native Son,* 1955

End the influence of white seminaries with their middle-class white ideas. Replace them with Black consciousness—that is, with Nathaniel Paul, Daniel Payne, Nat Turner, Marcus Garvey, Elijah Muhammad, and Malcolm X, instead of courses dealing with the theology of Reinhold Niebuhr. We need to deal with the theology of Henry Garnet and other Black revolutionaries.

JAMES CONE, *Black Theology and Black Power,* 1969

[The fact that] the Beatles were influenced by Chuck Berry and the Rolling Stones listened to Muddy Waters shows the obvious influence of rhythm and blues.

ALFRED PASTER, *The Roots of Soul,* 1982

The most influential person in my life was my grandmother. How did she influence me? With a switch.

CHUCK JACKSON, in the *Michigan Chronicle,* 22 August 1987

I don't see how you cannot have influence on somebody whose pillow you share at night.

OPRAH WINFREY, in "Opinionated Oprah," *Woman's Day,* 4 October 1988

I have looked to the sonic warriors named (Richard) Wright, (Langston) Hughes, (Paul Lawrance) Dunbar, (Sterling) Brown . . . earth pounders. They are my influences, my standard bearers. I somehow learn most from them. I hear them like great echoes, reminding and informing and guiding me through. . . .

ED LOVE, in *Black Art: Ancestral Legacy,* 1989

INFORMATION

Let me pull your coat-tail.

TRADITIONAL

A diploma without information is deceptive.

JESSE JACKSON

I'd raise my daughter with a lot of information so she could be as grounded as possible about her sexuality.

OPRAH WINFREY, in "Opinionated Oprah," *Woman's Day,* 4 October 1988

INHUMANITY

The bells of man's inhumanity to man do not toll for one man. They toll for you, for me, for all of us.

MARTIN LUTHER KING, JR., c. 1963

It is utopian to try to evaluate different forms of inhumanity.

FRANTZ FANON, *Black Skin, White Masks,* 1967

[T]he terrors, the sufferings of my past have honed me into a better human being. I grind my raw suffering into a refined glass that enables me to get a good look at man's GENERAL inhumanity. Inhumanity is rampant everywhere.

GWENDOLYN BROOKS, *Report From Part One,* 1972

INJUSTICE

Find out what people will submit to and you have found out the exact amount of injustice and wrong which will be imposed upon them.

FREDERICK DOUGLASS, *Life and Times of Frederick Douglass,* 1892

I expected some cowardly retaliation from the lynching. I felt one had better be fighting against injustice than to die like a dog or a rat in a trap. I had already determined to sell my life as dearly as possible if attacked.

IDA B. WELLS, in Duster, ed., *Crusade for Justice,* 1928

There must always be a remedy for wrong and injustice.

Ibid.

The bones of injustice have a peculiar way of rising from the tombs to plague and mock the iniquitous.

MARCUS GARVEY, c. 1934

If only ten or twenty Negroes had been put into slavery, we could call it an injustice, but there were hundreds of thousands of them throughout the country. If this state of affairs had lasted for two or three years, we could say it was unjust, but it lasted for more than two hundred years. Injustice which lasts for three long centuries and which exists among millions of people over thousands of miles of territory is injustice no longer—it is an accomplished fact of life.

RICHARD WRIGHT, *Native Son,* 1940

The answer to injustice is not to silence the critic but to end the injustice.

PAUL ROBESON, "The Constitutional Right to Travel," *Freedom,* 8 July 1955

Injustice anywhere is a threat to justice everywhere.

MARTIN LUTHER KING, JR., *Letter from a Birmingham City Jail,* 1963

I am willing by any means necessary to bring an end to the injustices our people suffer.

MALCOLM X, *Malcolm X Speaks,* 1965

[I]njustice anywhere can lead to injustice everywhere; blind hatred and bigotry anywhere can lead to blind hatred and bigotry everywhere.

SAMUEL B. MCKINNEY, "The Hot Winds of Change," in Philpot, ed., *Best Black Sermons,* 1972

[T]he injustice in justice [is] kicking the weak and protecting the strong.

RAY CHARLES, *Brother Ray,* 1978

You cannot have wholeness, you cannot have spiritual well-being or physical well-being in a situation of injustice.

DESMOND TUTU, c. 1984

Injustice wears ever the same harsh face wherever it shows itself.

RALPH ELLISON, "If the Twain Shall Meet," *Going to the Territory,* 1986

INNOCENCE

I have not committed iniquity against men. I have not oppressed the poor. I have not laid labor upon any free man beyond that which he wrought for himself. I have not defaulted, I have not committed that which is an abomination to the gods. I have not caused the slave to be ill-treated of his master. I have not starved any man, I have not made any to weep, I have not assassinated any man. I have not committed treason against any. I have not in aught diminished the supplies of the temple; I have not spoiled the show-bread of the gods. I have done no carnal act within the enclosure of the temple. I have not blasphemed. I have not falsified the balance, I have not taken the milk away from the mouths of sucklings, I have not taken with nets the birds of the gods. I am pure. I am pure. I am pure.

THE DECLARATION OF INNOCENCE, *The Book of the Dead,* c. 1550–1080 B.C.

And time, men, and something within me conspired against me and my innocence.

PETER ABRAHAMS, *Tell Freedom,* 1954

Experience, which destroys innocence, also leads one back to it.

JAMES BALDWIN, c. 1962

If I had to do it again, knowing the pitfalls, I'm so naive, I'd probably go out and fall right in them all over again.

RUTH BROWN, c. 1990

I was ambushed by the innocence—the alarming trust—in her eyes.

CHARLES JOHNSON, *Middle Passage,* 1990

INSPIRATION

The inspiration of the race is the race.

EDWARD BLYDEN, c. 1890

My men and my race are the inspiration of my work. I try to catch the character and the mood and feeling of my people. The music of my people is something more than the American idiom. It is the result of our transportation to American soil and was our reaction to plantation days—to the life we lived. What we could not say openly, we expressed in music. The characteristic melancholic music of my race has been forged from the very white heat of our sorrows and from our groping.

DUKE ELLINGTON, *Music Is My Mistress,* 1973

From Bessie Smith's records I learned to look at the people around me differently . . . [and that] as Black Americans we all had a song that was in us.

AUGUST WILSON, in "Spotlight: August Wilson," *Essence,* August 1987

You don't have to be Magic to be special. You're already special, you're you.

MAGIC JOHNSON, in *Michigan Living,* April 1989

INSTRUMENTS

Mighty drums echoing the voice/ of spirits determining the movements/ of human forms/ These sounds are rhythmatic/ The rhythm of vitality,/ The rhythm of exuberance/ and the rhythm of life/ These are the sounds of blackness/ Blackness—the presence of all color.

TED WILSON

A flugelhorn is a trumpet before taxes.

CLARKE TERRY, c. 1970

In playing the organ you have to wear narrow shoes or your feet get stuck.

ERROLL GARDNER, 24 October 1972

The drumbeat can summon tears from the springs of our eyes and drive our soul deep into the caverns of sorrow, or it can raise us to the very peak of elation. Drums can be sounded in such a way that they have a soothing effect and create a restful feeling. The beat of the drums can cure what no medicine can cure. It can heal the ills of the mind—it can heal the very soul. Where America and Europe have their evil drugs and the couches of their psychiatrists, the Africans still have their drums.

VUSUMAZULA CREDO MUTWA, c. 1976

There were many spasm bands, they played all sorts of gadgets that produced sound; musical saws, washboards, spoons, bells, pipes, sandpaper, xylophone, sets of bottles, harmonica, jew harp, string fiddle, guitar, small bass fiddle, tub basses, kazoos, ram horns, steer horns, tin flutes.

DANNY BARKER, *A Life in Jazz,* 1987

A violinist had his violin, a painter his palette. All I had was myself. I was the instrument that I must care for.

JOSEPHINE BAKER, in Rose, *Jazz Cleopatra,* 1989

The front men, the sax and the trumpet players, get to rest. They come out, play, and all the women go crazy. Then they go back, chill, and stand pretty holding their horns. But a bass player plays from beginning to end, every time. It's dogged work. . . . Bass playing is just a hell of a sacrifice.

BILL NUNN, in Lee, *Mo' Better Blues,* 1991

INTEGRATION

Integration is the great issue of our age, the great issue of our nation and the great issue of our community. We are in the midst of a great struggle, the consequences of which will be world-shaking.

MARTIN LUTHER KING, JR., in the *New York Times*, 27 February 1956

Integration means self-destruction, death, and nothing else.

ELIJAH MUHAMMAD, in Essien-Udom, *Black Nationalism*, 1962

Integration begins the day after the minds of the people are desegregated.

JOHN KILLENS, *Beyond the Angry Black*, 1966

Integration comes after liberation. A slave cannot integrate with his master. In the whole history of revolts and revolutions, integration has never been the main slogan of the revolution. The oppressed fights to free himself from his oppressor, not to integrate with him. Integration is the step after freedom when the freedman makes up his mind as to whether he wishes to integrate with his former master.

Ibid.

Integration is an opportunity to participate in the beauty of diversity.

MARTIN LUTHER KING, JR., *Where Do We Go From Here?* 1968

Go home and work and fight for the integration of male and female—human and human.

SHIRLEY CHISHOLM, speech given to Congress, 1970

We don't want to get integrated into a burning building.

LOFTON MITCHELL, "I Work Here to Please You," in Gayle, ed., *The Black Aesthetic*, 1971

[T]he faith I have in integration comes from the days I spent in schoolboy's cap and knickers chasing around the quiet tree-shaded lanes that stretched off and away from our little cottage. . . . Swedes and Norwegians, Poles, Germans, and Irish—first-and second-generation immigrants.

ROY WILKINS, *Standing Fast*, 1982

Once we became an integrated society, we became selfish and tried to forget the past.

MARTIN LUTHER KING, III, in *USA Today*, 24 August 1983

I don't fit in with whites, and I don't fit in with Blacks. We're in a mixed-up generation, those of us who were sent out to integrate society.

CLARENCE THOMAS, in *Legal Times*, 1984

Negro parents in the South never speak of sending their children to the "integrated" school; they say, "My child is going to the white school." No white children are "integrated" into Negro schools. Since integration is only a one-way street that Negroes travel to a white institution, then inherent in the situation itself is the implied inferiority of the Black man.

ALVIN POUSSAINT, c. 1987

There was so much pressure to accept that integration was wonderful—our parents told us it was, our leaders told us it was.

NA'IM AKBAR, in "Growing Up Integrated (Did Momma Do the Right Thing?)" *Crisis*, March 1988

In the period of integration we turned our backs on our institutions and communities and said, "Gee whiz! Now we can mainstream!"

MICHAEL LOMAX, in *Ebony*, May 1988

INTELLECTUAL

Everyone thinks himself perfect in intellect, and his child in beauty.

The Gulistan of Sadi, 1184–1292

You should not attempt to outwit a woman.

ALEXANDRE DUMAS, *Le Demi-Monde*, 1855

Our intellect is an ascetic who wears no clothes, takes no food, knows no sleep, has no wishes, feels no love or hatred or pity for human limitations, who only reason, unmoved. . . . It burrows to the roots of things because it has no personal concern with the thing itself.

RABINDRANATH TAGORE, *Nationalism*, 1912

The intellect is one way of avoiding yourself. One must find a way to get through life or to experience, but that can't be done intellectually.

JAMES BALDWIN, in *Who Speaks for the Negro?* 1965

The intellectuals must gain respect through their efficiency, their taste for unselfish work on behalf of the people, and their clarity. They must be sincere and truly feel themselves animated by an ideal that will stand come what may. They must set themselves apart from these minds which shine only with deceptive light, as artificial as it is sterile, the flash pseudo-intelligences that so readily prove to be insignificant.

CHEIKH ANTA DIOP, *Black Africa—The Economic Third World,* 1978

JAZZ

Jazz is a marvel of paradox: too fundamentally human, at least as modern humanity goes, to be typically racial, too international to be characteristically rational, too much abroad in the world to have a special home.

J. A. ROGERS, *Jazz at Home,* 1917

Jazz to me is one of the inherent expressions of Negro life in America: the eternal tom-tom beating in the Negro soul—the tom-tom of revolt against weariness in a white world, a world of subway trains, and work, work, work; the tom-tom of joy and laughter, and pain swallowed in a smile.

LANGSTON HUGHES, "The Negro Artist and the Racial Mountain," *Nation,* 23 June 1926

Do those Congress people feel I am not as good an artist as Mr. Sousa? Why, they're crazy. I have always been an admirer of Mr. Sousa's work. Of course, it isn't jazz, but it's all right for that kind.

FATS WALLER, c. 1940

Forget the rules. You have to play all twelve notes of your solo anyway.

JOHN COLTRANE, c. 1950

Jazz is making do with taters and grits, standing up each time.

BILLIE HOLIDAY, c. 1952

We all do "do, re, mi," but you have got to find the other notes yourself.

LOUIS ARMSTRONG, c. 1956

The history of Jazz is written in the memories of men and women.

Ibid.

You had your Shakespeare and Marx and Einstein and Jesus, but we came up with jazz, and all pop music in the world is from that prime cause.

CHARLIE MINGUS, *Black Maturation and the Revolution in Music,* 1970

If jazz means anything at all, which is questionable, it means the same thing it meant to musicians fifty years ago—freedom of expression. I used to have a definition, but I don't think I have one anymore, unless it is that it is a music with an African foundation which came out of an American environment.

DUKE ELLINGTON, *Music Is My Mistress,* 1973

Jazz is the music of the people who are privileged to live in a land with mountains of gold, rivers of oil, billions of bushels of surplus food, and freedom of expression.... It is an American idiom with African roots—a trunk of soul with limbs reaching in every direction....

Ibid.

Classical music is already written. It's a matter of interpretation. But with jazz ... you get to compose as you go [a]nd ... follow the chord changes along the way.

RAY CHARLES, *Brother Ray,* 1978

What do you think we were doing up there, kidding?

DIZZY GILLESPIE, 1980

[P]oetry is more like ... improvisational jazz, where each person blows the note that she hears.

ALICE WALKER, *In Search of Our Mothers' Gardens,* 1983

Jazz functions better underground.

ROY BROOKS, 1984

Jazz is American classic music.

WILLIE CONOVER, 1984

Jazz is music that really deals with what it means to be an American. The irony is when they wrote the Declaration of Independence and the United States Constitution, they didn't even think of a Black man. Yet Louis Armstrong, the grandson of a slave, is the one more than anybody else could translate into music that feeling of what it is to be an American.

WYNTON MARSALIS, "We Must Preserve Our Jazz Heritage," *Ebony,* February 1986

Jazz is the nobility of the race put into sound, it is the sensuousness of romance in our dialect, it is the picture of the people in their glory.

Ibid.

I was minding my own business when something says to me, "you ought to blow trumpet." I have just been trying ever since.

MILES DAVIS, "EM in Profile," *Ebony Man,* April 1987

Jazz is the ancestral down home voice at its highest level of refinement. Jazz tells us what we African Americans have done with our experience on these shores.

ALBERT MURRAY, "The Soul of Jazz," *Ebony Man,* April 1987

Jazz is self-expression, creativity, and freedom. It's total conversation with the music. Through jazz the bandstand stays happy.

JIMMY SMITH, in "Jazz Men: A Love Supreme," *Ebony Man,* April 1987

To be a jazz musician you have to have a very strong belief in yourself. You have to be true to yourself in ways that other people are not. You have to speak with your own voice.

CHICO FREEMAN, in *ibid.*

Jazz is very democratic musical form. It comes out of a communal experience. We take our respective instruments and collectively create a thing of beauty. Everybody's allowed to be out front and supportive during a composition. Everybody's free.

MAX ROACH, in *ibid.*

Jazz takes all the elements in our culture and puts them into perspective. It celebrates the individual freedom that we prize so dearly in our society.

BILLY TAYLOR, in *ibid.*

Jazz is the father of hipness, the mother of invention, and a Black philosophy of life without words. Jazz is about the business of the isness of being.

KHEPHERA BURNS, in *ibid.*

Jazz in its purest form is dynamic and changing. It will never be the jazz of the 1930s and 40s, because it's changing and responding to its environment.

AL JARREAU, c. 1988

It's always jazz. You can put a new dress on her, a new hat on her, but no matter what kind of clothes you put on her, she's the same old broad.

LIONEL HAMPTON, *Hamp,* 1989

Jazz creates a hunger within.

DIANNE REEVES, in "Spotlight: Dianne Reeves," *Essence,* January 1989

People are convinced that jazz is just some magic thing that happens with Negroes. We just wake up with horns in our mouths. But to play what we play, you have to be a supreme musician. The art form requires it. It requires the discipline of a classical musician, the emotional feeling any good musician should bring to this music, and knowledge of the blues. You must have the ability to create melody on the spur of the moment, which is what improvisation is all about. Musicians who are best at improvisation are those who can create melody.

BRANFORD MARSALIS, in Lee, *Mo' Better Blues,* 1991

JEW

If Jews object to the Ghetto and the Pale, does it prove them ashamed of themselves or afraid of those oppressors who find oppression easier when the victims are segregated and helpless?

W. E. B. DU BOIS, "The Jim Crow Argument," *Crisis,* May 1913

The Negro must strive to follow in the example of the Jews—they cling to their customs and traditions, no matter whether they live in Timbuctoo [Timbuktu] or in the highest Andean mountains; they cling together and behold the maxim that "in unity there is strength."

ARTHUR A. SCHOMBURG, in *Racial Integrity,* July 1913

Anti-Semitism is a disease of Europe and white Christianity. And Afro-American victims of the fiery cross must not be dragged into the vortex of anti-Semitism.

CLAUDE MCKAY, in "Claude McKay Replies to Poston on Solution to the Negro Problems," *New Leader,* 7 December 1940

Whenever the Jews were barred from a neighborhood they pooled their economic power and purchased that neighborhood. If they were banned from a hotel, they bought the hotel.

MALCOLM X, *The Autobiography of Malcolm X,* 1965

Anti-Semitism hits me head on: I am enraged, I am bled white by an appalling battle, I am deprived of the possibility of being man. I cannot disassociate myself from the future that is proposed for my brother.

FRANTZ FANON, *Black Skin, White Masks,* 1967

Blacks and Jews are hooked up and bound together by a common history of persecution.

RAY CHARLES, *Brother Ray,* 1978

Jews as a minority in America have been the model par excellence of the ability to achieve the ambitions of the mainstream, but at the same time not lose sight of their group identity and the difficulties of their underclass.

HAROLD CRUSE, "The Buppies," *Crisis,* April 1986

Most Jewish people don't live in totally Jewish communities, yet there is a connectedness with the Jewish community that sustains a cultural identity.

HARRY EDWARDS, in "Hardline," *Detroit Free Press,* 8 May 1988

As with the persecuted Jews in Germany, somebody is always trying to pin the Star of David on your clothes, but in this country it's very convenient. You wear the Star of David on your skin.

ISHMAEL REED, "Maligning the Male," *Life,* Spring 1988

We must remember lives lost in the struggle against racism. We have to take a lesson from the Jewish people. They did not take the Holocaust and lie down. They are constantly bringing it forth, not only to the attention of their children and people, but to the entire world.

MAMIE TILL MOBLEY, in *Jet,* 19 August 1991

JIM CROW

Jim Crow laws have been put on the books for a purpose and that purpose is . . . to promote in the mind of the smallest white child the conviction of First by Birth, eternal and irrevocable, like the place assigned to the Levites by Moses over the tribes of Hebrews.

ZORA NEALE HURSTON, "Crazy for This Democracy," *Negro Digest,* 1945

The whole world has watched with admiration the courage of Autherine Lucy, and the militant protest of 50,000 Negroes in Montgomery, Alabama, against Jim Crow.

PAUL ROBESON, "Message to National Conference," speech given in Manchester, England, 27 May 1956

It's going to take a lot of punching. Jim Crow won't be easy to stop. But I think there are enough thinking people in this fight, and enough ready to join to help bring real democracy to America.

JOE LOUIS, *My Life,* 1981

Kansas City . . . a Jim Crow town . . . nearly ate my heart out. . . . It was a melodramatic thing. It was a slow accumulation of humiliations and grievances. It was constant exposure to Jim Crow in the schools, movies, stores, hotels, and restaurants.

ROY WILKINS, *Standing Fast,* 1982

[I]t always surprised me to hear Southern racists talk about the sanctity of Jim Crow, as if he had been around forever. Actually, he didn't gain full strength until the years after *Plessy* v. *Ferguson.*

Ibid.

I was offered the ambassadorship of Liberia once. Then that post was earmarked for a Negro. I told them I wouldn't take a Jim Crow job.

RALPH BUNCHE, in "Black Americans as Participants in the Foreign Service," *Crisis,* November 1986

In the '60s, it was Jim Crow. In the '80s, it's Mr. James Crow, Esquire.

HARRY EDWARDS, in "Hardline," *Detroit Free Press,* 8 May 1988

JOB

See also WORK, LABOR

We must become mechanics; we must build as well as live in houses; we must make as well as use furniture; we must construct bridges as well as pass over them, before we can properly live or be respected by our fellow man. We need mechanics as well as ministers. We need workers in iron, clay, and leather. We have orators, authors, and other professional men, but these reach only a certain class, and get respect from our race in certain select circles.

FREDERICK DOUGLASS, letter to Harriet Beecher Stowe, 8 March 1853

Every hour sees [the black man] elbowed out of some employment to make room for some newly arrived emigrant . . . whose hunger and whose color entitle man to special favor.

Ibid.

One of my most important jobs was to be a beggar.

MARY MCLEOD BETHUNE, 1930

Not a small part of the task of the Negro in America is learning to work without timidity, neither looking for trouble nor avoiding it, and taking full advantage of the privilege of citizenship wherever he may be.

WILLIAM HASTIE, in *Personal Affairs,* 11 March 1934

If it falls your lot to be a street sweeper, sweep streets like Michelangelo painted pictures, like Shakespeare wrote poetry, like Beethoven composed music; sweep streets so well that all the host of Heaven and earth will have to pause and say, "Here lived a great sweeper, who swept his job well."

MARTIN LUTHER KING, JR., "Facing the Challenge of a New Age," speech given in Montgomery, Alabama, 19 December 1956

We intend to finish the journey that somebody else so rudely started us on—and we intend to finish the job that they so foolishly left undone.

SHIRLEY CHISHOLM, *Unbought and Unbossed,* 1970

You can predict a depression by how many black people start losing their jobs.

JOE LOUIS, *My Life,* 1981

If the federal government can pay farmers for not raising food, they can subsidize honest jobs for people.

COLEMAN YOUNG, 1984

It's a thankless job being a GOP Black appointee. You get bashed in the head by your own brothers and sisters and sometime you are cut to pieces by conservatives on the inside.

CLARENCE THOMAS in *Jet,* 26 November 1984

All of us are seeking, in many fitful ways, to be agents of the kingdom.

DESMOND TUTU, in *Message,* June 1986

I see myself as a regular person, I just do a different job than others.

MICHAEL JACKSON, c. 1987

Too much emphasis is placed on how others should do their jobs instead of how one should do his/her own job. If you pay too much attention to the pitcher or the batter, the next thing you know the ball is between your legs and rolling. You have missed the ball because your mind is on the pitcher and the batter and not on third base. If you're on third base, play third base.

MELVIN CHAPMAN, 1987

Dance is vulnerability, it's about giving your love, light, generosity. If an audience can pick up on all these things when you're on stage, then you're doing your job.

JUDITH JAMISON, 1988

As things now stand, the overwhelming majority of young Blacks who seek to fill the shoes of O. J., Dr. J, Reggie J, and Magic J, in all likelihood will end up with no "J" at all—no job whatever.

HARRY EDWARDS, in "Hardline," *Detroit Free Press,* 8 May 1988

[Handling my career is like] when you're the queen, but you have to blow your own horn and say, "Here she comes, here she comes!" You have to give your own announcement, and then you roll out your own red carpet, and then you go back and put your crown on. And then you say, "The Queen, the Queen!" And you walk. You just can't do all of those things.

ROBERTA FLACK, in "An Intimate Talk with Roberta," *Essence,* February 1989

Not only should we be great consumers but we must begin to be great entrepreneurs. This is mandatory to enable us to establish jobs and training positions so that our youth will have a future. We need to acquire and muster the survival instinct—an instinct that has to begin with "Unity."

DON DAVIS, 1989

We must learn to rear sons who will learn from the cradle that their major function as men is not to get a good job and a fine car, but to defend, protect, and support their people, even should death be the consequence.

FRANCES CRESS WELSING, *The Isis Papers,* 1991

JUDGMENT

You who judge others, at sometimes be also a judge of yourself. Look into the recesses of your own conscience.

ST. CYPRIAN, "Address to Demetrian," c. 252

Climin up the mountain, chillun,/ Didn't come here for to stay/ If I ever gonna see you agin,/ It'll be on judgment day.

SPIRITUAL

God wields national judgment on national sins.

FRANCES E. W. HARPER, letter to John Brown, 25 November 1859

You are not judged by the height you have risen, but from the depth you have climbed.

FREDERICK DOUGLASS, *Life and Times of Frederick Douglass,* 1881

If tomorrow anything should happen to those being judged today, tomorrow this will affect you, too.

PAUL ROBESON, "Two Worlds—Ten Years of Struggle," *Komsomolskaia, Pravda,* 16 June 1949

It is very easy to sit in judgment upon the behavior of others, but often difficult to realize that every judgment is a self-judgment.

HOWARD THURMAN, *Meditations of the Heart,* 1953

The thing to judge in any jazz artist is, does the man project and does he have ideas.

MILES DAVIS, c. 1962

No nation is judged by the position of their men, but by the position of its women.

ELIJAH MUHAMMAD, *Muhammad Speaks,* 1962

Every day is judgment day, and we, through our deeds and words, our silence and speech, are constantly writing in the Book of Life.

MARTIN LUTHER KING, JR., 1964

I believe in human rights for everyone, and none of us is qualified to judge each other and that none of us should therefore have that authority.

MALCOLM X, "Letter from Cairo," *Malcolm X Speaks,* 1965

I believe in judgment. Not a last judgment . . . but a continuing judgment. I am not the least bit concerned with the judgment of man. It means nothing.

ADAM CLAYTON POWELL, JR., *Adam by Adam,* 1971

Both man and men are under judgment, and with them all society—whether in the form of an era, a civilization, a culture, or a nation—is judged. And because of this I tremble for my country.

Ibid.

People in the West who have crawled into bed with Pretoria have no moral right to sit in judgement of Black people who can no longer accept it.

ALLAN BOESAK, in "Who Can Speak for South Africa?" *Crisis,* November 1986

People will judge you according to your own convictions.

DEXTER KING, c. 1988

JUSTICE

Righteousness means justice practiced between men and between nations.

IROQUOIS

I demand simple justice. I am not here as beggar. I do not care so far as I am personally concerned whether you give me my seat or not. I will go back to my people and come here again.

PINCKNEY PINCHBACK, Washington, D.C., 1873

Don't be deceived, there is no justice except strength.

MARCUS GARVEY, *Philosophy and Opinions of Marcus Garvey,* 1923

Let the justice be done to all mankind. If the strong oppress the weak, confusion and discontent will ever mark the path of man, but with love, faith, and charity toward all, the reign of peace and plenty will be heralded into the world—generations of men shall be called blessed.

Ibid.

Justice for the slave is not the same as justice for the freeman. Treatment of a thoroughbred is not the same for a workhorse.

A. PHILIP RANDOLPH, speech given to March on Washington Movement, Detroit, Michigan, 26 September 1942

It is not right to ask a man with elephantiasis of the scrotum to take on smallpox as well when thousands of other people have not had their share of small diseases.

CHINUA ACHEBE, *No Longer at Ease,* 1961

We refuse to believe that there are insufficient funds in the great vaults of opportunity of this nation. And so we've come to cash this check, a check that will give us upon demand the riches of freedom and the security of justice.

MARTIN LUTHER KING, JR., "I Have a Dream," speech given at the Lincoln Memorial, Washington, D.C., 28 August 1963

Who blindfolds justice on the courtroom roof/
While the lawyers weave the sleight of hand of proof.

MELVIN TOLSON, *Harlem Gallery,* 1965

I was a drum major for justice.

MARTIN LUTHER KING, JR., sermon given at Ebenezer Church, Atlanta, Georgia, February 1965

To demand freedom is to demand justice. When there is no justice in the land, a man's freedom is threatened. Freedom and justice are interdependent. When a man has no protection under the law it is difficult for him to make others recognize him.

JAMES CONE, *Black Theology and Black Power,* 1969

Just like you can buy grades of silk, you can buy grades of justice.

RAY CHARLES, *Brother Ray,* 1978

KILL

Because a man has injured your goat, do not go out and kill his bull.

IVORY COAST

For the freedom of my 22 million black brothers and sisters here in America, I do believe that I have fought the best that I know how, and the best that I could, with the shortcomings that I have had. . . . I know that societies often have killed people who have helped to change those societies. And if I can die having brought any light, having exposed any meaningful truth that will help destroy the racist cancer that is malignant in the body of America—then, all of the credit is due to Allah. Only the mistakes have been mine.

MALCOLM X, *The Autobiography of Malcolm X,* 1965

Killing is not bad or good in itself. It can be bad if you kill a person for no reason, but it gets you a Medal of Honor if you kill a person in another situation.

NATHAN HARE, JR., *U.S News and World Report,* May 1967

We are tired of the best of our brilliance and of promise-in-embryo coming to early grief—chopped and pinned to official chests as medals.

GWENDOLYN BROOKS, *Report from Part One,* 1972

The most fundamental truth to be told in any art form . . . is that America is killing us. But we continue to live and love and struggle and win.

SONIA SANCHEZ, "Ruminations/Reflections," in Evans, ed., *Black Women Writers,* 1984

There is a new Ku Klux Klan out there called Killer Crack and Cocaine, and the new lynch mob is sweeping all through the Black neighborhood.

JOSEPH LOWERY, "Home at Last," *Crisis,* November 1986

I saw the police rehearsing their roles in the drama of murder unfolding before us; it was a cool, calculated, cold-blooded dress rehearsal.

YOUTH LEAGUER, in Mandela, *Higher Than Hope,* 1991

KINDNESS

Do not feel badly if your kindness is rewarded with ingratitude. It is better to fall from your dream clouds than from a third-story window.

JOAQUIM MACHADO DE ASSIS, *Epitaph for a Small Winner,* 1881

To a haughty belly, kindness is hard to swallow and harder to digest.

ZORA NEALE HURSTON, *Moses, Man of the Mountain,* 1939

KING, MARTIN LUTHER, JR.

His grace, like Gandhi's, grows out of a complicated relation not to oppression, but the ancient scourges of man to pain, to suffering, to death. Men who conquer the fear of these things in themselves acquire extraordinary power over themselves and over others.

LERONE BENNETT, *What Manner of Man,* 1964

I perceived immediately that this boy—15 years old—was mature beyond his years, that he spoke as a man who should have had ten more years experience than was possible. He had a balance and a maturity that were far beyond his years and grasp of life and its problems that exceeded that.

BENJAMIN MAYS, eulogy of Dr. Martin Luther King, Jr., given at Ebenezer Church, Atlanta, Georgia, 9 April 1968

He did not belong to us, he belonged to all the world.

MARTIN LUTHER KING, SR. in Coretta Scott King, *My Life with Martin Luther King, Jr.*, 1969

King saw clearly the meaning of the gospel with its social implications and sought to instill its true spirit in the hearts and minds of Black and white in this land. He was a man endowed with the charisma of God; he was a prophet in our own time. And like no other Black or white American he could set Black people's hearts on fire with the gospel of freedom in Christ which would make them willing to give all for the cause of Black humanity. Like the prophet of old, he had a dream, a dream grounded not in the hopes of white America but in God. Nor did the dream of the future relieve him of responsibilities in the present; instead it made him fight unto death in order to make his dream a reality.

JAMES CONE, *Black Theology and Black Power*, 1969

He was a son of the South. He was steeped in and nurtured by familiar religious traditions. He had charisma, that intangible quality of personality that gathers up in its magic the power to lift people out of themselves without diminishing them. . . . His star shot across the heavens like Halley's comet, making a mighty radiance in the light of which ancient dwellers in darkness could find their way to brotherhood.

HOWARD THURMAN, *A Search for Common Ground*, 1971

King hated violence. He'd prefer never to see it. But in order to be a true participant in America, he believed that you needed a dramatic entrance.

RAY CHARLES, *Brother Ray*, 1978

King showed Black people they could make things change by working together.

JOE LOUIS, *My Life*, 1981

The face of Dr. Martin Luther King, Jr., was the first black face I saw on our new television screen. And, as in a fairy tale, my soul was stirred by the meaning for me of his mission—at the time he was being rather ignominiously dumped into a police van from having led a protest march in Alabama—and I fell in love with the sober and determined face of the Movement.

ALICE WALKER, *In Search of Our Mothers' Gardens*, 1983

My grandmother said he was a great man way before *Time* put him on the cover, long before the Nobel people even knew Black Americans, let alone a specific one, existed.

Ibid.

Through the combination of spiritualism, realism and nonviolent confrontation, Dr. King infiltrated the American political system and shook it at its deepest roots, making a lasting impact on life in America.

ADRIENNE JOHNSON, "The Political Legacy of Dr. King," *Crisis*, February 1986

I love Dr. King because he made $600,000 in one year and died a pauper.

HOSEA WILLIAMS, c. 1987

When Martin Luther King first began marching there were no television cameras, no white reporters. The only way he got his message across was through *Jet*.

JOHN H. JOHNSON, in "Interview: John H. Johnson," *Crisis*, January 1987

The dream is over. It's time to demand justice, demand equality, demand that the drug pushers leave our streets, demand that the homeless sleeping in our subways be housed. King would be appalled today if he knew we allowed crack and drugs to entertain our children. Wake up, America. The sleeping period is over.

BEN VEREEN, in *Community Access News*, January 1987

KINSHIP

Once African art is known and appreciated, it can scarcely have less influence upon the blood descendants, bound to it by a sense of cultural kinship, than those who inherit it by tradition.

ALAIN LOCKE, c. 1928

We have been told by the forefathers that there are many of us from this place who are in exile in that place called America—and in other places.

ALEX HALEY, *Roots,* 1977

The bond of black kinship—so sturdy, so resilient—has finally been broken in the cities of the North. There is no mutual caring, no trust.

ALICE WALKER, *In Search of Our Mothers' Gardens,* 1983

There is a kinship among wanderers, as operative as the bond between bishops or the tie between thieves.

MAYA ANGELOU, *All God's Children Need Traveling Shoes,* 1986

I feel a kinship with the ancient architects of the past. I relate to ancient forms, images and monuments. . . . This has enabled my art to be viable as social commentary on the present.

JEAN LACY, in *Black Art: Ancestral Legacy,* 1989

KNOWLEDGE

The lack of knowledge is darker than night.

AFRICA

He that knows not and knows not that he knows not is a fool; shun him./ He that knows not and knows that he knows not is a child; teach him./ He that knows and knows not that he knows is asleep; awaken him./ He that knows and knows that he knows is wise; follow him.

ARABIA

It is the wife who knows her husband.

ASHANTI

Knowledge is better than riches.

CAMEROON

She who doesn't know how to walk cannot climb a ladder.

CONGO

To one who does not know, a small garden is a forest.

ETHIOPIA

Knowledge is like a garden: if it is not cultivated, it cannot be harvested.

GUINEA

Not to know is bad. Not to want to know is worse. Not to hope is unthinkable. Not to care is unforgivable.

NIGERIA

Knowledge is learned. When one does not learn, that is humiliation.

SENEGAL

Nobody tells all he knows.

SENEGAL

Repetition is the mother of knowledge.

TRADITIONAL

There is nothing in race or blood, in color or features, that imparts susceptibility of improvement to one race over another. The mind left to itself from infancy, without culture, remains a blank. Knowledge is not innate. As the Greeks and Romans and Jews drew knowledge from the Egyptians three thousand years ago, and the Europeans received it from the Romans, so must the Blacks of the land rise in the same way. As one man learns from another, so nation learns from nation.

WILLIAM WELLS-BROWN, in the *Liberator,* 13 June 1862

We have to know as far as possible the things that actually happened in the world; with that much clear and open to every reader, the philosopher and prophet have a chance to interpret these facts.

W. E. B. DU BOIS, c. 1920

Not to know what one's race has done in former times is to continue always a child.

CARTER G. WOODSON, *The Story of the Negro Retold,* 1935

[T]he world [was] cryin[g] extry and [I] ain't read [the] common news yet.

ZORA NEALE HURSTON, *Their Eyes Were Watching God,* 1937

One never know, do one?

FATS WALLER, c. 1940

We must educate ourselves and our children to the rich power of knowledge which has elevated every people who have sought and used it. We must give the benefit of our knowledge to the elevation of our people.

ELIJAH MUHAMMAD, in Essien-Udom, *Black Nationalism,* 1962

Man cannot live without some knowledge of the purpose of life. If he can find no purpose in life he creates one in the inevitability of death.

CHESTER HIMES, *Beyond the Angry Black,* 1966

I think it rains/ That tongues may loosen from the porch/ Uncleave roof tops of the mouth, hang/ heavy with knowledge.

WOLE SOYINKA, *Idioms and Other Poems,* 1967

Armed with the knowledge of our past, we can with confidence charter a course for our future.

MALCOLM X, in *Malcolm X on Afro-American History,* 1971

I have always worshipped at the shrine of knowledge knowing that regardless of how much I study, read, travel, expose myself to enriching experiences, I still remain an intellectual pauper.

ADAM CLAYTON POWELL, JR., *Adam by Adam,* 1971

A man without knowledge of himself and his heritage is like a tree without roots.

DICK GREGORY, *No More Lies,* 1971

They who humble themselves before knowledge of any kind generally end up the wiser and as voices with something meaningful to say.

HAKI MADHUBUTI, in *Black Poetry Writing,* 1975

Only a real knowledge of the past can keep in one's consciousness the feeling of historical continuity.

CHEIKH ANTA DIOP, *The Cultural Unity of Black Africa,* 1978

Man only truly lives by knowing; otherwise he simply performs, copying the daily habits of others, but conceiving nothing of his creative possibilities as a man, and accepting someone else's superiority and his own misery.

ALICE WALKER, *In Search of Our Mothers' Gardens,* 1983

To know is to exist; to exist is to be involved, to move about, to see the world with my own eyes.

Ibid.

When a man gains knowledge through the observation of the truth, his view of the world changes.

KILINDI IYI, *African Presence in Asia,* 1985

I have never been to a university, but I do have common sense. I got it from my mother's breast.

MIRIAM MAKEBA, *My Story,* 1987

I beg of you to study. Your knowledge, your education is your husband. Your husband may leave you, but what you have in your mind will never leave you.

MIRIAM MAKEBA, "My Story," *Essence,* May 1988

Knowledge is not power, it is only potential power that becomes real through use.

DOROTHY RILEY, "Genealogy," speech given to Michigan Association of Media School Educators, Detroit, Michigan, May 1988

Ledge of the Nile. Nile edge = knowledge.

ED LOVE, in *Black Art: Ancestral Legacy,* 1989

The purpose of knowledge is to liberate the person from restrictive limits while simultaneously maintaining contact with the perceptible and ponderable universe.

WADE NOBLES, speech given in Detroit, Michigan, January 1989

LABOR

See also JOB, WORK

Labor is the fruit of civilization, not the basis of it.

ALEXANDER CRUMMELL "The Dignity of Labor, Its Values to a New People," speech given to Working Men's Club, Philadelphia, Pennsylvania, 1881

I have been in many labor battles. It has seemed strange to some that, having attained some status and acclaim as an artist, I should devote so much time and energy to the problems and struggles of working men and women. To me, of course, it is not strange at all. I have simply tried never to forget the soil from which I spring.

PAUL ROBESON, "The Battleground Is Here," *Freedomways,* 21 November 1952

You are demanding that this city respect the dignity of labor. So often we overlook the work and the significance of those who are not in professional jobs, of those who are not in so-called big jobs. Let me say to you whenever you are engaged in work that serves humanity and is for the building of humanity, it has dignity it has worth.

MARTIN LUTHER KING, JR., speech given to AFSME members during Memphis Sanitation Strike, Memphis, Tennessee, 3 April 1968

The main object is to create a huge army of migrant laborers by enclosing them in compounds at the center of the work and housing them in rural locations when they return home; it is hoped to prevent the emergence of a closely knit, powerful and articulate African industrial proletariat who might acquire the rudiments of political agitators and struggles. What is wanted by the ruling circle is a docile, spineless, unorganized and inarticulate army of workers.

NELSON MANDELA, *The Struggle Is My Life,* 1978

LAND

The land is shrunk—its rulers are many,/ It is bare—its taxes are great;/ The grain is low—the measure is large.

NEFERTARI, 2600–2450 B.C.

We want no white men here. The Black Hills belong to me. If the whites try to take them, I will fight.

TATANKA YOTANKA (SITTING BULL), speech given to Congress, 1874

Do not misunderstand me, but understand me fully with reference to my affection for the land. I never said the land was mine to do with it as I chose. The one who has the right to dispose of it is the one who has created it. I claim a right to live on my land, and accord you the privilege to live on yours.

HIGHN'MOOT TOOYALAKET (CHIEF JOSEPH) OF THE NEZ PERCES, "An Indian's View of Indian Affairs," *North American Review,* 1879

You say we must return to the land. But where is the land to which we must return?

ARTHUR FULA, *Johannes giet die Beeld,* 1954

Man depends on land for the necessities, food, clothing, and shelter for survival. A prime requisite for freedom and independence is having one's own land. There can be no freedom without a people having its own land.

ELIJAH MUHAMMAD, in Essien-Udom, *Black Nationalism,* 1962

Look at the American Revolution of 1776. That revolution was for what? For land. Why did they want land? Independence. How was it carried out? Bloodshed. Number one, it was based on land, the basis of independence. And the only way they could get it was bloodshed. The French

Revolution—what was it based on? The landless against the landlord. . . . The Russian Revolution—what was it based on? Land; the landless against the landlord. . . . You haven't got a revolution that doesn't involve bloodshed.

MALCOLM X, "Message to the Grass Roots," speech given 10 November 1963

Revolution is based on land.

Ibid.

To be landless can be a crime, and weekly we interviewed the delegates of grizzliest weather-worn peasants who came to tell us how many generations their families had worked a little piece of land from which they were now being ejected.

NELSON MANDELA, c. 1965

Where does one run when he's already in the promised land?

CLAUDE BROWN, *Manchild in the Promised Land,* 1965

He's allowed me to go up to the mountain. And I've looked over. And I've seen the promised land. I may not get there with you. But I want you to know, that we, as a people, will get to the promised land.

MARTIN LUTHER KING, JR., "I Have Been to the Mountaintop," sermon given in Memphis, Tennessee, 3 April 1968

Black people are land people, they jived us into the city.

JOHN WILLIAMS, *The Junior Bachelor Society,* 1976

This is our land, as much as it is any American's—every square foot of every city and town and village. The talk of winning our share is not the easy one of disengagement and flight, but the hard one of work, of short as well as long jumps, of disappointments, and of sweet success.

ROY WILKINS, *Standing Fast,* 1982

If it is true that land does not belong to anyone until they have buried a body in it, then the land of my birthplace belongs to me, dozens of times over.

ALICE WALKER, *In Search of Our Mothers' Gardens,* 1983

LANGUAGE

In the study of language in school pupils were made to scoff at the Negro dialect as some peculiar possession of the Negro which they should despise rather than directed to study the background of this language as a broken-down African tongue—in short to understand their own linguistic history, which is certainly more important for them than study of French Phonetics or Historical Spanish Grammar.

CARTER G. WOODSON, *The Mis-education of the Negro,* 1933

I have the map of Dixie on my tongue.

ZORA NEALE HURSTON, *Dust Tracks on a Road,* 1942

All cultivated people spoke English, straight English; the Jamaican dialect was considered a vulgar tongue. It was the language of the peasants.

CLAUDE MCKAY, *My Green Hills of Jamaica,* 1946

I have always loved verbal battles, and challenge. . . . I love languages. I wish I were an accomplished linguist. . . . I would just like to *study.* I mean ranging study, because I have a wide-open mind.

MALCOLM X, *The Autobiography of Malcolm X,* 1965

At the base of our language, and our songs and dances, there are rhythms of the drum, of the tom-tom, that underline and sustain them.

LEOPOLD SENGHOR, speech given at First World Festival of Negro Art, Dakar, Senegal, 1966

Mastery of language affords remarkable power.

FRANTZ FANON, *Black Skin, White Masks,* 1967

For the rest of his life, Malcolm made a fantastically effective effort to master the English language, not to become a precious little intellectual and impress people with his learning—he was bigger than that—but to shape words into bullets that would strike home at the center of his targets: American racism and the historic weakness of black men which permit such racism to persist without serious challenge.

JULIAN MAYFIELD, "You Touch My Black Aesthetic and I'll Touch Yours," in Gayle, ed., *The Black Aesthetic,* 1971

Paul [Robeson] spoke twenty-five languages not as an exercise but as a source through which he could absorb the many cultures into which he had not been born, but to which he was instinctively determined to belong. He consumed a language for the cultural essence it contained and became in practice, in custom, and in habit a loyal member of all the groups whose songs he sang.

OSSIE DAVIS, "To Paul Robeson," *Freedomways,* 1971

[I]t may turn out that the great restive underground language rising from the American slums and fringe communities is the real American poetry and prose, that can tell you the way things are happening now.

ISHMAEL REED, "19 Necromancers From Now," in Chapman, ed., *New Black Voices,* 1972

Every man prays in his own language and there is no language that God does not understand.

DUKE ELLINGTON, *Music Is My Mistress,* 1973

They had taken a language imposed upon them, and infused it with their own incisive rhythms and syntax, brought to bear upon it the few African words and sounds that had been retained, made it their own.

PAULE MARSHALL, *New Letter,* 1973

His diction reveals he doesn't know the principle of economy, and uses swollen language.

DUDLEY RANDALL, in *Black Poetry Writing,* 1975

It seemed to me that Black people's grace has been with what they do with language.

TONI MORRISON, in *The New York Times,* 11 September 1977

Linguistic unity based on a foreign language is cultural abortion.

CHEIKH ANTA DIOP, *The Cultural Unity of Black Africa,* 1978

The language of soul—or, as it might also be called, "Spoken Soul" or "Colored English"—is simply an honest vocal portrayal of Black America. It generally possesses a pronounced lyrical quality, which is frequently incompatible to any music other than that ceaseless and relentlessly driving rhythm that flows from poignantly spent ideas.

CLAUDE BROWN, c. 1983

Language is the building block of consciousness. To accurately understand the soul of a people, you not only search for their outward manifestations . . . but you examine their language.

HAKI MADHUBUTI, "Lucille Clifton: Warm Water, Greased Legs, and Dangerous Poetry," in Evans, ed., *Black Women Writers,* 1984

Part of the difficulty in communication between Blacks and whites is that whites do not listen to or respect serious communication from Blacks, and that whites do not understand, or prefer to ignore, voices of the majority of Blacks.

HAKI MADHUBUTI, "Sonia Sanchez: The Bringer of Memories," in *ibid.*

It [is] necessary to acquire the skills needed for communicating in a mixed society, and . . . this requires a melting and blending of vernacular and . . . standard speech and a grasp of the occasions in which each, or both, [are] called for.

RALPH ELLISON, "Going to the Territory," *Going to the Territory,* 1986

LAUGHTER

We have fashioned laughter out of tears and pain,/ But the moment after—/ Pain and tears again.

CHARLES BERTRAM JOHNSON, c. 1880

Those who laugh and dance and sing are better off even in their vices than those who do not.

J. A. ROGERS, c. 1931

[T]he fact that a sick man laughs is surely no reason for not attempting to cure his sickness.

PAUL ROBESON, "I Want to Be African," *What I Want From Life,* 1934

I am especially glad of the divine gift of laughter; it has made the world human and lovable, despite all its pain and wrong.

W. E. B. DU BOIS, *Dusk of Dawn: An Essay Toward an Autobiography of Race Concept,* 1940

Yes, friends, your untamed laughter, your lizard laughter in their walls, your heretics' laughter in their dogmas, your incorrigible laughter, your whirlpool laughter, into which their cities fall spellbound, your time bomb laughter under their lordly feet, your laughter will conquer them! Laugh, laugh, till the world, conquered by your laughter, falls at your naked feet.

AIMÉ CÉSAIRE, *Miraculous Weapons,* 1946

[W]e knew "Laugh" personally on that night, because as every one of them stopped laughing at us, "Laugh" did not stop for two hours. As "Laugh" was laughing at us on that night, my wife and I forgot our pains and laughed with him, because he was laughing with curious voices that we never heard before in our life. We did not know the time that we fell into this laugh. But we were only laughing at "Laugh's" laugh and nobody who heard him when laughing would not laugh, so if somebody continued to laugh with "Laugh" himself, he or she would die or faint at once for long laughing, because laugh was his profession and he was feeding on it. Then they began to beg "Laugh" to stop, but he could not.

AMOS TUTUOLA, *Palm Wine Drunkard,* 1952

There is laughter among the people in the morning. It is as though they find themselves surprised to be alive that they cannot help laughing.

PETER ABRAHAMS, *Tell Freedom,* 1954

And my raining laughter beats down the fury.

PAUL VESEY, *Elefenbeinzahne—Ivory Tusks,* 1956

[T]he Lord, who with a saxophonic laugh,/ created heaven and earth in six days

LEOPOLD SENGHOR, "New York," *Ethiopics,* 1956

Laughter has its limits, its risks. It can be a screen, a blinder, a way to avoid putting a bold eye on an uncomfortable reality.

TONI CADE BAMBARA, "Salvation Is the Issue," in Evans, ed., *Black Women Writers,* 1984

He who laughs, lasts.

MARY POOLE, c. 1987

A laugh like the edges of an April sunset—translucent and mystifying.

GLORIA NAYLOR, *The Women of Brewster Place,* 1988

Laugh I say for laughing is happiness,/ leave behind your sorrows,/ Laugh to heal your wounds, laugh to/ send away your troubles,/ Laugh to allow the body to grow in health and vigor,/ Laugh in order to rise should you fall.

SHABAAN ROBERTS, "Laugh with Happiness," in Chinweizu, ed., *Voices From Twentieth-Century Africa,* 1988

LAW

If men, though they know that the law protects all, will dare, in defiance of law, to execute their hatred upon the defenseless Black, will they not by the passing of this bill believe him still a mark for their venom and spleen? Will they not believe him completely deserted by authority, and subject to every outrage brutality can inflict—too surely they will and the poor wretch will turn his eyes around to look in vain for protection .

JAMES FORTEN, *Letters from a Man of Colour on a Late Senate Bill before the Senate of Pennsylvania,* 1813

It's a moot law that won't work both ways.

FREDERICK DOUGLASS, speech given in Boston, Massachusetts, 8 June 1849

There is a law above all statutes written on the heart, and by that law, unchangeable and eternal, no man can be or hold a slave.

FREDERICK DOUGLASS, *My Bondage and My Freedom*, 1855

If the school law provides that all the children in every state where there is a school system supported in whole or in part by general taxation shall have equal advantage of school privileges . . . then any child has the right to go to school anywhere they exist.

JAMES RAPIER, in the *Congressional Record*, 9 June 1874

Laws which determine the destinies of individuals and nations are impartial and eternal. We shall reap as we sow.

FREDERICK DOUGLASS, in the *North American Review*, 1881

Mob law is the most forcible expression of an abnormal public opinion; it shows the society is rotten to the core. Many of the laws intended to secure our rights as citizens are nothing more than dead letters.

T. THOMAS FORTUNE, "Political Independence of the Negro," speech given to Colored Press Association, Washington, D.C., 27 June 1882

Human society could not exist one hour except on the basis of law which holds the baser passions of men in restraint.

KELLY MILLER, *The American Negro*, 1908

The fundamental issue of life is the appeal of race to race, the appeal of clan to clan, the appeal of tribe to tribe, of observing the rule that self preservation was the first law of nature.

MARCUS GARVEY, *Philosophy and Opinions of Marcus Garvey*, 1923

They're going to pass a bill against lynching in the United States if we are to build a civilized nation.

NANNIE BURROUGHS, "With All They Getting," *The Southern Workman*, July 1927

I have firmly believed all along that the law was on our side and would, when we appealed to it, give us justice. I feel shorn of that belief and utterly discouraged, and just now, if it were possible, would gather my race in my arms and fly away with them. O, God, is there no redress, no peace, no justice in the land for us?

IDA B. WELLS, in Duster, ed., *Crusade for Justice*, 1928

It is important and right that all privilege of the law be ours, but it is vastly more important that we be prepared for the exercise of these privileges.

BOOKER T. WASHINGTON, *Speeches of Booker T. Washington*, 1932

Unless we can have the substance of law, it doesn't matter whether a person is hanged by an unauthorized mob or by a mob known as the "law."

WILLIAM HASTIE, in the *Afro-American*, 18 April 1936

Law is always nullified by practice and disdain, unless the minds and hearts of a people sustain law.

JAMES M. LAWSON, "From a Lunch-Counter Stool," speech given at SNCC Conference, Raleigh, North Carolina, April 1960

Freedom without law is anarchy.

KWAME NKRUMAH, *I Speak of Freedom*, 1961

Whenever you have to pass a law to make a man let me have a house. When you have to pass a law to let me go to school. When you have to pass a law to let me walk down the street—you have to enforce that law—then you'd be living in a police state. America right now is moving toward the police state.

MALCOLM X, c. 1963

There are laws that, little by little, are invalidated under the Constitution. There are other laws that forbid certain forms of discrimination. And we can be sure that nothing is going to be given free.

FRANTZ FANON, *The Wretched of the Earth*, 1963

One may well ask, "How can you advocate breaking some laws and obeying others?" The answer is found in the fact that there are two types of laws: there are *just* and there are *unjust* laws. . . . One has not only a legal but a moral responsibility to disobey unjust laws.

MARTIN LUTHER KING, JR., *Letter from a Birmingham City Jail,* 1963

You can't legislate integration, but you can certainly legislate desegregation. You can't legislate morality, but you regulate behavior. You can't make a man love me, but the law can restrain him from lynching me.

MARTIN LUTHER KING, JR., in *U.S. News & World Report,* 24 February 1964

Despite new laws, little has changed in . . . the ghetto. . . . The law pronounces him equal, abstractly, but his condition of life is still far from equal to those of other Americans.

MARTIN LUTHER KING, JR., "Negroes Are Not Moving Too Fast," *Saturday Evening Post,* 7 November 1964

[L]aws will not eliminate prejudice from the hearts of human beings. But that is no reason to allow prejudice to continue to be enshrined in our laws to perpetuate injustice through inaction.

SHIRLEY CHISHOLM, *Unbought and Unbossed,* 1970

[The] law of liberation and [the] spirit of freedom are of such heavenly concern that no ruler, power structure, system, or government can outlaw or overrule them. Any attempt to suspend, abridge, or obstruct these basic inherent rights of liberation causes divine intervention. Before God allows any defiance against his ongoing purpose of love and freedom, he will wreck any power or system.

D. E. KING, "The God Who Takes Off Chariot Wheels," in Philpot, ed. *Best Black Sermons,* 1972

Apartheid laws turn innumerable innocent people into criminals.

NELSON MANDELA, *The Struggle Is My Life,* 1978

Martin worked with the law. Sometimes he broke it intentionally; other times he didn't; but he always had the law in mind. His aim was to get the law on *our* side.

RAY CHARLES, *Brother Ray,* 1978

We are the only racial group within the United States ever forbidden by law to read and write. The law also forbade any white to teach us to read. After generations of such laws, while slave labor made profits and founded fortunes for others, we are besieged with accusations of "inferiority" in learning skills. We and the Native American were the only citizens or aliens legally forbidden to enter libraries, concert halls, theaters, and public schools.

ALICE CHILDRESS, "A Candle in a Gale Wind," in Evans, ed., *Black Women Writers,* 1984

Law and order mean something deeper than the prevention of violence and the control of crime. They mean that every citizen in every neighborhood is safe and secure.

TOM BRADLEY, *The Impossible Dream,* 1986

Only laws are suppressing the undercurrent of racism that still exists in America today.

BILL COSBY, c. 1987

Law does not exist for lawyers or for judges or for professors in law schools. Law is all that stands between the common man and every tyranny and degradation to which he is subjected wherever his leaders have unbridled power.

THOMAS SOWELL, c. 1988

After seven long, hard, difficult years of opposing this administration's efforts to dismantle affirmative action and reverse civil rights laws, there is a need now to go on the offensive.

REV. JOSEPH LOWERY, in "Words of the Week," *Jet,* 29 August 1988

When people ask why a separate Black law organization is needed at this late date, the answer is simple. It's not that late.

THURGOOD MARSHALL, in *Jet,* 29 August 1988

LEADER/LEADERSHIP

See also MARTIN LUTHER KING, MARCUS GARVEY, MALCOLM X, NELSON MANDELA, BOOKER T. WASHINGTON

If you are a leader who controls the affairs of the many, seek out every good deed so your conduct may be blameless.

PTAH HOTEP, c. 2340 B.C.

I was one who cultivated grain and loved the harvest god. The Nile greeted me and every valley. None was hungry in my years, none thirsted then. Men dwelt in peace through that which I wrought, and conversed in me.

AMENENHET, c. 760–657 B.C.

A tyrant does not remain in the world but the curse on him abides forever.

The Gulistan of Sadi, 1184–1292

Son you will have a warrior's name/ And be a leader of man/ And your sons, and your son's son/ will remember you long after you have slipped into darkness.

SUDAN, *Song of a Mother to Her First-Born*

We can get at the throat of treason and slavery through the State of Massachusetts. She was the first in the War of Independence, first to break the chains of her slaves, first to make the black man equal before the law, first to admit colored children to her common schools, and she was first to answer with her blood the alarm-cry of the nation.

FREDERICK DOUGLASS, *Life and Times of Frederick Douglass,* 1892

Some look to Booker T. Washington to lead them,/ Some yell for Trotter, some for Kelly Miller/ Some want Du Bois with fat ideas to feed them/ Some want Jack Johnson, the big white hope killer/ Perhaps some want Carranga, some want Villa/ I guess they want social equality to marry and mix in white society.

REGINOLD MARGRETSON, c. 1910

Frederick Douglass was the cataract that roared. His imagery was fine, vivid. Douglass was the lecturer, the powerful invective. He told the story of his wrongs so that they stood out in their naked ugliness.

ARTHUR A. SCHOMBURG, *Racial Integrity,* 1913

Our leaders, like Caesar's wife, must be above suspicion.

HUBERT HARRISON, "The Descent of Du Bois," *When Africa Awakes,* 1918

Leadership means everything—pain, blood, death.

MARCUS GARVEY, *Philosophy and Opinions of Marcus Garvey,* 1923

Our leader will not be a white man with a Black heart, nor a Black man with a white heart, but a Black man with a Black heart.

Ibid.

Chloroform your "Uncle Toms." Unload the leeches and parasitic leaders who are eating the life out of the struggle.

NANNIE BURROUGHS, "Unload Your Uncle Toms," *The Southern Workman,* December 1933

[W]hen you find a man who has lost his way, you don't make fun of him and scorn him and leave him there. You show him the way. If you don't do that you just prove that you're sort of lost yourself.

ZORA NEALE HURSTON, *Moses, Man of the Mountain,* 1939

Precious Lord, take my hand/ Lead me on, let me stand/ I am tired, I am weak, I am worn/ Through the storm, through the night/ Lead me on to the light.

THOMAS DORSEY, "Precious Lord," 1940

Gone are the days when a Negro can openly betray his people and still remain their leader.

CLAUDE MCKAY, *Harlem: Negro Metropolis,* 1940

Garvey was . . . an astonishing popular leader, . . . a master of propaganda. Within a few years, news of his movement, of his promises and plans, reached Europe and Asia, and penetrated every corner of Africa.

W. E. B. Du Bois, *Dusk of Dawn: An Essay Toward an Autobiography of Race Concept,* 1940

I do not wish to secure any job from the President of the United States or anybody else that can give political favors. A leader of the masses must be free to obey and follow the interests of the masses.

A. Philip Randolph, speech given at the March on Washington Movement, Detroit, Michigan, 26 September 1942

The leaders of the Democratic and Republican Parties are united in preparing for war . . . which means they must destroy civil rights.

Paul Robeson, "Vote for Peace," address given to the National Convention of the Progressive Party, Chicago, Illinois, 4 July 1952

Reading people are ruling people.

Melvin Chapman, speech given at Miller Junior High School, Detroit, Michigan, 1962

I always had a very high opinion of both the late Noble Drew Ali and Marcus Garvey and admired their courage in helping our people . . . and appreciated their work. Both of these men were fine Muslims. [Their] followers . . . should now follow me and co-operate with us in our work because we are only trying to finish up what those before us started.

Elijah Muhammad, in Essien-Udom, *Black Nationalism,* 1962

From the people heaving in action will come the leaders, not the isolated Black at the Sorbonne, the dabbler in surrealism, or the lawyer.

C. L. R. James, *The Black Jacobins,* 1963

When leaders have fulfilled their functions, it's time for them to retire.

Nathan Hare, *Black Scholar,* May 1967

[W]hen . . . I see the leaders of nations again talking peace while preparing for war, I take fearful pause. . . . A nation that continues year after year to spend more money for military defense than on programs of social uplift is approaching spiritual death.

Martin Luther King, Jr., *Where Do We Go From Here?* 1968

Far too often we become cowards when faced with individuals who have strong leadership abilities, individuals who often do not want social revolution as much as they want personal power. Far too often we follow blindly—without questioning their motives—without examining their actions. We follow blindly because what they say they want to do sounds right. We follow because we are afraid that those around us will misunderstand our questions and put us down.

Shirley Chisholm, speech given at Federal City College, Washington, D.C., 1969

[F]alse leaders and sick movements . . . must be stopped in the beginning, for they turn humanity against itself.

Jesse Owens, *Blackthink,* 1970

They thought he was the leader because he was loud and black and crude and he probably had ten people as followers, nine of them members of his family. . .

Whitney Young, 1971

The people of the streets, the failures, the misfits, the despised, the maimed, the beaten, the sightless, and the voiceless had made a captive of me. . . . Whenever they commanded, I followed, but followed only to lead.

Adam Clayton Powell, Jr., *Adam by Adam,* 1971

Our greatest fighters for freedom were religious leaders—Denmark Vesey, Nat Turner, David Walker, Henry Highland Garnet, and many others.

Gayraud Wilmore, "Black Theology," in Philpot, ed., *Best Black Sermons,* 1972

Dr. Carver was a really great man—a man who sacrificed so much for his people. He was obsessed with working for his people. If everyone who pretended to lead felt that, the Black race would be galloping.

AMY GARVEY, in "Mrs. Marcus Garvey Talks With Ida Lewis," *Encore,* May 1973

Jesus, the Black Messiah, was a revolutionary leader, sent by God to rebuild the Black nation, Israel, and to liberate Black people from powerlessness and from the oppression, brutality, and exploitation of the white gentile world.

BLACK CHRISTIAN NATIONALIST, 1979

Strong people don't need strong leaders.

ELLA BAKER, c. 1980

David Walker in 1830 and Frederick Douglass in 1850 had revealed the anguish and the pain of life for blacks in the United States. Martin Delaney and Harriet Tubman, Marcus Garvey and [W. E. B.] Du Bois, and Martin King and Malcolm X had explained with anger, passion and persuasion that we were living precariously on the ledge of life, and that if we fell, the entire structure, which had prohibited us living room, might crumble as well.

MAYA ANGELOU, *The Heart of a Woman,* 1981

Women, in general, are not a part of the corruption of the past, so they can give a new kind of leadership, a new image for mankind.

CORETTA KING, in Walker, *In Search of Our Mothers' Gardens,* 1983

Over the years, our Black leaders have been forced to act as intermediaries between Blacks and the President of the United States. I wonder why no President considers himself our leader.

ALICE CHILDRESS, "A Candle in a Gale Wind," in Evans, ed., *Black Women Writers,* 1984

Readers are leaders. Thinkers succeed.

MARVA COLLINS, 1986

I watched Adam Powell lead a depressed people to high spirits with intellect and savvy; Dr. King, with sheer power of his personality, intellect, and commitment, lift people, Dr. Benjamin Mays take patience and mold and shape young minds. John Johnson take a one-thousand-dollar loan from his mother and build a publishing empire. Percy Sutton, with his grace and class, go into public service, then into business. I drew strength from the shadows of these giants and tried to absorb into my own being the highest and best they had to offer.

JESSE JACKSON, in "Reverend Jesse Jackson," *Ebony Man,* December 1986

We need leadership that thinks about the future and encourages us to invest ourselves.

ANITA DE FRANTZ, in *American Visions,* 1988

How many Martin Luther Kings, how many Ralph Bunches, how many of these great minds are being wasted away on some back lot practicing the between-the-legs dribble and the behind-the-back pass, or trying to beat out the cornerback, or trying to turn a single into a double?

HARRY EDWARDS, in "Hardline," *Detroit Free Press,* 8 May 1988

This generation had no Douglass, no Powell, no King, no Malcolm to break things down for them.

SUSAN TAYLOR, "In the Spirit," *Essence,* August 1988

You must genuinely like and respect those who are performing under your command, for neither the liking nor the respect can be successfully faked.

BENJAMIN DAVIS, *Benjamin Davis, Jr.: An Autobiography,* 1991

LEARN/LEARNING

Learn by others' mistakes because you do not live long enough to make them all yourself.

TRADITIONAL

A little learning, indeed, may be a dangerous thing, but the want of learning is a calamity to any people.

FREDERICK DOUGLASS, speech given at the Colored High School commencement, Baltimore, Maryland, 22 June 1894

Give a man tools and let him commence to use them, and in time he will learn a trade.

BEVERLY NASH, c. 1900

Few [are] too young, and none too old, to make the attempt to learn.

BOOKER T. WASHINGTON, *Up From Slavery,* 1901

Learn to do uncommon things in an uncommon manner. Learn to do a thing so thoroughly that no one can improve upon what has been done.

Ibid.

She had learned how to talk some and leave some. She was a rut in the road. Plenty of life beneath the surface but it was kept beaten down by the wheels.

ZORA NEALE HURSTON, *Their Eyes Were Watching God,* 1937

Learning without wisdom is a load of books on a donkey's back.

ZORA NEALE HURSTON, *Moses, Man of the Mountain,* 1939

If I have learned anything in my life, it is that bitterness consumes the vessel that contains it.

RUBIN HURRICANE CARTER, 1960

One of the first things I think young people, especially nowadays, should learn is how to see for yourself and listen for yourself and think for yourself.

MALCOLM X, "To Mississippi Youth,"speech given at the Hotel Theresa, New York City, 31 December 1964

There are many things one must learn and read in elementary school and high school, otherwise it is too late, for each passing day makes its own new demands.

BENJAMIN MAYS, *Born to Rebel,* 1971

A child must learn early to believe that he is somebody worthwhile and that he can do many praiseworthy things. Without this hope, there would be nothing for him to do but to commit suicide.

BENJAMIN E. MAYS, "What Man Lives By," in Philpot, ed., *Best Black Sermons,* 1972

Our appeal, as Black people, is to learn more about us as a race. We are not asking charity of you, because we believe in self-help. We believe that as a race of people struggling onward and upward, we must of ourselves lift ourselves up, and all we ask you is that you treat us kindly and decently.

AMY GARVEY, in "Mrs. Marcus Garvey Talks with Ida Lewis," *Encore,* May 1973

I try to learn as much as I can because I know nothing compared to what I need to know.

MUHAMMAD ALI, in "Ali Begins a New Era," *Class,* April 1984

Learn enough about a given phenomenon and the "unexpected" becomes fairly predictable.

RALPH ELLISON, "Going to the Territory," *Going to the Territory,* 1986

She has touched me in the palm of my mind.

NETTIE JONES, "Colour, Sex and Poetry," *City Arts Quarterly,* Fall 1987

Look inside to find out where you're going, and it's better to do it before you get out of high school.

PRINCE, 1988

While my brothers and I were paying dues on the so-called "chitlin circuit" opening for other acts, I carefully watched all the stars because I wanted to learn as much as I could.

MICHAEL JACKSON, in *Jet,* 5 May 1988

[At college] you develop the process of learning and become a perennial student the rest of your life, which . . . is the key to youth, vitality, and longevity.

MELBA MOORE, in "Education," *Jet,* 29 August 1988

LEAVE

Some of these mornings and it won't be long, you gonna wake up calling me and I'll be gone.

BLUES

We do not mean to go to Liberia. Our minds are made up to live here if we can or die here if we must; so every attempt to remove us, will be, as it ought to be, a labor lost. Here we are and here we shall remain.

FREDERICK DOUGLASS, *The North Star,* 26 January 1849

It would seem that education and emigration go together with us, for as soon as a man rises amongst us, by his genius and learning, to do us great service, just as soon as he finds he can serve himself better by going elsewhere . . . Individuals emigrate—nations never.

FREDERICK DOUGLASS, letter to Harriet Beecher Stowe, 8 March 1853

I elect to stay on the soil of which I was born and on the plot of ground which I have fairly bought and honestly paid for. Don't advise me to leave, and don't add insult to injury by telling me it's for my own good; of that I am to be the judge.

ROBERT PURVIS, letter to Senator S. C. Pomroy, 1862

I left because at a certain moment in social proceedings I am on FIRE to leave; I have a leaving-FIT.

GWENDOLYN BROOKS, *Report From Part One,* 1972

O, Sugarman, don't leave me here/ Cotton balls to choke me/ O, Sugarman don't leave me/ Buckra's arms to yoke me.

TONI MORRISON, *Song of Solomon,* 1977

LEGEND

So all across Africa, America, the West Indies, there are tales of the powers of Moses and great worship of him and his powers. But it does not flow from the Ten Commandments. It is his rod of power, the terror that he showed before all Israel and to Pharaoh, and THAT MIGHTY HAND.

ZORA NEALE HURSTON, *Moses, Man of the Mountain,* 1939

Every legend contains its residuum of truth, and the root function of language is to control the universe by describing it.

JAMES BALDWIN, *Notes of a Native Son,* 1955

People surrounded by a legend rarely look the parts they have been assigned.

JAMES BALDWIN, *Nobody Knows My Name,* 1961

What is really sad is when a legend begins to fade. I think about the cowboys who carved notches in their guns for every man they killed. Everything the person has done is right there. You can see the experience in them. But sometimes, though the gun still has bullets and the aim is still good, the world stops the carving of the notches. It is so sad to see a legendary performer cut off from his audiences, even though the basic talent is still there, seasoned by experience. Who throws away a beautiful old bottle of wine?

PEARL BAILEY, *The Raw Pearl,* 1968

People always get excited about meeting a living legend. But I always ask myself the same question. What does a living legend do?

PEG LEG BATES, in "Peg Leg Bates:A Living Legend," *Crisis,* December 1985

I know what I've done for music, but don't call me a legend. Just call me Miles Davis.

MILES DAVIS, in *Jet,* 9 June 1986

I'm too young to be a legend. I'm still the lady next door. That keeps my feet on the ground.

ARETHA FRANKLIN, 1988

My birth was never recorded. I have no birth certificate, therefore I do not exist, that is why I am a legend.

EARTHA KITT, 1988

It is unfortunate that people have an image of me as a legendary figure and if they see me as anything less than Superman, they can't accept it.

MUHAMMAD ALI, in *Jet,* 16 May 1988

Being called a legend is another way of saying you survived.

JOE WILLIAMS, 1989

After twenty-five years, I guess you are either out of it or you're a legend.

MARTHA REEVES, 1990

LESSONS

The lessons of all the ages upon this point is, that a wrong done to one man is a wrong done to all men. It may be . . . delayed, but so sure as there is a moral government of the universe, so sure will the harvest of evil come.

FREDERICK DOUGLASS, *Life and Times of Frederick Douglass,* 1895

Let lessons of stern yesterdays . . . be your food, your drink, your rest.

JOSEPH COTTER, *Negro Tales,* 1912

The best lessons, the best sermons are those that are lived.

YOLANDA KING, *Ebony,* August 1987

LIBERTY

Too much liberty corrupts an angel.

TERENCE, *Self-Tormentor,* 161 B.C.

Do they think men who have been able to enjoy the blessings of liberty will calmly see it snatched away?

TOUSSAINT L 'OUVERTURE, *Lettres de Toussaint L'Ouverture,* 1802

Liberty is a spirit sent from God and like its great Author is no respecter of persons.

H. HIGHLAND GARNET, "An Address to the Slaves of the United States," speech given at National Negro Convention, Buffalo, New York, August 1843

The liberty of no man is secure, who controls not his political destiny . . . to suppose otherwise is that delusion which at once induces its victims to every species of wrong; trusting against probability and hoping against all reasonable expectations, for the privileges and enjoyment of rights, that will never be attained.

MARTIN DELANY, *The Condition, Elevation, Emigration, and Destiny of the Colored People of the United States,* 1852

Liberty exists in the very idea of man's creation. It was his even before he comprehended it. He was created in it, endowed with it, and it can never be taken away.

FREDERICK DOUGLASS, *My Bondage and My Freedom,* 1855

The price of liberty is eternal vigilance.

FREDERICK DOUGLASS, speech given at Bethel Literary Historical Association, Washington, D.C., 4 April 1889

I know the bitterness of being accused and harassed by prosecutors. I know the horror of being hunted and haunted. I have dashed across continents and oceans as a fugitive, and have matched my wits with the police and secret agents seeking to deprive me of one of the greatest blessings a man can have—liberty.

JACK JOHNSON, *Jack Johnson in the Ring and Out,* 1927

Eternal vigilance is the price of liberty, and it does seem that notwithstanding all those social agencies and activities there is not vigilance, which should be exercised in the preservation of our rights.

IDA B. WELLS, in Duster, ed., *Crusade for Justice,* 1928

In overthrowing me, you have cut down in San Domingo only the trunk of the tree of liberty. It will spring up again by the roots for they are numerous and deep.

TOUSSAINT L'OUVERTURE, in James, *The Black Jacobins,* 1963

Sweetest fruits of liberty are plucked by those who readily display boldness and daring.

ROBERT WILLIAMS, "USA: The Potential of a Minority Revolution," *The Crusader Monthly Newsletter,* May–June 1965

"Seek first the Kingdom of God and its righteousness and all these other things will be added unto you." This meant endurance now, liberty later.

JAMES CONE, *Black Theology and Black Power,* 1969

The move toward liberation from slave to serf to self, for Black folk, has meant a long, arduous trip.

SARAH WEBSTER FABIO, "Tripping with Black Writing," in Gayle, ed., *The Black Aesthetic,* 1971

[T]here can be no true black political liberation without religious and cultural liberation.

GAYRAUD S. WILMORE, "Black Theology," in Philpot, ed., *Best Black Sermons,* 1972

There have always been liberated women. Some are liberated because they demand it, some because they can afford it.

JOE LOUIS, *My Life,* 1981

African and Black Theology must be concerned—and vitally concerned—with liberation. . . .

DESMOND TUTU, *Hope and Suffering,* 1983

Liberation means you don't have to be silenced.

TONI MORRISON, in "Toni Morrison Now," *Essence,* October 1987

Liberty—the engine of our prosperity and the foundation of our national harmony—is under siege today by those who would strangle it on the name of one grandiose ideal or the other; "orderly markets," "a level playing field," "social justice." They offer us Old World–style trade restrictions, socialist-style income redistribution, and tribal-style ethnic privileges.

WALTER E. WILLIAMS, "Why We're Number One," *Success,* March 1989

LIES/LYING

When falsehood walks around it goes astray. It does not cross over in the ferry nor does it go forward. One who becomes rich by it has no children or heirs on earth. Those who sail with it do not reach dry land and their boat does not drop anchor at the intended town.

EGYPT

A lie betrays its mother tongue.

LIBERIA

Ninety-nine lies may save you, but the one-hundredth one will give you away.

WEST AFRICA

Lies, however numerous, will be caught when they rise up. The voice of truth is easily known.

AFRICA

We wear the mask that grins and lies,/ It hides our cheeks and shades our eyes.

PAUL LAURENCE DUNBAR, "We Wear the Mask," *Collected Poems,* 1913

Her tongue is hung in the middle and works both ways.

ZORA NEALE HURSTON, *Mules and Men,* 1935

They certainly lied up a mess. The men would start telling stories and one man would stop another and say, "Wait a minute, let me put my dime on your dollar."

Ibid.

We were once friends with the whites, but you nudged us out of the way by your intrigues, and now when we are in council you keep nudging each other. Why don't you talk straight, and let all be well?

MOTAVATO (BLACK KETTLE) in Brill, *Conquest of the Southern Plains,* 1938

The female companion of man has the gift of the soothing—balm of lies.

ZORA NEALE HURSTON, *Moses, Man of the Mountain,* 1939

I love the man, I'm a lie if I say I don't. But I'll quit my man, I'm a lie if I say I won't.

BILLIE HOLIDAY, c. 1940

The formula created by the necessity to find a lie more palatable than the truth has been handed down and memorized and persists yet with a terrible power.

JAMES BALDWIN, *Notes of a Native Son,* 1955

All of the Western nations have been caught in a lie, the lie of their pretended humanism.

JAMES BALDWIN, *Nobody Knows My Name,* 1961

We have to undo the millions of little white lies that America told itself and the world about the American Black man.

JOHN KILLENS, "Black Revolt and the White Backlash," Town Hall Forum, New York City, 15 June 1964

Malcolm kept snatching our lies away. He kept shouting the painful truth we whites and blacks did not want to hear from all the housetops. And he wouldn't stop for love nor money.

OSSIE DAVIS, in *The Autobiography of Malcolm X,* 1965

One has to lie sometimes to get closer to the truth.

JOHN KILLENS, "The Cotillion," in Clarke, ed., *American Negro Short Stories,* 1966

You have to prop a lie up with another lie and that one with another until nothing remains clear or simple.

FRANK YERBY, *Judas, My Brother,* 1967

You cannot subjugate a man and recognize his humanity, his history, and his personality, so systematically you must take this away from him. You began by telling lies about the man's role in history.

JOHN HENRIK CLARKE, speech at the Jewish Currents Conference, New York City, 15 February 1969

The national pastime in this country is not sex and it's not baseball. It's lying.

DICK GREGORY, *No More Lies,* 1971

It is one thing to tell a lie and another thing to believe it.

Ibid.

A device is a device, but that also has consequences: once invented it takes on a life, a reality of its own. So, in one country, men evoke the device of religion to cloak their conquests; in another, race. In both cases we recognize the fraudulence of the device, but the fact remains that a man who has a sword run through him because he will not become a Moslem or a Christian—or is lynched in Mississippi or Zatembe because he is black—is suffering the utter reality of that device of conquest. And it is pointless to pretend that it doesn't exist—merely because it is a lie.

LORRAINE HANSBERRY, *Les Blancs,* 1972

The lie of the artist is the only lie for which a mortal of good should die.

MELVIN TOLSON, in Redmond, *Drumvoice,* 1976

LIFE

Life is a shadow and a mist; it passes quickly by, and is no more.

CONGO

Without life, there is nothing.

ZULU

Alas! The journey of life is beset with thorns to those who have to pursue it alone.

ALEXANDRE DUMAS, *Le Demi-Monde,* 1855

A life without fighting is a dead sea in the universal organism.

JOAQUIM MACHADO DE ASSIS, *Epitaph for a Small Winner,* 1881

Life is won, the battle is still lost.

JOAQUIM MACHADO DE ASSIS, *Dom Casmurro,* 1881

I would set no limits to the attainments of the Negro in arts, in letters, or statesmanship, but I believe the surest way to reach those ends is by laying the foundation in the little things of life that lie immediately about one's door.

BOOKER T. WASHINGTON, *Up From Slavery,* 1901

A crust of bread and a corner to sleep in,/ A minute to smile and an hour to weep in,/ A pint of joy to a peck of troubles/ And never a laugh but the moans come double;/ And that is life.

PAUL LAURENCE DUNBAR, *Complete Poems,* 1913

How far you go in life depends on your being tender with the young, compassionate with the aged, sympathetic with the striving, and tolerant of the weak and the strong. Because someday in life you will have been all of these.

GEORGE WASHINGTON CARVER, c. 1920

Life for me ain't been no crystal stair.

LANGSTON HUGHES, "Mother to Son," 1926

There is more to life than increasing its speed.

MOHANDAS GANDHI, c. 1930

The purpose of life is to know oneself.

MOHANDAS GANDHI, 1932

Life is one of the clear fine tones in our medley of harsh discordant sounds. Life is measured by your own glowing, and you find life, you find its possibilities deeply hopeful and beautiful.

JEAN TOOMER, c. 1934

It was like sewing ruffles on a fence of nails. The will to make life beautiful was so strong.

ZORA NEALE HURSTON, *Their Eyes Were Watching God,* 1937

I find I cannot portray the life nor express the living hopes and aspirations of the struggling people from which I come.

PAUL ROBESON, "Why I Joined Labor Theatre," *Daily Worker,* 24 November 1937

Life is the fullest, most complete enjoyment of the possibilities of human existence. It is the development and broadening of the feelings and emotions, through sound and color, line and form . . . [L]ife is the free enjoyment of every normal appetite . . . giving rein to the creative impulse, in thought and imagination.

W. E. B. DU BOIS, "The Revelation of Saint Orgone the Damned," speech given at Fisk University, 1938

Life has its pain and evil—its bitter disappointments; but like a good novel and in healthful length of days, there is infinite joy in seeing the World, the most interesting of continued stories, unfold, even though one misses the end.

W. E. B. DU BOIS, *Dusk of Dawn: An Essay Toward an Autobiography of Race Concept,* 1940

Life is sufficient unto life if it is lived and felt directly and deeply enough.

RICHARD WRIGHT, *12 Million Black Voices,* 1941

No matter how joyful or how sad the case, there is sufficient poise for drama.

ZORA NEALE HURSTON, *Dust Tracks on a Road,* 1942

And above all, my body as well as my soul, beware of assuming the sterile attitude of spectator, for life is not a spectacle, for a sea of miseries is not a proscenium, a man screaming is not a dancing bear.

AIMÉ CÉSAIRE, *Notes on a Return to the Native Land,* 1947

To love life is to be whole in all one's parts; and to be whole in all one's parts is to be free and unafraid.

HOWARD THURMAN, *Meditations of the Heart,* 1953

All theories are suspect, the finest principles have to be modified, or may even be pulverized by the demands of life, and one must find one's own moral center and move through the world hoping that this center will guide us aright.

JAMES BALDWIN, *Notes of a Native Son,* 1955

My name is Life; certain people know me in going who won't recognize me on my return. I go and I come. When I return here, I shall present myself to you. You won't recognize me, for Life is prolific in its change.

BERNARD DADIE, "A Parable," *Dance of the Days,* 1956

[B]elieve in life! Always human beings will live and progress to greater, broader and fuller life.

W. E. B. DU BOIS, "Last Message to the World," 26 June 1957

People pay for the lives they lead and the crimes they commit and the blood from which they flee, whether they know they do or not.

JAMES BALDWIN, *Nobody Knows My Name,* 1961

The people in one's life or merely continually in one's presence reveal a great deal about one's needs and terrors.

Ibid.

Someone told me life is a water wheel. It turns. The trick is to hold your nose when you're under and not get dizzy when you're up.

Ibid.

No one can demand more of life than the honor to demand that he learn to live with his fears, and learn to live, every day, both within his limits and beyond them.

Ibid.

[W]e have allowed the means by which we live to outdistance the ends for which we live.

MARTIN LUTHER KING, JR., "The American Dream," speech given at Lincoln University, Oxford, Pennsylvania, 6 June 1961

Life at its best is a coherent triangle. At one angle is the individual person. At the other angle are other persons. At the tiptop is the Infinite Person, God. Without the development of each part of the triangle, no life can be complete.

MARTIN LUTHER KING, JR., *Strength to Love,* 1963

If a man hasn't discovered something that he will die for, he isn't fit to live.

MARTIN LUTHER KING, JR., speech given in Detroit, Michigan, 23 June 1963

The most extraordinary characteristic of current American life is the attempt to reduce life to buying and selling. Life is not love unless sex is bought and sold. Life is not knowledge save knowledge of technique, of science for destruction. Life is not beauty except beauty for sale. Life is not art unless its price is high and it is sold for profit. All life is production for profit, and for what is profit but for buying and selling again?

W. E. B. DU BOIS, *The Autobiography of W. E. B. Dubois: A Soliloquy on Viewing My Life from the Last Decade of Its First Century,* 1964

We search for the meaning of life in the realities of our experiences, in the realities of our dreams, our hopes, our memories.

CHESTER HIMES, *Beyond the Angry Black,* 1966

Life is an obscene farce, never a tragedy! Pain's the first principle on which the universe is built. Terror is the second. Lust is third, followed by madness, followed by death.

FRANK YERBY, *Judas, My Brother,* 1967

Life commences not with birth, but with the onslaught of awareness.

Ibid.

Life puts no greater burdens upon a man than the necessity of making decisions.

Ibid.

My life is caught in the lasso of existence.

FRANTZ FANON, *Black Skin, White Masks,* 1967

Life's piano can only produce the melodies of brotherhood when it is recognized that the black keys are as basic, necessary, and beautiful as the white keys.

MARTIN LUTHER KING, JR., *Where Do We Go From Here?* 1968

This the urging: Live!/ and have your blooming
in the noise of the whirlwind. . . ./ Define and/
medicate the whirlwind.

GWENDOLYN BROOKS, "The Second Sermon on the Warpland," *In the Mecca,* 1968

Life is more than fun and games/The thought/after
all/that either of us is capable of being
assassinated/at any moment/for absolutely
nothing/and relatively little/is of course unnerving.

AL YOUNG, *Dancing,* 1969

We get what we deserve, and we live by the grace of God.

BENJAMIN MAYS, c. 1970

Life doesn't give you all the practice races you need. . . .

JESSE OWEN, *Blackthink,* 1970

Man shall not live by bread alone. Man must live by affection and love; by forgiveness . . . of man and the forgiveness of God; by God's grace, by the labors of many hands, by faith, faith in himself, faith in others, and by faith in God. . . . [M]an must live by his dreams, his ideals, the unattainable goal, and what he aspires to be.

BENJAMIN MAYS, "What Man Lives By," in Philpot, ed., *Best Black Sermons,* 1972

Life is not intended to be safe. A safe life has too small a name for a creature of eternity. Life at its noblest and highest has a hazard about it; it ponders tomorrow but does not know it; it sounds the depths of the ocean, but knows not the hazards of the bottom. Life at its best takes a chance on righteousness no matter the hazard, no matter the cost. Life, when answering to its true name, lifts on wings, feeling no invisible hands supporting it.

HERMAN WATTS, "What Is Your Name?" in *ibid.*

Life's adventure with eternity is too long to be chained with transient and material things.

Ibid.

I wish to live because life has with it that which is good, that which is beautiful, and that which is love.

LORRAINE HANSBERRY, "What Use Are Flowers?" *Les Blancs,* 1972

Dissonance is our way of life in America. We are something apart, yet an integral part.

DUKE ELLINGTON, *Music Is My Mistress,* 1973

Life and death are all one, and life is constantly being reborn from itself.

ERNESTO CARDENAL, "Love," *Vida en al Amor,* 1974

Those things in life that matter will give you pain as you learn to understand life.

KEORAPETSE KGOSITSILE, in *Black Poetry Writing,* 1975

Life loves the liver of it. Life loves to be taken by the lapel and be told: "I am with you kid. Let's go."

MELVIN CHAPMAN, c. 1976

Life is a gamble; one had to keep gambling right from the day one was born.

BUCHI EMECHETA, *The Joys of Motherhood,* 1979

Life is a short walk from the cradle to the grave and it behooves us to be kind to one another along the way.

ALICE CHILDRESS, *A Short Walk,* 1979

If you don't know what you want from life, you will accept anything.

DOROTHY RILEY, *It's Up to You,* 1980

[I]t's foolish to determine what your life will be before you've even had a chance to live it.

NIKKI GIOVANNI, "An Answer to Some Questions on How I Write: In Three Parts," in Evans, ed., *Black Women Writers,* 1984

Life is very short and what we have to do must be done in the now.

AUDRE LORDE, "My Words Will Be There," in *ibid.*

Ads in magazines told her Americans would do anything to avoid life.

RICHARD PERRY, *Montgomery's Children,* 1984

This life is not real. I conquered the world and it did not bring me satisfaction.

MUHAMMAD ALI, in "Muhammad Ali: Champion of the Ring," *Class,* April 1984

Life is finding different taskmasters.

MARVIN GAYE, in Ritz, *Divided Soul,* 1985

What's so frightening about the diminished life chances of young Black Americans at home is not that so many of our citizens are not aware, but that so many are aware and do not care.

JULIAN BOND, c. 1986

Each must live within the isolation of his own senses, dreams, and memories; each must die his own death.

RALPH ELLISON, "A Very Stern Discipline," *Going to the Territory,* 1986

Continue on the yam level and life will be sweet.

RALPH ELLISON, *Going to the Territory,* 1986

Life doesn't run away from nobody. Life runs at people.

JOE FRAZIER, in *Newsweek,* 18 March 1986

From the day you're born till the day you ride in a hearse, there's nothing so bad that it couldn't be worse.

SMOKEY ROBINSON, in "Words of the Week," *Jet,* 8 September 1986

I gave my life to learning how to live. Now that I have organized it all/ now that/ I have finally found out how to keep my clothes in order, when to wash and when to sew, how/ to control my glands and sexual impulses/ How to raise a family,/ which friends to be loyal to, who is phony, and who is live,/ how to get rid of ambition and how to be thrifty,/ Now that I have/ Finally learned how to be closer to the nude and secret silence,/ my life is just about over.

LUCILLE CLIFTON, *Postscripts,*1987

The most important thing in life is each other. When you get that together, then all the material bull that we cling to doesn't mean anything, because you've got to leave it here. You take nothing away. Everything on earth stays here, including the body we rent.

SHERMAN HELMSLEY, in "Words of the Week," *Jet,* 22 June 1987

Life is like a butterfly. You can chase it, or you can let it come to you.

RUTH BROWN, c. 1988

If a man can reach the latter days of his life with his soul intact, he has mastered life.

GORDON PARKS, 1988

Life is accepting what is and working from that.

GLORIA NAYLOR, *The Women of Brewster Place,* 1988

As we go through life, our perceptions become calcified.

CHARLES JOHNSON, in "Word Star," *Essence,* April 1988

We are here, charged with the task of completing . . . ourselves. The process is jazz. It requires improvisation, the daring to strike out on your own coupled with a sure grounding in and respect for the tune on which you are working changes.

WILLIAM COOK, in "The Meaning of Life," *Life,* December 1988

[S]taying alive [is] the meaning of life.

ISHMAEL REED, in *ibid.*

To live is to suffer; to survive is to find some meaning in the suffering.

ROBERTA FLACK, in "An Intimate Talk with Roberta," *Essence,* February 1989

LIGHT

What's done in the dark will soon come to light.

AFRICA

Let the light of history enable us to see that enough of good there is in the lowest estate to sweeten life, enough of evil in the highest to check presumption; enough there is of both in all estates to bend us in compassionate brotherhood, to teach us impressively that we are of one dying and one immortal family.

CARTER G. WOODSON, c. 1935

Light has come into the world, and every man must decide whether he will walk in the light of creative altruism or the darkness of destructive selfishness.

MARTIN LUTHER KING, JR., *Strength to Love,* 1963

The lights gathering/ on the night lake/ sing a thousand songs/ of the sleeping sun.

HENRY DUMAS, "Images," *Play Ebony Play Ivory,* 1974

Thirst to become a light in this world, and the protection and support you need will be given.

SUSAN TAYLOR, c. 1987

His smile is like sunshine and fills me with light.

MIRIAM MAKEBA, *My Story,* 1987

LIMIT

I transcend earthly bound, I never cease to amaze myself. I haven't yet found my limit. I am ready to accept my limit, but every time I feel that way, boom! God touches me and I do something even more stupendous.

DON KING, in *Jet,* 25 April 1987

LINE

The problem of the twentieth century is the problem of the color line.

W. E. B. DU BOIS, *The Souls of Black Folk,* 1903

Weren't no sign that said black or white, it was an imagination line.

E. D. NIXON, c. 1965

There is a thin line between politics and theatrics.

JULIAN BOND, in *Newsweek,* 16 August 1976

LISTEN

Listen patiently to the speech of the petitioner. Do not rebuff him for his gut accusation. One who feels the weight of injustice wants to pour out his heart even more than the results coming from it. But if a petition is rebuffed, one says why does he reject it? Not all requests can be granted but a good hearing heals the heart.

EGYPT

Always listen. Be careful when you speak because the bush has ears.

GUYANA

Add a third to your two ears even if it be an imaginary one, for the news is so enchanting that two ears is not enough.

HAUSA

Advise and counsel him. If he does not listen, let adversity teach him.

CONGO

The earliest instruction was imparted orally, a system still extant in Africa and the Orient. It trains the mind to listen.

ARTHUR A. SCHOMBURG, in *Racial Integrity,* 1923

I am listening through the cracks of my skull. It rises, it rises, the black flood rises.

AIMÉ CÉSAIRE, *Miraculous Weapons,* 1946

Listen more often/ To Things than to Beings,/ Hear the voice of fire,/ Hear the voice of water./ Listen in the wind to/ The bush that is sobbing:/ This is the ancestors breathing/ It is the breathing of our forefathers.

BIRAGO DIOP, "Spirits," 1967

Anybody who listens to a beautifully performed symphony for the first time gains something from it. The next time he hears it, he gains more; when he hears the symphony for the hundredth time, he is benefited to the hundredth power. . . . The spectator can't get it all the first time; repeated viewings multiply the satisfaction.

DUKE ELLINGTON, *Music Is My Mistress,* 1973

We are a tongued folk. A race of singers. Our lips shape words and rhythms which elevate our spirits and quicken our blood. . . . I have spent over fifty years listening to my people.

MAYA ANGELOU, "Shades and Slashers of Light," in Evans, ed., *Black Women Writers,* 1984

LITERATURE

The folk literature of the American Negro has a rich inheritance from its African background. They brought with them no material possessions to aid in preserving the arts and customs of their homelands. Yet though empty-handed perforce, they carried on their minds and hearts a treasure of complex musical forms, dramatic speech, and imaginative stories, which they perpetuated through the vital art of expression. Wherever the slaves were ultimately placed, they established an enclave of African culture that flourished in spite of environmental disadvantages.

J. MASON BREWER

Fiction is of great value to any people as a preserver of manners and customs—religious, political, and social. It is a record of growth and development from generation to generation. No one will do this for us; we must ourselves.

PAULINE E. HOPKINS, *Contending Voices,* 1900

Temples fall, statues decay, mausoleums perish, eloquent phrases declaimed are forgotten, but good books are immortal.

WILLIAM T. VERNON, "The Upbuilding of a Race," speech given in Quindaro, Kansas, 1900

I sit with Shakespeare and he winces not. Across the color line I move arm in arm with Balzac and Dumas, while smiling men and welcoming women glide in gilded halls. From out the caves of evening that swing between the strong-limbed earth and the tracery of the stars, I summon Aristotle and Aurelius and what soul I will, and they come all graciously with no scorn nor condescension. So, wed with Truth, I dwell above the Veil.

W. E. B. DU BOIS, *The Souls of Black Folk,* 1903

Folklore is the boiled-down juice, or pot-likker, of human living.

ZORA NEALE HURSTON, *Folklore Field Notes,* 1925

Folklore does not belong to any special area, time, or people. It is a world and an ageless thing, so let us look at it from that viewpoint.

Ibid.

Othello in the Venice of that time was in practically the same position as a colored man in America.

PAUL ROBESON, "How it Feels for an American Negro to Play *Othello* to an English Audience," *Pearson's Weekly* (London), 15 May 1930

But certain things have seemed to me to be here as I heard the tongues of those who had speech, and listened to the lips of books.

ZORA NEALE HURSTON, *Dust Tracks on a Road,* 1942

With Shakespeare and poetry, a new world was born. New dreams, new desires, a self consciousness was born. I desired to know to know myself in terms of the new standards set by these books.

PETER ABRAHAMS, *Tell Freedom,* 1954

The story of Othello jumped at me and invaded my heart and mind. . . . I was transported to the land where the brave Moor lived and loved and destroyed his love.

Ibid.

Why should there not be "African Humanities"? Every language, which means every civilization, can provide material for the humanities, because every civilization is the expression, with its own peculiar emphasis, of certain characteristics of humanity.

LEOPOLD SENGHOR, *Prose and Poetry,* 1965

In Black Africa, literary art is an anonymous art because it is a social art, it is a social art because it is functional art, and it is functional because it is humanistic.

BASILE JULIET FOUDA, speech given at First World Festival of Negro Arts, Dakar, Senegal, 1966

Afro-American literature is food for a deep lifetime study, not something to be squeezed into a quarter or semester.

ISHMAEL REED, "19 Necromancers from Now," in Chapman, ed., *New Black Voices,* 1972

[B]lack literature is literature By blacks, ABOUT blacks, directed TO blacks. ESSENTIAL black literature is the distillation of black life.

GWENDOLYN BROOKS, in *Black Poetry Writing*, 1975

In the ... library ... I discovered ... Richard Halliburton's *Complete Marvels of the World.* I loved to browse through his stories about the pyramids, the Hanging Gardens of Babylon, the Taj Mahal, and the other marvels he visited around the world ... I came upon the chapter on Christophe's Citadel.

BILL RUSSELL, *Second Wind*, 1979

Literature is a unique resource that articulates and preserves a people's culture ... an understanding of the past to gain insight into the present and develop perspectives for the future.

CORETTA SCOTT KING, *Listen Children*, 1982

Literature should not be judged good or bad according to its imitation of the styles and taste of Europeans, but according to its presentation of the styles and traditions stemming from Africa and Afro-American culture.

DARWIN T. TURNER, "Theme, Characterization, and Style in the Works of Toni Morrison," in Evans, ed., *Black Women Writers*, 1984

I stumbled upon James Baldwin. In *Go Tell It on the Mountain*, I found for the first time the story of my life. Like John Grimes, the oldest son in the novel, I was caretaker of my siblings, confused and frightened by my relationship with my parents, and drawn to and repelled by religion. Like John, I had, by age thirteen, sadly retreated into the sanctuary of my intelligence.

RICHARD PERRY, in *Essence*, November 1985

[T]he function of literature ... is to remind us of our common humanity and the cost of that humanity.

RALPH ELLISON, "On Initiation Rites and Power," *Going to the Territory*, 1986

Black literature is taught as sociology, as tolerance, not as a serious, rigorous art form.

TONI MORRISION, in "The Pain of Being Black," *Time*, 22 May 1989

It is a tragic flaw in Black literature and drama that so much responsibility is put upon the artist to present images that are positive. It's not fair that more projects don't cover a wide span of Black life.

LYNN WHITFIELD, in the *Detroit News*, 20 March 1990

LONELINESS

You never miss your water until your well runs dry.

TRADITIONAL

We live amid swarms of people, yet there is a vast distance between people, a distance that words cannot bridge.

RICHARD WRIGHT, *12 Million Black Voices*, 1941

I always felt a sense of cosmic companionship. So that the loneliness and fear have faded away because of a greater feeling of security.

MARTIN LUTHER KING, JR., in "Interview," *Playboy*, January 1965

Escaping, evading, and avoiding are responses which lie at the base of much that is peculiarly American—the suburbs, the automobile, the self-service store and so on.

ROBERT SLATER, *The Pursuit of Loneliness*, 1971

It's a very lonely thing to be one of the first.

ARTHUR MITCHELL, in *New York Post*, February 1971

Loneliness is a constant companion to loving.

BETTYE J. PARKER-SMITH, "Alice Walker's Women: In Search for Some Peace of Mind," in Evans, ed., *Black Women Writers*, 1984

There is a loneliness that can be rocked. Arms crossed, knees drawn up; holding on the motion ... then there's a loneliness that roams. No rocking can hold it down. It is alive, on its own. A dry and spreading thing that makes the sound of one's feet going seem to come from a far-off place.

TONI MORRISON, *Beloved*, 1987

Loneliness is random; solitude is ritual.

PEARL CLEAGE, "In My Solitude," *Essence*, February 1989

LONGEVITY

Even though the old man is strong and hearty, he will not live forever.

ASHANTI

Like anybody, I would like to live a long life. Longevity has its place. But I'm not concerned about that now. I just want to do God's will. And He's allowed me to go up to the mountain. And I've looked over. And I have seen the promised land.

MARTIN LUTHER KING, JR., "I Have Been to the Mountaintop," speech given in Memphis, Tennessee, 3 April 1968

I didn't prepare myself to be seventy-one. We should begin earlier to think about later on, because we are all living longer.

LENA HORNE, in "Day by Day: A Profile," *Parade*, 30 April 1989

LOOK

Look before you leap.

AESOP, "The Fox and the Grapes," c. 300 B.C.

Only prosperity looks backward. Adversity is afraid to look over its shoulder.

ALAIN LOCKE, in *Opportunity*, February 1924

Never look behind you, something may be gaining on you.

SATCHEL PAIGE, c. 1940

If you are not afraid to look back, nothing you are facing can frighten you.

JAMES BALDWIN, "Why I Left America," *Essence*, October 1970

You can't look forward and backward at the same time.

COLEMAN YOUNG, 1972

LOVE

I have spread no snares today/ I am caught in my love of you.

EGYPT

Hearing your voice is pomegranate wine,/ I live by hearing it./ Each look with which you look at me/ Sustains me more than food and drink.

EGYPT

Love is like a baby, it needs to be treated gently.

CONGO

To love someone who doesn't love you is like shaking a tree to make the dew drops fall.

CONGO

When one is in love, a cliff becomes a meadow.

ETHIOPIA

A javelin without blood is not a javelin! Love without kisses is not love.

ETHIOPIA

Let your love be like the misty rains, coming softly, but flooding the river.

MADAGASCAR

When I make love with my lover, it is as if I were cleaning grain to feed myself: I eat and eat, a whole field full, yet my heart is not satisfied.

MOROCCO

It is better to be loved than feared.

SENEGAL

O how big is my beloved,/ More than all the ones I know./ O how lovely does my heart beat,/ When I only see him glow./ Love can never be forced; Treat it fondly, it will grow!

ZANZIBAR, *Swahili Love Song*

Love, you know, is strangely whimsical, containing affronts, jabs, parleys, wars then peace again. Now, for you to ask advice to love by, is as if you ask advice to run mad by.

TERENCE, *The Eunuch,* 192–157 B.C.

There is no greater invitation to love than loving first.

ST. AUGUSTINE OF HIPPO, 354–430 A.D.

The luster of your teeth, bright as the moon, scatters the darkness of my fear. The fire of desire burns in my soul: let me quench it in the honey of your lips. If you are angry, stab with your eyes, chain me in your arms, and rip me to tatters with your teeth. You are the pearl in the ocean of my being. You are the woman of my heart. . . . There is no power in my heart but love.

JAYADEVA, "Krishna in Paradise," *The Song of the Goatherd,* c.1175 A.D.

But I, in love, was mute and still.

ALEXANDER PUSHKIN, c. 1840

The less one loves a woman, the surer one is of possessing her.

Ibid.

Love without esteem cannot go far or reach high. It is an angel with only one wing.

ALEXANDRE DUMAS, *To a Sin, Man—Woman,* 1872

Pandemonium broke loose in the guard-room of love. My heart was caught like a thief by the greatest of lovers who had set snares in the air.

LALAN, c. 1885

I seem to have loved you in numberless forms, numberless times,/ In life after life, in age after age forever.

RABINDRANATH TAGORE, from *Unending Love,* 1890

It is the high function of love to welcome all limitations and to transcend them. For nothing is more independent than love, and where else, again, shall we find so much of dependence?

RABINDRANATH TAGORE, *Sadhana,* 1912

Love can only be bought by love: the king cannot buy it with power, the rich cannot buy it with gold, the woman cannot buy it with seduction.

Ibid.

I love the things I never had along with the things I have no more.

GABRIELA MISTRAL, "Things," *Desolación,* 1922

I could love her with a love so warm/ You could not break it with a fairy charm;/ I could love her with a love so bold/ It would not die, e'en tho' the world grew cold.

FENTON JOHNSON, "The World is a Mighty Ogre," in Kerlin, *Negro Poets and Their Poems,* 1923

I love you for your brownness/ And the rounded darkness of your breast./ I love you for the breaking sadness in your voice/ And shadows where your wayward eyelids rest.

GWENDOLYN BENNETT, "To A Dark Girl," in Kerlin, *Negro Poets and Their Poems,* 1923

[H]alt the tides, reshape the course of day through night; still the wheel of the universe, yet only death can rob me of my will to love the one I love.

JOSHUA HENRY JONES, *By Sanction of Law,* 1924

When Napoleon was winning battles he was loved by his people, but when he lost, he lost his friends. I want my friends to love me if I lose or win a battle tomorrow or a year hence.

JACK JOHNSON, c. 1925

My love is dark as yours is fair,/ Yet lovelier I hold her/ Than listless maids with pallid hair,/ And blood that's thin and colder.

COUNTEE CULLEN, "A Song of Praise," *Color,* 1925

Never love with all your heart,/ It only ends in aching;/ And bit by bit to the smallest part/ That organ will be breaking.

COUNTEE CULLEN, "Song in Spite of Myself," *The Black Christ and Other Poems,* 1929

Your love to me was like an unread book . . .

COUNTEE CULLEN, "Bright Bindings," in *ibid.*

Love is lak de sea. It's a "moving" thing, but still and all, it takes its shape from de shore it meets, and it's different with every shore.

ZORA NEALE HURSTON, *Their Eyes Were Watching God,* 1937

I have a strong suspicion, but I can't be sure, that much that passes for constant love is a golded-up moment walking in its sleep . . . so the moment has authority over all their lives. . . . They pray constantly for the miracle of the moment to burst its bond and spread out over time.

Ibid.

[Love makes your] soul crawl out from its hiding place.

Ibid.

The Negro now loves his own, cherishes his own, teaches his boy about black heroes, and honors and glorifies his own black woman. A whole race has been reborn; a whole race has found the soul.

BEN BRAWLEY, *Negro Builders and Heroes,* 1937

Young man, how many loves have you? I have hardly any, cousin, for they are only seven: the first, who cuts my fingernails; the second, who takes over for the one who stays at home when we go out; the third, who replaces the second in emergencies; the fourth, who follows me with longing eyes when I depart; the fifth, who comes to meet me when I return; the sixth, who nourishes my life as much as rice; the seventh, who doesn't mix with the crowd, and even if she does, always manages to make herself distinguished.

JEAN-JOSEPH RABÉARIVELO, "LVII," *Old Songs of Imerina Land,* 1939

[S]he just has the look of never having been loved. She has that terrible look of never having been nuded by a man.

ZORA NEALE HURSTON, *Moses, Man of the Mountain,* 1939

If my love and I must part/ May the earth and sky be joined.

JEAN-JOSEPH RABÉARIVELO, *Old Songs of Imerina Land,* 1939

Romance without finance is no good.

WILLIE "THE LION" SMITH, c. 1940

Do not love me, cousin,/ like a shadow/ for shadows vanish with the evening/ and I would keep you with me/ all night long;/ or like pepper/ which makes the belly hot/ for then I couldn't/ satisfy my hunger;/ or like a pillow/ for then we'd be together/ while we're sleeping/ but hardly see each other/ once it's day;/ or like rice/ for once swallowed/ you think no more of it:/ or like sweet words/ for they evaporate;/ or like honey/ sweet enough but all too common.

FLAVIEN RANAIVO, "The Common Lover's Song," *The Darkness and the Wind,* 1947

Love me like a lovely dream,/ your life in the night,/ my hope by day;/ like the silver coin/ I keep close on earth.

Ibid.

Don't threaten me with love, baby. Let's go walking in the rain.

BILLIE HOLIDAY, c. 1950

Love has no awareness of merit or demerit; it has no scale by which its portion may be weighed or measured. It does not seek to balance giving and receiving. Love loves; this is its nature.

HOWARD THURMAN, *Meditations of the Heart,* 1953

Why, loving him, did she leave him?

PETER ABRAHAMS, *Tell Freedom,* 1954

Perhaps it was more happiness than love, though the one cannot exist without the other. . . . Happiness and passion. Maybe that is what love really is.

CAMARA LAYE, *The Dark Child,* 1954

With you I have refound my name,/ My name long hidden 'neath the salt of distances.

DAVID DIOP, "With You," *Poundings,* 1956

You knew all the books but knew not love.

DAVID DIOP, "Vultures," in *ibid.*

Love does not begin and end the way we seem to think it does. Love is a battle, love is a war; love is growing up.

JAMES BALDWIN, c. 1961

Like hibiscus/ still unopened/ preening in the sun;/ Like water-lily petals/ shimmering gold and flame,/ springboard of the/ water nymphs,/ Love/ blossoms/ from a glance!

FILY DABO SISSOKO, "Like a Flower," *Poèms de l'Afrique noire,* 1963

To love is to make of one's heart a swinging door.

HOWARD THURMAN, *Disciplines of Spirit,* 1963

If we love a child, and the child senses that we love him, he will get a concept of love that all subsequent hatred in the world will never be able to destroy.

Ibid.

Love is the most durable power in the world. This creative force is the most potent instrument available in mankind's quest for peace and security.

MARTIN LUTHER KING, JR., *Strength to Love,* 1963

Many people are plunged into an abyss of emotional fatalism because they do not love themselves in a wholesome way.

Ibid.

No matter what . . . it is with God. He is gracious and merciful. His way is through love in which we all are. It is truly—A Love SUPREME.

JOHN COLTRANE, *A Love Supreme,* 1964

I cannot prevent myself from loving him./ It is something too powerful for me./ I am ashamed of myself, but I can neither resist it nor remain silent. . . . I am suffering from a love/which burns more than fire,/ which wounds more than arrows,/ which cuts more than a razor edge.

A BAMBARA EPIC OF OLD MALI, "Monzon and the King of Kore," *Présence Africaine,* 1966

Love stretches your heart and makes you big inside.

MARGARET WALKER, *Jubilee,* 1966

No love is innocent. There does not exist a relation between man and woman that does not have its deep hidden, graying ember of carnality, stubbornly aglow.

FRANK YERBY, *Judas, My Brother,* 1967

Most chastity is accidental, depending largely upon one not encountering any of the various loves who could melt it with a look, a smile.

Ibid.

I've decided to stick with love. Hate is too great a burden to bear.

MARTIN LUTHER KING, JR., 1968

Given the three-hundred-years war against Black manhood and womanhood, and given the circumstances under which most Black fathers and mothers are forced to live, the mystery is that so many still stand and love.

LERONE BENNETT, JR., *The Challenge of Blackness,* 1968

Baby, baby, where did our love go?

BRIAN HOLLAND, LAMONT DOZIER, EDDIE HOLLAND, "Where Did Our Love Go?" c. 1968

listen children/ keep this in the place/ you have for the keeping/ always/ keep it all ways/ we have never hated black/. . . . we have always loved each other/children/pass it on.

LUCILLE CLIFTON, *Good News About the Earth,* 1970

Love rejected hurts so much more/than love rejecting.

LUCILLE CLIFTON, *Good Times,* 1970

Love takes off the mask that we fear we cannot live with and know we cannot live without.

ROBERT SLATER, *The Pursuit of Loneliness,* 1971

That was why everyone "loved" him, because he loved no one, could love no one except himself.

GWENDOLYN BROOKS, *Report From Part One,* 1972

When you love a man, he becomes more than a body. His physical limbs expand, and his outline recedes, vanishes. He is rich and sweet and right. He is part of the world, the atmosphere, the blue sky and the blue water. If he happens to be dead, he is still what you love, and your big pity is for yourself, not for him.

Ibid.

[T]his world is terrible & that one must, above all,/ hold onto the love & the hearts of others.

AL YOUNG, "Dance of the Infidels," in Chapman, ed., *New Black Voices,* 1972

Love, like electricity or revolution or becoming, is a process (not a thing).

AL YOUNG, "Statement on Aesthetics, Poetics, Kinetics," in *ibid.*

Unconditional love not only means I am with you, but also I am for you, all the way, right or wrong. . . . Love is indescribable and unconditional. I could tell you a thousand things that it is not, but not one that it is. Either you have it or you haven't, there's no proof of it.

DUKE ELLINGTON, *Music Is My Mistress,* 1973

A lost love is like a toothache. It'll hurt you and it'll hurt so much you'll finally get rid of it. You'll miss it but you'll feel better.

Ibid.

We love you madly.

Ibid.

[L]ove as deeply/ as if it were/ forever/ only nothing is eternal.

AUDRE LORDE, "For Each of You," *From a Land Where Other People Live,* 1973

Or maybe the purpose of being here, wherever we are, is to increase the durability and the occasions of love among and between peoples. Love, as the concentration of tender caring and tender excitement, or love as the reason for joy. . . . [L]ove is the single, true prosperity of any moment and that whatever and whoever impedes, diminishes, ridicules, opposes the development of loving spirit is "wrong"/ hateful.

JUNE JORDAN, in Walker, *Revolutionary Petunias,* 1973

Great art can only be created out of love.

JAMES BALDWIN, c. 1974

When we feel we are loved by the person we love, we love more, and nothing inflames our love so much as to know we are loved by the person we love, and being loved more makes the other love more too. When we think about the person we love, we love him more until we are nothing but one burning flame of love.

ERNESTO CARDENAL, "Love," *Vida en al Amor,* 1974

The circle moon/ fell upon your face,/ The circle moon/ spilled powdered upon your shape./ The moon, the circle moon/ argued with me/ . . . told me that I could/ gather up all the dust of/ the circle night/ and I could tell you/ woman/ I love you.

HENRY DUMAS, "Full Moon," *Play Ebony Play Ivory,* 1974

May the love in the art that made you fill your heart.

LUCILLE CLIFTON, *An Ordinary Woman,* 1974

Love will open your mind like the chaste leaf in the morning when the sun first touches it.

WOLE SOYINKA, *The Lion and the Jewel,* 1975

Romance is the sweetening of the soul/ with fragrance offered by the stricken heart.

Ibid.

The Black experience is 360 degrees. Love and sex are probably two of them, but there are 358 more.

GIL SCOTT-HERON, in "Midnight News," *Newsweek,* 10 February 1975

I have only two loves, Paris and my own country.

JOSEPHINE BAKER, 12 April 1975

Love is in need of love today/ Don't delay/ Send yours right away.

STEVIE WONDER "Love's in Need of Love Today," 1976

[M]ost people have a harder time letting themselves love than finding someone to love them.

BILL RUSSELL, *Second Wind,* 1979

All my life I had had one main quest;. . . I have been moved by inner impulse, my turns, returns, leaps and crossings have followed love.

JEAN TOOMER, "Reflections of an Earth-Being," in Turner, ed., *Wayward Seeking,* 1980

Applause is a kind of love, and when people applaud you, that's love.

JOE LOUIS, *My Life,* 1981

[L]ove is like a virus. It can happen to anybody at any time.

MAYA ANGELOU, *The Heart of a Woman,* 1981

We always have fantasies about making love with our old lovers.

ALICE WALKER, *In Search of Our Mothers' Gardens,* 1983

Most of us love from our need to love, not because we find someone deserving.

NIKKI GIOVANNI, "An Answer to Some Questions on How I Write: In Three Parts," in Evans, ed., *Black Women Writers,* 1984

The perfect relationship is the one between Jesus and heavenly Father.

MARVIN GAYE, in Ritz, *Divided Soul,* 1985

Just because you have been married doesn't mean you're in love.

RICK JAMES, c. 1987

Love is or it ain't. Thin love ain't love at all.

TONI MORRISON, *Beloved,* 1987

Through a love-experience I discovered the reality of the soul. . . . My flood-gates were thrown open by inward surging and out poured the accumulated suffering of my entire life . . . as though my innermost pockets were being opened and the contents washed out; and all became sweet before it left me, so that what I gave back to the world was not hurt but tenderness, not hate but love.

JEAN TOOMER, in Kerman and Eldridge, *Lives of Jean Toomer,* 1987

[In love] there was transport, there was rapture, once or twice there was revelation. . . . But it came to an end. I want it to last, never ending. I want to rise there and remain there. I have no taste for anything else. I want to *be* there.

Ibid.

[L]ove has never cared about my schedule. It just barges in whenever it wants.

MIRIAM MAKEBA, *My Story,* 1987

Maybe I could learn to love if I was just close to something, closer to my higher self, closer to Heaven, closer to God.

PRINCE, in "Spotlight: Prince—What U See Is What U Get," *Essence,* November 1987

He said, "I will build you a castle with a tower so high it will reach the moon and I'll gather melodies from birdies that fly." Can you imagine being loved like *that?*

MARSHA WARFIELD, in "Introducing Marsha Warfield: Actress/Comedian," *Ebony,* May 1988

Love means exposing yourself to the pains of being hurt, deeply hurt by someone you trust.

RENITA WEEMS, in *Essence,* October 1988

You cannot love people who refuse to help themselves.

OPRAH WINFREY, in *Woman's Day,* 4 October 1988

Love is never ending. Love is always.

SMOKEY ROBINSON, c. 1989

My life is a very, very happy one. It's a happiness of being connected, of knowing that there is someone I can trust completely, and that the one I trust is the one I love. I also know that the one she loves is definitely the one she can trust.

BILL COSBY in *USA Weekend,* 7 April 1989

[Pe]ople fell in love as they might fall into a hole; it was something . . . a smart man avoided.

CHARLES JOHNSON, *Middle Passage,* 1990

I keeps fallin' in love with the same kinda woman ovah and ovah again. They all look like my wife. . . .

Ibid.

Love is the force by which God binds man to himself and man to man. Such love goes to the extreme; it remains loving and forgiving even in the midst of hostility.

JAMES LAWSON, in *Jet,* 14 May 1990

I love you more than my own skin.

FRIDA KAHLO, in Herrera, *Frida Kahlo: The Paintings,* 1991

Your love and devotion has created a debt which I will never attempt to pay back. So enormous is it that even if I had to pay regular installments for another century I would not settle it.

NELSON MANDELA, *Higher Than Hope,* 1991

LYNCHING

No savage nation can exceed the atrocities which are often heralded through the country and accepted by many as an incidental consequence. Men are hung, shot, and burnt by bands of murderers who are most invariably represented as the most influential and respectable citizens, while the evidence of guilt of what is charged against the victims is never established in any court.

H. M. TURNER, *20th Century Negro Literature or a Cyclopedia of Thought on the Vital Topics Relating to the American Negro,* 1902

Lynching is the aftermath of slavery.

MARY CHURCH TERRELL, "Lynching from a Negro's Point of View," *North American Review,* June 1904

Either the law must destroy lynching or lynching will destroy the law, involving the whole nation in anarchy and red ruin.

KELLY MILLER, *The American Negro,* 1908

They've lynched a man in Dixie./ O God, behold the crime./ And midst the mad mob's howling/ How sweet the church bells chime!/ They've lynched a man in Dixie./ You say this cannot be?/ See where his lead-torn body/ Mute hangs from yonder tree.

JOSHUA HENRY JONES, *The Heart of the World,* c. 1919

And so this Christian mob did turn/ From prayer to rob, to lynch and burn./ A victim helplessly he fell/ To tortures truly kin to hell;/ They bound him fast and strung him high . . .

WALTER E. HAWKINS, "A Festival in Christendom," *Chords and Discords,* 1921

A feast of moon and men and barking hounds,/ An orgy for some genius of the South/ With blood-hot eyes and cane-lipped scented mouths,/ Surprised in making folk songs from soul-sounds/ . . . Smoke from the pyramidal sawdust pile/ Curls up, blue ghosts of trees, tarrying low/ Where only chips and stumps are left to show/ The solid proof of former domicile.

JEAN TOOMER, "Georgia Dusk," *Cane,* 1923

Lynching and race riots all work to the advantage by teaching the Negro that he must build a civilization of his own or forever remain the white man's victim.

MARCUS GARVEY, *Philosophy and Opinions of Marcus Garvey,* 1923

Nowhere in the civilized world, save the United States, do men go out in bands, to hunt down, shoot, hang to death a single individual.

IDA B. WELLS, in Duster, ed., *Crusade for Justice,* 1928

I am only a mouthpiece through which to tell the story of lynching and I have told it so often that I know it by heart. I do not have to embellish: it makes its own way.

Ibid.

The loveliest lynchee was our Lord.

CLAUDE MCKAY, *Selected Poems,* 1953

And little lads, lynchers that were to be,/ Danced round the dreadful thing in fiendish glee.

Ibid.

Lynching is a practical demonstration of racial hysteria; it is actuated through fear, a guilty conscience, or a retributive foreboding.

AMY GARVEY, *Garvey and Garveyism,* 1963

Forgive thine erring people, Lord, who lynch at home and love abroad.

CHARLES R. DINKINS, "Invocation," c. 1900, in *Negro Poetry and Drama,* 1969

What bothered me was the way 5,000 white Northerners had gotten together on the lynching. The mob was in touch with something—an awful hatred. . . .

ROY WILKINS, *Standing Fast,* 1982

Normally, the individual dies his own death, but because lynch mobs are driven by a passionate need to destroy the distinction between the actual and the symbolic, its victim is forced to undergo death for all his group.

RALPH ELLISON, "An Extravagance of Laughter," *Going to the Territory,* 1986

MADNESS

I may be crazy, but I'm not stupid.

TRADITIONAL

Desire for a woman took hold of me in the night oo like madness, Desire for a woman took hold of me in the night oo like madness.

AZANDE (ZAIRE)

Insanity is a matter of degree.

JOAQUIM MACHADO DE ASSIS, *Epitaph for a Small Winner,* 1881

Whom the gods wish to destroy they first make mad. . . . First he begins to scoff and there is no truth in his views nor depth in his laugh. But, by and by, from mere pretending, it becomes real. He becomes callous. After that he goes to the devil cheerfully.

PAUL LAURENCE DUNBAR, *The Sport of the God,* 1901

Life is half insanity as we choose to make it.

GEORGE MARGRETSON, *Songs of Life,* 1910

Treasure, let's count:/ the madness that remembers/ the madness that howls/ the madness that sees/ the madness that is unleashed/ And you know the rest/ That 2 and 2 are 5/ that the forest miaows/ that the tree plucks the maroons from the fire/ that the sky strokes its beard. . . .

AIMÉ CÉSAIRE, *Notes on a Return to the Native Land,* 1947

[C]areless love may fool the eye,/ uncertain love brings madness.

FLAVIEN RANAIVO, "Old Merina Theme," *The Darkness and the Wind,* 1947

Each time he thought that he was mad he met someone else with a head full of sane socially acceptable madness.

RICHARD WRIGHT, *The Outsider,* 1953

I shall never be adjusted to lynch mobs, segregation, economic inequalities, "the madness of militarism."

MARTIN LUTHER KING, JR., "The Death of Evil upon the Seashore," sermon given at the Cathedral of St. John the Divine, New York City, 17 May 1956

When confronting madness it is best to hold one's peace.

JAMES BALDWIN, *Nobody Knows My Name,* 1961

The sickness and madness of those days. I'm glad to be free of them.

MALCOLM X, *The Autobiography of Malcolm X,* 1965

She was lost without realizing it./ Her frantic mind plunged into the darkness and she forgot the rest of the world.

"Love Strikes Queen Saran," *Monzon and the King of Kore,* 1966

We reclaim ourselves with precocious insanity, with blazing madness, with tenacious cannibalism. Accommodate yourselves to me. I do not accommodate myself to you.

AIMÉ CÉSAIRE, speech given at the African Forum, Dakar, Senegal, Summer 1967

There is something a little mad about sitting in London or Versailles, looking at the map of Africa and drawing lines as though there were no people living there.

JAMES BALDWIN, *A Rap on Race,* 1971

Perhaps to be sane in this society is the best evidence of insanity.

ADDISON GAYLE, JR. "The Son of My Father," in Chapman, ed., *New Black Voices,* 1972

[T]o understand madness is to be a bit mad.

ADDISON GAYLE, JR., *The Way of the New World: The Black Writer in America*, 1975

The full moon is not yet, but the women cannot wait, they must go mad without it.

WOLE SOYINKA, *The Lion and the Jewel*, 1975

Don't let yourself be governed by ephemeral sciences/ for they are the flower of human madness./ Life is not only appearances.

JOSÉ CARRERA ANDRADE, "Each Thing is a World in Itself," *Latin American Tales*, 1977

MAGIC

He got the black cat bone and snake wisdom. He's a two-headed man. He ain't like nobody on earth.

ZORA NEALE HURSTON, *Moses, Man of the Mountain*, 1939

There is no witchcraft except in the mind.

PETER ABRAHAMS, *Wild Conquest*, 1950

[T]he real magic is the magic of growth itself.

HOWARD THURMAN, *Disciplines of the Spirit*, 1963

There is a magic which theater images project in the mind.

WOODIE KING, JR. *Negro Digest*, April 1970

[Art is] about . . . mystique. . . . I've had an opportunity to respond to a form of magic and, in my response, recreate my own form of magic.

ROOSEVELT WOODS, in *Black Art: Ancestral Legacy*, 1989

Even if the magician is gone, there should be magic.

PERCY SUTTON, in "It's Showtime!" *Black Enterprise*, April 1989

Magic and imagination are a necessary reaction to rage.

REGINOLD MCKNIGHT, in *American Visions*, February 1990

MALCOLM X

One of the last times I saw him we had been talking about the children, not his in particular, but of all the children, growing up, and Malcolm said, "I'm the warrior of this revolution and you're the poet."

JAMES BALDWIN, *Nobody Knows My Name*, 1961

Malcolm was refreshing excitement; he scared hell out of the rest of us, bred as we are to caution, to hypocrisy in the presence of white folks, to the smile that never fades.

OSSIE DAVIS, in *The Autobiography of Malcolm X*, 1965

He was and is—a Prince—our own black shining Prince—who didn't hesitate to die, because he loved us so.

Ibid.

Master spellbinder that he was, Malcolm in death cast a spell more far-flung and more disturbing than any he cast in life.

ROY WILKINS, 7 March 1965

Malcolm is worthy of comparison with Plato and Aristotle of the Greeks.

MARCUS BOULWARE, "Minister Malcolm: Orator Profundo," *Negro History Bulletin*, November 1967

He had the hawk-man's eyes./ We gasped. We saw the maleness./ The maleness raking out and making guttural the air/ and pushing us to walls./ He opened us—/who was a key,/ who was a man.

GWENDOLYN BROOKS, "Malcolm X," *In the Mecca*, 1968

The essence of Malcolm was growth, change, and a seeking after truth.

WILLIAM GRIER AND PRICE COBB, *Black Rage*, 1968

In the beginning was the word,/ And in the end the deed./ Judas did it to Jesus/ For the same Herd. Same reason./ You made them mad, Malcolm./ Same reason.

ETHERIDGE KNIGHT, "It Was a Funky Deal," *Poems from Prison*, 1968

When and Where will another come to take your holy place?/ Old man mumbling in his dotage, or crying child, unborn?

MARGARET WALKER, "For Malcolm X," *Prophets for a New Day,* 1970

He X'd his name, became his people's anger,/ exhorted them to vengeance for their past;/ rebuked, admonished them.

ROBERT HAYDEN, "El-Haji Malik El-Shabazz," *Words in the Mourning Time,* 1970

He fell upon his face before/ Allah the raceless in whose blazing Oneness all/ were one. He rose renewed renamed, became/ much more than there was time for him to be.

Ibid.

Malcolm's presence among us had been a detonation and he died in the explosion, lying on a public platform for all the world to see, his life flowing in crimson rivulets from bullet punctures.

JULIUS LESTER, in Hansberry, *Les Blancs,* 1972

He spoke more truth, with less pretense, than any other Black leader . . . [he] opened eyes. His sense of justice was so keen that he pointed out areas of cultural bias that even its victims had been unaware of.

BILL RUSSELL, *Second Wind,* 1979

Malcolm was a path, a way into ourselves.

MAYA ANGELOU, *The Heart of a Woman,* 1981

Malcolm was a charismatic speaker who could play an audience as great musicians play instruments.

Ibid.

Malcolm is a saint and he means different things to many people.

SPIKE LEE, c. 1991

Blacks today who are proud to affirm their African heritage should thank Malcolm. More than anyone else he created a space for them to affirm their blackness. More than anyone else he taught Blacks that there can be no freedom in the United States without self-esteem, a high regard for themselves as *Black people.*

JAMES CONE, *Malcolm and Martin and America,* 1991

MAN/MANHOOD

A man does not appreciate the value of immunity from misfortune until it has befallen him.

ALGERIA

For you are father to the orphan, husband to the widow, brother to the rejected woman, apron to the motherless.

KHUN ANUP, *The Eloquent Peasant,* 2040–1650 B.C.

Are we MEN?—I ask you, O my brethren! are we MEN? . . . Have we any Master but Jesus Christ alone? Is he not their Master as well as ours?—What right then, have we to obey and call any other Master, but Himself? How we could be so *submissive* to a gang of men, whom we cannot tell whether they are as *good* as ourselves or not, I never could conceive.

DAVID WALKER, *Appeal to the Coloured Citizens of the World,* 1829

A man is sometimes lost in the dust of his own raising.

DAVID RUGGLES, *The "Extinguisher" or the Extinguished,* 1834

Men are whipped oftenest who are whipped easiest.

FREDERICK DOUGLASS, *Life and Times of Frederick Douglass,* 1895

If we make money the object of man-training, we shall develop money-makers but not necessarily men. . . .

W. E. B. DU BOIS, "The Talented Tenth," 1903

I walked down the street didn't have on no hat,/ asking everybody I meet,/ Where's my man at.

MA RAINEY, c. 1923

Man is not satisfied or moved by prayer or petitions, but every man is moved by that power of authority which forces him to do even against his will.

MARCUS GARVEY, *Philosophy and Opinions of Marcus Garvey,* 1923

Men who are in earnest are not afraid of consequences.

Ibid.

When men spoke she knew that their words were larger than hers, their interests broader. She could not bear knowing that there were many things she didn't know; that a man could introduce a subject and she would have to be silent. Her defense was to shut out of her mind the didactic sound of their voices.

DOROTHY WEST, c. 1924

Oh, it was hell to be a man of color, intellectually and naturally human in the white world. Except for a superman, almost impossible.

CLAUDE MCKAY, *Banjo,* 1929

One thing they cannot prohibit—The strong men
. . . coming on/ The strong men gittin' stronger/
Strong men . . . Stronger. . . .

STERLING BROWN, "Strong Men," *Southern Road,* 1932

Man is like a prisoner, and he's never satisfied.

ROBERT JOHNSON, "From Four Until Late," 1937

Men do not gather grapes of thorn nor figs of thistle.

MARY CHURCH TERRELL, *Confessions of a Colored Woman in a White World,* 1940

Men are many and each has his work to do.

RICHARD WRIGHT, *12 Million Black Voices,* 1941

High John de Conquerer came to be a man, and a mighty man at that. But he was not a natural man in the beginning. He was a whisper, a will of hope, a wish to find something worthy of laughter and song.

ZORA NEALE HURSTON, "High John de Conquerer," *American Mercury,* 1943

[M]ake me into a man for the beginning/ make me into a man of meditation/ but also make me into a man of germination/ make me into the executor of these lofty works/ the time has come to gird one's loins like a brave man.

AIMÉ CÉSAIRE, *Notes on a Return to the Native Land,* 1947

Man, if he wills, can do much for man, but only in the natural and human order. We can be men only if we help each other.

JEAN TOOMER, *The Flavor of Man,* 1949

I am an invisible man. No, I am not a spook like those who haunted Edgar Allan Poe; nor am I one of your Hollywood-movie ectoplasms. I am a man of substance, of flesh and bone, fiber and liquids—and I might even be said to possess a mind. I am invisible simply because people refuse to see me. . . . When they approach me they see only my surroundings, themselves, or figments of their imagination—indeed everything and anything except me.

RALPH ELLISON, *Invisible Man,* 1952

Man is a promise that he must never break.

RICHARD WRIGHT, *The Outsider,* 1953

I have told you all these things . . . because you are my son, the eldest of my sons, and because I have nothing to hide from you. There is a certain form of behavior to observe, and certain ways of acting in order that the guiding spirit of our race may approach you also.

CAMARA LAYE, *The Dark Child,* 1954

[H]e was a man and had his share of human frailties—but he was always uncompromising in his respect for ritual observance.

Ibid.

One's sense of manhood must come from within.

MARTIN LUTHER KING, JR., *Stride Toward Freedom,* 1958

The importance of having one of our sons in the vanguard of this march of progress is nothing short of axiomatic. By repaying his debt to the village our illustrious son and guest of honor will make it possible that an endless stream of students will be enabled to drink of the Spring of Knowledge.

CHINUA ACHEBE, *No Longer at Ease,* 1961

A race of people is like an individual man: until it rises on its own talent, takes pride in its own history, expresses its own culture, affirms its own selfhood, it can never fulfill itself.

MALCOLM X, "Message to the Grass Roots," speech given in Detroit, Michigan, 10 November 1963

I refuse to accept the idea that the "isness" of man's nature makes him morally incapable of reaching up for the "oughtness" that forever confronts him.

MARTIN LUTHER KING, JR., Nobel Prize Acceptance Speech, 10 December 1964

This thing of being a man, Booker, is a big thing. The Supreme Court can't make you a man. The NAACP can't do it. God Almighty can do a lot, but even He can't do it. Ain't nobody can do it but you.

LERONE BENNETT, JR., "The Convert," in Clarke, ed., *American Negro Short Stories,* 1966

Decolonization is quite simply the replacing of a certain "species" of men by another "species" of men.

FRANTZ FANON, *Wretched of the Earth,* 1967

[I] wanta say just gotta say something/ bout those beautiful beautiful beautiful outasight/ black men.

NIKKI GIOVANNI, "Beautiful Black Men," *Black Judgement,* 1968

Everything in this society is geared to keeping a Black boy from growing to manhood, but he has to try for himself.

JOHN KILLENS, 1970

[W]hen a man stands erect in the world, only the bottoms of his feet touch the ground and the rest of him will be mingled with the stars, communing with eternity.

OTIS MOSS, JR., "Going from Disgrace to Dignity," in Philpot, ed., *Best Black Sermons,* 1972

Men, all men belong to each other, and he who shuts himself away diminishes himself, and he who shuts another away from him destroys himself.

HOWARD THURMAN, *Search for a Common Ground,* 1973

First man wasn't Black or white—he was hairy.

WILLIAM J. SLATTERY, in *Encore,* May 1973

Man is the perfection of the visible creation and we cannot think him low and vile ("vile worm of the earth"), for this would mean calling all God's work low and vile.

ERNESTO CARDENAL, "Love," *Vida en al Amor,* 1974

Sons are very often mother's sons.

BUCHI EMECHETA, *The Joys of Motherhood,* 1979

We must cherish our old men. We must revere their wisdom, appreciate their insight, love the humanity of their words.

ALICE WALKER, *In Search of Our Mothers' Gardens,* 1983

[A] Black man is always a Black man. . . . No matter how far up the ladder you go, you are still black. . . . We think we've made it because we've moved uptown, but we are still the last hired and the first fired.

PHILIP R. COUSINS, in "Bishop Philip R. Cousins: Spiritual Leader of 40 Million Christians," *Ebony,* March 1985

To be born Black and male in America is a double jeopardy. [We are] a threat to those who control this society.

LELAND HALL, in "The Black Male in Jeopardy" *Crisis,* March 1986

We have to . . . teach Black boys social demands to add significance to the process of becoming a man.

NATHAN HARE, in "Interview: Dr. Nathan Hare," *Crisis,* March 1986

[A] man has a special kind of relationship with a woman who has borne him children, which is itself the supreme demonstration [of love].

ESKIA MPHAHLELE, "Chirundu," in Chinweizu, ed., *Voices From Twentieth-Century Africa,* 1988

We get so caught up in what a man isn't. It's what he is that counts.

GLORIA NAYLOR, *The Women of Brewster Place,* 1988

But for the black man with the attache case, or the black boy on the needle, it has always been the intention of the Republic to promulgate and guarantee his dependence on this Republic. For although one cannot really be educated to believe a lie, one can be forced to surrender.

JAMES BALDWIN, "Dark Days," *City Arts Quarterly,* Spring 1988

[T]hroughout our history black women could depend upon their men when they were unemployed or underemployed.

GLORIA NAYLOR, in "The Myth of the Matriarch," *Life,* Spring 1988

Being a black man in America is like being a spectator at your own lynching.

ISHMAEL REED, in "Maligning the Male," *Life,* Spring 1988

The penis has really become the authority in the sense that that's the most immediate, identifiable symbol of one's unmistakable masculinity.

NA'IM AKBAR, in "Free Your Mind," *Essence,* February 1989

You had to *work* at being manly; it took more effort . . . than rigging sails.

CHARLES JOHNSON, *Middle Passage,* 1990

Jesus was a black male who was lynched by uniformed white male Roman soldiers 2,000 years ago. . . . [That war against black males] has continued into the present day. . . .

FRANCES CRESS WELSING, *The Isis Papers,* 1991

MANDELA, NELSON

Nelson is the power, that he is because he is a great man. Our tragedy is that he has not been around to help douse the flames that are destroying our beautiful country.

DESMOND TUTU, 1984

Mandela is the father, the leader.

WINNIE MANDELA, in "The Soul of Nonzano Winnie Mandela," *Crisis,* November 1985

[Mandela's] spirit remains untouched. All those men are just as untouched. . . . Such total dedication, such total commitment. . . . They are totally liberated. It is a government in exile.

WINNIE MANDELA, "A Part of My Soul Went with Him," *Ebony,* December 1985

Nelson Mandela is unique to this world. The personal sacrifices he made for his convictions and for his people is beyond comprehension. Far less is required of us.

SUSAN TAYLOR, c. 1990

At seventy-one, Mandela is still a lion of a man . . . he still lives up to his Xhosa name Rolihlahla, which means "stirring up trouble" for the supporters of apartheid.

SUSAN WATSON, in the *Detroit Free Press,* 24 June 1990

What intrigues me is that he is not vindictive, he shows no bitterness, hatred, or malice. How unusual that is for a man who spent twenty-seven years in prison.

DAMON KEITH, speech given in Detroit, Michigan, 28 June 1990

African-Americans . . . have a long way to go in the same fashion Nelson Mandela is out of jail but he's still not free.

DAVID DINKINS, in "Inside Gracie Mansion with New York's First Black Mayor," *Ebony,* September 1990

MARRIAGE

Rank creates its rules: A woman is asked about her husband, a man is asked about his rank.

SCRIBE ANY of the Palace of Nefertari, 1554–1070 B.C.

I'm married no longer./ For I married too soon, you see./Thinking, there were no other men,/But, if only I'd known.

CONGO

Marriage is not a fast knot but a slip knot.

MADAGASCAR

He who marries a beauty marries trouble.

NIGER

If one's husband dies one will not sleep./ She will lie down as if she sleeps, and if sleep overcomes her she will sleep./ But after a little while she will wake, and will not sleep. . . . When one's husband dies there is no happiness.

ZUNI MOURNING SONG

Marriage castrates the soul.

ALEXANDER PUSHKIN, letter to Peter Vyazemsky, 1826

So heavy is the chain of wedlock that it needs two to carry it sometime.

ALEXANDRE DUMAS, c. 1856

She knew now that marriage did not make love. Janie's first dream was dead, so she became a woman.

ZORA NEALE HURSTON, *Their Eyes Were Watching God,* 1937

The spirit of the marriage left the bedroom and took to living in the parlor.

Ibid.

The daughter had come to meet me/ When her parents tried to prevent it./ I spoke soft words to her./ She did not answer./ You will grow old there, you and remorse:/ We and love /Shall go home to our house.

JEAN-JOSEPH RABÉARIVELO, *Old Songs of Imerina Land,* 1939

A wife is like a blade of grass: she stands upon her feet but is easily withered. A husband is like a clump of seaweed: he flourishes in water but is easily shredded.

Ibid.

Modern ice and iron marry, and offer presently a frightening progeny.

GWENDOLYN BROOKS, *Report From Part One,* 1972

Heaven is marriage, hell is disappointed love.

ERNESTO CARDENAL, "Love," *Vida en al Amor,* 1974

I change my wrestlers when I have learnt to throw them. I also change my wives when I have learnt to tire them.

WOLE SOYINKA, *The Lion and the Jewel,* 1975

I like my players to be married and in debt. That's the way you motivate them.

MAURY WILLS, in the *New York Times,* 11 April 1976

. . . when in walked a man with a belly like a pregnant cow . . . why, marrying such a jelly of man would be like living with a middle-aged woman.

BUCHI EMECHETA, *The Joys of Motherhood,* 1979

Marriage is a sane form securing one from insane sex impulses and their consequences.

JEAN TOOMER, in Kerman and Eldridge, *The Lives of Jean Toomer,* 1987

Marriage is like a piece of cloth, and like cloth, its beauty passes with wear and tear.

AMA ATA AIDOO, "Anowa," in Chinweizu, ed., *Voices From Twentieth-Century Africa,* 1988

If you want to grow up real quick, get married.

MIKE TYSON, in *Time,* 26 December 1988

One of the realities after years of marriage is that whatever changes you had planned to make for that person are going to happen slowly or not happen at all.

BILL COSBY, in *USA Weekend,* 7 April 1989

A husband should go with the flow of his marriage, even when that flow leads over a cliff.

Ibid.

Real marriage is the sacrificing of your ego, not for the other person, but for the relationship.

OPRAH WINFREY, in *Ladies' Home Journal,* May 1990

Fifty years. . . . I guess she must like my music.

DIZZY GILLESPIE, in "Horn of Plenty," *Modern Maturity,* December 1990

I cannot speak of Diego [Rivera] as my husband, because that term, when applied to him, is an absurdity. He never has been, nor will he ever be, anybody's husband.

FRIDA KAHLO, in Herrera, *Frida Kahlo: The Paintings,* 1991

Being the wife of Diego is the most marvelous thing in the world . . . I let him play matrimony with other women.

Ibid.

MASS

We can't give up, we have got to continue. . . . We are not here to hold a position or to be head of this, or that, or one or the other; we are here to mass our power and our thinking and our souls to see what we can do to make it better for that mass that can't speak out there.

MARY MCLEOD BETHUNE, speech given to the National Council of Negro Women, 26 November 1938

Mass social pressure in the form of marches and picketing will not only touch and arrest the attention of the powerful public officials but also the "little man" in the street.

A. PHILIP RANDOLPH, speech given to March on Washington Movement, Detroit, Michigan, 26 September 1942

Massive civil disobedience is a powerful weapon under civilized conditions, where the law safeguards the citizen's right of peaceful demonstration.

ROBERT WILLIAMS, "USA, The Potential of a Minority Revolution," *The Crusader Monthly Newsletter,* May–June 1965

No matter how many celebrities we may accrue, they cannot substitute for the masses of human beings.

ALICE CHILDRESS, "A Candle in a Gale Wind," in Evans, ed., *Black Women Writers,* 1984

The only power, legitimacy, and justice that we are going to receive as Black people in America is going to be because the Black masses exist.

HARRY EDWARDS, in "Hardline," *Detroit Free Press,* 8 May 1988

MATERIAL

Those too impressed with material things cannot hold their place in the world of culture; they are relegated to inferiority and ultimate death.

ALEXANDER CRUMMELL, c. 1880

In a material world we easily forget that life is lived from within, not from without.

SUSAN TAYLOR, c. 1989

MATURITY

To accept all experience as raw material out of which the human spirits distill meanings and values is a part of the meaning of maturity.

HOWARD THURMAN, *Meditations of the Heart,* 1953

Only hopelessly insecure, tragically immature people need to surround themselves with sameness. People who are secure and mature, people who are sophisticated, want diversity. One doesn't grow by living and associating only with people who look like oneself, have the same backgrounds, religion, and interests.

WHITNEY YOUNG, *To Be Equal,* 1964

Once you mature, you begin to see oppression for what it is, and if you are a champion of liberation for Black people and you're successful in freeing your people to a measure, you cannot stop until oppression and tyranny are rooted from the face of the earth. Anything less will cause you to support the very thing that you have condemned.

LOUIS FARRAKHAN, in *National Alliance,* 1985

MEASURE

In the economy of God there is but one standard by which an individual can succeed—there is but one race. This country demands that every race shall measure itself by the American standard . . . my race must pass through the severe American crucible.

BOOKER T. WASHINGTON, speech given at Harvard Alumni Dinner, 24 June 1896

Greatness is one part character and is measured by its possessors not so much by what they achieve for themselves as by what they achieve for others.

GILBERT WARE, in *Afro-American,* 11 August 1934

When you start measuring somebody, measure him right, child, measure him right. Make sure you done taken into account what hills and valleys he come through before he got to wherever he is.

LORRAINE HANSBERRY, *A Raisin in the Sun,* 1959

MELTING POT

There is a magic melting pot/ where any girl or man/ can step in Czech or Greek or Scot,/ step out American. . . . And every time Sam tried that pot/ they threw me out again.

DUDLEY RANDALL, "The Melting Pot," *Cities Burning,* 1968

I hear that pot stuff a lot, all I can say is we haven't melted yet.

JESSE JACKSON, in *Playboy,* November 1969

The melting pot has never been a reality, not even for whites.

GENEVA SMITHERMAN, *Talkin' and Testifying,* 1977

Where there's a melting pot there's smoke, and where there's smoke it is not simply optimistic to expect fire, it's imperative to watch for the phoenix's vernacular, but transcendent, rising.

RALPH ELLISON, "The Little Man at Chehaw Station," *Going to the Territory,* 1986

The melting pot is finished. America is a patchwork quilt where all ethnic groups stand side by side.

JANICE HALE BENSON, *Black Child in Education,* 1986

The melting pot is being promoted verbally, but it is never implemented institutionally. What does exist is assumed cultural vision that is Eurocentric in reality.

FELICIA KESSELL, in "Growing Up Integrated (Are You Black?)" *Crisis,* March 1988

MEMORY

Oh, the good times when we were so unhappy.

ALEXANDRE DUMAS

For memories of days that nothing can recall,/ To song or tears is dead and voiceless now.

ALEXANDER PUSHKIN, *Elegy,* 1826

When the last red man shall have perished from the earth and his memory among the white men shall have become a myth, these shores shall swarm with the invisible dead of my tribe. At night when the streets of your cities and villages shall be silent, and you think them deserted, they will throng with the returning hosts that once filled and still love this beautiful land.

CHIEF SEATHE OF THE DUWAMISH INDIANS, c. 1855

The kiss of his memory made pictures of love and light against the wall. Here was peace. She pulled in her horizon like a great fish-net. Pulled it from around the waist of the world and draped it over her shoulder. So much of life in its meshes! She called in her soul to come and see.

ZORA NEALE HURSTON, *Their Eyes Were Watching God,* 1937

The memory of things gone is important to a jazz musician. Things like old folks singing in the moonlight in the backyard on a hot night or something said long ago.

LOUIS ARMSTRONG, in the *New Yorker,* 8 July 1944

Morning memories benumb,/ daytime memories tire,/ evening memories are delicious . . .

FLAVIEN RANAIVO, "Old Merina Theme," *The Darkness and the Wind,* 1947

When all about me memories arise,/ Memories of anxious hangings on the edge of cliffs/ Of icy seas where harvests drown;/ When drifting days come back to me,/ Ragged days with a narcotic taste . . .

DAVID DIOP, "For My Mother," *Poundings,* 1956

I have simply tried never to forget the soil from which I sprang.

PAUL ROBESON, *Here I Stand,* 1958

It is the lingering melody of a song that moves me more than the initial experience itself; it is the lingering pain of a past insult that rankles and hurts me more than the insult itself.

EZEKIEL MPHAHLELE, *Down Second Avenue,* 1959

I would speak if only I had memories./ Go on—don't tell me who I was like yesterday./ I console myself with being mortal here;/ tomorrow very soon absence will come to my black brow.

TCHICAYA U TAM'SI, "Headline to Summarize a Passion," *Epitome,* 1962

Nostalgia has a sweetness too/but not from he-who-rubs-his-nose in it./ So sink, young man, collapse!/ Go founder in your dreams. / Tomorrow's sunrise will be rather late/for I and pining/ will be gone/ tonight.

FLAVIEN RANAIVO, "Distress," *Return to the Fold,* 1963

In every country of the world there are climbers, "the ones who forget who they are," and in contrast to them, "the ones who remember where they came from."

FRANTZ FANON, *Black Skin, White Masks,* 1967

Come and get these memories, since you've gone out of my heart.

EDDIE HOLLAND, LAMONT DOZIER, BRIAN HOLLAND, "Come and Get These Memories," 1968

History is a people's memory, and a people have a habit of remembering the very best about themselves. It is an all too human trait. But, in the final analysis, people must face their history squarely in order to transcend it.

JOHN KILLENS, 1969

[Soul] is in our racial memory, and the unshakable knowledge of who we are, where we have been, and, springing from this, where we are going.

JULIUS MAYFIELD, "You Touch My Black Aesthetic and I'll Touch Yours," in Gayle, ed., *The Black Aesthetic,* 1971

You have to write it down when it comes to you. You can remember the notes the next day, but not the values and the rhythm.

DUKE ELLINGTON, *Music Is My Mistress,* 1973

. . . give me my memories how i wuz when i wuz there.

NTOZAKE SHANGE, *For Colored Girls Who Have Considered Suicide When the Rainbow Is Enuf,* 1975

An individual who loses his or her memory is disabled. So it is with a people. African and African diasporan people have, in large measure, been deprived of the most important memories of history.

ASA HILLIARD, *Wonderful Ethiopians of the Ancient Cushite Empire,* 1985

they ask me to remember/ but they want me to remember/ their memories/ and I keep remembering/ mine.

LUCILLE CLIFTON, "Why Some People Be Mad at Me Sometimes," *Next,* 1987

Time's passage through the memory is like molten glass that can be opaque or crystallized at any given moment at will; a thousand days are melted into one conversation, one glance, one hurt, and one hurt can be sprinkled over a thousand days. It is silent and elusive, refusing to be damned and dripped out day by day; it swirls through the mind while an entire lifetime can ride like foam on the deceptive transparent waves and get sprayed into the consciousness at ragged unexpected intervals.

GLORIA NAYLOR, *The Women of Brewster Place,* 1988

I can't just remember a sound. I can't learn a text pidgin fashion because if I do, I can't even vary the emphasis anyway, because I don't know where I am—where the verbs are, where the nouns are, and why the sentence sounds like this.

JESSYE NORMAN, in "The Norman Conquest," *American Visions,* April 1988

Memories shouldn't serve to weaken us, but empower us, to energize and to inspire us . . . across all the years and miles and choices that cannot be taken back no matter how hard you try.

PEARL CLEAGE, "Introduction," *Catalyst,* Summer 1988

The genes remember.

CHUCK DAVIS, in "People," *Essence,* October 1988

My memories are of moving, constantly moving.

ALVIN AILEY, in "Alvin Ailey Celebrates 30 Years of Dance," *Essence,* November 1988

Memories of our lives, of our works and our deeds will continue in others.

ROSA PARKS, in "The Meaning of Life," *Life,* December 1988

The body remembers what the mind forgets.

GLORIA HULL, *Young Girls' Blues,* 1989

MESSAGE

I heard it through the grapevine.

TRADITIONAL

Please never despise the translator, he's the mailman of human civilization.

ALEXANDER PUSHKIN

MIND/MENTALITY

We should look to the mind, and not to the outward appearance.

AESOP, 570 B.C.

Change your mind and you will change your life.

TRADITIONAL

As the wound inflames the finger, so thought inflames the mind.

ETHIOPIA

Do not say the first thing that comes to your mind.

IVORY COAST

Men's minds are raised to the level of the women with whom they associate.

ALEXANDRE DUMAS, *My Memoirs,* 1826

Slaves, though we be enrolled/ Minds are never to be sold.

DAVID RUGGLES, *Appeals,* 1835

In every man's mind the good seeds of liberty are planted, and he who brings his fellow down so low, as to make him contented with a condition of slavery, commits the highest crime against God and man.

HENRY HIGHLAND GARNET, "An Address to the Slaves of the United States of America," speech given at the National Negro Convention, Buffalo, New York, August 1843

It is the mind that rules the body.

SOJOURNER TRUTH, c. 1877

Mr. Lincoln had told our race we were free, but mentally we were still enslaved.

MARY MCLEOD BETHUNE, c. 1915

We have outgrown slavery, but our minds are still enslaved to the thinking of the master race. Now take the kinks out of your mind, instead of out of your hair.

MARCUS GARVEY, *Philosophy and Opinions of Marcus Garvey,* 1923

[T]he mind of the Negro seems suddenly to have slipped from under the tyranny of social intimidation and to be shaking off the psychology of imitation and implied inferiority . . . The multitude perhaps feels as yet only a strange relief and a new vague urge, but the thinking few know that in the reaction the vital inner grip of prejudice has been broken.

ALAIN LOCKE, *The New Negro*, 1925

He can read my writing, but he can't read my mind.

ZORA NEALE HURSTON, *Mules and Men*, 1935

The white man is always trying to know somebody else's business. All right, I'll set something outside the door of my mind for him to play with and handle . . . I'll put his toy in his hand, and he will seize it and go away. Then I'll say my say and sing my song.

Ibid.

[T]he men were saving with the mind what they lost with the eye.

ZORA NEALE HURSTON, *Their Eyes Were Watching God*, 1937

There is a basin in the mind where words float around on thought and thought on sound and sight. Then there is a depth of thought untouched by words, and deeper still a gulf of formless feelings untouched by thought.

Ibid.

After the storm the earth is wet and fresh, the old rotten trees are down. There must be a new sowing, new planting, and the new maize and new trees must be nursed. So it is with the earth and so with the minds of men.

PETER ABRAHAMS, *The Path of Thunder*, 1948

The Black man in America has been colonized mentally, his mind has been destroyed. And today, even though he goes to college, he comes out and still doesn't even know he is a Black man; he is ashamed of what he is because his culture has been destroyed; he has been made to hate his skin; he has been made to hate the texture of his hair; he has been made to hate the features that God gave him.

MALCOLM X, in "Malcolm and James Farmer: Separation and Integration," *Dialogue*, May 1962

A man's mind is the activating force that directs him. He does as he thinks.

AMY GARVEY, *Garvey and Garveyism*, 1963

The most enduring freedom is freedom of the mind.

Ibid.

Stretch your mind and fly.

WHITNEY YOUNG, speech given before the House of Representatives, Washington, D.C., 14 April 1964

It is difficult for the American mind to adjust to the realization that the Rhetts and Scarletts were as much monsters as the keepers of Buchenwald—they just dressed more attractively.

LORRAINE HANSBERRY, speech given at Town Hall, New York City, 15 June 1964

[P]ersons who are narrow-minded, because their knowledge is limited, think that they're affected only by things happening in their block.

MALCOLM X, speech given at the Organization for Afro-American Unity Rally, Audubon Ballroom, New York City, 24 January 1965

One cannot have a slave's mentality and hope to be free, or one can hope, but that will not make anything really happen. The freeing of the mind must occur before anything else can happen. The people must actually want to be free. Want it bad enough to be it.

LEROI JONES, *Home: Social Essays*, 1966

I met a lot of guys in the Navy who didn't have as much "upstairs" as I did, yet here they were struggling for an education. I finally realized I was committing a sin—a mental sin.

BILL COSBY, c. 1968

We must not allow the outer chains of oppressive society to shackle our minds.

MARTIN LUTHER KING, JR., *Where Do We Go From Here?* 1968

As long as the mind is enslaved the body can never be free. Psychological freedom, a firm sense of self-esteem, is the most powerful weapon against the long night of physical slavery.

Ibid.

Like many still possessing a slave mentality, he boasted of his employer's possessions as though they were his own.

CHESTER HIMES, *The Quality of Hurt,* 1972

Gray skies are just clouds passing over.

DUKE ELLINGTON, *Music Is My Mistress,* 1973

The mind is the only place I can exist and feel free. In my mind I am absolutely free.

MARGARET WALKER, "On Being Female, Black and Free," in Trimmer and Hairston, eds. *The Riverside Reader,* 1983

[T]here would be less confusion in my mind, had I sense enough to keep a diary all those years I was traveling around. . . .

ALICE NELSON DUNBAR, *Give Us Each Day,*1984

[T]he white mentality [has] created a fool's paradise for themselves.

WINNIE MANDELA, in "The Soul of Nonzamo Winnie Mandela," *Crisis,* November 1985

Many parents have this free mentality they want the government to do everything.

MARVA COLLINS, in "Marva Collins: Teaching Success in the City," *Message,* February 1987

What never ceases to amaze me about American society is the mental closure, even among the most intelligent people.

WOLE SOYINKA, in "Nobel Laureate Wole Soyinka," *Essence,* August 1987

When bright young minds can't afford college, America pays the price.

ARTHUR ASHE, 1988

Sprinting is a mental thing. You don't want to think about anything else. If I commune with other runners I'll lose my killer instinct. I never want to do that.

EVELYN ASHFORD, 1988

There's so much mental training and yet twenty seconds after you start a race you're almost halfway finished. It's like driving a car real fast down a bumpy road. You don't have time to think—you're on autopilot, right on the edge of control.

EDWIN MOSES, in *American Visions,* 1988

The world we live in is first and foremost shaped by the mind.

CHARLES JOHNSON, "An Interview with Charles Johnson," *The World and I,* 1991

MINORITY

America gives her minority groups more of a chance than just about any country on earth.

PAUL ROBESON, in *PM,* September 1943

As minorities, we have been on the begging end too long. That strips me of my dignity.

MARVA COLLINS, in "Marva Collins: Teaching Success in the City," *Message,* February 1987

In some people's eyes, the time is never right for minorities. . . . So when is the time right?

GEORGE HOWARD, JR., 1989

When you belong to a minority group . . . you have to walk so that you don't upset the people who are in a position to give you the next step so you can eventually walk by yourself.

CARL ROWAN, c. 1989

A minority group has "arrived" when it has the right to produce some fools and scoundrels without the whole group paying for it.

Ibid.

Minorities are the targets of a disproportionate threat from toxins, both in the work place where they are assigned the dirtiest and most hazardous jobs, and in their homes, which tend to be in the most polluted community.

JOHN CONYERS, in *Community Access News,* June 1989

As minorities, we must be concerned with the preservation of our culture, traditions, and identity, but we must also learn how to understand and get along with members of other groups if we are to swim successfully in the mainstream.

CLARENCE PAGE, in the *Chicago Tribune,* 2 June 1991

MIRACLE

Garvey performed a spiritual miracle in getting colored people together and inculcating race pride.

JOHN HOPE FRANKLIN, *From Slavery to Freedom,* 1947

This is the first miracle, a man becomes his dreams; then it is that the line between what he does and is and his dream melts away.

HOWARD THURMAN, *Meditations of the Heart,* 1953

The greatest miracle Christianity has achieved in America is that the Black man in white Christian hands has not grown violent. It is a miracle that twenty-two million Black people have not risen up against their oppressors in which they would have been justified by all moral criteria and even by the democratic traditions.

MALCOLM X, in *Malcolm X on Afro-American History,* 1971

[E]very time God's children have thrown away fear in pursuit of honesty—trying to communicate themselves, understood or not—miracles have happened.

DUKE ELLINGTON, *Music Is My Mistress,* 1973

When you think of what some black women have gone through, and then look at how beautiful they still are! It is incredible that they still believe in the values of the race, that they have retained a love of justice, that they can still feel the deepest compassion, not only for themselves but for anyone who is oppressed; this is a kind of miracle, something we have that we must preserve and must pass on.

CORETTA SCOTT KING, in Walker, *In Search of Our Mothers' Gardens,* 1983

The miracle is that some have stepped out of the rags of the Republic's definition to assume the great burden and glory of their humanity and their responsibility for one another. It is an extraordinary achievement to be trapped in the dungeon of color and to dare to shake down its walls and to step out of it leaving the jailkeeper in the rubble.

JAMES BALDWIN, *The Price of the Ticket,* 1985

Most people in actuality are not worth very much, and yet every human being is an unprecedented miracle.

Ibid.

[Don't] gasp at a miracle that is truly miraculous because the magic lies in the fact that you knew it was there for you all along.

TONI MORRISON, *Beloved,* 1987

MISTAKE

The humble pay for the mistakes of their betters.

AFRICA

Truth tellers make no mistakes.

KENYA

Reminiscence alone may dare to visit the mistakes of burial sites on breathing sons or adjust the accounts between the living and the dead.

WILLIAM VERNON, "A Plea for Suspension of Judgement," speech given in Kansas City, Kansas, 1905

[H]e had made his mistakes and had his regrets. But every heart has its graveyard.

ZORA NEALE HURSTON, *Moses, Man of the Mountain,* 1939

We black men have a hard enough time in our struggle for justice, and already have enough enemies as it is, to make the drastic mistake of attacking each other and adding more weight to an already unbearable load.

MALCOLM X, speech given in Los Angeles, California, 25 March 1960

A person who has not made a mistake has not done anything.

MELVIN CHAPMAN, speech given at Miller Junior High School, Detroit, Michigan 1961

People make a mistake in believing they're going to be in paradise if they have more money.

MAHALIA JACKSON, c. 1965

To err is human; but a human error easily slips into three crimes; the initial mistake becomes deliberate wrong; attempt is then made to cure the wrong by force rather than reason; finally the whole story is so explained and distorted as to preserve no lesson for posterity, and thus history seldom guides us aright.

W. E. B. DU BOIS, foreword to *Freedom Road,* 1969

A parent's mistake is taking kids for granted.

BILL COSBY, c. 1975

It is a mistake for anyone to believe the American dream is apple pie and a happy ending.

COLEMAN YOUNG, 1981

[Do not] mistake (false) signs for (true) symbols.

SAMUEL HAY, "Alice Childress's Dramatic Structure," in Evans, ed., *Black Women Writers,* 1984

One of the big mistakes of young Blacks is that some of them are living in a white world and are associating only with white people who know who they are ... they think they are free ... And they're not.

JOHN H. JOHNSON, in "Interview: John H. Johnson," *Crisis,* January 1987

The fatal mistake of many young people is believing that what never existed was just cleverly hidden beyond reach.

GLORIA NAYLOR, *The Women of Brewster Place,* 1988

I've done some things I wish I could erase.... I invented mistakes. But the mistakes must be seen in context, and they must be weighed along with the positives.

SAMMY DAVIS, JR., in "Sammy Davis Jr., The Legacy of the World's Greatest Entertainer," *Ebony,* July 1990

MODEL

Can't tell you how it felt to see somebody that look like me in an airplane!

RALPH ELLISON, *Flying Home,* 1944

A truly horrible thing was that I grew up to womanhood and went through womanhood believing that the gleaming white family life on the motion picture screens should be my model.

GWENDOLYN BROOKS, *Report From Part One,* 1972

The absence of models, in literature as in life ... is an occupational hazard for the artist, simply because models in art, in behavior, in growth of spirit and intellect—even rejected—enrich and enlarge one's view of existence.

ALICE WALKER, *In Search of Our Mothers' Gardens,* 1983

MONEY

See also FINANCE

The eagle flies on Friday.

TRADITIONAL

People ravin' about hard times./ Tell me what it's all about?/ Hard times don't worry me. I was broke when they started out.

BLUES

Men may not get all they pay for in this world, but they must certainly pay for all they get.

FREDERICK DOUGLASS, *Life and Times of Frederick Douglass,* 1881

A race which cannot save its earnings can never rise in the scale of civilization.

FREDERICK DOUGLASS, in *North American Review,* 1884

Dollars not only count, but they rule.

CHARLES T. WALKER, "An Appeal to Caesar," speech given at Carnegie Hall, New York City, 1901

We are money-mad. Greed and wealth have chained the beast of power.

W. E. B. DU BOIS, "What Is Wrong with the United States?" address given to American Labor Party, Madison Square Garden, New York City, 13 May 1952

The only thing that was going to make these white people treat you like human beings was to fool with their pocketbooks.

E. D. NIXON, speech given during Montgomery Bus Boycott, Montgomery, Alabama, December 1955

Money is life. Once upon a time freedom used to be life. Now it's money.

LORRAINE HANSBERRY, *A Raisin in the Sun,* 1959

[M]oney, it turned out, was exactly like sex, you thought of nothing else if you didn't have it and thought of other things if you did.

JAMES BALDWIN, *Nobody Knows My Name,* 1961

Everything costs a lot of money when you haven't any.

JOE LOUIS, c. 1965

You can't ever be a big success without having money.

Ibid.

I don't like money actually, but it quiets my nerves.

Ibid.

Over the centuries the sheer energy of creating a valley for the Negroes to stay in drained us of untold ideas, has cost us billions of dollars, has branded the American dream, Lie.

JOHN WILLIAMS, *Beyond the Angry Black,* 1967

Money is the manifestation of power.

S. E. ANDERSON, in *Negro Digest,* September 1967

Where there is money, there is fighting.

MARIAN ANDERSON, *Marian Anderson, A Portrait,* 1970

Not poor, just broke.

DICK GREGORY, 1971

Money is the sun that makes you shine.

JUNE JORDAN, *Some Changes,* 1971

The Great Father has a big safe, and so have we. The hill is our safe. . . . We want seventy million dollars for the Black Hills. Put the money away some place at interest so we can buy livestock. That is the way the white people do.

MATO GLESKA (SPOTTED DOG), in Brown, *Bury My Heart at Wounded Knee,* 1971

We have sat and watched them pass here to get gold out and have said nothing . . . My friends, when I went to Washington I went into your money-house and I had some young men with me, but none of them took any money out of that house while I was with them. At the same time your people come into the Black Hills and take money out.

MAWATANI HANSKA (LONG MANDAN), in *ibid.*

Affluence separates people. Poverty knits 'em together.

RAY CHARLES, *Brother Ray,* 1978

I was making money and she had a beautiful funeral. Thank God for that. Didn't have to put the saucer on her. I've seen that happen to many of 'em, didn't have no insurance or belong to no club. While you was laying out there was the wake, they put a saucer on your chest and everybody who comes in, drops a nickel or dime or a quarter to try to make up for the undertaker.

LOUIS ARMSTRONG, *Autobiography,* 1979

Money and children don't go together: if you spent all your time making money and getting rich, the gods wouldn't give you any children; if you wanted children you had to forget money and be content to be poor.

BUCHI EMECHETA, *The Joys of Motherhood,* 1979

Accumulating money is so easy, I'm surprised more people aren't rich. That's the way money works. The important thing is not how much money a person makes, it is what he does with it that matters.

A. P. GASTON, c. 1983

Without money, an illness, even a simple one, can undermine the will. Without money, getting into a hospital is problematic and getting out without money to pay for the treatment is nearly impossible. Without money, one becomes dependent on other people, who are likely to be—even in their kindness—erratic in their support and despotic in their expectations of returns.

ALICE WALKER, *In Search of Our Mothers' Gardens,* 1983

All the money in the world will not buy you a kid who will do homework, or maturity for a kid who needs it. It may buy a kid who knows how to buy.

BILL COSBY, 1985

Politics doesn't control the world, money does. And we ought not to be upset about that. We ought to begin to understand how money works and why money works. . . . If you want to bring about . . . feeding the hungry, clothing the naked, healing the sick—it's going to be done in the free market system. You need capital.

ANDREW YOUNG, in "Words of the Week," *Jet,* 14 October 1985

[E]ven a feminist wants a man with some money.

NATHAN HARE, in "Interview: Dr. Nathan Hare," *Crisis,* March 1986

A basketball player averages $243,000 and an NFL player averaging $93,000 isn't going back to classes to listen to some $13,000 associate professor tell him how to succeed in life.

HARRY EDWARDS, in "Hardline," *Detroit Free Press,* 8 May 1988

All the money in the world doesn't mean a thing if you don't have time to enjoy it.

OPRAH WINFREY, in "Oprah's Wonder Year," *Ladies' Home Journal,* December 1988

The issue is no longer, can you check into the hotel? It's whether you've got the money to check out. The issue is no longer whether you can go to the University of Mississippi, but whether you can pay the tuition. The issue is no longer whether you sit on the bus or whether you can drive it; it's whether you can develop the capital to own the bus company.

WILLIAM GRAY, in *Life,* 1989

When you can count your money, you ain't got none.

DON KING, c. 1990

Every business has two financial objectives. One is to make money and the other is to make money consistently.

DON DAVIS, c. 1990

Donald Trump doesn't have an agent, the President of the United States doesn't have an agent, and neither do the top executives of General Motors. It doesn't make good business sense to give someone twenty percent of your salary right off the top.

ISAIAH THOMAS, c. May 1990

Economics do not dictate a level of intelligence. However, economics do dictate opportunity.

BILL COSBY, speech given in Washington, D.C., August 1991

MOTHER

See also FATHER, FAMILY

Thou shalt never forget thy mother. For she carried thee long beneath her breast and after thy months were accomplished she bore thee. Three long years she carried thee upon her shoulder. She nurtured thee, and took no offense from thy uncleanliness.

SCRIBE ANY of the Palace of Nefertari, 1550–1070 B.C.

In the eyes of its mother every beetle is a gazelle.

MOROCCO

Sometimes I feel/ Like a motherless child,/
Sometimes I feel/ Like a motherless child,/
Sometimes I feel like a motherless child,/A long way from home/ A long way from home.

SPIRITUAL

She is a mother, pale with fear,/ Her boy clings to her side,/ And in her kirtle vainly tries/ His trembling form to hide./ He is not hers, although she bore/ For him a mother's pain;/ He is not hers, although her blood/ Is coursing through his veins!

FRANCES E. W. HARPER, "The Slave Mother," *Poems on Miscellaneous Subjects,* 1854

Mothers are the lives which move education.

FRANCES E. W. HARPER, c. 1875

Oh ye mothers, what a responsibility rests on you! You have souls committed to your charge, and God will require a strict account of you.

MARIA W. STEWART, *Meditations from the Pen of Mrs. Maria W. Stewart,* 1879

We were stolen from our mother country and brought here. We have tilled the ground and made fortunes for thousands. This land which we have watered with our tears and our blood, so it is now our mother country.

RICHARD ALLEN, *The Life Experience and Gospel Labors of Richard Allen,* 1887

I do not recollect of ever seeing my mother by the light of day. She would lie down with me and get me to sleep, but long before I waked she was gone.

FREDERICK DOUGLASS, *Life and Times of Frederick Douglass,* 1895

Black mother of the iron hills that/ guard the blazing sea/ Wild spirit of a storm-swept soul/ a struggling to be free.

W. E. B. DU BOIS, *The Burden of Black Women,* 1896

Blushing, full of confusion, I talked with her about my worries and the fear in my body. I fell on her breast, and all over again I became a little girl sobbing in her arms at the terror of life.

GABRIELA MISTRAL, "Mother," *Desolación,* 1922

Motherhood is a profession by itself, just like school teaching and lecturing.

IDA B. WELLS, in Duster, ed., *Crusade for Justice,* 1928

Mother was of royal African blood, of a tribe ruled by matriarchs. . . . Throughout all her bitter years of slavery she had managed to preserve a queenlike dignity. She supervised all the business of the family.

MARY MCLEOD BETHUNE, "Faith That Moved a Dump Heap," *WHO,* June 1941

The worship of the Black woman as the mother of the human race goes back to the dimmest antiquity . . . the portal through which life passes in and emerges out into the world is black among all oriental nations.

J. A. ROGERS, *Nature Knows No Color Line,* 1952

The mother is there to protect you. She is buried in Africa and Africa is buried in her. That is why she is supreme.

CAMARA LAYE, *The Dark Child,* 1954

When the word becomes aristocrat/ To overcome the emptiness/ Behind closed blinds;/ Then Mother I think of you,/ Of your beautiful eyelids burnt by the years,/ Of your smile on my hospital nights,/ Your smile that told of old and vanquished miseries,/ O Mother mine Mother of us all.

DAVID DIOP, "For My Mother," *Poundings,* 1956

The person who brings children into the world is highly honored. You are performing a divine duty and responsibility. . . . You cannot always determine what they will do, but you can do your best to imbue certain ideas that will be guideposts and warnings and stops in their lives.

C. L. FRANKLIN, "Hannah, the Ideal Mother," sermon given in 1958

My mother first took us south to visit her Tennessee birthplace one summer when I was seven or eight. I woke up on the back seat of the car while we were still driving through . . . Kentucky and my mother was pointing out to the beautiful hills and telling my brothers about how her father had run away and hidden from his master in those very hills when he was a little boy. She said that his mother had wandered among the wooded slopes in the moonlight and left food for him in secret places. They were very beautiful hills and I looked out at them for miles and miles after that wondering who and what a "master" might be.

LORRAINE HANSBERRY, *To Be Young, Gifted and Black,* 1959

. . . I wonder about my Momma sometimes, and all the other mothers who got up at 6:00 A.M. to go to the white man's house with sacks over their shoes because it was so wet and cold. I wonder how they made it. They worked very hard for the man, they made his breakfast and they scrubbed his floors and they dispersed his babies. They didn't have much time for us.

DICK GREGORY, *Nigger, An Autobiography,* 1964

My mother wanted me to be a star and I worked hard for her goal.

LENA HORNE, *Lena,* 1965

My mother, religious-negro proud of,/ having waded through a storm, is, very obviously,/ a sturdy Black bridge that I/ crossed over, on.

CAROLYN RODGERS, *Songs of a Black Bird,* 1969

To describe my mother would be to write about a hurricane in its perfect power.

MAYA ANGELOU, *I Know Why the Caged Bird Sings,* 1969

There is no place I'd rather be tonight, except in my mother's arms.

DUKE ELLINGTON, speech given at the White House, 29 April 1969

My mother knit the family together, subtly pounding into us to care about each other.

COLEMAN YOUNG, in *Community Access News,* June 1976

When I was small and she would take me out for a walk where the curtains were clean and things were nice and pretty, she used to tell me that hope lived in those windows. Her teaching me that hope comes from within, that it grows inside you, was one of the main reasons I hung on for twenty-three years.

VIRGINIA CAPERS, c. 1978

I'll be with you always, and even when you don't want me to be.

DIANA ROSS, in Smith, *The Mother Book,* 1978

Africa is herself a mother. The mother of mankind. We Africans take motherhood as the most sacred condition human beings can achieve.

MAYA ANGELOU, c. 1979

Even today, when I think about my mother for any reason, what first jumps to mind are memories of her telling me that she loved me more than anyone else in the world. . . .

BILL RUSSELL, *Second Wind,* 1979

I hope they are still making women like my Momma. She always told me to do the right thing, to have pride in myself and that a good name is better than money.

JOE LOUIS, *My Life,* 1981

[I]n search of my mother's garden, I found my own.

ALICE WALKER, *In Search of Our Mothers' Gardens,* 1983

And for the three magic gifts I needed to escape the poverty of my hometown, I thank my mother, who gave me a sewing machine, a typewriter, and a suitcase. . . .

Ibid.

They dreamed dreams that no one knew—not even themselves, in any coherent fashion—and saw visions no one could understand. They wandered or sat about the countryside crooning lullabies to ghosts, and drawing the mother of Christ in charcoal on courthouse walls.

Ibid.

They forced their minds to desert their bodies and their striving spirits sought to rise, like frail whirlwinds from the hard red clay. And when those frail whirlwinds fell, in scattered particles, upon the ground, no one mourned. Instead, men lit candles to celebrate the emptiness that remained, as people do who enter a beautiful but vacant space to resurrect God. . . . Our mothers and grandmothers, some of them: moving to music not yet written.

Ibid.

Mothers forget to tell their sons not to bring babies home. We talk about how our daughters suffer from motherhood, but out sons suffer from fatherhood. It stops their dreams too.

NIKKI GIOVANNI, c. 1984

She made so many sacrifices to keep the family provided for. She was not home except late at night when she would return from work every day exhausted from cooking someone else's meals and washing clothes. She would then fix our next day's meal and ask about our schoolwork.

TOM BRADLEY, *The Impossible Dream,* 1986

Some mothers raise their daughters and love their sons.

JANICE HALE BENSON, in "Interview: Dr. Nathan Hale," *Crisis,* March 1986

Momma was home. She was the most totally human, human being that I have ever known; and so very beautiful. She was the lighthouse of her community. Within our home, she was an abundance of love, discipline, fun, affection, strength, tenderness, encouragement, understanding, inspiration, support.

LEONTYNE PRICE, in "The Most Unforgettable Person in My Family," *Ebony,* August 1986

[Mother] infused me with what Socrates taught . . . —"Know your right, then proceed"—and let no one dissuade you from that. . . . Respect for self as well as others was her byword; and not to ask of others until you have exhausted all means of doing for yourself was her belief.

L. DOUGLASS WILDER, in *ibid.*

My mother never gave up on me. I messed up in school so much they were sending me home, but my mother sent me right back.

DENZEL WASHINGTON, in "Spotlight: Denzel Washington," *Essence,* November 1986

My mother realized she was dying and would not have the chance to give me as much as she would have liked before she departed. So she crammed as much into me as she possibly could in those fourteen years. I didn't know exactly what she was doing at the time, but years later I realized how that care and love, the moral support sustained me.

GORDON PARKS, c. 1987

My mother was the influence in my life. She was strong; she had great faith in the ultimate triumph of justice and hard work. She believed passionately in education. She sacrificed to bring me to the North and a cold climate. Hardly a day goes by that I don't reach back and gain sustenance from something she said.

JOHN H. JOHNSON, in "Interview," *Crisis,* January 1987

I always wondered about where "kingdom come" might be, since my mother threatened so many times to knock me there.

BILL COSBY, c. 1988

She's like E. F. Hutton. When she speaks, we listen.

MARLON JACKSON, 1988

The woman she had been and was to become. . . .

GLORIA NAYLOR, *The Women of Brewster Place,* 1988

My mother means a great deal to me. In the early days, she would try to prevent me from going to the gym, but I'd go anyway. Some years later, when I decided to go for the Golden Gloves and Amateur Championships, she realized there was no stopping me.

THOMAS HEARNS, in "Famous Men and Their Moms," *Ebony,* May 1988

Mama was my greatest teacher, a teacher of compassion, love and fearlessness. If love is sweet as a flower, then my mother is that sweet flower of love.

STEVIE WONDER, in *ibid.*

Biology is the least of what makes someone a mother.

OPRAH WINFREY, in *Woman's Day,* 4 October 1988

My mom was the most fantastic woman in the world. She only went to the fifth grade, but she knew there was nothing wrong with my brain, I just couldn't see.

RAY CHARLES, in "Ray Charles Sees the Beauty," *Parade,* 10 October 1988

We got lots of negative messages in society. But my mother just put an end to those kinds of thoughts quickly—you might say she brainwashed us into believing that we could do anything.

BENJAMIN CARSON, in the *Detroit Free Press,* 25 December 1988

My mother was an abused child, and literature shows that abused children tend to grow up and abuse their own children. But she reversed this, gave affection and support to her family. She demanded excellence and got it.

JAMES COMER, c. 1990

Growing up without a father put a heavy burden on my mother. She didn't complain, and she didn't feel sorry for herself. She tried to carry the whole load, and somehow I understood what she was doing. No matter how many hours she had to be away from us at work, I knew she was doing it for us. That dedication and sacrifice made a profound impression on my life. It would be impossible to tell about my accomplishments without starting with my mother's influence.

BENJAMIN CARSON, *Gifted Hands,* 1990

MOTIVATION

Laughs, kidding and ridicule are often great for a player's motivation, and motivation is the greatest mystery in any champion athlete.

BILL RUSSELL, *Second Wind,* 1979

Pushkin's motivation and inspiration sprang from the spirit of freedom deeply embedded in him. His love of liberty made it impossible for him to sit idly by and passively accept a regime that exploited the people.

JAMES LOCKETT, "Alexander Sergeivich Pushkin: An Interpretation of the Russian Renaissance," *Negro History Bulletin,* July–September 1982

I'm motivated. The spirit hits me and I just keep going and don't stop. The more I play, the more I can invent, the more ideas come to me.

LIONEL HAMPTON, *Hamp: An Autobiography,* 1989

In my youth in the Transkei, I listened to the elders telling stories of the old days. . . . tales of wars fought by our ancestors in defense of the fatherland. The names of Dingane, Bambata, Hintsa, and Makana, Squngatha and Dalasile, Moshoeshoe, and Sekukhuni were praised as the pride and glory of the entire African nation. I wanted to serve my people . . . this is what motivated me.

NELSON MANDELA, *Higher Than Hope,* 1991

Hecklers just give me an incentive to do better.

JESSE BARFIELD, in "You (Bleep)," *Sports Illustrated,* 3 June 1991

MOUTH

If your mouth turns into a knife, it will cut off your lips.

AFRICA

No fish ever got caught with his mouth shut.

CURAÇAO

Open your mouth and God will speak for you.

TRADITIONAL

[H]abitual use of the superlative makes the mouth prolix.

JOAQUIM MACHADO DE ASSIS, *Dom Casmurro,* 1900

Just because my mouth opens up like a prayer book it does not have to flap like a Bible.

ZORA NEALE HURSTON, *Dust Tracks on a Road,* 1942

I don't let my mouth say nothing my head can't stand.

LOUIS ARMSTRONG, in *Life,* 15 April 1956

Some who criticize haven't done a thing but run their mouths.

COLEMAN YOUNG, in *Native Detroiter,* 1987

MOVE

If you stand still long enough, people throw dirt on you.

TRADITIONAL

I will not retreat one thousandth of an inch.

PAUL ROBESON, *Here I Stand,* 1958

I never stand still and I ain't running after no one.

RAY CHARLES, *Brother Ray,* 1978

The picket was the first time we got Black ministers and other Black professionals together with working-class people in a movement.

COLEMAN YOUNG, 1980

When blacks move into an urban neighborhood where the houses were built by European-Americans before them, one of the first things the African-Americans do is add on front porches. This turns the street into a wholly different cultural situation with dialogues crossing streets, porch to porch.

ROBERT F. THOMPSON, in *Black Art: Ancestral Legacy,* 1989

MOVEMENT

We shall not fully realize it until the inevitable reaction comes; when the popular interest flags, the movement will lose thousands of supporters who are now under its spell, but who tomorrow would be equally hypnotized by the next craze.

ALAIN LOCKE, "1928: A Retrospective View," *Opportunity,* 1929

Marcus Garvey's movement received amazing support from the Negro masses of the North and South. No other American Negro organization has ever been able to reach and stir the masses to the same degree or receive from them such generous financial support.

RALPH BUNCHE "Programs, Ideologies, Tactics and Achievements," 1940

The treadmill is moving backwards faster than we're able to go forward in this direction. We're not even standing still—we're going backwards.

MALCOLM X, "To Mississippi Youth," speech given at the Hotel Theresa, New York City, 31 December 1964

We are a movement, not an organization. And we move when the spirit says move. Anything outside is God's business. We are incorporated by the Lord, Resurrection City, and baptized by all this rain.

ANDREW YOUNG, speech given in Washington, D.C., 1968

[T]he very class that owes its new affluence to the Movement now refuses to support the organizations that made its success possible, and has retreated from its concern for black people who are poor.

ALICE WALKER, *In Search of Our Mothers' Gardens,* 1983

I've been marching since I was seventeen, long before there was a Civil Rights Movement. I was marching through the lobby of the Waldorf-Astoria, of the Sands, the . . . to a table at the Copa. And I marched alone. Worse. Often to Black derision.

SAMMY DAVIS, JR., in "Sammy Davis, Jr.: The Legacy of the World's Greatest Entertainer," *Ebony,* July 1990

MUSIC

Why, man, most of that modern stuff I just heard in 1918. Ain't no music out of date as long as you play it perfect.

LOUIS ARMSTRONG, 1948

My career was launched on the appendectomies of Italian sopranos.

LEONTYNE PRICE, 1957

There's only music, brother, and it's music we're going to sing where the rainbow ends.

RICHARD RIVE, "Where the Rainbow Ends" in Sissoko, ed., *Poems from Black Africa,* 1962

There is no music like that music, no drama like the drama of saints rejoicing, the sinners moaning, the tambourines racing, and all those voices coming together and crying holy unto the Lord. . . . I have never seen anything to equal the fire and excitement that sometimes, without warning, fill a church, causing the church, as Leadbelly and so many have testified, to "rock."

JAMES BALDWIN, *The Fire Next Time,* 1963

It was either live with music or die with noise—and we chose, rather, to live.

RALPH ELLISON, *Shadow and Act,* 1964

He carried off the healthiest child of Negro Music and starved it of its spirit until its parents no longer recognized it.

THELONIOUS MONK, in *Time,* 20 June 1964

Music is born with each child and accompanies him throughout life.

FRANCES BEBY, *African Music: A People's Art,* 1969

Black music unanimously recreates the Universe each time that thought is transformed into sound.

Ibid.

[Black] music is not only conspicuous within, but *CRUCIAL TO,* BLACK CULTURE. . . . [M]usic is not only a reflection of the values of black culture, but . . . the basis upon which it is built . . . the investigation of the Black mind, the Black social orientation, and, primarily, the Black culture.

BEN SIDRAN, *Black Talk,* 1971

We all go "do, re, mi," but you got to find the other notes for yourself.

LOUIS ARMSTRONG, in "The Unforgettable 'Satchmo,'" *Reader's Digest,* December 1971

All music is folk music, I ain't never heard no horse sing.

Ibid.

What we play is life.

Ibid.

The function of the music is to raise both performer and audience far above routine emotion; the elderly throw away their sticks and dance.

JOHN LOVELL, *Black Song,* 1972

Music . . . began with man, primitive man, trying to duplicate Nature's sounds—winds, birds, animals, water, the crescendo of fire—after which great systems of learning were set up, only to discover that music is limitless.

DUKE ELLINGTON, *Music Is My Mistress,* 1973

While waiting for my mother to finish cooking dinner . . . in fifteen minutes I wrote the score "Mood Indigo." "Black and Tan Fantasy" was written in a taxicab on the way to a recording session. In each case it was a matter of deadlines. Standing up against the studio's glass enclosure I wrote the score for "Solitude" in twenty minutes.

Ibid.

[My favorite tune?] The next one. The one I'm writing tonight or tomorrow, the new baby is always the favorite.

Ibid.

All musicians [who write] reflect their time.

Ibid.

Music is my mistress, and she plays second fiddle to no one.

Ibid.

[I]t is becoming increasingly difficult to decide where jazz starts or where it stops, where Tin Pan Alley begins and jazz ends, or even where the borderline lies between classical music and jazz.

Ibid.

Music itself is a category of sound, but everything that goes into the ear is not music. Music is music. If it sounds good, it's good music, and it depends on who's listening how good it sounds.

Ibid.

Music makes an image, summons, and describes where its energies were gotten.

IMAMU AMIRI BARAKA, c. 1975

Folk music straightened my spine, and kinked up my hair. It has given me a sense of us as people.

ODETTA, c. 1976

Music is the most shared experience—the most vital commodity among Afro-Americans. And poetry is music's twin.

EUGENE REDMOND, *Drumvoice,* 1976

Music is a world within itself/ With a language we all understand.

STEVIE WONDER, in "Stevie Wonder: The Genius of the Man and His Music," *Ebony,* January 1977

Music needs to make sense, needs to have order. From what some people consider the lowest stuff—a cat in the middle of a cotton field shouting the blues—to what's considered the highest—a symphony or an opera—it has to be structured.

RAY CHARLES, *Brother Ray,* 1978

I get way down in the music/ Down inside the music/ I let it wake me/ take me/ Spin me around and make me/ Uh get down.

ELOISE GREENFIELD, *Honey, I Love and Other Love Poems,* 1978

[Music can be used to] soothe slavery's torment or to propitiate God, or to describe the sweetness of love, and the distress of lovelessness, but . . . no race [can] sing and dance its way to freedom.

MAYA ANGELOU, *The Heart of a Woman,* 1981

Music serves life in all its manifestations. The unborn, the living, and the physically dead are served by music.

ALFRED PASTER, *The Roots of Soul,* 1982

Music . . . is the art I most envy.

ALICE WALKER, *In Search of Our Mothers' Gardens,* 1983

The jam session, the ultimate formal expression of the jazz musician, is, on one hand, a presentation of all the various ways, past and present, that a tune may be heard; on the other it is a revision of the past history of a tune ensuring what is lasting and valuable and useful.

ELEANOR TRAYLOR, "Music as Theme: The Blues Mode in the Works of Margaret Walker," in Evans, ed., *Black Women Writers,* 1984

Music is my addiction. When I get into it, I just fly.

PHILIP MICHAEL THOMAS, in "Spotlight: The Spice of Vice," *Essence,* November 1985

[A]nyone who listens to a Beethoven quartet or symphony and can't hear *soul* is in trouble.

RALPH ELLISON, "A Very Stern Discipline," *Going to the Territory,* 1986

[Music allows] "men [to] escape from their human condition, not by means of an evasion, but through a possession, [for] art is a way of possessing destiny."

RALPH ELLISON, "The Little Man at Chehaw Station," in *ibid.*

Music is to Black people what oil is to Arabs.

MELBA MOORE, c. 1987

We're in a period of the McDonalds' of music.

Ibid.

In the beginning was the beat, and the beat was the rhythm of God, and the rhythm of God became the harmony of humanity, and where there is harmony there is peace.

CLARENCE GLOVER, in "Spirituality: An African View," *Essence,* December 1987

My music will always be rooted in the streets.

TEDDY RILEY, c. 1988

The relationship of the Black listener to the music that he regards as "his" always has been a very deep and personal one, quite often reflecting a great deal about his subordinate position in the society. In contrast to all the things the Black man has not had in this country, he has always had his music.

PHYL GARLAND, c. 1988

In the African tradition, music had three basic functions: moral and spiritual order and as a means of self expression.

DANIEL ALDRIDGE, 1988

Hungry people work hard. I prefer a new act to be hungry.

PRINCE, 1988

We have to teach the younger generation to keep our foundation and organizations going that perpetuate the old gospel.

JAMES CLEVELAND, in *Ebony,* May 1988

Music allowed me to eat. But it also allowed me to express myself. I played because I had to play. I rid myself of bad dreams and rotten memories.

RAY CHARLES, in "Ray Charles Sees the Beauty," *Parade,* 10 October 1988

The key to Black music has been how we sing and approach singing, and the magic of the Black voice, which even instrumentalists copy.

NELSON GEORGE, 1989

From birth we've been hearing this music the way the heart pumps the blood.

SHARON MARLEY, 1989

Music can never become static. Once it does, it's a museum piece. Music is organic.

JULIUS HEMPHILL, 1989

Taking James Brown out of the music business is like taking Moses out of the Bible and saying it was a complete book.

JAMES BROWN, in *Detroit Free Press,* 12 February 1989

Music is all around me and in me, as I am in it.

AVERY BROOKS, in "Spotlight: Not Just Another Pretty Face," *Essence,* April 1989

We didn't invent anything. We just repeated it.

LUTHER CAMPBELL, in *Detroit Free Press,* 5 March 1992

MYSTERY

Who is there that can grasp the will of the gods in heaven?/ The plan of a god, full of mystery—who can understand it?

ENLIL, c. 1750 B.C.

Science is a system of exact mysteries.

JEAN TOOMER, *Essentials,* 1931

MYTH

Some unknown natural phenomenon occurs which cannot be explained and a new local demigod is named.

ZORA NEALE HURSTON, 1925

[U]ntil there is full freedom for *all* of colored America our democracy is a myth, a bad myth, a confusing myth.

PAUL ROBESON "An Evening in Brownsville," *Freedom,* May 1952

History demands united action on the part of the people . . . to put an end to the myths of white superiority.

PAUL ROBESON, in "Robeson Urges Government Defend Constitution Against Racists," *Daily Worker,* 23 September 1957

Myths are a way of solving the problem of making intelligible to the marketplace conclusions arrived at in the ivory tower.

ADESANYA ADEBAYO, 1958

For in the beginning of literature is the myth, and in the end as well.

JORGE LUIS BORGES, "Parable of Don Quixote," *Labyrinths,* 1962

The old myths must be cleared away. They are like cobwebs in your mind.

MARCUS GARVEY, in *Garvey and Garveyism,* 1963

The real victim of bigotry is the white man who hides his weakness under his myth of superiority.

JAMES BALDWIN, *Going to Meet the Man,* 1965

The artist . . . is the guardian of [the] image; the writer is the myth-maker of his people.

CAROLYN GERALD, "The Black Writer and His Role," in Gayle, ed., *Black Aesthetic,* 1971

To credit Abraham Lincoln with being the Great Emancipator or the supreme abolitionist of his time is pure myth.

DICK GREGORY, *No More Lies,* 1971

A myth is whatever concept of truth or reality a whole people has arrived at over years of observation. It cannot be manufactured by a handful of people. It must be the collective creation of—and acceptance by—hordes of anonymous people.

TONI MORRISON, "Behind the Making of the Black Door," *Black World,* 19 February 1974

Let the myth persist!

COLEMAN YOUNG, in the *Detroit Free Press,* 4 January 1976

We have myths like freedom, justice, equality for all.

JANICE HALE BENSON, *Black Child in Education,* 1986

[T]he human imagination finds it necessary to take exemplary people—charismatic personalities, cultural heroes—and enlarge upon them . . . [as a] mythmaking tendency.

RALPH ELLISON, "On Initiation Rites and Power," *Going to the Territory,* 1986

So important have . . . stories been to mankind that they . . . will be found following human societies as they recreate themselves through vicissitudes of their history, validating their social organizations, their political systems, their moral attitudes and religious beliefs, even their prejudices. Such stories serve the purpose of consolidating whatever gains people or their leaders have made or imagine they have made in their existing journey thorough the world.

CHINUA ACHEBE, "What Has Literature Got to Do With it?" Nigerian National Merit Award Lecture, Sokoto, 23 August 1986

In the proportion as Americans and Europeans become removed from such nonsense as the Nordic myth and race superiority, they will increase their interest in the history of other peoples. . . . However, they still lack the sense of humor to see the joke in thinking that one race has been divinely appointed to do all the great things on this earth and enjoy most of its blessings.

WILLIAM SIMMONS, c. 1987

The first myth that was dispelled was that on stage we were clowns. The minstrel thing hung over for a long time. My first stage performance was in 1936. We also changed the concept of beauty. We weren't pushing Black is beautiful. We just showed it.

KATHERINE DUNHAM, in "She Danced to Teach—and They Loved It," *American Visions,* February 1987

People don't want to admit that they owe much to Black culture. That goes back to slave systems, racism, distorted thinking, and how people like to perpetuate the myth that there is no such thing as Black culture.

TEVIS WILLIAMS, in "Black Dance in Perspective," *City Arts Quarterly*, Spring 1987

Myths galvanize people and direct their form of culture. They are the fullness and depth of the people. Myths are the projections of their learned fears, anxieties, frustrations, hopes, and the deepest unconscious contradictions of a civilization.

PAT ROBINSON, c. 1988

A myth always rises to fill a need.

GLORIA NAYLOR, "The Myth of the Matriarch," *Life*, Spring 1988

There was one thing in which the adherents of the scriptures as well as the atheists were agreed: belief in the existence of beings with superhuman powers.

NELSON MANDELA, *Higher Than Hope*, 1991

Take away myth and fallacies, and you take away the livelihoods of a whole class of people. We have overdosed on political fallacies, myths, and hysteria. The question now is: Will we suffer withdrawal symptoms if we suddenly give them up cold turkey?

THOMAS SOWELL, "Fallacies, Myths and Hysteria Abound," *Detroit News*, 15 July 1991

NAACP

The struggle of the NAACP against educational disadvantages in the South has attracted more attention during the past ten years. We have seen sensational victories in the courts.

WILLIAM H. HASTIE, "A Look at the NAACP," *Crisis*, September 1939

The NAACP is the only organization which has struggled with admirable singlemindedness and skill to raise us to the level of citizen.

JAMES BALDWIN, c. 1970

We employed the late Clarence Darrow in 1926 to defend a man and his family when a member of a mob threatening his newly purchased Detroit home was shot and killed. The NAACP has subscribed to nonviolence as a human as well as a practical necessity in the realities of the American scene, but we have never required this as a deep personal commitment for our membership.

ROY WILKINS, *Standing Fast*, 1982

Charles Houston was the Moses who led us through the wilderness of second-class citizenship toward the dimly perceived promised land of legal equality.

WILLIAM HASTIE, *Grace Under Pressure*, 1984

Thurgood Marshall was Mr. Civil Rights in those early days. He led the argument before the United States Supreme Court against racial segregation in the public schools which led to *Brown* v. *Board of Education.*

LEON SULLIVAN, c. 1986

Whether we call ourselves Urban League, Rainbow Coalition or PUSH, we have NAACP in our bloodstream.

JESSE JACKSON, in "NAACP Focus," *Crisis*, November 1986

In spite of the fact that *Forbes* rates my corporation as one of the top five hundred corporations in the country, I still need the NAACP. There is no security in success for a Black person.

JOHN H. JOHNSON, in "Interview: John H. Johnson," *Crisis*, January 1987

Whether it be Army, Air Force, Marines, or Navy, you don't think about writing your Congressman first. You write the NAACP. They've established the reputation because they get action.

ROBERT L. TONEY, in "Interview: Rear Admiral Robert L. Toney, *Crisis*, February 1987

There certainly is a need for the NAACP. All you have to do is read of Blacks moving into neighborhoods that were all white. Our schools are more segregated than ever before.

DAMON KEITH, in the *Detroit News*, 28 April 1991

NAME

So how shall we name you, little one?/ Are you your father's father, or his brother, or yet another?/ Whose spirit is it that is in you, little warrior?

UGANDA, A MOTHER TO HER FIRST BORN

There is nothing that there is not, whatever we have a name for, that is.

YORUBA

I told Jesus it would be all right if he changed my name.

SPIRITUAL

For a new master might often change a slave's name and this indicated that the slave had absolutely no rights which a white person were bound to respect.

WILLIAM WELLS-BROWN, *Narrative of William W. Brown, A Fugitive Slave*, 1847

When I left the house of bondage I left everything behind. I wasn't going to keep nothing of Egypt on me, an' so I went to the Lord an' asked him to give me a new name. And he gave me Sojourner because I was to travel up and down the land showing the people their sins and bein' a sign unto them. I told the Lord I wanted two names 'cause everybody else had two, and the Lord gave me Truth, because I was to declare the truth to the people.

SOJOURNER TRUTH, *Narrative of Sojourner Truth,* 1850

Africa is the land of our origin, and since she is, by fact of history and archaeology, the mother of the oldest civilization, the oldest science, the oldest art, she is by eminent fitness placed first in the compound title, Afro-American.

J. C. EMBRY, "Afro-American vs. Negro," *Afro-American Encyclopedia,* 1896

All the children had two names and some of them indulged in what seemed to me the extravagance of having three.

BOOKER T. WASHINGTON, *Up From Slavery,* 1901

These are my plans: to make a name in science, to make a name in literature, and thus to raise my race.

W. E. B. DU BOIS, *The Souls of Black Folk,* 1903

The name of Deadwood Dick was given to me by the people of Deadwood, South Dakota, July 4, 1876, after I had proven myself worthy to carry it, and after I had defeated all comers in riding, roping, and shooting, and I have always carried the name with honor since that time.

NAT LOVE, *Life and Adventures of Nat Love,* 1907

My good name is all that I have in the world and I was bound to protect it from attack by those who felt that they could do so with impunity because I had no brother or father to protect it for me.

IDA B. WELLS, in Duster, ed., *Crusade for Justice,* 1928

Suppose we arose tomorrow morning and lo! instead of being "Negroes," all the world called us "Cheiropolidi"—do you really think this would make a vast and momentous difference to you and to me? Would you be any less ashamed of being descended from a black man, or would your schoolmates feel any less superior to you? The feeling of inferiority is in you, not in any name. The name merely evokes what is already there. Exorcise the hateful complex and no name can ever make you hang your head.

W. E. B. DU BOIS, "Letter to Roland A. Barton," *Crisis,* March 1928

Up until 1912 when the French took over Morocco, Jews there lived under a form of fascism in their ghettoes, quite as Negroes in the South. And since then, the Moors have under the French lived under a form of colonial fascism. The name changes, but there is nothing new under the sun.

CLAUDE MCKAY, letter to Max Eastman, 21 March 1945

I have nothing but my word. It is enough to name the thing, and the sense appears in the sign.

LEOPOLD SENGHOR, c. 1952

Mylitta, Queen of the Gods, originally Assyrian, was Black . . . from her comes the word Mulatto. Other black Venuses were Melainis, from which is derived melanin; and Scotia, Egyptian princess, from whom the name Scot-land originated.

J. A. ROGERS, *Nature Knows No Color Line,* 1952

My name—an offense; my Christian name—humiliation; my age—the stone age.

AIMÉ CÉSAIRE, c. 1956

With you I refound my name, my name long hidden under the salt of distances.

DAVID DIOP, "With You," *Poundings,* 1956

Our fathers knew that Chukwa was the Overlord and that is why many of them gave their children the name Chukwuka—Chukwa is Supreme.

CHINUA ACHEBE, *No Longer at Ease,* 1961

Can you sense a man's hurt at not knowing the name he's called by, or to what his name calls him?

AIMÉ CÉSAIRE, *Tragedy of King Christophe,* 1963

Remember that there is only one Toussaint L'Ouverture in San Domingo and that at his name everybody must tremble.

TOUSSAINT L'OUVERTURE, in James, *The Black Jacobins,* 1963

It doesn't give you a country, because there is no such thing as a Negro country. It doesn't give you a culture—there is no such thing as a Negro culture, it doesn't exist. The land doesn't exist, the culture doesn't exist, the language doesn't exist, and the man doesn't exist.

MALCOLM X, speech given at Organization of Afro-American Unity Rally, Audubon Ballroom, New York City, 24 January 1965

The Western World has created me, given me my name, has hidden my truth as a permanent and historical fact. I may recover from this and I may not.

JAMES BALDWIN, in "James Baldwin . . . in Conversation," *Arts in Society,* Summer 1966

It is through our names that we first place ourselves in the world.

RALPH ELLISON, c. 1969

Every person I knew had a hellish horror of being "called out of his name." It was a dangerous practice to call a Negro anything that could be loosely construed as insulting because of the centuries of having been called nigger, jigs, dingoes, blackbirds, crows, boots, and spade.

MAYA ANGELOU, *I Know Why the Caged Bird Sings,* 1969

[B]lack is . . . the generalized term which we use to symbolize unity of origin, whether we are called Anglophone, Francophone, coloured, mulatto, West Indian or American Negro by the white image-makers. *Black* is the highly imagistic term we use to do away with all such divisionary euphemisms.

CAROLYN GERALD, "The Black Writer and His Role," in Gayle, ed., *The Black Aesthetic,* 1971

In Spanish Negro is the word for black, and brown cannot be black.

MALCOLM X, *On Afro-American History,* 1971

Every person comes into this world seeking his name. This is the centrality of life. By one's name is not meant the name upon a birth certificate, nor the name by which one's parents call him. Rather, what is the name by which God knows you?

HERMAN WATTS, "What Is Your Name?" in Philpot, ed., *Best Black Sermons,* 1972

You've got to have a name that appeals to the imagination . . . because it is a thing of the spirit.

WOLE SOYINKA, *The Trials of Brother Jeroboam,* 1973

We are not Black Muslims and never have been. We're a world community—a community that encompasses everybody.

WALLACE D. MUHAMMAD, in the *Cleveland Plain Dealer,* 10 October 1976

Funny Papa, T-Bone, Black Ace, Washboard, Cleanhead, Tampa Red, Juke Boy, Shine, Staggerlee. Names they got from yearnings, gestures, flaws, wins, mistakes, weaknesses. Names that bore witness. Macon Dead, Sing Bird, Crowell Bird, Pilate, Hagar, Ice Man, Muddy Waters, Jelly Roll, Fats, Leadbelly, Bo Diddley, Peg Leg, Son, Shortstuff, Smokey Babe.

TONI MORRISON, *Song of Solomon,* 1977

By ancient customs, for the next seven days there was but a single task with which Omoro would seriously occupy himself, the selection of a name for his first-born son. It would have to be a name rich with history and with promise for the people of his tribe—the Mandinkan believed that a child would develop seven of the characteristics of whomever or whatever he was named for.

ALEX HALEY, *Roots,* 1977

I don't think I would have chosen either name for myself. I mean, the sounds of them—Pinchback, Toomer—do not strike my ear well. In fact, few names strike my ear well. . . . [T]he names we human beings attach to ourselves are among the most ridiculous features of our existence.

JEAN TOOMER, "Earth Being," in Turner, ed., *Wayward Seeking,* 1980

The Dark Destroyer, Alabama Assassin, Detroit Destroyer, Michigan Mauler, Sepia Socker and the Brown Bomber. The Brown Bomber was the name that stuck the rest of my career.

JOE LOUIS, *My Life,* 1981

My great-great-great-grandmother walked as a slave from Virginia to Eatonton, Georgia—which passes for the Walker ancestral home—with two babies on her hips. She lived to be a hundred and twenty-five years old and my own father knew her as a boy. (It is in memory of this walk that I choose to keep and to embrace my "maiden" name, Walker.)

ALICE WALKER, *In Search of Our Mothers' Gardens,* 1983

Call a place Slidell, Zachary, Balatusha, Natchez, or Valese. Then when you said a name, you'd be saying something.

RICHARD PERRY, *Montgomery's Children,* 1984

Look what they have done to my name . . . the wonderful name of my great-great-grandmothers *Nomgqibelo Ncamisile Mnqhibisa/*. . . . My name is so simple/ and yet so meaningful,/ but to this man it is trash. . . . He gives me a name/ Convenient enough to answer his whim:/ I end up being Maria. . . .

MAGOLENG WA SELEPE, "My Name," in Chinweizu, ed., *Voices From Twentieth-Century Africa,* 1988

[Bleek, Big Stop, Gem, Rhythm Jones] . . . I collect names for characters. Names are valuable; they can be your first source of insight into a character.

SPIKE LEE, *Mo' Better Blues,* 1991

NATURE

Obscurity knows nature will light the way.

DAHOMEY

The sun does not go into hiding in the season of drought.

DAHOMEY

The history of the world, civil, sacred, and profane, show that some men have, in all ages, espoused popular and benevolent causes, more or less influenced by prejudice or selfishness, Human nature, with its imperfections, remains the same.

AUGUSTUS WASHINGTON, "African Colonization—By a Man of Color," *New York Daily Tribune,* 9–10 July 1851

The earth was created by the assistance of the sun, and it should be left as it was . . . The country was made without lines of demarcation, and it is no man's business to divide it.

HIGHN'MOOT TOOYALAKET (CHIEF JOSEPH) OF THE NEZ PERCES, "An Indian's View of Indian Affairs," *North American Review,* 1879

The woods are drugging. They are too powerful. I can't describe the grandeur of it all. Nature has upended her horn of plenty here.

ZORA NEALE HURSTON, 7 March 1927

The American Indian is of the soil, whether it be the region of forests, plains, pueblos, or mesas. He fits into the landscape, for the hand that fashioned the continent also fashioned the man for his surroundings. He once grew as naturally as the sunflowers; he belongs just as the buffalo belonged.

LUTHER STANDING BEAR, *Land of the Spotted Eagle,* 1933

She knew things that nobody had ever told her. For instance, the words of the trees and the wind. She often spoke to falling seeds and said, "Ah hope you fall on soft ground," because she had heard seeds saying that to each other as they passed.

ZORA NEALE HURSTON, *Their Eyes Were Watching God,* 1937

Human nature will find itself only when it fully realizes that to be human it has to cease to be beastly or brutal.

MOHANDAS GANDHI, in *Harijan,* 8 October 1938

The man who interprets Nature is always held in great honor. I am going to live and talk with Nature and know her secrets. Then I will be powerful, no matter where I may be.

ZORA NEALE HURSTON, *Moses, Man of the Mountain,* 1939

Nature was being thwarted and opposed by perverse and corrupt man.

ARNA BONTEMPS, *Drums at Dusk,* 1939

Hear the prayer of an earth stricken with pain: In the green woods, O may the birds/ Sing supreme again.

RABINDRANATH TAGORE, *Flying Man,* 1940

A river rises in the heights and goes into the depths. It carries gold and silver and mud and glass, always different, never tiring, full of goodness. It is a prolonged laugh on the dark face of the forest.

ADALBERTO ORTIZ, *Juyungo,* 1943

Nature is so made that we do not see our backs, it is reserved for others to see. Hence it is wise to profit by what they see.

MOHANDAS GANDHI, Prayer Speech in *Delhi Diary,* 1 December 1947

To you, tropics, I owe that childlike enthusiasm of running, laughing over mountains and clouds, while an ocean of sky is shattered in innumerable star—waves at my feet.

NICOLAS GUILLÉN, *Songoro Cosongo,* 1952

A long time ago this land belonged to our fathers; but when I go up to the river I see camps of soldiers on its banks. These soldiers cut down my timber; they kill my buffalo; and when I see that, my heart feels like bursting; I feel sorry . . . Has the white man become a child that he should recklessly kill and not eat? When the red men saw game, they do so that they may live and not starve.

CHIEF SATANTA OF THE KIOWAS, in Stanley, *Satanta and the Kiowas,* 1960

It is in the nature of the American Negro, the same as all other men, to fight and try to destroy those things that block his path to greater happiness in life.

ROBERT WILLIAMS, "USA, The Potential of a Minority Revolution," *The Crusader Monthly Newsletter,* May–June 1965

One does not sell the earth upon which the people walk.

TASHUNKO WITKLO (CRAZY HORSE) in Brown, *Bury My Heart at Wounded Knee,* 1971

You have driven away our game and our means of livelihood out of the country, until now we have nothing left that is valuable except the Black Hills that you ask us to give up . . . The earth is full of minerals of all kinds, and on the earth the ground is covered with forests of heavy pine, and when we give up these we know that we give up the last thing that is valuable to us or the white people.

WANIGI SKA (WHITE GHOST), in *ibid.*

Man is a child of nature. He cannot long separate himself from nature without withering as a cut rose in a vase.

HOWARD THURMAN, *A Search for Common Ground,* 1971

NECESSARY

Necessity is the mother of invention.

AESOP, "The Cow and the Pitcher," c. 600 B.C.

Necessity has no law.

TERENCE, *The Eunuch,* 167 B.C.

Throw aside every non-essential and cling only to the essential—his pillar of fire by night and his pillar of cloud by day shall be property, economy, education, and Christian character.

BOOKER T. WASHINGTON *Future of the American Negro,* 1889

When you hear me say "by any means necessary," I mean exactly that. I believe in anything that is necessary to correct unjust conditions—political, economic, social, physical, anything that is necessary.

MALCOLM X, answer to question at the Militant Labor Forum, 7 January 1965

You can see how necessary, how perfect, it was that Christianity came first, that the African was given something to take his mind off Africa; that he was forced if he wished to escape the filthy paternalism and cruelty of slavery, to work at least until he died, when he could be transported peacefully and majestically to the "promised land."

LEROI JONES, *Home: Social Essays,* 1966

A necessary act of liberation within myself was to acknowledge the beauty of the black, black woman.

ALICE WALKER, *In Search of Our Mothers' Gardens,* 1983

NEED

If I am all you have, then I'm all you need.

TRADITIONAL

But for ourselves who know our plight too well, there is a need of great patterns to guide us, great lives . . . to inspire us, strong men and women to lift us up and give us confidence in the powers we, too, possess.

LANGSTON HUGHES, in *Crisis,* June 1941

Fanatics . . . are boring and . . . unreliable. They tend to burn out just when you need them.

NIKKI GIOVANNI, "An Answer to Some Questions on How I Write: In Three Parts," in Evans, ed., *Black Women Writers,* 1984

Humans have a great and profound need to debate the heat while ignoring the sun; to need the rain while decrying the clouds.

NIKKI GIOVANNI, in *Catalyst,* Summer 1988

It's bad for a 71-year-old broad to be singing about how bad she needs it.

LENA HORNE, 28 October 1988

NEIGHBOR

The bedrock of individual success in life is securing the friendship, the confidence, the respect of your next-door neighbor in your little community in which you live.

BOOKER T. WASHINGTON, *Future of the American Negro,* 1899

All inhabitants of the globe are now neighbors. The large house in which we live demands that we transform this worldwide neighborhood into a worldwide brotherhood.

MARTIN LUTHER KING, JR., *Where Do We Go from Here?* 1968

When I grew up we lived in what was recognized as a neighborhood. Everybody vaguely knew everybody else.

JAMES BALDWIN, *A Rap on Race,* 1971

Our neighborhood is one large extended family. Every adult is every child's parent, and every child is every adult's son or daughter. What this means . . . is that if I do something wrong, any adult has the right to spank me, to discipline me, to tell me to cut it out.

MIRIAM MAKEBA, *My Story,* 1987

We send children to schools to study dance, but we can't all dance in the ballet. There have to be other avenues available to them. It's not up to Hollywood. It's up to the neighborhood. Let Hollywood come and get them.

MARLA GIBBS, in "Spotlight: Marla Gibbs," *Essence,* October 1988

We didn't have space to walk then. Now we have a beach. When you're walking on the beach, it's not like walking through the neighborhood where people can look at you and stare at you.

DICK GREGORY, in the *Detroit News,* 2 November 1988

NEW YORK

Folks in New York City/Ain't like the folks down South/They never say, "Have dinner,"/'Cause they live from hand to mouth.

BLUES

I'd rather drink muddy water, sleep in a hollow log than be in New York City treated like a dirty dog.

BLUES

I miss New York but I can't work there. I can't write. . . . Pressures are too much in New York. You spend all your time resisting. You don't find what you are thinking or dreaming.

JAMES BALDWIN, in "James Baldwin . . . in Conversation," *Arts in Society,* Summer 1966

New York is its people, and its people are *the city.* Among its crowds, along its streets, and in its high-piled buildings can be found . . . every custom, thought, and tradition, every color, flavor, religion, and culture of the entire earth. It is as if each of the world's greatest chefs had sent a pinch of his nation's most distinctive flavoring to contribute to the richness of taste of this great savory *pot au fev* called New York.

DUKE ELLINGTON, *Music Is My Mistress,* 1973

New York is the dream of a song. New York is a place where the rich walk, the poor drive Cadillacs, and beggars die of malnutrition with thousands of dollars hidden in their mattresses.

Ibid.

New York, whose people I love for their grace under almost continual unpredictable adversity. . . .

ALICE WALKER, *In Search of Our Mothers' Gardens,* 1983

Life in the Apple doesn't allow much time for reminiscing and pining for the good old days. The snap, pop, and hassle of tomorrow hits faster than a rimshot from Tubbal's tom-tom and is upon you as persistently as a landlord with the rent receipt.

HERB BOYD, in *City Arts Quarterly,* Summer 1988

NIGHT

No matter how long the night, the day is sure to come.

CONGO

Moon fell at the feet of morning,/ Loosened from night's fading necklace.

RABINDRANATH TAGORE, *Unyielding,* 1935

Night was striding across nothingness with the whole round world in his hands.

ZORA NEALE HURSTON, *Their Eyes Were Watching God,* 1937

The moon was a white canoe moored to the night.

FRANK MARSHALL DAVIS, "Midsummer," *Golden Slippers,* 1941

And the Spirits' milky splendor in the infinite celestial tann. But here as veils of darkness fall is the Goddess Moon's intelligence. African night, my black night, mystical and bright black and brillant.

LÉOPOLD SENGHOR, *Songs of Darkness,* 1945

[T]here is silver under/ The veils of the darkness/ But few care to dig in the night/ For the possible treasure of stars.

GWENDOLYN BROOKS, "intermission," *Annie Allen,* 1949

Night is a curious child, wandering/ Between earth and sky, creeping/ In windows and doors, daubing/ The entire neighborhood. . . .

FRANK MARSHALL DAVIS, "Four Glimpses of Night," in Bontemps, ed., *Poetry of the Negro,* 1949

Night and on all sides only the folding quiet,/ In the sky the wide staring eyes of the stars;/ Looking from them maybe the earth shines too, as winking softly they watch in their delight/ This loveliness that lies asleep in all its peace.

SAM SUTER, "Night," in *ibid.*

I came as a shadow,/ I stand now a light;/ The depth of my darkness/ Transfigures your night.

LEWIS ALEXANDER, "Nocturne Varial," in *ibid.*

. . . night I entered a world in which the dividing line between reality and dream was so fine as not to exist. . . .

PETER ABRAHAMS, *Tell Freedom,* 1954

On those nights with no name/ on those nights with no moon/ the pain that inhabits me/ presses/ the pain that inhabits me/ chokes.

LEON DAMAS, "There Are Nights," *Pigments,* 1956

The world was silent, except for the shrill cry of insects, which was part of the night.

CHINUA ACHEBE, *Things Fall Apart,* 1959

Like the closing of a lid on a kettle, night covered the earth.

OUSMANE SEMBANE, *God's Bit of Wood,* 1970

Night life is cut out of a very luxurious, royal-blue bolt velvet. It sparkles with jewels, and it sparkles in tingling and tinkling tones. . . . Night life seems to have been born with all its people in it, the people who never had been babies, but were born *grown,* completely independent.

DUKE ELLINGTON, *Music Is My Mistress,* 1973

Only the night is watching and the night was made for desire.

JAMES BALDWIN, c. 1975

Night covered my spirit like a gentle blanket. . . . When there was no moon, the stars hung like lanterns, so close I felt that I could reach up and pluck them from the heavens. . . . The night seemed to have movement in it, as if it were a great ocean wave. Other times, it was deathly still, no rhythm, no movement. At such times I could hear the night think, and feel the night feel . . . I found myself wishing the night would come, for under its cover, my mind would roam.

HOWARD THURMAN, *With Head and Heart,* 1979

NONVIOLENCE

Nonviolence is the greatest force at the disposal of mankind. It is mightier than the mightiest weapon of destruction devised by the ingenuity of man.

MOHANDAS GANDHI, in *Harijan,* 5 July 1935

Nonviolence cannot be taught to a person who fears to die and has no power of resistance.

Ibid.

Nonviolent resistance is not a method for cowards; it does resist.

MARTIN LUTHER KING, JR., *Stride Toward Freedom,* 1958

I left India more convinced than ever before that nonviolent resistance is the most potent weapon available to oppressed people in their struggle for freedom.

Ibid.

Nonviolence is a powerful and just weapon. It is a weapon unique in history which cuts without wounding. It is a sword that heals.

Ibid.

Through nonviolence, courage displaces fear; love transforms hate. Acceptance dissipates prejudice; hope ends despair. Peace dominates war; faith reconciles doubt. Mutual regard cancels enmity. Justice for all overthrows injustice. The redemptive community supersedes systems of gross social immorality.

SNCC, 1960

The effect of nonviolence on the offender is apt to be so threatened that the security he feels in the violent acts deserts him and he is thrown back upon the naked hunger of his own heart. . . .

HOWARD THURMAN, *Disciplines of the Spirit,* 1963

Let's not burn America down. Let's take her like she is and rebuild her. We must maintain and advocate and promote the philosophy of nonviolence.

MARTIN LUTHER KING, JR., in *Jet,* 4 April 1968

Let it be thoroughly understood that our deceased brother did not embrace nonviolence out of fear or cowardice. Moral courage was his noblest virtue.

BENJAMIN MAYS, eulogy of Martin Luther King, Jr., Atlanta, Georgia, 9 April 1968

[N]onviolence is . . . a spiritual discipline that requires a great deal of strength, growth, and purging of the self so that one can overcome almost any obstacle for the good of all without being concerned about one's own welfare.

CORETTA SCOTT KING, in Walker, *In Search of Our Mothers' Gardens,* 1983

It could not be denied that our policy to achieve a nonracial state by nonviolence had achieved nothing, and that our followers were beginning to lose confidence.

NELSON MANDELA, *Higher Than Hope,* 1991

We are not going to fight or attempt to fight, insult, or attempt to insult, provoke or attempt to provoke the police in their duties. We are not going to throw stones or anything that is going to obstruct the police . . . nobody is carrying money, knives, or any dangerous weapons. We have the continent on our side. We have history on our side. We will win.

ROBERT SOBUKWE, in Mandela, *Higher Than Hope*, 1991

NORTH

[S]omething more than a hope of reaching heaven. We meant to reach the *North,* and the North was our Canaan.

FREDERICK DOUGLASS, *Life and Times of Frederick Douglass*, 1882

I've seen them come dark/ wondering/ wide eyed/ dreaming/ out of Pennsylvania Station/ but the trains are late/ The gates open/ but there're bars/ at each gate.

LANGSTON HUGHES, c. 1940

I see so many hang-ups in the North that I don't see in the South. In the South men don't expect their wives to be seen and not heard and not doing anything. We've always been used to standing by our husband's side and doing whatever is necessary to help the family survive.

FANNIE LOU HAMER, in "Fannie Lou Hamer Speaks Out," *Essence*, October 1971

His control of the young Black man is more despotic than that of the southern plantation owner over Blacks in the South: for him, the weapons of control are economic, social, and political.

ADDISON GAYLE, JR., in Chapman, *New Black Voices*, 1972

The battleground is definitely in the North now—Detroit, New York, Chicago, most of these cities are settling on a powder keg of neglect. The problems in the major cities across the country are the problems of America in miniature.

CORETTA SCOTT KING, 1975

The whole family moved North together, almost like a tribe. Although I was an only child, I had thirty cousins, aunts, uncles, and grandparents all living within two or three blocks.

LOUIS GOSSETT, JR., in "I Was Swallowing a Kind of Poison," *Parade*, 17 July 1988

OBJECT/OBJECTIVE

Policies change, and programs change, according to time. But objective never changes. You might change your method of achieving the objective, but the objective never changes. Our objective is complete freedom, complete justice, complete equality, by any means necessary.

MALCOLM X, speech given at the Audubon Ballroom, New York City, 20 December 1964

There is no objective anything.

IMAMU AMIRI BARAKA, c. 1968

True "objectivity" where race is concerned is as rare as a necklace of Hope diamonds.

HOYT W. FULLER, "Towards a Black Aesthetic," in Gayle, ed., *The Black Aesthetic,* 1971

I've learned over a period of years there are setbacks when you come up against the immovable object; sometimes the object doesn't move.

COLEMAN YOUNG, c. 1980

OBLIGATION

You can place anyone under obligation to you, if you can induce him to accept gifts and favors.

TRADITIONAL

OBSTACLES

A partner in the business will not put obstacles to it.

CONGO

It's like a lion barring your road. You either turn back, because you cannot cope with it, or you kill it, and go on.

PETER ABRAHAMS, *Tell Freedom,* 1954

My hesitancy in speech, which was once annoyance, is now a pleasure. Its greatest benefit has been to teach me the economy of words. A thoughtless word hardly ever escapes my tongue. I do not recollect ever having to regret anything in my speech or writing.

MOHANDAS GANDHI, in Fischer, ed., *The Essential Gandhi,* 1962

[A]lmost anyone else can come into this country and get around barriers and obstacles that we cannot get around; and the only difference between them and us [is] they know something about the past.

MALCOLM X, speech given at the Organization of Afro-American Unity Rally, Audubon Ballroom, New York City, 24 January 1965

The Negro faces another stone wall when he presents such scientific productions to the publishing house. They may not be prejudiced, but they are not interested in the Negro.

CARTER G. WOODSON, *The Negro in Our History,* 1966

There are many barriers people try to break down. I try to do it with poetry.

LANGSTON HUGHES, in "Langston Hughes Memorial Service," *New Yorker,* 30 December 1967

To be a true reformer is to take obstacles in stride, hence many abolitionists found comfort in the belief that the Dred Scott decision was so monstrous as to boomerang against slavery, making for the ultimate downfall.

BENJAMIN QUARLES, *Black Abolitionists,* 1969

Of my two "handicaps," being female put many more obstacles in my path than being Black.

SHIRLEY CHISHOLM, *Unbought and Unbossed,* 1970

Walls go . . . back in history. . . . There is the wall of love that Romeo climbed to Juliet, and there is the

Wailing Wall in Jerusalem. But did God ever build a wall?

DUKE ELLINGTON, *Music Is My Mistress,* 1973

The school, for a great many Black teenagers, is just another obstacle that society has put in their way.

JOHN CONYERS, "The Politics of Unemployment: Lost—Another Generation of Black Youth," *Freedomways,* Third Quarter, 1975

[C]olorism, like colonialism, sexism, and racism, impedes us.

ALICE WALKER, *In Search of Our Mothers' Gardens,* 1983

We've broken barriers, we've climbed mountains, and Black America would not be Black America without *Ebony* and *Jet.*

JOHN H. JOHNSON, in "Interview: John H. Johnson," *Crisis,* January 1987

There may be obstacles, but keep going because the struggle is continuous.

RACHEL ROBINSON, in *Ebony,* May 1987

Whatever reason you have for not being *somebody,* there's somebody who had that same problem and overcame it.

BARBARA REYNOLDS, 1988

You can overcome any obstacle in this country. It may be a little harder for you than someone else. Like when Jackie Robinson got into baseball, he couldn't just be an average second baseman, 'cause there were plenty of them around. He had to be better than what was already there.

RAY CHARLES, in "Ray Charles Sees the Beauty," *Parade,* 10 October 1988

OPPONENT

You must be willing to suffer the anger of the opponent and yet not return anger. No matter how emotional your opponents are, you must remain calm.

MARTIN LUTHER KING, JR., *Stride Toward Freedom,* 1958

Negotiation means getting the best of your opponent.

MARVIN GAYE, in Ritz, *Divided Soul,* 1985

Being black in America is often like playing your home games on the opponent's court.

JAMES P. COMER, c. 1990

OPPORTUNITY

The opportunity that God sends doesn't wake up the sleeping.

SENEGAL

Let our opportunities overshadow our grievances.

BOOKER T. WASHINGTON, speech given at Atlanta Exposition, Atlanta, Georgia, 1895

The opportunity to earn a dollar is worth infinitely more than the opportunity to spend a dollar in an opera house.

BOOKER T. WASHINGTON, *Up From Slavery,* 1901

As the world is at present, the United States with all its limitations offers the millions of Negroes within its borders greater opportunity than any other land.

JAMES WELDON JOHNSON, *Black Manhattan,* 1930

Take advantage of every opportunity; where there is none, make it for yourself, and let history record that as we toiled laboriously and courageously, we worked to live gloriously.

MARCUS GARVEY, in *Garvey and Garveyism,* 1963

[L]et us move on in these powerful days, these days of challenge to make America what it ought to be. We have an opportunity to make America a better nation.

MARTIN LUTHER KING, JR., "I Have Been to the Mountaintop," speech given in Memphis, Tennessee, 3 April 1968

Just when the pendulum seemed to be clearly within his grasp, the Black man jumped and missed and the pendulum began to swing back the other way. To add insult to injury, each time the pendulum completed its swing, it picked up another rider—the Irishman, the Italian, the Jew—still the Black man could not climb on board.

DICK GREGORY, *No More Lies,* 1971

Every intersection in the road of life is an opportunity to make a decision, and at some time I had only to listen.

DUKE ELLINGTON, *Music Is My Mistress,* 1973

You have greater opportunities than my generation had, but the demands are greater as well.

COLEMAN YOUNG, in *Ebony,* April 1981

Wherever I have knocked, a door has opened. Wherever I have wandered, a path has appeared. I have been helped, supported, encouraged, and nurtured by people of all races, creeds, colors, and dreams.

ALICE WALKER, *In Search of Our Mothers' Gardens,* 1983

Civil Rights opened the windows. When you open the windows, it does not mean that everybody will get through. There are people of my generation who didn't get through. We must create our own opportunities.

MARY FRANCES BERRY, in *USA Today,* 1 June 1984

To think that the doors of opportunity will fly open out of a sense of good will and brotherhood is naive.

PARREN MITCHELL, in "Interview," *Crisis,* February 1986

Opportunities are there, but we can't start out as vice-president. Even if we landed such a position, it wouldn't do us any good because we wouldn't know how to do our work. It's better to start where we fit in, then work our way up.

BENJAMIN CARSON, *Gifted Hands,* 1990

OPPRESSION

Cock roach nebber in de right befo' fowl. (The oppressor always justifies his oppression of the weak.)

JAMAICA

For as we are an oppressed people wishing to be free, we must evidently follow the examples of the oppressed nations that have preceded us; for history informs us that liberties of an oppressed people are obtained only in proportion to their own exertions in their own cause. Therefore, in accordance with this truth, let us come up, and like the oppressed people of England, Scotland, and Ireland, band ourselves together and wage increasing war against the high-handed wrongs of the hideous monster Tyranny.

STATE CONVENTION OF COLORED CITIZENS, Michigan, 1843

Whenever and wherever men have been oppressed and enslaved, their oppressors and enslavers have, in every instance, found a warrant in the character of the victim.

FREDERICK DOUGLASS, "The Proclamation and a Negro Army," speech given in New York City, 6 February 1863

Only base men and oppressors can rejoice in a triumph of injustice over the weak and defenseless, for weakness ought itself to protect from assaults of pride, prejudice, and power.

FREDERICK DOUGLASS, *Life and Times of Frederick Douglass,* 1882

I can take no part in oppressing or persecuting any variety of the human family. Whether in Russia, Germany, or California, my sympathy is with the oppressed, be he Chinese or Hebrew.

Ibid.

Oppression does not always crush the spirit of progress. Men will achieve in spite of it.

CARTER G. WOODSON, *Negro Makers of History,* 1928

All oppressed people must assume the responsibility and take the initiative to free themselves. Jews must wage their battle to abolish anti-Semitism, Catholics must battle to abolish anti-Catholicism. The workers must wage their battle to advance and protect their interests and rights.

A. PHILIP RANDOLPH, speech given at March on Washington Movement, Detroit, Michigan, 26 September 1946

We are all brothers of oppressions and today brothers of oppression are identified with each other all over the world.

MALCOLM X, 1964

When an oppressed people show a willingness to defend themselves, the enemy, who is a moral weakling and coward, is more willing to grant concessions and work for a respectable compromise.

ROBERT WILLIAMS, "USA, The Potential of a Minority Revolution," *The Crusader Monthly Newsletter,* May–June 1965

When I turn on my radio, when I hear that Negroes have been lynched in America, I say that we have been lied to: Hitler is not dead; when I turn on my radio, when I learn that Jews have been insulted, mistreated, persecuted, I say that we have been lied to: Hitler is not dead; when, finally, I turn on my radio and hear that in Africa forced labor has been inaugurated and legalized, I say that we have certainly been lied to: Hitler is not dead.

AIMÉ CÉSAIRE, in Fanon, *Black Skin, White Masks,* 1967

Black power is part of the world rebellion of the oppressed against the oppressor, of the exploited against the exploiter.

KWAME NKRUMAH, *The Spectre of Black Power,* 1968

We are a colonized nation, albeit "the fanciest of all oppressed people."

MARI EVANS, in *Negro Digest,* May 1968

The effects of more than three centuries of oppression cannot be obliterated by doing business as usual.

WHITNEY YOUNG, in *Parks and Recreation,* April 1969

Whenever the oppressed, for whatever reason, begin to feel too weak to fight their real enemy, the oppressor himself, they turn upon themselves, squabbling over this or that theory while leaving the oppressor free to do anything he chooses.

NATHAN HARE, in *Black Scholar,* November 1969

In any enslaved people ignorance is a prerequisite for their oppression.

ARTHUR LITTLETON, *Black Viewpoints,* 1971

I have a daughter/ mozambique/ i have a son/
angola our twins/ salvador and johannesburg/
cannot speak the same language/ but we fight the
same old man/ in the new world.

NTOZAKE SHANGE, *From Okra to Greens,* 1979

Oppression places identifiable constrictions on the natural rhythm of man.

ALFRED PASTER, *The Roots of Soul,* 1982

In a society where you have the oppressed and the oppressor, . . . the oppression is primarily directed toward the male.

ALVIN POUSSAINT, in "The Black Man in Jeopardy," *Crisis,* March 1986

African people here created an antithesis of hope and possibility that gave birth to a synthesis of freedom and liberation out of a thesis of oppression.

CLARENCE GLOVER, in "Spirituality: An African View," *Essence,* December 1987

The greatest weapon that the oppressor has in his hand is the mind of the oppressed.

Ibid.

Mentally ill people, persons who do not respect themselves and have self/group-negating patterns of logic, thought, speech, action, emotional response and perceptions, never can liberate themselves from their oppressors.

FRANCES CRESS WELSING, *The Isis Papers,* 1990

ORGANIZATION

Organization is a sacrifice. It is sacrifice of time, of work and money, but it is after all the cheapest way of buying the most priceless of gifts, freedom and efficiency.

W. E. B. DU BOIS, 1915

If we must have justice, we must be strong; if we must be strong, we must come together; if we must come together, we can only do so through the system of organization.

MARCUS GARVEY, *Philosophy and Opinions of Marcus Garvey,* 1923

Organize yourself inside. Teach your children the internals and the externals, rather than just the externals of clothing and money.

NANNIE BURROUGHS, "Unload Your Uncle Toms," *Louisiana Weekly,* 23 December 1933

Organize as a group . . . those who realized the strength of their cultural group, their political demands were considered and determined by the force of their cultural grouping.

CLAUDE MCKAY, *Harlem, Black Metropolis,* 1940

No organization can do everything. Every organization can do something, and each organization is charged with the social responsibility to do that which it can, it is built to do.

A. PHILIP RANDOLPH, speech given at March on Washington Movement, Detroit, Michigan, 26 September 1942

In a multiracial society no group can make it alone. Organized strength will be effective only when it is consolidated through constructive alliances with the majority group.

MARTIN LUTHER KING, JR., c. 1965

Walking downtown saying that we protest means nothing if you are not organized.

MALCOLM X, in *Malcolm X Speaks,* 1965

ORIGINALITY

Originality is the essence of true scholarship. Creativity is the soul of the true scholar.

NNAMDI AZIKIWE, speech given in Lagos, Nigeria, 11 November 1934

He who must do/ Something altogether new/ Let him swallow his own head.

O. J. CHINWEIZU, "Originality," in *Voices From Twentieth-Century Africa,* 1988

PAIN

If I am losing my capacity for shock absorbing, if privation is beginning to terrify me, you will appreciate the situation and see that it isn't cowardice but that being pounded so often on the anvil of life I am growing less resilient.

ZORA NEALE HURSTON, letter to Annie Nathan Meyer, 17 October 1925

The pain of life may teach us to understand life and in our understanding of life, to love life.

HOWARD THURMAN, *Meditations of the Heart,* 1953

It is the lingering pain of a past insult that rankles and hurts me more than the insult itself.

EZEKIEL MPHAHLELE, *Down Second Avenue,* 1959

There is no pain equal to that of being forced to think.

FRANK YERBY, c. 1960

[W]here there is no experience of pain, there can be no suffering.

HOWARD THURMAN, *Disciplines of the Spirit,* 1963

The hurt was in the soul of a man who asks nothing but to look for meaning to his life.

RENE MARQUES, "A Body Abaft," *Latin American Tales,* 1977

An aspirin can cure a headache for an hour or two, but if the pain's really deep, nothing short of brain surgery is going to make it go away.

RAY CHARLES, *Brother Ray,* 1978

Have you ever been hurt and the place tries to heal a bit, and you just pull the scar off of it over and over again.

ROSA PARKS, 1980

Maybe to grow you have to hurt somebody.

JOHN MCCLUSKEY, JR., "And Called Every Generation Blessed," in Evans, ed., *Black Women Writers,* 1984

Pain is another word for fear. True believers have no fear.

MARVIN GAYE, in Ritz, *Divided Soul,* 1985

My life has been painful. And this body of mine has had all that it could do to survive the pressure it has been subjected to. But from it all I've won to a certain extent spiritual clarity which is still many spaces ahead of my ability to express it. One illusion after another has fallen off. God after God has died. But, unlike the generation which preceded me, in loosing these I have built up an edifice on which reverence and mystery may still find their altar. I kneel and pray before new gods come into a godless age.

JEAN TOOMER, in Kerman and Eldridge, *The Lives of Jean Toomer,* 1987

It's the little hurts that build up.

ISHMAEL REED, in "Maligning of the Male," *Life,* Spring 1988

I can't remember ever feeling such a desperate loss before. The pain hurt so deeply it seemed as if everybody in the world that I loved had died at one time.

BENJAMIN CARSON, *Gifted Hands,* 1990

Besides learning to withstand physical hardships, I had become hardened to personal abuse. When people hurt me, either by ignoring me or outright maltreatment, I gave no indication that I had been hurt, and an impassive look in response to insult became one of my useful strategies.

BENJAMIN DAVIS, JR., *Benjamin Davis, Jr.: An Autobiography,* 1991

Pain never goes away. We even tend to wallow in it. We're slightly masochistic. . . . We were never taught to feel it, identify it, and step out of it . . . release it and keep going.

BEN VEREEN, "Dealing with Adversities," *Body Mind Spirit,* Summer 1991

PARENT

If you are parents of worth and wisdom, train your children so they will be pleasing to God. And if they do what is right, following your example, and handle your affairs as they should, do for them all that is good.

PTAH HOTEP, c. 2340 B.C.

Pumpkin neba bear watermelon. (Children resemble parents.)

WEST INDIES

A school system without parents at its foundation is just like a bucket with a hole in it.

JESSE JACKSON, 1982

Our parents seemed to know that an extreme negative emotion held against other human beings for reasons they do not control can be blinding.

ALICE WALKER, *In Search of Our Mothers' Gardens,* 1983

There is no such thing as a parental aide to teachers. The teacher is an aide to the parents. It's the parents who rear the children.

JESSE JACKSON, 1984

As parents and role models . . . we must treat our children as potential academic superstars; they will not disappoint us.

CHRISTOPHER EDGE, in *Ebony,* August 1986

Part of our responsibility as parents, as adults, is to set examples for children. But we have to like children in order to be really happy fulfilled adults.

BOBBY MCFERRIN, 1988

Parenthood was always a very expensive affair. But it seems that now there is no man or woman created in nature who is endowed with enough powers to be a mother or a father.

AMA ATA AIDOO, "Anowa," in Chinweizu, ed., *Voices from Twentieth-Century Africa,* 1988

I didn't grow up in one of those families where people sat around and read the *Wall Street Journal.* My parents worked in Detroit public schools and were educated in the South and the church. It was quite an awakening when I entered Harvard Business School and found I was competing against people who grew up with that kind of business experience.

MARILYN DAVIS, in *Essence,* March 1989

You are the product of the love and affection of your parents, and throughout your life you have drawn strength and hope from that love and security.

NELSON MANDELA, *Higher Than Hope,* 1991

PASSION

Even the gods forget virtue when their passions are fully awake. But they are not to be blamed for this any more than fire when it burns.

JAYADEVA, *The Song of the Goatherd,* c. 1175 A.D.

Who is the more in fault in an erring passion, she who falls through entreaty, or he who entreats her to fall?

JUANA DE LA CRUZ, "Roundels," 1670

Human passion is the hallucination of a distempered mind.

WILLIAM WHIPPER, "An Address on Non-resistance to Offensive Aggression," *The Colored American,* 16 September 1837

Close by . . . there were two oranges: one was ripe, the other so beautiful it made one happy. I gave the ripe fruit to the Cherished One and the one-so-beautiful-as-to-bring happiness to the Beloved. But I cherish the one and truly love the other in vain. If either had a passion to subdue me, I would not know what to do.

JEAN-JOSEPH RABÉARIVELO, "XVIII" *Old Songs of Imerina Land,* 1939

In every desire, in every appetite we have there is a huge quantity of energy, passion and fire. And how great is this energy and fire when the soul surrenders entirely to wanting one thing only, loving one thing only?

ERNESTO CARDENAL, "Love," *Vida en al Amor,* 1974

To experience the passion of hatred is to know the force of love.

ALFRED PASTER, *The Roots of Soul,* 1982

Passions are dangerous. They cause you to lust after other men's wives.

MARVIN GAYE, 1983

PAST

We have to do with the past only as we can make it useful to the present and to the future.

FREDERICK DOUGLASS, "What to the Slave is the Fourth of July?" speech given at Corinthian Hall, Rochester, New York, 5 July 1852

We must remember his past in order to make his future.

ARTHUR A. SCHOMBURG, in *Racial Integrity,* July 1913

[T]he present was an egg laid by the past that had the future inside its shell.

ZORA NEALE HURSTON, *Moses, Man of the Mountain,* 1939

That past is . . . still quite near: it was only yesterday. But the world rolls on, the world changes, my own world perhaps more rapidly than anyone else's; so that it appears as if we are ceasing to be what we were, and that truly we are no longer what we were.

CAMARA LAYE, *The Dark Child,* 1954

The past is all that makes the present coherent, the past will remain horrible for exactly as long as we refuse to assess it honestly.

JAMES BALDWIN, *Notes of a Native Son,* 1955

To accept one's past—one's history—is not the same thing as drowning in it; it is learning how to use it. An invented past can never be used; it cracks and crumbles under the pressures of life like clay in a season of drought.

JAMES BALDWIN, *The Fire Next Time,* 1961

I no longer need the past to stand up in the present.

EDOUARD MAUNICK, "Seven Sides and Seven Syllables," *Carousels of the Sea,* 1964

[A]lmost anyone else can come into this country and get around barriers and obstacles that we cannot get around; and the only difference between them and us, they know something about the past, and in knowing something about the past, they know something about themselves, they have an identity.

MALCOLM X, speech given at the Organization for Afro-American Unity Rally, Audubon Ballroom, New York City, 24 January 1965

This fugitive return into the recent past tempered the exile, softened for a while the tenacious nostalgia, and brought back the bright and hot hours which one only learns to appreciate once one is far away.

BIRAGO DIOP, "The Stories Which Cradled My Youth," *Tales of Amadou Koumba,* 1966

We cannot remain in the past for we have too much at stake in the present, our future, much too much rewarding to be rejected.

RON KARENGA, in "Ron Karenga and Black Cultural Nationalism," *Negro Digest,* January 1968

They call me from their tombs and thrones;/ From many distant climes;/ They whisper old and sacred names:/ Each intonation chimes/ An ancient and familiar rite. . . .

MARGARET WALKER, "How Many Silent Centuries Sleep in My Sultry Veins," *Prophets for a New Day,* 1970

In the West the past is like a dead animal. It is a carcass picked at by the flies that call themselves historians and biographers. But in my culture the past lives.

MIRIAM MAKEBA, *My Story,* 1987

Walking into Forsyth County was a return to the past, to a time older people thought was behind them and younger people had never known.

JAMES WILLIAMS, "The Road to Cumming," *Crisis*, March 1987

These glorious names from the past cement our unity today. These links with legend lend present fame a lustre that extends to the clan, the tribe as a whole. There are still praise-singers to single out deeds and facts to feed our pride. A people needs these . . . stamps of approval.

SEMBANE OUSMANE, "The Last of the Empire," in Chinweizu, ed., *Voices From Twentieth-Century Africa*, 1988

Instead of always looking at the past, I put myself ahead twenty years and try to look at what I need to do now in order to get there then.

DIANA ROSS, in "Diana Ross: Down-to-Earth," *Essence*, October 1989

PATIENCE

One endures with patience the pain in the other fellow's stomach.

JOAQUIM MACHADO DE ASSIS, *Epitaph for a Small Winner*, 1881

I believe in Patience—patience with the weakness of the Weak and the strength of the Strong, the prejudice of the Ignorant and the ignorance of the Blind; patience with the tardy triumph of Joy and the mad chastening of Sorrow; patience with God.

W. E. B. DU BOIS, *Darkwater*, 1920

The eye that looks downward will certainly see the nose. The hand that dips into the bottom of the pot will eat the biggest snail. The sky grows no grass but if the earth calls her barren it will drink no more milk. The foot of the snake is not split in two like a man's or in hundreds like a centipede, but if Agere could dance patiently like the snake he will uncoil the chain that leads into the dead.

WOLE SOYINKA, *A Dance of the Forest*, 1963

PAY

What goes around comes around.

TRADITIONAL

Men may not get all they pay for in this world, but they certainly pay for all they get. If we get free from the oppression and wrongs heaped upon us, we must pay for their removal. We must do that by labor, suffering, by sacrifice, and if needs be, by our Lives and the Lives of others.

FREDERICK DOUGLASS, 1857

Our crown has been bought and paid for, all we have to do is wear it.

JAMES BALDWIN, c. 1961

People pay for what they do, and still more for what they have allowed themselves to become. And they pay for it very simply: by the lives they lead.

JAMES BALDWIN, *Nobody Knows My Name*, 1961

This country would go bankrupt in a day if the Supreme Court suddenly ordained the powers that be to pay back wages to children of slaves and to women who have worked all their lives for half pay or no pay.

ELEANOR HOLMES NORTON, in the *New York Post*, 25 March 1970

Ask for what you want and be prepared to pay for what you get.

MAYA ANGELOU, *The Heart of a Woman*, 1981

I danced, I paid the piper and left him a big fat tip.

JOE LOUIS, *My Life*, 1981

We must pay our debts to the past by putting the future in debt to ourselves.

ALICE WALKER, *In Search of Our Mothers' Gardens*, 1983

PEACE

Peace is costly, but it's worth the expense.

BAGUIRMI

A loose tooth will not rest until it's pulled out.

CONGO

I don't want to run over the mountains anymore; I want to make a big treaty . . . God made the white man and God made the Apache, and the Apache has just as much right to the country as the white man. I want to make a treaty that will last, so that both can travel over the country and have no trouble.

DELSHAY OF THE TONTO APACHES, in a report to the U.S. Secretary of the Interior, 1871

Peace is better than war, but some people will not solve their problems any other way.

CARTER G. WOODSON, *Negro Makers of History,* 1928

Public peace is the act of public trust, it is the faith that all are secure and will remain secure.

RICHARD WRIGHT, *Native Son,* 1940

Peace is the highest patriotism. Peace is our most sacred responsibility.

PAUL ROBESON, in *Freedom,* January 1953

True peace is not merely the absence of tension; it is the presence of justice.

MARTIN LUTHER KING, JR., *Stride Toward Freedom,* 1958

If there is to be peace on earth and good will toward man we must finally believe in the ultimate morality of the universe and believe that all reality hinges on moral foundations.

MARTIN LUTHER KING, JR., c. 1961

The only road to world peace and to a climate of respect for nature is to render the concept of killing irrelevant. A peaceful world order cannot exist where any form of killing is allowed or justified.

DICK GREGORY, 1969

We never did the white man any harm; we don't intend to . . . The buffalo are diminishing fast. The antelope, that were plenty a few years ago, they are now thin. When they shall all die we shall be hungry; we shall want something to eat, and we will be compelled to come into the fort. Your young men must not fire at us; whenever they see us they fire, and we fire on them.

TANKASHASKA (TALL BULL), in Brown, *Bury My Heart at Wounded Knee,* 1971

There can be no peace without justice, and justice without love is brutality. Love without justice is weak sentimentality.

OTIS MOSS, JR., "Going from Disgrace to Dignity," in Philpot, ed., *Best Black Sermons,* 1972

Peace of the world depends upon a pluralistic, egalitarian society throughout the world. In this process no group need be despised by the opposition or the means of developing and maintaining pride in its cultural heritage.

ROY WILKINS, 1975

We defeat oppression with liberty. We cure indifference with compassion. We remedy social injustices with justice. And if our journey embodies these lasting principles, we find peace.

PATRICIA ROBERTS HARRIS, 1985

PEOPLE

Treat all people as though they were related to you.

NAVAJO

The people of the United States are the boldest in their pretensions to freedom, and the loudest in their profession of love of liberty, yet no nation upon the face of the globe can exhibit a statute book so full of all that is cruel, malicious, and infernal as the American code of laws.

FREDERICK DOUGLASS, "What to the Slave is the Fourth of July?," speech given at Corinthian Hall, Rochester, New York, 5 July 1852

These are my people, I have built for them/ A castle in the cloister of my heart . . .

FENTON JOHNSON, "These Are My People," *A Little Dreaming,* 1914

For my people thronging 47th Street in Chicago and Lenox/ Avenue in New York and Rampart Street in New/ Orleans, lost disinherited dispossessed and happy/ people filling the cabarets and taverns and other/ people's pockets . . .

MARGARET WALKER, "For My People," *For My People,* 1942

People do not wish to be worse, they really wish to become better, but they often do not know how.

JAMES BALDWIN, c. 1965

PERFORMANCE

Going on stage to sing is like stepping into a perfect world. The past means nothing. Worries about the future do not exist. All that matters is the music. . . . This is the one place where I am most at home, where there is no exile.

MIRIAM MAKEBA, *My Story,* 1987

It used to be going up on stage was survival; I had no other world.

SAMMY DAVIS, JR., in *USA Weekend,* 2 March 1989

PERSISTENCE/PERSEVERANCE

Rain beats a leopard's skin, but it does not wash out the spots.

ASHANTI

What can't be cured must be endured.

IGNATIUS SANCHO, letter to Mrs. M, 16 September 1777

Keep on moving, keep on insisting, keep on fighting injustice.

MARY CHURCH TERRELL, in *Journal of Negro History,* January 1938

Every step toward the goal of justice requires sacrifice, suffering, and struggle; the tireless exertion and passionate concerns of dedicated individuals. Without persistent effort, time becomes an ally of the insurgent and primitive forces of irrational emotionalism and social destruction.

MARTIN LUTHER KING, JR., *Stride Toward Freedom,* 1958

[P]ersistence and a positive attitude are necessary ingredients for any successful venture.

L. DOUGLASS WILDER, in "Virginia's Lieutenant Governor," *Ebony,* April 1986

PHILOSOPHY

Philosophy is best practiced by the easy and affluent.

IGNATIUS SANCHO, letter to Mrs. L, 16 October 1775

It is a narrow and perverted philosophy which condemns as a nuisance, agitators.

T. THOMAS FORTUNE, speech given to the Afro-American League, Chicago, Illinois, January 1890

He was something of a philosopher. He had long ago had the conclusion forced upon him that an educated man of his race, in order to live comfortably in the United States, must either be a philosopher or a fool; and since he wished to be happy, and was not exactly a fool, he had cultivated philosophy.

CHARLES W. CHESTNUTT, *The Marrow of Tradition,* 1901

The political philosophy of black nationalism means: we must control the politics and the politicians of our community. They must no longer take orders from outside forces. We will organize, and sweep out of office all Negro politicians who are puppets for the outside forces.

MALCOLM X, "A Declaration of Independence," speech given 12 March 1964

We must exchange the philosophy of excuse—what I am is beyond my control for the philosophy of responsibility. We should tell the citizens that a man of liberty does not burn down the neighborhood store, then beg for his supper. We should tell him that a citizen of dignity does not wait for the world to give him anything.

BARBARA JORDAN, speech given to the Black National Bar Association, 1967

Do unto others. Be fair. It pays, not only as a moral imperative, [but as] common sense.

HAROLD WASHINGTON, in "Mayor Washington Eulogized as Symbol of Hope for Blacks," *Jet,* 14 December 1987

My philosophy has always been to get a little bit today and come back to get the rest tomorrow.

L. DOUGLASS WILDER, in "L. Douglas Wilder Makes History," *Crisis,* January 1990

Philosophy is about the asking of questions.

CHARLES JOHNSON, "Interview with Charles Johnson," *The World and I,* 1991

PIONEER

See also BALDWIN, KING, MALCOLM X, LEADER, HURSTON

Carter G. Woodson was always the lone pioneer and remained [so] until his death.

W. E. B. DU BOIS, c. 1953

Pioneers are special people. "First" is always difficult. We don't know that things can be done, that dreams can be fulfilled, that great accomplishments can be realized until somebody takes that first step.

GERALDINE NECKIMAN, c. 1973

Ralph Bunche gave Black youths new pride and, as a result of his extraordinary diplomatic statesmanship, settled the Israeli-Arab crisis in 1967 and became the first Black American recipient of the Nobel Peace Prize.

LEON SULLIVAN, "The Dream of the Future," *Negro History Bulletin,* March 1983

Baldwin went into that forbidden territory and decolonized it, robbed it of the jewel of naivete and ungated it for Black people so that in your wake we would enter it, occupy it, restructure it in order to accommodate our complicated passion and not our vanities, but our intricate, difficult demand, our tragic insistent knowledge, our livid reality, our classical imagination.

TONI MORRISON, "Goodbye James Baldwin," *Crisis,* January 1988

I'm happy to be a pioneer. When I say, "Don't think of me as Black or white," all I'm saying is, view me as person. I know my race.

MICHAEL JORDAN, in "Michael Jordan in His Own Orbit," *GQ,* March 1989

PLACE

There is a place in God's sun for the youth "farthest down" who has the vision, the determination, and the courage to reach it.

MARY MCLEOD BETHUNE, c. 1935

You don't want to stand on a corner and be told to get off it when you got nowhere else to go. And we want somewhere else to go.

ARNA BONTEMPS, *Anyplace But Here,* 1966

A place where I can find out again—where I am—and what I must do. A place where I can stop and do nothing in order to start again.

JAMES BALDWIN, *Istanbul,* 1970

There are roads out of the secret place within us along which we must all move as we go to touch others.

ROMARE BEARDEN, 1975

[T]o stay willingly in a beloved but brutal place is to risk losing the love and being forced to acknowledge only the brutality.

ALICE WALKER, *In Search of Our Mothers' Gardens,* 1983

To get to a place where you could love anything you chose, not to need permission for desire, that was freedom.

TONI MORRISON, *Beloved,* 1987

I can put myself into another person's place just by thinking about it.

OPRAH WINFREY, in *Ladies' Home Journal,* December 1988

Know your place, but let no one tell you what your place is.

JANICE HALE BENSON, speech given at African-American Child Conference, Detroit, Michigan, January 1989

PLAN

Strategic planning for the future is the most hopeful indication of our increasing social intelligence.

WILLIAM HASTIE, *Afro-American,* 1945

Make your plans big enough to include God and large enough to include eternity.

MARTIN LUTHER KING, JR., c. 1963

It's the plan, not the man.

SLOGAN OF CONGRESSIONAL BLACK CAUCUS, c. 1970

PLEASE

The new pleases and the old satisfies.

GHANA

You can't please everybody if you are going to make a difference in this world.

MELVIN CHAPMAN, speech at Miller Junior High, Detroit, Michigan, 1962

The Lord Himself could not please everyone; and some of those He displeased nailed Him to a cross.

ROBERT E. FARMER, in Hughes, ed., *Book of Negro Humor,* 1966

Most people are so hard to please that if they met God, they'd probably say yes, she's great, but . . .

DIANA ROSS, in "Diana Ross: Down-to-Earth," *Essence,* May 1989

POET/POETRY

O Black and unknown bards of long ago,/ How came your lips to touch the sacred fire?

JAMES WELDON JOHNSON, "O Black and Unknown Bards," *St. Peter Relates an Incident,* 1917

Poetry is religion brought down to earth and it is of the essence of the Negro soul.

ALBERT BARNES, "Negro Art and America," in Locke, ed., *The New Negro,* 1925

My poems are indelicate. But so is life.

LANGSTON HUGHES, in the *Pittsburgh Courier,* 1927

Poets may dream, but dreams are ferment of the stuff of experience.

CLAUDE MCKAY, "A Negro Writer Responds to His Critics," *New York Herald Tribune,* 6 March 1932

Paul Laurence Dunbar soared above race and touched the heart universal. He came on the scene at a time when America was being launched on the machine age and when the country was beset with problems. In a world of discord, he dared to sing his songs about nights bright with stars, about the secret of the wind and the sea, and the answer one finds beyond the years. Above the dross and strife of the day, he asserted the right to live and love and be happy. That is why he was so greatly loved and why he will never grow old.

BENJAMIN BRAWLEY, *Paul Laurence Dunbar,* 1936

Out of the sky, the birds, the parrots, the bells, silk, cloth, and drums, out of a touch of drunkenness and wild endearments, out of copper clanging and mother of pearl, out of Sundays dancing, children's words and love words, out of love for the little fists of children, I will build a world, my world with round shoulders.

AIMÉ CÉSAIRE, *Miraculous Weapons,* 1946

Poetry is music made less abstract.

IMAMU AMIRI BARAKA, in Gayle, ed., *The Black Aesthetic,* 1971

Black poetry is becoming what it has always been but has not quite been.

CAROLYN RODGERS, in *ibid.*

[A]ll Black poems ain't the same, certain poets hip you to something, pulls the covers off of something or run it down to you, or ask you to just dig it—your coat being pulled, every poet has written a being poem. Just writing the way they be, they lovers be, the world be. We do not want subhumans defining what we be doing.

Ibid.

A poem only lives when it has a soul to reside in.

JULIUS LESTER, introduction to Jordan, *Some Changes,* 1971

The poetry of a people comes from the deep recesses of the unconscious, the irrational and the collective body of our ancestral memories.

MARGARET WALKER, in *Black World,* December 1971

So much is involved in the writing of poetry—and sometimes, although I don't like suggesting it is a magic process, it seems you really do have to go into a bit of a trance, self-cast trance, because "brain-work" seems unable to do it all, to do the whole job. The self-cast trance is possible when you are *importantly* excited about an idea, surmise, or emotion.

GWENDOLYN BROOKS, *Report From Part One,* 1972

One virtue of poetry is that it makes us more alive. . . .

DUDLEY RANDALL, in *Black Poetry Writing,* 1975

The function of the poet is to write poetry.

Ibid.

Black poetry is like a razor; it's sharp and will cut deep.

HAKI MADHUBUTI, in *ibid.*

Poetry at its most expressive can be a prayer, an appeal, condemnation, encouragement, affirmation, the list is endless. And if it is authentic, as anything else expressive of a people's spirit it is always social.

KEORAPETSE KGOSITSILE, in *ibid.*

Poets sign their own signatures on the world.

HAKI MADHUBUTI, in i*bid.*

Poetry is a friend to whom you can say too much.

GWENDOLYN BROOKS, in *ibid.*

The Black artist. The Black man. The holy man. The man you seek. The climber, the striver. The maker of peace. The lover. The warrior. We are they whom you seek. Look in. Find yourself. Find the being, the speaker.

IMAMU AMIRI BARAKA, c. 1976

Poetry is applied science;/ Rewrapped corner rap . . .

EUGENE REDMOND, "Parapoetics," *Drumvoice,* 1976

A Black poet is a preacher.

HENRY DUMAS, in *ibid.*

Are you a poet first and then Black; or are you Black first and then a poet?

MELVIN TOLSON, in *ibid.*

Poetry's best measured by the depth and lucidity of its artistic perceptions, by the bold and subtle light it throws and engenders upon the ever upward spiraling struggles of humanity to shake off all oppressive shackles.

ANTON MBERI, in Paster, *The Roots of Soul,* 1982

One wants to write poetry that is understood by one's people, not by the Queen of England.

ALICE WALKER, *In Search of Our Mothers' Gardens,* 1983

Fill you up with something/ would make you swoon, stop in your tracks/ change your mind or make it up/ a poem should happen to you like/ cold water or a kiss.

NTOZAKE SHANGE, c. 1984

[P]oetry is *subconscious conversation,* it is as much the work of those who understand it and those who make it.

SONIA SANCHEZ, "Ruminations/Reflections," in Evans, ed., *Black Women Writers,* 1984

The ax I have to grind is the ax of the poet. You tell the truth as you see it. The reality is in the songs.

OSCAR BROWN, JR., in *Jet,* 27 May 1988

POINT

A sword does not pierce well with many points; it needs a single stabbing point.

HERMAN WATTS, "What Is Your Name?" in Philpot, ed., *Best Black Sermons,* 1972

POINT OF VIEW

Finger nebber say, "look here," him say "look dere." (People always point out the shortcomings of others but never their own.)

JAMAICA

If you knew the state of the ant under my foot,/It is like my condition under the foot of an elephant.

The Gulistan of Sadi, 1184–1292

To the man in the tower the world below is likely to look very small.

BOOKER T. WASHINGTON, *The Man Farthest Down,* 1912

History is too often what we want it to be and what we are determined men shall believe rather than a grim record of what has taken place in the past.

W. E. B. DU BOIS, *The World and Africa,* 1947

Some times before I didn't know when, my mind had rejected all reality as I had known it and I had begun to see the world as a cesspool of buffoonery.

CHESTER HIMES, c. 1964

When blacks are unemployed, they are considered lazy and apathetic. When whites are unemployed, it's considered a depression.

JESSE JACKSON, in *Time,* 6 April 1970

In the South the Black man was abused physically, in the North he was abused mentally. The enemy in the South was a man, in the North the enemy was a system.

DICK GREGORY, *No More Lies,* 1971

I'm the first, second and third person my own damn self. And I will intrude, protrude, obtrude or exclude my point of view any time it suits my disposition.

JOHN KILLENS, foreword to "The Cotillion," in Chapman, ed., *New Black Voices,* 1972

What you know is merely a point of departure. So let's move.

KEORAPETSE KGOSITSILE, in *Black Poetry Writing,* 1975

POLITICS

He sits on both sides of the fence and in the middle.

TRADITIONAL

Effective horsemanship is accomplished by straddling.

KELLY MILLER, "Come Let Us Reason Together," *The Voice of the American Negro,* January 1906

A conservative is satisfied with existing conditions and advocates their continuance while a "radical" clamors for amelioration of conditions through change.

KELLY MILLER, *The American Negro,* 1908

May God write us down as asses if ever again we are found putting our trust in either the Republican or the Democratic parties.

W. E. B. DU BOIS, "Education," *Crisis,* 1922

The trading of permission, license, monopoly, and immunity in return for money was engineered by politicians; and through their hands the pay went to voters for votes. Sometimes the pay was in cash, sometime in jobs, sometimes influence, sometimes in better streets, houses, or schools.

W. E. B DU BOIS, *Dark Princess,* 1928

A political party is a government of the government. It is an agency set up to get control of the government.

CARTER G. WOODSON, *Negro Makers of History,* 1928

They have sold us for a mess of pottage. We got the mess, but not the pottage.

NANNIE BURROUGHS, "Unload Your Uncle Toms," *Louisiana Weekly,* 23 December 1933

In politics, as in other things, there is no such thing as one getting something for nothing. The payoff may involve compromises that may strike at the ideals and principles one has held dear all his life.

A. PHILIP RANDOLPH, "Why I Can't Run for Congress on the Old Party Ticket," speech given 28 April 1944

Whether elected or appointed, public officials serve those who put and keep them in office. We cannot depend upon them to fight our battles.

CHARLES HAMILTON HOUSTON, c. 1945

In politics all abstract words conceal treachery.

C. L. R. JAMES, *The Black Jacobins,* 1963

No people ever became great and prosperous by devoting their infant energies to politics. We were literally born into political responsibility before we had mastered the economic conditions which underlie these duties.

T. THOMAS FORTUNE, in Meier, *Negro Thought in America,* 1964

Politics is class struggle.

KWAME NKRUMAH, *Dark Days in Ghana,* 1968

What we need is more women in politics . . . and not just to stuff envelopes, but to run for office. It is women who can bring empathy, tolerance, insight, patience, and persistence to government—the qualities we naturally have or have had to develop because of our suppression by man. Our country needs women's idealism and determination, perhaps more in politics than anywhere else.

SHIRLEY CHISHOLM, *Unbought and Unbossed,* 1970

Any candidate, Republican or Democrat, who sets his mind on the Presidency of the United States and misses it is never the same again.

BENJAMIN MAYS, *Born To Rebel,* 1971

Some politicians are political pimps. They endorse candidates not because they're good, but because they'll win. They respect no party or principles, but owe allegiance only to themselves; you cannot engage them in a battle of wits for they are unarmed men.

JULIAN BOND, speech given in Atlanta, Georgia, 13 January 1975

Any fool can be a politician. You just have to teach yourself how to tell convincing lies.

BUCHI EMECHETA, *The Bride Price,* 1976

Politicians are necessary, and it'd be foolish to blame them for our troubles. They're just doing what they've always done—looking to survive, looking to climb, trying to please everyone at once and grinning and lying while they're doing it.

RAY CHARLES, *Brother Ray,* 1978

Politics is the art of the possible.

DESMOND TUTU, *Hope and Suffering,* 1983

Politics doesn't control the world, money does.

ANDREW YOUNG, in "Words of the Week" *Jet,* 14 October 1985

All political parties are basically concerned with power and with maintaining power, not with humanitarian issues in the raw and abstract state.

RALPH ELLISON, *Going to the Territory,* 1986

[T]oo many Democrats are taking Republican positions.

PARREN MITCHELL, in "Interview with Parren Mitchell," *Crisis,* February 1986

Political influence is the cornerstone of group progress in America.

KENNETH JONES, "Quest for Power," *Crisis,* February 1986

If you run for office you have to represent *all* the people.

L. DOUGLASS WILDER, in "Virginia's Lieutenant Governor," *Ebony,* April 1986

Support candidates, run candidates, and retire candidates.

JESSE JACKSON, in *Essence,* October 1986

It makes no sense for a Black to hold a political office if he or she will not help to elevate his or her own people.

JOHNNY FORD, in "NAACP Focus" *Crisis,* November 1986

Neither the Republicans nor the Democratics are capable of providing honest representation for people of color or for the working classes as a whole.

ANGELA DAVIS, in "Angela Davis: Good Health Advocate," *Essence,* January 1988

We blame the politicians, when actually we ourselves—everybody—contributed.

TESS ONWUEME, in "The Broken Calabash," *City Arts Quarterly,* Spring 1988

We made the mistake of thinking we had enough when we got political power.

WILLIAM JUDSON KING, in the *Detroit News*, 3 September 1988

POSSIBILITY

It is possible for men to trample on justice and liberty so long and become entirely oblivious of the principles of justice and liberty.

FREDERICK DOUGLASS, *My Bondage and My Freedom*, 1855

The possibilities of man are infinite. So indeed is his cruelty and backwardness and it is a long march about.

LORRAINE HANSBERRY, "Black Revolution and White Backlash," speech given at Town Hall Forum, New York City, June 1964

I had to bring the possibilities the books I read suggested and the impossibilities of the life around me together.

JAMES BALDWIN, *A Rap on Race*, 1971

We can overcome the temporary setback of slavery, if in our minds we remain free. All is possible.

HAKI MADHUBUTI, "Sonia Sanchez: The Bringer of Memories," in Evans, ed., *Black Women Writers*, 1984

The potential in this country is so great that it makes me tremble and weep to see it go awry.

MAYA ANGELOU, in *USA Today*, 5 March 1985

I am where I am because I believe in all possibilities.

WHOOPI GOLDBERG, in *Essence*, August 1987

POSTERITY

You who after long years shall see the monuments, who shall speak of what I've done, you will say, "We do not know, we do not know how they can have made a mountain of gold." To gild them I have given gold measured by the bushel as though it were sacks of grain.

QUEEN HATSHEPSUT

Let us labor to acquire knowledge, to break down the barriers of prejudice and oppression believing, that if not for us, for another generation there is a brighter day in store.

CHARLOTTE FORTEN, *The Journal of Charlotte Forten*, 1854

Let our posterity know that we their ancestors, uncultured and unlearned, amid all trials and temptations, were men of integrity.

ALEXANDER CRUMMELL, "The Dignity of Labor, Its Value to a New People," speech given at Working Men's Club, Philadelphia, Pennsylvania, 1881

[I]f the great battle of human right against poverty, against disease, against color prejudice is to be won, it must be won not in our day, but in the day of our children's children.

W. E. B. DU BOIS, "The Children's Number," *Crisis*, 1912

Men and women of the Negro race, rouse up in the name of your posterity, summon your every sense, collect your every faculty, thrust the scales from your eyes and be converted to the cause of the Negro advancement, Negro power, and sovereignty; Negro freedom and integrity, thereby becoming the giants of your own destiny; your posterity is crying out to you.

GARVEYITE, c. 1923

The music of my race is something that is going to live, something which posterity will honor in a higher sense than merely that of music of the ballroom.

DUKE ELLINGTON, *Music Is My Mistress*, 1973

The people are generally not yet prepared to understand their own interests in the great work to be done for themselves and their children. We shall be obliged to work sometimes without the popular sympathy we ought to have, but with utterly inadequate resources.

EDWARD BLYDEN, in United Nations Special Committee Against Apartheid, "W. E. B. Du Bois: The Scholar Reconsidered," April 1978

People will not look forward to posterity who never looked back to their ancestors.

ALI MAZURI, c. 1985

I sought to be superior in whatever I did—not for me but for those who must follow.

MARVA COLLINS, 1988

POVERTY

Being well dressed doesn't prevent one from being poor.

CONGO

Let poverty be a stranger in my household; For if I have no wife, then I am poor; if I lack possessions, then I am poor; if my cloth is torn, then I am poor.

DAHOMEY

Poverty is a terrible disease; it penetrates the sides, it bends the vertebrae, it dresses one in rags, it makes people stupid. Poverty makes every desire remain in the breast. Those who are long it shortens; those who are short it destroys wholly.

ETHIOPIA

Three kinds of people die poor: those who are divorced, those who incur debts, and those who move around too much.

SENEGAL

Poverty is slavery.

SOMALIA

A poor man is a snake—his brothers avoid him because of the misery of the poverty stricken.

ZANZIBAR

Poverty breeds envy.

TRADITIONAL

You don't have a pot to piss in or a window to throw it out of.

TRADITIONAL

Poverty is a hellish state to be in. It is no virtue. It is a crime.

MARCUS GARVEY, *Philosophy and Opinions of Marcus Garvey*, 1923

We live in respectable poverty.

JOHN HOPE, c. 1930

The underprivileged are the shyest. They are most reluctant to reveal that which the soul lives by.

ZORA NEALE HURSTON, *Mules and Men*, 1935

[G]ot to look at the sole of his shoe everytime he cross the street to see whether he got enough leather to make it across.

ZORA NEALE HURSTON, *Their Eyes Were Watching God*, 1937

There is something about poverty that smells like death. Dead dreams dropping off the heart like leaves in a dry season and rotting around the feet; impulses smothered too long in the fetid air of underground caves. The soul lives in a sickly air.

ZORA NEALE HURSTON, *Dust Tracks on a Road*, 1942

Poverty had done its best to do him in. It had hollowed out the orbit, filled it with a camouflage of rheumy dust. It had stretched the empty space between the solid hinge of jaws and cheekbones of an old worn face. It had planted tiny, shining stakes of a several-day-old beard. It had disconnected the heart, and stooped the back.

AIMÉ CÉSAIRE, *Notes on a Return to the Native Land*, 1947

Anyone who has ever struggled with poverty knows how extremely expensive it is to be poor; and if one is a member of a captive population, economically speaking, one's feet have simply been placed on the treadmill forever. One is victimized, economically speaking, in a thousand ways. . . .

JAMES BALDWIN, *Nobody Knows My Name*, 1961

Poverty perpetuates itself in ever widening disability.

NATIONAL URBAN LEAGUE, 1965

Our family was so poor we would eat the hole out of a doughnut.

MALCOLM X, *The Autobiography of Malcolm X,* 1965

It is not practical to separate the problem of Black poverty from poverty as such. It makes it look as if we're asking for special privileges unless we do it within the context of elimination of poverty for all.

BAYARD RUSTIN, 1967

The poor have been ignored—and trapped in the bonds of their own poverty.

FLOYD MCKISSICK, c. 1968

The curse of poverty has no justification in our age. It is socially as cruel and blind as the practice of cannibalism at the dawn of civilization, when men ate each other because they had not learned to take food from the soil or to consume the abundant animal life around them.

MARTIN LUTHER KING, JR., *Where Do We Go from Here?* 1968

For I am you staring back from a mirror of poverty and despair, of revolt and freedom. Look at me and know that to destroy me is to destroy yourself.

GORDON PARKS, "The Cycle of Despair," *Life,* 8 March 1968

We will place the problems of the poor at the seat of government of the wealthiest nation in the history of mankind. If that power refuses to acknowledge its debt to the poor, it will have failed to live up to its promise to insure "life, liberty and the pursuit of happiness" to its citizens.

MARTIN LUTHER KING, JR., in "Showdown for Nonviolence," *Look,* 16 April 1968

We are on the side of the wealthy and secure while we create a hell for the poor. Somehow this madness must stop. We must stop now. I speak as a child of God and brother to the suffering. I speak for those whose land is being laid waste, whose homes are being destroyed, whose culture is being subverted. I speak for the poor of America who are paying the double price of smashed hopes at home and death and corruption. I speak as a citizen of the world, for the world as it stands aghast at the path we have taken.

Ibid.

No one can communicate to you/ The face of poverty—/ Can tell you neither shape,/ Nor the depth,/ nor the breadth/ Of poverty—/ Until you have lived with her intimately.

LUCY SMITH, "Face of Poverty," in Bontemps, ed., *Poetry of the Negro,* 1970

We prefer the poverty in freedom to riches in slavery.

SEKOU TOURE, in *Ebony,* August 1976

If you find humor in anything—even poverty—you can survive it.

BILL COSBY, in "Interview with Bill Cosby," *Scholastic,* 17 November 1977

[W]e were Poor. I'm spelling it with a capital P . . . we were on the bottom of the ladder looking up at everyone else. Nothing below us 'cept the ground.

RAY CHARLES, *Brother Ray,* 1978

It's going to take an act of Congress to deal with poverty and hunger, not only in this country, but throughout the world. We have the resources but we don't have the will.

CORETTA SCOTT KING, in Walker, *In Search of Our Mothers' Gardens,* 1983

[P]oor or whatever your circumstance, you are capable of being the best of people and that best, as a human, does not come from the outside in, it comes from the inside out.

LUCILLE CLIFTON, "A Simple Language," in Evans, ed., *Black Women Writers,* 1984

Not surprisingly, to be pushed out first were those who are quickly becoming irrelevant to the productive process—the uneducated young, the useless aged, and many of those whose skins are dark.

JULIAN BOND, in *American Visions,* February 1986

I've been rich and I've been poor and I have to admit that rich is better. I'm from the welfare rolls of Chicago, and poverty is always with me. It's what gets me up early in the morning and it is what keeps me up late at night.

JOHN H. JOHNSON, in "Interview with John H. Johnson," *Crisis,* January 1987

The easiest way to deal with poor people is to close our eyes and believe they aren't there.

WEARY FLETCHER, in *American Visions,* October 1987

Who among us can expect the homeless to remain silent forever, the unemployed to accept their lot quietly forever, the despairing to control their anger forever?

JOHN JACOBS, in *Congressional Clearinghouse,* 30 March 1988

The true definition would have to include the poverty of the spirit which is so deep, so awful that no amount of material goods poured into that sinkhole would make the difference.

OSSIE DAVIS, "It's on Us," *City Arts Quarterly,* Spring 1988

[T]he ultimate poverty is the poverty that tears families apart.

ELEANOR HOLMES NORTON, in "Barriers," *Life,* Spring 1988

Poverty makes people angry, brings out their worst side.

PRINCE, in "Spotlight: Prince—What U See Is What U Get," *Essence,* November 1988

I lived with my fifth-grade teacher for a while. But no matter how bad things got, my mother made it clear that we were not defined by our financial situation. We were defined by our ability to overcome it.

ANNA PEREZ, 1989

Only poor men put on a show.

CHARLES JOHNSON, *Middle Passage,* 1990

No matter how poor you are, poverty is no excuse for crime and violence. The quick buck will usually take a long time to pay back.

EMMETT C. BURNS, sermon given at the United Baptist Convention, Maryland, 1990

The children of poverty can be effectively educated despite segregation and other social injustices. Poverty has nothing to do with why children learn.

GEORGE MCKENNA, in *Association Supervisors and Curriculum Developers Update,* May 1991

Poverty is not about color.

QUEEN LATIFAH, in the *Detroit Free Press,* 8 March 1992

POWER

Those in power never give way and admit defeat. They plot and scheme to regain their lost power and privilege.

EGYPT

Power means authority, the authority of law and custom, backed by such force as necessary to make justice prevail.

IROQUOIS

Men have exercised authority over our nation as if we were their property, by depriving us of our freedom as though they had a command from heaven thus to do. But, we ask, if freedom is the right of one nation, why not the right of all the nations of the earth?

AFRICAN SOCIETY, Boston, Massachusetts, 1808

The love of power is one of the greatest human infirmities, and with it comes the usurping influence of despotism, the mother of slavery.

WILLIAM WHIPPER, "An Address on Non-resistance to Offensive Aggression," *The Colored American,* 16 September 1837

Power is the highest object of respect. . . . We pity the impotent and respect the powerful everywhere.

FREDERICK DOUGLASS, *The New National Era,* October 1870

Everywhere on earth men like to hold on to power; like to use their inferiors as tools and instruments; plume and pride themselves as superior beings; look with contempt upon the laboring classes and strive by every possible means to use them to their own advantage.

ALEXANDER CRUMMELL, "The Dignity of Labor, Its Value to a New People," speech given at Working Men's Club, Philadelphia, Pennsylvania, 1881

Through history, the powers of single black men flash here and there like falling stars, and die sometimes before the world has rightly gauged their brightness.

W. E. B. DU BOIS, *The Souls of Black Folk,* 1903

The Negro must have Power; the power of men, the right to do, to know, to feel, and to express that knowledge.

W. E. B. DU BOIS, "The Immediate Program of the Negro," *Crisis,* April 1915

Political power is the beginning of all permanent reform and the only hope for maintaining gains.

Ibid.

Nothing is so calculated to ruin human nature as absolute power over human beings.

Ibid.

Possession of power makes men blind and deaf, they cannot see things which are under their very noses and cannot hear things which invade their ears.

MOHANDAS GANDHI, in *Yeravda Mandir,* 13 October 1921

Power is the only argument that satisfies man.

MARCUS GARVEY, *Philosophy and Opinions of Marcus Garvey,* 1923

Get power of every kind. Power in education, science, industry, politics, and higher government. That kind of power will stand out signally.

Ibid.

I approach the future in a happy and rather adventuresome spirit. It is within my power to make this unknown path a somewhat beaten path.

PAUL ROBESON, in "Robeson in London Can't Explain His Success," *Baltimore Afro-American,* 22 September 1928

[Power] is a whirlwind among breezes.

ZORA NEALE HURSTON, *Their Eyes Were Watching God,* 1937

He had a bow-down command in his face.

Ibid.

Power superimposed always needs the help of the military and police, power generated from within should have little or no use for them.

MOHANDAS GANDHI, 4 September 1937

I made up my mind to fight your power with mine. But I found out I was no more against you than a grain of sand against a mountain, because you beat me and then bottled me up inside my own body and you been keeping me in jail inside myself ever since.

ZORA NEALE HURSTON, *Moses, Man of the Mountain,* 1939

You who play the zigzag lightning of power over the world, with the grumbling thunder in your wake, think kindly of those who walk in the dust. And you who walk in humble places, think kindly too, of others. There has been no proof in the world so far that you would be less arrogant if you held the lever of power in your hands. Consider that with tolerance and patience, we godly demons may breed a noble world in a few hundred generations or so.

ZORA NEALE HURSTON, *Dust Tracks on a Road,* 1942

Be not dismayed in these terrible times. You possess power, great power. Our problem is to hitch it up for action on the broadest daring and most gigantic scale.

A. PHILIP RANDOLPH, speech given to March on Washington Movement, Detroit, Michigan, 26 September 1942

We know now that the sun turns around our earth lighting the parcel designated by our will alone and that every star falls from sky to earth at our omnipotent command.

AIMÉ CÉSAIRE, *Notes on* a *Return to the Native Land,* 1947

[H]ow is it that we, the great majority of the people, struggling as we have for generation after generation forward to some better life, how can it happen that everywhere in history a few seem to take the power in their hands, confuse the people themselves and there they remain?

PAUL ROBESON, speech given at International Fur and Leather Workers Union Convention, 20 May 1948

Drunk with power, we are leading the world to hell.

W. E. B. DU BOIS, in *The New York Times,* 4 April 1949

Power always involves a man in a network of compromise.

HOWARD THURMAN, *Meditations of the Heart,* 1953

Powerlessness breeds a race of beggers.

RICHARD WRIGHT, 1957

We ourselves have the power to end the terror and win for ourselves peace and security. We have the power of numbers, the power of organization, and the power of spirit.

PAUL ROBESON, *Here I Stand,* 1958

A people deprived of political sovereignty finds it very nearly impossible to re-create, for itself, the image of its past . . . the definition of a living culture.

JAMES BALDWIN, *Nobody Knows My Name,* 1961

When power translates itself into tyranny, the principles of that power are bankrupt.

Ibid.

[P]ower is international, real power is international; today real power is not local.

MALCOLM X, speech given at Audubon Ballroom, New York City, 20 December 1964

The tremendous surges of the people of Russia and Asia and Africa may prove more powerful than tanks or guns. The urgent necessity for the building of a peace between the Western Powers and the rest of the world, founded upon respect for the peoples outside the Anglo-American fold, will be a span not to be lightly evaluated.

ROY WILKINS, c. 1965

Power never takes a back step—only in the face of more power.

MALCOLM X, "Prospects for Freedom in 1965," speech given at the Militant Labor Forum, 7 January 1965

Power in defense of freedom greater than power in behalf of tyranny and oppression, because power, real power, comes from conviction which produces action, uncompromising action. It also produces insurrection against oppression. This is the only way you end oppression—with power.

Ibid.

A dog is a dog except when he is facing you. Then he is Mr. Dog.

HAITIAN FARMER, in "Haiti: Pistol Packing Papa," *Newsweek,* 27 June 1966

Black power is organizing the rage of Black people and putting new hard questions and demands to white America.

CHARLES HAMILTON, *Black Power,* 1967

Power is the ability to influence another person—even against his will, if necessary.

NATHAN HARE, JR., in *U.S. News and World Report,* May 1967

There is nothing essentially wrong with power. The problem is American power is unequally distributed.

MARTIN LUTHER KING, JR., *Where Do We Go From Here?* 1968

One of the greatest problems of history is that love and power are usually contrasted as polar opposites. Love is identified with resignation of power and power with denial of love.

Ibid.

Power is the ability to achieve purpose.

Ibid.

Black Power gives the African-American an entirely new dimension. It is a movement of Black people, but it opens the way for all oppressed people.

KWAME NKRUMAH, *The Spectre of Black Power,* 1968

What is Black Power? The power of the four-fifths of the world population, which has been systematically damned into a state of undevelopment by colonialism and neocolonialism. It is the sum total of the economic, cultural, and political power which the Black man must have to achieve his survival in a highly developed technical society and in a world ravaged by imperialism, colonialism, neocolonialism, and fascism.

KWAME NKRUMAH, "Message to the Black People of Britain," in *The Struggle Continues,* 1969

Black power is an affirmation of the humanity of Blacks in spite of white racism. It is an attitude, an inward affirmation of the essential worth of blackness.

JAMES CONE, *Black Theology and Black Power,* 1969

I can change a river into a burning sand/ I can make a ship sail on dry land.

TEMPTATIONS, "I Can't Get Next To You," 1969

Power comes not from the barrel of a gun, but from one's awareness of his or her own cultural strength and the unlimited capacity to empathize with, feel for, care, and love one's brothers and sisters.

ADDISON GAYLE, JR., *The Black Aesthetic,* 1971

Power comes from bending nature to one's will.

WOLE SOYINKA, *Madmen and Specialists,* 1971

When power translates itself into tyranny, the principles on which that power depended are bankrupt . . . then the power is defended by thugs and mediocrities.

JAMES BALDWIN, *No Name In the Street,* 1972

There was a man who was blessed with the vision to see God. But even this man did and does not have the power . . . to show God to a believer, much less an unbeliever.

DUKE ELLINGTON, *Music Is My Mistress,* 1973

Education for Black people in America is a question of life and death, a question of power.

MELVIN CHAPMAN, speech given at Mercy College, Detroit, Michigan, June 1974

Do not call for Black power or green power. Call for brain power.

BARBARA JORDAN, *Barbara Jordan,* 1977

Any form of art is a form of power, it has impact, it can affect change—it can not only move us, it makes us move.

OSSIE DAVIS, in Noble, *Beautiful, Also, Are the Souls of My Black Sisters,* 1978

Economic power must be coupled with political power to form real power.

COLEMAN YOUNG, *Ebony,* April 1981

Nobody is as powerful as we make them out to be.

ALICE WALKER, *In Search of Our Mothers' Gardens,* 1983

[W]riting is a legitimate way, an important way, to participate in the empowerment of the community that names me.

TONI CADE BAMBARA, "Salvation Is the Issue," in Evans, ed., *Black Women Writers,* 1984

Being physically close to extreme power causes one to experience a giddiness, an intoxication.

MAYA ANGELOU, *All God's Children Need Traveling Shoes,* 1986

He would rely on the power of Jesus Christ to deal with things older, but not stronger, than He Himself was.

TONI MORRISON, *Beloved,* 1987

People who are empowered in this society have no leaders at all.

ELEANOR HOLMES NORTON, in "Barriers," *Life,* Spring 1988

When we empower one another, we free ourselves. When we empower one another, we diesempower those who certainly will not empower us. History should have taught us that by now.

CAMILLE COSBY, in *Delta Newsletter,* April 1989

Black purchasing power is now at $200 billion . . . but Black economic influence and benefits aren't commensurate with this purchasing power.

MARIAN WRIGHT EDELMAN, speech given to the Congressional Black Caucus, 26 September 1989

There is a lot of power in the word never. And it's mostly negative power.

PEARL CLEAGE, in "Never Say Never," *Essence,* October 1990

PRACTICE

Human law may know no distinction among men in respect of rights, but human practice may.

FREDERICK DOUGLASS, speech given at National Convention of Colored Men, Louisville, Kentucky, September 1883

Everybody else seems to want everybody else to practice what he preaches and nobody seems to be able or willing to practice what everybody else preaches.

LOREN MILLER, c. 1950

Practice without thought is blind; thought without practice is empty.

KWAME NKRUMAH, *Consciencism,* 1964

John Coltrane's music would not have been what it is, had he not spent many hours perfecting his ability to project the purest thing he felt.

STANLEY CROUCH, *Journal of Black Poetry,* Fall 1968

The historic practice of bowing to other men's gods and definitions has produced a crisis of the highest magnitude, and brought us culturally to the limits of racial Armageddon.

ADDISON GAYLE, JR., *The Black Aesthetic,* 1971

There's no such thing as a "natural." A natural dancer has to practice hard. A natural painter has to paint all the time and a natural fool has to work at it.

JOE LOUIS, *My Life,* 1981

PRAYER

See also THANKS

God is most high, I witness that there is none to worship except God. I witness there is none to worship except Muhammad the apostle of God. Arise to prayer, arise to divine power.

BILAL, 600 B.C.

O God, From whom to be turned is to fall,/ To whom to be turned is to rise,/ And with whom to stand is to abide forever;/ Grant us in all our duties/ Your help,/ In all our perplexities your guidance/ In all our dangers Your protection,/ And in all our sorrows Your peace.

AUGUSTINE OF HIPPO, 354–430

An' I couldn't hear nobody pray,/ O Lord, Way down yonder by myself,/ I couldn't hear nobody pray.

SPIRITUAL

Lord we ain't what we ought to be/ And we ain't what we want to be/ We ain't what we gonna be, but Thank God/ We ain't what we were.

TRADITIONAL

May the Great Spirit shed light on yours, that you may never experience the humiliation that the power of the American government has reduced me to.

BLACK HAWK OF THE SACS, *Farewell, My Nation! Farewell,* 1833

For the happy man prayer is only a jumble of words, until the day when sorrow comes to explain to him the sublime language by means of which he speaks to God.

ALEXANDRE DUMAS, *The Count of Monte Cristo,* 1844

I kneel and pray before new gods come into a godless age.

JEAN TOOMER, *Earth Being,* 1925

O Lord, we come this morning/ Knee-bowed and body bent/ Before thy throne of grace./ O Lord—this morning—/ Bow our hearts beneath our knees,/ And our knees in some lonesome valley./ We come this morning—/ Like empty pitchers to a full fountain,/ With no merits of our own./ O Lord—open up a window of heaven,/ And lean out far over the battlements of glory,/ And listen this morning.

JAMES WELDON JOHNSON, "Listen, Lord—A Prayer," *God's Trombones,* 1927

Pray if you believe in prayer for those shipwrecked by love else pity them; the sunburst of your compassion may heal their broken stems/ may restore their crushed tendrils.

DENNIS BRUTUS, "Pray," in Bontemps, ed., *Poetry of the Negro,* 1949

I learned how to pray from my mother, her faith in God was contagious for me.

C. L. FRANKLIN, "Hannah, the Ideal Mother," sermon given in 1958

Jesus Savior Pilot Me/ Over Life's Tempestuous Sea.

ROBERT HAYDEN, "Middle Passage," *A Ballad of Remembrance,* 1966

Lord, keep her safe since you can't keep her sane.

GLORIA NAYLOR, *The Women of Brewster Place,* 1988

The quilt was a prayer of poor women. They didn't have anything else to cover their children with.

JOHN BIGGERS, in *Black Art: Ancestral Legacy,* 1989

PREACHER

The Devil is a very successful preacher. He draws a great number after him. No preacher can command hearers like him—he was successful with our first parents—with the old world.

LEMUEL B. HAYNES, "Universal Salvation—A Very Ancient Doctrine," 1795

As to the preacher, he has many names given him in the sacred writings; the most common is the Devil . . . He was once an angel of light . . . he is an old preacher. It is now five thousand eight hundred and nine years since he commenced preaching. By this time he must have acquired great skill in the art.

Ibid.

What we need is not more but fewer ministers, but in that lesser number we certainly need earnest, broad, and cultured men; men who do a good deal more that they say; men of broad plans and far-seeing thought; men who will extend the charitable and rescue work of the churches, encourage home getting, guard the children, not on Sundays, but on weekdays, make the public use saving banks, and in fine, men who will really be active agents of social and moral reform in their communities.

W. E. B. DU BOIS, Commencement address, Fisk University, Nashville, Tennessee, 1898

The Preacher is the most unique personality developed by the Negro on American soil. A leader, a politician, an orator, a "boss," an intriguer, an idealist—all these he is, and ever, too, the center of a group of men, now twenty, now a thousand in number. The combination of a certain adroitness with deep-seated earnestness, of tact with consummate ability, gave him his preeminence, and helps him maintain it.

W. E. B. DU BOIS, *The Souls of Black Folk,* 1903

He strode the pulpit up and down in what was actually a very rhythmic dance, and he brought into play the full gamut of his wonderful voice, a voice—what shall I say?—not of an organ or a trumpet, but rather of a trombone, the instrument possessing above all others the power to express the wide and varied range of emotions encompassed by the human voice—and with greater amplitude. He intoned, he moaned, he pleaded—he blared, he crashed, he thundered. I sat fascinated; and more, I was, perhaps against my will, deeply moved; the emotional effect upon me was irresistible.

JAMES WELDON JOHNSON, *God's Trombones,* 1927

Merely being a good man is not enough to hold an important charge. He must also be an artist. He must be both a poet and an actor of a very high order, and then he must have the voice and the figure.

ZORA NEALE HURSTON, C. 1940

It strove to lift up; without coming down and while the good Presbyterian parson was writing his discourse, rounding off the sentences, the Methodist itinerant had traveled forty miles with his horse and saddle bags; while the parson was adjusting his spectacles to read his manuscript, the itinerant had given hell and damnation to his repentant hearers; while the disciple of Calvin was waiting to have his church completed, the disciple of Wesley took to the woods and made them re-echo with the voice of free grace, believing.

CARTER G. WOODSON, *History of the Negro Church,* 1945

A prophet is a preacher, and a preacher ought to be a prophet . . . a prophet born of God. For a prophet is one who knows the past, understands the present; he's able to predict the future. A prophet has sight, insight, and foresight. With sight he looks on things. With insight he looks into things. With foresight he looks beyond things.

C. L. FRANKLIN, "The Prophet and the Dry Bones in the Valley," sermon given c. 1957

I preached my trial sermon. It was a strange crowd that listened—all the girls from the Cotton Club, others from the downtown nightclubs, girls of every color, bootleggers, gamblers, all the fantastic array of acquaintances I had accumulated through the years. Adam's going to preach! Adam who played one of the best games of stud poker, who had slept with more women than anyone could count, and who could hold more liquor than anybody in his circle, was going to be a preacher.

ADAM CLAYTON POWELL, JR., *Adam by Adam,* 1971

One of the secrets of political success is recognizing the power of ministers.

COLEMAN YOUNG, *Blacks in Detroit,* 1980

If you're a preacher, you talk for a living, so even if you don't make sense, you learn to make nonsense eloquently.

ANDREW YOUNG, in "Words of the Week," *Jet,* 7 March 1988

PREJUDICE

We meet the monster prejudice everywhere. We have not power to contend with it, we are so downtrodden. We cannot elevate ourselves. . . . We want light; we ask it, and it is denied us. Why are we thus treated? Prejudice is the cause.

CLARISSA LAWRENCE, Proceedings, Anti-Slavery Convention of American Women, Philadelphia, Pennsylvania, May 1838

If prejudice were not unnatural, it would show itself everywhere. In the Southern states where it exists in its greatest form, violence is not innate.

PHILIP BELL, in *Pacific Appeal,* 19 April 1862

Prejudice is bound to give way before the patent influence of character, education, and wealth.

GEORGE WASHINGTON WILLIAMS, c. 1870

Race prejudice can't be talked down, it must be lived down.

FRANCIS JAMES GRIMKE, *Stray Thoughts and Meditations,* 1914

Prejudice is cultivated.

A. PHILIP RANDOLPH, *Messenger,* March 1919

Sometimes, I feel discriminated against, but it does not make me angry. It merely astonishes me. How can anyone deny themselves the pleasure of my company?

ZORA NEALE HURSTON, *The World of Tomorrow,* 1928

Our own history begins with it and though India tried some kind of race adjustment she has failed in giving birth to a political organism owing to this abnormal caste consciousness that obstructs the strain of human sympathy and spirit of human sympathy and mutual cooperation. This is why

India has not produced a great organic history; and it has yet to be seen if such history is in the making in which people of different colors can have a perfect bond of life from across the seas.

RABINDRANATH TAGORE, in the *Spectator,* 9 May 1931

[T]he most absurd results can be produced, not merely by prejudice itself, but by respect for prejudice.

PAUL ROBESON, "Thoughts on the Colour Bar," the *Spectator,* 8 August 1931

I will not allow one prejudiced person or one million or one hundred million to blight my life. I will not let prejudice or any of its attendant humiliations and injustices bear me down to spiritual defeat. My inner life is mine, and I shall defend and maintain its integrity against all the powers of Hell.

JAMES WELDON JOHNSON, *Negro American, What Now?* 1934

America's race prejudice must be destroyed.

JOHN H. SENGSTACKE, c. 1935

Racial prejudice is usually blind . . . [more] the result of reason and personal experience than of inherited ideas, and a hasty American tendency to lump all things which look alike into a single category.

PAUL WILLIAMS, in *American Magazine,* 1937

I return without fearing prejudice that once bothered me. . . . [F]or I know that people practice their cruel bigotry in their ignorance. . . .

PAUL ROBESON, in "Paul Robeson Told Me," *Theatre Arts Committee,* July–August 1939

A very singular fact about color prejudice. Where you would expect to find it most, it is least, namely in Europe, homeland of the whites.

J. A. ROGERS, *Nature Knows No Color Line,* 1952

Dealing with people very different from myself caused a shattering in me of preconceptions I scarcely knew I had.

JAMES BALDWIN, *Nobody Knows My Name,* 1961

The prejudice of race is superficially the most irrational of all prejudices.

C. L. R. JAMES, *The Black Jacobins,* 1963

Show me a person who is full of prejudice and I will show you a sick, unhappy, fearful individual, who is not going anywhere and is not growing. People don't shut others out, they fence themselves in.

WHITNEY YOUNG, *To Be Equal,* 1964

Prejudice is like a hair across your cheek. You can't see it, you can't find it with your fingers, but you keep brushing at it because the feel of it is irritating.

MARIAN ANDERSON, c. 1966

I had rationalized my environment, but it had rejected me in the name of color prejudice. Since there was no understanding on the basis of reason, I threw myself into the arms of the irrational. I became irrational up to my neck. The tom-tom drummed out my cosmic mission. The arteries of the world, torn open, have made me fertile. I found, not my origin, but the origin. I wedded the world.

FRANTZ FANON, *Black Skin, White Masks,* 1967

Bigotry always begins with a hurt. . . . And the hurt was soul-shattering sometimes. It was rougher than a cancer because, once you had it, you couldn't cut it out even for a single minute.

JESSE OWENS, *Blackthink,* 1970

All of us have prejudices that grow out of our egos. . . . Show me a person with no prejudice and I'll show you a person with no taste. The struggle is to keep the prejudice from turning into bigotry and hatred. Bigotry takes possession of people, and is mankind's biggest enemy.

BILL RUSSELL, *Second Wind,* 1979

I've often wondered how many punches my chin can take from prejudice. But someday I'll be able to counter with a KO punch myself. I know it's a hard fight. Hate just won't take the count overnight. But the toughest fights are the kind you like to win best.

JOE LOUIS, *My Life,* 1981

There is too much bigotry of the old holding back the spirit of togetherness of the young.

LEON SULLIVAN, *Crisis,* March 1983

The present surge of bigotry warns us that the enemy is regrouping.

GORDON PARKS, "What Became of the Prophets of Rage?" *Life,* Spring 1988

You must realize music has no prejudice itself; it's the people who make the difference. And when entertainers get together, they don't think in terms of who's old, who's young, who's white, who's Black. We think in terms of combining the talents and making it good and enjoyable to each other.

B. B. KING, in the *Dallas Morning News,* 24 June 1990

PREPARATION

To make preparation does not spoil the trip.

GUINEA

The day on which one starts out is not the time to start one's preparation.

NIGERIA

Hibernation is a covert preparation for a more overt action.

RALPH ELLISON, *Invisible Man,* 1952

Education is our passport to the future, for tomorrow belongs to the people who prepare for it today.

MALCOLM X, speech given at Founding Rally of Organization of Afro-American Unity, 28 June 1964

[The writer] must be prepared for the hatred and antagonism of many of his own people, for attacks from his leaders, the clergy and the press; he must be ready to have his name reviled at every level, intellectual or otherwise. The American Negro seeks to hide his beaten, battered soul, . . . his scars of oppression.

CHESTER HIMES, "Dilemma of the Negro Novelist in the U.S.A.," in Chapman, ed., *New Black Voices,* 1972

There is no obstacle in the path of young people who are poor or members of minority groups that hard work and preparation cannot cure.

BARBARA JORDAN, *Barbara Jordan,* 1977

You have to be insightful. Prepare yourself for the transitions you will have to undertake in life.

BEVERLY JOHNSON, in *Right On,* May 1979

You have to be there at the right time and you've got to be equipped.

WILLIAM HASTIE, *Grace Under Pressure,* 1984

Black Americans must understand that you don't wait for an inner-city child to prepare for college when he's in high school. That's too late.

MARVA COLLINS, in "Marva Collins: Teaching Success in the City," *Message,* February 1987

Preparation is hard work, running is the easy part.

EDWIN MOSES, *American Visions,* 1988

Luck is where opportunity meets preparation.

DENZEL WASHINGTON, in "Words of the Week," *Jet,* 7 March 1988

Prepare yourself with options. Go to school and get yourself an education

AHMAD JAMAL, in "Words of the Week," *Jet,* 30 May 1988

Life . . . is only a preparation for the eternal home, which is far more important than the short pleasures that seduce us here.

MUHAMMAD ALI, in "The Meaning of Life," *Life,* December 1988

PRESERVATION

[I]t is our duty to conserve our physical powers, our intellectual endowments, our spiritual ideals;

as a race we must strive by race organization, by race solidarity, by race unity to the realization of that broader humanity which freely recognizes differences in men, but sternly deprecates inequality in their opportunities of development.

W. E. B. DU BOIS, *The Conservation of Races,* 1897

On ourselves alone will depend the preservation of our liberties and the transmission of them in their integrity to those who will come after us.

PAUL ROBESON, "The New Idealism," *Targum,* June 1919

The race does not advance; it is only better preserved.

CHARLES OLSEN, c. 1960

PRESS

Among the multitudes of public prints, it is hard to say which lies the most.

IGNATIUS SANCHO, letter to Mrs. W E, 15 January 1780

Establish and maintain the Press, and through it, speak out in THUNDER TONES, until the nation repents and renders to every man that which is just and equal.

EDITORIAL, *The Colored American,* 4 March 1837

The press and our whole country is vexed and agitated on subjects pertaining to us.

AUGUSTUS WASHINGTON, "African Colonization—By A Man of Color," *New York Daily Tribune,* 9–10 July 1851

Our name, *The Elevator,* is indicative of our object; we wish to elevate the oppressed of all nations and of every clime to the position of manhood and freedom.

PHILIP BELL, in *The Elevator,* 7 April 1865

Ida B. Wells has become famous as one of the few of our women who handle a goose quill with diamond point as easily as any man in newspaper work.

T. THOMAS FORTUNE, 1890

There is a "Conspiracy of Silence" in the American press so far as presenting the colored American side of the story. Anybody who makes him ridiculous or criminal can get a hearing, but his struggles and heartaches are tabooed.

MARY CHURCH TERRELL, "What It Means to Be Colored in the Capital of the United States," *The Independent,* 24 January 1907

Always remember the press is a mighty power.

MARCUS GARVEY, *Philosophy and Opinions of Marcus Garvey,* 1923

What is the use of knowing things if they cannot be published to the world? If the Negro is to settle down to publishing merely what others permit him to bring out, the world will never know what the race has thought and felt and attempted and accomplished and the story of the Negro will perish with him.

CARTER G. WOODSON, c. 1928

[R]eason can and will prevail; but of course it can only prevail with publicity—pitiless, blatant publicity. You have got to make the people of the United States and of the world know what is going on in the South. You have got to use every field of publicity to force the truth into their ears, and before their eyes.

W. E. B. DU BOIS, "Behold the Land," speech given in Columbia, South Carolina, 20 October 1946

The Black press's primary focus was to serve as platforms for the Black abolitionist community and to fight the widespread conception of Black inferiority.

JOHN HOPE FRANKLIN, *From Slavery to Freedom,* 1947

The American Press has set out on its own campaign of deliberate misquotation and distortion of the things I say and do, trying to set my people against me, but they can't win because what I say is the unadulterated truth which cannot be denied.

PAUL ROBESON, in "My Answer," *New York Age,* 17 September 1949

I'm in the headlines and they're saying all manner of things about me such as "enemy" of the land of my birth, "traitor" to my country, "dangerous radical". . . . But they can't say that I'm not 100 percent for my people.

Ibid.

I have the greatest contempt for the press. Only something within me keeps me from smashing your cameras.

PAUL ROBESON, c. 1950

The Negro paper is current history of the Negro people, who need very much to know their history and achievements. At the same time, there is a grave necessity that sound critical thinkers should have a hearing in the Negro press.

HORTENSE HARLIN, *Indianapolis Recorder,* 1951

They do all their dirt with the press. They take the newspapers and make the newspapers blow you and me up as if all of us are criminals, all of us are racists, all of us are drug addicts, or all of us are rioting. . . . When you explode legitimately against the injustices that have been heaped upon you, they use the press to make it look like you're a vandal. . . . That's the image-making press . . . [it] is dangerous if you don't guard yourself against it.

MALCOLM X, speech given at Audubon Ballroom, New York City, 13 December 1964

Let us not forget the Black press, like the drums of Africa, are the main communication tool within our community. As such, they are not just business enterprises, they are a necessary key to our survival.

CHARLES COBB, c. 1970

When the white world embraced me and made me the first Black director, newspaper reporters came from all over the country to at last proclaim that they had a Black director.

GORDON PARKS, in "The State of the Arts: Film," *Crisis,* January 1986

I choose to fight for quality and most of all, for the historical, adversary role upon which the black press was founded.

ETHEL L. PAYNE, c. 1987

Most people in this country trust the press. They might not like some of the things we do, or the way we do them, but they trust the press. And most people in this country value a free press.

ED BRADLEY, in "Words of the Week," *Jet,* 19 January 1987

I felt like a morsel of red meat being thrown to a pack of wolves.

WOLE SOYINKA, in "Wole Soyinka: Nigerian Playwright is First Black Nobel Laureate in Literature," *Ebony,* April 1987

Ida Wells was a bold and tireless investigative reporter long before that term was coined.

MARGARET WALKER, 1988

[A] touch of mystery never hurts. I'm never going to reveal too much about myself [when I'm interviewed].

IMAN, in "Iman: By Her Own Rules," *Essence,* January 1988

How much license does the press have to destroy people's reputations?

COLEMAN YOUNG, in the *Detroit News,* 27 October 1988

Don't let the media get under your skin. And frankly avoid reading your press clippings—even the good ones.

MARJORIE JUDITH VINCENT, 14 January 1991

Knowing the country lives with a deep-seated racist-sexist mind-set, the media have an obligation to help remove it, not reinforce it. For example, the media never report that Blacks are only a third of the nation's poor. So when you talk to average citizens, their view is only Blacks are poor.

MARTIN KILSON, in *USA Weekend,* 28 June 1991

The media usually look for one person—spokesperson—to be representative of black people.

VANESSA WILLIAMS, in *USA Weekend,* 28 June 1991

PRIDE

A man can't ride you unless your back is bent.

TRADITIONAL

Nothing you know is worth anything if you don't know how to be proud of yourself.

TRADITIONAL

Envy and pride are the leading lines to all the misery that mankind has suffered from the beginning of time to the present day.

JOHN MARRANT, 1789

I maintain my pride in the face of men, but I abandon it before God, who drew me out of nothingness to make me what I am.

ALEXANDRE DUMAS, *The Count of Monte Cristo,* 1844

We have no reason to complain until we take pride in our own.

C. H. J. TAYLOR, in the *People's Advocate,* 3 March 1883

There is enough history to make one proud of his race. Why not then teach the child more of himself and less of others, more of his elevation and less of his degradation? This can produce true pride of race, which begets mutual confidence and unity.

D. A. STRAKER, "New South Investigated," *Gazette,* 13 January 1887

I believe in pride of race and lineage and self; in pride of self so deep as to scorn injustice to other selves; in pride of lineage so great as to despair no man's father; in pride of race so chivalrous as neither to offer bastardy to the weak nor beg wedlock of the strong, knowing that men may be brothers in Christ, even though they be not brothers in law.

W. E. B. DU BOIS, *Darkwater,* 1920

Be as proud of your race today as our fathers were in the days of yore. We have beautiful history, and we shall create another in the future that will astonish the world.

MARCUS GARVEY, *Philosophy and Opinions of Marcus Garvey,* 1923

I stand before you as a proud Black man, honoured to be a Black man, who would be nothing else in God's creation but a Black man.

Ibid.

Teach the children pride. Nothing learned is worth anything if you don't know how to be proud of yourself.

NANNIE BURROUGHS, "With All They Getting," *Southern Workman,* July 1927

Never in my life did I feel prouder of being an African, a Black, and no mistake about it, from Moscow to Petrograd I went triumphantly from surprise to surprise, extravagantly feted on every side . . . I was like a black ikon in the flesh.

CLAUDE MCKAY, *A Long Way from Home,* 1937

If our people are to fight their way out of bondage we must arm them with the sword and the shield and the buckler of pride—belief in themselves and their possibilities based upon a sure knowledge of the past. That knowledge and pride we must give them—if it breaks every back in the kingdom.

MARY MCLEOD BETHUNE, in the *Journal of Negro History,* January 1938

Alexandre Dumas the Elder was rather proud of his Negro ancestry. When his daughter married into an aristocratic family, he invited a large number of Negroes of Paris. The bridegroom's mother was shocked. Dumas told her, "They are my relatives who wish to be present."

J. R. ROGERS, *Nature Knows No Color Line,* 1952

The monster of pride feeds upon vermin. The hole in a poor man's garment is soon filled with the patchwork of pride, so resolutely does nature abhor a vacuum.

WOLE SOYINKA, *The Trials of Brother Jeroboam,* 1964

Say it loud, I'm black and I'm proud.

JAMES BROWN, c. 1965

We used to be "shiftless and lazy," now we are "fearsome and awesome." I think the Black man should take pride in that.

JAMES EARL JONES, in "Interview," *Newsweek,* 21 October 1968

Who/ can be born/ black/ and not exalt.

MARI EVANS, "My Father's Passage," *I Am A Black Woman,* 1970

I'm glad I didn't have to wait seventy years for someone in the '60s to teach me to appreciate what I am—Black.

BENJAMIN MAYS, *Born to Rebel,* 1970

Pride, like humility, is destroyed by one's insistence that he possess it.

KENNETH CLARK, *The Pathos of Power,* 1974

To say this is a proud day for me would be an understatement. If I had one wish in the world that wish would be to have Jackie Robinson here to see this happen. I don't think I would have stood the pressure or have gone through what Jackie had to.

FRANK ROBINSON, on becoming the first Black baseball manager, c. 1975

My pride has been starched by a family who assumed unlimited authority in its own affairs.

MAYA ANGELOU, *Singing and Swinging, and Getting Merry Like Christmas,* 1976

February, 1984, I blissfully floated on the ceiling of the space shuttle, Challenger, fast asleep. I was awakened by music piped up from mission control center. My eyes stretched wide in disbelief and my face lit up with delight for immediately I recognized the music as my college alma mater, North Carolina A&T.

RONALD MCNAIR, in *Choosing to Succeed,* 1986

Racial pride and self-dignity were emphasized in my family and community.

ROSA PARKS, in "The Meaning of Life," *Life,* December 1988

Never let pride be your guiding principle. Let your accomplishments speak for you.

MORGAN FREEMAN, in *Essence,* 1991

I have a sense of pride no different than that of Joe Louis when he was in the ring, or Paul Robeson acting, or Ralph Bunche practicing diplomacy. I am standing on the shoulders of some excellent giants.

BERNARD SHAW, in *USA Weekend,* 1 March 1991

PRISON

A prison has a door, but a grave hasn't.

ALEXANDRE DUMAS, *The Count of Monte Cristo,* 1844

I know why the caged bird sings, ah me,/ When his wing is bruised and his bosom sore,/ When he beats his bars and he would be free;/ It is not a carol of joy or glee,/ But a prayer that he sends from his heart's deep core. . . .

PAUL LAURENCE DUNBAR, "Sympathy," *Lyrics of Lowly Life,* 1896

My months of forcible removal from among you, being imprisoned as a punishment for advocating the cause of our real emancipation, have not left me hopeless or despondent; but to the contrary, I see a great ray of light and bursting of a mighty political cloud which will bring you complete freedom.

MARCUS GARVEY, speech given in Atlanta, Georgia, February 1927

You have sung and prayed about dying and forgiving your enemies and of feeling sure that you're going to the New Jerusalem because your God knows you're innocent. But, why don't you pray to live and ask to be freed? The God you serve is the God of Paul and Silas who opened their prison gates. You ought to believe that he will open your prison too.

IDA B. WELLS, in Duster, ed., *Crusade for Justice,* 1928

Men copied the realities of their hearts when they built prisons.

RICHARD WRIGHT, *The Outsider,* 1953

For in the dormitory it was as though they were in a cage with the doors flung open, but they couldn't release themselves. Nothing mattered outside the cage, because there was nothing. So they remained within the cage unaware of what was beyond, without a trace of desire for what was beyond.

GEORGE LAMMING, *The Emigrants,* 1954

What else can one do when he is alone in a narrow jail cell, other than write long letters, think long thoughts, and pray long prayers?

MARTIN LUTHER KING, JR., *Letter from a Birmingham City Jail,* 1963

Behind bars a man never reforms. He will never forget. He will never completely get over the memories of the bars.

MALCOLM X, *The Autobiography of Malcolm X,* 1965

Prison is the ultimate in oppression.

ETHERIDGE KNIGHT, 1968

South Africa has the dubious reputation of boasting one of the highest prison populations in the world. Jails are jam-packed with Africans—imprisoned for serious offenses—and crimes of violence are ever on the increase in an apartheid society—but also for petty infringements of statutory laws that no really civilized society would punish with imprisonment.

NELSON MANDELA, *The Struggle Is My Life,* 1978

Only free men can negotiate. Prisoners cannot enter into contracts.

NELSON MANDELA, February 1985

For many Black youths prison replaces the family as a primary source of socialization.

JOE JOHNSON, in Jones, "The Black Male in Jeopardy," *Crisis,* March 1986

The cell in which I was held at the beginning was so small that if I stretched my hands I touched both walls. I could barely exercise. In this cell, all I had was a plastic bottle with five glasses of water, a homemade sanitary bucket, and three blankets and a sisal mat. That is all, besides what I was wearing.

WINNIE MANDELA, "Solitary Confinement," *Mandela,* 1989

An hour was like a year. I was locked up in the bare cell, literally with nothing, nothing to read, nothing to write, nothing to do, and no one to talk to. . . . I suffered the isolation for two months and finally concluded that nothing was more dehumanizing than isolation from human companionship.

NELSON MANDELA, *Higher than Hope,* 1991

The prison is above all punitive. It operates to break the human spirit, to exploit human weakness, undermine human strength, destroy initiative, individuality, negate intelligence and process an amorphous, robot-like mass. The great challenge is not how to resist, but how not to adjust, to keep intact the knowledge of society outside and to live by its rules, for that is the only way to maintain the human in the social within you.

Ibid.

PRIZE

Two birds disputed about a kernel when a third swooped down and carried it off.

CONGO

The essential prize was freedom and the struggle was to provide choice for Black people.

JULIAN BOND, c. 1985

PROBLEM

When you see an arrow that is not going to miss you, throw out your chest and meet it head on.

CONGO

The real problem is not the Negro but the Nation. It is whether the republic shall be a republic in fact or in stupendous shame.

T. THOMAS FORTUNE, in *Freeman,* 9 October 1886

The problem of the twentieth century is the problem of the color line.

W. E. B. DU BOIS, *Souls of Black Folk,* 1903

Resolutions on paper will not solve people's problems.

LUANNA COOPER, 1949

You do not solve problems by drifting backwards; you solve them by tearing down barriers so you can get at them.

BENJAMIN MAYS, in the *Evening News,* 15 July 1950

A greater problem is that so many civilized persons are willing to live in comfort even if the price of this is poverty, ignorance, and disease of the majority of their fellowman.

W. E. B. Du Bois, preface to Jubilee edition of *The Souls of Black Folk,* 1953

The only way to solve a problem that is unjust is to take immediate action to correct it.

Malcolm X, in "Malcolm X and James Farmer: Separation and Integration," *Dialogue,* May 1962

Recognition of the problem is half the solution.

James Farmer, *The New Jacobins and Full Emancipation,* 1965

Never let blackness be your problem but somebody else's problem.

Adam Clayton Powell, Jr., speech given at Howard University, Washington, D.C., 29 May 1966

Liberation seems to be related to the distance people are from the problem.

Whitney Young, Jr., 2 September 1967

You are either part of the solution or part of the problem.

Eldridge Cleaver, c. 1968

Liberty and justice are in real danger in America. It is both curious and frightening to notice that what used to be minority problems have now become majority problems. Every time you turn around, you notice someone else is losing his civil liberty.

Dick Gregory, *No More Lies,* 1971

Everybody has an infirmity. Everybody has a weakness. Everybody has a defect. Everybody has a disease. Everybody has a problem. Everybody has an obstacle. Everybody has difficulty. It may be cancer. It may be mental frustration. It may be spiritual inequity. . . . Whatever it is, face it as a fact. Work within that limitation. That limitation is where your strength ends. It is where God's power begins.

William Holmes Borders, Sr., "Handicapped Lives," in Philpot, ed., *Best Black Sermons,* 1972

While the nation waltzed into the '70s believing that its Black problem had been blown or burned away, infant mortality rates remained twice as high for us, nearly half of all Black families earned less than $5,000 a year, and the average Black American was dying seven years earlier than others.

Julian Bond, speech given in Atlanta, Georgia, 13 January 1975

[I]f you isolate your problem from all others in society, your chances of solving it are slim; serious problems require wisdom, and wisdom requires perspective.

Bill Russell, *Second Wind,* 1979

Thinking your way through your problem is better than wishing your way through.

Coleman Young, 1980

The problem with me is I'm so good even my friends think I'm doing something wrong. Flair and flamboyance is not illegal. It may be detestable, it may be offensive, but it's not illegal.

Don King, in *Jet,* 19 November 1984

The problem with the criminal justice system is that it is inherently unjust. It leaves its victims at the mercy of institutionalized mental, physical, and spiritual harassment and abuse.

Safiya Henderson, in *Crisis,* March 1987

Two major problems are materialism and individualism. The idea that what provides me with the most immediate symbols of success is most important. So give me a gold chain, an automobile, and something that gives me the appearance of having arrived. This mentality is a real underminer of community values. The other problem is individualism—the attitude that "This is for me, this is mine, that's what counts." That has eroded the whole sense of family and community. There is a real loss of any sense of accountability.

Na'im Akbar, *Essence,* April 1988

White folks have historically not put Black folks over anything, or gotten them into anything that did not in some way connect to the "Black problem" in the country, and the Black problem is rapidly becoming synonymous with the Black underclass.

HARRY EDWARDS, in "Hardline," *Detroit Free Press,* 8 May 1988

I am not the problem. Man is the problem. Woman, anything capable of thought.

CHARLES JOHNSON, *Middle Passage,* 1990

The problem with a lot of Black writing—and American writing in general—is that we don't have the fiction opening up our understanding, our vision of the world.

CHARLES JOHNSON, in "Interview with Charles Johnson," *The World and I,* June 1991

Americans should not fall into the trap of blaming all the problems faced by Blacks or other minorities on others. We are not beggars or objects of charity. We don't get smarter just because we sit next to white people in class, and we don't progress just because society is ready with handouts.

CLARENCE THOMAS, *The Wall Street Journal,* 5 July 1991

PROGRESS

The whole history of the progress of human liberty shows that all concessions yet made to her august chains have been born of earnest struggle. If there is no struggle, there is no progress.

FREDERICK DOUGLASS, *My Bondage and My Freedom,* 1855

What stone has been left unturned to degrade us? What hand has refused to fan the flames of popular prejudice against us? What press has not ridiculed and condemned us? No other nation on the globe could have made more progress in the midst of such stringent disparagement. It would humble the proudest, crush the energies of the strongest, and retard the progress of the swiftest.

JAMES MCCABE SMITH, c. 1860

The moral, mental, and material condition of the race must be properly looked after before we can hope to establish any sort of status in the country.

T. THOMAS FORTUNE, in the *Freeman,* 26 March 1886

Time, patience, and constant achievement are great factors in the rising of a race.

BOOKER T. WASHINGTON, *The American Negro,* 1899

How shall man measure progress/ there where the dark-faced Josie lies?/ is it the twilight of nightfall/ or the flush of some faint-dawning day.

W. E. B. DU BOIS, *The Souls of Black Folk,* 1903

Out of abysses of Illiteracy,/ Through labyrinths of Lies,/ Across wastelands of Disease . . . / We advance!/ Out of dead-ends of Poverty,/ Through wildernesses of Superstition,/ Across barricades of Jim Crowism . . . / We advance!

MELVIN B. TOLSON, "Dark Symphony," *Rendezvous with Death,* 1944

Slowly we have lifted ourselves by our own bootstraps. Step by halting step, we have beat our way back. It has been a long and tortuous road since the Dred Scott decision of 1857, which branded us as non-citizens and by the Plessy decision, which gave the nation the green light to treat us as they pleased.

ROY WILKINS, "The Conspiracy to Deny," speech given to the NAACP, New York City, 1955

Progress is the attraction that moves humanity.

MARCUS GARVEY, *Garvey and Garveyism,* 1963

Self-progress brings its own reward.

Ibid.

Never at any time in the history of our people in this country have we made advances or progress in any way based upon the internal good will of this country. We have made advancement in this country only when this country was under pressure from forces above and beyond its control. The internal moral consciousness of this country is bankrupt.

MALCOLM X, "To Mississippi Youth," speech given in New York City, 31 December 1964

We began to boycott buses and form organizations, and go where we weren't wanted, or expected. We began to sit and march. We wanted to live our ideas, involved with various disciplines and religions. We came to understand that frustration was transferable, that energy was itself valuable. That the cool of death, of isolation, and self-imposed alienation was not what it meant.

IMAMU AMIRI BARAKA, c. 1967

[R]eappraise the past, re-evaluate where we've been, clarify where we are, and predict or anticipate where we are headed. . . .

TONI CADE BAMBARA, "Thinking About the Play *The Great White Hope,*" *Obsidian,* October 1968

We got our first colored hurricane—Beulah: when you can integrate that big breeze, that's progress.

DICK GREGORY, c. 1973

Don't let emotions interfere with our progress.

DUKE ELLINGTON, *Music Is My Mistress,* 1973

The one-time cotton picker was now the heavyweight champion of the world.

JOE LOUIS, *My Life,* 1981

When I came along in 1958, I was able to capture all of what was done before by men in segregated units denied the opportunity to advance. . . . but we still have a long way to go.

COLIN POWELL, in "Black General at the Summit of U. S. Powers," *Ebony,* July 1988

Here we are in the '80s, practically the '90s, talking about the same thing we were talking about in the '30s.

JAMES BROWN, in the *Detroit Free Press,* 12 February 1989

PROMISE

They made us many promises, more than I can remember, but they never kept but one; they promised to take our land, and they took it.

MANUELITO OF THE NAVAJOS, speech given to Congress, 1865

If a man loses anything and goes back and looks carefully for it he will find it, and that is what the Indians are doing now when they ask you to give them the things that were promised them in the past; and they should not be treated as beasts.

TATANKA YOTANKA (SITTING BULL), speech given to Congress, 1874

Life/ At fifteen/ Is a promise, a kingdom half glimpsed.

DAVID DIOP, "For a Black Child," *Poundings,* 1956

The shores of the great river, full of promises,/ Henceforth belong to you.

PATRICE LUMUMBA, *Weep, O Beloved Black Brother,* 1959

I had no idea of what I was going to make of my life, but I had given a promise and lost my innocence.

MAYA ANGELOU, *I Know Why the Caged Bird Sings,* 1970

What the people want is very simple. They want an America as good as its promise.

BARBARA JORDAN, speech given at Harvard University, Cambridge, Massachusetts, 16 June 1977

What Dr. King promised was not a ranch-style house and an acre of manicured lawn for every black man, but jail and finally freedom. He did not promise two cars for every family, but the courage one day for all families everywhere to walk without shame and unafraid on their own feet.

ALICE WALKER, *In Search of Our Mothers' Gardens,* 1983

PROPAGANDA

Truth comes to the market and could not be sold; we buy lies with ready cash.

NIGERIA

I have never seen things as bad as they are advertised.

BOOKER T. WASHINGTON, *The Man Farthest Down,* 1912

Propaganda has done more to defeat the good intentions of races and nations than even open warfare.

MARCUS GARVEY, *Philosophy and Opinions of Marcus Garvey,* 1923

Propaganda is used to convert people against their will.

Ibid.

He who has a message and no propaganda will not get very far.

J. A. ROGERS, "Critical Excursions and Reflections," *Messenger,* June 1924

Propaganda is a one-sided idea of life.

CLAUDE MCKAY, letter to W. E. B. Du Bois, 18 June 1928

Slogans can be worse than swords if they are only put in the right mouths.

ZORA NEALE HURSTON, *Moses, Man of the Mountain,* 1939

The whites told only one side. Told it to please themselves. Told much that is not true. Only his own best deeds, only the worst deed of the Indians, has the white man told.

YELLOW WOLF OF THE NEZ PERCES, in McWhorter, *Yellow Wolf: His Own Story,* 1940

In order to justify slavery and oppression in our times, the enslavers through their propagandists have to create the illusion that the enslaved people are subhumans and undeserving of human rights and sympathies. The first job is to convince the outside world of the inherent inferiority. The second job is to convince the citizen of the country where the enslavers hold forth and the third job, which is the cruelest, is to convince the slaves themselves that they deserve to be victims.

JOHN KILLENS, "Explanation of the Black Psyche," *The New York Times Magazine,* 7 June 1964

PROTECTION

The white men do not scalp the head; but they do worse—they poison the heart. His countrymen will not be scalped, but they will in a few years, become like the white men, so that you can not trust them. And there must be as in the white settlements, nearly as many officers as men, to take care of them and keep them in order.

BLACK HAWK OF THE SACS, c. 1804

I have no protection at home nor resting place abroad. I am an outcast from the society of my childhood, and an outlaw in the land of my birth. I am a stranger with thee and all my fathers were sojourners.

FREDERICK DOUGLASS, *My Bondage and My Freedom,* 1855

One afternoon the "troubles of the day come to visit the dead of the year" and the heaven is weakened by hidden beings; it is the heaven that all men fear who are in debt to the dead. And suddenly my dead approaches me. And he says to the dead: "You dead, who have always refused to die, who oppose death, protect from Sin to Seine, and in my fragile veins, my imperishable blood, protect my dreams like your sons, the birds of passages . . . "

LEOPOLD SENGHOR, *Songs of Darkness,* 1945

I shall probably never know my guardian angel, and though once I sought him earnestly, now I don't want to know him.

PAUL ROBESON, c. 1950

Never allow yourself to be cut off from the people. Predators use the separation tactic with great success. If you're going to do something radical, go to the masses. . . . That is your . . . protection.

VUSUMZI MAKE, in Angelou, *The Heart of a Woman,* 1981

If the men are oppressed, the women are oppressed. They depend on their men for protection and defense. Women do not have the muscle mass to liberate a people and protect the young. Women develop the young, but their men must provide protection and security.

FRANCES CRESS WELSING, *The Isis Papers,* 1991

PROTEST

"Walker's Appeal" was a remarkable brochure. Very few persons of this generation know of it, and those of the past have expressed a cold desire to inspect its pages.

ARTHUR A. SCHOMBURG, in *Racial Integrity,* July 1913

How like a spectre you haunt the pale devils! Always at their elbows, always darkly peering through the window giving them no rest, no peace! How they burn up their energies trying to keep you out! How apologetic and uneasy they are, yet, even the best of them, when you force an entrance, facetiously, incorrigibly smiling, disturbing, composed. Shock them out of their complacency, make them uncomfortable, make them unhappy. Give them no peace, no rest. How can they bear your presence, blackface, great unspeakable ghost of Western civilization.

CLAUDE MCKAY, review of "He Who Gets Slapped," *Liberator,* May 1922

If you protest courageously and yet with dignity, when the history books are written in future generations the historians will have to pause and say, "There lived a great people—a Black people—who injected new meaning and dignity into the veins of civilization." This is our challenge and our overwhelming responsibility.

MARTIN LUTHER KING, JR., speech given in Montgomery, Alabama, 5 December 1955

It is not enough to man the machinery of protest. Equally important today and twice as important tomorrow is participation in the responsibilities and opportunities of full citizenship in our democracy. This means moving, not only onto the picket line, but also the PTA meeting, moving into the libraries, community facilities and committee rooms, moving onto commissions and boards to exercise our rights and insure a fair share.

WHITNEY YOUNG, JR., *To Be Equal,* 1964

Negro protest and revolt is not new. It is as old as the slave trade. Negroes came here fighting back. They mutinied on the high seas; they organized hundreds of insurrections which were ruthlessly and predictably put down; they indulged in sabotage, mutilation, murder, and flight.

LORRAINE HANSBERRY, "White Backlash and the Black Revolution," speech given at Town Hall Forum, New York City, 15 June 1964

Other avenues of protest are ruled out. It's like a woman whose husband beats her and she doesn't cry out loud because she doesn't want the neighbors to know. If we play that role, we deserve to be beaten.

JOHN KILLENS, "White Backlash and the Black Revolution," speech given at Town Hall Forum, New York City, 15 June 1964

Every person of humane convictions must decide on the protest that best suits his convictions, but we must all protest.

MARTIN LUTHER KING, JR., "A Time to Break Silence," speech given at Riverside Church, New York City, 4 April 1967

Protest and pride in the Negro have been the most significant themes in what we've done.

DUKE ELLINGTON, *Music Is My Mistress,* 1973

PROVERB

Proverbs are the daughters of experience.

SIERRA LEONE

A proverb is the horse of conversation; when the conversation lags, a proverb will revive it.

YORUBA

A wise man who knows a proverb reconciles difficulties.

YORUBA

She is a proverb of propriety.

ALEXANDRE DUMAS, *Le Demi-Monde,* 1855

I got so tired of hearing those proverbs when I was a child. Now I use them all the time. Sometimes they are the best way to say what needs to be said. I teach them to my students. I have a collection of proverbs for class discussion and writing assignments.

MARVA COLLINS, c. 1987

PUNISH

There is scarcely a single fact more worthy of indelible record than the utter inefficiency of human punishments to cure human evils.

WILLIAM WHIPPER, "An Address on Non-resistance to Offensive Aggression," *The Colored American,* 16 September 1837

[T]he judge wished he could have sentenced Cherokee Bill to thirty days in the electric chair—with wet drawers on.

DICK GREGORY, *No More Lies,* 1971

If my daddy never spanked me what makes you think you can?

MARVA LOUIS, in Joe Louis, *My Life,* 1981

It's punishment to be compelled to do what one doesn't wish.

ALICE NELSON DUNBAR, in *Give Us Each Day,* 1984

Capital punishment has to be understood from an entirely new point of view. Race and class are important ingredients in the process that puts you on death row in the first place and determines if you go to the (electric) chair.

JOHN CONYERS, in "Words of the Week," *Jet,* 5 August 1985

PURPOSE

We come to a party to show teeth. We go to war to show our arms.

LIBERIA

We wanted to teach them what to eat, how to eat it, properly, and how to care for their rooms. Aside from this, we wanted to give them schooling and productive knowledge of some industry, thrift, and economy, that they would be sure of knowing how to make a living after they had left us. We wanted to teach them to study actual things instead of mere books alone.

BOOKER T. WASHINGTON, *Up From Slavery,* 1901

I am actually dying on my feet because I am giving every moment, almost night and day—every little crevice I can get into, every opportunity I can get to whisper into the ear of an upper official, I am trying to breathe my soul, a spiritual something, into the needs of our people.

MARY MCLEOD BETHUNE, speech given to the National Council of Negro Women, 26 November 1938

The less people have to live for, the less they have to risk losing—nothing.

ZORA NEALE HURSTON, *Moses, Man of the Mountain,* 1939

[T]here is a Purpose that invades all his purposes and a Wisdom that invades all his wisdoms.

HOWARD THURMAN, *Disciplines of the Spir't,* 1963

In no way should I derive my basic purpose from the past of the people of color.

FRANTZ FANON, *Black Skin, White Masks,* 1967

If the purpose of education is to make one person better off, it's going to take us forever to do what we need to do.

JOHNETTA COLE, c. 1971

And for ourselves, the intrinsic "Purpose" is to reach, and to remember, and to declare our commitment to all the living, without deceit, and without fear, and without reservation. We do what we can. And by doing it, we help ourselves trusting. . . .

JUNE JORDAN, in Walker, *Revolutionary Petunias,* 1971

Every man is born into the world to do something unique and something distinctive, and if he or she does not do it, it will never be done. If Lincoln had not emancipated the slaves, if Lincoln had not delivered those words in his inaugural address, those words would never have been written.

BENJAMIN MAYS, "I Knew Carter G. Woodson," *Negro History Bulletin,* March 1981

I have a purpose and a direction/ because yesterday I/ discovered me.

VAL GRAY, *Listen Children*, 1982

By childhood a person should have selected the purpose of his/her life.

MUHAMMAD ALI, in "Muhammad Ali: Champ of the Ring," *Class*, April 1984

Our lot on this earth is to seek and to search. Now and again we find just enough to enable us to carry on. I doubt that any of us will completely find and be found in this life.

JEAN TOOMER, in Kerman and Eldridge, *The Lives of Jean Toomer*, 1987

To have a purpose in life offsets any and all surrounding declines.

Ibid.

An inherent aim is in the soul of man, that it must seek and go after its destiny. God has given the soul a destiny: God has created man with an excellence—that excellence is his soul, is in him when he is born. Some people look at the fallacies in man, at the problems of man, the clumsiness of man, the lack of skills on the part of man, the ignorance of man; they look at all the shortcomings in man, and they judge him by his errors and not by his purpose.

IMAN DEEN MUHAMMAD, speech given in Los Angeles, California, 16 November 1987

Devoid of larger meaning and purpose, the schools have become the initial institution that too often fosters a lifelong pattern of antisocial behavior.

JOHN CONYERS, c. 1988

The purpose of all art is to make you see and reexperience things with unsealed vision.

CHARLES JOHNSON, in "Word Star," *Essence*, April 1988

QUARREL

A quarreler is a mindless person, if he is known as an aggressor. The hostile man will have trouble in the neighborhood.

PTAH HOTEP, c. 2340 B.C.

Quarrel is not a food which is eaten.

GHANA

Quarrels can end but words spoken never die.

SIERRA LEONE

A day of disputes, a day of insults.

WEST INDIES

There can't be an argument over the fact that we should have equality in America. But the white American doesn't want us to have it, because then he'll be giving up a freedom of his—to reject us because of color.

BILL COSBY, in *Playboy,* 1969

[Americans] have an on-going quarrel, with our lives, with the conditions that we live in.

RALPH ELLISON, "On Initiation Rites and Power," *Going to the Territory,* 1986

QUESTION

He who asks questions cannot avoid the answers.

CAMEROON

The real question is whether American justice, American liberty, American civil rights, American law, and American Christianity can be made to include all American citizens.

FREDERICK DOUGLASS, "What to the Slave is the Fourth of July?," speech given at Corinthian Hall, Rochester, New York, 5 July 1852

The question is not whether we will be extremist, but what kind of extremist we will be. Will we be extremist for hate or will we be extremist for love?

MARTIN LUTHER KING, JR., c. 1964

Question everything. Every stripe, every star, every word spoken. Question everything.

ERNEST GAINES, c. 1968

When I was told to do something, no questions would be tolerated. So I started to read and it was my salvation.

CAROLYN WARFIELD, in "Rising to the Light," *City Arts Quarterly,* Spring 1988

RACE

Slow and steady wins the race.

AESOP, "The Hare and the Tortoise," c. 600

Those who become inoculated with the vices of race hatred are more unfortunate than the victims of it. . . . Race hatred is the most malignant poison that can afflict the mind. It freezes up the fonts of inspiration and chills the higher faculties.

KELLY MILLER, *The American Negro,* 1908

[R]aces, like individuals, must stand or fall by their own merit: that to fully succeed they must practice their virtues of self-reliance, self-respect, industry, perseverance and economy.

PAUL ROBESON, "The New Idealism," *Targum,* June 1919

No race is richer in soul quality and color. Glorify them, popularize black.

NANNIE BURROUGHS, in *Southern Workman,* July 1927

The race rises as individuals rise . . . and individuals rise with the race.

ROSA BOWSER, *The Woman's Era,* c. 1928

Not to know what one's race has done in former times is to continue always a child.

CARTER G. WOODSON, *The Story of the Negro Retold,* 1935

Race is a blanket word for the entire human species and cannot be easily discarded. One may challenge the so-called scientific divisions of the human race, but we cannot abolish the instinct and the reality of race.

CLAUDE MCKAY, "Claude McKay vs Powell," *Amsterdam News,* 6 November 1937

Deal with me, and with the other men and women of my race as individual problems, not as a race problem, and the problem will soon cease to exist!

PAUL WILLIAMS, *American Magazine,* 1937

It never occurred to me to claim any merit because of it, and I have always resented the denial of anything on account of it.

CHARLES W. CHESTNUTT, "Post-Bellum—Pre-Harlem," *Breaking into Print,* 1937

I have no race prejudice of any kind. My kinfolks and my "skin-folks" are dearly loved. . . . I see the vices and virtues everywhere I look. . . . In my eyesight you lose nothing by not looking like me. . . .

ZORA NEALE HURSTON, *Dust Tracks on a Road,* 1942

No race has a monopoly on beauty, on intelligence, on strength. And there is room for everyone at the rendezvous of conquest.

AIMÉ CÉSAIRE, *Notes on a Return to the Native Land,* 1947

Othello's race since the days of Edmund Kean (1787–1833) has been in dispute. Here are some facts to remember: Shakespeare lifted his plot largely from the Hecatommithi (Novela, VII, 1608) by Cinthio, an Italian romancer. Cinthio only called his character "The Moor" and spoke of his "negrezza," or blackness of his skin. To "The Moor" Shakespeare gave a name, Othello.

J. A. ROGERS, *Nature Knows No Color Line,* 1952

The raceless American Christ has a light skin, brown hair, and sometimes—wonder of wonders—blue eyes. For whites to find him with big lips and kinky hair is as offensive as it was for the Pharisees to find him partying with the tax collectors. But whether whites want to hear it or not, Christ is black, with all of his features which are so detestable to white society.

JAMES CONE, *Black Theology and Black Power,* 1969

In our country, the authorities have made a third race: the Coloreds. According to the Immorality Act, no white can have any intimacy with a black, and vice versa. But even so, two million Coloreds have appeared. It just goes to show that you can not keep people from doing what they want.

MIRIAM MAKEBA, *My Story,* 1987

RACISM

Racism is a contempt for life, an arrogant assertion that one race is the center of value and object of devotion, before which other races must kneel in submission.

MARTIN LUTHER KING, JR., *Where Do We Go From Here?* 1958

The powerless can never be "racists" for they can never make the world pay for what they feel or fear except by suicidal endeavors which make them fanatics or revolutionaries, or both.

JAMES BALDWIN, *Nobody Knows My Name,* 1961

Racism shows the bankruptcy of man.

FRANTZ FANON, *The Wretched of the Earth,* 1963

Regardless of where or when one attends school in America, he receives along with legitimate educational experiences, a dose of pure, unadulterated racism. Since the earliest days of this nation's history, students attending its schools have achieved competence in the four, not three, "Rs," Reading, Riting, Rithmetic, and Racism.

MALCOLM X, in *Malcolm X Speaks,* 1965

[E]very Negro who did not challenge on the spot every instance of racism, overt or covert, committed against him and his people, who chose instead to swallow his spit and go on smiling, was an Uncle Tom and a traitor, without balls or guts, or any other commonly accepted aspects of manhood.

OSSIE DAVIS, in *The Autobiography of Malcolm X,* 1965

Afro-Americans have the right to direct and control our own lives, our history, and our future, rather than to have our destinies determined by American racists.

Ibid.

In his analysis . . . we aren't ready for freedom. . . . Africa wasn't ready for freedom. [Y]ou're not ready to go to a decent school . . . you're not ready to work on a decent job—they try and make it look like we never were ready.

MALCOLM X, speech given at the Organization for Afro-American Unity Rally, Audubon Ballroom, New York City, 24 January 1965

If this society fails, I fear that we will learn very shortly that racism is a sickness unto death.

MARTIN LUTHER KING, JR., in "Showdown for Violence," *Look,* 16 April 1968

I hate racism and I'm out to smash it or it's going to smash me.

STOKELY CARMICHAEL, in Cleaver, *Post-Prison Writings and Speeches,* 1969

Racism is so universal in this country, so widespread and deep-seated, that it is invisible because it is so normal.

SHIRLEY CHISHOLM, *Unbought and Unbossed,* 1970

We may not exterminate racism, but we must believe that different racial groups can live together in peace, and we must never cease to try to build a society in which the fatherhood of God and the brotherhood of man become realities.

BENJAMIN MAYS, "What Man Lives By," in Philpot, ed., *Best Black Sermons,* 1972

A bigot is a person who has no respect, no sympathy, no concern about any religion or any creed, person, race, except his religion, his creed, his color, and his race.

C. L. FRANKLIN, "The Conversion of Paul: A Bigot Meets Jesus," sermon recorded in 1973

Racism ... that peculiarly national disease, is an infection that's spread across the length and breadth of this land.

VERNON JORDAN, c. 1975

Most Negroes have a little Black militancy swimming around in them and most white people have a little of the Ku Klux Klan swimming around in them. If we'd be honest with each other, we would discover we are all victims of racism that is historically a part of this country.

BARBARA JORDAN, *Barbara Jordan,* 1977

The root cause of racism and its primary result is that whites refuse to see us [blacks] as people.

VUSUMZI MAKE, in Angelou, *The Heart of a Woman,* 1981

Racism is like the local creeping kudzu vine that swallows whole forests and abandoned houses; if you don't keep pulling up the roots it will grow back faster than you can destroy it.

ALICE WALKER, *In Search of Our Mothers' Gardens,* 1983

Nowhere else in the world is racism constitutionally enshrined. Put simply, in the Republic of South Africa, on the basis of race alone, more than seventy percent of the population is legally denied the basic right to vote or participate in any way in the national political process.

RANDALL ROBINSON, in Robinson and Kennedy, "The Case Against South Africa," *Ebony,* May 1985

Racism has always been alive, well, and living in America. But the real issue has always been: How are you going to let it or not let it affect you? I chose not to let it get to me by learning to do business.

BILL COSBY, c. 1986

Look at most of the major cities that have Black mayors and you'll find the same thing. What can we do about racism? We can talk about it, not in an acrimonious way, but in a clinical way. And maybe by talking about it, we can reach a few of those borderline white people who have never consciously thought about racism or prejudice to think about it and maybe want to do something about it.

HAROLD WASHINGTON, 1986

Racism took on the symbolic force of an American form of original sin....

RALPH ELLISON, "Perspective of Literature," *Going to the Territory,* 1986

Racism rests on an economic base. No group is pure and devoid of racism.

PARREN MITCHELL, in "Interview: Parren Mitchell," *Crisis,* February 1986

There will always be a need for the NAACP. Once we thought there would come a time when our work would be finished. But racism still exists and inequality is still built into this society.

BENJAMIN HOOKS, *Crisis,* June 1986

We leave the problem of racism for a period, but it returns. It always will. Race is a perpetual global dilemma.

GLOVER G. HANKINS, "Legal Comments," *Crisis,* November 1986

Racism has affected us so much that we are afraid of each other.

DOROTHY HEIGHT, in "NAACP Focus," *Crisis,* November 1986

A new country, but the same old racism. In South Africa, they call it apartheid. Here in the South, it is called Jim Crow.

MIRIAM MAKEBA, *My Story,* 1987

Racism is a scholarly pursuit, it's taught, it's institutionalized.

TONI MORRISON, in "Toni Morrison Now," *Essence,* October 1987

[Racists] ... have to negate the divinity and spirituality of the other person or group.

CLARENCE GLOVER, in "Spirituality: An African View," *Essence,* December 1987

[R]acism symbolizes a misunderstanding of the nature and reality of God.

Ibid.

Racism exists wherever slavery once built its house.

JULIO FINN, *Voices of Negritude,* 1988

Social climate in America today says that racism is tolerable again, and even fashionable in some neighborhoods.

CARL ROWAN, c. 1988

What's being sold today as "new ideas" is really just a new bottle to hold the old poison—the poison of neglect, of meanness, of throwing human beings into the ditch of permanent poverty.

JOHN E. JACOBS, speech at the Urban League Convention, Detroit, Michigan, 1988

Racism seems ageless—like the passion of those who war against it.

GORDON PARKS, "What Became of the Prophets of Rage?" *Life,* Spring 1988

We don't need to jive ourselves about the fact, this is a racist society with long traditions of racism. These are attitudes and dispositions deeply rooted in American society.

HARRY EDWARDS, in "Hardline," *Detroit Free Press,* 8 May 1988

Racism . . . leaves a shadow in one's sense of accomplishment, [and] it can make one feel like a perpetual outsider.

ALVIN AILEY, in "Alvin Ailey Celebrates 30 Years of Dance," *Essence,* November 1988

When I was turning from my teens to my twenties, I dealt with a lot of racism in Hollywood. I still have to persuade my way into offices and convince executives I'm right for certain roles. I put myself out there so far that when I fail it's very painful. Overcoming racism has certainly made me smarter and wiser.

RAE DAWN CHONG, c. 1989

We may be losing the battle for equality because racism is broader and stronger than ever before.

THURGOOD MARSHALL, 1989

Racism has evolved. Right-wing racism says, I'll let you in my corporation, but you'll never be president. I'll take you in my corporation, but you have to stay here twice as long to be a vice-president. I'll take you into my corporation, but I don't care how creative you are, you have to answer to white superiors.

DON DAVIS, 1989

Racism is deeply embedded in American religion and society. . . . Racism is a cancer. To get rid of this deadly disease requires radical surgery that cuts deep into not only the "body politic" but also the "body of Christ" as white and Black Christians like to call themselves.

JAMES CONE, *Martin and Malcolm and America,* 1991

Racism [began] as a form of self-alienation, [and] has evolved into the most highly refined form of alienation from others.

FRANCES CRESS WELSING, *The Isis Papers,* 1991

I'm always suspicious of people who say "I'm not racist." I feel on much better ground with people who say, "I'm working on overcoming my racism." We've got to approach this problem with as much humility and generosity as we possibly can.

ANDREW YOUNG, 7 January 1991

Racism is still very much a part of the American way of life; we do not live in a color-blind society.

DAMON KEITH, in the *Detroit News,* 26 April 1991

Racism can't be overcome. It will be there for the rest of your life. There will always be people who don't like you because you're Black, Hispanic, Jewish. You have to figure out how to deal with it. Racism is not an excuse to not do the best you can.

ARTHUR ASHE, in *Sports Illustrated,* July 1991

RADICAL

We need more radicalism among us before we can speak as becomes a suffering, oppressed, and persecuted people.

CHARLES LENOX REMOND, letter to a friend, 1841

We who for twenty-five years had been called radical were not radical at all.

W. E. B. DU BOIS, in the *Messenger,* March 1919

Radical is a label that is always applied to people who are endeavoring to get freedom. Jesus Christ was the greatest radical the world ever saw.

MARCUS GARVEY, c. 1925

Why, that man is a radical. He would have the common people talking about equality.

ZORA NEALE HURSTON, *Moses, Man of the Mountain,* 1939

I was born to be a radical.

ADAM CLAYTON POWELL, JR., "Once Upon a Time," *Marching Blacks,* 1945

I am a radical and I am going to stay one until my people get free to walk the earth.

PAUL ROBESON, "Let's Not Be Divided," *Baltimore Afro-American,* 30 July 1949

[A] radical change denotes the end of something . . . and the beginning of something . . . [a] revolution.

OTIS MOSS, "Going from Disgrace to Dignity," in Philpot, ed., *Best Black Sermons,* 1972

I consider myself a radical because I always wanted to understand what is at the root of the problems of Black people.

ANGELA DAVIS, in *USA Today,* 21 August 1986

READING

I have seen many beatings—Set your heart on books! I watched those seized for labor—There's nothing better than books! It's like a boat on water.

Instruction of Sile, c.1305–1080 B.C.

A good book is a garden carried in the pocket.

AFRICA

But who has ever seen good men spoiled by books?

AFRICA

I can't read a book, but I can read people.

SOJOURNER TRUTH, speaking at the 8th Anniversary of Negro Freedom, Boston, Massachusetts, 1 January 1871

A young colored boy who had learned to read in the state of Ohio came to Malden. As soon as the colored people found out that he could read, a newspaper was secured, and at the close of nearly every day's work this young man would be surrounded by a group who were anxious to hear him read the news.

BOOKER T. WASHINGTON, *Up From Slavery,* 1901

I read *Up From Slavery* and then my dream—if I may so call it—of being a race leader dawned.

MARCUS GARVEY, *Philosophy and Opinions of Marcus Garvey,* 1923

Make no sound, do not speak: eyes, heart, mind, dreams are about to explore a forest. . . . A secret but tangible forest.

JEAN-JOSEPH RABÉARIVELO, "Reading," *Near Dawn,* c. 1939

As I read, my ears are opened to the magic of the spoken word.

RICHARD WRIGHT, *12 Million Black Voices,* 1941

The whole world opened to me when I learned to read.

MARY MCLEOD BETHUNE, "Faith That Moved a Dump Heap," *WHO,* June 1941

But certain things have seemed to me to be here as I heard the tongues of those who had speech, and listened to the lips of the books.

ZORA NEALE HURSTON, *Dust Tracks on a Road,* 1942

It was the voice of the eternal storyteller, the trader in dreams who nursed the dreams of all the ages and clothed them with words.

PETER ABRAHAMS, *Tell Freedom,* 1954

Of all the literature that I studied, the book that did more than any other to fire my enthusiasm was the *Philosophy and Opinions of Marcus Garvey.*

KWAME NKRUMAH, *Autobiography of Kwame Nkrumah,* 1957

Garvey spent much of his time in the libraries reading of the rise and fall of empires, economics, and many other things.

AMY GARVEY, *Garvey and Garveyism,* 1963

[In prison,] in every free moment I had, if I was not reading in the library, I was reading on my bunk. . . . No university would ask any student to devour literature as I did.

MALCOLM X, *The Autobiography of Malcolm X,* 1965

My alma mater was books, a good library.

Ibid.

I started reading. I read everything I could get my hand on, murder mysteries, *The Good Earth,* everything. By the time I was thirteen I had read myself out of Harlem. I had read every book in two libraries and had a card for the Forty-Second Street branch.

JAMES BALDWIN, *A Rap on Race,* 1971

Reading [the] Declaration of Independence made me want to take a look at the United States Constitution to see what else I might have missed!

DICK GREGORY, *No More Lies,* 1971

Reading is important—read between the lines. Don't swallow everything.

GWENDOLYN BROOKS, c. 1975

I read everything I could about Black History.

COLEMAN YOUNG, speech given at Miller Junior High School, Detroit, Michigan, June 1978

Other than [my father], I relied on books. During [the] time of withdrawal in junior high I had my own private world, and my most prized possession was my library card from the Oakland Public Library.

BILL RUSSELL, *Second Wind,* 1979

The combination of Pushkin's genius and reading habits ultimately led to his crowning achievement, becoming the greatest poet in Russian history.

JAMES D. LOCKETT, "Alexander Sergeivich Pushkin: An Interpretation of the Russian Revolution," *Negro History Bulletin,* July–September 1982

I've been in . . . another college . . . a college of books—musty old books that went out of print years ago.

ALICE WALKER, *In Search of Our Mothers' Gardens,* 1983

I write the kind of books I want to read.

TONI MORRISON, "Rootedness: The Ancestor as Foundation," in Evans, ed., *Black Women Writers,* 1984

If you want to act, you've got to read scripts. That's why a lot of actors aren't working, they can't read.

ROBERT TOWNSEND, in *Jet,* 8 October 1984

What one reads becomes part of what one sees and feels.

RALPH ELLISON, "Remembering Richard Wright," *Going to the Territory,* 1986

While other students were out playing I would often slip into my seat during recess and read a book.

TOM BRADLEY, *The Impossible Dream,* 1986

I had the freedom to explore and develop my mind. I went to the library to read things I didn't know anything about. I read everything I wanted.

AUGUST WILSON, in "Spotlight: August Wilson," *Essence,* August 1987

I journeyed South to North with the nameless narrator of Ralph Ellison's *Invisible Man:* lived with elegant old Black men in the YMCA on 135th Street in Harlem; and had some of my illusions painfully stripped away. In Charles Chestnutt's *The Conjure Woman,* I sat spellbound at the feet of Julius, a master storyteller whose tales not only exposed the brutality of slavery but also were artfully designed to get exactly what he wanted from whites.

RICHARD PERRY, "My Expectations," *Essence,* January 1988

I read mythology a lot in the beginning. I read it to get some understanding of order. From there, I was able to delve into nonfiction, primarily history. Many of the images I draw I was exposed to through books.

CAROLYN WARFIELD, "Rising to the Light Within," *City Arts Quarterly,* Spring 1988

Being illiterate is like having handcuffs on all the time.

WILLIAM ROBINSON, *Life,* Spring 1988

My mother read me bedtime stories until I was six years old. It was a sneak attack on her part. As soon as I really got to like the stories, she said, "Here's the book, now you read."

OCTAVIA BUTLER, "Birth of a Writer," *Essence,* May 1989

Through the use of books I had the whole world at my feet, could travel anywhere, meet anyone, and do anything.

BENJAMIN CARSON, *Gifted Hands,* 1990

The doors of the world are open to people who can read.

SONYA CARSON, in *ibid.*

Developing good reading habits is something like being a champion. The champion didn't go into a gym one day and start lifting five-hundred-pound weights. He toned his muscles, beginning with lighter weights, always building up, preparing for more. It's the same with intellectual feats. We develop our minds by reading, thinking, by figuring things for ourselves.

Ibid.

There is nothing more important to the educational process than to have the ability to read and comprehend. It is the key. Otherwise you're always on the outside looking in.

WAYNE BUDD, in *Boston,* 7 December 1990

REALITY

Is this superiority? It is madness. We are the supermen who sit idly by and laugh and look at civilization. We, who frankly want the bodies of our mates and conjure no blush to our bronze cheeks when we own it. We who exalt the Lynched above the Lyncher and the Worker above the owner and the crucified above Imperial Rome.

W. E. B. DU BOIS, c. 1901

Illusion and reality often merged.

PETER ABRAHAMS, *Tell Freedom,* 1954

We take our shape within and against that cage of reality bequeathed us at our birth; and yet it is precisely by our dependence on this reality that we are most endlessly betrayed.

JAMES BALDWIN, *Notes of a Native Son,* 1955

Any upheaval in the universe is terrifying because it so profoundly attacks one's sense of one's own reality.

JAMES BALDWIN, *The Fire Next Time,* 1963

You face reality, not the lights. The lights go off as quickly as they go on.

JAMES BALDWIN, in "Conversation with James Baldwin," *Arts in Society,* Summer 1966

It is time for the Negro middle class to rise up from its stool of indifference, to retreat from its flight into unreality, and to bring its heart, its mind, and its checkbook to the aid of the less fortunate.

MARTIN LUTHER KING, JR., c. 1966

Reality is not the same to the doer as it is to the sayer.

HAKI MADHUBUTI, in *Black Poetry Writing,* 1975

Is there no reality that is unchanging, whatever the distance?

RENE MARQUES, "A Body Abaft," *Latin American Tales,* 1977

Reality has changed so chameleonlike before my eyes so many times, that I have learned, or am learning, to trust almost anything except what appears to be so.

MAYA ANGELOU, "Shades and Slashes of Light," in Evans, ed., *Black Women Writers,* 1984

Either you deal with what is the reality, or you can be sure that the reality is going to deal with you.

ALEX HALEY, 1985

You have to look at reality and see it like it is. Once you cloud your vision with sentimentality, you are in trouble.

COLEMAN YOUNG, 1987

The stories that we tell ourselves and our children function to order our world, serving to create both a foundation upon which each of us constructs our sense of reality and a filter through which we process each event that confronts us every day.

HENRY LOUIS GATES, JR., in Goss and Barnes, eds., *Talk That Talk,* 1989

REASON

If you can only find it, there is a reason for everything.

TRADITIONAL

If mankind ever expects to enjoy a state of peace, they must be ready to sacrifice on the altar the rude passions that animate them. This can only be done by exerting their reasoning powers.

WILLIAM WHIPPER, "An Address on Non-resistance to Offensive Aggression," *The Colored American,* 16 September 1837

When the human mind is once completely under the dominion of pride and selfishness, the reasoning faculties are inverted if not subverted.

FREDERICK DOUGLASS, in *Douglass Monthly,* 1863

Reasons are one thing, motives another.

CHARLES JOHNSON, in Locke, ed., *Negro Migration,* 1920

If prejudice could reason, it would dispel itself.

WILLIAM PICKENS, in Locke, ed., *The New Negro,* 1925

[W]hat is going to win in this world is reason if this ever becomes a reasonable world.

W. E. B. DU BOIS, "Behold the Land," speech given in Columbia, South Carolina, 20 October 1946

Reason, I sacrifice you to the evening breeze.

AIMÉ CÉSAIRE, *Notes on a Return to the Native Land,* 1947

Because there are no stars in the sky is no reason to assume that darkness is eternal.

PETER ABRAHAMS, *Return to Goli,* 1953

What lies beyond anger is reason.

JOHN WILLIAMS, *Beyond the Angry Black,* 1966

One cannot reason with those who have no use for reason.

Ibid.

Human existence cannot be mechanized or put into neat boxes according to reason. Human reason, though valuable, is not absolute, because decisions—those decisions which deal with human dignity—cannot be made by using the abstract.

JAMES CONE, *Black Theology and Black Power,* 1969

RECOGNITION

Let American and wrong, let American and cruelty, let American and prostitution, let American religion and piracy, let American and murder, cold-blooded and calculated, America's largest measure shake hands.

CHARLES LENOX REMOND, letter to the West Newberry Anti-Slavery Society, 16 September 1842

I know that my race must change. We cannot hold our own with the white man as we are. We only ask an even chance to live as other men live. We as to be recognized as men. We ask that the same law shall work alike on all men. If an Indian breaks the law, punish him by the law. If the white man breaks the law, punish him also.

HIGHN'MOOT TOOYALAKET (CHIEF JOSEPH) OF THE NEZ PERCES, "An Indian's View of Indian Affairs," *North American Review,* 1879

Recognition will do more to cement the friendship of the two races than any occurrence since the dawn of freedom.

BOOKER T. WASHINGTON, *Up From Slavery,* 1901

It seemed to me like trying to walk on the Atlantic Ocean to obtain recognition in the literary world.

FENTON JOHNSON, c. 1920

Recognition comes a little late.

MATTHEW HENSON, 1947

We have to keep in mind at all times that we are not fighting for integration, nor are we fighting for separation. We are fighting for recognition . . . for the right to live as free humans in this society.

MALCOLM X, "The Black Revolution," speech given at Hotel Teresa, New York City, 6 April 1964

He who is reluctant to recognize me opposes me.

FRANTZ FANON, *Black Skin, White Masks,* 1967

It is essential for a nation if they want recognition to be united and to enjoy self-control.

ELIJAH MUHAMMAD, *Muhammad Speaks,* 2 January 1971

I am America. I am the part you won't recognize. But get used to me, Black confident, cocky; my name, not yours; my religion, not yours; my goals, my own; get used to me.

MUHAMMAD ALI, *The Greatest,* 1975

Continue sending more and more representatives of your race against whom no negligibility can be found except the color of their skins, and unless human nature is basically rotten, recognition will come in time.

WILLIAM HASTIE, *Grace Under Pressure,* 1984

Recognition has come late. But you can never predict what's going to happen to you. My artistic nature was never dampened because the world didn't recognize me.

ADOLPH CAESAR, 1986

RECONSTRUCTION

Reconstruction was just as much a problem as the Civil War itself. Both the North and the South made mistakes in working out its solutions: but a thing of such difficulty cannot be perfectly done.

CARTER G. WOODSON, *Negro Makers of History,* 1928

The nation permitted a sordid bargain between Northern industry and Southern reaction; the former slaveholders submitting to commercial supremacy provided they were allowed to return the Negroes to slavery in all but name.

W. E. B. DU BOIS, *Reconstruction,* 1935

Gains made by Blacks during Reconstruction were literally drowned in rivers of blood.

COLEMAN YOUNG, in *Ebony,* April 1981

RELIGION

Hate sin; love God; religion be your prize;/ Her laws obeyed will surely make you wise,/ Secure you from the ruin of the vain,/ And save your souls from everlasting pain.

DANIEL PAYNE, *The Preceptor's Farewell,* 1835

I never had religion enough to keep me from running away from slavery in my life.

HENRY BIBB, *Narrative of the Life and Adventures of Henry Bibb,* 1849

Your religion was written on tablets of stone, by the iron finger of your God, lest you forget it. The red man could never remember it or comprehend it. Our religion is the tradition of our ancestors, the dreams of our old men, given them by the Great Spirit, and the visions of our sachems, and is written in the hearts of our people.

CHIEF SEATHE OF THE DUWAMISH, c. 1855

Religion! . . . that's always the cry with Black people. Tell me nothing about religion when the very man who hands you the bread at communion has sold your daughter away from you.

MARTIN DELANY, "Blakes, or The Huts of America," *Afro-Anglican Magazine,* 1859

Religion without humanity is poor human stuff.

SOJOURNER TRUTH, speech given in Battle Creek, Michigan, 1877

Were I to be reduced again to the chains I regard being the slave of a religious slaveholder the greatest calamity that could befall me . . . they are the worst, the basest, the meanest, the most cruel and cowardly of all others.

FREDERICK DOUGLASS, *Life and Times of Frederick Douglass,* 1892

A pretty good test of a man's religion is how it affects his pocketbook.

JAMES FRANCIS GRIMKE, *Stray Thoughts and Meditations,* 1914

We early imbibed the religion of the white man; we believed in it; we believe in it now. . . . But if that religion does not mean what it says, if God did not make of one blood all nations of men to dwell on the face of the earth, and if we are to be counted as part of the generation, by those who handed the oracle down to us, the sooner we abandon them or it, the sooner we find our place in a religious sect in the world.

C. E. MORRIS, sermon given at the National Baptist Convention, December 1922

If religion alone could win justice for the Black man, I would be a bishop.

MARCUS GARVEY, in *Negro World,* February 1924

I am sure that the missionaries from Abyssinia can teach the Italians more about the principles of Jesus than that ilk can teach the Ethiopians.

CARTER G. WOODSON, c. 1925

When you meet an American Negro who's not Methodist or a Baptist, some white man's been tampering with his religion.

BOOKER T. WASHINGTON, *Selected Speeches of Booker T. Washington,* 1932

The unreachable and therefore the unknowable always seem divine—hence, religion. People need religion because the great masses fear life and its consequences. Its responsibility weighs heavy.

ZORA NEALE HURSTON, *Dust Tracks on a Road,* 1942

Religion is very much like falling in love with a woman. You love her for her color and the music and the rhythm of her—for her Beauty, which cannot be defined. There is no reason to it, there may be other women more gorgeously beautiful, but you love one and rejoice in her companionship.

CLAUDE MCKAY, letter to Max Eastman, 16 October 1944

Theology, whether it be Jewish, Christian, Buddhist, Moslem, Shinto, or just plain heathen, is largely an excursion of the folk-mind into the realm of the unsubstantiated and the incoherent. Ideas picked up here and there are patched up into a system. The theologian of whatever faith is largely a romancer. For him miracles do happen as in pagan myths and in fairy tales.

J. A. ROGERS, *Nature Knows No Color Line,* 1952

When you've got so much religion that you can't mingle with people, that you're afraid of certain people, you've got too much religion.

C. L. FRANKLIN, "Without A Song," sermon given c. 1955

The first of us who came flocking to your religion came there as if to a revelation—that's it, as a revelation of your secret, the secret of your power, the power of your aeroplanes, your railways, and so on. Instead of that, you started to talk to them about God, the soul of the eternal life, and so forth. Do you think that they didn't know about that already long before your arrival?

MONGO BETI, *Le Pauvre Christ de Bomba,* 1956

[A]ny religion that professes to be concerned with the souls of men and is not concerned with the slums that damn them, and the social conditions that cripple them, is a dry-as-dust religion.

MARTIN LUTHER KING, JR., *Stride Toward Freedom,* 1958

My religion has come to mean more to me than ever before. I have come to believe more and more in a personal God—not a process, but a person, a creative power with infinite love who answers prayers.

MARTIN LUTHER KING, JR., in *Redbook,* September 1961

The Black man's pilgrimage in America was made less onerous because of his religion. His religion was the organizing principle around which his life was structured. His church was his school, his forum, his political arena, his social club, his art gallery, his conservatory of music. It was lyceum and gymnasium. His religion was his fellowship with man, his audience with God. It was the peculiar sustaining force which gave him the strength to endure where endurance gave no promise, and the courage to be creative in the face of his own dehumanization.

C. ERIC LINCOLN, c. 1962

Islam dignifies the Black man.

ELIJAH MUHAMMAD, in Essien-Udom, *Black Nationalism,* 1962

A divine libel suit would surely "hate and despise" a religious establishment which continues to build and decorate buildings while humans starve to death daily.

DICK GREGORY, *Nigger: An Autobiography,* 1964

Keep your religion in the closet, between you and your god. Because if it hasn't done anything more for you than it has, you need to forget it anyway.

MALCOLM X, speech given at Advanced Leadership meeting, Detroit, Michigan, 12 April 1964

America needs to understand Islam, because this is the one religion that erases the race problem from its society.

MALCOLM X, letter from Jedda, Saudi Arabia, 20 April 1964

The policies of every major religious institution, Protestant, Catholic, and Jewish, are in some way affected by what is economically expedient.

FLOYD MCKISSICK, *Three-Fifths of a Man,* 1969

[We] did not come into existence on the auction blocks of Richmond, Charleston, and New Orleans. Nor did our religious consciousness begin with the preaching of Christianity. The missionaries tried their best to stamp out the survivals of African religions . . . but they couldn't quite bring it off.

GAYRAUD WILMORE, "Black Theology," in Philpot, ed., *Best Black Sermons,* 1972

Christianity is the most materialistic of the major religions.

DESMOND TUTU, *Hope and Suffering,* 1983

Christianity can never be a merely personal matter. It has public consequences and we must make public choices.

Ibid.

Outcast to be used and humiliated by the larger society, the Southern Black sharecropper and poor farmer clung to his own kind and to a religion that had been given to pacify him as a slave, but which he soon transformed into an antidote against bitterness.

ALICE WALKER, *Living With the Wind,* 1985

When the Europeans came, they said we were nonbelievers. They denied the validity of our ancient religions.

MIRIAM MAKEBA, *My Story,* 1987

Religion in the African context is an understanding of nature.

CLARENCE GLOVER, in "Spirituality: An African View," *Essence,* December 1987

My Muslim belief tells me that the earth was created by a Supreme Being for mankind, given to Adam to do his thing.

KAREEM ABDUL JABBAR, in "The Meaning of Life," *Life,* December 1988

You don't need organized religion to connect with the universe. Often a church is the only place you can go to find peace and quiet. And where you bury the dead. But it shouldn't be confused with connecting with one's spirit. Spiritual zombies no longer hear their inner guide.

ALICE WALKER, in *USA Weekend,* 21 April 1989

My religion is my religion. My people are my people. They are not interconnected. My people are first. I happen to be a Black Jew. I am first Black and the religion I have chosen is Judaism.

SAMMY DAVIS, JR., in "Sammy Davis, Jr.: The World's Greatest Entertainer," *Ebony,* July 1990

RESERVATION

We will go north at all hazards and if we die in battle our names will be remembered and cherished by the people.

OHCUMGACHE (LITTLE WOLF) OF THE NORTHERN CHEYENNES, speech to Congress 1878

The soldiers came to the borders of the village and forced us across the Niobara to the other side, just as one would drive a herd of ponies. . . . We found the land there was bad and we were dying one after another, and we said. "What man will take pity on us?"

WHITE EAGLE OF THE PANCAS, speech to Congress, 1879

We bowed to the will of the Great Father and went south. There we found a Cheyenne cannot live. So we came home. Better it was, we thought, to die fighting than to perish of sickness. You may kill me here; but you cannot make me go back. We will not go. The only way to get us there is to come in here with clubs and knock us on the head, and drag us out and take us down there dead.

TAHMELAPASHME (DULL KNIFE) OF THE NORTHERN CHEYENNES, in Wright, "The Pursuit of Dull Knife from Fort Reno in 1878–1879," *Chronicles of Oklahoma,* 1968

RESISTANCE

Brethren, arise, arise! Strike for your lives and liberties. Now is the day and the hour. Let every slave throughout the land do this, and the days of slavery are numbered. You cannot be more oppressed than you have been—you cannot suffer greater cruelties than you have already. Rather die freemen than live to be slaves. Remember that you are four million! In the name of God, we ask, are you men? Where is the blood of your fathers? Has it all run out of your veins? Awake, awake! Let your motto be resistance, resistance, resistance!

HENRY HIGHLAND GARNET, "An Address to the Slaves of the United States of America," speech given at National Negro Convention, Buffalo, New York, August 1843

It is wrong for your lordly oppressors to keep you in slavery as it was for the man thief to steal our ancestors from the coast of Africa. You should, therefore, now use the same manner of resistance as would have been just in our ancestors when the bloody footprints of the first remorseless soul thief were placed upon the shores of our fatherland.

Ibid.

After resisting him, I felt as I had never felt before. It was a resurrection from the dark and pestiferous tomb of slavery. . . . When a slave cannot be flogged, he is more than half free.

FREDERICK DOUGLASS, *Life and Times of Frederick Douglass,* 1882

The whites were always trying to make the Indians give up their life and live like white men—go to farming, work hard and do as they did—and the Indians did not know how to do that and did not want to anyway. . . . If the Indians had tried to make the whites like them, the whites would have resisted, and it was the same way with many Indians.

WAMDITANKA (BIG EAGLE) OF THE SANTEE SIOUX, "Big Eagle's Story of the Sioux Outbreak of 1862," *Collections,* 1894

At the moment I saw King's resistance I knew I would never be able to live in this country without resisting everything that sought to disinherit me, and I would never be forced away from the land of my birth without a fight.

ALICE WALKER, *In Search of Our Mothers' Gardens,* 1983

Black people will not ride the caboose of society and we will not bring up the rear any more.

EDDIE MURPHY, in *Jet,* 2 May 1988

RESPECT

It is an abomination of the gods to show partiality. Look upon him who is known to thee like him who is unknown to thee.

EGYPT

The respect that is only bought by gold is not worth much. It is no honor to shake hands politically with men who whip women and steal babies.

FRANCES E. W. HARPER, *Anglo-African Man,* June 1859

Neither we, nor any other people, will ever be respected till we respect ourselves and we will never respect ourselves till we have the means to live respectfully.

FREDERICK DOUGLASS, in *North American Review,* 1881

[N]either the old-time slavery, nor continued prejudice need extinguish self-respect, crush manly ambition or paralyze effort.

PAUL ROBESON, "The New Idealism," *Targum,* June 1919

A race without authority and power is a race without respect.

MARCUS GARVEY, *Philosophy and Opinions of Marcus Garvey,* 1923

The longing of Black men must have respect, the rich and the strange readings of nations they have seen may give the world new points of view and make their loving, living, and doing precious to all human hearts.

W. E. B. DU BOIS, c. 1940

Respect me or put me to death.

MALCOLM X, speech given in New York City, 5 June 1964

I have more respect for the hippies than I have for the hypocrite.

HOSEA WILLIAMS, c. 1965

There are no degrees of human freedom or human dignity. Either a man respects another as a person or he does not.

JAMES CONE, *Black Theology and Black Power,* 1969

Do not confuse respect with knowledge. Remember, before one has white hairs, one must first have them black.

OUSMANE SEMBANE, *God's Bit of Wood,* 1970

[C]ommanding respect . . . is a social credit that will never become outdated, unless one is blinded by the blazing light of apparent freedom and overemphasized equality, the sugar-substitute meringue of what is actually being served to those who don't believe they are getting it.

DUKE ELLINGTON, *Music Is My Mistress,* 1973

You either cut the mustard or had mustard smeared all over your sorry face.

RAY CHARLES, *Brother Ray,* 1978

No Black American can have his or her self-respect and not be a member of the NAACP.

JESSE JACKSON, c. 1986

Perhaps I would get more respect from more people, but they see me as just another Black man. And if they don't respect Black people, in general, they won't respect me. And our country, in general, doesn't respect Black people.

JOHN H. JOHNSON, in "Interview," *Crisis,* January 1987

RESPONSIBILITY

No elephant ever found its trunk too heavy.

ZULU

It is a sad reflection . . . that a sense of responsibility which comes with power is the rarest of things.

ALEXANDER CRUMMELL, 1894

The writer who seeks to function within his race as a purposeful agent has a serious responsibility. In order to do justice to his subject matter, in order to depict Negro life in all of its manifold and intricate relationships, a deep, informed, and complex consciousness is necessary; a consciousness which draws for its strengths upon the fluid lore of a great people with the concepts that move and direct the force of history today.

RICHARD WRIGHT, c. 1940

Even an invisible man has a socially responsible role to play.

RALPH ELLISON, *Invisible Man,* 1952

History has thrust upon me a responsibility from which I cannot turn away. I have no choice.

MARTIN LUTHER KING, JR., sermon given at the Dexter Avenue Baptist Church, Montgomery, Alabama, January 1960

The Black woman has never been stronger than the Black man. The Black woman in the ghetto has been more responsible than the Black man.

DICK GREGORY, *No More Lies,* 1971

We are responsible for the world in which we find ourselves, if only because we are the only sentient force which can change it.

JAMES BALDWIN, *No Name in the Street,* 1972

Each person has a name that no other can bear. There is a beauty, a strength, and a glory that each person has of his own. The whole universe is thrown out of kilter when you shrink from your magnanimous responsibility.

HERMAN WATTS, "What Is Your Name?" in Philpot, ed., *Best Black Sermons,* 1972

He who made the cosmos had utter respect for law, order, and material, thus every person has a name, a place, and the responsibility for which no other can answer.

OTIS MOSS, "Going from Disgrace to Dignity," in *ibid.*

The responsibility for enforcement of the civil provisions of the civil rights statutes rests solely with the individual.

THURGOOD MARSHALL, c. 1975

Be responsible for our actions, and take responsible actions.

HAKI MADHUBUTI, c. 1975

We inherit a great responsibility . . . for we must give voice to centuries not only of silent bitterness and hate but also of neighborly kindness and sustaining love.

ALICE WALKER, *In Search of Our Mothers' Gardens,* 1983

We should neither ask nor accept that other races of people hold themselves responsible for what happens to our youth.

HORTENSE CANADY, in *Choosing to Succeed,* 1986

[E]ach writer has a triple responsibility—to himself, to his immediate group, and to his region.

RALPH ELLISON, "On Initiation Rites and Power," *Going to the Territory,* 1986

The role of the Black physician is to speak to the wide realm of healing . . . the burden has not gotten any lighter. You are not fixing a body, you are fixing a nation. You are players in this game of life—an extension of the omnipotent force.

OPRAH WINFREY, in *Jet,* 22 June 1987

I was taught by my mother and grandmother the responsibility of the penis.

GEORGE FOLKES, in "Is It True What They Say About Black Men?" *Ebony,* July 1987

Black Americans must begin to accept a larger share of responsibility for their lives. For too many years we have been crying that racism and oppression have to be fought on every front. But to fight any battle takes soldiers who are strong, healthy, committed, well-trained, and confident. I don't believe that we will produce strong soldiers by moaning about what the enemy has done to us.

JESSE JACKSON, 1988

The most worthwhile endeavor I have ever undertaken is responsibility for my own life. It's hard and it's worth it.

LEVAR BURTON, *Jet,* 29 August 1988

REVOLUTION

Every revolution has its catastrophes.

ALEXANDRE DUMAS, *The Count of Monte Cristo,* 1844

The Armistad triumphed against Oppression, under the leadership of Cinque, a prince of the Mendi people of Sierra Leone; these men refused to be enslaved.

Black Chronicle, 20 December 1864

Slavery and peaceful institutions can never live peaceably together. Liberty must either overthrow slavery, or be itself overthrown by slavery.

FREDERICK DOUGLASS, *Life and Times of Frederick Douglass,* 1881

The revolution is upon us, and since we are largely of the laboring population, it is very natural that we should take sides with the labor forces in the fight for a juster distribution of the results of labor.

T. THOMAS FORTUNE, in *Freeman,* 20 March 1886

Revolutions are of many sorts. They are silent and observable, noiseless, as the movement of the earth from center to circumference, making huge gaps in the map of the earth, changing the face of empires, subverting dynasties and breaking the fetters asunder or riveting them anew. Agitators are inevitable. They are as necessary to social organism as blood is to animal organism. Revolution follows as matter of course.

Ibid.

[N]ot until [the] revolution of mind is completed will there be a fair chance for the full development of those principles of brotherhood and liberty which we hold as ideals.

MARY MCLEOD BETHUNE, "Notes for Address before the Women's Club," c. 1930

Good morning, Revolution:/ You're the very best friend/ I ever had./ We gonna pal around together from now on.

LANGSTON HUGHES, "Good Morning Revolution," *The Dream Keeper and Other Poems,* 1932

Let a new earth rise. Let another world be born. Let a bloody peace be written in the sky. Let a second generation full of courage issue forth; let a people loving freedom come to growth. Let a beauty full of healing and a strength of final clenching be the pulsing in our spirits and our blood. Let the martial songs be written, let the dirges disappear. Let a race of men now rise and take control.

MARGARET WALKER, "For My People," *For My People,* 1942

Peace and revolution make uneasy bedfellows.

ALBERT LUTHULI, "The Dignity of Man," Nobel Peace Prize Acceptance Speech, 1961

Revolutions seldom go backward.

E. U. ESSIEN-UDOM, *Black Nationalism,* 1962

A great revolution is taking place in our world, a social revolution in the minds and souls of men. And it has been transformed into a unified voice, crying out, "We want to be free."

MARTIN LUTHER KING, JR., 1963

In a revolution one must choose his side and stick to it.

C. L. R. JAMES, *The Black Jacobins,* 1963

Revolution is like a forest fire, it burns everything in its path.

MALCOLM X, "Message to the Grass Roots," speech given in Detroit, Michigan, 10 November 1963

Revolution is necessitated by abusive and reactionary power.

ROBERT WILLIAMS, "USA: The Potential of a Minority Revolution," *The Crusader Monthly Newsletter,* May–June 1964

Things are never as simple and clear-cut as the shapers and revolutionaries would make us believe. There are no interest-free shortcuts. If you skip a stage in one way, you pay for it in another.

PETER ABRAHAMS, *This Island Now,* 1967

There is no violent revolution except as a result of the Black mind expanding, trying to take control of its own space.

IMAMU AMIRI BARAKA, c. 1968

Our war is not a war of conquest, it is a war of revolutionary liberation. We fight not only in self-defense but to free, unite, and reconstruct.

KWAME NKRUMAH, *Handbook of Revolutionary Warfare,* 1968

A revolutionary style always meshes with the demands of the masses at a given time and place.

LERONE BENNETT, JR., *The Challenge of Blackness,* 1968

And one of the great liabilities of life is that all too many people find themselves living amid a great period of social change and yet they fail to develop the new attitudes, the new mental responses that the new situation demands. They end up sleeping through a revolution.

MARTIN LUTHER KING, JR., "Remaining Awake Through a Great Revolution," sermon given at National Cathedral (Episcopal), Washington, D.C., 31 March 1968

All Black people are involved in the same struggle. Revolutionaries are not necessarily born poor or in the ghetto. There is a role for every person in the revolution.

H. RAP BROWN, *Die Nigger Die,* 1969

Every revolution that has been attempted in the name of bettering life for the total society has produced only a new ruling class. The vast majority of people who were "have nots" before the revolution were have nots after the revolution, precisely because they were in no position, politically, economically, or socially, to protect their own interests.

SHIRLEY CHISHOLM, speech given at Federal City College, Washington, D.C., 1969

Revolution is technical and economic and must encompass and connect itself very closely with scientific and economic discoveries.

NATHAN HARE, in *Black Scholar,* November 1969

Emasculated men don't revolt.

MARGARET WRIGHT, in "Storming the All-Electric Dollhouse," *Los Angeles Times,* 7 June 1970

In the last analysis, nearly all American revolutionaries, Black and white, can be bought. For this is a land where the dollar is God and many a one hundred pennies is hustled in His name.

LOFTON MITCHELL, "I Work to Please You," in Gayle, ed., *The Black Aesthetic,* 1971

When a woman becomes pregnant, the nine-month gestation period is evolution. But when that period of evolution is up, quick change occurs, the baby arrives and that is revolution. Anyone who thinks that he can stop a natural revolution by means of repression should muster all the National Guardsmen he can find, tell them to cross a pregnant woman's legs and see if they can stop the baby from being born.

DICK GREGORY, *No More Lies,* 1971

Revolution—replacing one ruling group and their system of government with another ruling group and a system of government.

JOHN O'NEAL, *Black Art Notebook,* 1971

One does not glorify in romanticizing revolution. One cries.

LORRAINE HANSBERRY, *Les Blancs,* 1972

Revolution arises out of need. Revolution is we need to change our ways of being with one another. Revolution is we need one another.

AL YOUNG, "Statement on Aesthetics, Poetics, Kinetics," in Chapman, ed., *New Black Voices,* 1972

The wonderful thing about revolution is that it gives one a chance to amend past crimes, to change, to be human.

TONI CADE BAMBARA, *Sea Birds Are Alive,* 1974

The two most revolutionary things Black people in America can do are to maintain a family and maintain a business.

SAFISHA MADHUBUTI, c. 1978

Only truth is revolutionary.

CHEIKH ANTA DIOP, *The Cultural Unity of Black Africa,* 1978

[M]ost ... revolutionaries ... do not really want change. They want exchange.

VUSUMZI MAKE, in Angelou, *The Heart of a Woman,* 1981

Not instant eradication of habits learned over a lifetime, but the abolition of everything that would foster those habits, and the creation instead of a new structure that would prevent them from returning.

ALICE WALKER, *In Search of Our Mothers' Gardens*, 1983

The real revolution is always concerned with the least glamorous stuff. With raising a reading level . . . with simplifying history and writing it down.

Ibid.

People are dying every day in South Africa. There is nothing that can be done gradually. A revolution is imminent.

JAMES M., in "South Africa: Peace Be Still," *Ebony Man*, December 1986

When Black men first went on the stage in the 1890s, it was a startling development, a revolutionary idea.

TEVIS WILLIAMS, "Black Dance in Perspective," *City Arts Quarterly*, Spring 1987

There are two revolutions going on in America, an economic and a political revolution. If you're in the political revolution, that's the one that's televised. The economic one is not. One is seeking freedom, the other finance. If you have economic power, you vote every day with your money. If you have political power, you vote only once every two years.

ROBERT WOODSON, c. 1988

RHYTHM

Something of old forgotten queens/ Lurks in the lithe abandon of your walk,/ And something of the shackled slave/ Sobs in the rhythm of your talk.

GWENDOLYN BENNETT, "To A Dark Girl," in Kerlin, *Negro Poets and Their Poems*, 1923

It is the thing that is most perceptible and least material. It is the archetype of the vital element. It is the first condition and the hallmark of Art, as breath is life: breath which accelerates or slows, which becomes even or agitated according to the tension in the individual, the degree and the nature of his emotion . . . rhythm in its primordial purity . . . in the masterpiece of Art . . . rhythm is alive, it is free . . . rhythm is that character of abandon which is ours, is itself rhythm.

LEOPOLD SENGHOR, "The Spirit of Civilization," *Présence Africaine*, 1956

Rhythm is the architecture of being, the inner dynamic that gives it form, the pure expression of the life force. Rhythm is the vibratory shock, the force which, through our sense, grips us at the root of our being. It is expressed through corporeal and sensual means; through lines, surfaces, colours, and volumes in architecture, sculpture, or painting, through accents in poetry and music, through movements in the dance. But, doing this, rhythm turns all these concrete things towards the light of the spirit. In the degree to which rhythm is sensuously embodied, it illuminates the spirit.

Ibid.

Black women, timeless,/ are sun breaths/ are crying mothers/ are snatched rhythms.

LARRY NEAL, "For Our Women," *Black Fire*, 1968

Rhythm is the element that infuses music with a biological force that brings forth a psychological fruit.

FRANCES BEBY, *African Music*, 1969

Rhythm is an invisible covering that envelops each note; a melodic phrase that is destined to speak of the soul or to the soul.

Ibid.

Rhythm—a basic creative principle. Rhythm—an experience or race memory.

LARRY NEAL, "The Black Art Movement," in Gayle, ed., *The Black Aesthetic*, 1971

I am the rhythm of my past, my present, I sing a song of the future/ I shall sing my rhythm.

EUGENE REDMOND, in Walton, *Music: Black, White & Blue*, 1972

We all share in the same cosmic rhythm. . . . For all natural laws are like the rhythm of the strings of the harp.

ERNESTO CARDENAL, "Love," *Vida en al Amor,* 1974

I want to proclaim out loud that life is only rhythm and rhythm within rhythm.

GUY TIROLIEN, "In Search of an Attitude," *Black Images,* Spring 1974

I set my own rhythm and it was usually a little faster than other people's.

RAY CHARLES, *Brother Ray,* 1978

Perfect rhythm brings perfect peace, perfect harmony, perfect joy.

ALFRED PASTER, *The Roots of Soul,* 1982

You change the rhythm of the talk and response and you change the rhythm *between* the talk and the response.

GAYL JONES, in Dixon, "Singing a Deep Song," in Evans, ed., *Black Women Writers,* 1984

RIGHTS

We will sooner bury ourselves beneath the ruins of our native country than suffer an infraction of our political rights.

HENRI CHRISTOPHE, *Manifesto of the King,* 18 September 1814

For even here, in the so-called free states, Blacks are denied the rights and privileges of citizenship. Foreigners, within a few years, receive these, but we native-born Black Americans, sons of the soil, are shut out.

Black Chronicle, September 1831

Before I go the bayonet should pierce me through. African rights and liberty is a subject that ought to fire the breast of every free man of color and excite in his bosom a lively deep, decided and heartfelt interest.

MARIA STEWART, 1833

Think of the undying glory around the ancient name of Africa, and forget not that you are native American citizens, and as such, you are justly entitled to all the rights.

HENRY H. GARNET, "Address to the Slaves of the United States of America," speech given at National Negro Convention, Buffalo, New York, August 1843

There is a great stir about colored men getting their rights, but not a word about colored women; and if colored men get their rights and not colored women theirs, you see the colored men will be masters over the women, and it will be just as bad as it was before. So I am for keeping the thing going while things are stirring; because if we wait till it is still, it will take a great while to get it going again.

SOJOURNER TRUTH, 1867

There was one or two things I had a right to, liberty or death. If I could not have one, I would have the other, for no man should take me alive. I should fight for my liberty as long as my strength lasted.

HARRIET TUBMAN, in Bradford, *Harriet, the Moses of Her People,* 1869

If we do not win we have certainly shown them that we were not cowards sleeping over our rights.

BOOKER T. WASHINGTON, 1879

The Bill of Rights is a Bill of Wrongs for the Negro.

FREDERICK DOUGLASS, c. 1881

The last struggle for our rights; the battle for our civilization is entirely with ourselves, and the problem is to be solved by us.

WILLIAM WELLS-BROWN, 1881

If we do not possess the manhood and patriotism to stand up in defense of these constitutional rights, and protest long, loud, and united against their continual infringement, we are unworthy of our heritage as American citizens and deserve to have fastened on us the wrongs about which many are disposed to complain.

J. C. PRICE, "The Negro in the Last Decade of the Century," *The Independent,* 1 January 1891

We will not be satisfied to take one jot or tittle less than our full manhood rights. We claim for ourselves every single right that belongs to a freeborn American, political, civil, and social; and until we get these rights we will never cease to protest and assail the ears of America with the story of its shameful deeds.

W. E. B. DU BOIS, speech given to Niagara Movement, Second Annual Meeting, Harper's Ferry, New York, 1906

If we fight we get our rights. We're second-class citizens because we sit idly by.

MARY CHURCH TERRELL, c. 1910

Human beings are equipped with divinely planted yearnings and longings. That's what the Constitution means by "certain inalienable rights."

NANNIE BURROUGHS, "Unload Your Uncle Toms," *Louisiana Weekly,* 23 December 1933

We do not intend to wait placidly for those rights which are already legally and morally ours to be meted out to us one at a time.

Advertisement in Greensboro, North Carolina, 1955

Political freedom and the rights of workers are indivisible.

KWAME NKRUMAH, speech given to African Trade Unions, Accra, Ghana, 5 November 1959

All men have the same rights. But some men have more duties than others.

AIMÉ CÉSAIRE, *Tragedy of King Christophe,* 1963

[R]ight temporarily defeated is stronger than evil triumphant.

MARTIN LUTHER KING, JR., Nobel Peace Prize Acceptance Speech, 10 December 1964

Human rights are God given. Civil rights are man made.

ADAM CLAYTON POWELL, JR., Commencement speech given at Howard University, Washington, D.C., 29 May 1966

I found myself in the world and I recognize that I have one right alone: That of demanding human behavior from the other. One duty alone: That of not renouncing my freedom from choice.

FRANTZ FANON, *Black Skin, White Masks,* 1967

I want the right to be Black and me.

MARGARET WRIGHT, in "Storming the All-Electric Dollhouse," *Los Angeles Times,* 7 June 1970

Civil rights don't take place in a vacuum. They are meaningful only in the real world where people have to survive, to work, to raise their families, to instill in their children hope for the future and the skills to function in a society where a broad back and a desire to work are no longer enough.

VERNON JORDAN, c. 1976

Chaos occurs when human rights are not respected.

ANDREW YOUNG, in *Playboy,* July 1977

[The] civil rights movement would never have taken off if some woman hadn't spoken up.

SEPTIMA CLARK, in "Righting Wrongs," *Life,* Spring 1988

No man has the right to consider his individual well-being when the survival of his race and his people are at stake.

HARRY EDWARDS, in "Hardline," *Detroit Free Press,* 8 May 1988

A lot of times you have civil rights groups whose business is mainly to stay in business. We're rehashing thirty-year-old rhetoric and not addressing the problems we have today, using old medicine on new diseases. A lot of doors have been kicked open, but I don't see groups leading people through them.

MARSHA WARFIELD, in *USA Weekend,* 28 June 1991

Since about 1980, the president and the Justice Department have failed to do much enforcement at all. Every time there is an employment complaint, the Justice Department is on the side of the people doing the discriminating.

MARY FRANCES BERRY, in *USA Weekend,* 28 June 1991

RITES

Elements in the initiates that I underwent in various cult groups in the Southern states in the 1930s corresponded with practices in West Africa. Among these were seclusion of novitiate, fasting, wearing of special clothing, dancing, spirit possession, sacrifices, acquiring a new name, reference to running water and to thunder and lightning.

ZORA NEALE HURSTON, *Mules and Men,* 1935

We must tell nothing of what we learned, either to women or to the uninitiated; neither were we to reveal any of the secrets of the rites of circumcision. That is the custom. Women, too, are not allowed to tell anything about the rites of excision.

CAMARA LAYE, *The Dark Child,* 1954

Primitive societies are much more efficient and consistent; they are much more concerned with guiding the young through each stage of their social development, while we leave much of this to chance. . . .

RALPH ELLISON, "On Initiation Rites and Power," *Going to the Territory,* 1986

An outdooring is the first African rite of passage. It always begins at dawn, eight days after the child's birth and gives family and friends a chance to see and welcome the newest soul.

MAYA ANGELOU, *All God's Children Need Traveling Shoes,* 1986

When I used to play basketball in the playground you didn't go to a stranger and introduce yourself. You had to prove yourself first.

HARRY EDWARDS, in "Hardline," *Detroit Free Press,* 8 May 1988

ROBESON, PAUL

. . . the tallest tree in the forest.

MARY MCLEOD BETHUNE, c. 1946

Robeson . . . more than any living man has spread the pure Negro folk song over the civilized world.

W. E. B. DU BOIS, "Tribute to Paul Robeson," 9 April 1958

Warning, in music-words/ devout and large,/ that we are each other's/ harvest:/ we are each other's/ business:/ we are each other's/ magnitude and bond.

GWENDOLYN BROOKS, "Paul Robeson," *Family Picture,* 1970

Paul Robeson needs to be studied. He was the most magnificent human being I have ever known of, heard of. A man of tremendous powers, a man of remarkable gifts. A man who had achieved a great deal, but was one of the simplest and one of the most gentle human beings.

C. L. R. JAMES, in "Interview: C. L. R. James," *The Black Scholar,* September 1970

Cynicism affects young people as detrimentally as drugs or crime, and a living faith that—with struggle—all things can be better is very much needed to medicine the times. Paul, in art and in life, was the living faith.

OSSIE DAVIS, "To Paul Robeson," *Freedomways,* First Quarter 1971

I have grown wiser and closer to painful truths about America's destructiveness. And I do have an increased respect for Paul, who over the span of that twenty years (since 1949) sacrificed himself, his career, and the wealth and comfort he once enjoyed because he was sincerely trying to help his people.

JACKIE ROBINSON, *I Never Had It Made,* 1972

Any organization that sponsored a Robeson appearance was threatened. . . . During the early 1950s a group of Harlem citizens organized to present Robeson in concert. Many prominent artists who had agreed to participate were threatened away by the powers in the entertainment world. And many citizens who did participate were witch-hunted on their jobs.

LOFTEN MITCHELL, *The New York Times,* 6 August 1972

If Paul Robeson had not been there, I would not be here. And so it is with the youth of today. The stand you took will help us with a stand in the days, weeks, months, and years ahead, for peace, for the rights and needs of the people.

SIDNEY POITIER, speech given at Tribute to Paul Robeson, Carnegie Hall, New York City, 15 April 1973

Your singing is a declaration of faith. You sing as if God Almighty sent you into the world to advocate the course of common man in song. You are truly the people's artist.

BENJAMIN MAYS, speech given at Tribute to Paul Robeson, Carnegie Hall, New York City, 15 April 1973

Here in the Valley of the Nile where men first lifted their eyes to the stars, we hail the day of your birth. Your life brings Peace on Earth and Goodwill to all men a little closer.

SHIRLEY GRAHAM DU BOIS, speech given at Tribute to Paul Robeson, Carnegie Hall, New York City, 15 April 1973

Kings will not be dethroned by fools. Giants will not be toppled by pygmies.

GEORGE W. CROCKETT, Paul Robeson Tributes, Carnegie Hall, New York City, 1976

How fortunate we were to have had Paul Robeson walk the earth among us! As artist and more he was a prophetic vision of how wondrously beautiful the human race may yet become.

LLOYD L. BROWN, Paul Robeson Tributes, Carnegie Hall, New York City, 1976

A titan whose free spirit could not be shackled.

CORETTA SCOTT KING, Paul Robeson Tributes, Carnegie Hall, New York City, 1976

Even in death, Paul Robeson stands as a monumental reminder that it is possible to find within oneself a purpose, and then to relentlessly and bravely pursue that purpose. Paul Robeson's purpose was to be a man.

PERCY SUTTON, Paul Robeson Tributes, Carnegie Hall, New York City, 1976

Although Paul is gone, his inspiration is eternal. We will continue to be instructed by his example, which was a source of our own theatrical birth.

DOUGLAS TURNER WARD, Paul Robeson Tributes, Carnegie Hall, New York City, 1976

Man does possess the capability to learn from his previous mistakes, as egregious as they may be. I hope that in the future we heed the words of the prophets and cries of the estranged. If so, we will have erected the only fitting monument to the life of Paul Robeson.

YVONNE BURKE, Paul Robeson Tributes, Carnegie Hall, New York City, 1976

He loved people of all colors and of many nations. He loved justice, freedom, compassion. Very few men in their lifetime bequeath a legacy to the living as Paul Robeson did. He was a giant among men.

ANDREW YOUNG, Paul Robeson Tributes, Carnegie Hall, New York City, 1976

The nobleness of Paul Robeson marked him as one of those rare individuals who deserve the accolade "Immortal." He strode across his time like a giant, fearless and ever willing to do and speak those things he believed in. He was a study in courage, a man of vast dignity and understanding.

VERNON JORDAN, Paul Robeson Tributes, Carnegie Hall, New York City, 1976

A great star. A truly great man, because greatness was his cloak.

WILLIAM (COUNT) BASIE, Paul Robeson Tributes, Carnegie Hall, New York City, 1976

The dimension of his talent made him our Renaissance man. He was the first American artist, Black or white, to realize that the role of the artist extends far beyond the stage and the concert hall. Early in life he became conscious of the plight of his people, stubbornly surviving in a racist society. This was his window on the world . . . he saw how the plight of his people related to the rest of the world.

JOHN HENRIK CLARKE, Paul Robeson Tributes, Carnegie Hall, New York City, 1976

Paul Robeson's dignity overrode the degradation heaped on him because of his color.

COLEMAN YOUNG, speech given at Paul Robeson Celebration, Detroit, Michigan, April 1976

Paul Robeson broke our hearts with beauty.

EDITORIAL, *Essence,* October 1977

Black he was, through and through, in feeling, thought, and act; maintaining by choice, at whatever the cost, his position in the struggle which had long ago become the central fact of his existence, and for which he had a strategy, a Black strategy.

OSSIE DAVIS, in "Paul Robeson Archives/Legacy of Change," *Essence,* October 1977

When I feel bad, when I get discouraged, when I feel frustrated, I go back and read Robeson.

HARRY EDWARDS, in "Hardline," *Detroit Free Press,* 8 May 1988

ROOTS

[We're] branches without roots.

ZORA NEALE HURSTON, *Their Eyes Were Watching God,* 1937

Having helped on many fronts . . . it is now time for me to return to the place of my origin—to those roots which, though embedded in Negro life, are essentially American. . . .

PAUL ROBESON, "A Great Negro Artist Puts His Genius to Work for His People," *Sunday Worker,* 4 June 1939

What a life it is we live! Our roots are nowhere! We have no home even upon this soil which we formed with our blood and bones.

RICHARD WRIGHT, *12 Million Black Voices,* 1941

[Y]ou come from sturdy, peasant stock, men who picked cotton and dammed rivers and built railroads, and in the teeth of the terrifying odds, achieved an unassailable and monumental dignity. You come from a long line of great poets, some of the greatest poets since Homer. One of them said, *The very time I thought I was lost, my dungeon shook and my chains fell off.*

JAMES BALDWIN, *The Fire Next Time,* 1963

Just as a tree without roots is dead, a people without history or cultural roots also becomes a dead people.

MALCOLM X, speech given at Organization for Afro-American Unity Rally, Audubon Ballroom, New York City, 24 January 1965

People find a sense of being, a sense of worth and substance being associated with land. Association with final roots gives us not only a history but proclaims us heirs to a future.

HAKI MADHUBUTI, c. 1975

All cultural explorers . . . start off from specific roots which color their vision and define the allegiances of the work of art they produce.

KEORAPETSE KGOSITSILE, in *Black Poetry Writing,* 1975

Let the roots of your motherhood caress your body,/
Let the naked skin absorb the home sun and shine ebony.

TSEGAYE MEDHEN, "Home-coming Son," in *Black African Voices,* 1975

Alienation implies a separation from the source, a loss of roots to sustain existence.

ALFRED PASTER, *The Roots of Soul,* 1982

. . . first in myth, later in reality, passion and violence watered my root soil.

ROY WILKINS, *Standing Fast,* 1982

He did not come from the ground like grass. He has risen like the banyan tree. He has roots.

MAYA ANGELOU, *All God's Children Need Traveling Shoes,* 1986

RUN

You may perhaps think hard of us for running away from slavery, but as to myself, I have but one apology to make for it . . . that I did not start at an earlier period. I might have been free long before I was.

HENRY BIBB, letter to Gatewood, 28 March 1844

A good run is better than a bad stand.

JAMES D. CARRUTHERS, *The Black Cat Club,* 1902

He that fights and runs away will live to fight another day.

Ibid.

The whole world is run on bluff.

MARCUS GARVEY, *Philosophy and Opinions of Marcus Garvey,* 1923

They can run, but they can't hide.

JOE LOUIS, c. 1940

Our godfathers and fathers had to run, run, run. My generation is out of breath. We ain't running no more.

STOKELY CARMICHAEL, c. 1963

He who starts behind in a race must forever remain behind or run faster than the man in front.

MARTIN LUTHER KING, JR., *Where Do We Go From Here?* 1968

I was a runaway from birth.

ESTEBAN MONTEJO, *Autobiography of a Runaway Slave,* 1968

Many Black people ran away from Mississippi in the twenties, some fleeing for their lives, but my father must be one of the few who ever ran to Mississippi.

BILL RUSSELL, *Second Wind,* 1979

SACRIFICE

Let not the natives of Africa be sacrificed to the greed of gold, their liberties taken away, their family life debauched, their just aspirations repressed, and avenues of advancement and culture taken from them.

W. E. B. DU BOIS, "To the Nations of the World," Address to Pan-African Conference, London, 1900

When I say sacrifice, I mean sacrifice. I mean a real and definite surrender of personal ease and satisfaction. I embellish it with no theological fairy tales of a rewarding God or a milk and honey heaven. I am trying to scare you into the duty of sacrifice by the fires of a mythical Hell.

W. E. B. DU BOIS, Howard University commencement address, 1930

Do not allow our brothers, our friends, to be sacrificed to men who wish to reign over the ruins of human species.

TOUSSAINT L'OUVERTURE, in James, *The Black Jacobins,* 1963

Isolated sacrifices are useless.

DOROTHY RILEY, in *Pelahatchee People,* 1986

I would not make the sacrifices for any job to stop doing what I enjoy doing.

WILLIE BROWN, in *GQ,* March 1990

SAVIOR

God deliver us from our friends and we will take care of our enemies.

AUGUSTUS WASHINGTON, "African Colonization—By A Man of Color," *New York Daily Tribune,* 9–10 July 1851

We should let our godliness exhale like the odor of flowers. We should live for the good of our kind, and strive for the salvation of the world.

ALEXANDER CRUMMELL, c. 1883

When the Bible says, "Work out your salvation with fear and trembling," I am tempted to believe that it means what it says. In the past we have had the fear and the trembling. We are to work out our salvation, work it out with pen and ink, work it out with rule and compass, work it out with horsepower and steam power, work it out on the farm, in the shop, school room . . . and in all life's callings.

BOOKER T. WASHINGTON, *Up From Slavery,* 1901

Human salvation lies in the hands of the creatively maladjusted.

MARTIN LUTHER KING, JR., "The Death of Evil Upon the Seashore," sermon given at Cathedral of St. John the Divine, New York City, 17 May 1956

We have been the finger in the dike for literally hundreds of issues.

JOHN CONYERS, in "The Congressional Black Caucus Seeking Power Beyond Their Numbers," *Crisis,* September 1986

Calling all brothers,/ crying for brothers,/ moaning for a brother,/ dying for a brother/ Ain't no brothers nowhere/ Calling the makers of babies to become their saviors.

ANEB KGOSITSILE, Words Against Weapons Conference, Detroit, Michigan, 1988

SCHOMBURG

The Schomburg Collection is one of the most important library of books by and about Negroes in the world.

CLAUDE MCKAY, *Harlem: Negro Metropolis,* 1940

The purpose is to reflect and reinforce the culture and works of African peoples all around the world.

JOAN HUTSON

The Schomburg Collection is so valuable that West Germany offered one million dollars for it to repose in one of their celebrated museums.

MARJORIE L. DAVIS

SECURITY

Let us gather around our children and give them the security that can only come from association with adults who mean what they say and share in deeds which are broadcast in words.

HOWARD THURMAN, *Meditations of the Heart,* 1953

Feeling secure in your worth often stems from knowing you belong to two very special groups—your family and your community.

DOROTHY STRICKLAND, *Listen Children,* 1982

You cannot get security through the barrel of a gun, nor through the draconian state of emergency.

DESMOND TUTU, c. 1988

Security is not an address. It's something you carry with you wherever you go.

ROZ RYAN, in *Guideposts,* April 1990

SEE

Seeing is different from being told.

IVORY COAST

Our eyes see something; we take a stone and aim at it. But the stone rarely succeeds like the eye in hitting the mark.

NIGERIA

[P]eople sat around on the porch and passed around the pictures of their thoughts for others to look at and see.

ZORA NEALE HURSTON, *Their Eyes Were Watching God,* 1937

[E]verything that we see is a shadow cast by that which we do not see.

MARTIN LUTHER KING, JR., *The Measure of Man,* 1959

Some people become and remain eternal spectators; they just go out to see. You can see them standing on the sidelines of every demonstration in history; they just want to see.

OTIS MOSS, "Going from Disgrace to Dignity," in Philpot, ed., *Best Black Sermons,* 1972

I am able to "see" in three dimensions . . . it is the most significant talent God has given me and the reason people say I have gifted hands.

BENJAMIN CARSON, *Gifted Hands,* 1990

SEED

My work is just begun; be assured that I planted well the seed of Negro or Black nationalism which cannot be destroyed.

MARCUS GARVEY, *Philosophy and Opinions of Marcus Garvey,* 1923

So in the dark we hide the heart that bleeds,/ And wait, and tend our agonizing seeds.

COUNTEE CULLEN, "From the Dark Tower," *Copper Sun,* 1927

We are mere journeymen, planting seeds for someone else to harvest.

WALLACE THURMAN, 1929

We've got to pick up the seeds again where they left off. It's no use worshiping the rottenest tacouba and tree-trunk in the historic topsoil. There's a whole world of branches and sensations we've missed, and we've got to start again from the roots up even if they look like nothing.

WILSON HARRIS, in James, *The Black Jacobins,* 1963

I have planted my seeds of dreams and visions and prophecies/All my fantasies of freedom and of pride,/ Here lie three centuries of my eyes and my brains and my hands. . . .

MARGARET WALKER, "Jackson, Mississippi," *Prophets for a New Day,* 1970

The entire Black Muslim philosophy is feeding upon the seeds that were planted by Marcus Garvey.

AMY GARVEY, in "Mrs. Marcus Garvey Talks with Ida Lewis," *Encore,* May 1973

Seeds of faith are always within us; sometimes it takes a crisis to nourish and encourage their growth.

SUSAN TAYLOR, c. 1988

SEGREGATION

They can put him in a smoking car or baggage car—take him or leave him at a railroad station, exclude him from inns, drive him from all places of amusement or instruction without the least fear of the national government interfering for the protection of his liberty.

FREDERICK DOUGLASS, c. 1875

Separation is impossible in a democracy. It means segregation, subordination and tyranny.

W. E. B. DU BOIS, "The Jim Crow Argument," *Crisis,* 1913

Now when the world is in a death grapple, agonizing to bring men together, shall we by supineness, quiescence, and cowardly submission retard the victory by clannishness, by living unto ourselves, by developing within the land a distinct civilization?

HERMAN DREER, *The Immediate Jewel of His Soul,* 1919

We must preach the end of segregating movements. When wars are upon us, Black and white die together. When peace comes, why can't they live together?

Ibid.

Segregation costs too much. It cannot be justified by law, cannot be justified by tradition. Neither justice nor money can justify it.

BENJAMIN MAYS, *Tampa Bulletin,* 7 April 1928

The opposition to segregation is an opposition to discrimination.

W. E. B. DU BOIS, "Segregation," *Crisis,* January 1934

We do not submit to discrimination simply because it does not involve actual and open segregation.

Ibid.

I wouldn't sing to segregated audiences, so I sang in Negro schools and white people came.

PAUL ROBESON, "'Democracy's Voice' Speaks," *People's Voice,* 22 May 1943

In 1896, the Supreme Court upheld segregation in its separate but equal doctrine set forth in Plessy v. Ferguson.

JOHN HOPE FRANKLIN, *From Slavery to Freedom,* 1947

Booker T. Washington financed some of the earliest court cases against segregation.

Ibid.

I felt as though a curtain had dropped on my selfhood. It was a bitter feeling going back to segregation. It was hard to understand why I could ride wherever I pleased on the train from New York to Washington and then had to change to a Jim Crow car at the nation's capital in order to continue the trip to Atlanta.

MARTIN LUTHER KING, JR., "Attack on the Conscience," *Time,* 18 February 1957

I had grown up abhorring not only segregation, but also the oppressive and barbarous acts that grew out of it. I had passed spots where men had been savagely lynched, and had watched the Ku Klux Klan on its rides at night. I had seen police brutality with my own eyes. . . .

MARTIN LUTHER KING, JR., *Stride Toward Freedom,* 1958

Separation is nothing but a form of slavery covered up with certain niceties of complexity.

Ibid.

Why should I confine myself/ to the image/ they would fix me in?/ for pity's sake,/ I'd suffocate/ segregated as exotic.

GUY TIROLIEN, "Ghetto," *Golden Bullets,* 1961

All segregation statutes are unjust because segregation distorts the soul and damages the personality.

MARTIN LUTHER KING, JR., *Why We Can't Wait,* 1963

White and Black, most of us, have arrived at a point where we don't know what to tell our children. The framework in which we operate weighs almost too heavily to be borne, and it's about to kill us. We're taught from grammar school up to accept segregation as a way of life. You lied to me, because you never intended that I should be free, and I lied to you because I pretended that it was all right. Small wonder our children are emotionally bankrupt and drifting toward disaster.

JAMES BALDWIN, "There's A Bill Due That Has to Be Paid," 24 May 1963

Nurtured by the fires of the controversy over segregation, I was soon aflame with indignation over my newly discovered social status and inwardly I turned away from America with horror, disgust, and outrage.

ELDRIDGE CLEAVER, *Soul On Ice,* 1968

We don't segregate, we marinate.

GEOFFREY HOLDER, 1981

The Cotton Club—smack dab in the middle of Harlem—but Black people couldn't go there. It was for whites only. The club featured Black entertainment and some of the most gorgeous Black women that could be found.

JOE LOUIS, *My Life,* 1981

When I went to Camp Upton in New York, I drove up in a chauffeured limousine—they gave me my uniform and sent me to the colored section.

Ibid.

[T]he treatment of black people in the United States is quite similar to the treatment of my people in South Africa. In the United States, Black[s] live in segregated areas that are not called townships but "ghettos." . . . It's the same thing in both countries, except that the American government condemns racism in its Constitution, and the South African constitution condones it.

MIRIAM MAKEBA, *My Story,* 1987

I didn't create segregation, didn't incubate it, didn't condone it, didn't develop it, but it's here.

HAROLD WASHINGTON, in "Mayor Washington Eulogized as Symbol of Hope for Blacks," *Jet,* 14 December 1987

I was raised to survive under the totalitarianism of segregation, not only without the active assistance of government, but with its active opposition.

CLARENCE THOMAS, speaking on the CNN television network, July 1990

The very nature of segregation was demeaning, and its effect upon its victim was deadening.

BENJAMIN DAVIS, *Benjamin Davis, Jr.: An Autobiography,* 1991

SELF

Never in my life/ did I once face/ the man who lives / in my own little body. My eyes blinded/ by the weight of storms, Can see nothing,/ even when he stirs. / My hands fail to reach his hands/ As he is forever engaged with the world. . . . Could I ever wish/ to know anyone else?/ I do not yet know /my own little body.

LALAN, c. 1885

Exaggerated self-importance is deemed an individual fault, but a racial virtue.

KELLY MILLER, *The American Negro,* 1908

Self-interest is the only principle upon which individuals or groups will act as if they are sane.

A. PHILIP RANDOLPH, "Lynching: Capitalism, Its Causes; Socialism Its Cure," *Messenger,* August 1919

I ain't never done nothing to nobody/ I ain't never got nothing from nobody, no time/ and until I get something from somebody, sometime/ I don't intend to do nothing for nobody, no time.

BERT WILLIAMS, "Nobody," c. 1922

Often when we have given to our child, we beg him to give us a little, not because we want to eat it but because we want to test the child. We want to know whether he is the kind of person who will give out or whether he will clutch everything to his chest when he grows up.

CHINUA ACHEBE, *Things Fall Apart,* 1959

People strive to lose themselves among other people. This they do because of their lack of knowledge of self.

ELIJAH MUHAMMAD, in Essien-Udom, *Black Nationalism,* 1962

Self knowledge comes too late and by the time I've known myself I am no longer what I was.

MABEL SEGUN, "Pigeonhole," in Ademola, *Reflections: Nigerian Prose and Verse,* 1962

The truth is that there is nothing noble in being superior to somebody else. The only real nobility is in being superior to your former self.

WHITNEY YOUNG, *To Be Equal,* 1964

If you're a cornbread baby, don't try to be a spice cake.

LANGSTON HUGHES, *Book of Negro Humor,* 1966

A child must have a sense of selfhood, a knowledge that he is not here by sufferance, that his forbears contributed to the country and to the world.

JOHN KILLENS, *Beyond the Angry Black,* 1966

I went to a masquerade/ Disguised as myself/ Not one of my friends/ Recognized.

BOB KAUFMAN, "Heavy Water Blues," *Golden Sandals,* 1967

Black is the selfhood and soul of anyone with one drop of black blood, in America, who does not deny himself.

SARAH WEBSTER FABIO, "Tripping with Black Writers," in Gayle, ed., *The Black Aesthetic,* 1971

Selfishness can be a virtue. Selfishness is essential to survival, and without survival we cannot protect those whom we love more than ourselves.

DUKE ELLINGTON, *Music Is My Mistress,* 1973

Black people are destroying themselves, their sense of humanity is being twisted into a philosophy of dog-eat-dog, get what you can and exploit each other if you have to.

AMY GARVEY, in "Mrs. Marcus Garvey Talks with Ida Lewis," *Encore,* May 1973

Turning into my own/ turning on into my own self at last.

LUCILLE CLIFTON, "Turning," *An Ordinary Woman,* 1974

We've got to stand by ourselves before we can make it. Nobody's going to help us.

KAREEM ABDUL JABBAR, c. 1975

Selflessness is necessary for a sense of collectivity.

ALFRED PASTER, *The Roots of Soul,* 1982

Self-acceptance means self-discovery.

RICHARD PERRY, *Montgomery's Children,* 1984

Selflessness is key for conveying the need to end greed and oppression.

SONIA SANCHEZ, "Ruminations/Reflections," in Evans, ed., *Black Women Writers,* 1984

I look at the past and I see myself.

MIRIAM MAKEBA, *My Story,* 1987

Self-plagiarization is even worse than copying from someone else, because you're denying yourself.

GILDA SNOWDEN, in "Interview with Gilda Snowden," *City Arts Quarterly,* Fall/Winter 1987

To define one's self is to give direction and this goes without saying, that this direction could be either positive or negative.

HAKI MADHUBUTI, c. 1988

Trust yourself. Think for yourself. Act for yourself. Speak for yourself. Be yourself. Imitation is suicide.

MARVA COLLINS, c. 1988

There is a war on Black men. There is [an] effort to disempower Black people, to have us implode, destroy ... our children, from within our own ranks.

SUSAN TAYLOR, c. 1988

Self is all we have. We are ourselves.

CAROLYN WARFIELD, in "Rising to the Light Within," *City Arts Quarterly*, Spring 1988

Find out who you are and what you stand for, and learn the difference between right and wrong, be able to weigh things.

PRINCE, in "Spotlight: Prince: What U See Is What U Get," *Essence*, November 1988

Self-esteem is at the foundation of our lives, mates, friends, religion, and political process. How we feel about ourselves follows us to the grave.

ALINE SMITH, in "Self-esteem Goes Political," *Crisis*, December 1990

Self-respect and self-love do not mean denigrating or hating other people.

JAMES CONE, *Malcolm and Martin and America*, 1991

SEX

A little pool without water! Yet men drown in it.

NIGER

Right is of no sex.

FREDERICK DOUGLASS, in *North Star*, 3 December 1847

He was seduced by her chastity. He would never be free as long as he knew he could be her first lover. Until he could see the face of her purity replaced by the face of surrender, her image would lie on his lids to torment him.

DOROTHY WEST, *The Living Is Easy*, 1924

He don't perform his duties like he used to do,/ He never holds my ashes 'less I tell him to/ Before he hardly gets to work, he says he's through,/ My Handy Man ain't handy no more.

EDITH WILSON, "My Handy Man Ain't Handy No More," 1925

The wife of another, O my elder brother,/ Is like a tree that grows by a ravine,/ The more one shakes it, the more it takes root,/ Take her at night, take her in the evening,/ Only he who takes her/ May have her altogether.

JEAN-JOSEPH RABÉARIVELO, *Old Songs of Imerina Land*, 1939

Sex can be got in the street. But companionship is something like a religion. A God.

PETER ABRAHAMS, *Dark Testament*, 1942

[T]here is a great space where sex ought to be; and what usually fills this space is violence.

JAMES BALDWIN, *Nobody Knows My Name*, 1961

Coitus is occasion to call on the gods of the clan. It is a sacred act, pure, absolute, bringing invisible forces into action.

FRANTZ FANON, *Black Skin, White Masks*, 1967

Sex and sensuality ... that youth of spirit; that innate respect for man and woman, that joy in living, that peace which is not disfigurement of imposed and suffered-through moral hygiene, but a natural harmony with the happy majesty of life.

Ibid.

To be sensual is to respect and rejoice in the force of life itself, and to be present in all that one does, from the effort of loving to the breaking of bread.

PHYL GARLAND, *Sound of Soul*, 1969

I must have been a puritan all my life. Then as now, I consider the sexual act private. I do not want my sexual experiences to be made public. I do not care for women who discuss the sexual behavior of men in public, or vice versa.

CHESTER HIMES, *The Autobiography of Chester Himes*, 1972

Sex is a symbol of divine love. It is a symbol and sacrament, and every profanation of it is sacrilege.

ERNESTO CARDENAL, "Love," *Vida en al Amor*, 1974

It's like living in a flower garden, you might pluck one, but that doesn't mean you remember it.

EUBIE BLAKE, *Eubie,* 1979

Sex is a kind of music with its own distinctive beat that thumps away pretense and the entrapment of modern life, a beat that ignites passion, hot beads of sexual excitement, burning pools of sweet funk.

ALFRED PASTER, *The Roots of Soul,* 1982

Beyond sex is God.

MARVIN GAYE, in Ritz, *Divided Soul,* 1985

I'm stuck with a romantic attitude about sex. I only go to bed with people I really love.

LENA HORNE, c. 1988

He was so passive, it was like a eunuch teaching a class on sex education.

LES PAYNE, c. 1988

The key was marvelously made and the lover made an easy entrance to the thirsty woman. This was how the man dipped his mouth into another man's soup and he came to enjoy her every day.

YORUBA, "Not Even God Is Ripe Enough to Catch a Woman in Love," in Chinweizu, *Voices From Twentieth-Century Africa,* 1988

Sexuality, just like sex, is in the head.

GLORIA NAYLOR, in "Sexual Ease," *Essence,* December 1988

Don't you feel dead without sex? I know I do.

GRACE JONES, c. 1989

The safest sex is on the shore of abstinence. The next is with one faithful partner. If you insist on wading out into the turbulent waters of multiple sex partners—wear a life jacket.

JOSEPH LOWERY, in *Jet,* 6 March 1989

My sexual energy goes into writing.

OCTAVIA BUTLER, "Birth of a Writer," *Essence,* March 1989

SHAME

Where there is no shame, there is no honor.

CONGO

It is hard to shame the devil.

TRADITIONAL

Shame has watchmen.

ZIMBABWE

How the facts of American history have in the last century been falsified because the nation was ashamed. The South was ashamed because it had fought to perpetuate human slavery. The North was ashamed because it had to call in the Black man to save the nation, abolish slavery, and establish democracy.

W. E. B. DU BOIS, c. 1910

We are not ashamed of the Race to which we belong and we feel sure that God made black skin and kinky hair because he desired to expose himself in that type.

MARCUS GARVEY, *Garvey and Garveyism,* 1963

You have already beaten him—you struck him where every human worthy of the name is most vulnerable. You have shamed him before his friends and before the world, and in doing that you have hurt him far more than you could by any bodily punishment.

OUSMANE SEMBANE, *God's Bit of Wood,* 1970

SHARE

Political, social, and industrial America will never become so converted as to be willing to share equitably among Blacks and whites.

MARCUS GARVEY, *Philosophy and Opinions of Marcus Garvey,* 1923

It wasn't necessary to kill the Indian. If we were going to steal the country, we could at least [have] shared it.

JAMES BALDWIN, 1971

I was a young energetic field researcher. I lived among the people. I took a recorder and played Duke Ellington records and the people would come around. I danced on toes and inevitably they would want to show me their dances, which I encouraged.

KATHERINE DUNHAM, in "She Danced to Teach—And They Loved It," *American Visions,* February 1987

You can have the number-one album, number-one-selling automobile, or whatever, but if you don't have somebody to run home to and jump up and down about it, then it's really empty.

ANITA BAKER, c. 1988

SHOW BUSINESS

Unless you really know what you want in this business you'd better not get involved. It can't be a little adventure, a matter of checking it out. When you start to make it people come around you for all kinds of reasons, just to take. There really are no givers, when you're up there. You have to love what you are doing with a passion.

GRACE JONES, in "An Interview with Grace Jones," *Black Stars,* May 1981

I've always done my act for myself, I've never really cared who didn't like it.

Ibid.

In my regular act, I never use dirty or raw materials. It limits you too much. How many times can you curse and swear in an act?

SLAPPY WHITE, in "Slappy White May Well Be the Greatest," *Black Stars,* May 1981

There will always be a need for *Soul Train.* The creativity never stops, and the need for folk to expose it never stops either.

DON CORNELIUS, in "Soul Train Has Arrived," *Essence,* November 1985

We had an effect on Hollywood. Hollywood wanted us to change the mixture of my company. They wanted the light-skinned ladies with straight hair. But some of them didn't dance. I saw no reason to change because of Hollywood.

KATHERINE DUNHAM, in "She Danced to Teach—And They Loved It," *American Visions,* February 1987

Coming to America is the first time Hollywood spent ten million dollars to do a positive movie about Black people, a positive love story.

EDDIE MURPHY, c. 1988

I thought you had to be magically appointed or birthed into a show-business family to go into show business.

MARSHA WARFIELD, "Introducing Comic Actress Marsha Warfield," *Ebony,* May 1988

Father and Will Mastin set me up so I'd be ready, a human being and a performer.

SAMMY DAVIS, JR., "Recalls Father With Joy, Music at Memorial Service," *Jet,* 13 June 1988

SILENCE

A silent tongue does not betray its owner.

AFRICA

When the heart speaks, the tongue is silent.

AFRICA

Silence is the door of consent.

LIBYA

The world in silence nods, but my heart weeps.

CLAUDE MCKAY, "J'Accuse," *Messenger,* October 1919

I went to the Harlem Renaissance and never said a word. I was young and a girl so they never asked me to say anything. I didn't know I had anything to say. I was just a little girl from Boston, a place of dull people with funny accents.

DOROTHY WEST, c. 1926

Moses consented by a freezing silence.

ZORA NEALE HURSTON, *Moses, Man of the Mountain,* 1939

Silence is all the genius a fool has and it is one of the things that a smart man knows how to use when he needs it.

Ibid.

Yet here I stand single in my loneliness, I cannot shout against the silence of the night.

SAM SUTER, "Night," *Poetry of the Negro,* 1949

Silence, the silence that roars like an indifferent cataract, the silence that reaches like a casual clap of thunder to the end of space and time.

RICHARD WRIGHT, *The Outsider,* 1953

Then one day, the Silence . . . / The sun's rays seemed to die out.

DAVID DIOP, "He Who Has Lost All," *Poundings,* 1956

You want to shut up every colored person who wants to fight for rights of his people.

PAUL ROBESON, *Here I Stand,* 1958

We will have to repent in this generation not merely for the vitriolic words and actions of the bad people, but for the appalling silence of the good people.

MARTIN LUTHER KING, JR., *Letter from a Birmingham City Jail,* 1963

I don't think that anybody should tell somebody else what they're going to do; they should go ahead and do it, and that's it.

MALCOLM X, *Malcolm X Speaks,* 1965

Those who they cannot convert, they silence.

H. RAP BROWN, c. 1968

Distance and silence may not set us free.

CONRAD KENT RIVERS, *Still Voice of Harlem,* 1968

For my only love/ I would stop the silence.

JUNE JORDAN, "For My Mother," *Some Changes,* 1971

The silence between your words/ rams into me/ like a sword.

ALICE WALKER, "Rage," *Revolutionary Petunias,* 1971

Silence at the right moment is a form of communication.

GEORGE KENT, in Brooks, *Report From Part One,* 1972

[S]ilence and invisibility go hand in hand with powerlessness. . . .

AUDRE LORDE, *The Cancer Journals,* 1980

Silence . . . blurs more truth than it reveals. . . .

MELVIN DIXON, "Singing a Deep Song," in Evans, ed., *Black Women Writers,* 1984

You see the sun making an appearance. It's absolutely silent. But the power it projects! The heat, the light, the radiation is so vast, so powerful.

ALICE COLTRANE, "Remembering . . . John Coltrane," *Essence,* November 1987

Her silence stole the last sanctuary for his rage.

GLORIA NAYLOR, *The Women of Brewster Place,* 1988

Push your tongue in your mouth and close it.

AMA AIDOO, "Anowa," in Chinweizu, *Voices from Twentieth-Century Africa,* 1988

Your silence will not protect you.

GLORIA HULL, "Poem for Audre," *Healing Hearts: Poems 1973–1988,* 1989

Silence as deep, as pervading, as the depths of the sea.

CHARLES JOHNSON, *Middle Passage,* 1990

When we turn our backs on feelings we should deal with, they fester and grow and ultimately consume us. Silence is denial. Silence is anxiety.

SUSAN TAYLOR, in "In the Spirit," *Essence,* July 1990

[T]hey were going to enforce an old West Point Tradition—"silencing"—with the object of making my life so unhappy that I would resign. Silencing had been applied in the past to certain cadets who were considered to have violated the honor code and refused to resign.

BENJAMIN DAVIS, JR., *Benjamin Davis, Jr.: An Autobiography,* 1991

SIN

He washed my sins away and that old account was settled long ago.

TRADITIONAL

Our sin has been not to demand our rights; even if to demand were to die. . . . Even for us there may be no remission of sin without the shedding of blood.

HERMAN DREER, *The Immediate Jewel of His Soul,* 1919

The sin of man asserts itself in racial pride, racial hatred, and persecution, and in the exploitation of other races.

BENJAMIN MAYS, in *Crisis,* November 1937

All sins are committed in secrecy. The moment we realize that God witnesses even our thoughts we shall be free.

MOHANDAS GANDHI, in *Harijan,* 17 January 1939

In our collective lives our sin rises to even greater heights. See how we treat each other. Race tramples over race; nations trample over nations. We go to war and destroy the values and the lives that God has given us. We leave the battlefield of the world painted with blood, and we end up with wars that burden us with national debts higher than mountains of gold, filling our nations with orphans and widows, sending thousands of men home psychologically deranged and physically handicapped.

MARTIN LUTHER KING, JR., speech given at Purdue University, West Lafayette, Indiana, 1958

Most fear stems from sin: To limit one's sins must assuredly limit one's fears, thereby bringing more peace to one's spirit.

MARVIN GAYE, in *Ebony,* November 1974

Original sin is responsible for all kinds of complications.

CLAUDE MCKAY, in Coopey, *Claude McKay,* 1989

SING/SONG

Slaves sing most when they are most unhappy. The song of the slave represents the sorrow of his heart, and he is relieved by them, only as an aching heart is relieved by its tears.

FREDERICK DOUGLASS, *Life and Times of Frederick Douglass,* 1881

One man opens his throat to sing, the other sings in his mind./ Only when waves fall on the shore do they make a harmonious sound;/ Only when breezes shake the woods do we hear a rustling in the leaves./ Only from a marriage of two forces does music arise in the world./ Where there is no love, where listeners are dumb, there can be no song.

RABINDRANATH TAGORE, *Broken Song,* 1894

Sing a song full of the faith that the dark past has taught us,/ Sing a song full of the hope that the present day has brought us,/ Facing the rising sun of our new day begun/ Let us march on till victory is won.

JAMES WELDON JOHNSON, "Lift Every Voice and Sing," 1900

"Lift Every Voice and Sing," came to be regarded as the Negro National Anthem. For this song, not once mentioning the Negro by name, shows a consciousness of suffering in the past, hopefulness for the future, belief in liberty, and faith in God and America. The last verse concludes, "May we forever stand,/ True to our God,/ True to our native land."

JAMES WELDON JOHNSON, *Along This Way,* 1933

My cradle song from Africa left traces in my sensitive music soul that were unlimitedly deep, and the Black churches and Black community were all part of my consciousness.

PAUL ROBESON, "The Related Sounds of Music," *Daily World,* 7 April 1937

When I sing "Let My People Go," I want it in the future to mean more than it has before. It must express the need for freedom not only of my own race, but of all the working class—here in America, all over. I was born of them. They are my people. They will know what I mean.

PAUL ROBESON, in "Paul Robeson Told Me," *Theater Arts Communication,* July–August 1939

[S]ing me your folk songs and I'll tell you about the character, customs, and history of your people.

PAUL ROBESON, "Songs of My People," *Soviet Music,* July 1949

I have to really feel a song before I'll deal with it and just about every song I do is based either on an experience I've had or an experience someone I knew had gone through.

ARETHA FRANKLIN, in *Right On,* February 1983

I don't sing anything I can't identify with.

ANITA BAKER, in "Spotlight," *Essence,* December 1987

When I sang in church, my singing helped others to witness and let go.

Ibid.

Singing isn't like playing the violin. We don't start having lessons at age three. The very best that could happen to a voice if it shows any promise at all is to leave it alone when it is very young, to let it develop naturally and let the person go on for as long as possible with the sheer joy of singing.

JESSYE NORMAN, in "The Norman Conquest," *American Visions,* April 1988

Singers are saying things that the public wants to be able to say, but they don't know how to express themselves. We're like the voice of the public.

OLETA ADAMS, in *Essence,* October 1990

SLAVERY

A slave has no choice.

KENYA

A slave's wisdom is in his master's head.

GHANA

[F]or weary centuries, despised, oppressed, /
Enslaved and lynched, denied a human place/ In the
great life line of the Christian West;/ And in the
Black Land disinherited,/ Robbed in the ancient
country of its birth . . .

CLAUDE MCKAY, "Enslaved," *Selected Poems,* 1953

One day we had a smooth sea and moderate wind; two of my countrymen were chained together; preferring death to such a life of misery, [they] somehow made it through netting and jumped into the sea: immediately another dejected fellow, who, on account of his illness, was suffered to be out of irons, also followed their example; and I believe many more would very soon have done the same if they had not been prevented by the ship's crew.

OLAUDAH EQUIANO, "Narrative of the Life of Olaudah Equiano or Gustavus Vassa," *The African,* 1789

The slave trade debauches men's minds, and hardens them to every feeling of humanity.

Ibid.

It seems almost incredible that the advocates of liberty should conceive of the idea of selling a fellow creature to slavery.

JAMES FORTEN, *Letters from a Man of Colour on a Late Senate Bill Before the Senate of Pennsylvania,* 1813

Must I dwell in slavery's night/ And all pleasure take its flight/ Far beyond my feeble sight,/ Forever?

GEORGE HORTON, "The Slave's Complaint," *Poems by a Slave,* 1829

Alas! and am I born for this? To wear this slavish chain?

GEORGE HORTON, "On Liberty and Slavery," *Poems by a Slave,* 1829

How can slaves be happy when they have the halter around their neck and the whip upon their back? and are disgraced and thought no more of than beasts?—and are separated from their mothers, and husbands, and children, and sisters, just as cattle are sold and separated?

MARY PRINCE, *The History of Mary Prince,* 1831

I could never be of any service to anyone as a slave.

NAT TURNER, *Confessions of Nat Turner,* 5 November 1831

I am opposed to slavery, not because it enslaves the Black man, but because it enslaves man. And were all the slaveholders in this land men of color, and the slaves white men, I would be as thorough and uncompromising an abolitionist as I now am, for whatever and whenever I may see a being, in the form of a man, enslaved by his fellowman, without respect to his complexion, I shall lift my voice to plead his cause against all the claims of his proud oppressor, and I shall do it not merely from the sympathy which man feels toward suffering man, but because God, the living God, whom I dare not disobey, has commanded me to open my mouth for the dumb, and to plead the cause of the oppressed.

DANIEL PAYNE, *A History of the African Methodist Episcopal Church,* 1839

Two hundred and twenty-seven years ago the first of our injured race were brought to the shores of America. They came not with glad spirits to select their homes in the New World. They came not with their own consent, to find unmolested enjoyment of the blessings of this fruitful soil. . . . They came with broken hearts, from their beloved native land, and were doomed to unrequited toil and deep degradation.

HENRY HIGHLAND GARNET, "An Address to the Slaves of the United States of America," speech given at National Negro Convention, Buffalo, New York, 15–19 August 1843

If a band of Christians should attempt to enslave a race of heathen men, and to entail slavery upon them and to keep them in heathenism in the midst of Christianity, the God of heaven would smile upon every effort which the injured might make to disenthrall themselves.

Ibid.

I come from another field—the country of the slave. They have got their liberty—so much good luck to have slavery partly destroyed; not entirely. I want it root and branch destroyed.

SOJOURNER TRUTH, *Narrative of the Life of Sojourner Truth,* 1850

Because God is not dead slavery can only end in blood.

Ibid.

Make me a grave where'er you will,/ In a lowly plain, or a lofty hill;/ Make it among earth's humblest graves,/ But not in a land where men are slaves.

FRANCES E. W. HARPER, "Bury Me in a Free Land," 1854

To make a contented slave you must make a thoughtless one.

FREDERICK DOUGLASS, *My Bondage and My Freedom,* 1855

I had much rather starve in England, a free woman, than be slave for the best man that ever breathed upon the American continent.

ELLEN CRAFT, *Running a Thousand Miles for Freedom,* 1860

Slavery is terrible for men; but it is far more terrible for women. Super-added to the burdens common to all, they have wrongs and sufferings and mortifications peculiarly their own.

LINDA BRENT, *Incidents in the Life of a Slave Girl,* 1861

If slave labor was an economic god, then the slave trade was its strong right arm. The Southern planters recognized this and with capital unfettered by a conscience, no laws were legislated to abolish the slave trade.

W. E. B. DU BOIS, "Reconstruction," *Atlantic Monthly,* December 1866

One of the bitterest fruits of slavery in our land is the cruel spirit of caste. Against this unchristian and hateful spirit, every lover of liberty should enter his solemn protest.

WILLIAM WELLS-BROWN, *The Negro in the American Rebellion,* 1867

Slavery has been the cancer of the Southern social system. . . . It rooted itself in the glands, terminating an ill-conditioned and deep disease, and causing the republic excruciating pain. It became schirrous and indurated. It brought disaster, grief, and evil.

Ibid.

My objection to slavery is not that it sinks a Negro to the condition of a brute, but that it sinks a man to that condition.

FREDERICK DOUGLASS, *Life and Times of Frederick Douglass,* 1881

A tale of woe with tones loud, long, and deep; they breathed the prayers and complaints of souls boiling over with the bitterest anguish. Every tone was a testimony against slavery, and a prayer to God for deliverance from chains.

Ibid.

When will all races and classes of men learn that men made in the image of God will not be the slave of another image?

SUTTON E. GRIGGS, *Imperium in Imperio,* 1899

O Negro slaves, dark purple ripened plums,/ Squeezed, and bursting in the pine-wood air,/ Passing, before they stripped the old tree bare/ One plum was saved for me, one seed becomes/ An everlasting song, a singing tree,/ Caroling softly souls of slavery. . . .

JEAN TOOMER, "Song of the Son," *Cane,* 1923

Trees are tall black slaves/ Driven by the stinging whip/ of the cruel north wind;/ And in the darkness of the night/ They sing sad songs/ Like I used to sing/ When I was a slave/ Driven by the whip of the world.

EDWARD SILVERA, *Slaves,* 1927

They dragged you from homeland,/ They chained you in coffles,/ They huddled you spoon-fashion in filthy hatches,/ They sold you to give a few gentlemen ease./ They broke you in like oxen,/ They scourged you,/ They branded you,/ They made your women breeders,/ They swelled your numbers with bastards. . . ./ They taught you the religion they disgraced.

STERLING BROWN, "Strong Men," *Southern Road,* 1932

For every hundred of us who survived the terrible journey across the Atlantic . . . four hundred of us perished. During three hundred years—the seventeenth, eighteenth, and nineteenth centuries—more than 100,000,000 of us were torn from our African homes.

RICHARD WRIGHT, *12 Million Black Voices,* 1941

Slavery was not abolished because it was bad and unjust. It was abolished because men fought, bled, and died on the battlefields in the Union Army and conquered the Confederate Forces in the Civil War.

A. PHILIP RANDOLPH, "Keynote Address to the Policy Conference of the March on Washington Movement," Detroit, Michigan, 26 September 1942

High John had come to live and work on the plantation, and all the slave folks knew him in the flesh.

ZORA NEALE HURSTON, "High John de Conquer: Negro Folklore Offers Solace to Sufferers," *American Mercury,* 1943

Why, of all the multitudinous groups of people in this country, [do] you have to single out the Negroes and give them this separate treatment? It can't be because of slavery in the past, because there are very few groups in this country that haven't had slavery some place back in the history of their group. It can't be color, because there are Negroes as white as drifted snow, with blue eyes, and they are just as segregated as the colored man. The only thing it can be is an inherent determination that the people who were formerly in slavery, regardless of anything else, shall be kept as near that state as possible.

THURGOOD MARSHALL, *Brown* v. *Board of Education,* 1953

The irons of slavery have rent my heart/ Tom-toms of my nights, tom-toms of my fathers.

DAVID DIOP, "He Who Has Lost All," *Poundings,* 1956

They fastened a people to merchant ships. They sold, leased, bartered flesh, old folk at the lowest price, men for the sugar harvests, women for the value of their children. There is no longer any mystery, any shock. The Indies were a marketplace of death.

EDOUARD GLISSANT, *The Indies,* 1958

They were packed like books on shelves into holds which in some instances were no higher than eighteen inches. . . . Here, for six to ten weeks of the voyage, the slaves lived like animals. Under the best conditions, the journey was intolerable. When epidemics of dysentery or smallpox swept the ships, the trip was beyond endurance.

LERONE BENNETT, *Before the Mayflower,* 1964

Capitalism is the gentlemen's method of slavery.

KWAME NKRUMAH, *Consciencism,* 1964

Slavocracy was neither gentle nor vague; it was a system of absolutism. He who stood up and preached "discontent" directly had his courageous head chopped off; his militant back flogged to shreds; the four points of his limbs fastened down to a sapling—or his eyes gouged out. Learning to read or write was variously corporally and capitally punished.

LORRAINE HANSBERRY, in the *Village Voice,* 11 January 1964

America has created a state of mood which is dangerous for the world. In order to buy and sell men like cattle, one had to pretend they were cattle. Being Christian, knowing it was wrong, they had to pretend it was not done to me but to animals. What has happened is that America, which used to buy and sell Black men, still isn't sure if they are animals or not. What I say applies to . . . to two-thirds of the globe.

JAMES BALDWIN, in "A Conversation with James Baldwin," *Arts in Society,* Summer 1966

I am not a slave of the Slavery that dehumanized my ancestors.

FRANTZ FANON, *Black Skin, White Masks,* 1967

Here was the way to produce a perfect slave. Accustom him to rigid discipline, demand from him unconditional submission, impress upon him a sense of innate inferiority, develop in him a paralyzing fear of white people, train him to adopt the master's code of good behavior, and instill in him a sense of complete dependence.

MARTIN LUTHER KING, JR., *Where Do We Go From Here?* 1968

As long as man is slave to another power, he is not free to serve God with mature responsibility. He is not free to become what he is, human.

JAMES CONE, *Black Theology and Black Power,* 1969

It isn't those who are taken by force, put in chains and sold as slaves who are the real slaves; it is those who will accept it, morally and physically.

OUSMANE SEMBANE, *God's Bit of Wood,* 1970

Every people, every race, has passed through a stage of slavery.

C. L. R. JAMES, in "Interview: C. L. R. James," *The Black Scholar,* September 1970

Oh, slavery, slavery, my daddy would say,/ It ain't something in a book, Lue/ Even the good part was awful.

LUCILLE CLIFTON, *Generations,* 1976

Her love and duty for her children were her chains of slavery.

BUCHI EMECHETA, *The Joys of Motherhood,* 1979

One of the most effective ways to keep people enslaved, in a scientific and technological state which is dependent upon a relatively high rate of literacy, is to create in that people a disrespect and fear of the written and spoken word.

HAKI MADHUBUTI, "Lucille Clifton," in Evans, ed., *Black Women Writers,* 1984

The auction is the platform on which I entered the Civilized World. Nothing that has happened since, from South Africa to El Salvador, indicates that the West has any real quarrel with slavery.

JAMES BALDWIN, *Evidence of Things Not Seen,* 1985

Central America is one large plantation: and I see the people's struggle to be free as a slave revolt.

ALICE WALKER, *Living With the Wind,* 1985

All Blacks over the age of sixteen in South Africa must carry passbooks, which are viewed by Blacks as badges of slavery.

RANDALL ROBINSON, "The Case Against South Africa," *Ebony,* May 1985

The Moors had been highly trained professionals in Spain . . . [t]hey had been in the Caribbean for over 113 years . . . and developed an elite class including doctors, lawyers and architects. . . . [A]bout 400 [were] visiting Boston [to refuel] on their way to England [for vacation], [were] later caught in a storm and sought refuge in Virginia. [Those Moors were traded as indentured servants.]

YOSEF BEN JOCHANNON, in "Interview: Dr. Yosef ben Jochannon," *Crisis,* June 1986

The "Doorway of No Return": The African who passed through it never saw home again. The door opened onto a two-hundred-foot pier where slavers docked and sharks lurked. Those who didn't survive the three months imprisonment in the House of Slaves were fed to the fish.

STEVEN BARBOZOA, in *American Vision,* February 1987

When you break the spirit of the people, you break their hope. Slavery was an attempt to break not only the back, but ultimately the spirit of Africans.

CLARENCE GLOVER, in "Spirituality: An African View," *Essence,* December 1987

[T]he African slave—despite the horrors of the Middle Passage—did not sail to the New World alone. These African slaves brought with them their metaphysical systems, their languages, their terms for order, [and] their expressive cultural practices which even the horrendous Middle Passage and the brutality of everyday life on the plantation could not effectively obliterate.

HENRY LOUIS GATES, JR., in Goss and Barnes, eds., *Talk That Talk,* 1989

I've been in slavery all my life. Ain't nothing changed for me but the address.

JAMES BROWN, in the *Detroit Free Press,* 12 March 1989

Slavery's requirement that we have no families, with men used solely as sources of seed and children sold away from their mothers, hovers over us even today.

CAMILLE COSBY, in *Delta Newsletter,* April 1989

SLEEP

Sleep has no master.

JAMAICA

I am going to take a long, deep and endless sleep. This is not a punishment, but a privilege to which I look forward for years.

W. E. B. DU BOIS, "Last Message to the World," 26 June 1957

Often I hear a person say, "I can't sleep in a strange bed." Such a person I regard with wonder and amazement, slightly tinged with envy . . . that such a small change as a strange bed would keep a person from sleeping, and envy that there are people who stay put so well that any bed other than their own upsets them. . . . At a conservative estimate, I figure I have slept in ten thousand strange beds.

LANGSTON HUGHES, "Ten Thousand Beds," *Langston Hughes Reader,* 1958

Sleep takes night beneath the arm/ and stumbles across the plain; a dog barks/ as the passer-by goes by/ telling fortunes to any taker/ among the hibernating/ . . . if they are asleep.

TCHICAYA U TAM'SI, "Headline to Summarize a Passion," *Epitome,* 1962

Some people sleep half their lives away. Sleep when you earn it.

GEOFFREY HOLDER, in "Geoffrey Holder Grabs for the Gusto," *Class,* April 1984

I slept deeply at first, then in pools of my own milky perspiration. Slept through the passing of light and patches of darkness in the portal above my head, and came awake into a conscious nightmare.

CHARLES JOHNSON, *Middle Passage,* 1990

SOCIETY

Biology transcends society.

JESSIE FAUSET, *The Chinaberry Tree,* 1913

Society is held together by our needs; we bind it together with myth, legend, coercion, fearing that without it we will be hurled into that void, within which like the earth before the Word was spoken, the foundations of society are hidden.

JAMES BALDWIN, *Notes of a Native Son,* 1955

You cannot appreciate the order of society unless you've been born and integrated into that society.

C. L. FRANKLIN, "Nicodemus Meets Jesus—Ye Must Be Born Again," sermon given in 1957

I had been born and brought up in a multiracial society where the present was ugly and the future promised to be uglier. There the problems of race and color, perhaps the key problems of our century, were so riddled with fear and hate they seemed beyond any but the most terrible and bloody solution.

PETER ABRAHAMS, *Jamaica: An Island Mosaic,* 1957

I have no mercy or compassion in me for a society that will crush people and then penalize them for not being able to stand up under the weight.

MALCOLM X, c. 1964

One of the paradoxes of education was that precisely at the point when you begin to develop a conscience, you must find yourself at war with your society. It is your responsibility to change society if you think of yourself as an educated person.

JAMES BALDWIN, "A Talk to Harlem Teachers," in Clarke, ed., *Harlem, USA,* 1964

If this is a great society, I'd hate to see a bad one.

FANNIE LOU HAMER, in *The Worker,* 13 July 1975

I concentrate on portraying have-nots in a *have* society, those seldom singled out by mass media, except as a source material for derogatory humor and/or condescending clinical, social analysis.

ALICE CHILDRESS, "A Candle in a Gale Wind," in Evans, ed., *Black Women Writers,* 1984

The greater the stress within society the stronger the comic antidote required.

RALPH ELLISON, "An Extravagance of Laughter," *Going to the Territory,* 1986

In order to live in any society, you must be a political being.

BILL SANDERS, in "Bill Sanders," *City Magazine,* December 1987

If I go to a restaurant, I am very likely to get that meal free. But poor people who go to the same restaurant got to wash dishes to eat. And I am the one that can afford it. Explain that, and then you can explain society.

MICHAEL JORDAN, in "Michael Jordan in His Own Orbit," *GQ,* March 1989

SORROW

Sadness came to us, and you laughed, Your day will come.

DAHOMEY

Ah done been in sorrow kitchen and ah done licked de pot clean.

GULLAH

Sorrow is like a precious pearl, shown only to a friend.

MADAGASCAR

I shall tell my grief to no one but a sympathizer. / It is useless to speak of bees to one/ Who never in his life felt their sting,/ As long as your state is not like mine,/ My state will be but an idle tale to you.

The Gulistan of Sadi, 1184–1292

Weep not, weep not,/ She is not dead;/ She's resting in the bosom of Jesus./ Heart-broken husband—

weep no more;/ Grief-stricken son—weep no more; Left-lonesome daughter—weep no more;/ She's only just gone home.

JAMES WELDON JOHNSON, "Go Down Death—A Funeral Sermon," *God's Trombones,* 1927

Tell all my mourners/To mourn in red—/ Cause there ain't no sense/ In my bein' dead.

LANGSTON HUGHES, "Wake," *Selected Poems,* 1942

Sorrow is the only faithful one:/ The lone companion clinging like a season/ To its original skin no matter what the variations.

OWEN DODSON, "Sorrow Is the Only Faithful One," *Powerful Long Ladder,* 1946

Sorrow clings to me more than to doomsday mountains/ Or erosion scars on a palisade./ Sorrow has a song like leech/ Crying because the sand's blood is dry.

Ibid.

If there be sorrow/ let it be/ for things undone. . . ./ undreamed/ unrealized/ unattained/ to these add one:/ Love withheld . . . / . . . restrained.

MARI EVANS, "If There Be Sorrow," *I Am a Black Woman,* 1970

They made sorrow come in our camps, and we went out like buffalo bulls when their cows are attacked.

PARRA-WA SAMEN (TEN BEARS) OF THE UAMPARIKA COMMANCHES, in Brown, *Bury My Heart at Wounded Knee,* 1971

Grief streams down my chest like spittle from the baby's mouth.

LANCE JEFFERS, "Grief Streams Down My Chest," in Chapman, ed., *New Black Voices,* 1972

Sorrows age even when the mortal/ is still young,/ Sorrows act as poison to life,/ so avoid sorrows, I say/ Sorrows are corrosive, they bring an/ early death. . . .

SHABAAN ROBERTS, "Laugh With Happiness," in Chinweizu, ed., *Voices From Twentieth-Century Africa,* 1988

Life does not stop for sorrow.

DOROTHY RILEY, *Family Reunion,* 1989

SOUL

It is offensive to the soul to waste time.

EGYPT

Sinner, please, don't let the harvest pass, and die and lose your soul at last.

SPIRITUAL

Fate has struck me down and God is trying my soul.

ALEXANDRE DUMAS, *The Count of Monte Cristo,* 1844

Men cannot be broken if their tormentors cannot invade and violate their souls. They cannot be broken in the flesh if they are not broken in the spirit.

FREDERICK DOUGLASS, *My Bondage and My Freedom,* 1855

The soul that is within me no man can degrade.

Ibid.

It is only by closing the ears of the soul, or by listening too intently to the clamor of the senses, that we become oblivious of their utterances.

ALEXANDER CRUMMELL, "Rightmindness," speech given at Lincoln University, Oxford, Pennsylvania, 1897

Invest in a human soul. Who knows? It might be a diamond in the rough.

MARY MCLEOD BETHUNE, speech given in Los Angeles, California, 21 September 1926

It is only what is written upon the soul of man that will survive the wreck of time.

FRANCIS JAMES GRIMKE, c. 1927

It is only the narrow people who live for themselves, who never read good books, who do not travel, who never open up their souls to permit them to come into contact with other souls—with the great world outside.

BOOKER T. WASHINGTON, *Speeches of Booker T. Washington,* 1932

How can I, who cannot control/ My own waking and dreaming, ever hope to make my voice/ heard in the wrangling for mankind's soul . . .

FRANCIS PARKES, *Blind Steersman,* 1965

We can cancel the captivity of our soul and destroy the enslavement of our minds by refusing to compromise any of our human rights.

ADAM CLAYTON POWELL, JR., Commencement address given at Howard University, Washington, D.C., 29 May 1966

I feel myself a soul as immense as the world, truly a soul as deep as the deepest rivers, my chest has the power to expand without limit. I am a master and I am advised to adopt the humility of the cripple. Yesterday, awakening to the world, I saw the sky turn upon itself utterly and wholly. I wanted to rise, but the disemboweled silence fell back upon me, its wings paralyzed. Without responsibility, straddling Nothingness and Infinity, I began to weep.

FRANTZ FANON, *Black Skin, White Masks,* 1967

America is in danger of losing her soul and can so easily drift into tragic anarchy and crippling fascism.

MARTIN LUTHER KING, JR., in Coretta Scott King, *My Life With Martin Luther King, Jr.,* 1969

Soul means so many things to so many people who are all so certain they know what they're talking about, that they may be all right, although their definitions contradict each other.

C. L. R. JAMES, c. 1970

Soul is the ability to feel oneness.

JOHNETTA COLES, in *Black Scholar,* June 1970

To the African singing and dancing are the breath of soul, no matter where he goes or what kind of life he is forced to live, these two things he will do, and in an African way.

JAMES LOVELL, *Black Song,* 1972

Soul is the way Black folks sing when they leave themselves alone.

RAY CHARLES, *Brother Ray,* 1978

Soul is like electricity—we don't know what it is, but it's a force that can light a room.

RAY CHARLES, c. 1988

Soul is like a heart: it's essential to being. You're either born with it or you're not.

REGINA BELLE, in *Jet,* 10 December 1990

They call me Lady Soul, so let me tell you something about soul. Soul is something creative, something active. Soul is honesty. I sing to people about what matters. I sing to the realists; people who accept it like it is. I express problems, there are tears when it's sad and smiles when it's happy. It seems simple to me, but to some, feelings take courage.

ARETHA FRANKLIN, speaking at the Grammy Legends Show, 1991

SOUTH

I'm going down South where the weather suits my clothes.

TRADITIONAL

I was born in the South, I have lived and labored in the South, and I expect to die and be buried in the South.

BOOKER T. WASHINGTON, on being told he had a few days to live, New York City, 1915

In the South of long ago whenever a new man appeared for work in any of the laborers' gangs, he would be asked if he could sing. If he could he got the job. The singing of these working men set the rhythm for the work.

W. C. HANDY, 1917

I shall forgive the white South much in its final judgment day; I shall forgive its slavery, for slavery is a world-old habit; I shall forgive its fighting for a well-lost cause, and for remembering that struggle with tender years; I shall forgive its so-called "pride of race," the passion of its hot blood, and even its dear, old, laughable strutting and posing; but one thing I shall never forgive . . . its wanton and continued persistent insulting of the Black womanhood which it sought and seeks to prostitute to its lust.

W. E. B. DU BOIS, *Darkwater,* 1920

The Southern planter suffered not only from his economic mistakes, the psychological effect of slavery upon him was fatal. The mere fact that a man could be, under the law, the actual master of the mind and body of human beings had to have disastrous effects.

W. E. B. DU BOIS, *Black Reconstruction,* 1935

Yet, deep down I knew I could never really leave the South, for my feelings had already been formed by the South, for there had been slowly instilled into my personality and consciousness, Black though I was, the culture of the South.

RICHARD WRIGHT, *12 Million Black Voices,* 1941

[W]e must expose ourselves unremittingly to the source of strength that makes the Black South strong!

PAUL ROBESON, "We Must Come South," speech given in New Orleans, Louisiana, 29 October 1942

The future of American Negroes is in the South. Here three hundred and twenty-seven years ago, they began to enter what is now the United States of America; here they have made their greatest contribution to American culture; and here they have suffered the damnation of slavery, the frustration of Reconstruction and the lynching of emancipation.

W. E. B. DU BOIS, "Behold the Land," speech given in Columbia, South Carolina, 20 October 1946

How big does a person have to grow down in this part of the country before he's going to stand up and say, "Let us stop treating other men and women and children with such cruelty just because they are born colored?

MAHALIA JACKSON, c. 1950

Those racial supremacy boys somehow think that little kids around six or seven are going to get funny ideas about sex and marriage, just from going to school together, but for some reason youngsters in law school aren't supposed to think that way. We didn't get it, but we decided that if that was what the South believed then the best thing for the moment was to go along.

THURGOOD MARSHALL, c. 1953

South means "south" of the Canadian border.

MALCOLM X, c. 1962

Our existence in the South has been one long travail steeped in terror and blood—our blood.

ROBERT WILLIAMS, "USA, the Potential of a Minority Revolution," *The Crusader Monthly Newsletter,* May–June, 1965

It's up South and down South, and it's no different.

FANNIE LOU HAMER, "The Special Plight of the Black Woman," speech given to the NAACP, New York City, 1971

The South is an ancestral home of Black Americans . . . slavery also existed in the North and Black people have lived from the beginning in all sections of this country. But collectively it is the South that is the nucleus of Black American culture. It is here that the agony of chattel slavery created the history that is yet to be written. The South is, in a sense, the myth in the landscape of Black America.

EUGENIA COLLIER, "The Closing of the Circle," in Evans, ed., *Black Women Writers,* 1984

The courageous and heroic fight of Southern Blacks for their suffrage rights stands in the forefront of the struggle of the oppressed for rights and liberation.

ANGELA DAVIS, c. 1985

No one here today would pretend the Old South is dead, that the events of the past twenty-five years, even my presence here today, has transformed our peculiar world beyond recognition.

The Confederate flag still flies in place on this campus.

CHARLAYNE HUNTER GAULT, c. 1987

In the South the community was self-contained and that led to a sense of the group. There were no homes to care for senior citizens, no orphanages, no doctors, not even an undertaker.

WILLIAM JUDSON KING, in the *Detroit News,* 3 September 1988

SOUTH AFRICA

We cannot afford to tolerate the advocates of White Supremacy in South Africa, any more than we can agree to the activities of the Ku Klux Klan in Georgia or Mississippi.

PAUL ROBESON, "Racialism in South Africa," speech given in London, 25 March 1949

It is later than they think in the procession of history, and that rich land must one day return to Africans, on whose backs the proud skyscrapers of the Johannesburg rich were built.

Ibid.

To allow the present situation in South Africa to continue means the preservation of one of the world's gravest danger spots. It is as necessary for the forces of progress to secure victory there as it is in Greece and Spain.

Ibid.

I wish I might do the impossible and speak for eight million Bantus who never had an opportunity to speak for themselves in Africa, who never had an opportunity to speak for themselves anywhere in the world.

BENJAMIN MAYS, in the *Buffalo Evening News,* 15 July 1950

The untenable claims of a minority in South Africa is steadily building a wall of intense hate, which will result in the most violent and regrettable consequences in the future unless this minority abandons the iniquitous racial policy which it pursues.

KWAME NKRUMAH, speech given to General Assembly of the United Nations, New York City, 23 September 1960

Is America the land of the free or only the land of the white free? If it is the latter, then we should prepare to join South Africa at the bottom of the list of nations, for there is no power or prestige for a Jim Crow Nation.

ROY WILKINS, speech given to the NAACP, Jackson, Mississippi, 7 June 1961

Outlawed, banned, censured, proscribed and prohibited; where to work, talk, or campaign for the realization in fact and deed of the brotherhood of man is hazardous, punished with banishment or confinement without trial or imprisonment; where effective democratic channels to peaceful settlement have never existed these three hundred years and where white minority power rests on the most heavily armed and equipped military machine in Africa.

ALBERT LUTHULI, "The Dignity of Man," Nobel Peace Prize acceptance speech, 1961

South Africa is a boiler in which millions of Blacks are clubbed and penned in by whites.

FRANTZ FANON, *The Wretched of the Earth,* 1963

This has nothing to do with mobs or color. It has to do with tyranny and oppression, with human cruelty: all the things minorities have always done throughout history to hold power against the will of the majorities. And here in our times, the issues have been reduced to the basic conflict between good and evil. . . . There is no hope of any good in white rule. . . . And when there is no hope of good, then the evil is complete.

PETER ABRAHAMS, *A Night of Their Own,* 1965

We have money and diplomats to crush Cuba, but not for South Africa. The day will come when the tide will turn in Johannesburg and one fine day we will hear about massacres. The Western world will be shocked.

JAMES BALDWIN, "In Conversation with . . . James Baldwin," *Arts in Society*, Summer 1966

South Africa is merely America with the pretty tinsel ripped off.

WILLIAM GRIER AND PRICE COBB, *Black Rage*, 1968

The hardship to which I was subjected was superficial—only a symptom of the deep disease of color prejudice.

MOHANDAS GANDHI, in Erikson, *Gandhi's Truth*, 1969

The government continues apartheid, which really enslaves thirty million South African Blacks who make up more than seventy-two percent of the population. The government enforces that subjugation through violent means aimed at stopping any social reform.

JOHN CONYERS, c. 1980

If Booker T. Washington could have lived now, he would probably have been asked to mediate the interracial belligerence in South Africa. His dialogue with them, ironically, would be similar to his one-hundred-year-old words spoken to the former American slave.

DAVID SMITH, c. 1980

There is no peace in South Africa, there is no peace because there is no justice.

DESMOND TUTU, *Hope and Suffering*, 1983

Today in the hands of those, South Africa is a lost land, sin sick and lonely, lost to all who dwell in her, black and white and brown grieved by some, mourned and wept over by others, fought for and died for by many, and simply indulged in by those whose status of privileged blindness expect it to go on forever.

ALICE WALKER, *Living With the Wind*, 1985

The whites through use of the most draconian measures have fashioned a society in which everyone watches everyone. The Blacks—voteless, landless, rightless—live under the boot of the world's most repressive government since Nazi Germany.

RANDALL ROBINSON, "The Case Against South Africa," *Ebony*, May 1985

The West refuses to understand what we mean by saying leave us alone. We are tired of being well-fed slaves. We want to fight for our freedom on empty bellies. Stop sustaining and maintaining apartheid. Again the white man prescribes for us. He tells us we will suffer, as if we have not been suffering.

WINNIE MANDELA, "The Soul of Nonzamo Winnie Mandela," *Crisis*, November 1985

Tyrannical regimes, over a period of time, collapse of their own weight because of their excessive repression.

RANDALL ROBINSON, in "Interview with Randall Robinson," *Crisis*, November 1986

I look at an ant and I see myself: a native South African, endowed by nature with a strength much greater than my size so I might cope with the weight of a racism that crushes my spirit. I look at a bird and I see myself: a native South African, soaring above injustices of apartheid on wings of pride, the pride of a beautiful people. I look at a stream and I see myself: a native South African, flowing irresistibly over hard obstacles until they smooth, and, one day, disappear—flowing from an origin that has been forgotten toward an end that will never be.

MIRIAM MAKEBA, *My Story*, 1987

In spite of appeals and protest and cries for change and justice within South Africa, repression against Blacks grows.

LEON SULLIVAN, in *Jet*, 22 June 1987

I feel a kindred to the people of South Africa as well as any other people who are being denied freedom, and as we try to free ourselves we must help those who are not free and are suffering all kinds of physical reprisals and denials.

ROSA PARKS, c. 1989

In order to transform South Africa into a united nonracial, democratic society, we must have one person, one vote in a nonracial voters' roll. If the vote is good enough for our white compatriots, it is also good enough for us.

NELSON MANDELA, speech given in Detroit, Michigan, 28 June 1990

South Africa is now a land ruled by the gun. The Government is increasing its army, navy, air force, and the police. Armaments factories are being set up in Johannesburg and other cities.

NELSON MANDELA, *Higher than Hope,* 1991

SPEECH

Nor shall any word that has been set down cease out of this land forever, but shall be made a pattern whereby princes shall speak well. My words shall instruct a man how he shall speak; yea, he shall become as one skillful in obeying, excellent in speaking. Good fortune shall befall him; he shall be gracious until the end of his life; he shall be contented always.

PTAH HOTEP, c. 2340 B.C.

There is none quick of speech who is free of hasty words and none light of heart and mind whose thoughts have weight.

EGYPT

No hen has a right to cackle who hasn't laid an egg.

AFRICA

Let him speak who has seen with his eyes.

CONGO

He who talks incessantly, talks nonsense.

IVORY COAST

Talking with one another is loving one another.

IVORY COAST

One must talk little and listen much.

MAURITANIA

Talk is cheap.

TRADITIONAL

If a man escapes from his own bad lusts he will not escape from the suspicions of accusers. It is proper to sit down to one's work, but it is impossible to bind the tongues of men.

The Gulistan of Sadi, 1184–1292

We wish to plead our own cause. Too long have others spoken for us. Too long have the public been deceived by misrepresentation. Daily slandered, we think that there ought to be some channel of communication in defense of five hundred thousand free people of color.

JOHN B. RUSSWURM, in *Freedom Journal,* 1829

Even an ambassador in bonds should speak with boldness.

KELLY MILLER, *The American Negro,* 1908

Now we have started to speak, and I am only the forerunner of an awakened Africa that shall never go back to sleep.

MARCUS GARVEY, *Philosophy and Opinions of Marcus Garvey,* 1923

Dialect or the speech of the people is capable of expressing whatever the people are.

STERLING BROWN, *The Negro Caravan,* 1929

My ancestors in Africa reckoned sound of major importance; they were all great talkers, great orators, and, where writing was unknown, folk-tales and an oral tradition kept the ears rather than the eyes sharpened.

PAUL ROBESON, in "An Exclusive Interview with Paul Robeson," *West Africa Review,* August 1936

You don't need to speak good English to be good. Our people didn't know English very well but they knew God.

MARTIN LUTHER KING, JR., "Something We Must Do," 1958

To speak means to assume a culture, every colonized people, every people in whose soul an inferiority complex has been created by the death and burial of its local cultural originality, finds itself face to face within the language of the civilizing nation.

FRANTZ FANON, *The Wretched of the Earth,* 1963

Black people have got to learn the white man's language if we're going to communicate with him.

MALCOLM X, *Malcolm X Speaks,* 1965

To talk like a book is to talk like a white man.

FRANTZ FANON, *Black Skin, White Masks,* 1967

Malcolm X's foundation for eloquent speaking was found in the poetical faculty for setting prose to music. The soul and breath of all speaking were striking simplicity and concreteness made luminous.

MARCUS BOULWARE, "Minister Malcolm: Orator Profundo" *Negro History Bulletin,* November 1967

He clung to his speech as the key to his success, as he might have clung to a magic cloak or talisman.

WILLIAM GRIER AND PRICE COBB, *Black Rage,* 1968

Speak the truth to the people/ Talk sense to the people/ Free them with reason/ Free them with honesty.

MARI EVANS, " Speak the Truth to the People," *I Am a Black Woman,* 1970

Never let anyone keep you contained and never let anyone keep your voice silent.

ADAM CLAYTON POWELL, *Adam by Adam,* 1971

When I got up to "speak" I suddenly decided to "speak" was irrelevant. I was a poet . . . a "poet *poets.*" So I merely read a few poems from my book.

GWENDOLYN BROOKS, *Report From Part One,* 1972

Every man prays in his own language and there is no language that God does not understand.

DUKE ELLINGTON, *Music Is My Mistress,* 1973

When you stand up to speak on behalf of your own people, you are classified as a Communist, as a race hater, as anything but good.

MUHAMMAD ALI, *The Greatest,* 1975

If I open my mouth to speak must I always be correct; and by whose standard.

ALICE WALKER, *In Search of Our Mothers' Gardens,* 1983

[I]f we talk about our room for improvement we should do it privately.

LUCILLE CLIFTON, "A Simple Language," in Evans, ed., *Black Women Writers,* 1984

My stammer made me very shy. . . . If you're young and a child with a speech impediment you turn inward. You concentrate on the visual.

GEOFFREY HOLDER, in "Geoffrey Holder: An Artist for All Times," *Class,* April 1984

In this country, business is conducted in white English. That is a fact of life. You don't "get down" when talking with the chairman of the board; you don't greet him with a big "Hey!" and a brothers' handshake. You don't punctuate every sentence that makes sense with a "right on."

BILL COSBY, c. 1985

To speak out against an unjust war was treasonous, to speak against the treatment of Blacks made you a Communist. But if you feel in your heart that you have a responsibility to advance justice and human rights, then do it.

HARRY BELAFONTE, in *Jet,* 20 May 1985

He had been trapped, without realizing it, by the demon of eloquence by which he stirred up and magnetized the crowds in the political arena.

AMINATA FALL, "The Beggar's Strike," in Chinweizu, ed., *Voices From Twentieth-Century Africa,* 1988

I had this thick Brooklyn accent. They paid me $300 a week to lose it tutoring me every day after school.

LOUIS GOSSETT, in "I Was Swallowing a Kind of Poison," *Parade,* 17 July 1988

SPIRIT

The spirit will not descend without song.

AFRICA

It is a dangerous thing to arouse the evil spirit. It will turn against and rend you.

KELLY MILLER, *The American Negro,* 1908

Lord, I will live persuaded by mine own./ I cannot play the recreant to these;/ My spirit has come home, that sailed the doubtful seas.

COUNTEE CULLEN, "The Shroud of Color," *Color,* 1925

Glorify things of the spirit and keep the things of the flesh under control.

NANNIE BURROUGHS, "Unload Your Uncle Toms," *Louisiana Weekly,* 23 December 1933

She knew things that nobody had ever told her. For instance, the words of the trees and the wind. She often spoke to falling seeds and said, "Ah hope you fall on soft ground," because she had heard seeds saying that to each other as they passed.

ZORA NEALE HURSTON, *Their Eyes Were Watching God,* 1937

But what exactly *was* a "guiding spirit"? What were these guiding spirits that I encountered almost everywhere, forbidding one thing, commanding another to be done? I could not understand it at all, though their presences surrounded me as I grew to manhood. There were good spirits, and there were evil ones; and more evil than good ones, it seemed.

CAMARA LAYE, *The Dark Child,* 1954

The spirit of African Negro civilizations, consciously or not, animates the best Negro artists and writers of today, whether they come from Africa or America.

LEOPOLD SENGHOR, "The Spirit of Civilization," *Présence Africaine,* 1956

There is an indomitable quality within the human spirit that cannot be destroyed; a face deep within the human personality that is impregnable to all assaults. They rest so deeply that prejudice, oppression, lynching riots, time, or weariness can never corrode or destroy them.

CHESTER HIMES, *Beyond the Angry Black,* 1966

Age might sap away the greater part of a man's physical strength, but a true warrior's spirit lives forever, eternally guiding the ideals and inspirations of the rising generation.

BUCHI EMECHETA, *The Bride Price,* 1976

Once the band starts, everybody starts swaying from one side of the street to the other, especially those who drop in and follow the ones who have been to the funeral. These people are known as the second line and they may be anyone passing along the street who wants to hear the music. The spirit hits them and they follow.

LOUIS ARMSTRONG, *Autobiography,* 1979

In the spirit of Dr. King and our national holiday of peace, I'll smile like the fox and cheer like the cheerleader, raging America to exhibit the character that will heal us as a nation.

STEVIE WONDER, in the *Detroit Free Press,* 2 November 1983

[T]he human spirit cannot be tamed and should not be trained.

NIKKI GIOVANNI, in Evans, ed., *Black Women Writers,* 1984

The spirit of the poor people who have been ground down to a fine powder of humanity and yet who stand like rocks and refuse to be blown away.

ALICE WALKER, *Living by the Wind,* 1985

When a Westerner is born, he or she enters a stream of time that is always flowing. When a point in life is passed, it is finished. When a Westerner dies, he leaves the stream, which flows on without him. But for us, birth plunges us into a pool in which the waters of past, present, and future swirl around together. Things happen and are done with, but they are not dead. After we splash about a bit in this life, our mortal beings leave the pool, but our spirits remain.

MIRIAM MAKEBA, *My Story,* 1987

[T]here is that in us, call it the spirit, which is not now and never has been all caught up in the earthy troubles of our bodies, emotions, and minds. And so it is free to undertake God's business for men on this earth. Whoever has this career has everything that he can have. Whoever lacks this career lacks everything, no matter what else he may apparently possess.

JEAN TOOMER, in Kerman and Eldridge, *The Lives of Jean Toomer,* 1987

It's really jarring and distressing to see how we've straightjacketed ourselves striving after externals and lost our spiritual balance in the process.

ALI ABDULLAH, in "An Interview With Ali Abdullah," *City Arts Quarterly,* Spring 1987

[T]he miracle of America is that Africans in bondage were able to transform their physical condition because of their innate spirituality.

CLARENCE GLOVER, in "Spirituality: An African View," *Essence,* December 1987

Welfare kills a man's spirit. It may give his body the vitamins to make him big and fat and he may be happy, but he doesn't have the spirit of initiative.

SAMUEL FULLER, in Terkel, *American Dreams: Lost and Found,* 1988

I have an old spirit.

ANITA BAKER, in Brown, *Anita Baker,* 1988

I am of old African descent. When old people go on back to where they came from for good their spirit and soul moves into a newborn baby. When Momma had me my body just received my soul and spirit, and way back then there was really a lot of African spirit here that wasn't mixed. I must claim some of that spirit and soul.

BESSIE HARVEY, in *Black Art: Ancestral Legacy,* 1989

SPIRITUAL

When, struck with sudden poverty, the United States refused to fulfill its promises of land to the freedmen, a brigadier-general went down to the Sea Islands to carry the news. An old woman on the outskirts of the throngs began singing ["Nobody Knows the Trouble I've Seen"]; all the masses joined with her, swaying. And the soldier wept.

W. E. B. DU BOIS, *The Souls of Black Folk,* 1903

The creation of the Spiritual was no accident. It was a creation born of necessity so that the slave might more adequately adjust himself to the conditions of the new world.

BENJAMIN MAYS, *Born to Rebel,* 1971

The spirituals, born in human and inhuman situations, give flesh to God's Word as they strengthen faith and affirm life for us in our time as they did for the believers who created, shaped, and preserved them.

MARIA LANNON, *Josephite Calendar,* 1978

They sang to forget the chains and misery. The sorrow will one day turn to joy. All that breaks the heart and oppresses the soul will one day give place to peace and understanding, and every man will be free. That is the interpretation of a true Negro spiritual.

SUSAN ROBESON, *Whole World in His Hand,* 1981

Black people from ancient Africa to now have always been a spiritual people, believing in an existence beyond the flesh. African art, the music of the slave culture, and the fervor of the urban storefront churches affirm the depth of this faith.

MARGARET WALKER, c. 1983

The quest for spiritual enrichment among Black people in the physical and cultural Diaspora has led to the adoption of the Holy Books of other peoples: the Torah, the Bible, and the Quran. Ironically the sacred literature of ancient Egypt, which predates those texts by thousands of years, is the source of much of the wisdom of those holy books.

JACOB CARRUTHERS, foreword to *The Husia,* 1984

SPORTS

Sports is the land of exaggeration, and the bigger the yarn the better people like it. You can have

"The Game of the Century" every week or so, and you can say "There is no tomorrow" in the heat of the finals.

BILL RUSSELL, *Second Wind,* 1979

Every time we lost a game, it was a real hard kick in the stomach. I don't sleep after we lose, and you know I've had a lot of sleepless nights.

Ibid.

I used to joke that if you could bottle all the emotion let loose in a basketball game you'd have enough hate to fight a war and enough joy to prevent one.

Ibid.

You ever hear of cycles? Basketball is now in its black cycle.

WILT CHAMBERLAIN, *Inside Sports,* 1980

Golf looked stupid to me. I couldn't see myself walking around in the hot sun chasing a golf ball.

CALVIN PEETE, c. 1986

Somebody's telling you how to coach when you've been coaching for twenty-two years, and the most athletic thing they've done is jump to a conclusion.

GEORGE RAVELING, c. 1986

The Olympics is the only time you can represent America and not have to carry a gun.

Ibid.

You can't win if you don't play as a unit.

KAREEM ABDUL JABBAR, in *Star,* May 1986

Boxing is the humble sport. Usually the underprivileged, the downtrodden, the poor and denied are part of the boxing arena. Boxing is the last vestige of the free enterprise system, supply and demand, where you go by ability and talent.

DON KING, c. 1988

I don't look at myself as being famous. I look at myself as an athlete. If the money is there, I'd be happy, but I have to be happy within myself first.

FLORENCE JOYNER GRIFFITH, 1988

Jesse Owens returned to a country in which he could not ride in the front of the bus or live where he wanted.

LOUIS STOKES, in *American Visions,* 1988

Football is about as close as you can get to war and still remain civilized.

HARRY EDWARDS, in "Hardline," *Detroit Free Press,* 8 May 1988

The athlete's role is praised and elevated above all others.

Ibid.

Sports were the way for the Negro, the way to respectability, acceptance by white folks, and, most of all, the way to make money, to own something.

Ibid.

The noblest sport of all is rowing.

ANITA DEFRANTZ, in *American Visions,* August 1988

It's becoming increasingly difficult to be a great athlete and not be smart.

EDWIN MOSES, in *Life,* October 1988

Had I not gone into show business I would have played football for the New York Giants. I would have tackled Jim Brown, and he would have broken my back. And I would have been paralyzed from here down, because I love football. I could have been paralyzed trying to tackle Jim, that's why I'm doing E. F. Hutton.

BILL COSBY, c. 1989

Sports is not physical. If you can handle it upstairs, everything is easy.

BO JACKSON, in "Only Bo Knows Bo," *GQ,* March 1990

I think I am the only Black athlete who can't play basketball. I can't dribble and run at the same time. I tend to want to tuck the ball under my arm and run down the court.

Ibid.

Soccer is one sport where no matter what your race, if you excel there will be some place in the world for you to play.

DESMOND ARMSTRONG, in the *Pittsburgh Courier,* 17 August 1991

STAND

The martyr must take the stand and refuse to yield . . . it is of the utmost importance that we not give in on any point.

CHESTER HIMES, *Crisis,* May 1944

Most of the people who have scaled the heights, who have climbed the mountains, who have gone through the valleys of their lives have not been people who were contented to just stand.

C. L. FRANKLIN, "The Moses and the Red Sea," c. 1957

Now is the time to make a newborn stand, it's up to us, even if we fall on our knees and creep to anchor ourselves before we get up.

WILSON HARRIS, *The Secret Ladder,* 1958

It's never the right time to take a particular stand.

ADAM CLAYTON POWELL, JR., "One Must Die for Many," *Keep the Faith, Baby,* 1967

STEREOTYPES

Our passion for categorization, life neatly fit into pegs, has led to an unforeseen, paradoxical distress; confusion, a breakdown of meaning.

JAMES BALDWIN, *Notes of a Native Son,* 1955

I could accept your labels/ and stay unidentified/ be tattooed by your numbers/ while remaining uncounted.

EDOUARD MAUNICK, "Seven Sides and Seven Syllables," *Carousels of the Sea,* 1964

[D]on't let people put labels on you—and don't put them on yourself. Sometimes a label can kill you.

MALCOLM X, answer to question, Militant Labor Forum, 7 January 1965

It's a curious way to find your identity, labeling yourself by labeling all the things that you are not.

JAMES BALDWIN, *A Rap on Race,* 1971

We cannot forever pigeonhole live people who refuse to die until they enjoy equality and the fruits of democracy in this country.

D. E. KING, "The God Who Takes Off Chariot Wheels," in Philpot, ed., *Best Black Sermons,* 1972

The category is a Grand Canyon of echoes. Somebody utters an obscenity and you hear it keep bouncing back a million times. Categories are sometimes used by a person who feels that the one he's talking to doesn't know enough about the language in which he speaks. So he uses lines, boxes, circles, and pigeonholes to help the less literate one to better understanding.

DUKE ELLINGTON, *Music Is My Mistress,* 1973

When you don't meet the approval or measure up to the standards that some people have set for you, they'll put all kinds of labels on you.

C. L. FRANKLIN, "The Conversion of Paul," *A Bigot Meets Jesus,* 1973

We are positively a unique people. Breathtaking people. Anything we do, we do big! Despite attempts to stereotype us, we are crazy, individual, and uncorral-able people.

LEONTYNE PRICE, in *Essence,* February 1975

Stereotypes are fabricated from fragments of reality, and it is these fragments that give life, continuity, and availability for manipulation.

RALPH ELLISON, "If the Twain Shall Meet," *Going to the Territory,* 1986

In my reading no one was talking about what it was like to be a little Black girl. There was a lot on civil rights. But there was no art about us. To a large part there still isn't. Black females are often represented as stupid stereotypes.

TONI MORRISON, c. 1987

Blacks have been fighting that stereotype about playing on pure instinct for so long, but it still exists.

ISAIAH THOMAS, c. 1988

Why should I be put in a box, when I don't belong in a box? I am a song stylist, which allows me to sing jazz, rhythm and blues, pop and blues.

NANCY WILSON, in "Words of the Week," *Jet,* 1 February 1988

STORY

It was impossible for me to repeat the same old story month after month and keep up my interest in it. It was an old story to me, and to go through with it night after night was a task altogether too mechanical for my nature. I was now reading and thinking. New views of the subject were being presented to my mind.

FREDERICK DOUGLASS, *My Bondage and My Freedom,* 1855

The fable of Aesop, the cherished and enjoyable book of our youth, was originally related as folklore by a Negro from Aethiopia to the Greeks, who in turn published them.

ARTHUR A. SCHOMBURG, in *Racial Integrity,* July 1913

All my life I have worked with youth. I have begged for them and fought for them and lived for them and in them. My story is their story.

MARY MCLEOD BETHUNE, c. 1920

We must give our own story to the world.

CARTER G. WOODSON, *Negro Makers of History,* 1928

I am a real storyteller, I identify myself with those who are really listening and tell my story.

CLAUDE MCKAY, *Banjo,* 1929

Stepped on a pin, the pin bent/ And that's the way the story went.

ZORA NEALE HURSTON, *Mules and Men,* 1935

Sit back and relax, dear listeners, and let the joy bells ring in your receptive minds as I attempt to do my thing.

J. MASON BREWER, c. 1940

The gusto and flavor of Hurston's storytelling, for example *Mules* and other books, became a local legend which might have spread further under different conditions. A tiny shift in our center of gravity could have made them best sellers.

ARNA BONTEMPS, c. 1949

Nobody can tell stories for hundreds of years and keep all the facts straight. Legend creeps in.

C. L. FRANKLIN, "The Preacher Who Got Drunk," c. 1954

They took me on strange adventures among strange people. And there were no words between me and the story, only the story, which was the reality.

PETER ABRAHAMS, *Tell Freedom,* 1954

Aunt Sue has a head full of stories./ Aunt Sue has a whole heart full of stories./ Summer nights on the front porch/ Aunt Sue cuddles a brown-faced child to her bosom/ And tells him stories.

LANGSTON HUGHES, "Aunt Sue's Stories," *Selected Poems,* 1959

I wanted, unskillful weaver that I am with a faltering weaver's shuttle, to put together a few strips so grandmother, if she returned, would find the thread which she was the first to spin, and where the Griot Amadou Koumba would recognize the colors of the beautiful fabrics which he wove for me.

BIRAGO DIOP, "The Stories Which Cradled My Childhood," *Tales of Amadou Koumba,* 1966

When you tell a story you automatically talk about traditions, but they're never separate from the people, the human implications. You're talking about politics and morality and economics and failure. You're talking about all your connections as a human being.

GAYL JONES, "Deep Song," *Chants of Saints,* 1979

No song or story will bear my mother's name. Yet, so many of the stories I write, that we all write, are my mother's stories. Only recently did I fully realize this, that through years of listening to my mother's stories of her life, I have absorbed not only the stories themselves, but something of the manner in which she spoke, something of the urging that involves the knowledge that her stories—like her life—must be recorded.

ALICE WALKER, *In Search of Our Mothers' Gardens,* 1983

Our lives preserved. How it was; and how it be. Passing it along in the relay. That is what I work to do: to produce stories that save our lives.

TONI CADE BAMBARA, "Salvation Is the Issue," in Evans, ed., *Black Women Writers,* 1984

Stories are important. They keep us alive. In the ships, in the camps, in the quarters, fields, prisons, on the road, on the run, underground, under siege, in the throes, on the verge—the storyteller snatches us back from the edge to hear the next chapter. In which we are the subjects.

Ibid.

It's not a ladder that we're climbing, it's literature we're producing. . . . We cannot possibly leave it to history as a discipline nor to sociology nor science nor economics to tell the story of our people.

NIKKI GIOVANNI, "An Answer to Some Questions on How I Write: In Three Parts," in *ibid.*

I hope that we are like the Jews in that we never get tired of telling our story and that people will be around to tell it over and over again.

MELBA MOORE, in "The Making of a Black Legacy in Film," *Ebony,* March 1985

Storytelling and story making are two of the most continued activities for a people's survival, endurance, and transcendence. Without the story, there is no continuity, there is nothing to grow to. There are no connectors with previous or future truths.

W. J. HARDEMAN, *Kemet and the African Worldview,* 1986

People create stories create people; or rather stories create people create stories.

CHINUA ACHEBE, "What Has Literature Got to Do With It?" Nigerian National Merit Award lecture, 1986

When you really read [*A Soldier's Story*], you'll see that Sergeant Waters is not really a real person but a composite and personification of all the positive values of the American black man caught up in the dilemma of a racist society.

ADOLPH CAESAR, in "The State of Arts: Film," *Crisis,* January 1986

One feels the excitement of hearing an untold story.

JOHN HOPE FRANKLIN, in "Book Review," *Crisis,* April 1986

I was unwanted as a Black in society and I still am. It's also why I could write for another hundred years and never run out of material. I've got a large story, the four-hundred-year autobiography of Black experience in America—and there are all kinds of ways to write about it.

AUGUST WILSON, c. 1987

Like an ebony phoenix, each in her own time and with her own season had a story.

GLORIA NAYLOR, *Women of Brewster Place,* 1988

What kind of people we become depends crucially on the stories we are nurtured on; which is why every sensible society takes pains to prepare its members for participation in its affairs by, among other things, teaching them the best and the most instructive from its inheritance of stories. These are . . . drawn from both the factual and the imaginative literature bequeathed by its ancestors, namely, its songs, poems, plays, myths, epics, fables, histories. . . .

CHINWEIZU, introduction to *Voices from Twentieth-Century Africa,* 1988

The story I have, nobody could steal.

DOUG WILLIAMS, 1989

Telling ourselves our own stories—interpreting the nature of our world to ourselves, asking and answering epistemological and ontological questions in our own voices and on our own terms—has as much as any single factor been responsible for the survival of African-Americans and their culture.

HENRY LOUIS GATES, JR., in Goss and Barnes, eds., *Talk That Talk,* 1989

There is something musical about the way the storyteller weaves the ups and downs of experience into the fabric of life. We are captured, enamored, by the twist of language, the turn of the phrase, the indirection of the truth.

MOLEFI KERE ASANTE, "Folk Poetry in the Storytelling Tradition," in *ibid.*

There are thousands of stories about Black people that need to be told. I've made three films, but I cannot make enough film to satisfy thirty million African-Americans.

SPIKE LEE, speech given at Northwestern University, Evanston, Illinois, April 1990

STRANGER

When a stranger wants to do too much for you, watch out.

TRADITIONAL

We reside among you, and yet are strangers; natives, and yet not citizens; surrounded by the freest people and most republican institutions in the world, and yet enjoying none of the immunities of freedom.

African Repository and Colonial Journal, 1827

Each day when you see us upon the dusty land of your farms or upon the hard pavement of your city streets, you usually take us for granted and think you know us, but our history is far stranger than you suspect, and we are not what we seem.

RICHARD WRIGHT, *12 Million Black Voices,* 1941

[T]he condition of the Afro-American writer in this country is so strange that one has to go to the supernatural for an analogy.

ISHMAEL REED, "19 Necromancers From Now," in Chapman, ed., *New Black Voices,* 1972

He was a stranger in a strange land, a poor pilgrim of sorrow. I don't know who I am. Some folks call me "nigger," but that's not my name; some folks call me "boy," and I've already lived three score and ten years; some folks call me "uncle," but they're not my nieces and nephews. My children simply say "him" and my wife just says "that man." Some folks call me "neurotic"; some call me "psychotic"; some call me "crazy"; some call me "foolish"; some call me "low-down"—I don't know who I am.

OTIS MOSS, JR., "Going from Disgrace to Dignity," in Philpot, ed, *Best Black Sermons,* 1972

STRENGTH

When a new cock comes to the poultry run the old cock picks a quarrel with him and the docile hens wait to see if the new arrival asserts himself or yields. Strength makes a law of its own and power allows no division.

MALI GRIOT MAMADOU KOUYATE, *Sundiata: An Epic of Old Mali,* 1217–1237

Strategy is better than strength.

HAUSA

There is more truth than mythology in the story of Antaeus and Hercules. Hercules in wrestling Antaeus found that each time the giant was thrown he arose stronger. The secret was that the earth was his mother, and each time he came in contact with her he gained renewed strength. So with races and peoples; it seems that after they have climbed to a certain height, they must fall back and lie close to the earth.

JAMES WELDON JOHNSON, "Africa and the World," speech given at the NAACP Annual Conference, 1919

Only the strong are free. Might may not make right, but there is no right nation without might.

RICHARD WRIGHT, *12 Million Black Voices,* 1941

When I studied the history of the great religions of the world, I saw that even in his religion, man carried himself along. His worship of strength was there. God was made to look that way too.

ZORA NEALE HURSTON, *Dust Tracks on a Road,* 1942

It takes no strength to give up, to accept shackles of circumstances, so they become shackles of soul, to shrug the shoulders in blind acquiescence.

HOWARD THURMAN, *Meditations of the Heart,* 1953

There is a strength beyond our strength, giving strength to our strength.

Ibid.

The strong man is the man who can stand up for his rights and not hit back.

MARTIN LUTHER KING, JR., c. 1967

It is no use painting the foot of the tree white, the strength of the bark cries out from beneath the paint.

AIMÉ CÉSAIRE, in Fanon, *Black Skin, White Masks,* 1967

The nettlesome task of Negroes today is to discover how to organize our strength into compelling power so that government cannot elude our demands. We must develop, from strength, a situation in which the government finds it wise and prudent to collaborate with us.

MARTIN LUTHER KING, JR., "Black Power Defined," *New York Times Magazine,* 11 June 1967

When the strength of a race depends on its beauty, when the focus is turned to how one looks as opposed to what one is, we are in trouble.

TONI MORRISON, "Behind the Making of the Black Door," *Black World,* February 1974

The strength of the artist is [the] courage to look at every old thing with fresh eyes and [the] ability to re-create, as true to life as possible, that great middle ground of people between Medgar Evers's murderer . . . and . . . John Brown.

ALICE WALKER, *In Search of Our Mothers' Gardens,* 1983

We cannot strengthen America with Black power alone or with white power alone; but with Black and white power and God's power working together, we can strengthen and build the kind of American power we all hope and pray for.

LEON SULLIVAN, "Dreams of the Future," *Negro History Bulletin,* January–March 1983

Go within every day and find the inner strength so that the world will not blow your candle out.

KATHERINE DUNHAM, in "She Danced to Teach—And They Loved It," *American Visions,* February 1987

A good head and good heart are always a formidable combination. But when you add to that a literate tongue or pen, then you have something very special.

NELSON MANDELA, *Higher than Hope,* 1991

STRUGGLE

I been swallowing bitter pills and chewing dry bones.

TRADITIONAL

If there is no struggle, there is no progress. Those who profess to favor freedom, and yet deprecate agitation, are men who want crops without plowing up the ground. They want rain without thunder and lightning. They want the ocean without the awful roar of its many waters. This struggle may be a moral one; or it may be physical; but itmust be a struggle. Power concedes nothing without a demand. It never did and it never will.

FREDERICK DOUGLASS, *Life and Times of Frederick Douglass,* 1881

The supreme struggle of mankind is one of life, of subsistence, of preventing death by starvation or exposure. All other objects of life are subordinated to this one.

T. THOMAS FORTUNE, "The Nationalization of Africa," speech given to the Africa and the Africans Congress, Atlanta, Georgia, 12–13 December 1896

No race of people ever got upon its feet without severe and constant struggle, often in the face of the greatest disappointments.

BOOKER T. WASHINGTON, "The Case of the Negro," speech given at the Tuskegee Institute, Alabama, 1902

[W]e are struggling on attempting to show that knowledge can be obtained under difficulties; that poverty may give place to affluence; that obscurity is not an absolute bar to distinction; and that a way is open to welfare and happiness to all who will follow the way with resolution and wisdom. . . .

PAUL ROBESON, "The New Idealism," *Targum*, June 1919

There comes a time when the most persistent integrationist becomes an isolationist, when he curses the white world and consigns it to hell. This tendency toward isolation is strong because it springs from a deep-seated natural desire—a desire for respite from the unremitting gruelling struggle; for a place in which refuge might be taken.

JAMES WELDON JOHNSON, 1934

Struggle between the morning and the night./ This marks our years; this settles, too, our plight.

MARGARET WALKER, "The Struggle Staggers Us," *For My People*, 1942

The struggle invades the cloistered halls of our universities and other seats of learning. The battleground is everywhere. There is no sheltered rear.

PAUL ROBESON, 1947

The struggle never seems to stop. It gets sharper and sharper.

PAUL ROBESON, "Remarks at Longshore, Shipclerks, Walking Bosses & Gatemen and Watchmen's Caucus," 21 August 1948

One's own struggle is individual, but it is not unique. All of life is involved, struggle is an inescapable aspect of life itself.

HOWARD THURMAN, *Meditations of the Heart*, 1953

The struggle for freedom on the part of oppressed people . . . is not going to disappear . . . there is no stopping point . . . until freedom is a reality for all of the oppressed peoples of the world.

MARTIN LUTHER KING, JR., "The Current Crisis in Race Relations," *New South*, March 1958

Struggle is a form of education.

MELVIN CHAPMAN, speech given at Miller Junior High School, Detroit, Michigan, 1961

Freedom is not a commodity which "gives" to the enslaved upon demand. It is a precious reward, the shining trophy of struggle and sacrifice.

KWAME NKRUMAH, *Africans Must Unite*, 1963

If there is meaning in the struggle in this country, it is the obvious point that freedom and liberation are indivisible, and that goes from Africa to Hungary to Mississippi to Manhattan.

JOHN KILLENS, "Black Revolution and White Backlash," speech given at the Town Hall Forum, New York, New York, 15 June 1964

We struggle in different ways.

MALCOLM X, speech given at Audubon Ballroom, New York City, 20 December 1964

The Black civil rights struggle against American racial segregation has the same spirit that led the Africans and Asians to overthrow European colonialism. Both are denials of human dignity.

MARTIN LUTHER KING, JR., c. 1965

We will struggle and there will be progress.

COLEMAN A. YOUNG, 1972

The struggle is my life.

NELSON MANDELA, *The Struggle Is My Life,* 1978

In the struggle, no allowance would be made for the deficient background of any advocates or for inferior early training or for inadequate grasp of subject matter. There could be no substitute for outstanding ability, resourcefulness, and years of rigorous preparation.

WILLIAM HASTIE, *Grace Under Pressure,* 1984

We're losing our togetherness. We don't feel that same togetherness that our parents did, so let's support our leaders and join them in the struggle.

CARL LEWIS, in "Focus on NAACP," *Crisis,* November 1986

The yearning of the Negro can only find expression and realization in the class struggle. For the Negro is in a peculiar position. In spite of a professional here and a businessman there, the maintenance of an all-white supremacy in the industrial and social life, as well as the governing bodies of the nation, places the entire race alongside the lowest section of the white working class. They are struggling for identical things. They fight along different lines simply because they are not as class conscious and intelligent as the classes they are fighting.

CLAUDE MCKAY, in Cooper, *Claude McKay,* 1987

We all end up in places and we cannot say how we got there or why. All we know is we must keep striving. I cannot hope to make sense of my life. I can only hope to continue the struggle and keep on singing.

MIRIAM MAKEBA, *My Story,* 1987

I had to believe that like all other living things, we would have our peaks and valleys. We celebrate our victories and the valleys we would negotiate.

BETTY SHABAZZ, 1988

Struggle is strengthening. Battling with evil gives us the power to battle evil even more.

OSSIE DAVIS, "It's On Us," *City Arts Quarterly,* Spring 1988

Some of the newer Black men and women in corporate America lack a real grasp of the bitter struggle that was waged to pry open the corporate doors. These "buppies" harbor the illusion that their good fortune is solely attributable to their own brilliance and their superior qualifications.

BENJAMIN HOOKS, Publisher's Foreword, *Crisis,* November 1988

Every day for the rest of my life is going to be a struggle not to succumb to the old buffet table.

OPRAH WINFREY, in *Woman's Day,* 19 December 1988

STUDY

Black studies will be revolutionary or it will be useless if not detrimental.

NATHAN HARE, in *Black Scholar,* September 1970

Anyone who loves to make music knows that study is necessary.

DUKE ELLINGTON, *Music Is My Mistress,* 1973

I have absolutely no sympathy for those athletes who can't handle the academic side. I've never met a star athlete who was dumb.

HARRY EDWARDS, in "Covering All the Bases," *Ebony Man,* October 1987

STYLE

When a guy invents a style, or becomes identified with a style, somebody else cannot come along and be a great member of the democratic world of sound which he has created.

DUKE ELLINGTON, *Music Is My Mistress,* 1973

Style is to gamble with your image, how others see you.

ALFRED PASTER, *The Roots of Soul,* 1982

Man [has the power] to define himself against the ravages of time through artistic style.

RALPH ELLISON, "Homage to Duke Ellington," *Going to the Territory,* 1986

When Black people are scarce, we are in style.

MAYA ANGELOU, *All God's Children Need Traveling Shoes,* 1986

SUCCESS

People fall low through greed. Those who prey on others achieve no real success. Their success is in truth a loss.

EGYPT

Nothing succeeds like success.

ALEXANDRE DUMAS, *Ange Pitou,* 1854

When we are noted for enterprise, industry, and success, we shall no longer have any trouble in the matter of civil and political rights.

FREDERICK DOUGLASS, in *North American Review,* 1881

I will not listen myself, and I will not have you listen to the nonsense that no people can succeed in life among people by whom they have been despised and oppressed.

FREDERICK DOUGLASS, *Life and Times of Frederick Douglass,* 1881

To be successful, grow to the point where one completely forgets himself; that is, to lose himself in a great cause.

BOOKER T. WASHINGTON, *Up From Slavery,* 1901

It is better for us to succeed, though some die, than for us to fail though all live.

WILLIAM PICKENS, 1922

There is no force like success, and that is why the individual makes all effort to surround himself throughout life with the evidence of it; as of the individual, so should it be of the nation.

MARCUS GARVEY, *Philosophy and Opinions of Marcus Garvey,* 1923

The greatest success of the Freedman Bureaus lay in the planting of the free school among Negroes and the idea of free elementary education among all classes in the United States.

W. E. B. DU BOIS, *Black Reconstruction,* 1935

Personal success can be no answer. It can no longer be a question of an Anderson, a Robinson, a Jackson, or a Robeson. It must be the question of the well-being and opportunities not of a few but for all of the great Negro people of which I am a part.

PAUL ROBESON, in "World Will Never Accept Racism, Robeson Asserts," *Milwaukee Journal,* 20 October 1941

It means little when a man like me wins some success. Where is the benefit when a small class of Negroes makes money and can live well?

Ibid.

Start from the bottom up and work like a son of a gun.

FATS WALLER, c. 1950

To dedicate oneself to the highest good that he knows, to hold on to the highest ideals that he knows, and to never compromise certain principles—reward and victory and success may be slow for you, but victory is surely yours if you do not allow your spirit, your ambition, your faith to be destroyed under the impact of trials and crises.

C. L. FRANKLIN, "Jacob Wrestling the Angel," c. 1957

My friends made fun of me. They thought it foolish of me to anticipate success in a field in which so many men before me had failed, but I went on fighting the opposition of my adversaries and the indifference of my friends; I emerged victorious.

ROBERT SENGSTACKE ABBOTT, in *The Lonesome Road,* 1958

American equation of success with the big times reveals an awful disrespect for human life and achievement. This equation has placed our youths among the most empty and bewildered.

JAMES BALDWIN, "Letter from Harlem," in Clarke, ed., *Harlem, USA,* 1964

Anytime you see someone more successful than you are, they are doing something that you aren't.

MALCOLM X, *The Autobiography of Malcolm X,* 1965

Early to bed, early to rise, work like a dog and advertise.

MELVIN VAN PEEBLES, c. 1970

Success is knowing what I have going for me, perfecting it, and simultaneously eliminating all weaknesses.

GRACE JONES, in "An Interview with Grace Jones," *Black Stars,* May 1981

In the ring, I give it all I've got. I box for money. To me it's just a job. People think I reached the top overnight; well, it took me fourteen years. I was twenty-nine before I really made it. Nobody gave me a thing. I've had my jaws and hands broken. One arm is out of place. I've paid my dues in this business.

LARRY HOLMES, c. 1983

[M]aking it . . . adopting the ethic of rash individualism, looking out for self and ignoring the unchanging condition of the community.

HOYT FULLER, *Homage to Hoyt Fuller,* 1984

If you're born with energy and drive, you'll succeed. I always get what I want. I work at it.

GEOFFREY HOLDER, in "Geoffrey Holder: An Artist for All Times," *Class,* April 1984

It takes a person with a mission to succeed.

CLARENCE THOMAS, in *Jet,* 26 November 1984

The true musician is to bring light into people's hearts. If I can bring joy into the world, if I can get people to stop thinking about their pain for a moment, or the fact that tomorrow morning they're going to get up and tell their boss off—if I can delay that for a moment and bring a little joy into that spat and help them to see things a little bit differently, then I'll be successful.

BOBBY MCFERRIN, c. 1985

Freedom from alien substances like drugs. Life is a secret lease from God and we should not allow ourselves to be bruised. Family life is our strength and success.

JOSEPH LOWERY, in *USA Today,* 8 March 1985

You can't sustain success on a gimmick and no talent.

SADE, 1986

Examine the histories of successful Black women and men who are in the forefront of serving their community or country; almost without exception one will find a strong connection to the Black college, the Black church, or both.

HORTENSE CANADY, in *Choosing to Succeed,* 1986

Black men who have succeeded have an obligation to serve as role models for young men entrapped by a vicious cycle of poverty, despair, and hopelessness.

BENJAMIN HOOKS, "Publisher's Foreword," *Crisis,* March 1986

I've had enough success for two lifetimes. My success is talent put together with hard work and luck.

KAREEM ABDUL JABBAR, *Star,* May 1986

Without love, children, race respect, one will find the air, at the top, is too thin to bring sweet satisfaction.

MAYA ANGELOU, "Save the Mothers: Black Mothers . . . Were All Their Sacrifices in Vain," *Ebony,* August 1986

If it gets any better, I may just go jump over the moon.

OPRAH WINFREY, in "Spotlight: Oprah Winfrey Stealing the Show," *Essence,* October 1986

To succeed, one must be creative and persistent. That is why the NAACP has succeeded. It has been creative and persistent over the years.

JOHN H. JOHNSON, in "Interview," *Crisis,* January 1987

I look at my books the way parents look at their children. The fact that one becomes more successful than the others doesn't make me love the less successful one any less.

ALEX HALEY, in Massaquoi, "Alex Haley's Hideway," *Ebony,* October 1987

It's a wonderful world. But you've got to work, you've got to think, you've got to study. If you do all these things, it's a pleasure.

HAROLD WASHINGTON, in "Mayor Washington Eulogized as Symbol of Hope for Blacks," *Jet,* 14 December 1987

Success is the result of perfection, hard work, learning from failure, loyalty, and persistence.

COLIN POWELL, in "Black General at the Summit of U.S. Power," *Ebony,* July 1988

Every time people become successful, they leave their community and go some place else. I'm staying because I want to show that if I can do it, they can do it at any of the Harlems across the country—or the world.

ARTHUR MITCHELL, in "Structure and Discipline Through Dance," *Smithsonian,* July 1988

One has to have an individual life fulfillment and self-image to succeed as a human being.

TESS ONWUEME, in "The Broken Calabash," *City Arts Quarterly,* Fall 1988

Everybody has barriers and obstacles. If you look at them as containing fences that don't allow you to advance, then you're going to be a failure. If you look at them as hurdles that strengthen you each time you go over one, then you're going to be a success.

BENJAMIN CARSON, in *Parade,* 25 December 1988

Make your success work to help others achieve their measures of success and hope they, in turn, will do likewise. This is the kind of chain reaction that is music to my ears.

BERRY GORDY, c. 1989

If there is a most likely to succeed, I was the least.

MICHAEL JORDAN, in "Michael Jordan in His Own Orbit," *GQ,* March 1989

Success has a power of its own.

CORDISS COLLINS, c. 1990

Success in life revolves around recognizing and using our abilities, our "raw material."

BENJAMIN CARSON, *Gifted Hands,* 1990

I know nobody who enjoys success as much as I do. I love it. I love tying up traffic when I go out. I love being recognized. I love getting the best table. I went through h— to earn this. This is what I worked for.

SAMMY DAVIS, JR., in "Sammy Davis, Jr.: The Legacy of the World's Greatest Entertainer," *Ebony,* July 1990

If you set out to be successful, then you already are.

KATHERINE DUNHAM, in "Living Legend: Katherine Dunham," *Essence,* October 1990

Success has nothing to do with money . . . it is having an education and nobody being able to take it from you.

DREW BROWN, in the *Pittsburgh Courier,* 17 August 1991

To be successful, you need to embrace change, learn to work with others, and make good choices.

DEBORAH MCGRIFF, in the *Detroit Free Press,* 25 August 1991

SUFFER

Rockatone at ribber bottom no know sun hot. (The person of wealth cannot appreciate the sufferings of the poor.)

JAMAICA

When elephants fight it is the grass that suffers.

AFRICA

Suffering is like life; that there is always something unknown beyond it.

ALEXANDRE DUMAS, *The Count of Monte Cristo,* 1844

The suffering that your people bear has been borne triumphantly before, and your fellow countrymen have shared that burdensome experience of having had their destinies dictated by alien powers.

RICHARD WRIGHT, "Open Letter to Kwame Nkrumah," *Black Power,* 1954

There will be no way to avoid a degree of suffering, of trial, of tribulation; suffering comes to all people, but you have within your power the means to make the suffering of your people meaningful to redeem whatever stresses and strains may come.

Ibid.

Because my mouth/ Is wide with laughter/ And my throat/ Is deep with song,/ You do not think/ I suffer after/ I have held my pain/ So long?

LANGSTON HUGHES, "My Early Days in Harlem," in Clarke, ed., *Harlem, USA,* 1964

When suffering knocks at your door and you say there is no seat for him, he tells you not to worry because he has brought his own stool.

CHINUA ACHEBE, *Arrow of God,* 1967

In our overindustrialized society there is no longer any place for your sensibility. One must be hard in order to survive. It is no longer a question of playing "the game of the world," but of subjecting oneself to the arrangements of integrals and atoms.

FRANTZ FANON, *Black Skin, White Masks,* 1967

Suffering stalks man, never losing the scent, and sooner or later seizes upon him to wreak devastation.

HOWARD THURMAN, *Meditations of the Heart,* 1976

To know the essence of suffering is to know the essence of joy.

ALFRED PASTER, *The Roots of Soul,* 1982

All the compassion and worry people have over me, I wish they had for people who are really hurting.

MUHAMMAD ALI, c. 1986

It is important to be sympathetic to the suffering of people because no people will indefinitely tolerate repression.

RANDALL ROBINSON, in "Interview: Randall Robinson," *Crisis,* November 1986

Don't just sit there/ gaping at me/ like an impotent observer/ because life/ is a/ serious matter,/ suffering is real,/ and the man writhing/ in pain/ is/ not/ dancing for amusement.

NAIWU OSAHON, "The Impotent Observer," in Chinweizu, *Voices From Twentieth-Century Africa,* 1988

SUPERSTITION

His knowledge may be your superstition.

JEAN TOOMER, *Essentials,* 1931

A baby born near midnight will be able to see ghost.

J. MASON BREWER, *American Negro Folktales,* 1968

Bringing a hoe in the house will cause bad luck.

Ibid.

A dream of death is a sign of marriage. To dream of marriage is a sign of death.

Ibid.

If you sweep someone's feet, he will run off.

Ibid.

SUPPORT

Why, gentlemen, I do not see why I need your endorsement. Under God I have done work without any assistance from my own people. And when I think that I have been able to do the work with His assistance that you could not do if you would, and you would not do if you could.

IDA B. WELLS, in Duster, ed., *Crusade for Justice,* 1928

Sanctions are supposed to produce a willingness on the part of the subject to negotiate towards a desirable end. They will not cause the downfall of the South African government and economy, but they will raise the cost to that government of the practice of apartheid.

RANDALL ROBINSON, in "The Case Against South Africa," *Ebony,* May 1985

SURPRISE

Anybody who hired me as a window dressing would be in for some very, very unpleasant surprises.

HARRY EDWARDS, in "Hardline," *Detroit Free Press*, 8 May 1988

I don't know, did I paralyze you?

NELSON MANDELA, interview with Ted Koppel, 26 June 1990

SURRENDER

I am tired of fighting. Our chiefs are dead. The old men are all dead. It is the young men who say yes or no. He who led the young men is dead. It is cold and we have no blankets. The little children are freezing to death. My people, some of them, have run away to the hills, and have no blankets, no food; no one knows where they are—perhaps freezing to death. I want to have time to look for my children and see how many of them I can find. Maybe I shall find them among the dead. Hear me, my chiefs! I am tired; my heart is sick and sad. From where the sun now stands I will fight no more forever.

HIGHN'MOOT TOOYALAKET (CHIEF JOSEPH) OF THE NEZ PERCES, "An Indian's View of Indian Affairs," *North American Review*, 1879

I have done everything within my power to defend my kingdom and deliver it from your hands. But as fortune has not favored me, take my life; it will be most fitting; and in so doing you will bring an end to the Mexican kingdom, for already you have ruined and destroyed my city and my people.

CUAUHTEMOC, *Surrender Speech of Cuauhtemoc*, 1891

I surrender. Once I moved like the wind. Now I surrender to you and that is all.

GERONIMO, in Barrett, *Geronimo's Story of His Life*, 1907

SURVIVAL

My soul looked back and wondered how I got over.

SPIRITUAL

We have passed through the furnace and not been consumed. During more than two centuries and a half, we have survived contact with the white race. We have risen from the small number of twenty to over five million, living and increasing, where other tribes are decreasing and dying.

FREDERICK DOUGLASS, in the *Douglass Monthly*, 1863

If America is to survive in this new world, she will have to deal with millions of Negroes who will no longer be in bondage.

PAUL ROBESON, in the *Milwaukee Journal*, 10 October 1941

Without discipline true freedom cannot survive.

KWAME NKRUMAH, *Ghana, Autobiography of Kwame Nkrumah*, 1957

For its very survival's sake, America must re-examine old presuppositions and relieve itself from many things that for centuries have been held sacred. For the evils of racism, poverty, and militarism to die, a new set of values must be born.

MARTIN LUTHER KING, JR., c. 1958

One cannot survive allowing other people to make your errors for you, discarding your own visions which you believe.

JAMES BALDWIN, *Nobody Knows My Name*, 1961

If you can come through the snow and the rain and the sleet, you know you can make it easily when the sun is out and everything is all right.

MALCOLM X, speech given at the Organization for Afro-American Unity Rally, Audubon Ballroom, New York City, 24 January 1965

When the prairie is on fire you see animals surrounded by the fire; you see them run and try to hide themselves so that they will not burn. That is the way we are here.

NAJINYANUPI (SURROUNDED) in Brown, *Bury My Heart at Wounded Knee*, 1971

We are one people, and we shall survive as one people, or we shall go, one by one, Baptist, Methodist, Catholic, Protestant, Republican, Democrat to that white doom this society is preparing.

LERONE BENNETT, JR., *Challenge of Blackness,* 1976

We didn't have any of what they called Civil Rights back then. It was just a matter of survival—existing from day to day.

ROSA PARKS, in *Blacks in Detroit,* 1980

Black people do not just endure, they triumph with the will of collective consciousness that Western civilization cannot extinguish.

SONDRA O'NEAL, "Reconstruction of the Composite Self: New Images of Black Women in Maya Angelou's Continuing Autobiography," in Evans, ed., *Black Women Writers,* 1984

The spirit of poor people who have been ground down nearly to a fine powder of humanity and yet who stand like rocks and refuse to be blown away.

ALICE WALKER, *Living With the Wind,* 1985

I am too important to myself not to survive.

BILL COSBY, c. 1986

Despite the murders, rapes, and suicides, we had survived the middle passage, and the auction block had not erased us. Not humiliations, nor lynchings, individual cruelties, nor collective oppression had been able to eradicate us from earth.

MAYA ANGELOU, *All God's Children Need Traveling Shoes,* 1986

If Blacks are alive and reasonably well today, it is not because of missionaries and welfare agents, it is because of the extended Black family and house rent parties and church suppers and Black schools and churches.

LERONE BENNETT, JR., "The 10 Biggest Myths About The Black Family," *Ebony,* August 1986

It is crucial to our continual existence that Black men be involved at every level of community activism because we are often being defined by people who have no desire to see us survive and prevail.

E. RANDALL OSBURN, in "The Greatest Gift: Yourself," *Ebony Man,* December 1986

We survive in a technological world by teaching our children to say no to drugs, and teaching them to say no to pregnancies, and teaching them to say no to disrespect. And we survive by having a "don't quit" attitude.

ARTHUR THOMAS, in *Jet,* 16 December 1986

I went in blind and I came out blind. I was none the worse for it. I survived.

RAY CHARLES, *Brother Ray,* 1987

Education is a precondition to survival in America today.

MARIAN WRIGHT EDELMAN, c. 1988

The survival of Black people in the Western Hemisphere is a great story of the triumph of spirit and the will to survive.

SUSAN TAYLOR, 1988

My mother made me do everything the other kids did. I had to make my bed, scrub the floor, wash the dishes, and cook.

RAY CHARLES, in "Ray Charles Sees the Beauty," *Parade,* 10 October 1988

The unjust society, nation, corporation, or university, will not succeed and cannot survive.

CHARLES G. ADAMS, c. 1989

I never thought I'd be working at my age, but you get caught up in the gratification of feeling you're a worker—you get into the habit of surviving.

LENA HORNE, "Day by Day," 1989

SUSPICION

If a man escapes from his own bad lust he will not escape the bad suspicions of accusers.

AFRICA

A thief is always under suspicion.

SOMALIA

He felt the bite of the tiny fear known as suspicion.

ZORA NEALE HURSTON, *Moses, Man of the Mountain,* 1939

All theories are suspect.

JAMES BALDWIN, *Notes of a Native Son,* 1955

I have always taken care to put an idea or emotion behind my words. I have made it a habit to be suspicious of the mere music of words.

LEOPOLD SENGHOR, *Ethiopics,* 1956

A leader of the oppressed becomes suspect to his people when the oppressors take him to their bosoms.

JOHN KILLENS, foreword to *An ABC of Color,* 1963

[I]f you're born Black in the United States, you're suspect of being everything, except white.

JOHN H. CLARKE, in Angelou, *The Heart of a Woman,* 1981

SYMBOL

Symbolism is the act of thinking in images, an act now lost to civilized man.

AFRICA

From the symbol of Joe's [Louis] strength they took strength, and in that moment all fear, all obstacles were wiped out, drowned.

RICHARD WRIGHT, "Joe Louis Uncovers Dynamite," *New Masses,* 8 October 1935

[W]ise men do not die. When they have attained a certain stage of wisdom they enter the serpents.

ZORA NEALE HURSTON, *Moses, Man of the Mountain,* 1939

The Ohio is more than a river. It is a symbol, a line that runs through our hearts, dividing hope from despair, just as once it bisected the nation, dividing freedom from slavery.

RICHARD WRIGHT, *12 Million Black Voices,* 1941

The symbol of the twentieth century is the man on the corner with a machine gun.

Ibid.

So they asked God for one more sign. Would he please make the sun shout so they could be sure. All that God got mad and said he had shown them all the signs he intended to. If they still didn't believe, He would send their bodies to the grave, where the worm never dies, and their souls to Hell where the fire is never quenched. So then they cried out "I believe! I believe!"

ZORA NEALE HURSTON, *Dust Tracks on a Road,* 1942

If we do not now dare everything, the fulfillment of that prophecy, re-created from the Bible in song by a slave, is upon us: *God gave Noah the rainbow sign, No more water, the fire next time!*

JAMES BALDWIN, *The Fire Next Time,* 1963

The triangle straight up symbolizes woman, the inverted triangle symbolizes man, and the two of them together are a six pointed star or the Star of David, which symbolizes life, because man and woman in their holy union symbolize life.

CLAUDE BROWN, *Manchild in the Promised Land,* 1965

Why don't they stop throwing symbols. The air is cluttered enough with echoes.

BOB KAUFMAN "Heavy Water Blues," *Golden Sandals,* 1967

The valley depicts our traditional position as the most completely oppressed people in America; the mountains, snowcapped, are our aspirations for the fulfillment of America's promise—ever before us, but totally beyond our reach.

EUGENIA COLLIER, "The Closing of the Circle: Movement from Division to Wholeness in Paule Marshall's Fiction," in Evans, ed., *Black Women Writers,* 1984

America has provided an enduring symbol of Freedom for generations of people from other countries who fear persecution in their native land on the basis of political beliefs.

COLEMAN YOUNG, "Proclaiming Detroit a City of Sanctuary," *City Arts Quarterly,* 30 September 1987

Three things I never wanted to own: a dog, a cane, a guitar. In my mind they each meant blindness and helplessness.

RAY CHARLES, in "Ray Charles Sees the Beauty," *Parade,* 10 October 1988

A snake communicates danger. But the dreaded reptile also symbolically binds persons in the town to the woods and the river, to realms where cures are hidden and wisdom concealed among the ancestors.

ROBERT F. THOMPSON, in *Black Art: Ancestral Legacy,* 1989

SYMPATHY

Truly generous men are always ready to become sympathetic when their enemy's misfortunes surpass the limits of their hatred.

ALEXANDRE DUMAS, *The Count of Monte Cristo,* 1844

SYSTEM

I was a slave in the system and he was a slave to the system.

FORMER SLAVE

The best way to destroy a system is from within.

TRADITIONAL

[T]he educational system as it has been developed both in Europe and America [is] an antiquated process which does not hit the mark even in the case of the needs of the white man himself . . . even if the Negroes do successfully imitate the white, nothing new has been accomplished. You simply have a larger number of persons doing what others have been doing.

Carter G. Woodson, The Mis-education of the Negro, 1933

An imposed system, however good it may be, is never valued as much as one that one has created for oneself. What is lacking is human dignity.

SEKOU TOURE, "What Colonialism Did to Africa," *Negro Digest,* December 1961

The system in this country cannot produce freedom for an Afro-American. It is impossible for this . . . economic system, this political system, this social system, this system, period.

MALCOLM X, "The Harlem 'Hate-Gang' Scare," speech given 29 May 1964

The power structure serves the system and the system is the thing which demands exploitation of the people.

H. RAP BROWN, *Die Nigger Die,* 1969

When you take on a system, you are subject to getting burned.

COLEMAN YOUNG, c. 1974

When you stand against a whole system and say you can do better, you've taken a very lonely road and you're going to suffer.

MARVA COLLINS, in "Marva Collins: Teaching Success in the City," *Message,* February 1987

There's something wrong with the system. It's designed for you not to make it. And if you make it, it's designed for you not to keep it.

JAMES BROWN, in the *Detroit Free Press,* 12 February 1989

TALENT

In the long run, there is not much discrimination against superior talent. It constrains men to recognize it.

CARTER G. WOODSON, *Negro Makers of History,* 1928

The talents of an artist, small or large, are God-given. . . . They are a sacred trust.

PAUL ROBESON, "Paul Robeson Speaks About Art and the Negro," *The Millgate,* December 1930

Any writer, I suppose, feels that the world . . . is nothing less than a conspiracy against the cultivation of his talent. . . . On the other hand, it is only because the world looks on his talent with such a frightening indifference that the artist is compelled to make his talent important.

JAMES BALDWIN, *Notes of a Native Son,* 1955

God has given each normal person a capacity to achieve some end. True, some are endowed with more talent than others, but God has left none of us talentless.

MARTIN LUTHER KING, JR., "Facing the Challenge of a New Age," speech given in Montgomery, Alabama, 19 December 1956

Nature never made a nobody. Everybody was born with some kind of talent.

MELVIN CHAPMAN, speech given at Miller Junior High School, Detroit, Michigan, 1960

The main thing about the poolroom, besides all the extraordinary talent, was the *talk* . . . [The] poolroom sounded as though the prime authorities on *every* subject had assembled there. Baseball, football, basketball, boxing, wrestling, racing, medicine, law, politics—everything was discussed with authority.

DUKE ELLINGTON, *Music Is My Mistress,* 1973

Talent and ability are neither young nor old. Agedness is only vaguely related to chronology. Without know-how, nobody is anything.

Ibid.

A waste of talent was a product of racial prejudice; Blacks and Mexican-Americans were channeled into service professions.

TOM BRADLEY, *The Impossible Dream,* 1986

I had marvelous poise and talent and could handle any question. I would always win in the talent part.

OPRAH WINFREY, in "Spotlight: Oprah Winfrey, Stealing the Show," *Essence,* October 1986

There is a brilliant child locked inside every student.

MARVA COLLINS, in "Marva Collins: Teaching Success in the City," *Message,* February 1987

My mother taught me that my talent for singing and dancing was as much God's work as a beautiful sunset or a storm that left snow for children to play in.

MICHAEL JACKSON, in *Jet,* 16 May 1988

The United States cannot afford to leave underdeveloped the talents of millions of children who happen to be born different by virtue of race, language, sex, or income status. Nor can it ignore, under the pretense of educational excellence, the unfinished national task of offering every child a fair chance to learn and become a self-sufficient citizen.

MARIAN WRIGHT EDELMAN, "Save the Children: They Are Our Most Precious Resource," *Ebony,* August 1988

They had all this talent, and they had no instruments. So they started rap music. They rhymed on their own. They made their own sounds and their own movements.

MAX ROACH, in "Hip-Hop Madness," *Essence,* April 1989

Learn to recognize your God-given talents (and we all have them). Develop these talents and use them in the career you choose.

BENJAMIN CARSON, *Gifted Hands,* 1990

[I]f it's a God-given talent, then nobody can take it from you. It's there for you to use, to express, and you give thanks. It doesn't come from you, it comes through you. It's wonderful to have that kind of talent in one's life, but it's almost blasphemous not to share it.

JOIE LEE, in Spike Lee, *Mo' Better Blues,* 1990

TASTE

Many musicians acquire great technique but taste is the final thing. Taste is something you're born with. Acquiring the skills is a matter of handling tools. Even a great hawk has to have good taste, because he has to know what to steal.

DUKE ELLINGTON, *Music Is My Mistress,* 1973

I'm trying to exhibit good taste. I prefer to leave standing up, like a well-mannered guest at a party.

LEONTYNE PRICE, in her farewell to opera

TEACH

Every man teaches as he acts.

PTAH HOTEP, 2340 B.C.

You do not teach the path of the forest to an old gorilla.

CONGO

Pupils, attend my last departing sounds;/ Ye are my hopes, and my mental crowns,/ My monuments of intellectual might,/ My robes of honor and my armor bright.

DANIEL PAYNE, *The Preceptor's Farewell,* 1835

Many a child called dull would advance rapidly under a patient, wise, and skillful teacher, and the teacher should be as conscientious in the endeavor to improve himself as he is to improve the child.

FRANCES COPPIN, *Reminiscences of School Life,* 1913

Can you expect to revolutionize the social order for the good of the community? Indeed we must expect this very thing. The educational system of a country is worthless unless it accomplishes this task. Men of scholarship, and prophetic insight, must show us the right way and lead us into light which is shining brighter and brighter.

CARTER G. WOODSON, 1931

A teacher is one who brings tools and enables us to use them.

JEAN TOOMER, *Essentials,* 1931

Afro-American history cannot be honestly taught without some reference to its African background and the Black American search for the meaning of that background and its relevance to their present-day lives.

W. E. B. DU BOIS, c. 1933

When they learn the fairy tales of mythical kings and queens, we must let them hear of the Pharaohs and African kings and the brilliant pageantry of the Valley of the Nile; when they learn of Caesar and his legions, we must teach them of Hannibal and his Africans, when they learn of Shakespeare and Goethe, we must teach them of Pushkin and Dumas.

MARY MCLEOD BETHUNE, "Clarifying our Vision with the Facts," *Journal of Negro History,* January 1938

Tell me, and then again show me, so I can know.

ZORA NEALE HURSTON, *Moses, Man of the Mountain,* 1939

While most girls run away from home to marry, I ran away to teach.

MARY CHURCH TERRELL, *Confessions of a Colored Woman in a White World,* 1940

The greatest of the teachers of mankind were all Asiatics and did not possess a white face.

MOHANDAS GANDHI, in *Harijan,* 30 June 1946

Teaching of Elijah Muhammad enables me to break the noose that ignorance and racism put around my neck.

MALCOLM X, *The Autobiography of Malcolm X,* 1965

The [priest] was really my teacher, because I reacted against the things he told me. I was a child. I had no reasoning. But I had an intuition about the black African civilization, the intuition that we had roots in a profound spiritual tradition.

LEOPOLD SENGHOR, address given at the World Festival of Negro Arts, Dakar, Senegal, 1966

A good teacher, like a good entertainer, first must hold his audience's attention. Then he can teach the lesson.

JOHN HENRIK CLARKE, "Race: An Evolving Issue," *Journal of Human Relations,* Third Quarter, 1970

A teacher cannot create a poet. But a teacher can explain the "wonders" of iambic pentameter, can explain how the Shakespearian sonnet differs from the Petrarchan. More important: a teacher can oblige the writing student to write.

GWENDOLYN BROOKS, *Report From Part One,* 1972

At my old school there is at least one teacher who loves me. She is the teacher who "knew me before I was born" and bought my first baby clothes. It is she who makes life bearable.

ALICE WALKER, *In Search of Our Mothers' Gardens,* 1983

My teachers treated me as a diamond in the rough, someone who needed smoothing.

MARY FRANCES BERRY, in *USA Today,* 1 June 1984

We can, whenever and wherever we choose, successfully teach all children whose schooling is of interest to us. We already know more than we need to do that. Whether or not we do it must finally depend on how we feel about the fact that we haven't so far.

RON EDMONDS, in the *Metropolitan Detroit Association of Black School Educators Newsletter,* September 1984

One of the worst things for a teacher to do to a Negro child is to treat him as though he were completely emasculated of potentiality.

RALPH ELLISON, "What These Children Are Like," *Going to the Territory,* 1986

If you can show me how I can cling to that which is real to me, while teaching me a way into the larger society, then I will not only drop my defenses and my hostility, but I will sing your praises and I will help to make the desert bear fruit.

Ibid.

A loving caring teacher took a liking to me. She noticed the potential and wanted to help shape it. She also brought me clothes and shoes.

TOM BRADLEY, *The Impossible Dream,* 1986

[O]nly a Black man can teach a boy how to be a man, and Black men seldom talk to their sons.

HAKI MADHUBUTI, in ". . . A Conflict of Reasons and Remedies," *Crisis,* March 1986

You cannot teach what you don't know. You cannot give energy if you're not on fire on the inside.

JESSE JACKSON, in "Reverend Jesse Jackson," *Ebony Man,* December 1986

I am a teacher. A teacher is someone who leads. There is no magic here. I do not walk on water, I do not part the sea. I just love children.

MARVA COLLINS, "Marva Collins: Teaching Success in the City," *Message,* February 1987

It seems perfectly plain that inner-city children should be taught in the same way other children are taught, because all children want the same things out of life. A ghetto child learns the same way as any other child and is equally capable of reading Dante, Homer, Pascal, or Chaucer. I don't hold with a ghetto approach to teaching.

Ibid.

Teach—while you can. Do—when you must.

CLAYTON RILEY, c. 1988

Here lies a teacher. That's all I ever was, that's all I am, that's the one thing I really do well.

HARRY EDWARDS, in "Hardline," *Detroit Free Press,* 8 May 1988

My first art teacher was neither a professional nor a professional artist. Instead he was a bricklayer and a stone mason.

EUGENE GRIGSBY, JR., in *Black Art: Ancestral Legacy,* 1989

You can't call it teaching if there is no learning, and the beginning of learning is order. There must be a sense of purpose before there's going to be any seriousness in learning.

MANFORD BYRD, 1990

[The teachers] realized that the contribution they might be able to make to [the] young students could not and would not be made elsewhere by anyone else.

BENJAMIN DAVIS, JR., *Benjamin Davis, Jr.: An Autobiography,* 1990

If you want to teach a child to be good, don't tell him how bad he is. Tell him how good he can be.

KWASI GEIGGAR, in *Jet,* 10 December 1990

To strengthen children's minds and to cultivate graces, to build strong bodies and to develop loveliness of character, are astonishing privileges. No king or head of state has a more noble calling.

RAYMOND S. MOORE, in *Message,* 1991

TELEVISION

The popular culture on television and in comic books and in movies is based on fantasies created by very ill people. Fantasies that have nothing to do with reality.

JAMES BALDWIN, "A Talk to Harlem Teachers," in Clarke, ed., *Harlem, USA,* 1964

Television is business and business is America.

BILL COSBY, in *Ebony,* September 1966

The Black child growing into adulthood through a series of weekend movies seeing white protagonists constantly before him projecting the whole gamut of human experiences is, in extreme cases, persuaded that he too must be white, or (what is more likely) he experiences manhood by proxy and in someone else's image. He sees, in other words, a zero image of himself. If there are Black people on the screen, they are subservient to, uncomfortably different from, or busy emulating the larger, all-inclusive white culture. In that case, our young person sees a negative image of himself.

CAROLYN GERALD, "The Black Writer and His Role," in Gayle, ed., *The Black Aesthetic,* 1971

People underestimate the power and influence of television. I don't know what kind of hoodlum I might have been if we had had television.

DICK GREGORY, *No More Lies,* 1971

We seldom appear in media as who we say we are, but as whites say we are.

ELLEN HOLLY, speech given at the Delta Sigma Theta convention, Seattle, Washington, 1975

Life makes no sense without television.

RENE MARQUES, "A Body Abaft," *Latin American Tales,* 1977

Television is one of the most potent weapons this nation has for keeping Blacks lulled, deceived, and impotent.

EUGENIA COLLIER, in Noble, *Beautiful, Also, Are the Souls of My Black Sisters,* 1978

Television has been by far the biggest influence on sports in my lifetime. But though it has made it richer and vastly more popular, it threatens to destroy some sports and ruin the way we think of others.

BILL RUSSELL, *Second Wind,* 1979

[F]ew people detected the cultural bias against Blacks that ran through all television programming. . . . They didn't see it because their habits kept them from being aware of details that are to them part of the background. Such things are virtually invisible.

Ibid.

Television in America is just media to sell goods.

JOHN WILLIAMS, in "Interview," *Catalyst,* Spring 1988

"Cosby" and "Amen" are successful because they show a view of the Black experience that isn't at odds with the white perception.

ST. CLAIR BOURNE, "Salute," *Life,* Spring 1988

It is racist to suggest that "The Cosby Show" is merely "Father Knows Best" in blackface. The Black style of the characters is evident in their speech, imitations, and nuances. Black art, music, and dance are frequently displayed. Black authors and books are often mentioned, Black colleges and other institutions have been introduced on the show perhaps for the first time on network television.

ALVIN POUSSAINT, "The Huxtables: Factor Fantasy," *Ebony,* October 1988

Television cannot be held responsible for our children. Parents can. Parents must.

CLARENCE PAGE, in the *Detroit News,* 26 December 1988

"The Cosby Show" is a show with a Black American family, but what's important in this show is that our family represents about ninety percent of all people out there in the audience. We are family and the humor comes out in our attitude towards each other and life in general.

BILL COSBY, c. 1989

Minds today have been placed at the disposal of TV; the poorer a person, the more television they watch.

GIL NOBLE, 1989

In television you don't have to fake real life.

OPRAH WINFREY, in "Oprah's Wonder Year," *Ladies' Home Journal,* May 1990

Television is a cool image. . . . The responsibility is so weighty it keeps me up at night.

BERNARD SHAW, in *USA Weekend,* 1 March 1991

TEMPTATION

We do not pray not to be tempted, but not to be conquered when we are tempted.

ORIGEN, *Concerning Power,* c. 233

The devil tempts, but he doesn't force.

BRAZIL

Temptation hence away,/ With all thy fatal train,/ Nor once seduce my soul away,/ By thine enchanting strain.

PHILLIS WHEATLEY, "A Farewell to America," 1774

In missionary and educational work among the underdeveloped, people yield to the temptation by doing that which was done one hundred years before, or is being done in other communities thousands of miles away. The temptation often is to run each individual through a certain educational mold, regardless of the condition or the end to be accomplished.

BOOKER T. WASHINGTON, *Future of the American Negro,* 1899

Never once in my life have I been tempted to cross the color line and deny my racial identity. I could not have maintained my self-respect if I had continually masqueraded as being something I am not.

MARY CHURCH TERRELL, *Confessions of a Colored Woman In a White World,* 1940

A man must live in this world and work out his own salvation in the midst of temptation.

FRANK YERBY, *Judas, My Brother,* 1967

There is always the understandable temptation to seek negative and self-destructive solutions. Some seek a passive way out by yielding to the feeling of inferiority; or allowing the floodgates of defeat to open with an avalanche of despair; or by dropping out of school; or by turning to the escape valves of narcotics and alcohol.

MARTIN LUTHER KING, JR., *Where Do We Go From Here?* 1968

TERROR

Better die once for all than to live in continual terror.

AESOP, *Fables,* 570 B.C.

Terror reigns like a new crowned queen.

LEWIS ALEXANDER, "Enchantment," in Bontemps, ed., *Poetry of the Negro,* 1949

Terror can produce its own antidote: an overwhelming pride and rage, so that, whether or not one is ready to die, one gives every appearance of being willing to die.

JAMES BALDWIN, *Nobody Knows My Name,* 1961

You'll see terrorism that will terrify you, and if you don't think you'll see it, you're trying to blind yourself to the historic development that's taking place on this earth today.

MALCOLM X, "The Harlem 'Hate-Gang' Scare," speech given to Militant Labor Forum, 29 May 1964

Terror does not belong to open day.

OWEN DODSON, "Counterpoint," in Bontemps, ed., *Poetry of the Negro,* 1970

The quiet terror brings on silent night./ They are driving us crazy.

CONRAD KENT RIVERS, "To Richard Wright," in Bontemps, ed., *American Negro Poetry,* 1974

Mob "justice" was the rule, creating a terror so great that its victims did not dare to light a single candle against the night.

ROY WILKINS, *Standing Fast,* 1982

THANKS

See also PRAYER

A man does not appreciate the value of immunity from a misfortune until it has befallen him.

The Gulistan of Sadi, 1184–1292

I thank you, Lord, for having made me Black,/ for having made me/ the sum of all griefs,/ for having put upon my head/ the World./ I wear the livery of the Centaur/ and I have carried the World since the first morning.

BERNARD DADIÉ, "I Thank You Lord," *Dance of the Day,* 1956

THEATER

See also ACTOR/ACTRESS

The classic function of the theater is to project and illuminate the feelings and concerns of the community which sustains it. Thus the theater, like the church, is a community retreat.

ROBERT ABRAHAMS, c. 1965

In the thirties and forties, the Communists tried to run theaters; in the fifties, the politicians tried to run theaters; in the sixties, social workers tried to run theaters. Theaters communicated directly and quickly.

WOODIE KING, in *Negro Digest,* April 1970

THINK

People may think you're a fool. Open your mouth and they'll know it.

TRADITIONAL

Then God sat down—/ On the side of a hill where he could think;/ By a deep, wide river he sat down;/ With his head in his hands,/ God thought and thought,/ Till he thought: I'll make me a man!

JAMES WELDON JOHNSON, "The Creation," *God's Trombones,* 1927

When you control a man's thinking you do not have to worry about his actions. You do not have to tell him not to stand here or go yonder. He will find his "proper place" and will stay in it. You do not need to send him to the back door. He will go without being told.

CARTER G. WOODSON, *The Mis-education of the Negro,* 1933

If we had a few thinkers we could expect great achievements on tomorrow. Some Negro with unusual insight would write an epic of bondage and freedom which would take its place with those of Homer and Virgil. Some Negro with esthetic appreciation would construct from collected fragments of Negro music a grand opera that would move humanity to repentance. Some Negro of philosophic penetration would find solace for the modern world in the soul of the Negro, and then men would be men because they are men.

Ibid.

[O]nce you wake up thought in a man, you can never put it to sleep again.

ZORA NEALE HURSTON, *Moses, Man of the Mountain,* 1939

One thought can put thousands to knowing, but knowing one thing don't put many to thinking.

Ibid.

Man was a feeling creature long before he was a thinking creature. The mind is younger than the body and younger than the emotions.

HOWARD THURMAN, *Meditations of the Heart,* 1953

Nothing pains some people more than having to think.

MARTIN LUTHER KING, JR., *Strength to Love,* 1963

I have lived througn disagreement, vilification, and war and war again. But in all that time, I have never seen the right of human beings to think so challenged and denied as today.

W. E. B. DU BOIS, *The Autobiography of W. E. B. DuBois: A Soliloquy on Viewing My Life from the Last Decade of Its First Century,* 1964

I still marvel at how swiftly my previous life's thinking pattern slid away from me, like snow off a roof. It made me very proud, in some odd way, to give up pork. One of the universal images was that we couldn't do without pork.

MALCOLM X, *The Autobiography of Malcolm X,* 1965

I feel like a man who has been asleep somewhat and under someone else's control. Now I think with my own mind.

MALCOLM X, in the *New York Times,* 22 February 1965

Clarity is not a thought process but a way of life.

KEORAPETSE KGOSITSILE, "Paths to the Future," *Negro Digest,* September 1968

A lot of people just don't want to think. They would rather forget.

ALBERT KING, in "Albert King's Blue Funk," *Essence,* October 1977

Many have been brainwashed into thinking that legally right and morally right mean the same thing.

DESMOND TUTU, *Hope and Suffering,* 1983

When you can put your thought on paper, you have a skill.

ALICE WALKER, *In Search of Our Mothers' Gardens,* 1983

[W]hat people think of me isn't any of my business.

OPRAH WINFREY, in "An Intimate Talk with Oprah," *Essence,* August 1987

Strategic thinking of a depth and intensity unparalleled in our history has become a matter of life and death of the inner city.

COLEMAN YOUNG, c. 1988

In my country they jail you/ for what they think you think./ My uncle once said to me:/ they'll implant a microchip/ in our minds/ to flash our thoughts and dreams/ on to a screen at John Vorster Square./ I was scared:/ by day I guard my tongue/ by night my dreams.

PITIKA NTULI, "In My Country," in Chinweizu, ed., *Voices From Twentieth-Century Africa,* 1988

If you think long enough about it, you'll do it.

THOMAS HEARNS, in *Jet,* 13 January 1989

If you learn to THINK BIG, nothing on earth will keep you from being successful.

BENJAMIN CARSON, *Gifted Hands,* 1990

I lead a life where I hardly have enough time to think.

NELSON MANDELA, *Higher than Hope,* 1991

You don't have to march in lockstep with someone to recognize what they're made of. There is not and should not be a correct African-American way of thinking. We are entitled to diversity of thought, opinion, and perspective.

GWENDOLYN KING, speech given at the Annual Blacks in Government Conference, Washington, D.C., August 1991

TILL, EMMETT

The mutilated body of Emmett Till, fourteen years old, of Chicago, Illinois, was taken from the Tallahatchie River, near Greenwood, on August 31, three days after he was kidnapped from the house of his uncle, by a group of whites armed with rifles. . . .

ROY WILKINS, in *Crisis,* October 1955

Where hands are placed upon the Bible/ Though the Bible is unopened,/ A fifteen-year-old life can allay the river's hunger.

DAVID DIOP, "For a Black Child," *Poundings,* 1956

They had five hundred years EMMETT TILL,/ five hundred years is the ageless age of the gallows of Cain./ EMMETT TILL I tell you/ in the heart zero/ not a drop left/ of blood.

AIMÉ CÉSAIRE, "State of the Union," *Shackles,* 1959

I die alone from pride/ I leave to Emmett Till his death/ from horror at myself./

TCHICAYA U TAM'SI, "Fragile," *Epitome,* 1962

I felt a kinship with Emmett Till. We were born on the same day and the same year.

MUHAMMAD ALI, *The Greatest,* 1975

And then Emmett Till's tragedy came about. Reading *Jet* magazine and looking at that situation, watching it unfold and talking to my father, it dawned on me that there was nothing that any Black man in American society could really do to protect me from that same type of end. I don't think it's safe for a Black male to feel safe in white America.

HARRY EDWARDS, in "From the Hearts of Men," *Essence,* November 1988

His untimely death was the call for freedom that was heard around the world. Emmett Till Road will be a symbol of hope and inspiration.

MAMIE TILL MOBLEY, in *Jet,* 19 August 1991

TIME

All the world fears time, but time fears the Pyramids.

EGYPT

Calm down, little brother,/ Time heals all wounds./ No matter how much one is weeping,/ The moon always follows the sun.

ETHIOPIA

Truth and morning become light with time.

ETHIOPIA

No man rules forever on the throne of time.

GHANA

Time destroys all things.

NIGERIA

Time flies, but it takes its own time in doing it.

TRADITIONAL

He may not come when you need Him, but He's right on time.

TRADITIONAL

Corruption in the land, people take your stand; time is winding up. 'Struction in the land, God's gonna move His hand. Time is winding up.

SPIRITUAL

Time leaves the marks of his rough fingers upon all things.

IGNATIUS SANCHO, letter to Mrs. S., 26 November 1774

Every once in a while I will come out and tell you what time of night it is.

SOJOURNER TRUTH, 1835

The time has come when you must act for yourselves.

HENRY HIGHLAND GARNET, 1865

Time is impartial, just and certain in its actions.

FREDERICK DOUGLASS, speech given in Washington, D.C., 14 April 1876

Time is an invisible web on which everything may be embroidered.

JOAQUIM MACHADO DE ASSIS, *Esau and Jacob,* 1904

All truly useful men must be, in a measure, time servers, for unless they serve their time, they can scarcely serve at all.

KELLY MILLER, *The American Negro,* 1908

It is the season to devote our time to kindling the torch that will inspire us to racial integrity.

ARTHUR A. SCHOMBURG, *Racial Integrity,* July 1913

Cherish your strength, my strong Black brother. Be not dismayed because the struggle is hard and long. O, my warm wonderful race. The fight is longer than a span of life; the test is great. Gird your loins, sharpen your tools! Time is on our side. Carry on in organizing and conserving your forces for a great purpose—for the Day.

CLAUDE MCKAY, review of "He Who Gets Slapped," *Liberator,* 5 May 1922

Let us not waste time in breathless appeals to the strong while we are weak, but lend our time, energy, and effort to the accumulation of strength among ourselves by which we will voluntarily attract the attention of others.

MARCUS GARVEY, *Philosophy and Opinions of Marcus Garvey,* 1923

. . . read on down to chapter 9, women must learn how to take their time.

BESSIE SMITH, c. 1925

But time to live, to love, bear pain and smile,/ Oh, we are given such a little while.

COUNTEE CULLEN, "Protest," *Copper Sun,* 1927

History is the witnesses of the times, the torch of truth, the life of memory, the teacher of life, the messenger of antiquity.

CARTER G. WOODSON, *The Story of the Negro Retold,* 1935

There are years that ask questions and years that answer.

ZORA NEALE HURSTON, *Their Eyes Were Watching God,* 1937

It was the meanest moment of eternity. A minute before she was just a scared human being fighting for its life. Now she was her sacrificing self . . . She had wanted him to live so much and he was dead. No hour is ever eternity, but it has its right to weep.

Ibid.

Time does not wait.

PAUL ROBESON, "The Artist Must Take Sides," *Daily Worker,* 4 November 1937

Time put tracks on Zipporah. . . . Time left its footprints all over Jethro, too.

ZORA NEALE HURSTON, *Moses, Man of the Mountain,* 1939

. . . years are a long time for millions of folk like us to be held in such subjection, so long a time that perhaps scores of years will have to pass before we shall be able to express what slavery has done to us, for our personalities are still numb from its long shocks; and as the numbness leaves our souls, we shall yet have to feel and give utterance to the full pain we shall inherit.

RICHARD WRIGHT, *12 Million Black Voices,* 1941

Who can reverse time?

RICHARD WRIGHT, *The Outsider,* 1953

You've got to have something to eat and a little love in your life. Everything goes smack back to that. I'd been hungry so long, just like the other cats. We try to live our hundred days in one, get all the feelings, bend all the notes—and you can't do all you want to in the time you've got.

BILLIE HOLIDAY, interview, *Night Beat with Ted Wallace,* 1955

There are times for dreaming/ In the peacefulness of nights with hollow silences/ And times for doubt/ When the heavy web of words is torn with sighs./

There are times for suffering/ Along the roads of war at the look in mother's eyes,/ There are times for love/ In lighted huts where one flesh sings./ There is what colors times to come/ As sunshine greens the plants./ In the delirium of these hours,/ In the impatience of these hours,/ Is the ever fertile seed/ Of times when equilibrium is born.

DAVID DIOP, "The Hours," *Poundings,* 1956

I know not when it was. I still confuse the present and the past/ The way I mix up Death and Life—a bridge of sweetness links them.

LEOPOLD SENGHOR, "I Know Not When It Was," *Ethiopics,* 1956

We stand in life at midnight, we are always on the threshold of a new dawn.

MARTIN LUTHER KING, JR., *Stride Toward Freedom,* 1958

The time has come ... for us to examine ourselves, but we can only do this if we are willing to free ourselves of the myth of America and try to find out what is really happening here.

JAMES BALDWIN, *Nobody Knows My Name,* 1961

The hour is late; the clock of destiny is ticking out.

MARTIN LUTHER KING, JR., "The American Dream," commencement speech given at Lincoln University, Oxford, Pennysylvania, 6 June 1961

Don't be in a hurry to condemn because he doesn't do what you do or think as you think or as fast. There was a time when you didn't know what you know today.

MALCOLM X, 1963

There comes a time when people get tired of being trampled over by the iron feet of oppression. There comes a time, when people get tired of being thrown across the abyss of humiliation where they experience the bleakness of nagging despair. There comes a time, when people get tired of being pushed out of the glittering sunlight of life's July, and left standing amidst the piercing chill of an Alpine November.

MARTIN LUTHER KING, JR., *Why We Can't Wait,* 1963

[T]ime is neutral. It can be used either destructively or constructively.

MARTIN LUTHER KING, JR., *Letter from a Birmingham City Jail,* 1963

[T]he time is coming for ballots or bullets. [I]t is useless to ask [the] enemy for justice.

MALCOLM X, "The Ballot or the Bullet," speech given in Cleveland, Ohio, 3 April 1965

[T]ime listens for you/ it knows I am naked/ it knows I am rich/ it knows that it knows/ I know that someone will turn over the hourglass.

EDOUARD MAUNICK, "This Strange Calculation of Roots," *The Book of Death and the Sea,* 1966

It is one minute to midnight. Time is running out not just on people who are economically and educationally deprived, but time is running out for people throughout the world.

WHITNEY YOUNG, 3 March 1968

No man is ahead of his time. Every man is within his star, each in his time. Each man must respond to the call of God in his lifetime and not in somebody else's time.

BENJAMIN MAYS, eulogy of Martin Luther King, Jr., Atlanta, Georgia, 9 April 1968

Time has to be experienced in order to make sense or become real. A person experiences time in his own life, and partly through the society which goes back many generations before his own birth. Since what is in the future has not been experienced, it does not make sense and cannot constitute time.

JOHN MBITI, *African/Religion Philosophy,* 1970

It is more important to be in time than on time.

Ibid.

Time has swift wings.

BENJAMIN MAYS, *Born To Rebel,* 1971

Time passes and passes. It passes backward and it passes forward and it carries you along, and no one knows more about time than this.

JAMES BALDWIN, *No Name in the Street,* 1972

I don't need time. What I need is a deadline.

DUKE ELLINGTON, *Music Is My Mistress,* 1973

But any Time is with us. And if we take control to shape our attitude and reshape our memories, that time is always *now—our time* for the best possible uses of our lives.

KEORAPETSE KGOSITSILE, in *Black Poetry Writing,* 1975

Time can be your enemy or your friend.

RAY CHARLES, *Brother Ray,* 1978

There are no weeks in nature, much less weekends. All divisions of time are man-made, and many of them have been settled by war.

BILL RUSSELL, *Second Wind,* 1979

[Y]ou will be timeless if you will *be* about constant work and change. Black people will have no beginning or end if each generation does the job it must do to change the world.

SONIA SANCHEZ, "Ruminations/Reflections," in Evans, ed., *Black Women Writers,* 1984

Let not our children die before they will have time to be children. Let not this cancer devour more of our people and destroy more of our world. Let not our hope and our struggle and our pain be in vain. Now is the time.

ALLAN BOESAK, "Who Can Speak for South Africa?" *Crisis,* November 1986

A battle had been raging that it was about time the third world was honored, the African continent in particular.

WOLE SOYINKA, in "Wole Soyinka: Nigerian Playwright is First Black Nobel Laureate in Literature," *Ebony,* April 1987

I've got to steal some time for myself.

LEONTYNE PRICE, 1988

There is only one time, infinite and definite. Definite by the sundial, by the drum. In fact, all music is nothing but an organization of sound and silence in relationship to time. And those who can take time and make it swing are in possession of a cosmic force more powerful than any other.

OSCAR BROWN, JR., Remarks: Open Dialogue Conference, Chicago, Illinois, 1988

Printer's errors may be corrected, a book revised/ Whole editions destroyed and reset/ But what is time that we cannot reverse it?

ONWUCHEKWA JEMIE, "Lament for Ellsworth Janifer," in Chinweizu, ed., *Voices From Twentieth-Century Africa,* 1988

We don't have eternity to realize our dreams, only the time we have here.

SUSAN TAYLOR, 1988

Because time has been good to me, I treat it with great respect.

LENA HORNE, in *Lears,* January–February 1989

Learn not to waste time, for time is money and time is effort. God gives some people the ability to manage time. The rest of us have to learn how. And we can.

BENJAMIN CARSON, *Gifted Hands,* 1990

The worst part of imprisonment is being locked up by yourself. You came face to face with time and there is nothing more terrifying than to be alone with sheer time. Then the ghosts come crowding in.

NELSON MANDELA, *Higher than Hope,* 1991

We must use time creatively, and forever realize that the time is always ripe to do right.

Ibid.

TIRED

I don't feel no ways tired. I've come too far from where I started from. Nobody told me the road would be easy. I don't believe He brought me this far to leave me.

SPIRITUAL

My feet is tired, but my soul is rested.

MOTHER POLLARD, in Montgomery bus boycott, 1955

We're tired of being kicked about by the brutal feet of oppression.

MARTIN LUTHER KING, JR., Montgomery Improvement Association meeting, 4 December 1955

I don't really know why I wouldn't move. There was no plan at all. I was just tired from shopping, my feet hurt.

ROSA PARKS, start of Montgomery bus boycott, 5 December 1955

I'm sick and tired of being sick and tired.

FANNIE LOU HAMER, c. 1972

The tired among us must recharge their batteries. The uninitiated must learn to gird their loins. We have not finished the job of making our country whole.

JAMES FARMER, *Lay Bare the Heart,* 1985

When you get into a fight with a bear, you don't get tired until the bear gets tired.

COLEMAN YOUNG, in the *Detroit Free Press,* 29 May 1988

TOMORROW

You do not know the plan of God and should not weep for tomorrow.

AMENENOPE

If you wait for tomorrow, tomorrow comes. If you don't wait for tomorrow, tomorrow comes.

SIERRA LEONE

We build our temples for tomorrow, strong as we know how, and we stand on top of the mountain, free within ourselves.

LANGSTON HUGHES, "The Negro Artist and the Racial Mountain," *The Nation,* 23 June 1926

And the . . . dancers who will dance like flame and the singers who will continue to carry our songs to all who listen—they will be with us in even greater numbers tomorrow.

Ibid.

[H]owever hard the road, however difficult today, tomorrow things will be better. Tomorrow may not be better, but we must believe that it will be. Wars may never cease, but we must continue to strive to eliminate them. We may not abolish poverty, but we must believe that we can provide bread enough and to spare for every living creature and that we can find the means to distribute it. We may not exterminate racism, but we must believe that different racial groups can live together in peace, and we must never cease to try. . . .

BENJAMIN MAYS, "What Man Lives By," in Philpot, ed., *Best Black Sermons,* 1972

Tomorrow is in the wings waiting for you to sound her entrance fanfare.

DUKE ELLINGTON, *Music Is My Mistress,* 1973

A believer is an optimist who thinks of tomorrow.

Ibid.

I have had tomorrow/ stripped from/ my soul./ When all seemed/ Certain./ The future/ No longer clutters my mind,/ Because there is none.

BARBARA WOLF BOOTH, "In the Shallows," *Akwesasne Notes,* Summer 1975

TOUCH

The touch among the loveless is that they must narcoticize themselves before they can touch any human being at all.

JAMES BALDWIN, *Nobody Knows My Name,* 1961

Not touching someone is a way of rejecting him.

JAMES BALDWIN, *A Rap On Race,* 1971

There are things sadder than you and I. Some people do not even touch.

SONIA SANCHEZ, *Love Poems,* 1973

A touch no heavier than a feather but loaded, nevertheless, with desire.

TONI MORRISON, *Beloved,* 1987

TRADITION

In 1619 twenty Africans were sold as slaves to settlers in Jamestown. In 1624, a Negro child was baptized and from that time on Negroes were baptized in most of the oldest churches in the South.

W. E. B. DU BOIS, c. 1900

A group tradition must supply compensation for persecution, and pride of race, the antidote for prejudice. History must restore what slavery took away for it is the damage of slavery that the present generation must repair and offset.

ARTHUR SCHOMBURG, c. 1925

If a race has no history, if it has no worthwhile traditions, it becomes a negligible factor in the thought of the world. The American Indian left no continuous record. He did not appreciate the value of tradition; and where is he today? The Hebrew keenly appreciates the value of tradition.

CARTER G. WOODSON, *The Story of the Negro Retold,* 1935

The survival of varying degrees of Africa in America does not suggest that there has been only a limited adjustment of the Negro to the New World. To the contrary, it merely points out that he came out of an experience that was sufficiently entrenched to make possible the persistence of some customs and traditions.

JOHN HOPE FRANKLIN, *From Slavery to Freedom,* 1947

[T]he legacy of struggle which might serve as inspiration to black youth has not been passed from one generation to the next.

NORMAN RILEY, "Footnotes of a Culture at Risk," *Crisis,* March 1986

The tradition of American music and the lineage of musicians that I'm trying to represent have created something very valuable and should be known and taught to all the students in this country.

WYNTON MARSALIS, "We Must Preserve Our Jazz Heritage," *Ebony,* February 1986

Tradition is important for reasons other than to re-create the past. When an actor studies Shakespeare, it's not because he wants to do Shakespeare for the rest of his life, it's for use of language. Having a concern for tradition doesn't mean that you merely want to copy something that was done thirty years ago, but expand what you're doing today.

SPIKE LEE, *Mo' Better Blues,* 1991

TRAGEDY

Not that men are poor—all men know something of poverty; that men are wicked—who is good? Not that men are ignorant—what is truth? Nay, but that men know so little of man.

W. E. B. DU BOIS, c. 1902

One of the worst tragedies in the world is the individual trained to do a specific thing and not in position to do it. Turn . . . on a bunch of redcaps. . . . you would find a score of Bachelors of Arts, Doctors of Law, Doctors of Medicine. . .

GEORGE S. SCHUYLER, in the *Pittsburgh Courier,* 14 February 1931

He is that tragic creature, a man without a nationality. He claims to be American . . . British . . . and French—but you cannot assume a nationality as you would a new suit of clothes.

PAUL ROBESON, "I Want to Be African," in *What I Want From Life,* 1934

When Paul sang "Were You There?" he sang not only of the crucifixion of Jesus, but also of the lynching crucifixion of the Negro people, the cremation of the Jewish people, and of the intolerance, fear, hatred, and brutality which caused the tragedies. One can almost hear him sing. Were you there when they crucified the Moors?

ESLANDA GOODE ROBESON, "Here's My Story," *Freedom,* 1953

Real tragedy is never resolved. It goes on hopelessly. Conventional tragedy is too easy. The hero dies and we feel a purging of the emotions. A real tragedy takes place in a corner, in an untidy spot. The rest of the world is unaware of it.

CHINUA ACHEBE, *No Longer At Ease,* 1961

This is the tragic plight of man, tragic, because he need not be so prodigal, tragic because man is made for something better.

MARTIN LUTHER KING, JR., speech given at Purdue University, West Lafayette, Indiana, 1968

It must be borne in mind . . . that the tragedy in life does not lie in not reaching your goal. The tragedy lies in having no goal to reach. It isn't a calamity to die with dreams unfulfilled, but it is a calamity not to dream. . . . It is not a disgrace not to reach the stars, but it is a disgrace to have no stars to reach for. Not failure, but low aim is the sin.

BENJAMIN MAYS, "What Man Lives By," in Philpot, ed., *Best Black Sermons,* 1972

The modern tragedy is the tragedy of a freedom that can err disastrously and evilly. I was caught in the bewildering realization that believing myself liberated from fate as an implacable, blind, and alien force, I could not separate myself from myself, a self subjected into the evil of the world I lived in and also to the sources of that evil within myself. I was in a total sense, my own fate.

CARLOS FUENTES, "Central and Eccentric Writing," *The American Magazine,* 21 October 1974

There can be no greater tragedy than to forget one's origin and finish despised and hated by people among whom one grew up.

PAUL ROBESON, in *The Whole World in His Hand,* 1981

Tragedy, no matter how sad, becomes boring to those not caught in its addictive caress.

MAYA ANGELOU, *All God's Children Need Traveling Shoes,* 1986

I've had tragedy, but I have had lots of joy and triumph.

CORETTA SCOTT KING, c. 1988

To want to learn, to have the capacity to learn and not be able to learn is a tragedy.

MICHAEL JACKSON, in *Jet,* 28 March 1988

One of the tragedies for many women is that our mothers told us nothing.

OPRAH WINFREY, in *Woman's Day,* 4 October 1988

TRAINING

Train your head and hands to do, your head and heart to dare.

JOSEPH COTTER, *Links of Friendship,* 1898

The training of the schools we need today more than ever—the training of deft hands, quick eyes and ears, and . . . a deeper, higher culture of gifted minds and pure hearts.

W. E. B. DU BOIS, *The Souls of Black Folk,* 1903

First you find the logical way, and when you find it avoid it, and let your inner self break through and guide you. Don't try to be anybody else but you.

WILL MARION COOK, in Ellington, *Music Is My Mistress,* 1973

I train myself for triumph by knowing it is mine no matter what.

AUDRE LORDE, *The Cancer Journals,* 1980

TRAVEL

He who does not travel will not know the value of men.

ALGERIA

The man who goes ahead stumbles, so that the man who follows may have his wits about him.

KENYA

We've come a distance, but we still have a distance to go.

TRADITIONAL

If you don't know where you want to go any road will take you there.

TRADITIONAL

Having traveled over a considerable portion of these United States, and having, in the course of my travels, taken the most accurate observation of things as they exist—the result of my observations has warranted the full and unshaken conviction, that we, (coloured people of these United States) are the most degraded, wretched, and abject set of beings that ever lived since the world began.... [T]he Israelites in Egypt, the Helots in Sparta, and ... the Roman Slaves ... whose sufferings under those ancient and heathen nations, were, in comparison with ours, no more than a cypher ... while wretchedness and endless miseries were reserved, apparently in a phial, to be poured out upon our fathers, ourselves and our children, by Christian Americans!

DAVID WALKER, *Appeal to the Coloured Citizens of the World,* 1829

Let us cheer the weary traveler,/ cheer the weary traveler./ Let us cheer the weary traveler/ Along the heavenly way.

W. E. B. DU BOIS, *The Souls of Black Folk,* 1903

Before taking steps the wise man knows the object and end of his journey.

W. E. B . DU BOIS, "Hail Columbia," *Crisis,* April 1913

Morality is largely a matter of geography.

GEORGE S. SCHUYLER, in *The Messenger,* August 1923

It's the long road to Guinea./ No bright welcome will be made for you/ in the dark land of dark men:/ Under a smoky sky pierced by the cry of birds/ around the eye of the river/ the eyelashes of the trees open on decaying light./ There, there awaits you beside the water a quiet village,/ and the hut of your fathers, and the hard ancestral stone/ where your head will rest at last.

JACQUES ROUMAIN, "Guinea," *Ebony Wood,* 1939

Not to go means lingering here to live out this slow death; to go means facing the unknown.

RICHARD WRIGHT, *12 Million Black Voices,* 1941

Mine has not been an easy road. Very few of my generation found life easy or wanted it that way. Your road may be somewhat less rugged because of the struggles we have made.

MARY MCLEOD BETHUNE, c. 1945

During my travels, I met native Africans, West Indians, Chinese, East Indians ... who are fighting for the same thing—freedom from bondage....

PAUL ROBESON, in "My Answer," *New York Age,* August–September 1949

The right to travel is a Constitutional right. And there's nothing in that document that says you have to be muzzled before you can pack your bag.

PAUL ROBESON, "The Constitutional Right to Travel," *Freedom,* July–August 1955

Man's journey is hazardous because the world in which he lives is grounded in order and held intact by an inner and irresistible logic, which also make living a dramatic risk.

HOWARD THURMAN, *Disciplines of the Spirit,* 1963

[I have made my pilgrimage to Mecca.] Never have I witnessed such sincere hospitality and ... brotherhood as is practiced ... here in this ancient holy land....

MALCOLM X, letter from Jedda, Saudi Arabia, 20 April 1964

We must get beyond textbooks, go out into the bypaths and untrodden depths of the wilderness of truth and explore and tell the world the glories of our journey.

JOHN HOPE FRANKLIN, c. 1967

To have been where we were, to have paid the price we have paid, to have survived, and to have shaken up the world the way we have is a rare journey.

JAMES BALDWIN, "Why I Left America," *Essence,* October 1970

[W]anderlust grew like a virus.

ADAM CLAYTON POWELL, JR., *Adam by Adam,* 1971

His wanderlust grew like a virus and it has infected me too.

Ibid.

To other countries I may go as a tourist. To India, I come as a pilgrim.

MARTIN LUTHER KING, JR., in *King, A Critical Biography,* 1978

It is the final voyage into oneself that is the most difficult.

HAKI MADHUBUTI, "Lucille Clifton: Warm Water, Greased Legs, and Dangerous Poetry," in Evans, ed., *Black Women Writers,* 1984

TREE

Not all the flowers of a tree produce fruit.

MADAGASCAR

The tree of love gives shade to all.

TRADITIONAL

We are like trees. We wear all colors naturally.

CLAUDE MCKAY, *Home to Harlem,* 1928

The custom of planting a tree after the birth of a child is common in Africa. If the tree whose shadow protects the child becomes tall and strong, it is a sign of vigor and posterity for the child.

PIERRE ERNY, "The Social Psychology of the Black African Child," *Childhood and Cosmos,* 1968

Jazz is a tree, a most unusual tree. Can't you just see it making its first break through, sprouting in its environment despite the climate, completely ignorant of the nature of its own existence, but continually growing up, until it is a strong healthy child, attractive and admired! Nobody ever warned it of the hazards of adulthood.

DUKE ELLINGTON, *Music Is My Mistress,* 1973

Black music is like a tree with many branches. From Jazz comes all the rock and roll, and rhythm and blues.

LESTER BOWIE, in "Jazz Men: A Love Supreme," *Ebony Man,* April 1987

We have stopped under this tree of life for a short while. We have stopped under a tree of temporary comfort. We have enjoyed its shade.

MUHAMMAD ALI, in "The Meaning of Life," *Life,* December 1988

Trees are soul people to me, maybe not to other people, but I have watched the trees when they pray, and I've watched them shout and sometimes they give thanks slowly and quietly. They praise God in their beautiful light, the flowers do too. All these things do, everything but man.

BESSIE HARVEY, in *Black Art: Ancestral Legacy,* 1989

The practice of bottle trees went hand in hand with having a grass-free yard. The devil could hide himself in a blade of grass, but if the yard was gravel or dirt, there was no place to hide.

ROBERT THOMPSON, in *ibid.*

The bottle pile besides your shotgun house grows bigger—empty bottle—the beers are brown. The whiskeys clear and milk of magnesia comes in translucent blue. But on this summer day you've cut a green bay tree/ Sheared the leaves away, stubbed the branches/ Stuck it upright in your yard./ Your bluebottle tree, a hard won/ Stay against confusion.

JAMES SEAY, "The Blue Bottle Tree," in *ibid.*

Trees possess great spiritual powers in traditional African cultures, and sacrificial offerings are placed before certain trees which are felled for use as sculpture.

REGENIA PERRY, in *ibid.*

TROUBLES

Wherever I turned there was evil upon evil./ Misery increased, justice departed/ . . . The like of this had never been seen:/ Wherever I turned, there was trouble in pursuit.

ENLIL, BABYLON, c. 1750 B.C.

Up above my head I see Trouble in the air,/ There must be a God somewhere.

SPIRITUAL

Don't trouble trouble till trouble troubles you.

TRADITIONAL

I'm alone every night and the lights are sinking low,/ I've never had so much trouble in my life before.

BERTHA "CHIPPIE" HILL, "Trouble in Mind," c. 1946

No one can leave a permanent mark on the world till he learns to be true to himself.

PAUL ROBESON, in "My Answer," *New York Age,* August–September 1949

That's the trouble with you and this country and all of us. We don't mean anything. We abuse, deny, outrage, insult, and don't mean anything.

PETER ABRAHAMS, *Tell Freedom,* 1954

I realize I'm saying some things that you think can get me in trouble, but, brothers, I was born in trouble. I don't even care about trouble.

MALCOLM X, speech given at Audubon Ballroom, New York City, 20 December 1964

Men are more inclined to hate trouble than to hate injustice.

CARL ROWAN, in *Who Speaks for the Negro?* 1965

Presentation of the truth is awesome; to speak it requires courage, to write it is dangerous, to live it guarantees an early death.

WYATT T. WALKER, in *Negro Digest,* December 1967

Nations, like men, are wary of truth, for truth is too often not beautiful.

ADDISON GAYLE, JR., *The Black Aesthetic,* 1971

There is nothing written in the Bible, Old or New Testament, that says: "If you believe in Me, you ain't going to have no troubles."

RAY CHARLES, in "Ray Charles Sees the Beauty," *Parade,* 10 October 1988

TRUST

In God we trust, all others pay cash.

TRADITIONAL

Whatever you tell me I mean to hold fast to. I will pick it up and hold it close to my heart.

CHIEF SATANTA OF THE KIOWAS, in Stanley, *Satanta and the Kiowas,* 1960

In the bush, "trust" no one you don't know.

ALEX HALEY, *Roots,* 1977

TRUTH

One falsehood spoils a thousand truths.

ASHANTI

The truth is like gold, keep it locked up and you will find it exactly as you first put it away.

SENEGAL

If I tell you a hen dip snuff, look under its wing and find a whole box.

TRADITIONAL

If I'm lying, I'm flying.

TRADITIONAL

Tell the truth and shame the devil.

TRADITIONAL

It profits nothing to show virtue in words and destroy truth in deeds.

ST. CYPRIAN, *On Morality,* c. 252

Everything I tell you is the truth, but there's plenty I can't tell you.

SLAVE

I will keep my word until the stones melt.

DELSHAY OF THE TONTO APACHES, in report to the U.S. Secretary of the Interior, 1871

Truth is proper and beautiful at all times and in all places.

FREDERICK DOUGLASS, 14 April 1876

Truth is patient and time is just.

Ibid.

Threats cannot suppress the truth.

IDA B. WELLS, *A Red Record,* 1895

What this nation needs is a Renaissance of reverence for the truth.

W. E. B. DU BOIS, "The Jim Crow Argument," *Crisis,* 1912

You must speak straight so that your words may go like sunlight to our hearts.

COCHISE OF THE CHIRICAHUA APACHES, in "Recollections of an Interview with Cochise, Chief of the Apaches," *Collections,* 1915

Truth comes to us from the past, then, like gold washed down from the mountains.

CARTER G. WOODSON, *Story of the Negro Retold,* 1935

Let truth destroy the dividing prejudices of nationality and teach universal love without distinction of race, merit, or rank.

Ibid.

[W]hat I say is the unadulterated truth which cannot be denied.

PAUL ROBESON, in "My Answer," *New York Age,* August–September 1949

In every age, among the people, truth is the property of the national cause.

FRANTZ FANON, *The Wretched of the Earth,* 1963

[U]narmed truth and unconditional love will have the final word in reality.

MARTIN LUTHER KING, JR., Nobel Peace Prize acceptance speech, 10 December 1964

I'm for truth, no matter who tells it. I'm for justice, no matter who is for or against it. I'm for whoever and whatever benefits humanity as a whole.

MALCOLM X, *The Autobiography of Malcolm X,* 1965

The truth can be quickly received, or received at all, only by the sinner who knows and admits that he is guilty of having sinned much. . . . The very enormity of my previous life's guilt prepared me to accept the truth.

Ibid.

[T]ruth pressed to earth will rise again.

MARTIN LUTHER KING, JR., speech at the March on Montgomery, Montgomery, Alabama, 25 March 1965

I face the possibility of annihilation so that two or three truths may cast their eternal brilliance over the world.

FRANTZ FANON, *Black Skin, White Masks,* 1967

Who loves Truth loves God, for God is Truth.

FRANK YERBY, *Judas, My Brother,* 1967

If the truth is not uttered by the anointed, and the seats of government become stools for injustice and impiety, even if the rocks have to cry out, the groanings of the suffering will be heard.

JESSE JACKSON, c. 1968

Truth needs witness, truth needs monuments.

LERONE BENNETT, JR., *Challenge of Blackness,* 1968

Truth alone is powerless against power, but truth fused with power is more powerful than power alone.

Ibid.

Truth is that which places a man in touch with the real; once found, he is prepared to give all for it.

JAMES CONE, *Black Theology and Black Power,* 1969

All truths proclaimed by man are relative. My search has been for the absolute truth.

ADAM CLAYTON POWELL, JR., *Adam by Adam,* 1971

I write to bear witness to the truth.

JAMES BALDWIN, *Rap on Race,* 1971

True Black writers speak as Blacks about Blacks to Blacks.

GWENDOLYN BROOKS, *Jump Bad,* 1972

When face to face with oneself or looking oneself in the eye, there is no cop out. It is the moment of truth. I cannot lie to me.

DUKE ELLINGTON, *Music Is My Mistress,* 1973

Truth is the baby of the world, it never gets old.

DICK GREGORY, interview, "NBC Wide World of Sports," 14 November 1975

Truth for me has been a wandering path that's crisscrossed all the shades of ecstasy, all the shadows of bitterness.

BUFFY SAINTE-MARIE, in *Akwesasne Notes,* Winter 1976

I keep alive by being the troublesome/
Indestructible stinkweed of truth.

NAOMI MADGETT, "Tree of Heaven," *A Student's Guide to Creative Writing,* 1980

I cannot tell the truth about anything unless I confess to being a student, growing and learning something new every day. The more I learn, the clearer my view of the world becomes.

SONIA SANCHEZ, "Ruminations/Reflections," in Evans, ed., *Black Women Writers,* 1984

They sat on the truth so long by now they've mashed the life out of it.

ALICE WALKER, *Living With the Wind,* 1985

The truth and the justice that we are fighting for are more enduring than the shallow, selfish, racist self-interests that seem to be inspiring America[n] policies toward [South Africa].

ALLEN BOESAK, "Who Can Speak For South Africa?" *Crisis,* November 1986

The preacher . . . must now share [his] power with people . . . who read and find out that some things propagated under the name of Christianity are not really true.

CLARENCE GLOVER, in "Spirituality: An African View," *Essence,* December 1987

I tell Black kids the truth: Don't look for pie in the sky when you die, get something on the ground while you're around. In this society, your Blackness is a shortcoming, and you better be able to deal with it, because you're going to run into prejudice, discrimination, and segregation. Instead of getting bitter, angry, and mad, get smart.

DON KING, in *Jet,* 16 May 1988

Truth, whether you perceive it or not, only brings light into your life.

OPRAH WINFREY, in *Essence,* November 1988

I, the old eagle, say to you young Turks, learn the truths of our glorious age of Songhai West Africa, then you will be shielded from the darts and arrows of the falsehoods portrayed on television and the motion pictures about Africa and Africans. You will find that there is no subject you cannot master, that there is no profession that you cannot claim, that there is no height to which you cannot climb because you have the strength of kings in your wings. Fly on!

EDWARD ROBINSON, "The Story of the Eagle," in Goss and Barnes, eds., *Talk That Talk,* 1989

UNDERGROUND

Termites live underground.

ETHIOPIA

On my underground railroad I never ran my train off the track. And I never lost a passenger.

HARRIET TUBMAN, c. 1840

The Underground Railroad helped others escape by secret methods through persons aiding the fugitives from place to place all the way to free soil.

CARTER G. WOODSON, *Negro Makers of History,* 1928

There's a lot of talk today about the underground. We Negro people must remember that we would not be talking anywhere without the underground struggles of our forefathers in the days of liberation here in America . . . my own father . . . escaped twice by the underground railroad.

PAUL ROBESON, "Tribute to William. L. Patterson," *Freedom,* August 1951

In going underground, I whipped it all except the mind.

RALPH ELLISON, *Invisible Man,* 1952

God blessed the Underground/ great praise to it shall ever resound./ The train, it never left the track./ No one was lost. No one turned back.

FRANK MORRIS, *Blacks in Detroit,* 1980

UNDERSTANDING

By and by when the morning comes, all the saints of God are gathered home. We'll tell the story of how we overcome, for we'll understand it better by and by.

SPIRITUAL

We should understand that we are still surrounded by quicksands.

HENRI CHRISTOPHE, *Proclamation,* 1 January 1816

Ain't no such thing as only "understanding." Under means action.

HARRIET TUBMAN, c. 1840

I will not do anything that I do not understand. I do not understand the psychology or philosophy of the Frenchmen, German, or Italian. Their history has nothing in common with the history of my slave ancestors.

PAUL ROBESON, in "Robeson Spurns Music He 'Doesn't Understand,'" *New York World-Telegram,* 30 August 1933

Unless you see [the] fur, a mink skin ain't no different from a coon skin.

ZORA NEALE HURSTON, *Their Eyes Were Watching God,* 1937

For then will be refound the unity of ancient times, the reconciliation of/ Lion, Bull, and Tree,/ Idea linked to act, ear to heart, and sign to sense

LEOPOLD SENGHOR, *Ethiopics,* 1956

[Americans] are, in effect, still trapped in a history which they do not understand; and until they understand it, they cannot be released from it. They have had to believe for many years, and for innumerable reasons, that black men are inferior to white men. Many of them, indeed, know better, but, as you will discover, people find it very difficult to act on what they know. To act is to be committed, and to be committed is to be in danger.

JAMES BALDWIN, *The Fire Next Time,* 1962

Shallow understanding from people of good will is more frustrating than absolute misunderstanding from people of ill will.

MARTIN LUTHER KING, JR., *Letter from a Birmingham City Jail*, 1963

Why am I as I am? To understand that of any person, his whole life, from birth must be reviewed. All of our experiences fuse into our personality. Everything that ever happened to me is an ingredient.

MALCOLM X, *The Autobiography of Malcolm X*, 1965

It disturbs the soul of man to truly understand what he invariably senses: that nobody really finds oppression or poverty tolerable.

LORRAINE HANSBERRY, *Les Blancs*, 1972

If you understood everything I say, you'd be me.

MILES DAVIS, in Ellington, *Music Is My Mistress*, 1973

It took me twenty years of study and practice to work up to what I wanted in this performance. How can she expect to listen five minutes and understand it?

Ibid.

Blacks believe that soul, feeling, emotional and spiritual, serve as guides to understanding life.

GENEVA SMITHERMAN, *Talkin' and Testifying*, 1977

Let us understand and revere all things,/ and penetrate into that secret world./ May the flower be your guiding light.

JOSÉ ANDRADE, "Each Thing Is a World in Itself," *Latin American Tales*, 1977

Men will never understand women. There is an age-old mystery that will always separate the two.

GRACE JONES, in "An Interview with Grace Jones," *Black Stars*, May 1981

That's what makes Magic Johnson such a great basketball player. He understands every position on the court, not just his position. And he understands those positions in transition as they change. He has in-depth understanding. You need that kind of complete understanding to be good at what you do, be it music or any other profession.

WYNTON MARSALIS, 1988

UNITY

Then spider webs unite—they can tie up a lion.

ETHIOPIA

All for one, one for all.

ALEXANDRE DUMAS, *The Three Musketeers*, 1844

We are one, our cause is one, and we must help each other; if we are to succeed.

FREDERICK DOUGLASS, editorial, *North Star*, 1847

We will never separate ourselves voluntarily from the slave population in this country; they are our brethren by the trees of consanguinity, of suffering and of wrong; and we feel there is more virtue in suffering privations with them than fancied advantage for a season.

RICHARD ALLEN, *The Life Experience and Gospel Labors of Richard Allen*, 1887

The dawn of a new day is upon us and we see things differently. We see now not as individuals, but as a collective whole, having one common interest.

MARCUS GARVEY, *Philosophy and Opinions of Marcus Garvey*, 1923

Whether you have a Ph.D, a D.D., or no D, we're in this together. Whether you're from Morehouse or No house we're in this bag together.

FANNIE LOU HAMER, "The Special Plight and Role of Black Woman," speech given at NAACP Legal Defense Fund Institute, New York City, 7 May 1954

In a time of chaos, in a time of trouble, we're asking for unity, as defense against these mad white people who continue to run the world.

LEROI JONES, speech given at Hotel Theresa, New York City, 1960

We cannot think of uniting with others, until after we have first united among ourselves. We cannot think of being acceptable to others until we have first proven acceptable to ourselves. One can't unite bananas with scattered leaves.

MALCOLM X, "A Declaration of Independence," press conference at Park Sheraton Hotel, New York City, 12 March 1964

We've got to change our own minds about each other. We have to see each other with new eyes. We have to see each other as brothers and sisters. We have to come together with warmth so we can develop unity and harmony.

MALCOLM X, "The Ballot or the Bullet," speech given in Cleveland, Ohio, 3 April 1964

In Birmingham in 1963, friends from my church were picketing. I went down, I didn't tote no signs, but my boss told me when I got back to work, not to tote. The next time I went and toted. The third time I toted I didn't have a job. But I'd rather work for $25 a week for Dr. King than $125 for my boss.

BIRMINGHAM RESIDENT

You don't fight racism with racism, the best way to fight racism is with solidarity.

BOBBY SEALE, in *Time,* 6 April 1970

Not to fight to liberate ourselves from the men—this is another trick to keep us from fighting among ourselves—but to work together with the Black man.

FANNIE LOU HAMER, c. 1970

The road to solidarity and strength leads inevitably through reclamation and indoctrination of Black art and culture.

HOYT W. FULLER, in Gayle, ed., *The Black Aesthetic,* 1971

I cannot allow the devious purpose of white supremacy to lead me to any conclusion other than what may be the most robust and important one of our time: that the ultimate destiny and aspiration of the African people and twenty million American Negroes are magnificently bound up together forever.

LORRAINE HANSBERRY, *Les Blancs,* 1972

The picket line was the beginning of cross-class unity among Blacks.

COLEMAN YOUNG, 1974

I am nostalgic for the solidarity and sharing a modest existence can sometimes bring.

ALICE WALKER, *In Search of Our Mothers' Gardens,* 1983

When it comes to the crunch, whatever the morality involved, whites will stick by their fellow whites.

DESMOND TUTU, c. 1984

Liberation is costly. It needs unity.

Ibid.

We can always stick together when we are losing, but tend to find means of breaking up when we're winning.

THURGOOD MARSHALL, in Hastie, *Grace Under Pressure,* 1984

For one lost, all lost—the chain that held them would save all or none.

TONI MORRISON, *Beloved,* 1987

Let nothing and nobody break your spirit. Let the unity in the community remain intact.

JESSE JACKSON, c. 1989

All of us [blacks worldwide] are bound to Mother Africa by invisible but tenacious bonds. She has nurtured the deepest things in us blacks. All of us have roots that go deep into the warm soil of Africa, so that no matter how long and traumatic our separation from our ancestral home has been, there are things we are often unable to articulate but which we feel in our very bones, things which make us different from others who have not suckled the breasts of our mother, Africa.

DESMOND TUTU, in *The Words of Desmond Tutu,* 1989

UNIVERSAL

Suffering is universal for mankind. There is no one who escapes. It makes demands alike upon the wise and the foolish, the literate and the illiterate, the saint and the sinner.

HOWARD THURMAN, *Meditations of the Heart,* 1953

To de-westernize in order to universalize is our desire.

ALIOUNE DIOP, speech given at the Second Congress of Negro Writers and Artists, Rome, 1959

Universality emerges from the truthful identity of what is.

LORRAINE HANSBERRY, *Les Blancs,* 1972

The God I pray to is as universal as the moon is universal.

DICK GREGORY, c. 1974

One must rise above the Earth to become universal.

JEAN TOOMER, in Kerman and Eldridge, *The Lives of Jean Toomer,* 1987

UNIVERSE

All things in the universe move in cycles; so who knows but that in the whirl of God's great wheel the torch may again flame in the upper valley of the Nile.

JAMES WELDON JOHNSON, "Africa and the World," speech given at the NAACP Annual Conference, 1919

We who talk of the knowledge of the universe cannot sense the exact nature of an apple.

JEAN TOOMER, *Essentials,* 1931

When you look at the universe on a starry night (one galaxy has three hundred thousand million stars with the brightness of three hundred thousand suns, and there are a hundred million galaxies in the universe to be explored) you should not feel your littleness and insignificance but your greatness. For the human spirit is much greater than those universes. Because we can look at those worlds and understand them, but they cannot understand us.

ERNESTO CARDENAL, "Love," *Vida en al Amor,* 1974

Whenever you set out to build a temple, you must face the fact that there is a tension at the heart of the universe between good and evil.

MARTIN LUTHER KING, JR., in Oates, *Let the Trumpet Sound,* 1982

The white man regards the universe as a gigantic machine hurtling through time and space to its final destruction: individuals in it are but tiny organisms with private lives that lead to private deaths: personal power, success, and fame are the absolute measure of values, the things to live for.

ANTON LEMBEDE, in Mandela, *Higher than Hope,* 1991

The African, on his side, regards the universe as one composite whole; an organic entity, progressively driving towards greater harmony and unity, whose individual parts exist merely as interdependent aspects of one whole, realizing their fullest life in the corporate life whose communal contentment is the absolute measure of values.

Ibid.

UPBRINGING

Your mother didn't raise you in a dog house.

TRADITIONAL

I was not raised that way and neither the promise of gain nor the threat of loss has ever moved me from my firm convictions.

PAUL ROBESON

I was brought up knowing that you don't let anybody get you down and you don't let anybody get the best of you.

CHARLAYNE HUNTER GAULT

I was the product of a strict Southern home, and even though I was a shade wild and restless I understood the meaning of rules.

RAY CHARLES, *Brother Ray,* 1978

I'm Black, but I'm an American, and representing a Black character as always having to be twice as good at something, or having to rise to his height because of the difficulties of being Black, seem the residual of slavery. I wasn't raised that way and I won't accept it.

Lou Gossett, in "I Was Swallowing a Kind of Poison," *Parade,* 17 July 1988

I grew up in the context of a Black community where ideas such as dignity and integrity and proper behavior still existed. I thought that was the way the whole world was; and I will insist that, ultimately, that's the way it still is.

Avery Brooks, in "Avery Brooks: Not Just Another Pretty Face," *Essence,* April 1989

UTOPIA

What color is Utopia?

Jesse Owens, *Blackthink,* 1970

Utopia is what the imagination of man has to say about the possibilities of the human spirit.

Howard Thurman, *A Search for Common Ground,* 1971

VALUE

You're not more than anyone else and you're not less than, but you're just as much as anyone else.

TRADITIONAL

The colored man needs something more than a vote in his hand; he needs to know the value of home life; to rightly appreciate and value the marriage relations, to know how to be incited to leave behind him the old shreds and shells of slavery; to rise in the scale of character, worth, and influence.

FRANCES E. W. HARPER, *The Underground Railroad,* 1872

Race prejudice decreases values both real estate and human; crime, ignorance and filth decrease values.

W. E. B. DU BOIS, "The Challenge of Detroit," *Crisis,* 1925

I wish I could buy you for what you are really worth and sell you for what you think you're worth. I sure would make money on the deal.

ZORA NEALE HURSTON, *Moses, Man of The Mountain,* 1939

[The] value of an-all Negro movement is that it helps to create faith by Negroes in Negroes, develops a sense of self-reliance with Negroes depending on Negroes. It breaks down the slave mentality, which comes and is nourished with Negroes relying on white people.

A. PHILIP RANDOLPH, speech at March on Washington Movement, Detroit, Michigan, 26 September 1942

When a person goes against his values in the choices he makes, the failure is automatic.

HOWARD THURMAN, *Meditations of the Heart,* 1953

Our nationalism is not aggressive force, but a way of preserving our values: we wish to enrich, not to impoverish, ourselves and others.

CARLOS FUENTES, "Central and Eccentric Writing," *The American Magazine,* 21 October 1974

Nothing of value is given up voluntarily.

ALICE WALKER, *In Search of Our Mothers' Gardens,* 1983

A man with fine aims and high values works and suffers for creative life—events of force, in an age when no one cares and the majority of the people simply do not respond to him, while those who care are not willing to do much and they soon forget him.

JEAN TOOMER, in Kerman and Eldridge, *The Lives of Jean Toomer,* 1987

[T]he value of a ragged basket is not realized/ Until the day/ When the remains of a sacrifice are thrown away.

NNAMDI OLEBARA, "At the End," in Chinweizu, ed., *Voices From Twentieth-Century Africa,* 1988

I can't tell a solid gold coin from a gold-plated penny. I also have never learned to tell the difference between time told by a $40 Timex and a $6,000 Rolex.

SUSAN WATSON, in the *Detroit Free Press,* 26 October 1988

When a black person understands his or her African past, accepts being African, he is different from one who does not know these things. Those of us who know, know our value.

D'JIMO KOUYATE, "The Role of the Griot," in Goss and Barnes, eds., *Talk That Talk,* 1989

VICTORY

If it had not been for the victory of the Union army, I should be on some plantation in the

South, manacled body and soul in the fetters of a slave.

MARY CHURCH TERRELL, c. 1888

Ralph Metcalfe was ahead of me at 70 meters and 120,000 people were roaring. Between 70 and 90 meters Ralph and I were streaking neck and neck. Then I was in front at the finish. My eyes blurred as I heard the "Star Spangled Banner" played first faintly and then loudly, and then I saw the American flag slowly raised for my victory.

JESSE OWENS, 1936

Our real victory is not so much the desegregation of the buses as it is a new sense of dignity and destiny.

MARTIN LUTHER KING, JR., c. 1959

The victory so courageously won in the street can easily become an empty hollow mockery if we do not simultaneously equip ourselves with the skills, the values which the future will demand.

WHITNEY YOUNG, "Social Revolution: Challenge of the Nation," speech given at the Urban League Conference, 1963

Every time a man has contributed to the victory of the dignity of the spirit, every time a man has said no to an attempt to subjugate his fellows, I have felt solidarity with his act.

FRANTZ FANON, *Black Skin, White Masks,* 1967

I came back from Berlin and the 1936 Olympics to a welcome few people have ever experienced. The streets of New York were lined with tens of thousands . . . wanting . . . to touch me. . . . [B]ut one omission stood out more . . . as the months passed. No one had offered me a job.

JESSE OWENS, *Blackthink,* 1970

Too many victories weaken you. The defeated can rise up stronger than the victor.

MUHAMMAD ALI, *The Greatest,* 1975

If you surrender to the wind, you can ride it.

TONI MORRISON, in "The Pain of Being Black," *Time,* 22 May 1989

VIOLENCE

If men's superiority over the brute creation consists only in his reasoning powers and rationality of mind, his various methods of practicing violence towards his fellow creatures has in many cases placed him on a level with, and sometimes below, many species of the quadruped race.

WILLIAM WHIPPER, "An Address on Non-resistance to Offensive Aggression," *The Colored American,* 16 September 1837

Beginning with the KKK the Negro has been constantly subjected to some form of organized violence ever since he became free.

MARY CHURCH TERRELL, "Lynching From a Negro's Point of View," *North American Review,* June 1904

To return violence for violence does nothing but intensify the existence of violence and evil in the universe. Someone must have sense enough and morality enough to cut off the chains of violence and hate.

MARTIN LUTHER KING, JR., "Advice for Living," *Ebony,* February 1958

The violent act is the desperate act. It is the imperious demand of a person to force another to honor his desire and need to be cared for, to be understood.

HOWARD THURMAN, *Disciplines of the Spirit,* 1963

If violence is wrong in America, violence is wrong abroad.

MALCOLM X, "Message to the Grass Roots," speech given in Detroit, Michigan, 9 November 1963

Riots are the voice of the unheard.

MARTIN LUTHER KING, JR., 1965

The ultimate weakness of violence is that it is a descending spiral, begetting the very thing it seeks to destroy. Instead of diminishing evil, it multiplies it.

MARTIN LUTHER KING, JR., *Where Do We Go From Here?* 1968

A word to the violent has never been sufficient/ They have a hard speech that shatters conversation./ Practically speaking, a word to the violent is wasted.

RAYMOND PATTERSON, "A Word to the Wise Is Enough," *26 Ways of Looking at a Black Man,* 1968

Violence is necessary and it's as American as apple pie.

H. RAP BROWN, *Die Nigger Die,* 1969

Black people are called "violent" these days as if violence is a new invention out of the ghetto. But violence against the Black minority is built in the established American society, brutalization is inherent in all the customs and practices which bestow privileges on the whites and relegate the Blacks to the status of pariahs.

HOYT A. FULLER, "Toward a Black Aesthetic," in Gayle, ed., *The Black Aesthetic,* 1971

Apartheid is the main cause of violence in South Africa and the South African government is the main perpetrator of violence.

ALLEN BOESAK, "Who Can Speak for South Africa?" *Crisis,* November 1986

A person coming out of an environment with a lot of violence and hatred needs to know what love is. I have seen some young people on TV and the news who were brought in for killing someone or some other violence and I could see in their little faces that they had never been loved.

MELBA MOORE, in *USA Today,* 17 September 1987

Violence is part of the landscape of our history.

AVERY BROOKS, in "Spotlight: Not Just Another Pretty Face," *Essence,* April 1989

When a government decides to ban political organizations of the oppressed, intensifies oppression, and does not allow any free political activity, no matter how peaceful and nonviolent, then the people have no alternative but to resort to violence.

NELSON MANDELA, speech given in Detroit, Michigan, 28 June 1990

Western culture has produced much violence and destruction on the planet. It is like a cancer destroying the body.

FRANCES CRESS WELSING, *The Isis Papers,* 1991

VISION

Not through height does one see the moon.

AFRICA

I can see farther over the mountain than the man who is standing atop of it.

GULLAH

After the revelation in the year of 1825, and the knowledge of the elements being made known to me, I sought more than ever to obtain true holiness before the great day of judgment should appear.

NAT TURNER, *Confessions of Nat Turner,* 5 November 1831

All great people glorify their history and look back upon their early attainments with a spiritualized vision.

KELLY MILLER, "The Artistic Gift of the Negro," *Voice of the Negro,* April 1906

With our short sight we affect to take a comprehensive view of eternity. Our horizon is the universe.

PAUL LAURENCE DUNBAR, *The Uncalled,* 1908

When I walk through the campus with its stately palms and well-kept lawns, and think back to the dump-heap foundation, I rub my eyes and pinch myself. And I remember my childish visions in the cotton fields.

MARY MCLEOD BETHUNE, "Faith That Moved a Dump Heap," *WHO,* June 1941

Ultimately the artist and the revolutionary pay whatever dues they must pay behind it because they are both possessed by a vision, and they do not so much follow this vision as find themselves driven by it. Otherwise they could never endure much less embrace the lives they are compelled to lead.

JAMES BALDWIN, *Nobody Knows My Name,* 1961

Where there is no vision, the people perish.

Ibid.

In this country today we are menaced—intolerably menaced—by a lack of vision.

JAMES BALDWIN, "A Talk to Harlem Teachers," in Clarke, *Harlem, USA,* 1964

If dying is a must for the vision to be, then dying must be done, for the loss of the vision would make a worse death for the seer.

JOHN O'NEAL, "Black Art: Notebook," in Gayle, ed., *The Black Aesthetic,* 1971

[W]ho I am is what fulfills me and what fulfills the vision I have of a world.

AUDRE LORDE, "My Words Will Be There," in Evans, ed., *Black Women Writers,* 1984

It's hard for young players to see the big picture. They just see three or four years down the road.

KAREEM ABDUL JABBAR, *Star,* May 1986

VISITOR

All my cows have a bone in their legs. All of my beds are full of folks so you can't snore in my ears no more.

ZORA NEALE HURSTON, *Moses, Man of the Mountain,* 1939

VOICE

He who seeks a favor uses a low voice./ You who come entreating,/ Give me a low voice.

DAHOMEY

Thicken the thunders of man's voice, and lo! a world awakes.

W. E. B. DU BOIS, *The Souls of Black Folk,* 1903

[I]f, deaf to the voice of the Zeitgeist, we refuse to use and develop these men, we risk poverty and loss.

Ibid.

I am but one man. I am the voice of my people. Whatever their hearts are, that I talk. I want no more war. I want to be a man. You deny me the right of a white man. My skin is red; . . . I am a Modoc.

KINTPUASH (CAPTAIN JACK) OF THE MODOCS, in Riddle, *The Indian History of the Madoc War,* 1914

I know my voice is too feeble to raise itself above the uproar of this bustling time. . . . I know what a risk one runs in being styled an idealist in these days when thrones have lost their dignity and prophets have become anachronism, when the sound that drowns all voices is the noise of the market-place.

RABINDRANATH TAGORE, *Nationalisrn,* 1916

Whose voice was first sounded on this land? The voice of the red people who had but bows and arrows.

MAHPIUA LUTA (RED CLOUD) OF THE OGLALA SIOUX, in Hyde, *Red Cloud's Folk,* 1937

I have heard in the voices of the wind the voices of my/ killed children.

GWENDOLYN BROOKS, "the mother," *A Street in Bronzeville,* 1945

[Y]our voice,/ your voice with its nostalgic sound,/ remembering/ trembling, weeping/ here tonight/ for the soul of the black land/ where the ancients sleep.

GUY TIROLIEN, "The Soul of the Black Land," *Golden Bullets,* 1961

Since 1912 and year after year the African people have discussed the shameful misdeeds of those who rule the country. Year after year they have raised their voices in condemnation of the grinding poverty, the low wages, the acute shortage of land, inhuman exploitation and the whole policy of white domination. But instead of more freedom, repression began to grow in volume and intensity.

NELSON MANDELA, c. 1963

Excuse me for raising my voice. As long as my voice is the only thing I raise, I don't think you should become upset.

MALCOLM X, speech given at Harvard University, Cambridge, Massachusetts, December 1964

History will say that my voice—which disturbed the white man's smugness, his arrogance, and his complacency—that my voice helped to save America from a grave, possibly fatal catastrophe.

MALCOLM X, *The Autobiography of Malcolm X,* 1965

The voice of an adult American black man has undeniable texture. It has a quality of gloss, slithery as polished onyx, or it can be nubby and notched with harshness. The voice can be sonorous as a bass solo or light and lyrical as a flute. When a black man speaks in a flat tone, it is not only intentional but instructional to the listener.

MAYA ANGELOU, *The Heart of a Woman,* 1981

VOTE

A man landless, ignorant, and poor may use the vote against his interests, but with intelligence and land he holds in his hand the basis of power and the element of strength.

FRANCES E. W. HARPER, *The Underground Railroad,* 1871

When women, because they are women, are hunted down through the cities of New York and New Orleans, when they are dragged from their houses and hung upon lamp posts; when their children are torn from their arms, and their brains dashed upon the pavement; when they are objects of insult and outrage at every turn; when they are in danger of having their homes burnt down over their heads; when their children are not allowed to enter schools; then they will have an urgency to obtain the ballot equal to our own.

FREDERICK DOUGLASS, in *The History of Woman Suffrage,* 1881

Courage, brothers, the battle for humanity is not lost or losing. The Slav is rising in his might, the yellow millions are tasting liberty, the Black Africans are writhing toward the light, and everywhere the laborer, with ballot in his hand, is voting open the gates of Opportunity and Peace.

W. E. B. DU BOIS, c. 1920

Innocently, we vote into office men to whom the welfare of our lives is of far less concern than yesterday's baseball score.

RICHARD WRIGHT, *12 Million Black Voices,* 1941

We can't afford to sit anything out, any more than we can afford to have so called leaders who sit and take it.

PAUL ROBESON, "We Can't Sit Out This Election," *Freedom,* August 1952

Give us the ballot and we will by the power of our vote write the law of the statute books of the Southern states and bring to an end the dastardly acts of the hooded perpetrators of violence.

MARTIN LUTHER KING, JR., 4 June 1957

Our only hope is to control the vote.

MEDGAR EVERS, c. 1963

We cannot be satisfied as long as a Negro in Mississippi cannot vote and a Negro in New York believes he has nothing for which to vote. No, we are not satisfied, and we will not be satisfied until justice rolls down like waters and righteousness like a mighty stream.

MARTIN LUTHER KING, JR., "I Have a Dream," speech given at the Lincoln Memorial, Washington, D.C., 28 August 1963

[W]here we have the right to register and vote, we don't register and vote. If all the people in Alabama could register and vote, they probably wouldn't register and vote.

MALCOLM X, speech given at the Organization for Afro-American Unity Rally, Audubon Ballroom, New York City, 24 January 1965

The idea one hundred and twenty years ago that Black votes would be the key to the presidential election would have seemed like wild-eyed conjecture.

HAROLD WASHINGTON, in "Speaking Out—The Black Vote," *Ebony,* November 1983

The history of Black suffrage is eternal struggle.

WILLIAM HASTIE, *Grace Under Pressure,* 1984

People who do not vote have no line of credit with people who are elected and thus pose no threat to those who act against our interests.

MARIAN WRIGHT EDELMAN, speech given before the Congressional Black Caucus, 26 September 1987

When you vote for the president you also vote for his wife.

OPRAH WINFREY, in *Woman's Day,* 4 October 1988

You've got to vote for someone. It's a shame, but it's got to be done.

WHOOPI GOLDBERG, in the *Detroit News,* 26 October 1988

"Don't vote": This is an insult to our common sense, to two centuries of struggle for full citizenship, to Black efforts over the past decades, to become power players in the political arena.

EDDIE WILLIAMS, in *Michigan Chronicle,* 27 October 1988

WAIT

She had waited all her life for something, and it had killed her when she found it.

ZORA NEALE HURSTON, *Their Eyes Were Watching God,* 1937

We are waiting for a new people,/ For the joining of men to men/ And man to God.

JEAN TOOMER, "The Blue Meridian," in Bontemps, ed., *Poetry of the Negro,* 1949

For years now I have heard the word "Wait!" It rings in the ear of every Negro with a piercing familiarity. This "Wait" has almost always meant "Never."

MARTIN LUTHER KING, JR., *Letter from a Birmingham City Jail,* 1963

Why should we have to wait for what other people have when they are born in America?

MALCOLM X, Paris, 1964

We can't . . . sit and wait for somebody else. We must go ahead—alone if necessary, but together in the end.

WHITNEY YOUNG, *To Be Equal,* 1964

"Seek first the Kingdom of God and its righteousness and all those other things will be added to you." This meant endurance now, liberty later.

JAMES CONE, *Black Theology and Black Power,* 1969

If I waited to be right before I spoke, I would be sending little cryptic messages on the Ouija board, complaints from the other side.

AUDRE LORDE, "My Words Will Be There," in Evans, ed., *Black Women Writers,* 1984

If you go there and stand in the place where it was, it will happen again; it will be there waiting for you, waiting.

TONI MORRISON, *Beloved,* 1987

WALK

Every time my baby walk, it's just like a leaf shaking on a tree.

BLUES

You got to walk that lonesome valley, you got to walk it for yourself. Nobody here can walk it for you, you got to walk it for yourself.

SPIRITUAL

Something of old forgotten queens/ Lurks in the lithe abandon of your walk.

GWENDOLYN BENNETT, "To a Dark Girl," c. 1920

Her walk is like the replica/ Of some barbaric dance/ Wherein the soul of Africa/ Is winged with arrogance.

COUNTEE CULLEN, "A Song of Praise," *Color,* 1925

Daisy is walking a drum tune. You can almost hear it by looking at the way she walks.

ZORA NEALE HURSTON, *Their Eyes Were Watching God,* 1937

You can't walk alone. Many have given the illusion but none have really walked alone. Man is not made that way. Each man is bedded in his people, their history, their culture, and their values.

PETER ABRAHAMS, *Return to Goli,* 1953

Yesterday he walked where angels feared to tread, today he walks with the angels.

HOYT W. FULLER, in *Negro Digest,* August 1968

When a man walks manly, he don't stumble even in the lion's den.

LUCILLE CLIFTON, *Good News About the Earth,* 1972

Many of us feel we walk alone without a friend/ Never communicating with the one who lives within.

STEVIE WONDER, in *Ebony,* January 1977

We did walk ten paces behind—and the reason was to tell you where to go.

BEA MEDICINE, "Roles and Functions of Indian Women," *Indian Education*, January 1977

WAR

Only three things are worthy of a man, to make love, to make war, and to make verse.

Antar, 600 B.C.

One doesn't throw the stick after the snake has gone.

LIBERIA

O you who ride to Segotta, the fighting men who set out for there full of life have not come back.

BERBER (Morocco)

The spirit of war can never be destroyed by all the butcheries and persecutions the human mind can invent.

WILLIAM WHIPPER, "An Address on Non-resistance to Offensive Aggression," *The Colored American*, 16 September 1837

Was it for this that wealth and life/ Were staked upon that desperate strife,/ Which drenched this land for seven years/ with blood of men, and women's tears.

JAMES WHITFIELD, "America," 1853

War begins where reason ends.

FREDERICK DOUGLASS, "Reconstruction," *Atlantic Monthly*, December 1866

The present disgraceful, cruel, and iniquitous war . . . grasping ambition, tyranny, usurpation, atrocious aggression, cruel and haughty. We beseech our countrymen to leave off the horrid conflict, abandon their murderous plans, and forsake the way of blood.

FREDERICK DOUGLASS, *Life and Times of Frederick Douglass*, 1882

A war undertaken and brazenly carried on for the perpetual enslavement of colored men calls logically and loudly for colored men to help suppress it. Only a moderate share of sagacity was needed to see that the arm of the slave was the best defense against the arm of the slaveholder.

Ibid.

If John Brown did not end the war that ended slavery, he did, at least, begin the war that ended slavery.

Ibid.

Since this ruthless war is wrong, it should stop. If we had no right to begin, we have no right to continue. There is no room at the bar of morals for the argument that because we have embarked on a career of crime, we must persevere. Nor is any man who is opposing this crime to be frightened by names. The "leader" is not he who is seeking to keep his country true to her highest ideas—who is fighting to save her from ruinous folly.

MOORFIELD STOREY, 1899

War with all its glorification of brute force is essentially a degrading thing. It demoralizes those who are trained for it. It brutalizes men of naturally gentle character. It outrages every beautiful canon of morality. Its path of glory is foul with the passions of lust, and red with the blood of murder.

MOHANDAS GANDHI, in *Indian Opinion*, 12 February 1910

The cause of war is preparation for war.

W. E. B. DU BOIS, "Of the Children of Peace," *Crisis*, 1914

We return from the slavery of uniform which the world's madness demanded us to don to the freedom of civil garb. We stand again to look America squarely in the face and call a spade a spade. We sing: This country of ours, despite all its better souls have done and dreamed, is yet a shameful land. It *lynches*. . . . It *disenfranchises* its own citizens. . . . It encourages *ignorance*. . . . *It steals* from us. . . . *It insults* us. . . . We *return from fighting*. We *return fighting*.

W. E. B. DU BOIS, "Returning Soldiers," *Crisis*, May 1919

Make way for Democracy! We saved it in France, and by Great Jehovah, we will save it in the United States, or know the reason why.

Ibid.

What, then, is this dark world thinking? It is thinking that as wild and awful as this shameful war was, it is nothing to compare with that fight for freedom which black and brown and yellow men must and will make unless their oppression and humiliation and insult at the hands of the White World cease. The Dark World is going to submit to its present treatment just as long as it must and not one moment longer.

W. E. B. DUBOIS, *Darkwater,* 1920

Violence seldom accomplishes permanent and desired results. Herein lies the futility of war.

A. PHILIP RANDOLPH, *The Truth About Lynching,* 1922

We may know how a war starts, but we never know how or when it will end until it ends.

CARTER G. WOODSON, *Negro Makers of History,* 1928

Sherman branded War for all times when he called it Hell. There is yet another gaping, abysmal Hell into which some of us are actually born or unconsciously sucked. The Hell that Sherman knew was a physical one—of rapine, destruction, and death. The other is a purgatory for the mind, for the spirit, for the soul of men. Not only War is Hell.

VICTOR DALY, *Not Only War,* 1932

War is murder, force, anarchy, and debt. Its end is evil, despite all incidental good.

W. E. B. DU BOIS, *Black Reconstruction,* 1935

In the Civil War nearly two hundred thousand Negroes fought for their own freedom and perhaps three hundred thousand others helped as laborers and servants so that their freedom was not given to them, it was earned.

Ibid.

[W]ar is fundamentally a collision between conservative and liberal forces. It is a clash between those who would enslave the common man and those who would give him freedom.

PAUL ROBESON, in "World Will Never Accept Slavery, Robeson Asserts," *Milwaukee Journal,* 20 October 1941

War knows no law, except that of might. The atom bomb brought an empty victory to the allied armies but it resulted for the time being in destroying the soul of Japan.

MOHANDAS GANDHI, in *Harijan,* 7 July 1946

In the name of God, we have indulged in lies, massacres of people, without caring whether they were innocent or guilty, men or women, children or infants. We have indulged in abductions, forcible conversions, and we have done all this shamelessly.

MOHANDAS GANDHI, "letter to a Disciple," 16 January 1948

War is the major evil of our time.

PAUL ROBESON, *Masses and Mainstream,* August 1951

We have committed more war crimes almost than any nation in the world . . . And we won't stop it because of our pride, and our arrogance as a nation.

MARTIN LUTHER KING, JR., " The Drum Major Instinct," sermon given at Ebenezer Baptist Church, 9 April 1958

We are in an untenable position morally and politically. We are left standing before the world glutted by our own barbarity. We are engaged in a war that seeks to turn the clock of history back and perpetuate white colonialism.

MARTIN LUTHER KING, JR., c. 1963

Men who war against each other, if they are effective in their undertaking, must hate.

HOWARD THURMAN, *Disciplines of the Spirit,* 1963

It was not until war was declared with Germany, and America became involved in a manpower shortage in regards her factories plus her armies, that the black man . . . was permitted to make a few strides forward.

MALCOLM X, "To Mississippi Youth," speech given in New York City, 31 December 1964

War is a poor chisel to carve out tomorrows.

MARTIN LUTHER KING, JR., "Our Struggle," *Liberation*, December 1965

We have escalated the war in Vietnam and deescalated the skirmish into poverty. It challenges the imagination to contemplate what lives we could transform if we were to cease killing.

MARTIN LUTHER KING, JR., "Beyond Vietnam," sermon given in Riverside Church, New York City, 2 May 1967

Life and history give eloquent testimony to the facts that conflicts are never resolved without trustful give and take on both sides.

Ibid.

[N]obody can go to war . . . and win.

JAMES BALDWIN, "Why I Left America," *Essence*, October 1970

My people have never first drawn a bow or fired a gun against the whites. There has been trouble between us and my young men have danced the war dance. But it was not begun by us. It was you who sent out the first soldier and we who sent out the second.

PARRA-WA SAMEN (TEN BEARS) OF THE UAMPARIKA COMMANCHES, in Brown, *Bury My Heart at Wounded Knee*, 1971

I hear the white man say there will be no more war. But this cannot be true. There will be other wars. Men have not changed, and whenever they quarrel they will fight, as they have always done.

ALEEK-CHEA-AHOOSH (PLENTY COUPS), in *ibid.*

Wars have been fought for power, for building empires, for enslaving minorities, for oppressing the masses and for countless other excuses.

D. E. KING, "The God Who Takes off Chariot Wheels," in Philpot, ed., *Best Black Sermons*, 1972

Wars of nations are fought to change maps. But wars of poverty are fought to map changes.

MUHAMMAD ALI, in *The New York Times*, 6 March 1978

Every person under the sound of my voice is a soldier. You are either fighting for your freedom or betraying the fight for freedom or enlisted in the army to deny somebody else's freedom.

MALCOLM X, in Angelou, *The Heart of a Woman*, 1981

[W]ars and the seeds of revolution do not skip over the Black community.

BENJAMIN HOOKS, Publisher's Foreword, *Crisis*, November 1986

This great catastrophe has come upon the world proving the hollowness of nationhood, patriotism, racial pride, and most of the things we were taught to revere and respect.

JEAN TOOMER, in Kerman and Eldridge, *Lives of Jean Toomer*, 1987

Bring on your tear gas, bring on your grenades, your new supplies of mace, your state troopers and even your national guards. But let the record show we ain't going to be turned around.

RALPH ABERNATHY, *The Walls Came Tumbling Down*, 1989

Black males must understand that contrary to what is said, the war being conducted in urban centers is not against drugs, but against Black men.

FRANCES CRESS WELSING, *The Isis Papers*, 1991

WARNING

When one's peers in age die it is a warning to oneself.

SENEGAL

You fall out of that tree and I'll break your neck.

TRADITIONAL

A whistling woman and a crowing hen don't ever come to no good end.

TRADITIONAL

Oh! be warned! Oh! be warned! A horrible reptile is coiled up in your nation's bosom; the venomous creature is nursing at the tender breast of your youthful republic; for the love of God, tear away and fling from you the hideous monster, and let the weight of twenty million crush and destroy it forever.

FREDERICK DOUGLASS, "What to the American Slave is Your Fourth of July," speech given at Rochester, New York, 5 July 1852

We must beware of those who seek, in words, no matter how urgent or crisis-charged, to interpose an alien and dubious curtain of reality between our eyes and the crying claims of a world which we see only too poignantly and briefly.

RICHARD WRIGHT, *12 Million Black Voices,* 1941

I'd like to close with a message to my dear little wife—get that man outta there, honey 'cause I'm coming home directly.

FATS WALLER, in CBS broadcast, c. 1950

WASHINGTON, BOOKER T.

Booker T. Washington lit a torch in Alabama, and darkness fled.

MARTIN LUTHER KING, Jr., commencement address given at Lincoln University, Oxford, Pennsylvania, 6 June 1961

Almost everything Washington said or did was shot through with a certain irony. He bowed before the prejudices of the meanest Southerner, but he moved in circles in the North which were closed to all but a few white men. He told Negroes that Jim Crow was irrelevant, but he himself violated the law by riding first class in a Pullman car with Southern white men and women. And he who advised Negroes to forget about politics wielded more political power than any other Negro in American history.

LERONE BENNETT, *Before the Mayflower,* 1962

He dedicated his life to lifting his people from the dirt to where they were responsible for themselves and had a sense of being somebody. He wanted them to be able to use their hands and earn a decent living.

AMY GARVEY, in "Mrs. Marcus Garvey Talks with Ida Lewis," *Encore,* May 1973

Booker T. Washington was a slave in 1856 and lived one for nine years. But despite poverty, illiteracy, and other disadvantages he always imagined a purposeful life for himself.

DAVID SMITH, c. 1986

WASTE

If you try to cleanse others—like soap, you will waste away in the process.

MADAGASCAR

Wrong reaching, wrong bleaching, and wrong mixing have most nigh ruint him.

NANNIE BURROUGHS, "With All They Getting," *Southern Workman,* July 1927

People . . . waste too much time putting their mouth on things they don't know nothing about.

ZORA NEALE HURSTON, *Their Eyes Were Watching God,* 1937

What deserts might be reborn, what cities built, what children saved with one-third wasted to build bombs we can't afford to use.

JAMES BALDWIN, "Conversation with . . . James Baldwin," *Arts in Society,* Summer 1966

We remember and feel in our bones the wasted lives of those generations of old people dead and gone and dying still, and there is nothing mystical about it.

JULIAN MAYFIELD, "You Touch My Black Aesthetic and I'll Touch Yours," in Gayle, ed., *The Black Aesthetic,* 1971

We waste our years on "making a living" instead of living.

HERMAN H. WATTS, "What Is Your Name?" in Philpot, ed., *Best Black Sermons,* 1972

The man who views his world at fifty the same way he did at twenty has wasted thirty years of his life.

MUHAMMAD ALI, in *Playboy,* November 1975

Such waste, such beauty, such a bundle of energy! How could anyone be so cruel as to cut short such a fruitful life?

WINNIE MANDELA, "A Part of My Soul Went With Him," *Ebony,* December 1985

How many grapes are you willing to crush to get that one glass of wine, to get one Magic Johnson? You'll have literally tens of thousands of our most competitive and inspired young people wasting their lives.

HARRY EDWARDS, in "Hardline," *Detroit Free Press,* 8 May 1988

In our country with all our wealth and our power, we Americans waste more minds than any other civilization on the earth.

OSSIE DAVIS, "It's On Us," *City Arts Quarterly,* Spring 1988

WATER

Stolen water is sweet.

AFRICA

It is the calm and silent water that drowns a man.

ASHANTI

A coward sweats in water.

ETHIOPIA

The toad likes water, but not when it's boiling.

GUINEA

When it rains, the roof always drips the same way.

LIBERIA

Wade in the water, children/ wade in the water, children/ wade in the water, children/ God gonna trouble the water.

SPIRITUAL

You never miss your water till your well runs dry.

TRADITIONAL

All water finds ultimate issue in a common source. The ultimate reunion in that source is the inevitable end of all striving.

JOHN O'NEAL, "Black Arts: Notebook," in Gayle, ed., *The Black Aesthetic,* 1971

It's not the front that pulls the river along. It's the rear guard that is the driving force.

TONI CADE BAMBARA, *The Sea Birds Are Still Alive,* 1974

Wind off the water was like a fist of fresh air, a cleansing blow.

CHARLES JOHNSON, *Middle Passage,* 1990

WEAKNESS

The pretender sees no one but himself, he has the veil of conceit in front of his face. If he were endowed with a God-discerning eye, he would see that no one is weaker than himself.

INDIA

Assistance given to the weak makes the one who gives it strong, and oppression of the unfortunate makes one weak.

BOOKER T. WASHINGTON, *Speeches of Booker T. Washington,* 1932

The weakness of most men/they do not know how to become a stone or tree.

AIMÉ CÉSAIRE, "First Problem," *Miraculous Weapons,* 1946

It's just like when you've got coffee that's too black, which means it's too strong. What do you do? You integrate it with cream, you make it weak. But if you pour too much cream in it, you won't even know you ever had coffee. It used to be hot, it becomes cool. It used to be strong, it becomes weak. It used to wake you up, now it puts you to sleep.

MALCOLM X, "Message to the Grass Roots," speech given in Detroit, Michigan, 9 November 1963

Greed is weakness that cripples.

BETTYE J. PARKER-SMITH, "Alice Walker's Women," in Evans, ed., *Black Women Writers,* 1984

WEALTH

Do not put trust in your wealth,/ Which came to you as a gift of God.

PTAH HOTEP, 2340 B.C.

When a man is wealthy, he may wear an old cloth.

ASHANTI

One cannot feast and become rich.

ASHANTI

A man's wealth may be superior to him.

CAMEROON

There is no wealth where there are no children.

LIBERIA

A wealthy man will always have followers.

NIGERIA

Get wisdom, but with all your getting, get wealth.

ROSA BOWSER, *The Woman's Era,* c. 1919

Only prosperity looks backward. Adversity is afraid to look over its own shoulder.

ALAIN LOCKE, "Apropos of Africa," *Opportunity,* February 1924

In the midst of your material wealth, you are spiritually and morally poverty-stricken, unable to speak to the conscience of the world.

MARTIN LUTHER KING, JR., speech given at Purdue, University, West Lafayette, Indiana, 1958

I wanted to become rich and famous simply so no one could evict my family again.

JAMES BALDWIN, "Why I Left America," *Essence,* October 1970

In show business you can be rich today and back in the projects tomorrow.

BILL COSBY, c. 1973

All you have to do is to get the first thousand dollars. When you get that, you will want another thousand. When you get to ten thousand you will want another ten. And when you get to a hundred thousand, it's just on and on to the million.

DUKE ELLINGTON, *Music Is My Mistress,* 1973

The pretense of wealth prevents the accumulation of real wealth.

NATHAN HARE, in "Interview: Dr. Nathan Hare," *Crisis,* March 1986

Wealth is really what you own and control, not how much you have in your pockets.

JOHN H. JOHNSON, in "Interview: John H. Johnson," *Crisis,* January 1987

The fundamental difference is the attitude white people have about acquiring wealth and the attitude Black people have. White people know that wealth brings power, so they do everything possible to gain more wealth and thus more power. Black people, too often, seek wealth to have enjoyment, to buy pleasure. There's a big difference between power and pleasure, and since power lasts longer than pleasure, whites have gained control of practically everything.

RAYMOND ST. JACQUES, c. 1988

[Y]our race sets much store by these things which you think are precious and which you call wealth. This is nothing but metal and useless stones from the earth. On the day you die you would not be able to purchase a single extra breath of air with this rubbish.

VUSAMAZULU CREDO MUTWA, "The Rout of The Arabi," in Chinweizu, ed., *Voices From Twentieth-Century Africa,* 1988

All the wealth on this earth, all the wealth under the earth, and all the wealth in the universe is like a mosquito's wing compared to the wealth we will receive in the hereafter.

MUHAMMAD ALI, in "The Meaning of Life," *Life,* December 1988

Wealth isn't what a man has, but what he is.

CHARLES JOHNSON, *Middle Passage,* 1990

WEAPONS

The only weapon of self-defense I could use successfully was that of deception.

HENRY BIBB, *Narrative of the Life and Adventures of Henry Bibb,* 1849

The Lord will preserve me without weapons. I feel safe even in the midst of my enemies, for the truth is all powerful and will prevail.

SOJOURNER TRUTH, *Narrative of Sojourner Truth,* 1850

When our fathers lived they heard that Americans were coming across the great river westward. . . . We heard of guns and powder and lead—first flintlocks, then percussion caps, and now repeating rifles.

MANUELITO OF THE NAVAJOS, speech to U.S. Congress, 1865

[A] tongue cocked and loaded [is] the only real weapon left to weak folks.

ZORA NEALE HURSTON, *Their Eyes Were Watching God,* 1937

My song is my weapon.

PAUL ROBESON, *Here I Stand,* 1957

Our greatest weapon is silence.

JAMES BALDWIN, *Nobody Knows My Name,* 1961

Protest we must. Demonstrate if necessary. These are the time-tested weapons for correcting injustices and righting historic wrongs.

WHITNEY YOUNG, "Social Revolution: Challenge of the Nation," speech given at the Urban League Conference, 1963

Fervor is the weapon of choice of the impotent.

FRANTZ FANON, *Black Skin, White Masks,* 1967

Martin Luther King, Jr., faced the dogs, the police, jail, heavy criticism, and finally death; and he never carried a gun, not even a knife to defend himself.

BENJAMIN MAYS, eulogy of Dr. Martin Luther King, Jr., Ebenezer Church, Atlanta, Georgia, 9 April 1968

Anything you don't control can be used as a weapon against you.

H. RAP BROWN, *Die Nigger Die,* 1969

[R]hetoric is perhaps the most bludgeoning weapon of all.

ADDISON GAYLE, JR., "The Son of My Father," in Chapman, ed, *New Black Voices,* 1972

Music is a weapon for living.

JAMES LOVELL, *Black Song,* 1972

The most vicious weapon is the tongue.

RAY CHARLES, *Brother Ray,* 1978

I don't know karate but I know karagon.

JAMES BROWN, c. 1978

He'll come at me like a bullet, but I'm three beats faster.

SUGAR RAY LEONARD, c. 1985

Arm yourself with common sense, not weapons.

OPRAH WINFREY, in *Woman's Day,* 4 October 1988

[R]ape is an act in which the genitals become a weapon.

FRANCES CRESS WELSING, *The Isis Papers,* 1991

WEATHER

When it's lightning, the angel is peeping in the looking glass, when it thunders, they're rolling out the rain barrels, when it rains, somebody dropped a barrel or two and bust it.

ZORA NEALE HURSTON, *Mules and Men,* 1935

[T]he wind and water had given life to lots of things that folks think of as dead and given death to so much that had been living things.

ZORA NEALE HURSTON, *Their Eyes Were Watching God,* 1937

The wind came back with triple fury, and put out the light for the last time. They sat in company with the others in other shanties, their eyes straining against crude walls and their souls asking if He meant to measure their puny might against His. They seemed to be staring at the dark, but their eyes were watching God.

Ibid.

The hot winds of change, blowing through the central city ghettos . . . are producing an articulate group of young people [who] possess the seeds of hope for tomorrow. . . .

SAMUEL B. MCKINNEY, "The Hot Winds of Change," in Philpot, ed., *Best Black Sermons,* 1972

Weather is a cunning low-down, just-won't-do-right woman, who in the middle of a winter marked by ice and barren landscapes so cold, so bitter it bred loneliness like garbage bred flies, would appear lush and brown and fertile, whispering that you should take your clothes off and lie down beside her, meeting your hesitation with the most lascivious promise of warmth and carnal delight.

RICHARD PERRY, *Montgomery's Children,* 1984

If our children run into bad weather on the way, they will not have the protective clothing to withstand the wind and the rain, lightning and thunder that have characterized the Black sojourn in America.

MARIAN WRIGHT EDELMAN, speech given before the Congressional Black Caucus, 26 September 1987

WINNING

It is the race or individual that exercises the most patience, forbearance, and self-control in the midst of trying conditions that wins.

BOOKER T. WASHINGTON, speech given to Afro-American Council, July 1903

What will win one person has no effect on another.

ZORA NEALE HURSTON, *Mules and Men,* 1935

A man is up against a hard game when he must die to beat it.

ZORA NEALE HURSTON, *Their Eyes Were Watching God,* 1937

Mass action in political life and elsewhere is power in motion, and it is the way to win.

PAUL ROBESON, *Here I Stand,* 1958

If we can't win here, can we win anywhere?

MELVIN CHAPMAN, speech given at Miller Junior High School, Detroit, Michigan, 1960

I know winning, I'm a winner, winning is inside me.

MARGARET AVERY, c. 1984

You have to have already convinced yourself that you are going to win no matter what the other influences are.

EDWIN MOSES, in *American Visions,* Olympic Issue, 1988

You have to know you can win. You have to think you can win. You have to feel you can win.

SUGAR RAY LEONARD, c. 1989

America looks at winners with a magnifying glass.

AL JOYNER, in "Spotlight: Life in the Fast Lane," *Essence,* March 1989

I play to win, whether during practice or a real game. And I will not let anything get in the way of me and my competitive enthusiasm to win.

MICHAEL JORDAN, in "Michael Jordan in His Own Orbit," *GQ,* March 1989

Jesse Jackson runs to inspire, I run to win.

L. DOUGLASS WILDER, c. 1990

WISDOM

Wisdom is rarer than emeralds, and yet it is found among the women who gather at the grindstone.

PTAH HOTEP, c. 2340 B.C.

A wise man sips the elixir of life, circumspectly, slowly, and heedful.

PANCHATANTRA, 2 A.D.

It is better to be wise than to seem wise.

ORIGEN, *Against Celsus,* c. 215

Should wisdom disappear from the face of the earth, still no one will acknowledge his own ignorance.

The Gulistan of Sadi, 1184–1292

A man with wisdom is better off than a stupid man with any amount of charm.

AFRICA

The heart of the wise man lies quiet like limpid water.

CAMEROON

Children are the wisdom of the nation.

LIBERIA

The wise man and the fool appear the same in a time of enjoyment, but in time of trouble, the wise man stands out clearly.

NIGERIA

Wisdom is like a goatskin bag, every man carries his own.

NIGERIA

Wisdom is like mushrooms that come after you have finished eating. Too late.

NYASALAND

The child looks everywhere and often sees nought; but the old man sitting on the ground sees everything.

SENEGAL

Wisdom does not come overnight.

SOMALIA

All human wisdom is summed up in two words, wait and hope.

ALEXANDRE DUMAS, *The Count of Monte Cristo,* 1844

Knowledge and wisdom are like links in a single chain. Wisdom is the gift, the endowments to know how to use power. Knowledge is only an instrument in the hand of wisdom.

DANIEL PAYNE, c. 1860

To be reconciled to the inevitable with good grace is wisdom.

RABINDRANATH TAGORE, speech given in Geneva, Switzerland, 1912

A man is born with all the wisdom he needs for life.

DICK GREGORY, c. 1974

Had I been born in Africa, I would have belonged to that family which sings and chants the glories and legends of the tribe. I would have liked in my mature years to have been a wise elder, for I worship wisdom and knowledge of the ways of men.

PAUL ROBESON, in *Whole World in His Hand,* 1981

A wise man who has the moment in his hand should not let that moment slip.

LOUIS FARRAKHAN, in *National Alliance,* 1984

WISH

Ships at a distance have every man's wish on board. For some they come in with the tide. For others they sail forever on the horizon, never out of sight, never landing until the Watcher turns his eyes away in resignation. . . .

ZORA NEALE HURSTON, *Their Eyes Were Watching God,* 1937

[N]othing can stop you from wishing. You can't beat nobody down so low till you can rob [th]em of the[ir] will.

Ibid.

For if he grows up expecting and regarding as his due that to wish is to have his wish fulfilled, then he is apt to become a permanent cripple.

HOWARD THURMAN, *Disciplines of the Spirit,* 1963

If we wish to live, to be healthy, we must will it. If we will it we must be willing to endure the act of transformation.

ELEANOR TRAYLOR, "Music as Theme," in Evans, ed., *Black Women Writers,* 1984

WOMAN

Beware of a woman from abroad, who is not known in her city. Look not upon her when she comes and know her not. She is like the vortex of deep waters, whose whirling is unfathomable. The woman whose husband is far away, she writes you every day. If there is no witness with her she arises and spreads her net. Oh deadly crime if one hearkens.

SCRIBE ANY of the Palace of Nefertari, c. 2300 B.C.

Women are like one's shadow. They follow at the heels of those who run away from them. They bully and boss and lead those who follow them.

SOMALIA

Woman without man is like a field without seed.

ETHIOPIA

If I have a headache, I have myself bled./ If I have a colic, I take some medicine./ If I am seized by the pox, I go down to the Hot Springs./ But where is there help, for what she does to me?

ETHIOPIA

The lineal descent of the people of the Five Nations shall run in the female line. Women shall be considered the progenitors of the nation. They shall own the land and the soil. Men and women shall follow the status of their mothers.

ARTICLE 44 OF THE IROQUOIS GREAT LAW OF PEACE

The woman I love is fat and/ Chocolate to the bone/ Every time she shakes/ Some skinny woman loses her home.

BLUES

Where did your Christ come from? From God and a woman. Man had nothing to do with it.

SOJOURNER TRUTH, *Narrative of the Life of Sojourner Truth,* 1850

Look at me! Look at my arms! I have plowed and planted, and gathered into barns, and no man could head me—and ain't I a woman? I could work as much and eat as much as a man (when I could get it) and bear de lash as well—and ain't I a woman? I have borne thirteen children and seen 'em mos' all sold into slavery, and when I cried out with mother's grief, none but Jesus heard—and ain't I a woman?

SOJOURNER TRUTH, speech given at the Women's Rights Convention, Akron, Ohio, 1851

Black women are the regenerative force to uplift the race.

LUCY CRAFT LANEY, c. 1880

I have done little in this world in which to glory except this one act—and I certainly glory in that. When I ran away from slavery, it was for myself; when I advocated emancipation, it was for my people; but when I stood up for the rights of women, self was out of the question, and I found a little nobility in the act.

FREDERICK DOUGLASS, *Life and Writings of Frederick Douglass,* 1881

I am a self-made woman.

SOJOURNER TRUTH, 1882

God said one woman is enough for a man, and two is a war on your hands.

JOHN JASPER, *Dem Seben Women,* 1889

Let woman's claim be as broad in the concrete as in the abstract. We take our stand on the solidarity of humanity, the oneness of life, and the unnaturalness and injustice of all special favoritisms, whether of sex, race, country, or condition.

ANNA JULIA COOPER, *A Voice from the South, by a Black Woman of the South,* 1892

If the fifteenth century discovered America to the Old World, the nineteenth is discovering woman to herself. . . . Not the opportunity of discovering new worlds, but that of filling this world with fairer and higher aims than the greed of gold and lust of power, is hers. Through weary, wasting years men have destroyed, dashed in pieces, and overthrown, but today we stand on the threshold of woman's era, and woman's work is grandly constructive.

FRANCES E. W. WATKINS, "Women's Political Future," 1893

But yet, as meanly as she is thought of, hindered as she is in all directions, she is always doing something of merit and credit that is not expected of her. She is irrepressible. She is insulted, but she holds up her head; she is scorned, but she proudly demands respect. Thus, it has come to pass that the most interesting girl of this country is the colored girl.

FANNIE BARRIER WILLIAMS, "A Northern Negro's Autobiography," *The Independent,* 14 July 1904

Were it mine to select a woman/ As queen of the hall of fame;/ One who has fought the gamest fight/ And climbed from the depths of shame;/ I would have to give the sceptre/ To the lowliest of them all;/ She, who struggled through the years with her back against the wall.

ANDREA RAZAFKERIEFO, "The Negro Woman," in Kerlin, *Negro Poets and Their Poems,* 1923

God and the devil still wrangling/ Which should have her, which repel;/ God wants no discord in his heaven;/ Satan has enough in hell.

COUNTEE CULLEN, "For a Mouthy Woman," *Color,* 1925

Wild women don't worry, wild women don't get the blues.

IDA COX "Wild Women Blues," c. 1928

I had to become a mother before I realized what a wonderful place in the scheme of things the Creator has given woman. She it is upon whom rests the jovial share of the work of creation, and I wonder if women who shirk their duties in that respect truly realize that they have not only deprived humanity of their contribution to perpetuity but that they have robbed themselves of one of the most glorious advantages in the development of their own womanhood.

IDA B. WELLS, in Duster, ed., *Crusade for Justice,* 1928

With the equatorial circle/ ties around her waist like a small world/ the Black woman, a new woman/ advances in her sheer serpent's gown.

NICOLAS GUILLEN, "Songoso Cosogo," *poemas ulatos,* 1932

It seems almost paradoxical, but nevertheless true, that the history of women and the history of Negroes are in the essential features of their struggle for status, quite parallel.

MARY McLEOD BETHUNE, "A Century of Progress of Negro Women," speech given in Chicago, Illinois, 30 June 1933

What was there to being a man? Men just worked. That was easier than what women did. It was women who did the lying awake, the planning, the sorrowing, the scheming to stretch a dollar. That was the hard part, the head part. A woman had to think all the time. A woman had to be smart.

DOROTHY WEST, c. 1934

Man has regarded woman as his tool. She has learnt to be his tool, and in the end found this easy and comfortable because when one drags another in his fall the descent is easy.

MOHANDAS GANDHI, in *Harijan,* 25 January 1936

He wanted to win a woman and hold her by love. The matter was smooth and round like a ball. There was his heart's desire inside the sphere but the outside presented no place of entry.

ZORA NEALE HURSTON, *Moses, Man of the Mountain,* 1939

. . . the consciousness of vast sections of Black women lies beyond the boundaries of the modern world, though they live and work in that world daily.

RICHARD WRIGHT, *12 Million Black Voices,* 1941

It is dangerous for a woman to defy the gods;/ To taunt them with the tongue's thin tip,/ Or strut in the weakness of mere humanity,/ Or draw a line daring them to cross. . . .

ANNE SPENCER, "Letter to My Sister," in Bontemps, ed., *Poetry of the Negro,* 1949

Naked woman, dark woman!/ Clad in the color that is life, in your form that is beauty! I have grown up in your shade, the sweetness of your hands bound my eyes/ And now in the heart of summer and noon, I discover you, promised earth, from the tower of your sun-scorched neck/ And your beauty smites me to the full of my heart like the flash of an eagle.

LEOPOLD SENGHOR, "Black Woman," *Ethiopics,* 1956

The wildness of your glance pleases me,/ Your mouth has the taste of mango,/ Rama Kam./ Your body is the black pimento/ That makes desire sing/ Rama Kam./ As you pass/ The handsomest woman is made jealous/ By the warm rhythm of your hips,/ Rama Kam.

DAVID DIOP, "Rama Kam," *Poundings,* 1956

The special plight and the role of Black women is not something that just happened three years ago. We've had a special plight for three hundred and fifty years.

FANNIE LOU HAMER, c. 1964

If you are in a country that reflects the consciousness of the importance of education, it's because the woman is aware of the importance.

MALCOLM X, Paris, November 1964

Women must come to realize that the superficial symbolisms that surround us as women are negative only when we ourselves perceive and accept them as negative.

SHIRLEY CHISHOLM, speech given at Federal City College, Washington, D.C., 1969

I am a Black woman/ the music of my song some sweet arpeggio of tears/ is written in a minor key/ and I/ can be heard humming in the night.

MARI EVANS, *I Am A Black Woman,* 1970

To be Black and be a woman. To be a double outsider, to be twice oppressed, to be more than invisible.

JULIUS LESTER, introduction to Jordan, *Some Changes,* 1971

Women have always spoiled me. And I have done everything within my power to assist them.

ADAM CLAYTON POWELL, JR., *Adam by Adam,* 1971

The alleged benefits of femininity did not accrue to her. She was not sheltered or protected; she would not remain oblivious to the desperate struggle for existence unfolding outside the home. She was also there in the field, alongside the man, toiling under the lash from sun-up to sun-down.

ANGELA DAVIS, in *The Black Scholar,* December 1971

Black Woman must remember, through all the prattle about walking or not walking three or twelve steps behind or ahead of "her" male, that her personhood precedes her femalehood; that, sweet as sex may be, she cannot endlessly brood on Black Man's blonds, blues, blunders.

GWENDOLYN BROOKS, *Report From Part One,* 1972

Lovers have come and gone, but only my mistress stays. She is beautiful and gentle. She waits on me hand and foot. She is a swinger. She has grace. To hear her speak, you can't believe your ears. She is ten thousand years old. She is as modern as tomorrow, a brand-new woman every day, and as endless as time mathematics. Living with her is a labyrinth of ramifications. I look forward to her every gesture.

DUKE ELLINGTON, *Music Is My Mistress,* 1973

Be not discouraged, Black women of the world, but push forward, regardless of the lack of appreciation shown you. A race must be saved, a country must be redeemed, and unless you strengthen the leadership of Negro men, we will remain marking time until the Yellow race gains leadership of the world, and we be forced to subservience under them or extermination.

AMY JACQUES GARVEY, in *Encore,* May 1973

From the days of slavery until now, we Black women have been given chores that sometimes were beyond our very strength, so we can no longer carry the burden alone. Black women must be allowed to be women.

Ibid.

Beloved,/ I have to adore the earth:/ The wind must have heard your voice once./ It echoes and sings like you./ The soil must have tasted you once./It is laden with your scent./ The trees honor you in gold/ and blush when you pass. I know why the north country/ is frozen,/ It has been trying to preserve/ your memory. I know why the desert burns with fever./ It has wept too long without you./ On hands and knees,/ the ocean begs up the beach,/ and falls at your feet./ I have to adore the earth/ the mirror of the earth./ You have taught her well how to be beautiful.

HENRY DUMAS, "Love Song," *Play Ebony Play Ivory*, 1974

i had expected more than this/ i had not expected to be an ordinary woman.

LUCILLE CLIFTON, *An Ordinary Woman*, 1974

A nation is not conquered until the hearts of its women are on the ground. Then it is done, no matter how brave its warriors or how strong its weapons.

CHEROKEE, "The Brave Hearted Woman," *Akwesasne Notes*, Summer 1976

The reign of Queen Candace, a contemporary of Augustus Caesar, was really historic. Augustus, after having conquered Egypt, drove his armies across the Nubian desert to the frontiers of Ethiopia.... The Queen herself took command of her army; at the head of her troops she charged the Roman soldiers, as Joan of Arc was later to do against the English army. This heroic resistance made a great impression on all classic antiquity, not because the Queen was a Negro, but because she was a woman; the Indo-European world was still not accustomed to the idea of a woman playing a political and social role.

CHEIKH ANTA DIOP, *The Cultural Unity of Black Africa*, 1978

You are a good daughter, but a good daughter must be a good wife.

BUCHI EMECHETA, *The Joys of Motherhood*, 1979

I called her Iodine because she was such strong medicine that she could clean all my wounds if I didn't mind the sting.

BILL RUSSELL, *Second Wind*, 1979

They stumbled blindly through their lives: creatures so abused and mutilated in body, so dimmed and confused by pain, that they considered themselves unworthy even of hope . . . exquisite butterflies trapped in an evil honey, toiling away their lives in an era, a century, that did not acknowledge them, except as "the mule of the world."

ALICE WALKER, *In Search of Out Mothers' Gardens*, 1983

Women's problems cut across race and countries.

BUCHI EMECHETA, c. 1987

Black women have always been society's best managers, because they have had to do the most with the least.

JESSE JACKSON, c. 1987

She is a friend to my mind. She gathers me. The pieces I am, she gathers them and gives them back to me in all the right order. It's good when you got a woman who is a friend of your mind.

TONI MORRISON, *Beloved*, 1987

And she had nothing to fall back on: not maleness, not whiteness, not ladyhood, not anything. And out of the profound desolation of her reality she may very well have invented herself.

Ibid,

She represented to me my mother, myself, all the women before me, as well as the ones yet to come ahead. She was the earth, Africa and all the races ever persecuted, abused, taken for granted, "dogged out," ignored, or denied an equal opportunity.

RACHEL BROWN, "Window on the Park," *City Arts Quarterly*, Fall–Winter, 1987

Women work overtime, do double triple duty, juggle ten balls at once—children, careers, husbands, schoolwork, housework, church work, and more work—and when one of the balls drops, we think something is wrong with us.

SUSAN TAYLOR, c. 1988

Women are simply a generalized-about human species more mysterious than Martians.

NURUDDIN FARAH, "Sweet and Sour Milk," in Chinweizu, ed., *Voices from Twentieth-Century Africa,* 1988

I spent years crying in my diary. But I finally stopped finding fault with myself. We're all different, yet the same. Why as women are we always feeling bad about ourselves?

JASMINE GUY, in "Spotlight: Jasmine Guy," *Essence,* August 1988

She doesn't date men, she dates growth industries.

MICHAEL JORDAN, in "Michael Jordan in His Own Orbit," *GQ,* March 1989

I never considered it a disadvantage to be a Black woman. I never wanted to be anything else. We have brains. We are beautiful. We can do anything we set our minds to.

DIANA ROSS, in "Diana Ross: Down-to-Earth," *Essence,* October 1989

Of all the things that drove men to sea, the most common disaster, I've come to learn, is women.

CHARLES JOHNSON, *Middle Passage,* 1990

Women are blessed with a jewel of strength that glows all the time.

JUDITH JAMISON, in "The Magic of the Spirit," *Essence,* December 1990

WOODSON, CARTER G.

I believed in Carter Woodson because he stirred the dormant pride in the souls of thousands ignorant or unmindful of our glorious heritage, and then struck the roots of his leadership deep to produce the orderly and keen-sighted evaluation and objective interpretation of the facts unearthed through his efforts. I believed in him because he was big. He was quiet to the point of being taciturn because he was shy. He was a man of the soil. He grew to young manhood, the hard self-taught way. But he was too big and too wise to underestimate or reject the tools of intellectual training and skill. He knew the value of both experience and training.

MARY MCLEOD BETHUNE, eulogy of Carter G. Woodson, Shiloh Baptist Church, Washington, D.C., 3 April 1950

Dr. Woodson did everything from editing the *Journal of Negro History* to banking the furnace and writing books to wrapping books. One never got the idea the boss would ask you to do anything that he would not do himself.

LANGSTON HUGHES, in the *Negro History Bulletin,* February 1967

Carter G. Woodson was a legend in his own time. He went up and down the length and breadth of this country urging Negroes to teach Negro history.

BENJAMIN MAYS, "I Knew Carter G. Woodson," *Negro History Bulletin,* March 1981

He was a discoverer of truth, a disseminator of truth, an organizer of truth, a contributor to truth, and a defender of truth.

CHARLES H. WESLEY, in *ibid.*

WORDS

Had I unknown phrases,/ Sayings that are strange/ Novel, untried words/ Free of repetition;/ Not transmitted sayings,/ Spoken by the ancestors!/ I wring out my body of what it holds,/ In releasing all my words;/ For what was said is repetition,/When what was said is said./ Ancestors' words are nothing to boast of,/ They are found by those who come after.

ANKHU, "The Complaint of Khakheperre-Sonb," 1550–1305 B.C.

Scandal is not like bread: there is never any shortage.

AFRICA

Great events stem from words of no importance.

CONGO

If you want fo' lick the old woman pot, you scratch him back. (Use flattery and you will succeed.)

JAMAICA

A cutting word is worse than a bowstring; a cut may heal, but the cut of the tongue does not.

MAURITANIA

There are some words that close a conversation like an iron door.

ALEXANDRE DUMAS, *The Count of Monte Cristo,* 1844

Action! action! not criticism, is the plain duty of this hour. Words are now useful only as they stimulate to blows. The office of speech is now only to point out when, where, and how to strike to the best advantage.

FREDERICK DOUGLASS, *Life and Times of Frederick Douglass,* 1882

The words "superiority" and "supremacy" are the only words that express what will be understood by the rank and file of people who live where lynchings take place.

NANNIE BURROUGHS, 1894

Never let the word "dumb" be used in your class or anything said disrespectful of parents or guardians.

FRANCES COPPIN, *Reminiscences of School Life,* 1913

That words have meanings is just the difficulty. That is why the poet has to turn and twist them in meter and verse, so that the meaning may be held in check, and the feeling allowed a chance to express itself.

RABINDRANATH TAGORE, *My Reminiscences,* 1917

Your words dropped into my heart like pebbles into a pool,/ Rippling around my breast and leaving it melting cool.

CLAUDE MCKAY, "Absence," *Selected Poems,* 1953

But if my father never actually spoke, I know that he was forming words in his mind. I could tell from his lips, which kept moving, bending over the pot, he stirred the gold and charcoal with a bit of wood that kept bursting into flame and had constantly had to be replaced by a fresh one. What sort of words did my father utter? I do not know . . . but could they have been anything but incantations?

CAMARA LAYE, *The Dark Child,* 1954

The words dripped on my consciousness, sank into my being, and carried me away to the magic long ago of once upon a time.

PETER ABRAHAMS, *Tell Freedom,* 1954

With words as our weapons, there are some few of us who will stand on the ramparts to fend off the evildoers, the slanderers, the greedy, the self-righteous! You are not alone.

RICHARD WRIGHT, "An Open Letter to Kwame Nkrumah," *Black Power,* 1954

All change, all production and generation are effected through the word.

LEOPOLD SENGHOR, *Présence Africaine,* 1956

Words were living things bestriding the air and charging the room with strong colors.

PAULE MARSHALL, *Brown Girl, Brownstones,* 1959

When old people speak it is not because of the sweetness of words in our mouths; it is because we see something which you do not see.

CHINUA ACHEBE, *No Longer At Ease,* 1961

Text without context is pretext.

HOWARD THURMAN, *Disciplines of the Spirit,* 1963

Diplomacy—species of lies and deceptions.

C. L. R. JAMES, *The Black Jacobins,* 1963

You can taste a word.

PEARL BAILEY, in *Newsweek,* 4 December 1967

We have written a Declaration of Independence, itself an accomplishment, but the effort to transform the words into a life experience still lies ahead.

MARTIN LUTHER KING, JR., *Where Do We Go From Here?* 1968

Words do wonderful things. They sound purr. They can urge, they can wheedle, whip, whine. They can sing, sass, singe. They can churn, check, channelize. They can be a hup, 2, 3, 4. They can forge a fiery army out of a hundred languid men.

GWENDOLYN BROOKS, afterword, *Contending Forces,* 1968

A word has power in and of itself. It comes from nothing into sound and meaning; it gives origin to all things. By means of the word can a man deal with the world on equal terms. And the word is sacred.

N. SCOTT MOMADAY, *The Way to Rainy Mountain,* 1969

As the Word came to prophets of old,/As the burning bush spoke to Moses, . . ./ So the Word of fire burns today/ On the lips of our prophets in an evil age. . . .

MARGARET WALKER, "Prophets for a New Day," *Prophets for a New Day,* 1970

You cannot wear the word *love* out.

AL YOUNG, "Statement on Aesthetics, Poetics, Kinetics," in Chapman, ed., *New Black Voices,* 1972

"Body African"—as opposed to "Body English."

GWENDOLYN BROOKS, *Report From Part One,* 1972

What you do is totally destroy somebody else with words. It's the whole competition thing again, fighting each other. There'd be forty or fifty dudes standing around and the winner was determined by the way they responded to what was said. The real aim of the dozens was to get a dude so mad that he'd cry or get mad enough to fight.

H. RAP BROWN, c. 1973

[T]he Word is at its most expressive in poetry. . . .

KEORAPETSE KGOSITSILE, in *Black Poetry Writing,* 1975

Preslavery background was one in which the concept of Nommo, the magic power of the Word, was believed necessary to actualize life and give man mastery over them. All activities of man, and all the movements in nature, rest on the word, on the productive power of the word which is water and heat and seed and Nommo, that is, life force itself. The force, responsibility, and commitment of the word and the awareness that the word alone alters the world.

GENEVA SMITHERMAN, *Talkin' and Testifying,* 1977

If we have the Word, let us say it/ If we have the Word, let us Be it/ If we have the Word, let us Do.

MARI EVANS, *Nightstar,* 1981

Because no matter what anyone says, it is the black woman's words that have the most meaning for us, her daughters, [who] [have] experienced life not only as a black person, but as a woman; and it was *different* being Frederick Douglass than being Harriet Tubman—or Sojourner Truth, who only "looked like a man," but bore children and saw them sold into slavery.

ALICE WALKER, *In Search of Our Mothers' Gardens,* 1983

I had a large vocabulary and had been reading constantly since childhood, I had taken words and the art of arranging them.

MAYA ANGELOU, "Shades and Slashes of Light," in Evans, ed., *Black Women Writers,* 1984

In the battle for peace the word will always be the winner.

NIKKI GIOVANNI, "An Answer to Some Questions on How I Write: In Three Parts," in *ibid.*

Words are alternately Life, Death, Silence, Truth. And they are the natural tools of the poet.

JOAN MARTIN, "The Unicorn Is Black," in *ibid.*

In 1948, pornographic would have been the mispronunciation of the machine on which records are played.

RICHARD PERRY, *Montgomery's Children,* 1984

[T]he word play of Negro kids in the South would make the experimental poets, the modern poets, green with envy.

RALPH ELLISON, "What These Children Are Like," *Going to the Territory,* 1986

Sticks and stones broke bones, mere words could be dismissed by considering the source, and keeping a cool eye on the odds against one.

Ibid.

Americans are given to eating, regurgitating, and alas, re-eating even our most sacred words.

RALPH ELLISON, "The Little Man at Chehaw Station," in *ibid.*

Words without deeds have no meaning.

TOM BRADLEY, *The Impossible Dream,* 1986

If we are not honest about words, it cripples us. We must filter everything.

JANICE HALE BENSON, *Black Child in Education,* 1986

I believe in the power of the spoken word.

ANITA BAKER, c. 1987

Be careful, think about the effect of what you say. Your words should be constructive, bring people together, not pull them apart.

MIRIAM MAKEBA, *My Story,* 1987

When I use the words I wish to create those things which can only come to life in them. I am violated to think of literature as nothing more than a vicarious experience of what one should be strong enough to wring from the social life.

JEAN TOOMER, in Kerman and Eldridge, *The Lives of Jean Toomer,* 1987

Wrestling, boxing, and football are rough contact sports. Yet one of the most brutal games we play is the "word game." It can nearly defeat a people.

R. P. STAFFORD, c. 1988

I have a particular affliction. I am unable to say a word I can't spell.

JESSYE NORMAN, in "The Norman Conquest," *American Visions,* April 1988

Words are too sweet for the vulgar horrors of South Africa. For Birmingham and Montgomery remembered. For the billy clubs and the bomb, the fire hoses and the rifles. Words between these two lay no testament to the pain.

DIANE BOGUS, "After A Kiss," *Catalyst,* Summer 1988

I found a way to make my peace with the recent past by turning it into WORD.

CHARLES JOHNSON, *Middle Passage,* 1990

WORK

There's no profession without a boss.

INSTRUCTION OF SILE, c. 1305–1080 B.C.

Whoever works without knowledge works uselessly.

AFRICA

We bake the bread, they give us the crust

TRADITIONAL

I don't want to rust out, I just want to work out.

TRADITIONAL

When God has a work to be executed he also chooses the man to execute it. He also qualifies the workman for the work. Frederick was fitted best for his work, Daniel Payne for his. . . . The hour for the man and the man for the hour. He who undertakes, through envy, jealousy, or any other motive or consideration, to reverse this divine law resists the purpose of the Almighty and brings misfortune upon himself.

DANIEL PAYNE, c. 1860

We worked, in a manner of speaking, from can to can't, from the time they could see until they couldn't see.

SLAVE

A man is worked upon by what he works on. He may carve out his circumstances, but his circumstances will carve him out as well.

FREDERICK DOUGLASS, *Life and Times of Frederick Douglass,* 189?

We have the record of kings and gentlemen ad nauseum and in stupid detail; but of the common run of human beings and particularly of the half or wholly submerged working group, the world has saved all too little authentic record and tried to forget or ignore even the little saved.

W. E. B. DU BOIS, c. 1903

We have been worked, now let us learn to work.

BOOKER T. WASHINGTON, *The American Negro,* 1908

Our day of work is not our day of joy—for that we require a holiday; for miserable that we are, we cannot find our holiday in our work. The river finds its holiday in its outward flow, the fire in its outburst of flame, the scent of the flower in its permeation of the atmosphere, but in our everyday work there is no such holiday. It is because we do not let outselves go, because we do not give ourselves joyously and entirely up to it, that our work overpower us.

RABINDRANATH TAGORE, *Sadhana,* 1912

We shall not always plant while others reap. . . .

COUNTEE CULLEN, "From the Dark Tower," *Copper Sun,* 1927

I die if I don't work, and if I do, I die, either way I die.

NICHOLAS GUILLÉN, *Blues,* 1930

We need workers, not leaders. Such workers will solve the problems which race leaders talk about.

CARTER G. WOODSON, *The Mis-education of the Negro,* 1931

Never let work drive you, master it and keep in complete control.

BOOKER T. WASHINGTON, *Speeches of Booker T. Washington,* 1932

It is necessary to learn the difference between being worked and working—to learn that being worked meant degradation, while working meant civilization.

Ibid.

As I worked with my children in school and met with their parents in the homes, on the farms, and in church, I found myself studying them all with sympathetic objectivity, as I could realize they were something apart; but in an instant's reflection, I could realize that they were me and I was they; that a force stronger than blood made us one.

JAMES WELDON JOHNSON, *Along This Way,* 1933

I know the unskilled worker of this city by working with him as a porter and a longshoreman and as a waiter on the railroad. I lived in the same quarters and caroused together in bars and at rent parties.

CLAUDE MCKAY, *A Long Way from Home,* 1937

[F]or it is not true that the work of man is done/ that we have no business being on earth/that we parasite the world/that it is enough for us to hee to the world/whereas the work has only just begun.

AIMÉ CÉSAIRE, Notes of a *Return to the Native Land,* 1947

The powerless must do their own dirty work. The powerful have it done for them.

JAMES BALDWIN, *Nobody Knows My Name,* 1961

Black and white workers did not fight each other because they hated each other, but they hated each other because they fought each other. They fought each other because they did not know each other. They did not know each other because they had no control or communication with each other because they were afraid of each other.

A. PHILLIP RANDOLPH, "The Struggle for the Liberation of the Black Laboring Masses in This Age of a Revolution of Human Rights," speech given at Negro American Labor Concil, 10–12 November 1961

The work of men is not durable.

TOUSSAINT L'OUVERTURE in James, *The Black Jacobins,* 1963

. . . there is no place on this earth without my fingerprint and my heel upon the skeleton of skyscrapers, and my sweat in the brilliance of diamond.

Ibid.

The hardest work in the world is being out of work.

WHITNEY YOUNG, JR., 3 December 1967

Not all men are called to specialized or professional jobs; even fewer to the heights of genius in the arts and sciences; many are called to be laborers in factories, fields, and streets. But no work is insignificant.

MARTIN LUTHER KING, JR., *Where Do We Go from Here?* 1968

[A] man must have his work. . . . [B]uild on what you know, what you love . . . there [is] something larger, something related to that part of your life, which you can use as an anchor for the new[.]

MARTIN LUTHER KING, JR., in Owens, *Blackthink,* 1970

I haven't seen much ballet or opera recently. I work. I'm a laborer.

DUKE ELLINGTON, *Music Is My Mistress,* 1973

[Jazz] has been a banner under which I have written and played most of my life, almost all the way around the world. . . . I have been received by presidents, first ladies, kings, queens, maharajahs, maharanees, champions, chief justices, *chefs de cuisine,* painters, sculptors, screen stars, butchers, bakers, doctors, lawyers, dishwashers, and street cleaners.

Ibid.

After Marcus Garvey had returned millions to Africa spiritually, he had done his work.

AMY JACQUES GARVEY, in "Mrs. Marcus Garvey Talks with Ida Lewis," *Encore,* May 1973

To deprive a person of work is to negate a portion of his/her humanity.

JOHN CONYERS, "The Politics of Unemployment," *Freedomways,* Fall 1975

If I didn't make good at Temple, I knew a lifetime as a busboy or a factory worker waited for me.

BILL COSBY, in "Interview," *Scholastic,* 17 November 1977

To be unemployed is a crime because no African can for long evade arrest if his passbook does not carry the stamp of authorized and approved employment.

NELSON MANDELA, *The Struggle Is My Life,* 1978

The first time I was at the Apollo, I threw my tie out to them, and they threw it back to me. I said, "James, you have got some work to do."

JAMES BROWN, c. 1980

Your work, that was done, to be done to be done to be done.

GWENDOLYN BROOKS, *To the Diaspora, To Disembark,* 1981

The day of the hustle is over; to make it in today's society, you must produce.

GEORGE C. COOPER, "It's Nice to Be Remembered," *Negro History Bulletin,* September 1982

Much of the satisfying work of life begins as an experiment; no experiment is ever quite a failure.

ALICE WALKER, *Living With the Wind,* 1985

A good piece of work shows you have taken a victorious position in the struggle with falsehoods.

WYNTON MARSALIS, "We Must Preserve Our Jazz Heritage," *Ebony,* February 1986

You work all the time, it's not workaholism—it's greed.

CAMILLE COSBY, c. 1987

It is ironic that in a society based upon the work ethic, the worth of an individual is often confused with the work that he or she performs.

JOHN CONYERS, 1987

The man who does just enough work to get by seldom gets more than "by."

SAMUEL B. FULLER, in Terkel, *American Dreams: Lost and Found,* 1988

Even a python grows old and weak. It is the man who goes under, not the work. There is always work.

ES'KIA MPHAHLELE, "Tirenje or Monde?" in Chinweizu, ed., *Voices From Twentieth-Century Africa,* 1988

I have not been waiting for stardom. I've been working. Stardom is people paying you an awful lot of money just because you're you. You don't really have to work anymore. Then you're worthless. If I see stardom looming on the horizon, I'm leaving. I'm going sailing.

MORGAN FREEMAN, in *Jet,* 22 June 1988

I love this sport, and with God's help I can continue to do it. I'd rather do this than a nine to five job. I'll know when to call it quits, and that is before they hit me more than I hit them.

SUGAR RAY LEONARD, *Jet,* 26 September 1988

[My mother] had to go wherever the work was, usually picking cotton or cleaning, washing and cooking for white folks.

ALVIN AILEY, in "Alvin Ailey Celebrates 30 Years of Dance," *Essence,* November 1988

Voluntary compliance does not work. If it did Moses would have come down the mountain with the Ten Guidelines. But he came down with the the Ten Commandments.

WILLIAM MCEVERS, c. 1989

Black people worked three hundred and fifty years without a paycheck.

JANICE HALE BENSON, speech given at African-American Child Conference, Detroit, Michigan, January 1989

WORLD

[T]he modern world must remember that in this age when the ends of the world are being brought so near together the millions of black men in Africa, America, and the Islands of the Sea, not to speak of the brown and yellow myriads elsewhere, are bound to have a great influence upon the world in the future, by reason of sheer numbers and physical contact.

W. E. B. DU BOIS, "To the Nations of the World," speech given to Pan African Conference, London, 1900

And God stepped out on space,/ And he looked around and said:/ I'm lonely—/ I'll make me a world.

JAMES WELDON JOHNSON, "The Creation," *God's Trombone,* 1927

The world today is in a state of semi-chaos. . . . We are floundering.

JAMES WELDON JOHNSON, *Negro Americans, What Now?* 1934

She knew the world was a stallion rolling in the blue pasture of ether. She knew that God tore down the old world every evening and built a new one by sun-up. It was wonderful to see it take form with the sun and emerge from the gray dust of its making. The familiar people and things had failed her so she hung over the gate and looked up the road towards way off.

ZORA NEALE HURSTON, *Their Eyes Were Watching God,* 1937

The world is before you and you need not take it or leave it as it was when you came in.

JAMES BALDWIN, *Nobody Knows My Name,* 1961

One way the world remains the same. The child still thinks she is wiser than the cotton head of age.

WOLE SOYINKA, *The Lion and the Jewel,* 1963

We're living in an awkward world. The whole race problem has made relations in America awkward.

MALCOLM X, speech given at Audubon Ballroom, New York City, 20 June 1964

For this is a beautiful world; this is a wonderful America, which the founding fathers dreamed until their sons drowned it in the blood of slavery and devoured it in greed. Our children must rebuild it!

W. E. B. DU BOIS, *The Autobiography of W. E. B. DuBois: A Soliloquy on Viewing My Life from the Last Decade of Its First Century,* 1964

Our world is no worse than yesterday's, nor will the world of tomorrow be any better. Moreover, there is no possible way of returning to the past.

OCTAVIO PAZ, *Alternating Currents,* 1967

This is a wicked world, but it can be made better.

WYATT T. WALKER, in *Negro Digest,* December 1967

The world is changing and anyone who thinks he can live alone is sleeping through a revolution.

MARTIN LUTHER KING, JR., "Remaining Awake Through a Great Revolution," sermon given at Washington Episcopal Cathedral, Washington, D.C., 31 March 1968

To be perfectly adjusted in a crazy, impractical, unreasonable society, hellbent for its own annihilation, seems tantamount to remaining blissful in a raging booby hatch.

JOHN KILLENS, "The Black Writer Vis-à-vis His Country," in Gayle, ed., *The Black Aesthetic,* 1971

One cannot live with sighted eyes and feeling heart and not know and read of the miseries which affect the world.

LORRAINE HANSBERRY, *Sign in Sidney Brustein's Window,* 1972

An old world is dying, and a new one, kicking in the belly of its mother, time, announces that it is ready to be born. The birth will not be easy, and many of us are doomed to discover that we are exceedingly clumsy midwives.

JAMES BALDWIN, *No Name in the Street,* 1972

The world goes on no matter what you do.

EUBIE BLAKE, *Eubie,* 1979

Everything in your world is created by what you think.

OPRAH WINFREY, 1988

. . . like you, living in a world with no address.

GLORIA NAYLOR, *Women of Brewster Place,* 1988

WRITING/WRITER

I think I must write a book. I am almost afraid to undertake a book so early and with so little experience in composition. But it has been my cherished dream . . . knowledge of the classics, acquaintance with the modern languages, an intimate friendship with literature, etc., seven years in the schoolroom, two years of married life, and a habit of studying character have not left me entirely unprepared to write even a book.

CHARLES CHESTNUTT, journal entry, 28 May 1880

From threads of fact and fiction I have woven a story whose mission will not be in vain if it awakens in the hearts of our countrymen a stronger sense of justice and a more Christlike humanity in behalf of those whom the fortunes of war threw homeless, ignorant, and poor on the threshold of a new era.

FRANCES E. W. HARPER, *Iola Leroy,* 1892

I find that I am actuated by a strong sense of race consciousness. This grows upon me as I grow older, and though I struggle against it, it colors my writing in spite of everything I can do. There may have been many things in my life that have hurt me and I find the surest relief from these hurts is in writing.

COUNTEE CULLEN, in "A Study of Countee Cullen," *Crisis,* March 1926

The books you write/ will wrestle with what's unreal,/ unreal from being too real/ like dreams.

JEAN-JOSEPH RABÉARIVELO, "Your Work," *Near Dreams,* 1934

One day some young poet/ will make your impossible wish come true/ by knowing your books,/ books as rare as flowers underground,/ written for a hundred friends.

JEAN-JOSEPH RABÉARIVELO, *Translated From the Night,* 1935

Negro writers must accept the nationalist implications of their lives, not in order to encourage them, but in order to change and transcend them. They must accept the concept of nationalism because in order to transcend it, they must possess and understand it.

RICHARD WRIGHT, "Blueprint For Negro Writing," *New Challenge,* Fall 1937

My method of writing is a method of "after thought." I mean that after all the details of commas, periods, spelling, there comes the final and to me the most important item of polishing and settling and even restating.

W. E. B. DU BOIS, c. 1940

Hughes tried every literary genre, he wrote some of the most revolutionary works by any American writer of his generation. He was called the "poet laureate of the Negro race," but never for reasons which included his radical verse. It did not fit his popular image.

FAITH BERRY, *The Big Sea,* 1940

My writing was more an attempt at understanding self than self-expression.

RICHARD WRIGHT, in *American Mercury,* July 1940

Richard Wright had a tremendous effect on countless numbers of people whom he never met, and multitudes whom he . . . will never meet. This means his responsibilities and his hazards were great.

JAMES BALDWIN, *Nobody Knows My Name,* 1961

If the writer exists for social good, his role is that of preserving in art those human values which can endure by confronting change.

RALPH ELLISON, *The Same Pain, The Same Pleasure,* 1961

Writers can die in many ways; some perish in obscurity and others in the light. They die in the street and the Waldorf Astoria sipping champagne.

JAMES BALDWIN, "A Conversation with James Baldwin," *Arts in Society,* Summer 1966

I remember those times, now so remote, when young and scuffling and afraid, I took a great long shot at being a writer to save my family. I couldn't do anything else. . . . No one could tell me what a writer looked like. . . . I made money and bought them a house. What's happened is fantastic. I'm probably the most photographed writer in the world. The trick is to survive it and I'm going to survive it.

Ibid.

If anyone's gonna write about me, I reckon it'll be me/myself.

LANGSTON HUGHES "Notes on Community Theater," *Freedomways,* 2nd Quarter 1966

I wrote about love, about the steel mills where my stepfather worked, the slums where we lived, and the brown girls from the South prancing up and down Central Avenue.

Ibid.

We can write another luminous moral chapter in American history. All of us are on trial in this troubled hour, but time still permits us to meet the future with a clear conscience.

MARTIN LUTHER KING, JR., in "Showdown for Nonviolence," *Look,* 16 April 1968

What is new is the deliberate desecration and smashing of idols, the turning inside-out of symbols—bitterness is being replaced by wrath; a sense of frustration giving way before a sense of power.

CAROLYN F. GERALD, "The Black Writer and His Role," in Gayle, ed., *The Black Aesthetic,* 1971

I am a writer perhaps *because* I am not a talker.

GWENDOLYN BROOKS, *Report From Part One,* 1972

A dramatist has to thoroughly inundate himself or herself in an awareness of the realities of the historical period. Then become absolutely dedicated to the idea that what you're going to do is create human beings whom you know in your own time.

LORRAINE HANSBERRY, *Les Blancs,* 1972

More than anything else, the compelling obligation of the writer and citizen of life is a participation in the intellectual affairs of all men, everywhere. The foremost enemy of the past has been—and in a large sense remains—"isolation."

Ibid.

We write not only to express our experiences, our intellectual process, but to interpret the meaning contained in them. We search for the meaning of life in the realities of our . . . dreams, our hopes, our memories. Beauty finds reality in the emotion it produces, but that emotion must be articulated before we can understand it. Anger and hatred require expression as do love and charity.

CHESTER HIMES, "Dilemma of the Negro Novelist in U.S.A.," in Chapman, ed., *New Black Voices,* 1972

No matter what I did or how I lived, I had considered myself a writer. . . . It was my salvation. The world can deny me all other employment, and stone me as an ex-convict . . . as a disagreeable, unpleasant person. But as long as I write whether it's published or not , I'm a writer . . .

CHESTER HIMES, *The Quality of Hurt,* 1972

Writing requires devotion and a bit of arrogance.

BUCHI EMECHETA, c. 1982

Writing really helps you heal yourself.

ALICE WALKER, c. 1983

I write . . . what I want to read—understanding fully and indelibly that if I don't do it no one else is so vitally interested, or capable of doing it to my satisfaction.

ALICE WALKER, *In Search of Our Mothers' Gardens,* 1983

Writing, like dreams, confronts, pushes you up against the evasions, self-deceptions, investments in opinions and interpretations, the clutter that blinds, that disguises that underlying, all-encompassing design within which the perceivable world—in which society would have us stay put—operates.

TONI CADE BAMBARA, "Salvation Is the Issue," in Evans, ed., *Black Women Writers,* 1984

Writing is a labor of love and also an act of defiance, a way to light a candle in a gale wind; 'In the beginning was the Word and the Word was with God, and the Word was God.'

ALICE CHILDRESS, "A Candle in a Gale Wind," in *ibid.*

I write for those women who do not speak; who do not have verbalization because they, we, are so terrified, because we are taught to respect our fears, but we *must* learn to respect ourselves and our needs.

AUDRE LORDE, "My Words Will Be There," in *ibid.*

I write the way women have babies. You don't know it's going to be like that. If you did, there's no way you would go through with it.

TONI MORRISON, "Rootedness: The Ancestor As Foundation," in *ibid.*

Writing requires intelligence. You have to want to do it. You have to make up your mind. You learn to handle defeat, loss, and even criticism. You can't let that interfere with what you want to write. You can't set up your own obstacles.

Ibid.

In 1957 it was hard to be a thirteen-year-old Black boy who wanted to be a writer. To begin with, I was oblivious to the fact that Black writers even existed. . . . Second, my rural community, whose center was the Pentecostal church, referred to writing as lying, regarding it with the same withering stares they reserved for short skirts, blues and jazz. Third, the arched eyebrows of my peers suggested that writing was not a very masculine occupation. And Lord knows above all I wanted to be a man.

RICHARD PERRY, in "Grapevine," *Essence,* November 1985

Writers are gorged in injustice as swords are forged.

RALPH ELLISON, *Going to the Territory,* 1986

A writer—one day in prison, one day being decorated by the head of state.

WOLE SOYINKA, in "Wole Soyinka: Nigerian Playwrite is First Black Nobel Laureate in Literature," *Ebony,* April 1987

Writing is a dialogue between the writer and the society.

TESS ONWUEME, in "The Broken Calabash," *City Arts Quarterly,* Fall 1988

We write to develop consciousness, not to entertain, there's enough entertainment going on.

Ibid.

Writing is one of the few professions in which you can psychoanalyze yourself, get rid of hostilities and frustrations in public, and get paid for it.

OCTAVIA BUTLER, in "Birth of a Writer," *Essence,* May 1989

Writing is my refuge. It's where I go. It's where I find that integrity I have.

CHARLES JOHNSON, in "Interview with Charles Johnson," *The World and I,* 1990

Writers began their lifelong odyssey in art with expression or experience interpreted by others, not, as popular wisdom sometimes has it, with an ensemble of events that already mean something.

Ibid.

WRONG

You are learned, skilled, accomplished, but not in order to plunder! You should be the model for all men, but your affairs are crooked! The standard for all men cheats the whole land!

KHUN ANUP, *The Eloquent Peasant,* 2040–1650 B.C.

The injuries we do and those we suffer are seldom weighed on the same scale.

AESOP, "The Partial Judge," 600 B.C.

Some of you have done us so much injury, that you will never be able to repent.

DAVID WALKER, *Appeal to the Coloured Citizens of the World,* 1829

And what is wrong in a woman's life/ In a man's cannot be right.

FRANCES E. W. HARPER, "A Double Standard," c. 1854

They who study mankind with a whip in their hand will always go wrong.

FREDERICK DOUGLASS, "Slavery and the Irresponsible Conflict," speech given in Geneva, New York, 1 August 1860

The lesson of all the ages upon this point is, that a wrong done to one man is a wrong done to all men. It may not be felt at the moment, and the evil may be long delayed, but so sure as there is a moral government of the universe, . . . so sure will the harvest of evil come.

FREDERICK DOUGLASS, *Life and Times of Frederick Douglass,* 1892

If they do you wrong, they invent a bad name for you, a good name for their acts and then destroy you in the name of virtue.

ZORA NEALE HURSTON, *Moses, Man of the Mountain,* 1939

If we are wrong, the Supreme Court is wrong. If we are wrong, the Constitution of the United States is wrong. If we are wrong, God Almighty is wrong. If we are wrong, Jesus of Nazareth was merely a Utopian dreamer who never came down to earth. If we are wrong, then justice is a lie.

MARTIN LUTHER KING, JR., speech given in Montgomery, Alabama, 5 December 1955

After forty years of doing good things, do one thing wrong and people will talk about that far more than all the good things you did for forty years.

C. L. FRANKLIN, "The Preacher Who Got Drunk," c. 1958

When you are wrong, you're wrong. But when you're right, you're wrong anyway.

BAYARD RUSTIN, *Down the Line,* 1971

Everybody wants somebody to be perfect. Well, if you're perfect how can you tell imperfect people what's right and what's wrong?

DREW BROWN, in the *Pittsburgh Courier,* 17 August 1991

YOUTH

Instruction in youth is like engraving in stone.

LIBYA

The child looks everywhere and often sees nought, but the old man, sitting on the ground, sees everything.

SENEGAL

Youth never despairs, for it is still in harmony with the Divine.

ALEXANDRE DUMAS, *My Memoirs,* 1802–1821

[T]he upstart of today is the elite of tomorrow.

FREDERICK DOUGLASS, speech given at the Colored High School commencement, Baltimore, Maryland, 22 June 1894

No greater injury can be done to any youth than to make him feel because he belongs to this or that race he will be advanced in life regardless of his own merits or efforts.

BOOKER T. WASHINGTON, *Up From Slavery,* 1901

A nation cannot teach its youth to think in terms of destruction and oppression without brutalizing and blunting the tender conscience and sense of justice of the youths of the country. More and more we must learn to think not in terms of race or color or language or religion or of political boundaries, but in terms of humanity. Above all races and political boundaries there is humanity.

Ibid.

We have Negro youth, with arresting visions and vibrant prophecies; forecasting in the mirror of art what we must see and recognize in the streets of reality tomorrow, foretelling in new notes and accents the maturing speech of full racial utterance.

ALAIN LOCKE, ed., *The New Negro,* 1925

Youth is the turning point in life, the most sensitive and volatile period, the state that registers most vividly the impressions and experience of life.

RICHARD WRIGHT, *12 Million Black Voices,* 1941

Denmark Vesey and Nat Turner were young men when they struck for freedom. And the incomparable Frederick Douglass was still a boy when he whipped the slave-breaker Covey, still a minor when he broke from Baltimore for freedom. . . .

PAUL ROBESON, speech to First National Convention of the Labor Youth League, 24 November 1950

When I was young and loved life's laughter./ I climbed tall hills and touched the sun;/ I did not know till long years after/ That ecstasy and pain are one.

NAOMI MADGETT, "When I Was Young," *The One and the Many,* 1956

You are young, gifted, and Black. We must begin to tell our young, There's a world waiting for you, Yours is the quest that's just begun.

JAMES WELDON JOHNSON, in Hansberry, *To Be Young, Gifted and Black,* 1959

The young are not likely to follow the example of past generations who were radical in their teens, liberal in their twenties, conservative in their thirties and reactionary in their forties.

WHITNEY YOUNG, JR., *To Be Equal,* 1964

He had but one life to live. He couldn't wait, even though he died young. How long do you think Jesus would have had to wait for the constituted authorities to accept him? Twenty-five years? A hundred years? A thousand? He died at thirty three. . . . It isn't how long one lives, but how well. It's what one accomplishes for mankind that matters. Jesus died at thirty-three; Joan of Arc at nineteen; Byron and Burns at thirty-three; Keats and Marlowe at twenty-nine; Shelley at thirty; Dunbar before thirty-five . . . and Martin Luther King, Jr., at thirty-nine.

BENJAMIN MAYS, eulogy of Dr. Martin Luther King, Jr., Ebenezer Church, Atlanta, Georgia, 9 April 1968

Black youth are in need of a secure sense of personal identity, self-confidence and racial pride. A racial minority in a society which deals harshly with them, they are too often unable to articulate satisfactory answers to the questions: Who am I? What is my group identity? What is my racial heritage?

I. A. NEWBY, "Historians and Negroes," *Journal of Negro History,* January 1969

We will die without our young people.

ALEX HALEY, *Roots,* 1977

African youth with distinguished scholastic records are not a credit to the country, but a serious threat to the governing circles, for they are not likely to descend to the bowels of the earth and cough their lungs out to enrich the mining magnates, nor will they elect to dig potatoes on farms for wretched rations.

NELSON MANDELA, *The Struggle Is My Life,* 1978

All young people were the same: they never imagined they would get old.

BUCHI EMECHETA, *The Joys of Motherhood,* 1979

If the old folk would get rid of their prejudice, the young folk would take care of the rest. Most young people of today do not understand the racism of their parents.

LEON SULLIVAN, "Dreams of the Future," *Negro History Bulletin,* January–March 1983

I've been involved since I was a kid in some sort of rebellion against circumstances in which I found myself.

COLEMAN YOUNG, c. 1984

How the young attempt and are broken/differ from age to age.

AUDRE LORDE, "My Words Will Be There," in Evans, ed., *Black Women Writers,* 1984

Young people today can't believe that there was a time when no hotel in New York would take Marian Anderson as a guest except the Algonquin.

AMINDA WILKINS, in "Interview: Aminda Wilkins," *Crisis,* January 1988

This young generation was the first not to know segregation and discover its ever-present manifestation of America's racial hatred. It was the first not to grow up with the ubiquity of lynching, the first to whom Mississippi, Georgia, and Alabama are only states and not dark terrifying symbols of our people's martyrdom.

WILLIAM STRICKLAND, in "Growing Up Integrated," *Crisis,* March 1988

I was young and I learned by listening to my elders and by drawing my own conclusions through experience.

COLEMAN YOUNG, in the *Detroit News,* 22 April 1988

If we can reach young people's minds deep enough, we can teach young minds deep enough so that they will change the negative concept they have of themselves from which most of the negative social consequences flow.

OSSIE DAVIS, "It's On Us," *City Arts Quarterly,* Spring 1988

BIBLIOGRAPHY

Abrahams, Peter. *Dark Testament.* Winchester, Mass.: Allen & Unwin, 1942.

———. *The Path of Thunder.* New York: Harper & Brothers, 1948.

———. *Wild Conquest.* New York: Harper & Brothers, 1950.

———. *Return To Goli.* London: Faber and Faber, 1953.

———. *Mine Boy.* London: Faber and Faber, 1954.

———. *Tell Freedom.* London: Faber and Faber, 1954.

———. *Jamaica: An Island Mosaic.* London: Her Majesty's Stationery Office, 1957.

———. *A Night of Their Own.* London: Faber and Faber, 1965.

———. *This Island Now.* London: Faber and Faber, 1967.

Achebe, Chinua. *Things Fall Apart.* New York: Fawcett Crest, 1958.

———. *No Longer At Ease.* New York: Fawcett Crest, 1961.

———. *Arrow of God.* New York: Doubleday, 1967.

Ademola, Frances. *Reflections: Nigerian Prose and Verse.* African University Press, 1962.

Ali, Muhammad. *The Greatest.* New York: Ballantine Books, 1975.

Allen, Richard. *The Life Experience and Gospel Labors of Richard Allen.* Philadelphia, 1887.

Angelou, Maya. *I Know Why the Caged Bird Sings.* New York: Random House, 1969.

———. *Gather Together In My Name.* New York: Random House, 1974.

———. *Singing and Swinging like Christmas.* New York: Random House, 1976.

———. *The Heart of a Woman.* New York: Bantam Books, 1981.

———. *All God's Children Need Traveling Shoes.* New York: Random House, 1986.

Armstrong, Louis. *Autobiography of Louis Armstrong.* New York: Doubleday, 1979.

Attaway, William. *Let Me Breathe Thunder.* New York: Doubleday, 1939.

Bailey, Pearl. *The Raw Pearl.* New York: Harcourt Brace and World, 1968.

Baldwin, James. *Notes of a Native Son.* Boston: Beacon Press, 1955.

———. *Nobody Knows My Name.* New York: Dial, 1961.

———. *The Fire Next Time.* New York: Dial, 1963.

———. *A Rap on Race.* New York: Dell, 1971.

———. *No Name in the Street.* New York: Dial, 1972.

———. *The Price of the Ticket.* New York: St. Martins Press, 1985.

———. *The Evidence of Things Not Seen.* New York: Holt, Rinehart & Winston, 1985.

Bambara, Toni Cade. *Gorilla, My Love.* New York: Random House, 1972.

———. *Sea Birds Are Still Alive.* New York: Random House, 1974.

———. *The Salt Eaters.* New York: Random House, 1980.

Bates, Daisy. *The Long Shadow of Little Rock.* New York: David McKay, Inc., 1962.

Beby, Francis. *African Music; A People's Art.* Westport, Conn.: Lawrence Hill, 1969.

Bennett, Jr., Lerone. *The Challenge of Blackness.* Chicago: Johnson Publishing, 1972.

Beti, Mongo. *Le Pauvre Christ de Bomba.* Paris, 1956.

Bibb, Henry. *Narrative of the Life and Adventures of Henry Bibb.* 1849.

Bontemps, Arna. *The Poetry of the Negro.* New York: Doubleday, 1949.

———. *Anyplace But Here.* New York: Hill & Wang, 1966.

Bontemps, Arna, and Langston Hughes, eds. *The Book of Negro Folklore.* New York: Dodd Mead, 1965.

Borges, Jorge Luis. *Labyrinths: Selected Stories and Other Writings.* New York: New Directions Publishing, 1962.

Bradley, Tom. *The Impossible Dream.* New York: Roundtable Publishing, 1986.

Brawley, Benjamin. *Early Negro American Writers.* Chapel Hill: University of North Carolina Press, 1935.

——— *Negro Builders and Heroes.* Chapel Hill: University of North Carolina Press, 1937.

Brewer, J. Mason. *American Negro Folklore.* New York: New York Times Books, 1968.

Brooks, Gwendolyn. *A Street in Bronzeville.* Harper & Brothers, 1945.

———. *Annie Allen.* New York: Harper & Brothers, 1949.

———. *In the Mecca.* New York: Harper & Row, 1968.

———. *Family Pictures.* Detroit: Broadside Press, 1970.

———. *World of Gwendolyn Brooks.* New York: Harper & Row, 1971.

———. *Report From Part One.* Detroit: Broadside Press, 1972.

Brown, Claude. *Manchild in the Promised Land.* New York: Signet, 1965.

Brown, H. Rap. *Die Nigger Die.* New York: Dial, 1970.

Brown, Sterling. *Collected Poems of Sterling Brown.* New York: Harper & Row, 1980.

Brown, William Wells. *Narrative of William W. Brown, A Fugitive Slave.* 1856.

———. *Negro in the American Rebellion.* Boston, 1867.

———. *My Southern Home.* Boston: The Gregg Press, 1880.

Caesar, Adolph. *Ma Rainey's Black Bottom.* New York: New American Library, 1985.

Cardenal, Ernesto. *Vida en al Amor.* London: Search Press Limited, 1974.

Carmichael, Stokely. *Black Power.* New York: Random House, 1967.

Carrera Andrade, Jorge. *Latin American Tales.* New York: New American Library, 1977.

Carson, Benjamin. *Gifted Hands.* Grand Rapids, Mich.: Zondervan Books, 1990.

Césaire, Aimé. *Les Armes Miraculeuses.* Paris, 1946.

———. *Notes on a Return to the Native Land.* Paris: Présence Africaine, 1947.

———. *The Tragedy of King Christophe.* 1963.

Chapman, Abraham. *New Black Voices.* New York: New American Library, 1972.

Charles, Ray, and David Ritz. *Brother Ray.* New York: Warner, 1978.

Chestnutt, Charles W. *Wife of his Youth.* 1899.

———. *The Marrow of Tradition.* 1901.

———. *Breaking into Print,* New York: 1937.

Chinweizu, Onwucheka Jemie. *Voices from Twentieth-Century Africa.* London: Faber and Faber, 1988.

Chisholm, Shirley. *Unbought and Unbossed.* Boston: Houghton Mifflin, 1970.

Clarke, John Henrik. *Rebellion in Rhyme.* Prairie City, Ill.: Dicker Press, 1948.

———. *Harlem, USA.* New York: Seven-Seas Press, 1964.

———, ed. *American Negro Short Stories.* New York: Hill & Wang, 1966.

———. *Tales From Harlem.* New York: New American Library, 1970.

Cleaver, Eldridge. *Soul On Ice.* New York: McGraw-Hill, 1968.

———. *Post-Prison Writings and Speeches.* New York: Random House, 1969.

Clifton, Lucille. *Good Times.* New York: Vintage, 1970.

———. *Good News About the Earth.* New York: Random House, 1972.

———. *An Ordinary Woman.* New York: Random House, 1974.

———. *Generations.* New York: Random House, 1976.

———. *Next.* Brockport, N.Y.: Boa Editions, Ltd, 1987.

Cloyd, Iris, ed. *Who's Who Among Black America.* Detroit: Gale Research, Inc.

Cone, James. *Black Theology and Black Power.* New York: Seabury Press, 1969.

———. *Martin and Malcolm and America.* Maryknoll, N.Y.: Orbis Books, 1991.

Courlander, Harold. *Negro Folk Music.* New York: Columbia University Press, 1963.

Cruse, Harold W. *The Crisis of the Negro Intellectual.* New York: Morrow, 1967.

Cullen, Countee. *On These I Stand.* New York: Harper & Brothers, 1927.

———. *Caroling Dusk: An Anthology of Verse by Negro Poets.* Harper & Brothers, 1927.

Dadie, Bernard. *Africa Arise.* Paris, 1950.

———. *Dance of the Days.* Paris, 1956.

Dallas Museum of Art. *Black Art: Ancestral Legacy.* Dallas: Museum of Art, 1989.

Damas, Leon. *Pigments.* Paris, 1937.

———. *Poetes d'expression Francaise.* Paris, 1947.

Danner, Margaret. *To Flower.* Detroit: Broadside Press, 1963.

Danquah, J. B. *Akan Laws and Customs.* London, 1928.

Dee, Ruby. *My One Good Nerve: Rhythms, Rhymes and Reasons.* Chicago: Third World Press, 1987.

Delaney, Martin. *The Condition, Elevation, Emigration and Destiny of the the Colored People of the United States.* Philadelphia, 1852.

Depestre, Rene. *Minerai Noir.* Paris, 1956.

Diop, Birago. *Gleams and Glimmers.* Paris: Présence Africaine, 1960.

———. *Tales of Amadou Kouyate.* New York: Oxford University Press, 1966.

Diop, Cheikh Anta. *Black Africa—The Economic.* Chicago: Third World Press, 1978.

Diop, David. *Poundings.* Paris: Présence Africaine, 1956.

———. *Modern Poetry of Africa.* London: Penguin, 1963.

Dodson, Owen. *Powerful Long Ladder.* New York: Farrar Strauss and Co., 1946.

Douglas, Frederick. *Narrative of the Life of Frederick Douglass, an American Slave, Written by Himself.* Boston: Anti-Slavery Office, 1845.

———. *My Bondage and My Freedom.* Miller, Orton and Mulligan, 1855.

———. *Life and Times of Frederick Douglas, Written By Himself.* Park Publishing, 1881.

———. *Life and Times of Frederick Douglas, Written By Himself: His early life as a slave, his escape from bondage, and his complete history to the present time.* Dewolfe and Co, 1892.

Drachler, Jacob, ed. *African Heritage: Intimate Views of Black Africans.* Collier Books, 1904.

Du Bois, W. E. B. *The Souls of Black Folk: Essays and Sketches.* Chicago: A. C. McClurg & Co., 1903.

———. *The Talented Tenth,* Potts and Co., 1903.

———. *Darkwater: Voices from Within the Veil.* 1920.

———. *Dark Princess.* 1928.

———. *Black Reconstruction in America 1860–1880.* S. A. Russell, 1935.

———. *Dusk of Dawn: An Essay Toward an Autobiography of Race Concept.* New York: Harcourt Brace, 1940.

———. *The World and Africa; An Inquiry into the Part which Africa Has Played in World History.* New York: Viking, 1947.

———. *An ABC of Color: Selections from over a Half Century of the Writings of W.E.B. Dubois.* New York: Seven-Seas Press, 1963.

Dumas, Alexandre. *The Count of Monte Cristo.* Paris, 1844.

———. *Le Demi-Monde.* Paris, 1855.

Dumas, Henry. *Play Ebony Play Ivory.* New York: Random House, 1974.

Dunbar, Alice Nelson. *Give Us Each Day.* New York: Norton, 1984.

Dunbar, Paul Laurence. *Complete Poems of Paul Laurence Dunbar.* New York: Dodd, Mead, 1913.

Dunham, Katherine. *A Touch of Innocence.* New York: Harcourt Brace, 1959.

Duster, Alfreda M. Barnett, ed. *Crusade for Justice: The Autobiography of Ida B. Wells.* Chicago: University of Chicago Press, 1970.

Ellington, Edward K. *Music Is My Mistress.* New York: Doubleday, 1973.

Ellison, Ralph. *Invisible Man,* New York: Random House, 1952.

———. *Shadow and Act.* New York: Random House, 1964.

———. *Going to the Territory.* New York: Random House, 1986.

Emecheta, Buchi. *The Bride Price.* New York: Braziller, 1976.

———. *The Joys of Motherhood.* New York: Braziller, 1979.

Erny, Pierre. *Childhood and Cosmos.* Maryland: Media Intellectuals, 1973.

Essien-Udom, E. U. *Black Nationalism: A Search for Identity.* Chicago: University of Chicago Press, 1962.

Evans, Mari. *I Am a Black Woman.* New York: Morrow, 1970.

———, ed. *Black Women Writers, 1950–1980.* New York: Anchor Press, 1984.

Fanon, Frantz. *The Wretched of the Earth.* New York: Grove Press, 1963.

———. *Black Skin, White Masks.* New York: Grove Press, 1967.

Farrakhan, Louis. *Africa's Cultural Revolution.* New York: Macmillan Books.

Finn, Julio. *Voices of Negritude.* Quartet Books, 1988.

Franklin, John Hope. *From Slavery to Freedom: A History of American Negroes,* 6th ed. New York: Knopf, 1987.

Fremantle, Anne. *Latin American Literature Today.* New York: New American Library, 1977.

Garland, Phyl. *The Sound of Soul.* Port Washington, N.Y.: Regency, 1969.

Garvey, Amy Jacques. *Philosophy and Opinions of Marcus Garvey.* 1923.

———. *Garvey and Garveyism.* Kingston, 1963.

Gayle, Jr., Addison. *From the Black Situations.* New York: Horizon, 1970.

———, ed. *The Black Aesthetic.* New York: Anchor Press, 1971.

Giovanni, Nikki. *Black Feeling Black Talk Black Judgement.* New York: Morrow, 1970.

———. *Cotton Candy on a Rainy Day.* New York: Morrow, 1978.

Glissant, Edouard. *La Lezarde.* Paris, 1958.

Goodison, Lorna. *I Am Becoming My Mother.* London: New Beacon, 1986.

Goss, Linda, and Marian Barnes, editors. *Talk That Talk.* New York: Simon and Schuster, 1989.

Greenburg, Jonathan. *Staking a Claim: Jake Simmons and the Making of an African-American Oil Dynasty.* New York: Penguin, 1991.

Greenfield, Eloise. *Honey, I Love and Other Love Poems*. New York: Harper & Row, 1978.

Gregory, Dick. *Nigger: An Autobiography*. New York: E. P. Dutton, 1964.

———. *No More Lies: The Myth and the Reality of American History*. New York: Harper & Row, 1971.

Grier, William H., and Price Cobb. *Black Rage*. New York: Bantam, 1968.

Guillén, Nicolas. *Motivos del son*, Havana: 1930.

Hale-Benson, Janice. *Black Children: Their Roots, Culture, and Learning Styles*. Baltimore: Johns Hopkins University Press, 1986.

Haley, Alex. *Roots*. New York: Doubleday, 1977.

———. *The Autobiography of Malcolm X*. New York: Grove Press, 1965.

Hampton, Lionel. *Hamp: An Autobiography*. New York: Warner Books, 1989.

Hansberry, Lorraine. *A Raisin in the Sun*. New York: Random House, 1959.

———. *To Be Young, Gifted and Black*. 1959.

———. *Les Blancs. The Collected Last Plays of Lorraine Hansberry*. New York: Vintage Books, 1972.

Harper, Michael S., and Robert Stepto, eds. *Chants of Saints: A Gathering of Afro-American Literature, Art, and Scholarship*. Champaign, Ill.: University of Illinois Press, 1979.

Harrison, Daphne Duval. *Black Pearls: Blues Queens of the 1920s*. New Brunswick, N.J.: Rutgers University Press, 1988.

Haskins, James. *Growing up in a World of Darkness*. New York: Lothrop, 1976.

Hayden, Robert E. *Kaleidoscope: Poems by American Negro Poets*. New York: Harcourt Brace and World, 1968.

Himes, Chester. *The Quality of Hurt: The Autobiography of Chester Himes*. Columbia, Mo.: University of Missouri Press, 1972.

———. *Black On Black*. New York: Doubleday, 1973.

Hoaglund, Everett. *Black Velvet*. Detroit: Broadside Press, 1970.

Horne, Lena. *Lena*. New York: Doubleday, 1965.

Hughes, Langston. *The Weary Blues*. New York: Knopf, 1926.

———. *The Dream Keeper and Other Poems*. New York: Knopf, 1932.

———. *Selected Poems*. New York: Knopf, 1942.

———. *Simple Speaks His Mind*. New York: Hill & Wang, 1950.

———. *Langston Hughes Reader*. New York: Braziller, 1958.

———. *Fight for Freedom: The Story of the NAACP*. New York: Norton, 1962.

———. *Poems from Black Africa*. Bloomington, Ind.: Indiana University Press, 1963.

———. *The Book of Negro Humor*. New York: Knopf, 1966.

Hull, Gloria. *Young Girls Blues*. New York: Kitchen Table/Women of Color Press, 1989.

Hurston, Zora Neale. *Jonah's Gourd Vine*. Philadelphia: Lippincott, 1934.

———. *Mules and Men*. Bloomington, Ind.: Indiana University Press, 1935.

———. *Their Eyes Were Watching God*. Bloomington, Ind.: Indiana University Press, 1937.

———. *Moses, Man of the Mountain*. Philadelphia: Lippincott, 1939.

———. *Dust Tracks on a Road*. Bloomington, Ind.: Indiana University Press, 1942.

Jackson, Bo. *Bo Knows Bo*. New York: Doubleday, 1990.

Jacobs, Harriet. *Incidents in the Life of a Slave Girl*. 1861.

Jahn, Jaheinz. *A Bibliography of Neo-African Literature from Africa, America, and the Caribbean*. 1965.

James, C. L. R. *The Black Jacobins*. New York: Random House, 1963.

Jeffers, Lance. *My Blackness Is the Beauty of this Land*. Detroit: Broadside Press, 1970.

Johnson, Charles. *Middle Passage*. New York: Viking, 1990.

Johnson, James Weldon. *The Glory of the Day Was in Her Face*. New York: Viking, 1917

———. *The Book of American Negro Poetry*. New York: Harcourt Brace, 1922.

———. *Second Book of Negro Spirituals*. 1926.

———. *God's Trombones: Some Negro Sermons in Verse*. New York: Viking, 1927.

———. *Black Manhattan*. New York: Arno, 1930.

———. *Along This Way: The Autobiography of James Weldon Johnson*. New York: Viking, 1933.

Jones, Gayl. *Eva's Man*. New York: Random House, 1976.

Jones, Joshua. *The Heart of the World*. c. 1919.

Jones, LeRoi. *Blues People: Negro Music in White America*. New York: Morrow, 1963.

———. *Home: Social Essays*. New York: Morrow, 1966.

Jordan, Barbara, with James Haskins. *Barbara Jordan*. New York: Dial, 1977.

Jordan, June. *Some Changes*. New York: E. P. Dutton, 1970.

Karanga, Maulana. *The Husia*. University of Sankore Press, 1989.

Kaufman, Bob. *Golden Sandals*. San Francisco: City Lights Books, 1967.

Kennedy, Ellen Conroy, ed. *Negritude Poets*. New York: Viking, 1975.

Kerlin, Robert. T. *Negro Poets and Their Poems*. Washington, D.C., 1923.

Kerman, Cynthia E. and Richard Eldridge. *The Lives of Jean Toomer: A Hunger for Wholeness*. Baton Rouge: Louisiana State University Press, 1987.

Killens, John. *And Then We Heard the Thunder*. New York: Knopf, 1963.

King, Coretta Scott. *My Life with Martin Luther King, Jr.* New York: Holt, Rinehart & Winston, 1969.

King, Martin Luther, Jr. *Stride Toward Freedom*. New York: Harper & Brothers, 1958.

———. *Letter from a Birmingham Jail*. 1963.

———. *Strength to Love*. New York: Harper & Row, 1963.

———. *Why We Can't Wait*. New York: Harper & Row, 1963.

———.*Where do We Go From Here: Chaos or Community?* Boston: Beacon Press, 1968.

Knight, Etheridge. *Poems from Prison*. Detroit: Broadside Press, 1968.

Kunjunfu, Jawanza. *Conspiracy to Destroy Fourth Grade Boys*. New York: African American Institute, 1983.

Lamming, George. *The Emigrants*. London, 1954.

———. *Season of Adventure*. London: Michael Joseph, 1960.

Laye, Camara. *The Dark Child*. New York: Farrar, Straus and Co., 1954.

Lee, Don L. (Madhubuti). *Dynamite Voices*. Detroit: Broadside Press, 1971.

Lincoln, C. Eric. *The Black Muslims in America*. Boston: Beacon Press, 1961.

Littleton, Arthur. *Black Viewpoints*. New York: New American Library, 1971.

Locke, Alain, ed. *The New Negro: An Interpretation*. Boni and Liveright, 1925.

Lomax, Alan, and Abdul Raoul, eds. *3,000 Years of Black Poetry*. New York: Dodd Mead, 1970.

Lorde, Audre. *From a Land Where Other People Live*. Detroit: Broadside Press, 1973.

———. *The Cancer Journals*. San Francisco: Spinster Press, 1980.

Louis, Joe. *Joe Louis: My Life*. New York: Berkley Books, 1981.

Lovell. John, Jr. *Black Song: The Forge and the Flame*. New York: Macmillan, 1972.

McKay, Claude. *My Green Hills of Jamaica*. New York: Schomburg Collection, 1919.

———. *Home to Harlem*. New York: Harper & Brothers, 1928.

———. *Banjo: A Story Without a Plot*. New York: Harper & Brothers, 1929.

———. *Harlem: Negro Metropolis*. New York: E. P. Dutton, 1940.

———. *Selected Poems of Claude McKay*. Bookman, 1953.

McKissack, Floyd B. *Three-fifths of a Man*. New York: Macmillan, 1968.

Madgett, Naomi Long. *Star by Star*. Detroit: Harlo Press, 1965.

Mandela, Nelson, with Fatima Meer. *Higher Than Hope: The Authorized Biography of Nelson Mandela*. New York: HarperCollins, 1991.

Maran, Rene. *Batoula*. Paris, 1921.

Mars, Jean Price. *Thus Spake Our Uncle*. Port au Prince, 1928.

Marshall, Paule. *Brown Girl, Brownstones*. New York: Random House, 1959.

Mays, Benjamin E. *Born to Rebel*. New York: Scribner, 1970.

Makeba, Miriam. *My Story*. New York: New American Library, 1987.

Maunick, Edouard. *Carousels of the Sea*, Paris: Présence Africaine, 1964.

Mbiti, John. *African Religion and Philosophy*. New York: Anchor Press, 1970.

Miller, Kelly. *The American Negro: His History and Literature*. Neale, 1908.

———. *Race Adjustment*. Neale, 1908.

Mingus, Charlie. *Black Maturation and the Revolution in Music*. New York: Pathfinders Press, 1970.

Morrison, Toni. *Sula*. New York: Bantam, 1975.

———. *Song of Solomon*. New York: Knopf, 1977.

———. *Beloved*. New York: Knopf, 1987.

Moton, Robert. *Finding a Way Out*. New York: Doubleday, 1920.

Mphahlele, Ezekiel. *Chirundu*. New York: Raven Press.

———. *Down Second Avenue*. London: Faber and Faber, 1959.

Muhammad, Elijah. *Message to the Black Man*. Chicago, 1965.

Naylor, Gloria. *The Women of Brewster Place.* New York: Penguin Books, 1988.

Noble, Jeanne. *Beautiful, Also, Are the Souls of My Black Sisters.* Englewood Cliffs, N.J.: Prentice-Hall, 1978.

Nkrumah, Kwame. *Ghana, Autobiography of Kwame Nkrumah.* Thomas Nelson and Sons, 1957.

———. *Africa Must Unite.* International Press, 1963.

———. *Consciencism.* London: Panaf, 1964.

———. *Neocolonialism.* London: Panaf, 1965.

———. *The Spectre of Black Power.* London: Panaf, 1968.

———. *Handbook of Revolutionary Warfare.* International Press, 1968.

Nyerere, Julius. *Ujamaa.* New York: Oxford University Press, 1968.

Obradovic, Nadezda. *Looking For A Rain God.* New York: Simon and Schuster, 1990.

Okot p'Bitek. *Horn of My Love.* London: Heinemann Educational Books.

Owens, Jesse. *Blackthink.* New York: Morrow, 1970.

Parks, Gordon. *A Choice of Weapons.* New York: Harper & Row, 1966.

———. *Voices in the Mirror.* New York: Doubleday, 1990.

Paster, Alfred. *The Roots of Soul.* New York: Doubleday, 1982.

Patterson, Raymond. *26 Ways of Looking at A Black Man.* Universal Publishers, 1968.

Payne, Daniel. *Recollections of 70 years.* New York: Arno Press, 1969.

Paz, Octavio. *Alternating Currents.* New York: Viking, 1973.

Perry, Richard. *Montgomery's Children.* New York: Harcourt Brace Johanovich, 1984.

Philpot, William M., ed. *Best Black Sermons.* Valley Forge, Penn.: Judson Press, 1972.

Powell, Adam Clayton, Jr. *Adam by Adam.* New York: Viking, 1971.

Pritchard, E. E. *Witchcraft, Oracles and Magic among the Azande.* New York: Oxford University Press.

Quarles, Benjamin. *Black Abolitionists.* New York: Oxford University Press, 1969.

Rabéarivelo, Jean-Joseph. *Old Songs of Imerina Land.* Madagascar, 1939.

———. *Twenty Four Poems.* Ibadan: Mbari, 1962.

Ranaivo, Flavien. *The Darkness and the Wind,* 1947.

———. *Return to the Fold.* Madagascar, 1955.

———. *Ebony Wood.* New York: Macmillan, 1971.

Randall, Dudley Felker. *Cities Burning.* Detroit: Broadside Press, 1968.

———. *Black Poetry.* Broadside Press, 1969.

Randall, Dudley Felker, and Margaret Burroughs, eds. *For Malcolm.* Detroit: Broadside Press, 1967.

Redding, Jay Saunders. *To Make A Poet Black.* McGrath, 1939.

———. *They Came in Chains: Americans from Africa.* Philadelphia: Lippincott, 1951.

Redmond, Eugene B. *Drumvoice: The Mission of Afro-American Poetry.* New York: Anchor Press, 1976.

Reed, Ishmael. *Nineteen Necromancers From Now.* New York: Doubleday, 1970.

Reed, Victor. *New Day.* London, 1949.

Ritz, David. *Divided Soul.* New York: McGraw-Hill, 1985.

Rivers, Conrad Kent. *The Still Voice of Harlem.* London: Paul Bremen, 1968.

Robeson, Paul. *Here I Stand.* Othello Associates, 1958.

Robeson, Susan. *Whole World in His Hand.* Secaucus, N.J.: Citadel Press, 1981.

Robinson, Jackie. *Baseball Has Done It.* Philadelphia: Lippincott, 1964.

Rose, Al. *Eubie Blake,* New York: Schirmer Books, 1979.

Rose, Phyllis. *Jazz Cleopatra: Josephine Baker in Her Time.* New York: Doubleday, 1989.

Roumain, Jacques. *Masters of the Dew.* 1947.

Roumer, Edward. *Poemes d'Haiti et de France.* Paris, 1925.

Russell, Bill with Taylor Branch. *Second Wind.* New York: Simon and Schuster, 1979.

Sedron, Ben. *Black Talk.* New York: Holt, Rinehart & Winston, 1971.

Sembane, Ousmane. *God's Bit of Wood.* New York: Doubleday, 1970.

Senghor, Leopold. *Prose and Poetry.* London, 1965.

———. *The Foundation of Africanite.* Paris: Présence Africaine, 1971.

———. *Negritude and Civilization.* Paris, 1977.

Shange, Ntozake. *For Colored Girls Who Have Considered Suicide When the Rainbow is Enuf.* New York: Macmillan, 1975.

———. *See No Evil.* San Francisco: Momo's Press, 1984.

Silberman, Charles. *Crisis in Black and White.* New York: Knopf, 1964.

Sissoko, Fily Dabo. *Poems from Black Africa.* Paris: Les Nouvelles Edition, 1962.

Slater, Robert. *The Pursuit of Loneliness.* Boston: Beacon Press, 1971.

Smith, Liz. *The Mother Book,* New York: Bantam, 1978.

Smitherman, Geneva. *Talkin' and Testifying.* Wayne State University Press, 1977.

Southern, Eillen. *The Music of Black America: A History.* New York: Norton, 1972.

Soyinka, Wole, ed. *A Dance of the Forest.* New York: Oxford University Press, 1963.

———. *Idioms and Other Poems.* New York: Oxford University Press, 1967.

———. *Kongi's Harvest.* New York: Oxford University Press, 1967.

———. *Collected Plays.* New York: Oxford University Press, 1974.

———. *Poems of Black Africa.* New York: Hill & Wang, 1975.

———. *The Lion and the Jewel.* New York: Oxford University Press, 1975.

Spradling, Mary, ed. *In Black and White.* Detroit: Gale Research, 1980.

Stewart, Maria W. *Meditations from the Pen of Mrs. Maria W. Stewart, Negro.* Washington D.C., 1879.

Terrell, Mary Church. *Confessions of a Colored Woman in a White World.* Washington, D.C.: Ransdell, 1940.

Thurman, Howard. *Meditations of the Heart.* Friends United Press, 1953.

———. *Disciplines of the Spirit.* New York: Harper & Row, 1963.

———. *The Search for a Common Ground.* New York: Harper & Row, 1971.

Tirolien, Guy. *Golden Bullets.* Paris: Présence Africaine, 1961.

Titon, John Todd, ed. *Give Me This Mountain.* Champaign, Ill., University of Illinois Press, 1989.

Tolson, Melvin. *Rendezvous with America.* New York: Dodd Mead, 1944.

Toomer, Jean. *The Flavor of Man.* Philadelphia, 1949.

Truth, Sojourner. *Narratives of Sojourner Truth, A Northern Slave.* Boston, 1850.

Turner, Darwin T., ed. *Wayward Seeking: A Collection of Writing by Jean Toomer.* Washington, D.C.: Howard University Press, 1980.

Tutu, Desmond. *Hope and Suffering.* W. B. Eerdman, 1983.

Tutuola, Amos. *The Palm Wine Drunkard.* London: Faber and Faber, 1952.

U Tam'si, Tchicaya Felix. *Brush Fire.* Paris, 1957.

———. *Epitome.* Paris: Jean Oswald, 1962.

Van Sertima, Ivan. *African Presence in Ancient America: They Came Before Columbus.* New York: Random House, 1976.

Van Sertima, Ivan, and Runoko Rashidi. *African Presence in Early Asia.* Brunswick, N.J.: Transaction Books, 1985.

Walker, Alice. *Revolutionary Petunias.* New York: Harcourt-Brace, 1971.

——— *Meridian.* New York: Harcourt Brace Jovanovich, 1976.

———. *In Search of Our Mothers' Gardens.* New York: Harcourt Brace Jovanovich, 1983.

Walker, David. *An Appeal to the Coloured Citizens of the World.* Boston, 1829.

Walker, Margaret. *For My People.* New Haven: Yale University Press, 1942.

———. *Jubilee.* Boston: Houghton Mifflin, 1966.

———. *Prophets for a New Day.* Detroit: Broadside Press, 1970.

Walton, Ortiz. *Music, Black, White & Blue.* New York: Morrow, 1972.

Ware, Gilbert, and William Hastie. *Grace Under Pressure.* New York: Oxford University Press, 1984.

Warren, Robert Penn. *Who Speaks for the Negro?* New York: Random House, 1965.

Washington, Booker T. *The Man Farthest Down: A Record of Observation and Study in Europe.* New York, 1912.

Washington, E. Davison, ed. *Selected Speeches of Booker T. Washington.* New York: Doubleday, 1932.

Wembridge, Eleanor. *Life Among the Lowbrows.* Boston, 1931.

Wilkins, Roy. *Standing Fast.* New York: Viking, 1982.

Williams, Chancellor. *The Destruction of Black Civilization.* Chicago: Third World Press, 1975.

Williams, John, ed. *Beyond the Angry Black.* New York: New American Library, 1967.

Woodson, Carter G. *Negro Makers of History.* Washington, D.C: Associated Publishers, 1928.

———. *The Mis-education of the Negro.* Washington, D.C: Associated Publishers, 1931.

———. *The Story of the Negro Retold.* Washington, D.C: Associated Publishers, 1935.

———. *The History of the Negro Church.* Washington, D.C: Associated Publishers, 1945.

———. *The Negro in Our History.* Washington, D.C: Associated Publishers, 1947.

Wright, Richard. *Native Son.* New York: Harper & Brothers, 1940.

———. *12 Million Black Voices: A Folk History of the Negro in the United States.* New York: Viking, 1941.

———. *The Outsider.* New York: Harper & Brothers, 1953.

X, Malcolm with Alex Haley. *The Autobiography of Malcolm X.* New York: Grove, 1965.

———. *By Any Means Necessary.* Merit, 1970.

———. *Malcolm X Speaks: Selected Speeches and Statements.* Merit, 1971.

Yarbrough, Camille. *Cornrows*. New York: Coward McCann, 1979.

Yerby, Frank. *Goat Song.* New York: Dial, 1967.

———. *Judas, My Brother*. New York: Dial, 1968.

Young, Whitney. *To Be Equal.* New York: McGraw-Hill, 1964.

———. *Black Manifesto: Religion, Racism, and Reparations.* Sheed and Ward, 1969.

INDEX BY SPEAKER

INDEX BY SUBJECT